A NEW
MUNICIPAL PROGRAM

NATIONAL MUNICIPAL LEAGUE SERIES

A NEW MUNICIPAL PROGRAM

EDITED BY

CLINTON ROGERS WOODRUFF

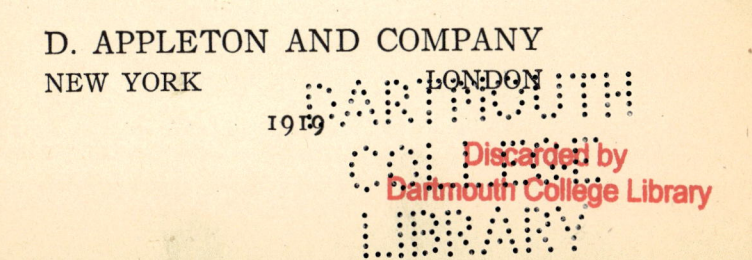

D. APPLETON AND COMPANY
NEW YORK   LONDON
1919

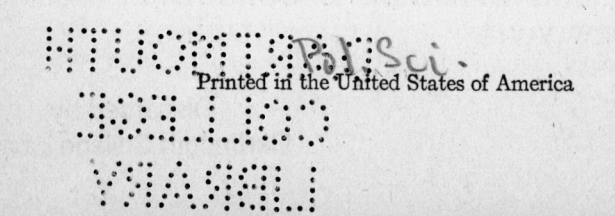

COPYRIGHT, 1919, BY
D. APPLETON AND COMPANY

Printed in the United States of America

PREFACE

To explain and justify their conclusions, the various members of the National Municipal League's Committee on Municipal Program have coöperated in producing this volume. To each was assigned a specific subject for treatment, and to the editor the welding of them together.

This new Municipal Program is put forward with a full appreciation of the difficulties to be met with, but with a consciousness that it represents years of patient thought and hard experience on the part of those who have labored incessantly to improve conditions; and that it has had the formal approval and endorsement of the National Municipal League after three years' discussion.

Municipal Government in America has assumed a leading position among questions of government and this report is offered as a contribution to the solution of those phases of the problem having to do with its machinery. Two other volumes in the National Municipal League Series deal with other portions of this phase, the first, Woodruff's "City Government by Commission" and Toulmin's "The City Manager." These may be regarded as preliminary to the present volume, which aims to give at once the philosophical and the practical arguments for the Committee's conclusions which are embodied in a Model City Charter and model constitutional provisions. So that the book is doubly valuable alike to the student and the charter draftsman.

There are numerous details to be filled in like those for a municipal court and the public library, but these are being taken care of by separate committees which have not yet concluded their labors. The report is substantially complete so far as the general framework of government is concerned.

The New Municipal Program is put forth with the hope that it may be as substantial a contribution to charter revision as its predecessor and a stimulating factor in developing American charter-making along sound lines.

CONTRIBUTORS

M. N. BAKER, Montclair, New Jersey, editor of the *Engineering News-Record;* chairman of the Executive Committee of the National Municipal League; for a number of years president of the Montclair Board of Health and later a member of the New Jersey Board of Health.

RICHARD S. CHILDS, New York City, secretary of the National Short Ballot Organization; vice-president of the National Municipal League, and author of "Short Ballot Principles."

JOHN A. FAIRLIE, Urbana, Illinois, professor of political science at the University of Illinois; secretary of the Illinois Municipal League; author of "Municipal Administration," "Local Government in Counties, Towns and Villages," "Essays in Municipal Administration," "The Taxation and Revenue System of Illinois"; editor, *American Political Science Review.*

MAYO FESLER, Brooklyn, N. Y., secretary, Brooklyn Chamber of Commerce and formerly secretary of the Cleveland Civic League, and of the St. Louis Civic League; secretary of the Convention that drafted the present Cleveland charter.

WILLIAM DUDLEY FOULKE, Richmond, Indiana, president of the National Municipal League from 1910 to 1915; United States civil service commissioner under President Roosevelt; for many years a member of the National Civil Service Reform League.

AUGUSTUS RAYMOND HATTON, Cleveland, Ohio, professor of politics at Western Reserve University; a member of the convention which drafted the present Cleveland charter, and field secretary, National Short Ballot Organization.

HERMAN G. JAMES, Austin, Texas, associate professor in the school of government at the University of Texas; author

CONTRIBUTORS

of "The Introductory Articles of the Illinois Constitution," "Applied City Government," "Handbook of Civic Improvement," "Municipal Functions"; secretary, League of Texas Municipalities.

A. LAWRENCE LOWELL, Cambridge, Mass., president of Harvard University; author of "Public Opinion and Popular Government," "The Influence of Party upon Legislation in England and America," "The Government of England"; a frequent contributor on the subject of administration to the *National Municipal Review* and other periodicals.

WILLIAM BENNETT MUNRO, Cambridge, Mass., professor of government at Harvard University; author of "The Government of European Cities," "The Initiative, Referendum and Recall," "The Government of American Cities," "Bibliography of Municipal Government," "Principles and Methods of Municipal Administration."

ROBERT TREAT PAINE, Boston, Mass., a long time student of economic problems; Democratic nominee for Governor of Massachusetts in 1896; formerly vice-president of the National Municipal League.

DELOS F. WILCOX, Elmhurst, New York City, deputy commissioner of water, gas and electricity under Mayor Mitchel; author of "The Study of City Government," "The American City," "The Government of Great American Cities," "Municipal Franchises."

CLINTON ROGERS WOODRUFF, secretary of the National Municipal League; editor, *National Municipal Review;* National Municipal League Series, and "City Government by Commission."

CONTENTS

CHAPTER		PAGE
I	THE MUNICIPAL PROGRAM: OLD AND NEW	1
	By Clinton Rogers Woodruff	
II	EXPERTS IN MUNICIPAL GOVERNMENT AND THE NEW MODEL CHARTER	28
	By Abbott Lawrence Lowell	
III	CIVIL SERVICE AND EFFICIENCY	46
	By William Dudley Foulke	
IV	CONSTITUTIONAL MUNICIPAL HOME RULE	73
	By Augustus Raymond Hatton	
V	ELECTORAL PROVISIONS OF THE NEW MUNICIPAL PROGRAM	95
	By Mayo Fesler	
VI	THE SHORT BALLOT PRINCIPLE IN THE MODEL CHARTER	109
	By Richard S. Childs	
VII	ADMINISTRATIVE ORGANIZATION	119
	By Herman G. James	
VIII	THE COUNCIL	145
	By William Bennett Munro	
IX	THE INITIATIVE, REFERENDUM AND RECALL	159
	By Clinton Rogers Woodruff	
X	THE FRANCHISE POLICY OF THE NEW MUNICIPAL PROGRAM	173
	By Delos F. Wilcox	

CONTENTS

CHAPTER		PAGE
XI	Financial Provisions of the New Municipal Program	199
	By John A. Fairlie	
XII	City Planning	218
	By M. N. Baker	
XIII	Business Management for City Courts . . .	228
	By Herbert Harley	
XIV	Municipal Development in the United States Since 1900	251
	By Clinton Rogers Woodruff	

The Model City Charter 295

Table of Contents 297

Report of Commitee on Municipal Program . . . 301

Appendix 367

Index 379

A NEW
MUNICIPAL PROGRAM

A NEW MUNICIPAL PROGRAM

I

THE MUNICIPAL PROGRAM: OLD AND NEW

AT the Philadelphia Conference for Good City Government (January, 1894) jointly called by the City Club of New York and the Municipal League of Philadelphia, the feeling on the part of students of municipal government and those interested in its improvement was largely one of hopelessness. The papers read at the Philadelphia meeting set forth a condition of affairs sufficient to fill the most stout-hearted with a feeling of dismay. Nevertheless, the thought was present in the minds of many that a careful study of municipal conditions and a frequent exchange of views would not only clear the atmosphere, but might eventually lead to the adoption of a program of action upon which union for definite work might be possible. Several of the speeches looked toward this end. Indeed, the proposition was advanced that there should be formed an organization having for its object the study of American municipal conditions as a precedent to the formulation of "a municipal program." One speaker thus outlined the thought:

NEED FOR EXCHANGE OF VIEWS

"One important lesson of this Conference must have been impressed on the minds of all who have taken part in it. The municipal reformers have for many years been duplicating one another's work unnecessarily. We have had no means of intercommunication; we have not been able to share one another's knowledge. In this country of ours there are examples of almost every kind of political experiment. If we only knew of these experiments, if we had some means of interchanging our dearly bought knowledge, we should save ourselves a deal of time and futile effort. I look to the formation or growth out of this municipal conference, and as its most favorable result, of some kind of national municipal league or national municipal council, call it what you please, but a central body to which information can be sent, and which will make it its business to gather information on its own account; to revise, condense, and compare reports made to it, and to keep the local centers of reform throughout the country in touch with one another. If you have a good thing in Philadelphia, a point in your charter, which we should have in New York, we should know it. If New York's experience will prove of any value to Chicago, Chicago should have the benefit of it, if only by way of awful example. We have no desire to try experiments that have been tried and have failed already."

There was a conviction, however, shared quite as much by those who held this view, as by those who were doubtful of its wisdom or expediency, that the time was not ripe for the formulation of a Municipal Program. Sentiment had not crystallized. This preamble and resolution, as expressive of the sentiment of the meeting, was adopted without opposition:

" Whereas, the elements brought together in this conference should not be allowed to separate without providing some permanent agency for continuing its work and promoting a comparison of views, the exchange of experiences, the discussion of methods, and that mutual confidence and sympathy which adds so much to the strength and enthusiasm of fellow-workers in a great cause; it is therefore

" Resolved, that the President of this conference is requested to appoint a representative committee of seven to prepare a plan for the organization of a national municipal league, which shall be composed of associations formed in American cities, and having as an object the improvement of municipal government. Upon the completion of the plan and its approval by such associations, or as many of them as the said committee may deem necessary, the committee shall declare the proposed league to be fully organized, and prepared to enter upon its work."

THE NATIONAL MUNICIPAL LEAGUE ORGANIZED

Out of the Philadelphia meeting and of the Committee of Seven, appointed by the president thereof, in accordance with this resolution, grew the National Municipal League, formally organized in New York City in May,

1894. It at once entered upon its work, and proceeded to bring together through its affiliated membership the leading municipal reform organizations of the country; through its associate membership the leading students of municipal government; and through its annual conferences both these elements for a mutual exchange of views and a detailed study of the situation.

Four conferences, those held in Minneapolis (1894), Cleveland (1895), Baltimore (1896) and Louisville (1897), were devoted to a consideration of actual municipal conditions. The papers presented formed an important contribution to the study of municipal government as it actually existed in the United States, and furnished a substantial basis for municipal publicists in their efforts to better American municipal conditions.

In some respects, the Louisville conference, the fifth of the series, may be considered the most important held up to that time. In the first place, the meeting marked the beginning of a new era in the work of the National Municipal League. Theretofore the meetings had been devoted to a statement of municipal conditions and to a discussion of the lessons which they taught. There had been no attempt to formulate a program for adoption, or to construct a platform upon which municipal campaigns should be waged. No such effort had been made because in the minds of those actively identified with the League's management the time had not arrived when such a step was deemed either wise or feasible. Publicists and students were not in a position to agree upon a statement of belief, mainly because they had not given to the general plans

OLD AND NEW 5

of the problem the necessary attention and study. Their particular experiences had been purely local.

The American people had been led by the educational work of the League, its conferences, and its published proceedings to a realization that there was an American municipal problem; that the question of good city government was something more than a merely local issue; that it was, perhaps, the most important single problem confronting the American people at that time.

A MUNICIPAL PROGRAM COMMITTEE

In the second place, the following resolution had been adopted at Louisville:

"Resolved, That the Executive Committee appoint a committee of ten to report on the feasibility of a Municipal Program which will embody the essential principles that must underlie successful municipal government, and which shall also set forth a working plan or system consistent with American industrial and political conditions, for putting such principles into practical operation; and such committee, if it finds such municipal program to be feasible, is instructed to report the same, with its reasons therefor, to the league, for consideration."

Accordingly the Executive Committee secured the consent of the following to serve on the "Municipal Program Committee": Horace E. Deming, New York; George W. Guthrie, Pittsburgh (later Ambassador to Japan); Charles Richardson, Philadelphia; Frank J. Goodnow, New York, now President Johns Hopkins University;

Prof. Leo S. Rowe, Philadelphia, now Assistant Secretary of the Treasury; Dr. Albert Shaw, Editor *Review of Reviews*, New York; Clinton Rogers Woodruff, Philadelphia. An exchange of suggestions through informal personal meetings and correspondence was the first step taken by the members of the committee. These were consolidated and embodied in a series of preliminary reports and criticisms which were laid before a session of the committee lasting nearly a week. At this meeting, the views of the committee were reduced to the form of definite propositions, tentatively adopted. A sub-committee was then appointed to elaborate these propositions into drafts of proposed constitutional amendments, and a general municipal corporations act for further examination, criticism and suggestion; and a revised draft was submitted to the Indianapolis meeting of the League, in November, 1898.

A MUNICIPAL PROGRAM FOUND TO BE FEASIBLE

In presenting this preliminary report, the committee took occasion to say that it did not " apologize for presenting this outline sketch of its labors to fulfill the commission intrusted to it. The fact that a body of men of widely divergent training, of strong personal convictions, and who approached the matter in hand from essentially different points of view, should and did come to unanimous agreement that a Municipal Program was feasible and practicable, and had conferred, and by comparison of opinion, were able to embody the result of their agreement in definite propositions, is a hopeful augury that the general body of the League, after a full opportunity for discussion, criticism, and interchange of views, can and will adopt either the committee's propositions, or some improvement upon them. The committee therefore presents its report with the confident expectation that after sufficient time and opportunity shall have been given for such further consideration which the importance of the subject demands, the members of the League will be able formally to present to their fellow-citizens in the United States a definite Municipal Program that will embody the essential principles that must underlie successful municipal government, and which shall also set forth a working plan or system, consistent with American industrial and political conditions, for putting such principles into practical operation.

" The resolution of the League under which the committee acted involved a task for which few, if any, precedents existed. The committee was working to crystallize the result of the experiences of American and European cities, and at the same time to make the results of its labors practically applicable to our present conditions. Under such circumstances it became necessary to proceed with care, caution, and conservatism. The committee keenly felt the necessity of bringing any system they might recommend into organic relation with the traditions and accepted political ideas of the American people."

Sundry papers discussing the more important underlying principles that controlled the preparation of the amendments and acts were submitted to and approved by the several members of the committee, and constituted an essential part of its report. These were read at the Indianapolis Conference, as a part of the preliminary report of the committee. These principal papers were in turn discussed in subsidiary papers by a number of students of the municipal problem, all of which were published in the proceedings of the Conference. At this meeting the report of the committee and criticisms and suggestions which had been made were referred back to the committee with instructions to complete their work for action at the next meeting of the League.

MUNICIPAL PROGRAM ADOPTED

In connection with the final draft presented the next year at Columbus, several additional explanatory papers were presented and like those of the preceding year were constituted an essential part of the committee's report. These papers and the text of the Constitutional Amendments and the Municipal Corporations Act, adopted by an unanimous vote at Columbus (1900), were the logical outcome of six years of effort on the part of the National Municipal League and the result of two years of unremitting and painstaking endeavor to present, in accordance with the original resolution, " a working system consistent with American industrial and political conditions, and embodying the essential principles that must underlie successful municipal government in this country." The Amendments and the Municipal Corporations Act, together with explanatory papers already referred to, and certain others, including one on " Municipal Development in the United States," by Professor John A. Fairlie, were published by The Macmillan Company in a volume entitled "A Municipal Program." It was widely utilized by charter makers and constitutional conventions. It was nowhere enacted into law as a whole, but, as Dr. Delos F. Wilcox pointed out at the Chicago (1904) meeting, its influence "has been felt practically everywhere that charters have been framed, constitutions revised or municipal reform agitated 'under the flag.'" It was published in full in Honolulu for the benefit of the Hawaiian legislature. It was used by the Havana Charter Commission and, I believe, by the Porto Rican and Philippine Commissions. It has left marked traces in the new constitutions of Virginia and Alabama, and formed the basis for a sweeping amendment to the Colorado constitution. The Charter Commission of Portland, Oregon, used it. The Charter Revision Commission of New York adopted some of its provisions. The Duluth and St. Paul charters are in line with it in important respects. It has formed the basis of agitation for charter reform in Wisconsin, Michigan, Delaware, and doubtless many other states. Its experience in Ohio, however, has been unfortunate. The Municipal Code Commission in that state was at work at the time of the Columbus Conference for Good City Government, at which the Program was adopted. Perhaps on account of their proximity, the commissioners absorbed so many reform ideas that their code was rejected by the Ohio politicians."

FUNDAMENTAL PRINCIPLES INVOLVED

This Municipal Program embodied five fundamental principles of municipal government, which were defined by Dr. Wilcox in the same address to be:

1. That every city or other local community should have the right of self-government in its local affairs without the interference of outside governmental or party machinery.

2. That the city's public property in land, with especial reference to franchise rights, should be so safeguarded as to be preserved unimpaired for the use of all the people in this and future generations.

3. That all barriers should be removed which prevent the popular will from freely and effectively expressing itself as the public will.

4. That municipal administration should be conducted in the main by a class of public servants who by reason of experience and special training are particularly fitted for their official duties.

5. That official responsibility should be so placed through simplification of governmental machinery and full publicity of accounts that the people may hold their public servants to the execution of the public will with the least possible delay and uncertainty.

THE COMMISSION FORM OF GOVERNMENT

In the same year (1900) in which the first Municipal Program was officially and finally adopted occurred the Galveston flood which well nigh destroyed the city, physically and financially. Among other things swept away was the typical old style mayor and council form of government, which was replaced by a commission of five men appointed by the Governor of Texas. This commission worked swiftly and efficiently, to quote from a report of a committee of the National Municipal League,

OLD AND NEW

and soon had the municipal government working and at much less annual cost. "After the emergency passed, an attempt was made to continue the same government with three members appointed by the governor and two chosen by popular vote, as it was supposed that so simple and powerful a form of organization would be unsafe if manned entirely by elective representatives. A court decision declared the continued appointment of city officers in this way to be unconstitutional, and the entire commission forthwith became elective. To the surprise of many observers, no demoralization ensued, and through successive elections the changes in the personnel have been very slight. Galveston began to claim that it was the best governed city in the United States, and Houston, Texas, in 1905, copied the Galveston charter with similar satisfaction."

In 1907 Des Moines adopted the Galveston plan, with the addition of the initiative, referendum, recall and nonpartisan primary. This plan was widely copied, largely on the strength of the Des Moines experience, the number of cities adopting this form having increased until, on May 1, 1918, there were 111 cities and towns of 2,000 and over which had changed their governments to the new type.[1] Few changes of importance were made in the Des Moines model for several years (except the pref-

[1] The history of the movement is described in Bradford's "Commission Government in American Cities," Hamilton's "Dethronement of the City Boss" and Woodruff's "City Government by Commission." The latter contains a symposium of the comments of various authoritative observers. Analyses of the charters, together with the texts of the more significant ones, are to be found in Beard's "Digest of Short-Ballot Charters," a loose leaf volume on the subject. A study of the administrative workings of commission government is to be found in Bruere's

erential ballot added first by Grand Junction, Colo.) until the appearance in 1913 of the city manager, or commission manager modification.

Commission government, as it came to be popularly known, has been a success as compared with the older forms, in the opinion of a committee of the National Municipal League appointed in 1910, consisting of Charles A. Beard, Professor of Politics, Columbia University; Ernest S. Bradford, Washington, D. C.; Richard S. Childs, Secretary, National Short Ballot Organization; William Bennett Munro, Professor of Municipal Government, Harvard University; and Clinton Rogers Woodruff, Editor, *National Municipal Review*. This committee reported at Richmond (1911) that it found itself in agreement on the following interpretations of the major features of commission government:

THE BENEFICIAL FEATURES OF COMMISSION GOVERNMENT

" The people who live under it are generally more content. They feel that they are more effective politically and that commission government is an asset of their town. Substantial financial improvements have generally resulted, demonstrating a striking increase in efficiency and a higher standard of municipal accomplishment, and this may fairly be credited to the better working of the new plan.

" This relative success of commission government results primarily because it is more democratic (i.e., sen-

"The New City Government," comprising intensive examinations by representatives from the New York Bureau of Municipal Research.

sitive to public opinion) than the old form. Among the features which undoubtedly are responsible for this increased sensitiveness are:

"1. Its *unification of powers* as contrasted with the old undesirable separation of powers. The commission having all the power, has no one to blame for failure to please the public, cannot evade full responsibility, and having ample power to remedy each abuse, can be held responsible for any failure to do so. This stripping away of the old-time protective confusion-of-responsibility exposes the commission to the direct fire of public opinion and makes its members personally targets for public criticism. The unification of powers unifies the whole governmental system, gives the government the single controlling brain which is necessary to a successful organism, prevents lost motion, 'pulling and hauling,' deadlocks, and ill feeling.

"2. *The short ballot.*— This makes each elective official conspicuous on election day and after; makes intelligent voting so easy that practically every citizen can vote intelligently without any more conscious effort than he expended on his business of citizenship under the old plan.

"Being acutely sensitive and therefore anxious to please, commission government has been giving the people better government because the people are and always have been ready to applaud honest and progressive government. A contributing factor undoubtedly is the fact that the radical change has usually awakened a fresh civic interest among the citizens, which runs along of its own momentum for a considerable time and does much to tone up every branch of administration."

ONE MUNICIPAL PROGRAM AND COMMISSION
GOVERNMENT

It will be seen that the commission form succeeded because it embodied certain of the fundamental principles of the Municipal Program. There might be a difference as to the form, but very little difference in the underlying thought of responsibility, responsiveness and simplicity. It is true that the first Municipal Program provided for a longer ballot than is now considered ideally desirable, but it was a short ballot as compared with what went before, inasmuch as only three kinds of elective officers were provided for: the mayor, the legislators and the auditor. It did provide for a non-partisan ballot, as do the best types of commission government, although in the opinion of the committee already quoted from, this was "highly desirable, but not absolutely indispensable, as the short ballot by making the party label a superfluous convenience, thereby destroys much of the label's influence anyway."

Neither the initiative, referendum nor recall were provided for in the original Municipal Program, although it was placed within the power of the council to establish them with the consent of the voters, as well as either preferential voting or proportional representation (Article V, Section 11, Municipal Corporations Act). "The initiative and referendum-by-protest have proved useful as provisions," in the judgment of the special committee, "for allaying the time-honored popular fear of entrusting large power to single bodies. The sensitiveness of commission government reduces the necessity for these devices and instances of their use in commission governed cities are very uncommon. It should not be forgotten that Galveston and Houston, the first two cities to have the plan, made their success without these features." It might also have been pointed out that the initiative and the referendum were instruments whereby the policy-determining and the policy-executing functions of a city government could be kept apart. This was a distinction forcibly pointed out and persistently emphasized and insisted upon by the Committee on Municipal Program, and as in commission government the same group of men were both legislators *and* administrators, it looked as if the principle were ignored in the new form of government. As a matter of fact, in those commisson governments which have the initiative and referendum, there is an undoubted, even though unconscious and in a way imperfect recognition of the principle enunciated in the Program of 1900.

The Municipal Program and commission government agree in the abolition of ward lines as necessary to put an end to numerous petty abuses; as tending to prevent petty log-rolling and emphasizing the unity of the city. They also agree in providing for an independent auditor.

Thus it will be seen that, unconsciously or otherwise, the commission form of government embodied many important features of the National Municipal League's Program of 1900; but of course it did not embody the principle of home rule, for that is a constitutional, and not a charter principle; and there was a difference in form, and in the observing of the distinction between legislation and administration, and more important still, in the diffusion of administrative responsibility.

THE COMING OF THE COMMISSION-MANAGER PLAN

While the committee of five was of the opinion that the commission form had led to a cleaning up of many ancient abuses, it recognized that it was by no means the ultimate form, but only a transitional form. In its second report (at Toronto, in 1913) it hailed "The Coming of the Commission-Manager Plan," pointing out that the first city in America to commit its administrative affairs to the charge of an appointive executive or city manager was Staunton, Va. This action was taken by ordinance in 1909. The Staunton manager, however, is responsible to a mayor and council of the old-fashioned type. Other cities have created managers under similar circumstances; but the city manager plan was more exactly described by the committee as the "*commission*-manager" plan, with the manager subordinate to a *single* governing body which is vested with all the powers of local government (like the commission in commission-governed cities). The committee defined the commission-manager plan to be " a single elective board (commission) representative, supervisory and legislative in function, the members giving only part time to municipal work and receiving nominal salaries or none; an appointive chief executive (city manager) hired by the board from anywhere in the country and holding office at the pleasure of the board. The manager appoints and controls the remaining city employees, subject to adequate civil service provisions. . . . This variation has both of the great basic merits which our earlier report ascribed to the original commission plan, namely, the 'unification of powers' and 'the short ballot.'"

At this point, however, the committee divided, and four (Messrs. Beard, Childs, Munro and Woodruff) united in a majority which maintained that:

THE ADVANTAGES OF THE CITY MANAGER PLAN

"The city manager feature is a valuable addition to the commission plan, and we recommend to charter-makers serious consideration of the inclusion of this feature in new commission government charters. Its advantages are:

"1. It creates a single-headed administrative establishment instead of the five separate administrative establishments seen in the Des Moines plan. This administrative unity makes for harmony between municipal departments, since all are subject to a common head.

"2. The commission manager plan permits expertness in administration at the point where it is most valuable, namely, at the head.

"3. It permits comparative permanence in the office of the chief executive, whereas in all plans involving elective executives, long tenures are rare.

a. This permanence tends to rid us of amateur and transient executives and to substitute experienced experts; gives to administrative establishment the superior stability and continuity of personnel and policies which is a necessary precedent to solid and enduring administrative reforms; makes more feasible the consideration and carrying out of far-sighted projects extending over long terms of years; makes it worth while for the executives to educate themselves seriously in municipal affairs, in the assurance that such education will be useful over a long period and in more than one city.

"4. The commission manager plan permits the chief executives to migrate from city to city, inasmuch as the city manager is not to be necessarily a resident of the city at the time of his appointment, and thus an experienced man can be summoned at an advanced salary from a similar post in another city.

a. This exchangeability opens up a splendid new profession, that of " city managership."

b. This exchangeability provides an ideal vehicle for the interchange of experience among the cities.

"5. The commission manager plan, while giving a single-headed administration, abolishes the one-man power seen in the old mayor-and-council plan. The manager has no independence and the city need not suffer from his personal whims or prejudices since he is subject to instant correction, or even discharge, by the commission. Likewise, in the commission, each member's individual whims or prejudices are safely submerged and averaged in the combined judgment of the whole commission, since no member exerts any authority in the municipal government save as one voting member of the commission.

a. This abolition of one-man power makes safer the free-handed extension of municipal powers and operations unhampered by checks and balances and red tape.

b. More discretion can be left to administrative officers to establish rulings as they go along, since they are subject to continuous control and the ultimate appeal of dissatisfied citizens is to the fairness and intelligence of a group (the commission) rather than to a single and possibly opinionated man (an elective mayor). Inversely, laws and ordinances can be simpler, thus reducing the field of legal interpretation and bringing municipal business nearer to the simplicity, flexibility and straightforwardness of private business.

"6. The commission manager plan abandons all attempts to choose administrators by popular election. This is desirable because:

a. It is as difficult for the people to gauge executive and administrative ability in candidates as to estimate the professional worth of engineers and attorneys. As stated in our 1911 report, such tasks are not properly popular functions.

b. By removing all requirements of technical or administrative ability in elective officers, it broadens the field of popular choice and leaves the people free to follow their instinct which is to choose candidates primarily with reference to their representative character only. Laboring men, for instance, can then freely elect their own men to the commission, and there is no requirement (as in the Des Moines charter) that these representatives shall, despite their inexperience in managing large affairs, be given the active personal management of a more or less technical municipal department.

"7. The commission manager plan leaves the lines of responsibility unmistakably clear, avoiding the confusion in the Des Moines plan between the responsibility of the individual commissioners and that of the commission as a whole.

" 8. It provides basis for better discipline and harmony, inasmuch as the city manager cannot safely be at odds with the commission, as can the Des Moines commissioners in their capacity as department heads, or the mayor with the council in the mayor-and-council plan.

" 9. It is better adapted for large cities than the Des Moines plan. Large cities should have more than five members in their commission to avoid overloading the members with work and responsibility and to avoid conferring too much legislative power per individual member. Unlike the Des Moines plan, the commission manager plan permits such enlarged commissions, and so opens the way to the broader and more diversified representation which large cities need.

" 10. In very small cities, by providing the services of one well-paid manager instead of five or three paid commissioners, it makes possible economy in salaries and overhead expenses.

" 11. It permits ward elections or proportional representation as the Des Moines plan does not. One or the other of these is likely to prove desirable in very large cities to preserve a district size that will not be so big that the cost and difficulty of effective canvassing will balk independent candidates, thereby giving a monopoly of hopeful nominations to permanent political machines.

" 12. It creates positions (membership in the commission) which should be attractive to useful citizens, since the service offers opportunities for high usefulness without interruption of their private careers."

THE SECOND MUNICIPAL PROGRAM COMMITTEE

This extended quotation from the report of the League's Committee on Commission Government is given because in reality it constitutes the connecting link between the old and new Programs, as well as gives in concise form the arguments in favor of the city manager form over the commission form of city government. Moreover, it foreshadows and leads up to the fuller report of the second Committee on Municipal Program, giving the reasons for recommending the commission manager form in preference to the commission form, notwithstanding the wide vogue which the latter had, and is still having. This is not to be taken as undervaluing the importance of that form as an evolutionary step. It has wiped out where adopted many deep-seated abuses of long standing, such as ward representation; partisan nominations and domination; complexity and lack of concentration, with a large measure of success. It has served a further purpose in that it eventually led up to the next step of a carefully selected expert official, the embodiment of that principle of the first Municipal Program that " municipal administration should be conducted in the main by a class of public servants who by reason of experience and special training are particularly fitted for their official duties."

The second Committee on Municipal Program was appointed in 1913 to consider the original " Municipal Program " adopted in 1900 and if desirable to draft a new model charter and home rule constitutional amendments embodying the result of subsequent study and developments. It was composed of William Dudley Foulke,

Richmond, Indiana, then president of the National Municipal League, Chairman; M. N. Baker, of the *Engineering News;* Richard S. Childs, secretary of the Short Ballot Organization; John A. Fairlie, professor of political science, University of Illinois; Mayo Fesler, secretary, Cleveland Civic League; Augustus Raymond Hatton, professor of politics, Western Reserve University, Cleveland; Professor Herman G. James, University of Texas, and secretary of League of Texas Municipalities; President A. Lawrence Lowell, Harvard University; William Bennett Munro, professor of municipal government, Harvard University; Robert Treat Paine, Boston; Dr. Delos F. Wilcox, Assistant Commissioner of Water, New York City; Clinton Rogers Woodruff, secretary of the League.

This committee presented a partial report to the meeting of the League in Baltimore, in November, 1914, in the form of sections dealing with the council, the city manager and the civil service board. Two day sessions in New York, April 8 and 9, 1915, were then held, at which time these sections were carefully revised and other sections dealing with the initiative, referendum, recall and other electoral provisions were considered and added, and a partial draft of the constitutional provisions, which had been presented at the Baltimore meeting, was completed. Another meeting of the committee was held in New York September 14, 1915, at which time further revisions were made, and the financial provisions added as well as the two appendices treating of proportional representation and franchise provisions, all of which were included in the tentative draft. The Program was again submitted to the League at its annual meeting in Dayton on November 19, 1915, and after extended discussion, the sections were approved by the members there present. The document was referred back to the Committee on Municipal Program for further amendments, which were adopted at a meeting of the Committee in Philadelphia, December 27 and 28, 1915. Then the whole was submitted in pamphlet form to the entire membership of the National Municipal League with the following letter of explanation:

THE ADOPTION OF THE SECOND MUNICIPAL PROGRAM

Enclosed you will find a copy of "The Model City Charter and Municipal Home Rule," as prepared by the Committee on Municipal Program of the National Municipal League. This final report represents the results of three years' labor. The first report was presented at the Baltimore meeting of the League in November, 1914; the second report was presented to the Dayton meeting, November, 1915. In the meantime several editions of the conclusions reached by the committee had been published and distributed.

At Dayton the principles underlying the report were approved, and the committee given authority to make such final revisions as further study seemed to make necessary and to transmit the whole to the members of the League, the action of the League being as follows:

The Secretary: I move that after the Committee on Municipal Program has completed its draft, that it be instructed to have the same printed and a copy sent to each member of the League of record at that date for an expression of approval or disapproval, with the understanding that the Committee may fix a time limit for the expression of opinion, to publish the fact of approval or disapproval.

This action was carried unanimously.

In accordance with the authority vested in the Committee, the chairman has fixed May 1 as the time limit for the expression of opinion.

The Committee desires to call attention to the fact that the subjects of taxation, libraries, education, special assessments and public improvement are to be considered subsequently by special committees which are now at work on the subjects. The Committee felt that as these were separate and separable subjects, the publication of the model charter need not be further delayed until reports on them were received, considered and approved.

As there were no votes cast against the adoption of the charter within the prescribed time (and for that matter, none since), the Municipal Program as set forth in the Appendix of this volume [1] was finally promulgated as the League's "Model City Charter."

There have been sundry suggestions offered since, several having been prepared by the Committee on Budgets. These have to do with detail of procedure rather than principle, and may be made the subject of future consideration as possible amendments. There is one exception, that presented by Lieutenant Shaw, in a note which has been attached to the chapter on civil service.[1] The Charter and Constitutional provisions as presented represent the careful judgment of a group of twelve men of varied training and great experience in public life as well as in academic work, and life-long students of the problems involved. They do not assert that the Model Char-

[1] See page 295.

ter is the last word, but the latest, and that it embodies the form and content which it is believed will at the present state of public mind and practice on the subject yield the largest measure of efficient, democratic government.

THE NEW MODEL CITY CHARTER

As was the case in the first Program, the present one is presented in two parts: one a set of Constitutional Amendments designed to give cities the largest possible power of self-government. The charter in the first was in the form of a municipal corporations act, that is to say, a statute or act of assembly which would apply to all the cities in the state. The new model is assumed to be a home rule charter based upon some such provisions for constitutional home rule as those suggested in the report. When this or a similar charter is made available for cities by statute a comprehensive grant of powers may be and should be included in the act itself. Otherwise cities securing such a charter will have only the powers enumerated in the general law of the state and be subject to all the restrictions and inconveniences arising from that method of granting powers. It was suggested, therefore, by the Committee, that the following grant of powers be included in any such special statutory charter or optional charter law. The changes of language necessary to adapt it to a special statutory charter readily suggest themselves:

"Section.— Cities organized under this act shall have and are hereby granted authority to exercise all powers relating to their municipal affairs; and no enumeration of powers in any law shall be deemed to restrict the general grant of authority hereby conferred.

"The following shall be deemed to be a part of the powers conferred upon cities by this section:

"(a) To levy, assess and collect taxes and to borrow money within the limits prescribed by general law; and to levy and collect special assessments for benefits conferred.

"(b) To furnish all local public services; to purchase, hire, construct, own, maintain, and operate or lease local public utilities; to acquire, by condemnation or otherwise, within or without the corporate limits, property necessary for any such purpose, subject to restrictions imposed by general law for the protection of other communities; and to grant local public utility franchises and regulate the exercise thereof.

"(c) To make local public improvements and to acquire, by condemnation or otherwise, property within its corporate limits necessary for such improvements; and also to acquire an excess over that need for any such improvement, and to sell or lease such excess property with restrictions, in order to protect and preserve the improvement.

"(d) To issue and sell bonds on the security of any such excess property, or of any public utility owned by the city, or of the revenues thereof, or both, including in the case of a public utility, if deemed desirable by the city, a franchise stating the terms upon which, in case of foreclosure, the purchaser may operate such utility.

"(e) To organize and administer public schools and

libraries, subject to the general laws establishing a standard of education for the state.

"(f) To adopt and enforce within their limits local police, sanitary and other similar regulations not in conflict with general laws.

"Except as otherwise provided in this act, the council shall have authority to determine by whom and in what manner the powers granted by this section shall be exercised."

Similar changes will easily convert the "Model Charter" into the form of a municipal corporations act.

II

EXPERTS IN MUNICIPAL GOVERNMENT AND THE NEW MODEL CHARTER

THE need of using experts in the administration of American cities requires demonstration less than it did formerly. Until a few years ago, their importance in securing good government was little perceived, even by people deeply interested in improving the condition of our cities and willing to adopt wide departures from traditional methods. But now, men holding very divergent views on political questions have come to see that their objects cannot be effectively attained, and, indeed, that no advance in the public welfare can be fully secured, unless the public makes use of the best tools it can find, and that the best tool of modern civilization is the trained human brain.

All thoughtful men agree to-day that, whatever our political merits in other respects, American cities have been on the whole less well administered than those of the most advanced countries in Europe; that the waste here has been greater, while the people have been less well served; and a careful study of the actual methods of operation shows that the contrast is due in great part to the use made of experts.

But the term itself is liable to misconception. Most people think of experts only as the members of the older professions or of the highly skilled trades — the lawyers, the physicians, the engineers, the watchmakers, the gasfitters, the men, in short, whom we must consult when something goes wrong, because they deal with things that we do not understand, and can do for us what we cannot do for ourselves at all. We think of the expert as the man without whom we are quite helpless. There is, however, another kind of expert, the man who can do things we can to some extent do for ourselves, but who can do them a great deal better. Every one can use a hammer and saw after a fashion, yet if he wants really good work done he employs a carpenter. Now all this is true of the public service. We have long realized that every city solicitor must be a lawyer, every city physician a doctor, and we are learning that no one is competent to design a steel bridge unless he is an engineer. But many people do not appreciate the fact that, although an intelligent man without special experience can after a fashion administer the police, the fire department, the streets, the schools, the poor relief, or the finances; can coördinate and keep in working order all these parts of the public service; and in rare instances can do these things remarkably well; yet an equally intelligent man who has had experience in the work and has been thoroughly trained therefor will, as a rule, do it much better, to the great benefit of the city and its inhabitants. The public administration of a large city is at least as difficult and complex as that of a railroad, and a railroad employs not only lawyers to conduct its law-suits, and engineers to lay out its lines and design its bridges, but also administrative experts — that is, men who have a special knowledge of railroad management and make it their career for life — and except for young men who are learning to be experts, it will employ no one else.

It is in this larger sense, that of men trained in municipal administration, and not alone in the limited meaning which includes only members of recognized civic professions, that the cities in the progressive countries of Europe employ experts. The forms of city government in these countries differ widely, but they all agree in giving to the experts a wide field and substantial influence; whereas the cities in the United States, whatever their type of charter, have for the most part been alike in making a comparatively slight use of officials with an expert knowledge of municipal administration.

In Germany, which is almost ostentatiously the land of experts, the actual, as well as the official, head of the city government is the Burgomaster. He is a municipal administrator by profession, being often called if successful in one place to a larger one, just as the president of a railroad is in America. He is assisted by a corps of subordinate professional administrators in the various departments, and he is advised by citizens who are not experts and are chosen by the electorate of the city; but the business, as the saying goes, is mainly done at the head of the table. That the German cities are well governed no one doubts; that the excellence of their management is chiefly due to the use of experts few men would venture to deny. Their ways are not altogether our ways, but we can learn something of the secret of their efficiency, and adapt it to our own conditions.

English traditions and methods are more like our own.

In form the city government is democratic, the whole power being vested in a council which issues from a popular vote. But the council works through a body of expert administrative officers, who are virtually permanent, and for whom municipal service is a lifelong career. Moreover, although in outward appearance the city business is conducted by the council and its committees, one cannot go very far under the surface without finding that in fact the influence of the experts, both on current administration and on civic policy, is very great. It is exerted quietly, inconspicuously, in the committee rooms, and especially through the chairmen of the committees who have usually served some years in the council and appreciate the weight that should be given to the opinions of men thoroughly familiar with the problems that arise. The influence of the permanent officials is not due to any political authority. It is simply that which expert knowledge, when given a fair chance, will properly command and it makes for efficiency, honesty, and progress in civic welfare. The example of England is especially valuable for us because here, as there, the form must be democratic, the popular element must be strongly in evidence, and the expert had better not be too prominent. Above all he must take no part in politics, for politics naturally involves a not infrequent change of personnel which is quite inconsistent with permanence of tenure. The most important thing for the improvement of city government in the United States to-day is to learn to make a large use of experts and to use them in a form consistent with popular institutions.

That the permanent officials in the English cities are by no means out of harmony with democratic conditions, that they are the ministers, not the masters, of the public, no one familiar with the facts will doubt. A recent change, indeed, in English civic administration is noteworthy in this connection. Under the former school-boards the influence of the clerks of the boards, who corresponded to our superintendents of schools, was as a rule distinctly less than that of other permanent officials in the city; but with the abolition of these boards, and the transfer of their powers to the city or borough councils, there has been a marked increase in the importance of the professional school administrators. The city councils from their experience understood better their value and how to make use of it. Curiously enough a similar change has taken place in the position of superintendents of schools here. Within a generation their occupation has become much more of a profession, their tenure has become more permanent, their influence in the management of the public schools has greatly increased, they have more control over the qualifications and the selection of teachers, and their opinions on educational policy have far greater weight with the school committees. All this has taken place, not by legislative enactment, but by a growth of opinion among all people interested in education, among the members of the school boards and in the public at large. At the same time it may be observed that the management of the schools has not become bureaucratic, in the sense of getting out of touch with popular aspirations. On the contrary there has never been a time when the school authorities were

EXPERTS IN GOVERNMENT

striving so earnestly as they are now to discover the real needs of the public, to work out plans for vocational and other training that will prepare the children for their occupations in life. It is a case where the people have learned to use good tools for a most important public object.

In order to make good use of a piece of machinery, one must understand it. Men did not learn to manage gasoline engines without running at first a risk of breaking their arms in cranking them or of getting the machinery out of order. This is not less true of a human mechanism or institution than of physical machinery. The conditions of its existence and functions must be comprehended or it will fail to fulfill its purpose and may become at best useless, at worst mischievous. The first condition of expert public service is permanence. A temporary expert is a contradiction in terms. An expert is one who has learned his business by long experience, who makes it his work in life, the profession to which he devotes his chief thought and labor until he obtains a command of its problems that other men do not possess. But in order that a man of ability should give up the chance of other occupations to devote himself wholly to a certain field of work, he must have a reasonable expectation that if successful he can make it a career, respected, enduring and fairly remunerated. The salary need not be very large if the employment is constant and there is a good prospect of promotion for efficient service. But if, when meritorious, a man is likely to be dropped for reasons unrelated to his own work; if, for example, a superintendent of streets, or of schools, or a city treasurer is in danger of losing his office because the citizens have changed their minds about a national tariff, or the granting of liquor licenses; his occupation cannot be a career. It cannot have the nature of a profession, nor can there be any certainty that the incumbent will remain long enough in office to give the real service needed from an expert. In fact, it is morally certain that under such conditions the men in the offices of the city will not be experts in city administration, that they will not devote their whole lives to the study and practice of municipal service.

It follows that if we hope to use experts in our cities they must not hold elective offices, that their positions must be independent of political change. The duty of a superintendent of streets, or of schools, for example, is to furnish good streets or good schools, and keep them in proper condition. After hearing the advice of the expert, the public, through its political representatives, must decide what streets or what schools it will have and how much it will spend upon them; and the superintendent must do the best he can with the means given him. He must not be held responsible for the political decision, with which he may not have agreed, but for the way it has been carried out. Another conclusion follows with equal certainty. If the officer is to be an expert, and therefore, if he is to be permanent, he must keep entirely out of politics, both national and local. He must take no part in electoral campaigns, although the issues may be ones that affect his department or his plans. This may seem to be going very far. If, for instance, a Superintendent of Schools has been urging on his board a larger expenditure on high schools, and it happens that this becomes one of the issues in a city election, it may seem absurd to say that he ought not to make speeches at campaign meetings in its favor; and yet if he does, he may well lose his place if the election goes against him. He can speak at other times but not then. Extraordinary cases may, of course arise, where corruption is involved, when a permanent official must speak out, whatever the consequences, cases where his duty as a citizen overrides his duty as a permanent expert. But in such a case he is compelled not only to risk his own career but also to impair the certainty of tenure of all permanent experts. Instances of this kind should be exceedingly rare where the position of the expert is well recognized and understood. The permanent expert must not lay his hands on politics and elections if they are not to lay their hands on him; he must keep himself free from politics if his office is to be free from politics. Nor must he in a democracy strive for political notoriety or public applause. A truly ambitious and worthy permanent official is abundantly satisfied by recognition from his employers and the members of the profession to which he belongs. This is one of the few cases where a man must forego the exercise of some of the privileges of citizenship to render a greater public service.

Finally, in order that the country may enjoy the benefits of a corps of permanent municipal experts, some adequate system of recruiting and training them must exist, and some method of promotion which opens a prospect of a desirable career in life. The recruiting and training may be provided in various ways. Men may be brought in young from other occupations and learn their duties in the service of the city, as they do in England, and as is usually the case in commercial and industrial life here; or they may be specially trained by instruction in schools and colleges, and this would seem to be more in accord with the growing tendency of American education. But no plan of recruiting or training will avail anything if the subsequent career is not inviting. To provide a career worth pursuing it is essential that there should be sufficient certainty of promotion for merit, and in all but the largest cities this means that men who prove valuable must have a chance of advancement in other places than their own. We shall never have efficient municipal administration by expert officials until our cities, like our business, educational and other institutions, outgrow the idea that offices should be a perquisite of local citizens instead of a means of serving the public.

But, above all, we cannot have expert administration until a large part of the intelligent citizens appreciate the need of it; until they realize that it is the only method of making our cities more comfortable for their inhabitants. For some time to come, the effort must be in a large part a campaign of education, teaching as much as possible by example. We must strive to disabuse the public of the impression that permanent officials involve government by a rigid and unpopular bureaucracy. It is only by educating the electorate in the proper use of such men that progress can be made; for the main difficulty before us lies in the fact that the true functions of experts in government cannot be prescribed by law.

Americans are prone to rely on legal provisions, on constitutional machinery, and to trust to that alone for results. But this cannot be done in the case of permanent administrative officials, because in the very nature of things the functions of the expert and the layman cannot be exactly defined. They must rest to some extent upon mutual confidence and respect; upon a free interchange of views, and incessant compromises of opinion voluntarily made. In every form of administration, and especially in a democracy, both expert and lay elements are indispensable for the best results; the expert for his knowledge of the most effective means of attaining the results desired; the layman to keep the expert in touch with public opinion, to preserve him from falling into ruts, to prevent the trees from obscuring his view of the forest. They are not two antagonistic elements, each seeking to enlarge its sphere of action at the expense of the other. They are not even independent powers in the government, each working in a distinct field, performing its appropriate acts, and having for these purposes an authority of its own. On the contrary, they are two parts of the same mechanism, or we may liken them to two elements in one chemical compound whose combined qualities give the character to the substance. In a sense, they take part jointly in every act performed. On everything that is done the expert should be consulted, and every act, however minute, technical or in the nature of routine, should be done with the approval, express or implied, of the lay controlling body which must assume to the public the responsibility therefor. The lay body must never cast the blame upon the expert. If convinced that he is unfit for his position it may remove him; for permanence does not mean incompetence in office. But a removal must only mean a search for a better man to hold permanently, that is by a tenure dependent only upon his professional work. The expert, on the other hand, must realize that he is not the ultimate authority; that everything which ought in his opinion to be done cannot be accomplished; that he has a double function, the conduct of current administration, and persuading the representatives of the public so far as he can that his plans are wise.

It may seem that such a delicate interlacing relationship must be very difficult to create and maintain, but experience shows that this is not true. If the laymen in control recognize that they are not experts, and the expert that he is not an independent authority, still less a dictator, but an employee,— a servant not a master of the public,— it is astonishing how naturally the relations of the two adjust themselves, and with how little friction the result works itself out. There is only one serious danger in our cities, that of the use of appointments to offices as political patronage. Unless this can be eliminated from municipal government; until the citizens feel that the city ought to be managed in their interest, and not in the interest of a small group of office holders and office seekers; the use of experts will certainly be unsatisfactory and probably a failure.

If the foregoing is a fair statement of the functions of permanent experts and their relation to the representatives of the public it is evident that no charter can regulate their powers and duties rigidly, or even prescribe their appointment in a way that will ensure the result

EXPERTS IN GOVERNMENT

desired. The utmost that can be done is to provide conditions which will render their employment obvious and natural, and have a tendency to educate public opinion on the subject. This is what the new model charter prepared by the National Municipal League seeks to do. It provides for a city council, elected at large, which has full power and authority to conduct the public business except as otherwise prescribed by the charter. The council is to elect one of its members chairman with the title of mayor. He is the official head of the city and represents it on all public occasions, but except in case of danger or emergency he is not its administrative head and acts only as chairman of the council. He is the presiding member of a body which is not intended to administer directly the affairs of the city, but to select, direct and control the officers who do so. For this purpose the council is to appoint a city manager as the chief executive officer of the city; and it is provided that " he shall be chosen solely on the basis of his executive and administrative qualifications," and that the " choice shall not be limited to inhabitants of the city or state." Clearly these provisions governing the selection cannot be enforced by law. There is nothing to prevent the council from appointing a mere political wire-puller or the candidate of the local boss, and asserting that he was chosen solely on the basis of his executive and administrative qualifications. Nor could any provision be devised that would really restrict the choice, and yet leave to the council the freedom in selection that is necessary if the relations between the manager and the council are to be such as to produce good government. When expert municipal administration has become an established profession it will be possible, and may be wise, to prescribe that the city manager shall be a member thereof, but no such profession exists to-day. Nevertheless the provisions of the charter are by no means useless. They give notice to the council and to the public of the kind of man who ought to be chosen; they constrain the council to justify the appointment on those grounds, and they give to every member of the council and to every citizen a good ground for criticism of a selection made for political reasons. They indicate the selection of an expert, and in cities that desire good government they not only make the selection of an expert administrator possible, but tend to encourage and promote it. In short they provide a plan for expert administration and have an educational value for the public in that direction.

The same may be said about the city manager's tenure of office. If incompetent or negligent there must be some means of removing him, and as the council is responsible for his administration, and must work with and through him, the power of removal must rest with its members. But to discourage removal for political motives his appointment is to be made for an indefinite period, and hence there is no time when the question of reëlection comes up. He cannot be quietly dropped at the end of a term, but must be formally removed for cause. Moreover it is provided that he may demand written charges and a public hearing. This again does not fetter the council, but has a strong tendency to enlighten the public and prevent abuse.

Then comes the subject of his functions. The charter provides that he " shall be responsible to the council for the proper administration of all affairs of the city, and to that end shall make all appointments"; that he "shall prepare and submit to the council the annual budget"; and that, "except when the council is considering his removal, he shall be entitled to be present at all meetings of the council and of its committees and to take part in their discussions." The provisions express very clearly the general principles that ought to govern the work of the expert administrator, and his relations to the representatives of the public. He is to have the direct charge of all the city business, and in fact, it is especially provided in section 3 of the charter that "Except for the purpose of inquiry the council and its members shall deal with the administrative service solely through the city manager, and neither the council nor any member thereof shall give orders to any of the subordinates of the city manager either publicly or privately"— any such order being made a criminal offense. Nevertheless he is responsible for his management to the council, which can approve or disagree with what he does, and may by ordinance or resolution give him directions. He submits the budget for the ensuing year which they are not bound to accept, but which they must receive and therefore consider, and which in the main they will almost inevitably adopt.

In general the relation of the city manager to the council are those which ought to prevail between the expert and the laymen in any well regulated enterprise or institution. In the case of appointments to office it was thought necessary to go farther. Normally appointments to the higher posts in a service might well be subject to approval by the board of trustees or directors, but the danger of using city offices as political spoils, and the pressure that is sure to be brought to bear upon the council for that purpose, are so great that it was deemed wise to remove appointments from the control of the council altogether. It was therefore provided, not only that the city manager shall make all appointments, but also in the section already referred to that " Neither the council nor any of its members shall dictate the appointment of any person to office or employment by the city manager, or in any manner interfere with or prevent the city manager in exercising his own judgment in the appointment of officers and employees in the administrative service,"— any such dictation or interference being likewise made a punishable offense.

Finally the provision that the city manager shall be present at all meetings of the council and its committees is absolutely essential for the proper relations between them. If he is not present he cannot exert the influence upon their opinions that he ought to have, nor can they exercise so constant and comprehensive a supervision as they should. He will be to some extent an outside authority. There cannot be the free interchange of views, the mutual give and take that ought to exist. It will be observed that, except for the appointment of subordinate officials and employees, the provisions about the city manager are mainly designed to create the conditions under which an expert administrator should work, to indicate what his position should be, and to lead the public to understand it.

This is no less true of the provisions relating to the

EXPERTS IN GOVERNMENT

heads of departments, called in the charter directors. Each of them must be chosen "on the basis of his general executive and administrative experience and ability and of his education, training and experience in the class of work which he is to administer." As in the case of the city manager this has a moral rather than a legal value. But for the directors the charter goes on to be more specific. It provides as follows: "The director of the department of law shall be a lawyer, of public health a sanitary engineer or a member of the medical profession, of public works an engineer, of education a teacher by profession, of public safety and welfare a man who has had administrative experience, and of public finance a man who has had experience in banking, accounting or other financial matters; or in each case the man must have rendered active service in the same department in this or some other city." The provision may not be, and probably no provision could wisely be, made legally enforceable; but it states very distinctly that the director must be an expert in a field closely related, at least, to the one for which he is appointed; and it will be very hard to evade this without provoking criticism which is obviously well founded. It is, indeed, by opening the door to obvious criticism whenever the spirit of the charter is violated that provisions for the employment of experts can be most effectively enforced.

The directors are appointed and removable by the city manager, to whom alone they are directly responsible for the management of their departments. This is in accordance with the policy of keeping the members of the council from interfering with the details of administration; while to indicate the position of the directors as real heads of the departments and at the same time their relations to the city manager as his subordinates and assistants, it is provided that they shall prepare departmental estimates, make other reports and recommendations, and give their advice whenever requested by him. In order to reduce as far as possible the danger of removal for political reasons, there is a provision in the case of the directors, as in that of the city manager himself, for written charges and a public hearing.

The appointment of officials and employees to positions of less importance in the service of the city is governed by elaborate provisions in the charter for a civil service board and selection by competitive examination. But that subject will be treated in a separate chapter in this book, and it would be out of place to discuss it here. It is well, however, to point out that the use of experts in city government can be a reality, and bring the improvement which it is capable of producing, only in case political patronage, the appointment to public office in consideration of service to a party or a candidate instead of service to the public, is wholly abolished; and experience has yet shown no way of doing this for the great mass of employments except competitive examinations conducted by a civil service board. The civil service rules are, therefore, essential to the plan for municipal government set forth in the new model charter.

In closing, let us remember that the plan proposed is able at the most to provide a method whereby American cities can obtain the use of experts in administration if they want it. Such a change must come if we are to enjoy as good city government as other progressive countries. But no charter can produce a system whereby the use of expert administrators may be enforced by law against the wishes of the voters or of the men they elect to represent them. The model charter does all that can be done by providing an organization in which the use of trained men will be as natural as possible, and which will tend to educate the public in their employment. If the city manager is himself a true professional administrator, and remains in office long enough to acquire a powerful influence, it is certain that he will draw to his aid, and maintain, a corps of expert subordinates with the same professional spirit that he has himself. And even if he is not at first a trained expert, yet if the regulations governing the directors of the departments are not grossly violated, these men will have an expert knowledge and a professional attitude that will in time almost inevitably extend itself to the post of city manager. No sensible man believes that human institutions can be regenerated instantly by the words of a statute or charter. We must be satisfied if the road is pointed out and made passable. The city manager plan of municipal government is not the only one for reaching the end in view, but it is the best that has yet been proposed for American cities, and the one most in harmony with the spirit of our institutions.

III

CIVIL SERVICE AND EFFICIENCY

THE dominant note in our model city charter is the elimination of the sytem of checks and balances in the organization of our cities and the substitution therefor of responsible government under a small legislative chamber which in its turn selects a single administrative head. The city manager plan represents not merely the type in common use in business corporations, but also in parliamentary government. This administrative chief is to be invested with the fullest powers and neither the council by which he is elected, nor its members are to interfere with him in his duties. He is merely to be accountable for the results of his stewardship and he is therefore to have the sole authority over his heads of departments and all subordinate officers and employees.

NECESSITY FOR THE COMPETITIVE SYSTEM

If this thought were pressed to its logical conclusion he should have the right to appoint as well as to promote, discipline and remove every official in the service. It has been found in practical experience, however, that the discretionary power of appointment lodged in a chief executive or in the heads of departments is quite sure to be abused and perverted to injurious political ends. The appointing officer is beset by persistent and often irresistible importunities for places by those who wield a controlling political power in the community. Political and personal services are rewarded by public office. The unworthy and the unfit are chosen and the entire community is infected with corruption. It has been found that the way to avoid this is to make appointments to purely administrative places by a system of competitive examinations. This system has been successfully tried not only in our federal government, in several of the states and in most of our principal cities, but it was long since so successfully grafted upon the parliamentary system of government in England that when the administration there is changed, very few places in the service are included in the change, and the officials who have been selected by competitive examinations remain undisturbed.

The evils of the political or patronage system in our municipalities have been particularly great and no city can hope to avoid these evils unless the competitive system of appointments is adopted. The manager's power to control his subordinates is amply secured so long as his right to discipline them and to dismiss the undesirable remains unimpaired. Hence administrative officers, if they be not politicians, generally look with satisfaction and relief upon a system which takes the place of an employment bureau, and furnishes them with the names of those who have shown the best qualifications after a competitive test.

So the committee drafting the model charter felt that it would be unwise to be the mere slaves of a formula in regard to the unlimited authority of the city manager, but that the results of general experience should be recognized in reference to appointments, transfers, promotions, reductions and removals by the adoption of the competitive system. We have therefore followed the best precedents of federal, state and municipal civil service laws.

Need of Detailed Provisions.— In drawing up these provisions we have departed in another respect from the plan adopted in other parts of this model charter. Elsewhere we have generally prescribed the mere framework of government, leaving each city to develop the details at its own will by means of its own ordinances, rules or regulations. But as to the competitive system experience has shown that in communities unfamiliar with that system the failure to include specific and detailed provisions has been followed by a laxity in the administration of the law which deprives it of much of its efficacy. These provisions therefore are set forth with greater detail than most others affecting municipal administration. It was felt that the doors to political intrigue and manipulation ought to be effectively closed before any efficient administration can be looked for in city government.

Method of Selecting the Civil Service Board

The initial difficulty in creating a system which shall eliminate politics and spoils is in securing in the first place a civil service board independent of political and personal manipulation and therefore independent of the council and even of the manager himself. For if council or manager can control the board and appoint and remove its members at pleasure such a board is likely to be the mere creature of the power to which it owes its existence, and if politics infects the course of appointments it may well infect all the branches of administration. Unnecessary and unreasonable exceptions may be made to the competitive principle and large numbers of "temporary appointments" may be allowed. Even the examinations may be perverted in the hands of unscrupulous men to secure certain desired political results.

It is not easy to divorce the civil service board from *all* political influence because the ultimate source of its power is bound, in a republican government, to be some person or body, whether governor, council, mayor or manager who has been either directly or indirectly chosen by political methods. In order to remove the board as far as possible from political control a plan has been suggested which is now under consideration by the National Civil Service Reform League, to appoint the members by competitive examinations. The plan is this: that the governor of the state shall appoint a special examining board of three persons, one a member, chief examiner or secretary of some civil service commission already in existence, a second person, one who has been engaged continuously for two or more years in selecting trained employees for positions involving professional or technical skill, and the third a judge of a court of record. The special examiners are to select by competitive examinations a state civil service commissioner or commissioners and the state commission is to select by similar competitive examinations the municipal civil service commission or board, and the members both of the state commission and the municipal board are to hold their places indefinitely unless removed for malfeasance in office upon written charges duly proved before a special board appointed for the purpose. This plan for the appointment and removal of a civil service board would undoubtedly do much to remove that body from political influence, but it has not yet been tried and your committee did not feel that they should recommend for adoption in the model charter a measure untested by practical experience.[1] The plan which offers the nearest approach to independence and which has been so tested is an independent appointment of three members of a civil service board by the city council for overlapping terms of six years each, so arranged that one member retires every two years, any member of the board to be removable for negligence, incapacity or malfeasance by a four-fifths vote of the council after written charges upon at least ten days' notice and after a public hearing. It is recognized that this does not furnish a perfect protection against all political influence, but it gives the members of the board a reasonable independence of the appointing power and where the public sentiment in a city is sufficiently strong to adopt the civil service provisions of our model charter it seems to offer a reasonable assurance that these provisions will be enforced and political appointments generally eliminated.

While the model charter provides that the civil service board shall consist of three members it is realized that in small towns a single civil service commissioner might be preferable. Moreover in those places where there is a state civil service commission the examinations and certifi-

[1] Full details as to this proposed model civil service law can be secured from the secretary of the National Civil Service Reform League, 79 Wall Street, New York.

cations might be made through the agency of that commission if the community in question felt disposed to relinquish to that extent the control of this part of its domestic administration.

The model charter provides that the board should employ a secretary and chief examiner, though the same person may perform the duties of both offices. It may be found desirable in some cases that the secretary and the chief examiner shall themselves constitute two out of the three members of the board, the third member being its president. It might also be provided that the places of secretary and chief examiner should be filled by competitive examination or by promotion or transfer from other positions in the competitive classified service. This would keep these places from political influence.

Scope of the Competitive Service.—It is provided that the superintendents, principals and teachers of schools as well as the heads of the various departments may be classified *if so directed by the council*. The question whether the public school service shall be included in the classified system is one which ought to be determined by local conditions.

The proposition that the heads of the different departments shall be selected by competitive tests is one that may be regarded as radical by those not familiar with the constant progress of the merit system, both in the federal government and in various states and cities. At the beginning of this reform movement large classes of employees were excepted, including those in expert and responsible administrative positions, because it was then considered that men of high grade would not submit to examinations. This, however, is no longer the case. It is found that men of excellent professional, scientific and administrative attainments actually do compete in these tests. The examinations for such places are no longer mere written scholastic question sheets and answers, and the examiners are not the ordinary subordinates and employees of the civil service board, but are experts of high rank and character specially called in to prepare the competitive tests and to pass upon the qualifications of the competitors. Professional men and administrators of large experience and high character no longer feel a reluctance in submitting to an investigation. Hence there is no dearth of competitors and those who stand at the top are found to be excellent material out of which to select competent public servants.

In the federal service the supervising architect of the treasury is thus chosen as well as the professor of chemistry in the public health and marine service, and engineers of all kinds and in all branches of the government, also the superintendent of the lighthouse service as well as Indian reservation superintendents.[1] The applicant is required to give the names and addresses of say ten persons, five of whom have been in superior or subordinate business relations with him and have personal knowledge of his qualifications. He submits a complete statement of his general education, the institutions where he has studied and for how long and the courses pursued. He must detail the facts of his life, his environments, and occupations

[1] See article on "Expert City Management," by W. D. Foulke, *National Municipal Review*, Vol. I, page 549. C. R. W.

and show what special training he has had. He must furnish an account of his experience in managing men and describe his methods of dealing with them, and show what work he has done in an executive capacity. He must submit an essay or article to test his general intelligence. Each of these things are given ratings proportionate to their probable value in the successful administration of his office.

Such competitive tests have been successful in city government as well as in the federal service. In New York the chief of the fire department was selected on a competitive promotion examination. In Philadelphia the superintendent of the general hospital and the chief of the bureau of highways and street cleaning was selected by competitive tests. In Chicago the librarian of the great public library was so chosen, and he was one of the most eminent expert librarians in America. It is hoped that in the near future the most important administrative city offices under the city manager will be selected generally by methods similar to these.

Non-Competitive Places

It is indeed prescribed in our model charter that the civil service board may by unanimous vote provide for non-competitive tests for any position requiring peculiar and exceptional qualifications of a scientific, managerial, professional or educational character, but all such actions of the board and the reasons therefor shall be published in its annual report. This provision recognizes that there may, under exceptional circumstances, sometimes be a need of selecting a man by some other means than competition. In practice, however, such selection has nearly always been found to be injurious. Personal or political motives are apt to creep in and it is of the utmost importance that such exceptions be closely limited to cases of the strictest necessity. Indeed in any city where the framers of the charter believe that such exceptions can be safely dispensed with, these provisions may very wisely be omitted.

Selection from the Eligible Lists

In regard to the selection from the eligible lists an important question arose whether the appointing officer ought to be allowed to choose from the three candidates graded highest as in the federal service, or from the two graded highest, or whether he should be required to appoint the one graded highest of all. Where the selection is made from one out of three there is still some ground for the exercise of political or personal favor which is undesirable. Considerable abuses have crept into the federal service by reason of this liberty of choice, in the case, for instance, of the fourth class postmasterships and among rural free delivery carriers, where the number of names upon the entire list will not average more than three and where the advice of congressmen in regard to these appointments has been unlawfully solicited and received. It is found that these appointments are very largely political. In cases where there are many applicants and the eligible lists are longer, this political influence is less apparent and it is felt that the appointing power ought to have some choice in selecting subordinates. Moreover, in some places the constitutional provisions vesting the power of appointment in the superior officer have been construed to require that some such power of selection should be left to him. Our model charter therefore still follows the federal rule to this extent that the selection must be made from *not more* than the three candidates graded highest. But the civil service board may provide in its rules that the selection may be from the two candidates graded highest or that the man who stands at the top must be appointed. In many places (for instance in Chicago and in the Illinois state service) the highest man must receive the appointment. This eliminates all political or personal choice and where it has been adopted it has generally worked very well. If therefore in any city which is not hampered by constitutional provisions, it is felt that it is wiser to provide in the charter itself that the appointment must be made of the candidate graded highest or that the selection should be from the two highest, such a provision could be appropriately substituted for the one in our model charter.

Publicity of Eligible Lists

Another important provision not contained in the federal civil service law is that each list of eligibles with their respective grades shall be open to public inspection. If these lists can be kept secret by the civil service board there may be often no means of discovering whether personal or political favor may have dictated appointments, and there will always remain suspicion of this, even if the fact is otherwise. The federal civil service commission leaves these appointments thus open to suspicion when it refuses, as it has done, to allow the eligible lists to be inspected by any one except the appointing officer or some member of Congress. This evil ought not to be permitted in city administration.

Promotions

The primary purpose of the civil service reform movement was the exclusion of political influence in making appointments to office; in other words it was the overthrow of the spoils system, a system that infected and corrupted not only the civil service itself, but also the legislative department of government and the community at large in all its political activities — primaries, conventions and elections. This elimination of patronage is measurably secured by open competitive examinations for admission, and in the early days of the reform movement very little attention was paid to the general conduct of the civil service in other particulars. The fact that better men were secured by the competitive system than by personal and political appointments was very justly regarded as a secondary consideration. There were no provisions in the law regarding promotions, transfers, reductions, suspensions and removals, although rules regulating these things naturally developed afterwards in the operation of the new system. It was felt at first that these things could safely be left to the discretion of the operating officers who were responsible for the work of their departments. But it is now realized that uniform rules in these matters also have a distinct advantage where they do not too greatly limit the power of superior officers to control their subordinates, and that the civil service board can greatly aid such officers by prescribing appropriate tests and regulations. Our model charter, therefore, provides that this board shall prescribe in its rules for promotion from the lower grades to the higher based upon competitive records of efficiency and seniority to be furnished by the various departments or else upon competitive promotion tests or upon both together.

Efficiency Records

Seniority alone ought to play a very small part in making promotions from one grade to another. Efficiency records, if they are accurately kept, furnish the best methods of determining who should be thus advanced where the higher grades of the service are not essentially different from the lower grades. But experience shows that these efficiency records are often improperly kept. One head of an office, for instance, unwilling to discriminate between his subordinates, gives them all an equal grade, perhaps the highest rating possible. Such an efficiency record gives no information as to the relative deserts of the subordinates in that office. Perhaps in a neighboring office the man who marks his employees has a stricter notion of his duty; he will discriminate between them or perhaps mark them all at a lower grade. In case the promotions should involve a transfer from one office to another it is evident that such ratings will be very misleading. In order to secure any kind of justice it is necessary that the work of all the different offices should be coördinated and that essentially the same standards should be applied in each and the same methods adopted of determining the efficiency of each employee. For this purpose the civil service board becomes not only a civil service, but also an efficiency bureau whose advice to the manager or heads of departments ought to be of the highest value. Provisions for these things are made in our proposed model law. (Sec. 43.)[1]

[1] Lieut. C. P. Shaw, one of the most valued members of the League, sent to the secretary in answer to the referendum after the distribution of the final edition of the charter on March 15th, the following criticism of a portion of Section 43:

"By this section the powers of the board are prescribed as follows: 'The board shall fix standards of efficiency and recommend measures *for coördinating the operation of the various departments* and for increasing individual, *group and departmental efficiency.*' This provision, I believe, is wholly destructive of the undivided responsibility which the city manager plan is intended to place on the city manager. In my opinion, the proper method of coördinating the various departments and securing their hearty coöperation would be to form the heads of the various departments into the manager's cabinet, as it might be called, or if preferred, call it the council of efficiency, and thus by advising among themselves, the heads of departments who are most radically concerned in promoting departmental and group efficiency would have the strongest impelling motive to secure harmony of action, which itself is an essential element of efficiency. No outside body could possibly do the necessary investigation without producing more or less friction and lack of harmony. With the heads of departments acting together to secure the result in which they are all interested, there should be a minimum of friction and a maximum of efficiency.

"With the city manager selected as an expert for the express purpose of securing efficiency through the elimination of politics and the selection of his subordinates for ascertained fitness, both the civil service commission and the bureau of efficiency become naturally *his subordinate agencies* for attaining these ends, and hence should be so organized as always to work with him, and not be placed in a position of possible antagonism. They should report to him, and he should have the final word in every case."

The reason for adopting in the charter the provision that the civil service board rather than any manager's cabinet shall fix standards of efficiency is due to the fact that it is the civil service board and not the manager or heads of departments which passes upon the qualifications for admission to the civil service. It is intended that this civil service board shall be an expert body upon the question of employment, including also the efficiency of the employees, and this being the special function of such a board it was believed that the work could be better done

But when a promotion involves new duties essentially different from those in the lower place a mere record of efficiency is not enough. The candidate for promotion ought also to show that he understands the duties of the new place to which he aspires and a competitive examination held for this purpose is highly desirable. In these cases part of the rating should be based upon the efficiency record of the candidate and part upon the knowledge of the new duties as shown in the competitive examination. The civil service board acting in conjunction with the operating officers can best determine how far the efficiency records and how far the competitive examination should determine such promotions.

When the competitive system was first adopted it was felt that admissions ought to be made only to the lower grades of the service and that the higher grades ought to be filled by promotion. This plan furnishes the strongest incentive to do good work and the idea of beginning at the bottom and working up is one which has always been popular in our industrial institutions and conforms to our ideas of democratic equality of opportunity. The entrance examinations, however, necessarily have to be arranged in reference to the particular duties of the position to which the applicant seeks admission and where these

---

by them than by a cabinet composed of the heads of departments who have so many other functions and duties to perform. The charter does not propose that the board shall have the final determination in "coördinating the different departments and for increasing group and departmental efficiency," but simply that they shall *recommend* measures for this purpose. They thus become, as Mr. Shaw desires, "the manager's subordinate agencies," and since he has the final authority, it is not seen why there is likely to be any antagonism to the injury of the service.

duties are of a special character involving expert or professional attainments they can not be filled appropriately from the mere clerical or other general grades of the service. For example, a mere clerical examination will not test the qualifications for an engineer's place. A man can not well be promoted from a clerk's position to that of an engineer. Therefore a special engineer's examination has to be held for the latter position, even though it involves more responsible duties, a higher grade and better pay than a mere clerical place.

Still for the general service it used to be considered that a man ought to go up step by step to the highest position attainable; for instance, from clerk to chief clerk, and then to chief of the division, or bureau, and that appointments to these higher places ought to be made from among those who held lower positions.

But it is realized to-day that sometimes the higher place, especially if it be an administrative office involving a wide knowledge of affairs and great responsibility, cannot be adequately filled by promotion from the lower grades, and that men of wider attainments than those who entered the service from mere clerical grades are necessary and therefore that a new and special examination ought to be given and while those filling lower positions should be admitted to the competition, yet such competition ought not to be confined to them alone.

In this matter the experience of the English civil service has been most instructive. It was found there that the intellectual qualifications of those in the lower grades did not always include that liberal education, that knowledge of men and that general information essential in the higher positions. Applicants were therefore divided into two classes, one for ordinary clerkships and the other composed of highly trained men for higher positions. It was found that the men thus admitted were generally better fitted for dealing with members of Parliament and people outside the service than those obtained by promotion.

The so-called Ridley investigation into the service (1888-90), showed that while purely clerical work should be done by those entering the lower examinations and while the door of promotion should be open to all, that it was necessary to introduce a very limited number of men by a higher examination to fill some of the more important posts so that men of broad liberal culture should be attracted to the public service.[1] This plan has the disadvantage that it does not furnish the strongest incentive to good work on the part of the clerical force who, although they may have done their duty well, occasionally see men appointed from the outside to places above them. But their dissatisfaction is hardly to be weighed in the balance with the necessity of having broad men with wide attainments in the highest grades. The question is the same as that presented in industrial life. If the higher administrative places can be properly filled by those below, the employer will find it to his interest to fill them by promotion. If not, he looks elsewhere for the man he needs.

Lord Haldane, formerly war secretary and afterward Lord Chancellor, thus sets forth the reason why a higher education is necessary for the superior post: "When a civil servant comes in contact with an outside citizen, he has to persuade him and make the outsider see

[1] "The Civil Service of Great Britain," by Robert Moses.

that the point of view which the civil service represents is a reasonable one. That depends on his power to take a large view and to get at the principle and reason of the thing; and my experience is that the highly trained first division clerk is quite admirable for getting alongside the mind of the soldier, for getting alongside the mind of the civilian in the county association, for getting alongside the minds of the one hundred and one people you have to deal with in a complicated organization. . . . While I am not without sympathy with the complaint of democracy that the entrance to the higher positions in the civil service is by far too much the monopoly of a class, I reply that a highly educated clerk is essential for a particular kind of work which the state needs."

The evidence taken in the recent investigation by the Royal Commission in which Lord Haldane testified, showed that while there ought to have been more promotions and fewer appointments than were actually made yet that some such appointments were necessary (Moses, p. 241).

We have therefore provided in our model charter that appointments to such higher positions as shall be specified by the civil service board may, if the city manager approves, be made after competitive tests in which persons not in the service of the city may compete also, as well as applicants from the lower grades and from other branches of the service.

Investigations

Another clause in our civil service provisions provides that the civil service board may make investigations, not only in regard to the execution of the civil service sections of the law and of the rules established thereunder, but also concerning the general condition of the civil service of the city or any branch thereof. Such a provision has been found of immense advantage in many places, notably in Chicago, where it has enabled the civil service commission of that city to uncover many defects of administration, to suggest appropriate remedies and to remove from the service those who have been guilty of corruption, inefficiency and other shortcomings. Such a provision enables the civil service board to act in the capacity of a bureau of municipal research and with the power to subpœna and examine witnesses and compel the production of documents, and it thus furnishes a far more effective method of uncovering abuses than where investigations are made by some outside body without the necessary legal authority.

Removals

Probably the question in our civil service provisions upon which the widest difference of opinion now exists is that regarding removals. In the early days of the civil service reform movement it was believed that the right of the appointing officer to suspend, reduce or remove his subordinates ought to be absolutely unrestricted. It was believed that so long as the entrance to the civil service was adequately guarded the exit might safely be left open. Political removals under the spoils system were principally made because the superior officer had some particular personal or political friend or protégé whom he wanted to put into the coveted place and when he could not do this, it was thought that temptation to remove a subordinate who was doing his duty would be taken away. This view has in the main been justified by experience and since the adoption of the federal civil service law the number of political removals from the competitive classified service has greatly diminished. It may be truthfully said in a general way that there are a great many more men who are improperly kept in the service than those who are improperly removed. Still there were some unjust removals, some of them for personal and some for political reasons and as a check upon these removals it was insisted by the advocates of the merit system that the appointing officer should in all cases be obliged to state the reasons for such removal and should inform the man to be removed of any charges against him and give him an opportunity to answer and put his answer on record, but that no trial or examination of witnesses should be required except in the discretion of the removing officer. It was realized that the power of the superior officer to discipline his subordinates and to remove those whom he regarded as objectionable ought not to be impaired. George William Curtis, the leader of the reform movement in this country, said in his annual address at the meeting of the National Civil Service Reform League, August 4, 1886, "Removal for cause, if the cause were to be decided by any authority except that of the superior officer, instead of improving, would swiftly and enormously enhance the cost and ruin the efficiency of the public service by destroying subordination and making every lazy officer or clerk twice as lazy and incompetent as before."

Carl Schurz said on the same occasion, " I would leave to the appointing officer entire discretion in removing subordinates, but I should oblige him in all cases to state the reasons."

In 1896, the resolutions of the National Civil Service Reform League declared: " The League fully recognizes the importance of preserving to responsible superior officers the power of removal of their subordinates whenever in their judgment this power should be exercised in the public interest, but the League deems it no less important that the officer exercising this power should do it with full and trustworthy information as to the facts, and that reasonable safeguards should be afforded to employees against the loss of their livelihood for personal or political causes."

The rule of the federal civil service commission is drawn substantially in accordance with the above principle and it is provided that the commission shall have no jurisdiction to review the finding of the removing officer if the proper procedure be followed, unless it can be shown that the removal was for political or religious reasons. Throughout a long series of years the general effect of this removal rule has been excellent. The chief evil, as already remarked, is that there are not enough removals made and that a considerable number of inefficient men are permitted to stay in the service, and it is realized that there ought to be some method (automatic so far as possible) of getting rid of those men whom the superior officer, whether from kindness of heart, the desire to avoid trouble or other reasons, is unwilling to remove. A method for this has been found in the Chicago civil service law, which gives the civil service commission the power to make such removals upon written charges and after hearing before a trial board appointed by the commission. These charges may be made by one of the officers of the commission itself. It also becomes the duty of the commission to establish a standard of efficiency for employees with a schedule of demerits based upon attendance and discipline and where the average of the employee for a certain established period falls below 70% charges must be made and unless a proper excuse is shown the employee is removed. This right of the commission to make removals has in the main operated well, though it must be said that of late years the number of removals thus made has been extremely small. Whether this is due to the efficiency of the service or to some laxity in keeping the records or in making removals cannot be definitely stated. The Chicago law, however, goes further and not only gives to the civil service commission the power to remove, but also takes away that power entirely from the appointing officer. He has only the power to suspend for thirty days and it was believed by the committee proposing this model charter that thus to take away the power of discipline, including removal, from the superior officer would lead to the destruction of all proper subordination. The federal removal rule has therefore been substantially incorporated into our model charter with the additional powers as above described granted to the civil service board.

Lieut. Shaw also objects to the provision in the charter which establishes " Three agencies for the removal of officers or employees from the city service, namely, the city manager, the head of a department and the civil service board," and he adds:

"Experience with our Norfolk charter during the ten years that it has been in operation has abundantly proved that such a provision is absolutely unworkable and productive only of friction, confusion and inefficiency. In this charter, the mayor, the head of a department or the board of control can each dismiss. The arrangement is simply destructive of efficiency, and I should most strenuously protest against its incorporation into what claims to be 'A Model Charter.' The term 'Model' as applied to such a charter is wholly inapplicable. Instead of being called a 'model' it would better deserve, so far as this feature is concerned, the appellation 'A horrible example of how NOT TO DO IT.'"

Of this criticism it may be said that the experience of the Norfolk charter can hardly be conclusive since in that charter there was neither a city manager, invested with full administrative control nor a civil service board invested with the special power of determining efficiency and of making removals where that efficiency does not exist. A general board of control is quite a different sort of an organization.

In our proposed charter where the manager not only has the power to appoint but to dismiss the heads of departments, he can naturally control removals made by these department heads and no serious conflict of authority can arise. It might indeed have been just as well to have omitted the words " or by the head of the department in which he is employed " (Sect. 44), thus taking away the right from the heads of departments who would then have to secure the manager's previous approval for every dismissal, but it is not perceived that the insertion of these words substantially affects the manager's ultimate power. The head of a department will certainly not dismiss any man whom the manager seriously wishes to retain when his own tenure of office depends upon the approval of his chief.

The reasons for giving the civil service board a concurrent power to remove or reduce an official or employee upon written charges of misconduct preferred by any citizen after hearing and also the power to dismiss those who fall below the minimum standard of efficiency established by them, have been set forth in the above article. There is one great advantage in giving this board the ultimate power of removing an employee proved to be inefficient or guilty of misconduct. So long as the manager only can remove, or an appeal to the manager can be entertained, he is constantly liable to pressure and importunities from the men removed and their friends, and whenever any political influences are present it has been found by experience that such pressure and importunities often prevail. It is believed that managers generally will welcome the power thus given to an independent body to discharge employees who have been proved to be unworthy and to relieve them of this pressure and political influence.

The remaining civil service provisions speak for themselves. They are based, it is believed, upon the best precedents obtainable at the present time. The desirability of the competitive system in cities as well as in the national and state governments has been so abundantly established by experience that no additional arguments seem necessary in support of that system.

NOTE

In the foregoing discussion of the civil service provisions no reference has been made to their relation to the provisions made upon this subject in the first Municipal Program adopted by the National Municipal League in 1900. Indeed the difference between the original sections and those above discussed in respect to civil service is by no means so great as in regard to many other provisions in the model charter.

It was, however, found desirable in the first place to condense considerably the civil service sections adopted in 1900 in the matter of phraseology; secondly, to adapt them to the new commission manager plan of government, and thirdly to take advantage of the experience of intervening years and perfect a number of their provisions in accordance therewith. The main difference between the two sets of provisions are the following:

According to our original provisions the appointment of the civil service commission was vested in the mayor, who was to be the political as well as the administrative head of the city and was directly elected by the people. By this model charter the mayor as a chief executive no longer exists. The council is the supreme representative body, and the duties of the city manager are wholly administrative. Therefore the question naturally arose whether the civil service board should be elected by the council or appointed by the manager. Since the manager controlled the whole administration, if he also appointed and removed the civil service board, that board would be so absolutely dependent upon him that its functions in restraining his political or personal appointments would be greatly limited. The experience of many cities where the civil service board or commission has been the mere creature of the mayor has shown that it is desirable that that board should have more independence, hence it was determined that the appointing power should be lodged in the council, and this independence secured by long terms of office, six years each, so arranged that the term of one member should expire every two years. The board is thus a continuing body and not subject to control by the manager, the members being only removable for neglect, in capacity or malfeasance in office after written charges and a public hearing, and then only by a four-fifths vote of the council.

Both our Municipal Program of 1900 and the present model charter provide that the civil service board (or commissioners as they were formerly called) shall promulgate civil service rules or regulations, but the present provisions are more specific as to character of these rules. Moreover it is now provided that they are to promulgate these rules only after public notice and hearing. The element of publicity is considered of value, it being believed that if public hearings are granted before the rules are made or amended many imperfections which might result from inadvertence or lack of skill will be avoided.

The Municipal Program of 1900 provided that such regulations should provide for the classification of offices and employments. The present provisions prescribe that the rules shall provide also for the standardization of these positions and that salaries shall be uniform for like service in each grade. The present charter also states what are the exceptions from such classification; it is not to include offices elected by the people, or judges, and may or may not include the directors of executive departments or the superintendents or teachers of the public schools as may be directed by council.

The provisions for open competitive examination in our model charter although quite different in form from those in our former Municipal Program, are much the same in substance, a clause being added that non-competitive tests can only be given by unanimous vote of the board for positions requiring peculiar and exceptional qualifications of a scientific, managerial, professional or educational character, and such action of the board, with the reasons therefor, is to be published in its annual report.

A provision has been added in our present model that eligible lists shall remain in force not longer than two years. In the former program an eligible list was accessible to each person whose name appeared upon it. By the model charter it is open to public inspection. Provision is also made for re-instatement on such lists of persons separated from the service without fault or delinquency. By the former program, temporary appointments were limited to thirty days, by our model charter such appointments are not to exceed sixty days. Under the former, the period of probation was not to exceed three months; under the present it must not exceed six months.

The provisions in regard to promotion are much more explicit and detailed in the new model than in the previous one, and provide for promotion from the lower grades to the higher upon competitive records of efficiency and upon seniority, or upon competitive promotion tests, or both, and that appointments to higher positions may also be made after competitive tests in which persons not in the service of the city may also compete. An increase in compensation within a grade may be granted upon the basis of efficiency and seniority records.

The former program provided that the civil service commissioners should keep records of their proceedings and of the markings and grading upon examinations as well as all recommendations. The present model charter adds to this that the board is also to keep a public record of the conduct and efficiency of each person in the service. As to investigations, the board may make them, not only in respect to the execution of the civil service sections and the rules (as was provided for by the former program) but also concerning the general condition of the civil service of the city or any branch thereof and may fix standards, and recommend measures for increasing efficiency and for coördinating the operation of the various departments.

The provisions of the former program as to the roster of employees has been considerably condensed in our new model, but the roster now also includes ordinary laborers.

As to removals, though the phraseology is altered, the methods provided are much the same, but it is added in the present model charter that an official or employee may be removed, not only by the manager or head of department, but by the civil service board upon written charges of misconduct preferred by any citizen and after reasonable notice and full hearing and that the board shall fix a minimum standard of conduct and efficiency, and if the employee falls below this he must show cause why he should not be removed, and if no satisfactory reason is given he is to be removed, suspended or reduced in grade as the board shall determine.

The sections against fraudulent practices and the prohibition of political activity are quite similar in the two in their general features, but a few new elements have been introduced. For instance *no person whatsoever* shall solicit political assessments or contributions from any one in the classified service, this prohibition being no longer limited to officials or employees; also no person about to be appointed to a classified position shall execute a resignation in advance of his appointment.

Any person violating any of the penal provisions of the Act is not only liable to fine and imprisonment, but if he be an applicant he shall be excluded from examination, if an eligible, his name shall be stricken from the list, and if an officer or employee he shall be removed from the service.

Any taxpayer may not only recover for the city all money paid in violation of the charter, but may enjoin the board from illegally certifying a payroll for services rendered and the rules are to have the force of law. These are the chief points of difference between the present model charter and the Municipal Program of 1900 in regard to the Civil Service.

IV

CONSTITUTIONAL MUNICIPAL HOME RULE

NOTHING is clearer than that people living in cities must be permitted wide freedom in the management of their municipal affairs if they are to develop any considerable political capacity. In this, they are not peculiar. Everywhere local self-government is the best, if not the indispensable school of effective citizenship. Furthermore, self-government is the only means of escape from ignorant, ill-advised and corrupt local government; the only method by which efficient local government can be permanently attained.

While no political theory has been more ardently proclaimed in America than this, no principle has been so persistently violated in American practice respecting cities. The reasons for this contradiction between profession and practice need not be detailed here. They are to be found in traditions attaching to political institutions founded among and for a people largely rural; in the nature and strength of American political parties; and in the influence of those forces which, desiring to exploit the people of the cities through the control of public utilities services, have seen their chances of success increased if the cities were kept in strict bondage to the state legislatures. The result is sufficiently marked. Of the nations boasting free institutions America has, in general, granted her cities the smallest measure of local autonomy. In this respect she has lagged behind Great Britain and France and has been even less liberal than autocratic Prussia.

Upon the establishment of American independence, municipalities in America found themselves dependent on the legislatures of their respective states for the form of their governments and the powers which they might exercise. Legislative control of cities was unlimited. It should be said in passing that this was, and is, in no sense unusual. The most progressive and freest cities of Great Britain and Europe receive their systems of governments and derive their powers from legislative grants. Moreover, the power of these legislatures over the municipalities within their jurisdiction is not limited by any provisions of superior law such as may be afforded by our state constitutions. In Great Britain and Europe this power has, on the whole, been generously used. Cities have been provided with simple and flexible forms of government, granted broad powers, and then " through a wise and salutary neglect," permitted to settle their own problems. The result is a large measure of municipal freedom in the exercise of which the cities have not only made great progress, but have provided the chief training ground for self-government.

The history of legislative control of cities in the United States has been very different. Through a combination of the forces already mentioned, legislative treatment of cities became increasingly harassing and illiberal during the last three-quarters of the nineteenth century. So long as there were no cities of considerable size and the total urban population was relatively small this was not of great moment. However, by the middle of the century, the municipal problem had become of such importance that it was no longer possible to remain indifferent as to how cities were governed. By that time, also, the state legislatures had begun to lose some of their original high repute because of their action regarding other matters than cities. To meet these growing legislative defects resort was had to the state constitutions. A cure was sought in constitutional provisions prohibiting the state legislatures from passing certain laws.

One of the most flagrant abuses during the period of unrestricted legislative power was the enactment of special city charters. Properly employed, this power might have been put to the laudable use of meeting the peculiar needs of individual cities. In actual practice, special legislation became a favorite weapon in the armory of national party politics. The governments of cities were frequently ripped up and reconstructed with the sole end in view of strengthening the majority party in the state legislature, or at least for the purpose of weakening the rival party. By dealing with cities individually, municipal offices and other patronage could be made to contribute to the strength of the dominant party. This pernicious use of legislative power did not always take the form of a complete city charter. It also came to be used for the purpose of making unsolicited amendments to city charters varying in importance from changing the name of the municipality to granting local public utility franchises.

Almost exactly at the middle of the nineteenth century, states began to insert provisions in their constitutions prohibiting their legislatures from passing special laws for the incorporation and organization of municipalities or for changing or amending their charters. In some states, these provisions were practically nullified by dividing the cities into classes and passing laws applicable to each class. There were instances in which the state supreme court upheld classifications of such a nature that the old era of special legislation was abolished only in name. On the other hand, where legislation by classification was prevented, another difficulty arose. Municipalities, large and small, were required to conform to one rigid system regardless of special circumstances or needs. Furthermore, it was found that the requirement of general legislation did not entirely preclude political manipulation by the state legislatures. Municipal codes, general in form, frequently had a decidedly partisan cast and the same could be said of amendments thereto. It was also found that the requirement of general legislation hindered rather than aided the cities in their struggle to secure adequate powers.

The movement for constitutional restriction of state legislatures did not end with the prohibition of special legislation. There was a tendency to add specific prohibitions against the passage of specified laws respecting cities. On the whole, this policy of negation served a useful purpose. It did stop a certain amount of political tampering, and cut off a good deal of corrupt legislation, but enough interference was still possible to be annoying and hampering. Municipal powers were ridiculously inadequate, and the very constitutional restrictions inserted to protect the municipalities sometimes offered a plausible excuse for legislative inaction when relief was sought. As a result of these experiments, it became increasingly clear that a mere policy of negation on legislative action was insufficient.

Even under the most severe constitutional restrictions, the state legislatures could still dictate the form of city government in minute detail and give, withhold or take away powers at will. As a result, city governments remained complex and rigid in form, unadaptable to cities of varying sizes, tied to national party organizations and without adequate power to deal with local needs. An enlightened legislature could have avoided these difficulties. France and England have found it possible to provide a simple and flexible form of organization which is applicable to municipalities of great diversity in population. The same nations by legislative act have given their municipalities ample power to deal with local affairs. Unfortunately, an intelligent and sympathetic conception of the municipal problem has rarely manifested itself in an American state legislature.

Out of this situation, the movement for constitutional municipal home rule was a logical development. The policy of restricting legislative power over cities had produced only negative results and even those not all that had been expected. In addition to protection from legislative interference, the cities needed positive action which would enable them to meet their growing needs and emancipate themselves from the corrupting forces which were preying upon them. There appeared to be no reasonable hope of securing such action from a state legislature. It is not strange, therefore, that the idea arose of carrying the American doctrine of federalism one step farther by granting certain powers to cities through the fundamental law of the state. Constitutional municipal home rule is, thus, but an expansion into a sort of intra-state federalism of the earlier practice of restricting legislative power over cities. Its purpose was to continue and extend such restrictions by adding a positive quality which they had previously lacked. It was a reply to the refusal of state legislatures to grant municipalities a reasonable degree of freedom in the management of local affairs.

The first home rule provision was embodied in the Missouri Constitution of 1875. In the light of more than forty years of experience since acquired, and of the later conception of municipal freedom, this was an awkward and timorous effort. Its operation was restricted to cities of more than 100,000 inhabitants. Any such city was authorized to " frame a charter for its own government, consistent with and subject to the constitution and laws " of the state. A further restriction required that any such charter should provide for a mayor and two houses of legislation. The work of framing a charter was placed in the hands of a board of thirteen freeholders chosen by the voters of the city. A charter so framed would supersede any existing charter and amendments thereto, if approved by four-sevenths of the voters at a general or special election. These provisions of the Missouri constitution have not been changed since their adoption, except that in 1902 St. Louis was released from the necessity of having a council of two houses.

In 1875, St. Louis was the only city in Missouri having more than 100,000 inhabitants. In the course of time Kansas City also exceeded that number, but so far only those two cities come within the Missouri home rule provisions. In many other respects this first attempt to free cities by constitutional grant left much to be desired. The essential grant of power was that which authorized a city " to frame a charter for its own government," which, when properly adopted, should " supersede any existing charter and amendments thereto." However, this grant of power was qualified by the provision that any charter so framed must " be consistent with and subject to the constitution and laws " of the state. This language raised a series of perplexing questions: What might a city properly include in a charter for its own government? Was a home rule charter subject to all general laws of the state or only to those dealing with other than municipal matters? Would a law dealing with municipal affairs repeal a conflicting provision of a home rule charter previously adopted? These and many other questions could only be answered by appeal to the courts as cases arose. Unfortunately, the decisions of the Supreme Court of Missouri in such cases have been vacillating in the extreme. However, it is easy to be overcritical of this first attempt to free cities by constitutional process. The proponents of the idea had no precedent to guide them and the provisions which they secured were only such as could be wrung from a cautious and reluctant constitutional convention. It was no inconsiderable achievement to have introduced a method of dealing with cities which, though imperfect in form, reversed the Anglo-Saxon practice of centuries. Moreover, in spite of the defective character of the provisions and of the sometimes inconsistent course of the Supreme Court, probably no one acquainted with the municipal history of St. Louis and Kansas City would deny that the Missouri experiment has been of positive value. As a result of it those two cities have acquired fuller control of their destinies than is permitted to most municipalities in the United States.

The first state to follow the lead of Missouri was one whose people are less fearful of experimentation and more persistent in their efforts to achieve any purpose which they have set for themselves. In 1879 a provision for constitutional municipal home rule was written into the constitution of California. In its original form, this was practically a duplicate of the home rule sections of the Missouri constitution. Its operation was restricted to cities of over 100,000 population, which made it applicable at that time only to San Francisco. However, the people of California cities did not rest content with this imperfect charter of liberty. In 1887, home rule powers were extended to cities having over 10,000 inhabitants and they were again widened in 1892 to include cities of over 3,500 population. Furthermore, as the cities acquired experience under the home rule sections, and especially as the supreme court of the state rendered decisions adverse to municipal aspirations, amendment after amendment to the constitution was adopted extending and consolidating the sphere of local autonomy. Thus, when it appeared that the Supreme Court would hold that any provision of a home rule charter would be subject to a general law subsequently passed dealing with the same matter, the constitution was amended to provide that home rule charters should be subject to and controlled by general laws "*except in municipal affairs.*" In this manner, an attempt was made to make it clear that within a certain sphere, cities which had framed and adopted charters were not subject to state control. Not content with establishing the supremacy of a home rule charter within the general domain of municipal affairs, an amendment was adopted at the same election making it competent for any such charter to deal with certain specified measures. These included the constitution, regulation, government and jurisdiction of police courts; the election or appointment of boards of education; the establishment of boards of police commissioners, and the constitution, regulation, compensation and government of such boards and of the municipal police force, and finally the election or appointments of boards of election, their regulation, compensation, etc. In this manner, cities framing and adopting charters were authorized by specific enumeration to deal with matters which there was reason to fear the courts would hold were not strictly municipal in character.

In 1894, an amendment was adopted authorizing the consolidation of city and county government into one municipal government with one set of officers. Three years later, a further amendment made it clear that any charter framed for a consolidated city and county could provide for the manner in which county officers should be elected or appointed, for their terms of office and their compensation. Finally by amendments adopted in 1911 and 1914, charter-making powers were conferred upon counties. Altogether in the twenty-seven years from 1887 to

1914, the home rule provisions of the California constitution were amended or extended no less than fifteen times. As a result of this growth by accretion the California provisions give an impression of unnecessary length and complexity. However, this defect in form should not be permitted to obscure the fact that the cities of California have probably acquired a larger measure of freedom than has been granted to cities elsewhere in the world. It is also true that of the states which have placed home rule provisions in their constitutions, the experience of California has been the most varied and valuable.

Since the adoption of home rule in California, eleven other states have followed in the same path.[1] In general, it may be said of the later provisions that, in scope and effectiveness, they lie somewhere between those of Missouri and California.[2] From the experience of these thirteen states, extending over the period from 1875 to 1918, it is possible to deduce certain valid conclusions concerning this peculiarly American practice.

In the first place, in giving cities a sphere of constitutional autonomy, the states have not been prevented from exercising the needed control over matters of general state concern. Constitutional municipal home rule does not constitute the city an *imperium in imperio* as its oppo-

---

[1] Washington, 1889; Minnesota, 1896; Colorado, 1902; Oregon, 1906; Oklahoma, 1908; Michigan, 1909; Ohio, 1912; Arizona, 1912; Nebraska, 1912; Texas, 1912; Maryland, 1915. Among the home rule provisions of the various states, those of Ohio are best as to form. They also grant broader powers than those of any state except California.

[2] For the law of home rule as developed under the various constitutional provisions see Professor Howard Lee McBain's exhaustive study, "The Law and Practice of Home Rule."

nents never tire of saying in constitutional conventions; on the contrary it has certain positive advantages from the standpoint of state government. It saves the time of the legislature by reducing the number of bills to be considered dealing with purely local matters. In states without municipal home rule, it is not uncommon to have as much as one-third of the legislative time taken up with bills of no importance except to the municipalities to which they apply.[1] Such bills not only consume time which should be given to matters of importance to the state as a whole, but they become one of the chief factors in the general scheme of legislative log-rolling. Moreover, home rule removes from the legislature the temptation to enact laws affecting cities having either corrupt or partisan purposes. When municipalities can escape from such laws by the simple process of adopting or amending a charter, their passage is no longer attempted or urged. This purifying effect of municipal home rule upon both the legislature and the city is attested by the fact that the powerful forces tending to corrupt municipal government always oppose it. They thus make it clear that they can secure more from the legislature than from city authorities.

As to the cities themselves the advantages which have been gained from their varying degrees of freedom are manifold. It is noticeable, for instance, that home rule cities develop a high civic spirit more frequently than

[1] At the session of the Iowa Legislature held in 1913, 397 laws were enacted. Of that number 108 had to do with cities and towns. This takes no account of bills introduced and not enacted into law. The Iowa situation is fairly typical of non-home rule states.

others. This naturally results from the knowledge that their form of government and the conduct of their business is in their own hands. Such responsibility encourages action on the part of the city electorate when municipal affairs are wrongly conducted. Furthermore the very process of providing a charter for their local government is of great educational value and helps to arouse the people to a sense of community obligation. Consequently, taking the country as a whole, the outstanding cities in point of civic spirit and civic pride are those which have framed and adopted charters.

That home rule cities have derived great benefits as a result of their comparative immunity from legislative tinkering may be deduced from what has been above stated. In addition they have also been, in general, more secure in their powers and have profited greatly by their ability to construct governments suited to their peculiar needs.

The fear, sometimes expressed, that local charter making will result in a collection of badly constructed and slipshod charters has proven to be unfounded. In point of ability, local charter commissions are usually superior to the average state legislature, and they are much more likely to make use of expert assistance. They also show a greater inclination than state legislatures to familiarize themselves with work done elsewhere similar to that upon which they are engaged. This is evidenced by their tendency to consult the experience of other municipalities and to make use of language found in other city charters. As a result, city-made instruments of government compare favorably in draftsmanship with the best product of our state legislatures and some of them have set a distinctly high standard of excellence.

Without overstating the case, it may be said that the most numerous and substantial contributions to the progress of municipal government in the United States are being made by the cities of the home rule states. These cities have led the way in simplifying the complicated systems of government which state legislatures fastened upon American municipalities; they have given the country its fullest demonstration of the manager plan of government and, having control of their own structure, they have been enabled readily to introduce improved methods of organization and administration. In the domain of electoral reform the contributions of the home rule cities have been striking. No such city has adopted a long ballot charter in years; partisan designations have been swept from the ballot with almost complete unanimity; preferential voting, permitting nomination by petition, has been given a trial, and the highly promising experiment with proportional representation has been inaugurated. The recall of elective offices was introduced by a home rule city, and the most complete and practical development of the initiative and referendum has been worked out in city-made charters.

This enumeration might give the impression that, if left to their own devices, city electorates lean too much toward innovation. Such is far from the case. Scores of cities are now operating under charters of their own construction and, in general, their attitude in charter making has been distinctly conservative. No city in framing a charter has shown an inclination to fill its fundamental law with promising, but experimental, provisions; but here and there, in widely separated cities, experiments have been made singly. In this manner a large body of trustworthy evidence available for all cities has been accumulated, without involving the stability of municipal institutions anywhere.

When the National Municipal League issued its " Municipal Program" eighteen years ago, it already felt justified in committing itself to the principle of constitutional municipal home rule. With a view to unshackling cities, certain constitutional and statutory provisions were at that time suggested. Since then the number of states granting home rule privileges to cities through their constitutions has trebled and a wealth of experience has been acquired. In the light of this experience, the League has reëxamined the position which it took in 1900 and, as a result, now puts forward the revised and amplified constitutional provisions printed elsewhere in this volume. This new suggestion is based on the following principles which are regarded as having been well established as a result of the actual practice of constitutional municipal home rule in the various states, viz.:

1. The legislature should be left in a position to work out a broad and comprehensive system of home rule based on statutes. (Secs. 1 and 2.)

2. The constitution should authorize cities to frame and adopt charters for their own government and to amend such charters. (Secs. 3 and 4.)

3. The constitution should, in general terms, grant authority to cities to exercise all powers relating to municipal affairs. (Sec. 5.)

4. As a reassurance to those who fear the disintegration of state power, and in order to make it clear to the courts that a distinction between local and general matters is intended, the constitution should indicate that the legislature retains power to pass general laws, applicable alike to all cities of the state, in matters relating to state affairs. (Sec. 5.)

5. To avoid the uncertainty attaching to a grant of powers in general terms, an enumeration of the more important powers which it is thought should be comprehended within the general grant should be inserted in the constitution. (Sec. 5.)

6. Authority should be reserved to the state government to require full publicity as to the financial conditions and transactions of cities. (Sec. 6.)

7. The constitutional provisions, through which cities are authorized to frame and adopt charters and acquire home rule powers, should be self-executing in all essential particulars.

8. The constitution should authorize the consolidation of city and county governments and the framing of a charter by and for any such consolidated city and county. (Sec. 8.)

A detailed discussion of these principles as embodied in the proposed constitutional provisions is unnecessary. For the most part, the meaning and purpose of the various sections will be evident to the reader. In a few instances, however, brief comment may be of some value.

The first principle is established by Sections 1 and 2 of the constitutional provisions. In accordance with these sections, the legislature would be required to pass a general law for the incorporation of cities and villages. It is obvious that the conditions under which a given territory and population shall be permitted to pass from a rural to a municipal status politically must be established by some general authority. It would not be practicable to leave communities to decide this matter for themselves. The provision here suggested, however, leaves it to the legislature to determine what municipalities shall be classed as cities and what as villages. In view of the greater power which the legislature is permitted to retain over villages, this might, in some states, be considered an unwise concession. Where such a feeling exists, the difficulty may be avoided by stating in the constitution the point in population at which a municipality shall pass out of the village class.[1]

The legislature would also be required to provide by a general law for the organization and government of such cities and villages as did not adopt some special form of government made available by other features of the suggested provisions. It was not thought desirable to cut off the legislature by rigid constitutional restrictions from the opportunity of dealing generously and wisely with cities. For that reason, the legislature is authorized to enact other laws relating to the organization and government of cities and villages, with the proviso that no such law shall go into effect except when submitted to the electors of the municipality concerned and approved by a majority of those voting on the question. Under these simple provisions, any legislature which so desired could provide the municipalities of its state with such ample

[1] See the constitution of Ohio, Art. XVIII, Sec. 1.

powers, and make available for their adopting such a variety of optional charters, that it would scarcely be necessary for any city to frame and adopt a charter for its own government. This plan reserves all the benefits of special legislative charters without opening the way for any of their evils. Provisions similar to these are found in the home rule sections of the Ohio constitution [1] and, in that state, have proved to be of some value. While it is true that the legislature has not risen to its full opportunity, it has made a good beginning. Under such provisions there is hope that, in time, state legislatures may forget the bad habits acquired in the days of their complete supremacy and establish themselves as authorities which can be trusted to determine the structure of municipal government and establish the limits of municipal powers.

A sufficient guaranty that the legislature would not abuse its power over municipalities is afforded by the provision which authorizes cities [2] to frame and adopt their own charters. The procedure for such action laid down in the New Program is based on the experience of the more advanced home rule states. Probably in most states, these provisions in their present form would be operative without any assisting legislation. It should be noticed, however, that they assume the existence of election authorities constituted by the state and of laws which provide for the verification of signatures to petitions.

[1] Constitution of Ohio, Art. XVIII, Sec. 2.
[2] It will be noted that charter-making powers are conferred only upon cities. In at least one state, Ohio, such power is granted to all municipalities. Constitution of Ohio, Article XVIII, Sec. 7.

In these and other particulars, any state thinking of adopting these provisions should make sure that legislation is well established which would enable a city to act upon the constitutional authorization without further legislative assistance. If thought desirable, complete provisions as to the ballot and the filing and verifying of petitions can be embodied in the constitution itself. Whenever possible, however, it is desirable to avoid the duplication of administrative machinery such as that for the conduct of elections.

The provisions for granting powers to cities are found in Section 5. The first part of this section is designed to accomplish the purpose always intended, but not always achieved, by constitutional provisions for home rule. That purpose is to permit cities greater freedom of action in the management of their affairs by releasing them from the limitations of a strictly enumerated grant of powers. In seeking this end the method has been to grant to cities through the constitution, either by specific statement or by implication, the authority to exercise all powers which are municipal in character. The establishment of such a method of granting power to cities reverses the practice, which we have inherited from the English law, of naming municipal powers in detail, with the result that powers not so named are held by the courts to be denied. Any one at all acquainted with the operation of city governments is aware how awkward and unsatisfactory the old system frequently proves to be. There is no legislative body, no matter how wise or well intentioned, which can possibly foresee all the needs of a growing city. It is this system which occasions the most frequent appeals to state legislatures for amendments to charters and municipal codes. The vast majority of such appeals are requests for authority to do things which are of no importance whatever to the state as a whole. The net result is an enormous waste of legislative time, and great inconvenience — sometimes great loss — to the municipalities. Experience in the home rule states indicates the necessity of extreme care in drawing the constitutional provision intended to authorize cities in one general grant to exercise all local or municipal powers. Accustomed to the long established English and American practice of enumerated powers, the courts are not inclined to recognize the new doctrine unless the constitutional intention is clear. In some states, judicial interpretation has all but eliminated any grant of municipal powers in general terms. It is not believed that the general grant of authority to "exercise all powers relating to municipal affairs," as set forth in section 5, could be called in question.

The enumeration of powers following the general grant of authority calls for particular attention. It is well known that, unless there is clear intimation to the contrary, the courts will hold that, where powers are enumerated, it is intended that only those named may be exercised. As a safeguard against this danger, it is provided in the first paragraph of the section that "no enumeration of powers in this constitution or any law shall be deemed to limit or restrict the general grant of authority hereby conferred." The further precaution is taken of prefacing the enumeration of powers with the declaration that the powers named, "shall be deemed to be *a part* of the powers conferred upon cities by this section." By these statements, it is made clear that the powers enumerated are by way of partial definition of the general grant of authority to "exercise all powers relating to municipal affairs."

This enumeration of powers should make unnecessary most of the appeals to the courts which would otherwise be required to determine whether this or that power falls within the domain of municipal affairs. In the home rule states in which the cities have been largely dependent for their powers upon a general authorization to frame charters for their own government or to exercise all powers of local self-government, the content of the general grant of powers has been established only after tedious litigation. The list here given, though occupying a relatively small amount of space includes all the more important powers usually granted to cities and at least two which are somewhat unusual. The latter are the grant of the power of "excess condemnation" in section 5c, and the authorization to sell bonds on the security of excess property condemned, or of any public utility owned by the city, found in section 5d. These are likely to prove useful powers to the cities in years to come and, in the absence of a specific grant in the constitution, might be held by the courts to be outside the domain of municipal affairs.

It will be noted that some of the powers granted in the home rule provisions of the California constitution are not included in this enumeration. The two prominent instances are the failure to specify control by the city of the local police and of the authorities conducting local elections. There is no doubt that, in the absence of some constitutional provision to the contrary, the legislature can provide for taking the local police entirely out of the hands of city authorities. In Missouri, this has been done in large measure in the case of both St. Louis and Kansas City. In most states, however, the tradition in favor of the local control of police is so well established that the legislature is not apt to violate it. One of the great needs of the immediate future is a better coördination of state and local police efforts. For that reason it does not seem best, except in extreme cases, to exclude the state entirely from the right to intervene in local police matters. But when the situation is such as now prevails in Missouri, as regards St. Louis and Kansas City, it would be justifiable, through the home rule provisions of the constitution, to exclude the state government from participation in the organization and control of the local police.

As regards the authorities for conducting elections, if those set up by the state do their work efficiently and honestly, there is no reason why the city should provide a duplicate piece of administrative machinery. There have been instances, however, where cities have found it practically impossible to secure an honest count of the ballots by a state appointed board. Where such a condition seems likely to continue, it would be proper to specify the right to constitute and control local boards of election among the powers relating to municipal affairs. From the foregoing it will be observed that, under the plan for home rule here suggested, the enumeration in the constitution of the powers comprehended within the term "municipal affairs" can be broadened or narrowed to suit conditions in the individual state.

It is with considerable confidence that the National Municipal League offers the draft of these constitutional provisions for consideration in those states where a grant of home rule powers to cities is contemplated. Of course, it is not expected that they would fit into the constitutional system of any state without at least some changes in detail. In fact, it is particularly important that such provisions be brought into harmony with other phases of the fundamental law. But with such necessary concessions in mind, it is believed that this draft can be used with the assurance that it is superior in form and principle to the provisions for constitutional municipal home rule now found in any state constitution.

V

ELECTORAL PROVISIONS OF THE NEW MUNICIPAL PROGRAM

In its first municipal program, issued in 1898, the National Municipal League emphasized the desirability of eliminating from local elections both the party primary and the party form of ballots. Nothing has developed since then from experience which would lead this committee to suggest any change in the policy then adopted. The League has consistently stood for non-partisanship in city elections. By the use of the term "non-partisan" it has not meant that there should be no parties in municipal affairs, but rather that state and national political parties and issues should be eliminated, and local issues be made paramount, in purely local elections. Local municipal parties with definite political platforms based upon local issues are entirely consistent with the principle of non-partisanship in local affairs. In order to separate as far as possible local issues from national parties and issues, the new program provides that municipal elections shall be held only in the years when there are no state or national elections, or, if held in the same year, that they shall be held some thirty or sixty days before or after the state and national elections.

PREFERRED METHOD OF ELECTION

Three methods of electing candidates to public office are presented in this program, namely:

(a) Nominations by petition — no primary — election by a non-partisan proportional representation system.
(b) Nominations by petition — no primary — election by a non-partisan preferential ballot.
(c) Nominations (and election if a candidate receives more than half the votes) at a non-partisan primary and a single choice non-partisan ballot at the election.

The method of electing the council preferred by a substantial majority of the members of the committee is the Hare method of proportional representation, otherwise called the "single transferable vote." This method has been included in the text of the proposed charter.

THE HARE SYSTEM OF PROPORTIONAL REPRESENTATION

The object of this system is to give every element in the community, and every individual voter, an opportunity to share equitably in the election to the council of their most trusted spokesmen. It also gives each political group representation in proportion to its relative voting strength.

Nominations are made by petition, each petition being signed by a specified number of voters. No voter is allowed to sign more than one. The number of signatures required should depend not only on the number of

ELECTORAL PROVISIONS

voters in the city, but on the number of seats in the council. The more the voters, and the fewer the seats, the more the signatures that should be required. Usually the number required should be from one half of one per cent to two per cent of the voters.

The Hare ballot gives the voters the opportunity of expressing their preferences for the council by means of numerals, 1 for first choice, 2 for second choice, etc. They are permitted to express thus as many preferences as they please, with the assurance that the indication of a lower choice will in no case operate, when the votes are counted, to reduce the chances of election of a candidate indicated as a higher choice.

At the voting precincts no attention is paid to anything on the ballots except the first choices. This makes the work of the local election officials very easy. After the polls are closed the precinct election officials sort the ballots according to the first choices of the voters. The ballots for each candidate are put up in separate packages, showing the total number of ballots in each and the name of the candidate for whom cast as a first choice. All of the ballots and records are then forwarded to the election authorities, who proceed to add and tabulate all of the first choice votes, in accordance with the Hare rules outlined in the proposed model charter. The whole number of valid ballots is then divided by a number greater by one than the number of places to be filled. The next whole number larger than the quotient thus obtained is the "quota." All candidates who receive a number of first choice votes equal to or greater than the quota are declared elected. All surpluses above the required quota cast for the elected candidates are then transferred to the candidates receiving the voter's second choice, each surplus ballot beng transferred to the credit of the candidate marked on that ballot as second choice (or next available choice in case the second choice is already elected).

After these transfers have been completed and any candidates declared elected who have received the quota, the lowest candidate on the ballot is dropped and his ballots are transferred, each according to the next available choice marked on it. Thus the count proceeds, by the dropping of the lowest candidates, one by one, until the quota has been received by as many candidates as are to be elected or until the number of candidates has been reduced to that number.

This method of counting gives each voter, with few exceptions, a share in the election to the council of the candidate whom he prefers to help elect. To express it in another way, the count sorts the voters out, by means of their ballots, into as many unanimous and approximately equal constituencies as there are councilmen to be elected, and lets each such constituency elect the candidate whom it is united in desiring to elect.

The most obvious result of such a system of election, of course, is the one which is suggested by its name of "proportional representation," namely that it gives to each group of voters in the community as many seats in the council as it is entitled to, based upon the number of votes it casts. In this respect the method differs radically from the two alternative methods mentioned above, both of which are intended to accomplish the election of the entire membership of the council by a majority or plurality of the voters.

Advantages of Hare Election System

Besides the "proportional" apportionment of the seats, however, the Hare system has other results which, though less obvious, appear to be no less important. The advantages claimed for it are as follows:

1. It makes primary elections unnecessary.

2. It gives the voters real freedom to nominate independent candidates when the candidates nominated by their group are not all to their liking. This freedom is due to the fact that the preferences which the voter may express on the Hare ballot are so treated in the count that he runs no risk, provided only he marks a sufficient number of preferences, of throwing his vote away by giving a high preference to a candidate supposed to lack support.

3. It brings out as candidates strong men, who might not be nominated by any organized party or group, but whom many voters would gladly support when they could do so without danger of throwing their votes away.

4. It gives the voters freedom to mark their ballots according to their real will, regardless of any candidate's expected chances of election.

5. It greatly increases interest in voting. This is because it makes practically every ballot effective in the election to the council of a person really wanted by the voter.

6. It opens within each organized group or party free competition for the seats to be won by it, depriving the

group's "machine" of all power except the legitimate power that comes from leadership.

7. It gives a seat to each sufficient number of like-minded voters whether organized or not.

8. It makes minority rule impossible. Under the Hare system a majority of the seats in the council can be filled only in accordance with the real will of a majority of the voters. The rule of the majority is by no means assured, of course, under the old ward system of election, for under that system the value of any group of votes is dependent largely on how the votes of the several groups happen to be distributed among the wards. Moreover, unless an excellent method of preferential voting be used in the ward elections, a small well-organized minority in a ward may easily force its candidate upon the ill-organized majority.

Even the above-mentioned alternative methods of electing the council at large do not insure majority rule in any such sense as that in which the Hare system insures it, for under either of those methods the voters must often consider, when marking their ballots, not only their own will but the different candidates' relative chances of election, so that many of the ballots that count with the majority in electing members are really those of voters who would have marked their ballots differently if they could have done so without risk of thwarting their will thereby.

9. The Hare system insures fair representation of all large minorities.

10. The Hare system makes for stability and continuity of policy, for under it a change of view on the part

of a small percentage of the voters cannot result in a sweeping, but only in a corresponding, change in the complexion of the council. It is believed that councils elected by this method will prove capable of developing a continuous and growing program of public policy instead of rocking violently back and forth between radicalism and reaction.

11. The Hare system makes the manager plan of government thoroughly democratic by making the council, which selects and oversees the manager, truly representative of all elements and groups of opinion.

Arguments Against the Hare System

Although a majority of the committee preferred the Hare system of proportional representation, for the election of a council, to either of the majority-plurality systems suggested as alternatives, the committee is well aware that arguments are often offered against it. Some of these arguments, with the rejoinders made by supporters of the proportional system, are as follows:

The opponents say that the Hare system tends to divide the city into factions. Its supporters, however, say that it merely condenses the city into its true leaders, and, by giving every voter an effective voice in the government, tends to secure the coöperation of all. The voting system that divides the city into factions is the majority (or plurality) system applied to the representative body at large, as in most cities governed under the commission and commission-manager plans; for under that system some of the voters may elect all the members, the others none.

Under the Hare system, the opponents say, all the councilmen may live in one part of the city. Its supporters reply that this might happen, but that it could not happen unless nearly all of the voters of the city preferred residents of that part of the city as their councilmen. Under the Hare system voters can favor near-by candidates if they wish, and a quota of voters in any locality always has it in their power to elect a local candidate.

Under the Hare system, the opponents say, there is danger that a council which represents all elements will become a mere debating society. Its supporters reply that this is not the result where the system is used. As soon as a vote is taken on an issue before the council, the decision of the majority, which prevails, can be executed just as efficiently if the various views held in the community have been voiced fully as it can if some of these views have been misrepresented or unexpressed.

The Hare system, the opponents say, tends to maintain national party lines in city elections. Its supporters reply that it gives the voters an entirely new freedom to make their will count whether they vote on party lines or not. It will, it is true, tend to weaken the dominating influence and control of party machines and bosses, but it will at the same time tend to direct party activities into their legitimate channel of formulating and promoting political principles and policies.

The Hare system, its opponents say, is too complicated. Its supporters say it is less complicated for the voter than the old single-choice plurality system, for he is relieved of any concern about any candidate's chances of election and does not have to pay any attention to any candidates whom he does not want or does not know. For the precinct election official the Hare system is simplicity itself. The only persons who have to understand the counting of the votes are those who count them at the central electoral office. And this means, in practice, simply that one man in the city must master the count, which any capable man can do in a day, and then train in a number of clerks in connection with a practice count.

ALTERNATIVE METHODS OF ELECTING THE COUNCIL

First Alternative: Elimination Primary with Majority Election at Large

This method provides for a primary election and a final election. At both each elector is allowed to vote for as many candidates as there are places in the council to be filled. The names of the candidates are put on the primary ballot by petitions signed by a specified number of voters and filed with the election authorities. Any candidate who is voted for at the primaries by more than half of those who vote on that occasion is declared elected at once. If the required number of members are all thus elected at the primary, the second election is not held. At the second election the ballot contains the names of the candidates, other than those already declared elected, who receive most votes in the primary up to twice the number still to be chosen. At this second and final election the required number of candidates who receive most votes are declared elected.

Of course, the outstanding difference between this method and the Hare is that this method aims not at equal representation of all groups but at the election of the entire council by the majority.

Three disadvantages of this method, as compared with either of the others that we are considering, are (1) the additional expense and trouble of the second election, (2) the tendency of voters to remain away from one of the elections when two are required, and (3) the limitation on the voter's power to express an opinion on all candidates.

The advantages claimed for this system are: (1) the ballot is simple, (2) the counting is easy, and (3) the double election offers the voter an opportunity for longer deliberation in his final choice.

Second Alternative: Preferential Voting System

This method provides for nomination by petition, without a primary, and for election by means of a system of preferential or "several choices" voting. It attempts to give to the voter the opportunity of weighing the relative merits of all candidates for an office, and registering his conclusions concerning each. It also attempts to elect to seats in the council candidates acceptable to the majority, or largest possible plurality, of the voters. Model provisions for carrying out this method will be found in the appendix to the Program.

The Preferential system differs fundamentally from the Hare system in object as well as method. The object of the Hare system is true representation of all elements and all voters; that of the preferential, the true representation of the majority or largest possible plurality. And as for method, though both systems use a preferential ballot, their principles of handling the preferences in the count are essentially different.

Advantages of the Preferential Ballot.— The supporters of this form of ballot maintain that it will more nearly insure a majority choice of candidates than will the single choice ballot. It will not always result in majority choice. Sometimes there will be no candidate upon whom a majority of the voters can unite. In that case, the candidate receiving the largest number of first and second choice votes will be declared elected if they constitute a majority; or in other cases the first, second, and other choices whether they constitute a majority or merely a plurality. Even under such circumstances the preferential ballot more nearly approximates a majority than does the single choice ballot.

The supporters further maintain that the preferential system is a sifting process. The addition of each successive choice tends to eliminate the less worthy. The preferential ballot enables the voter to register a vote against, as well as for, a candidate. The refusal to express a choice for a candidate is a vote against him. The successful candidate under the preferential system is usually the least objectionable on the ballot, if he is objectionable at all. Under the old plurality system the worst candidate often has the best chance of election because his support is usually compact and undivided, while the forces for good government are often split by the bipartisan trick of throwing into the race two or more good candidates for the purpose of splitting the vote.

Objections to the Preferential Ballot.— The chief objection advanced to the use of this ballot for the election of the council is that, in the opinion of the objectors, no plurality or majority system of any sort is suitable for that purpose: what is needed being a proportional or "condensing" system that will insure equal representation to all elements and all voters.

Objections are also made, by the opponents of this system of election, to its method of counting. It is pointed out that in making a second or other choice, the voter may, under certain circumstances, help to defeat the candidate whom he has marked with a higher choice. This imperfection results not only in limiting the confidence of the voters in the results of elections under this system but in reacting upon them to prevent their marking lower choices. Frequently the lower choices marked fall as low as twenty-five or even twenty per cent of the first choice, and sometimes they become so few as to be almost negligible. For example, in the municipal election of San Francisco in 1917, the first under the preferential system, the second choice votes numbered less than three per cent, and the second-and-third-choice votes together less than four per cent, of the first-choice votes. When the lower choices marked have no effect on the result, the preferential system becomes the same, of course, in its actual effects, as the old plurality system itself.

Two suggestions have been made to overcome this defect in the operation of the preferential system. The first one is to require the voter to mark several choices. Such a requirement is objectionable not only because some of the voters actually do not have the number of choices that the proposed requirements would force them to express, but because it is unreasonable to require a voter to express a preference, even if he has it, when he may perhaps be afraid of helping thereby to defeat a candidate whom he has marked as a higher choice. The second suggestion often made is to grade the values of the several choices; for example to count the first choice as a unit, the second choice as half a unit, and the third choice as a third of a unit, etc. Whether or not these changes would be a distinct improvement cannot be determined without careful testing by actual experience. The hope and belief, however, of the advocates of the preferential ballot is that the voters will in time remedy the above defect by voluntarily increasing the number of second and other choice votes cast.

In spite of these practical difficulties in its operation, the preferential system is considered a satisfactory majority-plurality system by many of the communities which are using it. The verdict is not unanimous, but the system has enough support where it is used to give it a claim to careful consideration by other cities which desire a majority-plurality, rather than a proportional method, of electing the council. When the preferential system is presented to a community for its approval, it should not be extolled as the last word in election methods: it should be offered only as a method of majority-plurality election which, it is believed, will prove far better than the old plurality system.

THE VOTER'S RESPONSIBILITY

Much is said about the apathy of the voter and his lack of interest in governmental problems. While this charge is, to some extent, true, the critics of the voter have apparently failed to realize that much of this apathy and lack of interest is probably traceable to the crude electoral system and the burdensome electoral task which has been placed upon the voter in the effort to remedy existing evils. The model charter seeks to simplify the election process, assure the elector that his vote will be given its full weight, and leave to him the responsibility for his own government. When his responsibility is made clear and distinct, when his task is unconfused and free from unnecessary complications, and when he sees that he can register his opinion and will effectively, then he will begin to exercise the authority which is his in a democratic form of government. These right electoral conditions, we believe, have been provided for in this charter. Under them, an alert, intelligent, and active electorate can make its will easily effective.

VI

THE SHORT BALLOT PRINCIPLE IN THE MODEL CHARTER

AMERICAN charter makers in the past, anxious to evade "politics" in administration, have often sought good government by undemocratic and devious routes. For instance: there is a scandal in the public works. A group of angry citizens rush to the capitol, get an amendment to the charter displacing the existing department head and substituting a board of public works of three heavily-bonded members appointed by the mayor for six year terms in rotation, the mayor's own term being two years. The first board appointed, following the scandal and reorganization, is a good one, selects a good superintendent and things go well. The device then, is declared a success. A few years pass, the complexion of the board of public works alters, corruption takes root, the new organization being intrinsically just as vulnerable as any other kind, and the town wakes up to another scandal only to find that it will require four years and two elections to clear out the corrupt board.

All such governmental inventions inevitably cut both ways. Many students will search this Model Charter to see what super-ingenuities we have devised on some ratchet system that can only work toward good government. They will find nothing of the sort here. They will discover that a city can easily roll headlong to the

Devil with the Model Charter. "The citizens can elect a bad council, the council can hire a crook, or the local boss, as manager, and the manager can put the City Hall in his vest pocket." No checks and balances, no veto, no charter limitations on the council's powers, no red tape except enough to compel an embarrassingly prompt and complete public display of all the facts at every stage of the progress of the City Hall toward the aforesaid vest pocket. Only in the matter of long term public utility franchises, do we provide checks to slow up and circumscribe the procedure, on the ground that delinquency in that field reacts not merely (and salutarily) upon the delinquent electorate, but upon the innocent next generation. Otherwise the voters can steer this modern automobile into any telegraph pole along the road and we guarantee simply that the car will obey the steering wheel and hit whichever pole they steer for, with a certainty and precision exceeding that of any old style loose-jointed charter. It is no legitimate function of a charter to be self-steering!

"But," insists the typical fearsome American mind, "suppose the people do get misled, as of course they sometimes do, and suppose they do elect a bad council?"

In that case, this charter provides the most fundamental of preventives against the repetition of the disaster by establishing and exhibiting a short and direct concussion between cause and effect. Their mistake brings its full consequences immediately and positively. A dog to be trained must receive his punishment or reward on the very heels of the commission of his act, so that he can see the connection.

The main message of this chapter, however, is to point out the precautions which the Model Charter takes to prevent the people from making mistakes. The unescapable hazard of democracy is not exactly that the voters may elect bad men, but that they may elect men whom they do not really want and whom they would not have selected if they had known more about them. To return to our automobile simile again, the hazard of a poor car is not that the driver will deliberately steer into the telegraph pole, but that he may hit it unintentionally because the steering gear is erratic or his head-lights insufficient in the gloom. Let me explain therefore what we have done to give the people a clear and easy view of the road, so that mistakes can only result from real recklessness. Real recklessness we believe to be rare. It is an old fashion for reformers to shrug their shoulders over bad political conditions and remark that "the people have only themselves to blame," but it is not usually true, for under our old style charters there are myriad contributing causes. Those contributing causes we have stripped away. If government goes wrong for any considerable length of time under the Model Charter, it will really be fair to blame the people.

The way to keep the people from electing men whom they really do not want is to have them elect only a few at a time, so that the people will get a good square leisurely look at every one of them. In foreign democracies, England, for instance, the voter's task at election time is simply to choose one man from a field of two or three to be the municipal councilor for the ward. The British voter gets to know his candidate and votes with the sane clear-cut convictions that an American voter does when he votes for president of the United States. One issue to decide, one mark to make on the ballot, and the voter is through for the year! Such a vote is not easily controlled by the politicians, or muddled by oratory, or confused and misled by partisan symbols.

We in America have departed far from such primitive simplicity! Our long and miscellaneous list of elective offices baffles, encumbers and entangles the whole elective process. It disfranchises the ordinary work-a-day citizen by the simple expedient of making politics too complex for him, with his scanty leisure, to master. The remaining five or ten per cent of the citizens, who for one reason or another choose to live and work in the political arena, acquire a rarely-disturbed control of the government. An outraged citizenry may sporadically "rise in its might and majesty" and invade the caucuses, conventions, primaries, etc., which constitute the devious lair of the professional politicians, but the politicians know that these meddlesome citizens cannot stay long and must soon return to their usual vocations and avocations. Whereupon the politicians — our modern ruling class — will resume their interrupted sway. The old remedy, "Let all good citizens go into politics," was sound in theory, but unworkable in practice, for a wholesome citizenry has much else to do. The new remedy is to bring politics to the citizen by making politics so simple and easy that every citizen will play his full part without conscious effort, leaving no mesh of detail to give footing to the politician.

THE SHORT BALLOT PRINCIPLE 113

The Model Charter does not reduce the number of offices on the ballot to one, as in England, but it carefully keeps the ballot very short. Only members of the council are elective, no separate mayor or clerk or treasurer or the like to be elected.

The council may be of any size from five to twenty-five, provided that the ballot is somehow kept short and popularly intelligible. The limit per ballot is five offices. If you want a council of fifteen, for instance, elect five at a time in rotation. Or divide a city in wards and choose five or less from each. Or, best of all, adopt our proportional representation option, wherein the voter votes for one with a series of secondary choices. His Majesty, the voter, has a delicate appetite. Thrust upon him more than he cares to eat and he may thank you for it, but he will go off and leave the surplus and the politicians will wax fat thereon.

A corollary of the Short Ballot principle that the number of officers to be chosen at any one election must be few, so as to permit adequate and unconfused examination of the candidates, is found in the further necessity that the elective officers must be of enough importance, both absolute and relative, to secure and deserve effective scrutiny by the voters. *E. G.* if at a given election the ballot carried only the office of coroner, the people would not bother to go to the polls. Quite rightly too! A citizen ought to be about better business than determining his insignificant share of that petty question. Or if the offices on the ballot were simply the mayor and coroner, the people would be drawn to the polls by the mayoralty contest, but their votes for the coronership would be so indifferent and half informed as to be an empty, meaningless formality rather than a genuine plebiscite. Many city charters provide ballots that are short as to actual number of offices, but suffer because some of the offices are little overshadowed offices that inevitably escape the public scrutiny necessary to the maintenance of healthy conditions.

In our Model Charter this pitfall is avoided. The councilors who alone are elective are all of equal and high importance. This is to be no ordinary city council — it is the supreme board of directors of the municipal corporation, a post of great opportunities for good or ill, subject to no veto, free from red tape, master of every power within the city's scope; a board of mayors, so to speak. The councilors are the head of the ticket and the tail of the ticket — the whole ticket. If elected by wards they may confidently be expected to tower above the petty sectionalism of present ward-elected councils in the mayor-and-council plan, for the littleness of the old style councilor was based not on the littleness of his ward, but on the littleness of his job in the city government. Strong men won't accept the nomination to an old-style council; the fact that they have only a ward to canvass will not prevent them from accepting the nomination to this new post of real honor.

The Wieldy-District Principle [1]

The application of the Short Ballot principle is enough to cut off both the function and the sustenance of the

[1] See article on "The Principle of Wieldy Districts," by Mr. Childs, in the "Proceedings of the Buffalo Conference on Good City Govt.," page 340. C. R. W.

political machines in small cities, leaving them only the diminished fare of county and state offices and a morsel of pork from the federal barrel. A multitude of experiences in commission-governed cities supports this expectation, although of course so long as other jurisdictions serve to keep it alive, the machine continues as a menace and sometimes manages to triumph. The story of commission governments in hundreds of minor cities is a story of political clubs dying out, machine headquarters getting forlornly empty, bosses losing influence and professional politicians going to work.

In the large Short Ballot cities,— St. Paul, Boston, Cleveland, Buffalo — the machines retain an important opportunity and continue to be so useful to their candidates that the machines survive.

Election in these cities is at large, and the electoral district unit is the whole city. This makes a district so large that an intermediary is needed between the electorate and the candidates. A candidate, unless he happens to be owner of a newspaper, like Hearst, or a millionaire, cannot readily come out for office and introduce himself to a million people single-handed. He must have an organization to do such wholesale work. Can he improvise one big enough and quickly enough? And if by sheer energy he can, who will pay the bills? Grant that he can manage it after a fashion, here comes the old political machine, its workers drilled, its ramifications complete, its organization experienced, its finances drawn by roundabout devices of patronage from the spacious city treasury. Will he make a treaty with it and thus get its help?

Forthwith he is its grateful servant. Will he fight it? It will beat him without half trying.

In Boston, for instance, the candidates nominate themselves by petition and the campaign opens. Canny reporters hang around the doors of the local good government league, the Republican city committee and the Democratic city committee. The league endorses Smith, the Democratic commitee says a kind word for Jones. Forthwith it is a duel. Smith and Jones become the only candidates worth considering. A vote for other candidates will be wasted and they drop out of the running. Smith and Jones each find a little well-financed standing army campaigning on their behalf. After election is it not dangerously like that Smith (or Jones) considers himself deeply in debt to that obscure little standing army and its captains, whose nod made all the difference between success and failure? So the government of Boston becomes a joint affair with control divided between the rank and file of the people, on the one hand, and a compact group, or groups, of self-constituted leaders on the other. Even if both the league and the Democratic committee be at present entirely controlled by high-minded unselfish men, such private groups holding the real though informal monopoly over hopeful nominations, are an undemocratic phenomenon, fraught with insidious danger. And if the people of Boston should acquire a distrust of both these nominating powers, they can do little about it except to create and support a new one!

Such is the unwieldy district. The principle runs far through our political life. It has done much, for instance, to upset the workings of direct primaries in state-wide elections.

By a wieldy district, we mean one small enough to permit really free competition for the elective office, small enough so that any suitable private citizen with an ordinary citizen's resources of acquaintance and money can canvass it adequately with the aid of such temporary organization as he can hastily improvise for the purpose. In such a district there will still be a machine perhaps, but its nominations, if unsatisfactory, will be subject to a very real danger from latent competition.

Chicago furnishes the best example of the value of such wieldy districts, in its aldermanic elections. These elections come separately — only one man to elect — and the districts are small and compact. Aided by the information of the voters' league, which rings the alarm-bell on due occasion, the citizens of Chicago have in numberless cases demonstrated the effectiveness and reality of latent competition under such circumstances. Thereby they have chased politics out of the board of aldermen, made it the one good board of its sort in America, and established, so far as this branch of their government is concerned, the most stable popular and good government to be found among our large cities. If the politicians could change the aldermanic election back to an obscure place on the long list of forty to fifty offices that grace the typical Chicago ballot at its general elections, and elect the aldermen at large or from much bigger districts, they would instantly recover complete control, such as they have in the case of the mayor and the county offices.

In small cities, election-at-large, if the ballot be short,

does not violate the wieldy district principle. Mr. Mac-Vicar of Des Moines, for instance, without organized help and against organized opposition, canvassed the city for himself and won the highest vote at a total cost of six dollars.

The size-limit of a wieldy district is not determinable with any precision. A homogeneous city of 100,000 is probably not too big for election at large, but a district of no natural unity embedded in a big city should be smaller than that — say 50,000, although that is a guess. In cities over the million class, that would be inconsistent with our desire to keep the council down to twenty-five members as a maximum and some kind of balance must be struck between the two principles.

Our goal is democracy. In the Model Charter that means a council composed regularly and entirely of members who enter office under no obligations to any private political authorities for their election, whether it be a political machine, a ring, a boss or a reform league, but who have been able to deal solely and directly with a free people.

On the stable democracy of such a council, efficiency can be boldly and swiftly developed.

VII

ADMINISTRATIVE ORGANIZATION

As the distinguishing characteristic of the form of city government advocated in the New Municipal Program is to be found in the concentration of administrative powers and responsibilities in the hands of a city manager, it is eminently fitting that the portion of the charter dealing with the administrative service should begin with a consideration of the manager, himself. Indeed, the initial sentence of this portion strikes the keynote of the entire administrative organization by declaring that the city manager shall be *the chief executive officer of the city*. It is true that this declaration in and of itself may mean much or nothing. Similar declarations are to be found, for instance, in nearly all of our state constitutions, and in many city charters of the mayor and council type. It is a matter of common knowledge, however, that our state governors are in no real sense the chief executive officers of the state in spite of the constitutional declarations to that effect, and that in most cities under the mayor and council form the mayor exercises a part only and not always by any means the major part of the executive powers of the city government. The trouble, therefore, has been in the past that the constitutions and charters, after making a declaration of a sound principle of governmental organization, have nullified that declaration by the distribution of functions actually made in the organic law. Fortunately, as will be seen, the New Municipal Program lives up to its confession of faith in this regard and the opening declaration as to the position of the city manager is a promise that it is fulfilled in the working out of the details of organization.

The city manager is to be chosen by the council solely on the basis of his executive and administrative qualifications. This departure from American political traditions involved in making the executive head of the government appointive, instead of elective, is epoch making. That the appointment of the city manager should lie with the council, the elective representative governing body of the city, would seem to be self-evident. There are, of course, other possible ways of choosing the city manager, but merely to name them is sufficient to realize their undesirability. To have the city manager chosen by some other local body, for instance, if such were provided, would be to strike at the fundamental principal of efficient governmental organization upon which both commission government and the commission manager plan are based, namely that there should exist a complete coördination and harmonious interrelation between legislation and administration. To have the city manager appointed by some central authority, on the other hand, such as the governor of the state, would not only preclude the possibility of responsible government by the council, but would be destructive of the most essential principles of home rule.

That the city manager shall be chosen solely on the basis of his executive and administrative qualifications would seem to be so obvious a consideration as not to require incorporation into the charter. Unfortunately, however, American political experience has taught us that no principle has been more consistently violated in our governments than that persons should be appointed to public office because of fitness for the office, and not because of political considerations. It is the almost universal disregard of that indispensable principle that makes necessary the incorporation of civil service merit provisions discussed in another chapter of this book. As a direct statement of an essential consideration in the filling of this important post the requirement under discussion is practically indispensable. As an effective provision for insuring that the consideration will have due weight in the actual choice of a manager it is unfortunately of little legal value, as the charter provides no way of enforcing it. To limit the council in its choice of the manager by definite requirements enforceable in a court of law would indeed have been quite possible, but not, on the whole, desirable. What would have been gained by the sanction of legal process would, it was felt, have been lost by the possibility of bringing up a legal controversy over the appointment of the manager by disappointed candidates or enemies of the council. For that reason the statement was left advisory rather than mandatory in effect.

Even more purely advisory and suggestive is the declaration to the effect that the choice of the city manager shall not be limited to inhabitants of the city or state. The idea that public offices, both elective and appointive, should be reserved for local men is as typically American as is the principle of the spoils system. In the case of such an office as that of city manager it is especially important that local residence be not taken into account, for the training and qualifications needed for a good city manager are such that in smaller cities especially it will frequently be impossible to find a suitable candidate. Furthermore, local men are almost sure to enter such an office with personal friendships and enmities of long standing, both of which might prove serious handicaps in the proper performance of their functions. What the native son, therefore, can adduce in the shape of a knowledge of local conditions will frequently be more than offset by local connections which may make it more difficult for him to profit by that knowledge. Other things being equal, therefore, a city council would do well to favor the candidate who is without a local past. Certainly the negative declaration contained in the provision under discussion is desirable as calling attention to the advisability of considering outside candidates, and the footnote commending the practice of publicly advertising for candidates suggests a way of increasing the likelihood of such candidates coming to the attention of the council.

The salary of the city manager is not specified in the charter for, of course, that will have to vary with the size of the city. At the same time it should be emphasized that the great possibilities of the city manager plan of government will never be realized unless adequate salaries are paid; that is, salaries that will attract men of the highest caliber. The qualifications that fit a man to be an efficient city manager are the same as those that fit him for success in business administration and the salaries must obviously be at least comparable to those paid to successful administrators in private business. Of course, the great possibilities for community service in the position of city manager will attract high-minded men from even better paying positions in private activities, and the dignity and influence which the chief executive office in the city carries with it will permit of a somewhat lower salary scale than that applied to men in private undertakings. But the discrepancy must not be too great or we shall, as usual in our governmental activities, be trying to do a first class work with third rate men, and the result will be a disappointment to every one interested in improved city government. The citation of the example of Dayton, a city of 117,000 inhabitants, paying its manager $12,500 a year serves to indicate what would seem to be a fairly liberal basis. It is said that Dayton was willing to pay even double that salary had it been possible to get a certain man of world-wide reputation as an administrator.

Charters should not specify the salary to be paid, but should set a liberal maximum, leaving it to the council to get the best man within the limit set.

The appointment of the city manager is to be for an indefinite period, which is intended to mean during good behavior. The other alternative was to make the appointment for a definite period, a term of years, with, of course, the possibility of terminating his employment at any time that his services were found to be unsatisfactory. The superiority of the indefinite term of appointment would seem to lie in the fact that if the city manager has to be reappointed at periodic intervals his enemies (comprising, of course, those who want the place for themselves or their friends) can concentrate their attacks upon the office at those strategic times. A majority being required to reappoint, there is greater likelihood that the incumbent will lose his place as the result of political intrigue, than if a majority vote is necessary to oust him, as is the case when the appointment is for an indefinite period. By the same token, however, it must be said, it might be more difficult to get rid of an incompetent or incapacitated city manager under the indefinite term than under the other arrangement. On this point opinions are divided and it can hardly be said to be a fundamental matter.

Of vital importance, however, is the next provision, which states that the city manager shall be removable by the council. One of the commonest objections urged against the city manager plan is that it is bureaucratic or autocratic instead of democratic. Were the city manager in any way independent of the representative body of the city, were it possible for him to disregard the wishes of the council with impunity, there would be considerable truth in the charge that we are setting up a one man government for our cities. It is essential, therefore, in order to avoid this serious charge and in order to insure absolute responsibility by the administration to the elected representatives of the people, that the city manager be at any time and for any cause, removable by the council. It has been urged that to let the dismissal of the city manager rest with the caprice of the council would be to discourage competent men from entering into such positions, and that therefore some limitations should be inserted in the charter to protect the manager from removal upon improper grounds. To this it must be replied that no considerations equal in importance the necessity of having absolute accountability by the manager to the representative body, and that the insertion of any sort of limitations enforceable in the courts would be to strike at the very root of the proper relation between council and manager.

Is there no way then in which the council can be held responsible to the people for the *abuse* of the absolute power of removal which it must have with regard to the manager? Obviously the only way to insure such a responsibility is to make certain that if the council is acting arbitrarily, the arbitrary nature of their action shall be made manifest. This can be done by providing that the city manager may demand written charges and a public hearing on the same, prior to the time that his removal is to take effect. The requirement of written charges insures that specific grounds shall be alleged, and the requirement of a public hearing insures that a defense to these charges may be made before the public.

It is true that these requirements in no way interfere with the removal of the manager by the council upon trumped up, ridiculous, or unproved charges. It does, however, provide a means whereby the manager may clear himself of blame, and the public may have means of learning how their representatives are discharging the solemn responsibility of getting and keeping good men in the position of manager. Obviously, if the public is alive and interested in that question, the necessity of written charges and a public hearing cannot but have a most beneficial moral effect upon the council. The provision that such written charges and public hearing may be demanded only after six months of service has the effect of making the first six months a purely probationary period, such as is provided in the case of appointments under civil service merit rules and regulations.

Section 35 of the charter, dealing with the powers and duties of the city manager, contains the provisions which give effect to the opening declaration that the city manager shall be the chief executive officer of the city. To the end that the city manager shall be really responsible for the proper administration of all affairs of the city he is given power to make all appointments, except as otherwise provided in the charter. Were it not for the exception qualifying this grant of the appointing power we could say that in the fundamental matter of filling the administrative offices of the city, the city manager had been given complete responsibility. As, however, provisos and exceptions not infrequently operate to annul previous general provisions, it will be necessary to see to what extent the charter provides otherwise before the full meaning of the grant of the appointing power to the city manager can be understood.

In the first place, the civil service board is not appointed by the city manager. The reason for this exception is obvious. This board being provided for the purpose of regulating and controlling, among other things, the manner of appointing persons to the classified service of the city, should not be appointed by the person whose appointing power is to be controlled, namely the city manager. In the next place the council is to appoint auditors for the independent auditing of the accounts of the city offi-

ADMINISTRATIVE ORGANIZATION

cers. Here again the reason for the exception is plain, being the same as existed in the case of the civil service board, viz., that officers of supervision or inspection must not be selected by the authorities to be supervised or inspected. These two cases are the only instances of municipal officers whose appointment is not lodged in the hands of the city manager. They constitute slight, but very necessary exceptions to the general rule.

Of much more significance, however, as a limitation upon the administrative power of appointment, than the two exceptions noted above, are the provisions dealing with the civil service board. The reasons for introducing these limitations and the manner in which they operate are fully discussed in the chapter dealing with the civil service provisions. It must be pointed out, however, that they constitute very important limitations upon the power of appointment here under discussion. All positions and employments in the civil service are made subject to the limitations imposed, excepting the councilors, the judges, the directors of departments, and superintendents, principals and teachers of the public schools. The four classes of officers last named may also be included in the service to which these limitations apply, if so directed by the council.

Now what is the character of these limitations upon the appointing power of the city manager? Briefly stated, they limit him in the matter of appointments to selecting one of the three highest candidates on the eligible list for any given position. Now courts have held that to limit an officer to whom is entrusted the appointing power to the selection of the highest candidate on such an eligible list is to deprive him of the appointing power because no discretion is left him. In the same way it is obvious that to limit him to three candidates for a place is to impose a very serious restriction on his power of appointment. What is true of the administrative power of appointment is equally true of the power of making promotions. This is a most important part of the administrative power, but is also restricted by the provisions relating to the civil service rules in such a way that the city manager is not left free to make promotions at his own discretion.

The other fundamental administrative powers in connection with the personnel of the service, namely, the power of discipline and removal, are not so limited, but are left to the city manager and the department heads under him, with the single requirement that the reasons for such action be furnished the person affected in writing and that he be given a reasonable time to reply in writing. As the power of discipline and removal is a more important administrative power than the power of appointment, it is fortunate from the point of view of giving effect to the responsibility of the city manager for the proper administration of the affairs of the city that he enjoys this power practically without limitation.

Taking up now the second part of section 35 we see a provision that the city manager shall be entitled to be present at all meetings of the council and of its committees and to take part in their discussions. The importance of this is to be found in the fact that successful government elsewhere has been the result of continued consultation between the governing body of laymen and the expert administrative officials. In European cities, as in America, the council is composed of laymen; but the council and its committees there do not take any important action except in consultation with the administrative experts. Many a proposal that is promising in theory presents well-nigh insuperable technical or administrative difficulties, and many a measure that seems on its face to offer little promise may be most desirable from an administrative point of view. To give proper weight and consideration to both points of view it is highly desirable that the chief administrative officer of the city be heard on every important matter that comes up for decision. Of course he does not have a vote in the council, and his opinions when given need not in any way be taken into consideration by the council in its action, but unless a provision of this nature is inserted in the charter a city council will be very likely to think that the city manager has no business in council meetings unless his presence is expressly requested. Since the charter gives the city manager the right to written charges and a public hearing before removal, it is quite proper that the council be permitted to discuss this one matter in his absence.

Section 36 imposes upon the city manager the duty of preparing the annual budget on the basis of estimates made by the directors of the departments and submitting it to the council. As the detailed provisions with regard to the character of the budget and its manner of presentation are included under another head and will therefore be discussed in a different chapter, these matters will not be taken up here. It is sufficient to point out that the preparation of the budget is a matter of considerable administrative difficulty, and should therefore be entrusted to the person who has continuous, first hand contact with all of the activities of the city. The lack of budget provisions in our state and national systems of government has long been properly decried as one great cause of inefficiency and extravagance. It is the more necessary in city government where the expenditure per capita is greater.

The preparation of the budget which is entrusted to the city manager is not, however, wholly a matter of finance administration. On the contrary it involves the expression of municipal policy for the coming year because almost all important measures involve expenditure of money, whether they be new undertakings or improvements in existing services. It is for that reason that an ideal city manager must be more than a first class executive, fundamental as that requirement is. He must be a man of broad vision and extensive training in the social sciences if he is to live up in the fullest measure to his possibilities and responsibilities. It is in the preparation of the budget more than in any other duty that he must show himself a leader, formulating policies and urging their adoption by the council. Therein, of course, lies also the danger of his becoming a political issue, a danger that can be guarded against only by tactful modesty on his part in keeping out of print and off the center of the stage. However, that is another story.

Coming now to a consideration of the administrative departments, we find the charter providing for six administrative departments: Law, health, works and utilities, safety and welfare, education, and finance. The division of the work of a city into departments presents no little difficulty, and presents also a possibility for varying opinions. Most city charters of whatever type have been especially weak and illogical in this regard, and have commonly adopted a division that could not well be justified from any point of view. The first consideration to be kept in mind with regard to such a distribution is that it is merely a matter of convenience and should be looked at from that point of view solely. The work of administering a city is an entity, a very complicated entity it is true, but nevertheless an entity. It is impossible, therefore, to adopt any kind of a division into departments, no matter how minute, which will make the individual departments separate and unrelated to each other. It is because of this fact that the single administrative head provided in the city manager is so fundamental a necessity for efficient city administration. It is the overlooking of this fact in the organization of the ordinary commission government which has been largely responsible for the failure of that form to attain a higher standard of administrative efficiency. The individual commissioners as department heads have been too prone, naturally and almost inevitably so, to regard their own departments as distinct fields of activity to be administered with respect to themselves alone, without proper regard for the interdependence of all the departments.

Under the city manager plan, providing as it does a central authority to coördinate the work of all the departments, it is no longer necessary to attempt the impossible in trying to divide the work of the city in such a way that each department can be run without reference to the rest. It is necessary only to adopt such main departments as will unite the activities most nearly related and most clearly distinguished from the other activities, and will demand a knowledge and training on the part of the director differing essentially from that demanded for the other departments. It is well to point out that the danger in the administrative organization of the city, or of any other governmental unit, either, for that matter, lies in the useless multiplication of departments. This is a danger which has made itself felt not only in the United States but in European governments as well, and its basis there as here lies in political considerations. The continual increase in the size of the British ministry, for instance, and especially of the cabinet, has been clearly due to political considerations, for each new cabinet post created gave the opportunity for rewarding more party leaders with posts of responsibility and honor, with little or no regard to the requirements of efficient administrative organization. In France still more, where the multiplicity of parties and the necessity of coalition governments demand a maximum number of cabinet posts as rewards for party support, the number of cabinet positions has been continually increasing with primary emphasis on the political rather than the administrative side. Other examples might be cited, among which must not be omitted the federal government of the United States. Every new cabinet position created makes one more berth for a loyal party supporter and the number of departments has increased from five in 1789 to ten at the present time. The same considerations have prompted the unnecessary increase of departments in our cities, for whether those department heads were elective or appointive the dominant political party enjoyed just that much more valuable patronage. It is worth noting, moreover, that while ten departments are considered sufficient to administer the affairs of our national government, most of our larger cities have found it desirable to exceed that number. Boston, for instance, had thirty departments, for the reason, as Professor Munro states, that for many years heads of departments were about the only higher administrative officers exempt from civil service regulations and new departments were frequently created by ordinance to provide for political spoilsmen.

An examination of all the different functions to be performed by the city would seem to lead naturally to a division into the six departments enumerated, on the basis of approximate inclusiveness and exclusiveness of functions and the training required of the department head. The legal work of the city, for instance, including the giving of legal counsel on all matters that arise, the drafting of ordinances in accordance with legal powers and to accomplish the desired ends, and the representation of the city in civil and criminal suits is quite distinct in character from the rest of the work of the city and demands at its head a man who has had a thorough legal training. The acquisition of a thorough legal training demands to-day about all of the time any man has for acquiring education and professional training and would leave little opportunity for a man thoroughly prepared for that work to become sufficiently familiar with the work of any of the other departments to undertake their immediate direction. The same considerations apply to the work of public health which demands a trained sanitarian; of public education, which demands an educational expert; of public works and utilities, which requires engineering training of a broad and thorough kind; and the work of public finance, which involves training as a professional accountant and expert on public finance. The remaining department, that of public safety and welfare, may on its face present less of a logical entity than the first five named departments. A moment's consideration, however, will show the close connection between the function of police protection and of social welfare activities. The neglect of social welfare activities in a city, such as proper housing, recreation facilities, charities and corrections, has a most immediate effect on the necessity of police activities. Indeed, social welfare work may from one important point of view be regarded as the positive or preventive side of police administration. For that reason the activities of preventing poverty, vice, and crime must logically go hand in hand with the activities of dealing with their manifestations. Consequently a well trained director of public safety should be a thorough sociologist as well, and the two phases of this activity should be under the direction of the same person.

It is believed that there is no activity of the modern city which cannot logically fall within one of these departments. It is true that there are many activities which partake to such an extent of the character of functions found in two or more of the departments that they might properly be placed in any one of them, but in such cases convenience will dictate the distribution to be made and the general logic of the scheme will not be destroyed. This power of determining in detail the functions of the various departments is expressly left to the council, by the charter.

The charter does indeed confer the power on the council of creating new departments, combining or abolishing existing departments, or establishing temporary departments for special work, and the footnote to this sentence suggests the directions in which such departures from the organization provided might best be made. But the general inadvisability of making such changes except for very good reasons is reflected in the requirement that a three-fourths vote of the entire membership of the council shall be required to make such changes. This safeguard is intended to resist the temptation to multiply departments unnecessarily for political reasons, particularly if the directors of departments are not put under the civil service regulations governing the classified service. The writer is personally of the opinion, however, that as regards the increase of departments the mere increase in the size of the city should never be regarded as a proper reason for multiplying the number of departments. The growing complexity of the department administration may properly demand sub-divisions into bureaus under the department heads; but if our analysis and grouping of functions were sound such increasing complexity would not demand new departments. The city manager must keep a watchful eye on the entire administration of the city through the department heads and his task will be simplified by having a minimum number of individuals to deal with. If the task of looking after the entire city administration in a general way is not considered beyond the possibilities of one man, surely no one of the single departments outlined would grow beyond the power of an efficient department head to direct. There would never appear to be, then, a necessity for increasing the number of departments beyond six.

The possibility of reduction in the number of departments and combining the functions of two or more, rests, however, on a clear necessity. In cities of the smaller class, in which the city manager plan is making its chief advances at the outset, it is obvious that the expense of retaining six expert administrators as department heads in addition to the city manager would be wholly unjustified when there is neither money to pay them nor work to keep them busy. In such cases the number of departments must of necessity be reduced, and the footnote suggests the logical way in which this is to be done.

One other matter remains for consideration in connection with the creation of departments. Although the department of education is enumerated as one of the regular city departments, a footnote declares that in places where the school system works well under a separate organization it had better not be disturbed. This declaration rests clearly on the doctrine of letting well enough alone. As a matter of administrative principle there would seem to be no reason, the writer is here again voicing his personal opinion, for excluding the administration of education from the general administrative organization of the city that would not apply with equal force to any one of the other departments of city work. The territorial jurisdiction of the educational authority is identical with that of the city, and the same persons are to be served, and the same property is to be taxed as in the case of public health, safety, works or any of the other departments. With equal reason, therefore, could the friends of public health administration, or of parks and playgrounds, or of libraries, water works, or what not, insist that these matters should be entrusted to separate authorities for their better administration. Indeed that is just what we are escaping from and trying to avoid under the city manager plan. We have been laboring for decades under separately elected health boards, library boards, park boards and other administrative authorities. This scattering of administrative authority has been generally deplored by students of municipal administration, and the concentration of these activities under the strong mayor type of mayor and council government, and even more now under the city manager plan has been welcomed as meeting a fundamental prerequisite of efficient administration. Certainly educational administration is no more independent or unrelated to the other work of the city than is public health, for instance, is no more vital to the welfare of the city, and is therefore no more entitled to be treated differently than the latter. In England, in Germany and in France educational administration is a function of the city council, not of a separate authority. In the United States, moreover, the beginnings of public elementary education were inaugurated by imposing the duty of providing it upon the town governments, not upon separate authorities.

The development of separate independent school authorities was due mainly to the general multiplication of elective authorities in our cities in what was believed to be the democratic movement during the early part of the nineteenth century. The argument in favor of keeping them separate from the general city administration today rests on the contention that educational matters are too important to be allowed to "become involved in municipal politics." Even supposing that independently elected school authorities insured the elimination of improper politics in the administration of school affairs, what argument can be advanced in favor of entrusting such important matters as public health and social welfare to a city government unfit to handle the educational problems of the community? The whole opposition to entrusting educational administration to the city council rests therefore on the hypothesis that this council will be inefficient, if not dishonest and corrupt; and that schools, at least, should be saved from their pernicious control. If we grant the soundness of that hypothesis, and of the further one that independently elected authorities for separate branches of administration will be more satisfactory than the union of municipal powers in the hands of a single body, how can we consistently advocate commission government and the city manager plan? In my opinion, therefore, logic and consistency demand that the inclusion of education in the general administration of the city be strongly advocated, instead of suggesting, as does the note in question, that matters had better not be disturbed.

The directors of departments are to be appointed by

the city manager. If the city council should make use of its power to include the directors of executive departments in the standardized and classified service, then the provisions with regard to appointment to office in that service set forth under the head of the civil service board and briefly considerd above will apply also to the selection of department heads. If the council does not take such action the department heads are to be chosen by the city manager at his discretion, subject only to the limitations expressed in section 38 of the charter. These provide that each director shall be chosen on the basis of his general executive and administrative experience and ability and of his education, training, and experience in the class of work which he is to administer. This general principle of selection is made more specific in the following requirements that the director of the department of law shall be a lawyer; of the department of health, a sanitary engineer or a member of the medical profession; of the department of works, an engineer; of the department of education, a teacher by profession; of the department of safety and welfare, a man who has had administrative experience; and of the department of finance, a man who has had experience in banking, accounting or other financial matters. As a general alternative to these specific requirements is the provision that the man must have rendered active service in the same department in this or in some other city. Obviously these requirements are to be considered in the light of minimum qualifications, not as satisfactory standards of fitness. Among all applicants or candidates showing at least these attainments the best equipped is to be chosen, whether or not they are submitted to the competitive tests of the civil service board. The director of the department of law should, of course, be a lawyer. But he should be more than that. He should be a lawyer especially versed in constitutional and municipal law, and skilled in the science of ordinance drafting. The director of the department of health should be more than a mere sanitary engineer or a mere member of the medical profession. He should be an expert in all the problems of public health, of which neither sanitary engineers nor doctors ordinarily have more than a smattering of knowledge. The director of education should be more than a mere teacher. He should have demonstrated his grasp of educational problems in the largest sense. The requirement with regard to the director of the department of safety and welfare means practically nothing. In practice he should be a man with university training in the social sciences. Administrative experience, and more than that, proved executive ability, with all that that implies, must of course be understood as an implied prerequisite to the headship of any department, although the head of the department of public safety and welfare may have a larger force of men and somewhat more difficult administrative problems on his hands. It is obvious that a director of finance should have had experience in accounting and finance administration. But a city that would be willing to permit any man who merely came up to the minimum requirements as set forth in this article to serve as head of a department would surely be disappointed in the outcome. The alternative requirement that the man must have rendered active service in the same department of the city or of another city is intended to insure only a minimum of practical acquaintance with the problems of administration in that department. As a matter of fact in the majority of cases today the man who could satisfy this requirement would be lacking in the broad training so necessary to the best accomplishment of his important functions. This alternative must therefore be considered in the light of a futurist requirement, looking ahead to the time when the subordinate officials of administration will have been properly trained to take their places as heads of departments after proving their administrative qualifications. The specific qualifications enumerated in the second half of the first paragraph of section 38 must therefore not be regarded as setting up a satisfactory standard for those positions.

The directors of departments are made removable by the city manager at any time. We have already pointed out that to charge an administrative officer with responsibility for the acts of subordinates whom he cannot remove, and consequently cannot control, is unjust and ineffective. But in case of removal of the department heads, as in the case of the removal of the city manager himself, it was felt desirable to provide some safeguard against purely arbitrary action by assuring the officer of the right to written charges and a public hearing. There would not seem to be quite the same necessity for such a provision to guard against arbitrary action by the city manager as was necessary with regard to his removal by the council. The responsibility of the city manager to the council for his acts in this regard as in all others is direct and complete, and he may be called to account at any time for an abuse of the removal power. The responsibility of the council to the public on the other hand is necessarily somewhat diffused and could be greatly obscured if the requirements for written charges and a public hearing were not insisted upon. But for the purpose of aiding the council in its judgment of any controversy between the manager and the head of a department resulting in the removal of the latter, the requirements that the charges and the director's reply thereto shall be filed with the clerk of the council are worth inserting.

The directors of departments are expressly made immediately responsible to the city manager for the administration of their departments, and he may require their advice in writing on all matters affecting their departments. It has been seen that the work of directing any one of the six departments is of a nature to require for its proper accomplishment professional training in that particular field. It is obvious, therefore, that the city manager cannot, in the nature of things, be a technical expert in more than one or at most two of the departments. In the conduct of the other departments he must consequently, in strictly technical matters, rely upon the expert advice of his departments heads. Without such advice the city manager, in any large city at any rate, would be hopelessly at sea and with the best of intentions would make the most serious of mistakes. That he should be able to require this advice is therefore most necessary, and that it should be in writing is important, both for the sake of insuring clarity and of providing him with information which can be kept continually on file and used as occasion demands.

Quite as important for the city manager as advice from his department heads is the necessary information on which he can base his own opinions. Formal reports at stated intervals are important, but even more valuable are reports on particular activities furnished upon request of the manager for special purposes, and it is well to grant the power of demanding such reports in the charter itself. In the work of making up the annual budget the departmental reports and estimates are, of course, the starting point on which the city manager bases his own recommendations to the council. For that reason a special section is devoted to the manner of preparing the budget under the head of financial provisions.

The last section under the head of the administrative service confers upon the council, the city manager and any officer or board authorized by them, or either of them, the power to make investigations as to city affairs, to subpœna witnesses, administer oaths and compel the production of books and papers. So far as the granting of this power to the council itself is concerned, the reason and necessity are obvious. Almost equally important is it, however, from the administrative point of view, that administrative acts and decisions which are so often dependent upon the obtaining of information that cannot be gotten without the application of compulsion, should be available to the city manager directly or through his subordinates by the means granted in this section.

To epitomize the provisions of the charter with regard to the administrative service, it may be said that they give the fullest possible recognition to the principle of administrative centralization. Every employee in the city is subordinate and responsible to some official, every subordinate official is in the same relation to some superior, every department is under the charge of a director and every director is in every way subordinate and responsible to the city manager. There is the administrative pyramid in desired perfection, incomplete only to the extent that the civil service provisions of the charter break the chain of complete control in the interests of preventing the abuse of the administrative powers of appointment, promotion, discipline and removal. Lest there be the slightest suspicion of our having erected a bureaucracy in creating the administrative hierarchy, the apex of the pyramid, the city manager, is made absolutely and completely subordinate to the city council, the elective body representing the people of the city.

It would not be proper to close a consideration of the administrative provisions of the charter without calling attention to the provisions of section 3 of the charter, which, though entitled "Powers of the Council," contains limitations on the dealings of the council and its members with the city manager that are of fundamental importance for the successful administration of the city under this plan. These provisions are discussed elsewhere. It is sufficient to emphasize here their prime importance in relation to the administrative service.

VIII

THE COUNCIL

In all branches of government, as President Goodnow pointed out in the Municipal Program of sixteen years ago, there are two primary functions to be performed. First, there is the general function of determining in a broad way what the public policy shall be, and, second, there is the function of executing this policy or carrying it into effect after it has been determined. The former we usually call legislation, the latter administration.

In American government, whether national, state, or municipal, it has been a generally accepted doctrine, moreover, that these two functions should be placed in separate hands. Congress is the policy-determining branch of the national government; but the work of national administration is devolved upon the president and upon the heads of the various executive departments who are appointed by him. The several state legislatures in their own sphere determine the course of state policy; but the governors and the heads of the state departments are intrusted with the function of carrying this policy into effect. In the American municipal system, taken as a whole, the same division of functions has been recognized. The city council has been the policy-determining organ of the municipality; the mayor and the heads of the city departments have been the custodians of administrative authority. The doctrine of division of powers, of checks and balances, has thus permeated every branch of American public life.

This principle, furthermore, did not stop with the mere functional division of powers. Its full recognition has required an organic division, in other words it has demanded that not only shall the policy-determining and the administrative authorities be separate, but that they should be independent as well. In short, it has meant that neither shall be subordinate to the other, but that each shall have its own orbit and be supreme within it. As applied to municipal government, however, this complete separation was not made at the outset; from colonial times down to about the middle of the ninteenth century the city council was not only the policy-determining organ in American municipal government, but possessed much authority in administrative matters as well. As the cities grew in size and importance, with increased administrative work to be done, the various committees of the city council became more important. The control of the police, fire protection, water supply, and other departments went virtually into the hands of these various committees, each doing its work subject to the authority of the whole council, but each in actual practice having its own determining voice in departmental affairs.

As an organ of administration, however, the city council seemed to be a failure. In many cities, especially in the larger ones, the council was a two-chambered body, large and unwieldy. The committees were made up of members from both chambers, with the result that they were often too large for the work which they had to do, and the representatives from the two branches of the council frequently failed to work in harmony. The vice of political patronage dominated the work of these committees; their appointments were made on a strictly partisan basis, and responsibility for waste was easily evaded by thrusting it upon the council as a whole. In the course of time, therefore, the control of some city departments was taken from the council and vested in the hands of independent administrative boards. This policy showed itself first in the police department, but it soon extended to such departments as streets, water supply and public health. In some cases these boards were elected by popular vote, in others their members were appointed by the mayor; in a few cases the control of the police department was transferred to commissioners appointed by the state.

This movement for the transfer of administrative authority from the council to special boards or commissioners made notable headway during the period following the Civil War, and especially after 1880. The New York charter of 1873, and the Boston charter of 1885 afford good examples of the changes which the movement brought in its train. In New York the framing of the city budget passed from the hands of the council to the new board of estimate and apportionment. In Boston the charter of 1885 swung the predominance of power in the city's administrative affairs from the council to the mayor, and there it has remained ever since. Other examples might be drawn from the municipal history of Pittsburgh, Chicago, St. Louis and many smaller cities.

It is worthy of note that in other countries, in England

and in the German empire, where a similar rapid growth in the size and administrative problems of cities took place, no movement for the transfer of powers from the council to independent administrative boards made headway during this period. The English borough still administers the affairs of its municipal departments, streets, water-supply, police, fire protection, public health, and so on, through the agency of council committees, just as it did a half century or more ago. The administrative affairs of German cities have been steadily handled for a hundred years by joint committees (*Deputationen*) of the two chambers of the city council. It was only in America that the principle of division of powers was permitted to run riot in municipal organization.

From several points of view this shearing of the American council's authority, while natural enough in the ordinary course of events, was unfortunate in its results. It caused a decline in the prestige of city councils throughout the land. The position of councilman lost its appeal to the better equipped men of the community. The work of governing a modern city is largely administrative in nature. Legislation as such forms but a small item in the annual program of a city government. The efficiency of a city's business depends chiefly upon the way in which appointments are made, the way in which the budget is framed, the way in which the departments are managed day by day, rather than upon the content of the municipal ordinances. Moreover, the field of local legislation has been greatly narrowed by the widening sphere of state law-making, which now reaches down into the minutiæ of urban life. Larger questions of municipal policy are often settled by state statutes, so that the city council, even though we call it a policy-determining body, deserves that title only in a humble sense. And finally, the use of the initiative and the referendum has transferred final discretion in many important questions of municipal policy directly to the hands of the voters themselves.

Putting all these things together, it is easy to see why membership in city councils throughout the United States gradually lost its appeal to men of ability and public spirit. The councils filled up with ward politicians, with the hirelings of public service corporations, with the minions of those who sought contracts from the city or who had supplies to sell, and with men of paltry caliber who could make no headway in private vocations. Others would not give up their time and energy to fruitless bickerings in a body which no longer possessed the constructive power to improve the conduct of the city's affairs. It is power and the promise of results that attract men of the right type to public office. When the city councils lost these things it was natural that they should everywhere suffer a serious impairment in personnel.

Let it be repeated that this decline in the authority and in the standards of city councils has been unfortunate. Without question there is a place in every sound municipal system for a deliberative body, provided it is properly made up, not too cumbersome, given definite powers and restrained from interference with matters which are not within its own sphere. There are things which ought to be settled by a meeting of minds, not by the decisions of one man. If there is no city council to handle them, they are altogether likely to be taken over by the state legislature. A council of some sort is therefore needed (1) to ensure to the city a reasonable degree of autonomy in the determination of local policy, and (2) to enable a proper distinction to be made between those things which require deliberation, and those which, being purely administrative in character, demand vigor and decision.

There has been in the public mind during the last fifteen years much confusion upon the question of separating local legislation from administrative work. A great deal of it has arisen from a failure to understand that the two functions can be kept separate without being independent. Friction, and a lack of coöperation between the two branches of city government, has been due, not to the fact of their separate existence, but to the irresponsibility of one to the other. This is a feature which many sponsors of the commission plan have been prone to overlook. From one system in which the legislative and administrative branches of city government were as independent as two watertight compartments, they have turned with eager expectation to another in which the two are completely fused. The commission is a legislative and executive board combined. The commission plan denies the need of the slightest separation of powers.

It is here that one finds the root of the troubles which confront the commission plan in actual operation. Save in small cities a commission of five men is not large enough to be a proper policy-determining body. The satisfactory determination of civic policy involves adequate representation of all the real interests concerned, and a body of five men does not, in larger municipalities, provide adequate representation. Four years ago a committee of the National Municipal League, in its report upon the merits and shortcomings of the commission plan of city government in actual operation, laid emphasis upon this point. "Five men are too few to represent the varied elements of a great population, and will be too far from the people to be able to analyze public opinion by direct contact. The commission plan should therefore be enlarged but in a manner which will retain the short ballot. For moderate-sized cities, the choice of only a part of the commission at a time would help, but in the larger cities a sub-division of the people by ward divisions or proportional representation seems advisable." It is urged on the other hand, that the use of the iniative, referendum and recall would be sufficient to keep even a few men in touch with the wants of the masses, but that would hardly be the case unless these things were used frequently and on a scale such as would ultimately break them down.

The commission plan, accordingly, provides a body which is too small to be "able to analyze public opinion by direct contact" in larger cities. On the other hand the commission of five is too large to be thoroughly efficient as an administrative body. Much has been said and written about the way in which a commission concentrates responsibility for the conduct of municipal business, unifying the whole governmental system, and providing the supervisory brain which is necessary to a successful organism. In truth there is far more unification of responsibility and far more coördination of energies under the commission plan than under the ramshackle of councils, boards, committees and commissioners which so many cities possessed two decades ago. But it is at the most a five-headed unification; it still leaves room for friction on a three-to-two basis, for wasted energy and for the management of departments in such way as to promote personal or political ends. That is not a mere possibility; many commission governed cities in the last few years have found it to be a disappointing reality. Almost every argument that can be used in favor of concentrating administrative functions in the hands of five men instead of fifty can be applied to the project of concentrating them in one rather than in five. Localization of responsibility in a city manager is more complete than it can ever be in any body of men however small.

Commission government, accordingly, has in some cases failed to meet expectations, because it tries to straddle two horses going in opposite directions. It provides a body which is, in many cases, too small to be a good local legislature and too large for efficient administration. It asks the voters to choose men who will adequately represent them in the general determination of city policy — men of broad views and general sympathies — but who will at the same time each be competent to take general charge of a special administrative department such as finance, public works or public safety,— who will, in other words, have highly specialized interests and sympathies as well.

So far as the composition and powers of the city council are concerned the plan set forth in the Model City Charter rests upon the conviction that there should be a place in the municipal framework for a body which will be avowedly deliberative, supervisory, and policy-determin-

THE COUNCIL

ing, which will be wieldy enough to perform these functions properly and yet large enough to be truly representative of the community's opinions. It rests upon the further conviction that deliberative and administrative functions cannot with the best results be vested in the hands of the same men. In other words the framers of this Model City Charter have come to the conclusion that functions can be and ought to be separated without being made independent. Many of the troubles which beset our cities before the advent of the commission plan resulted from the fact that authority was placed in independent hands and in too many of them, not from the mere fact that legislative and administrative powers were committed to separate authorities.

The Model City Charter accordingly provides for a council with a membership which can be enlarged or contracted according to the varying size and needs of different cities. This council is to be the pivot of the municipal system. It is to be the final source of local authority, not sharing its powers with some other body or official but delegating some of them. That is to say, to a city manager chosen by the council and holding office during the council's pleasure, it assigns the entire charge of administrative affairs. The two great functions of municipal government are thus placed in separate but not in independent hands. Legislation is intrusted to a body which is large enough to be adequately representative; on the other hand, the concentration of administrative functions is made complete. The councilors are laymen, without expert knowledge or special interests. The city manager is a professional administrator. There can be no confusion in this arrangement, no deadlocks or lost motion.

Now as to the composition and powers of the council. The number of councilors is advisedly left flexible, with a range from five to twenty-five, according to the size of the city. Councilors are to be chosen at large. The system of election by wards has long since proved itself to be an obstacle in the way of attempts to get councilors of adequate quality. But where a city is very large, where it would constitute, when taken as a whole, an unwieldy electoral area, there is a strong case for dividing it into districts of considerable size. "To express it in another way, an electorate may be so large that it cannot perform even a simple task without organizing for it. . . . In huge electorates it will have to be a more elaborate and costly organization than we can ask the candidates to construct. . . . Let the political unit of district be not so large, but that an adequate impromptu organization can be put together at short notice. . . . Enlarge the district beyond a certain point and the business of winning an election becomes a job for experts only."[1]

Provision is made for the nomination of candidates by petitions bearing a moderate number of signatures and for election on a short ballot bearing no party designations. Into this system a plan of preferential voting or of proportional representation may be readily adjusted if that should be desired.

As for the powers of the city council, these may be stated briefly. It is designed to embody, as it were, the

[1] R. S. Childs, "Short Ballot Principles" (Boston, 1911), pp. 54-56.

THE COUNCIL

sovereignty of the community. It is the legislative organ of the city exercising all the authority which the municipal corporation possesses — with one important exception only. This restriction is that the city council, once it selects a city manager, devolves all direct administrative authority upon him. "Neither the council nor any of its committees or members shall dictate the appointment of any person to office or employment by the city manager, or in any manner interfere with the city manager or prevent him from exercising his own judgment in the appointment of officers or employees in the administrative service"[1] The council appoints the city manager, it maps out his work; it may investigate his results, and it may remove him at any time; but while he is in office it may not interfere with the performance of his designated functions. Administration is given a place apart, but it is not an independent place. It is subject to control but not to factious interference.

On the other hand, a large range of authority is given to the city council. It enacts the ordinances, levies the taxes, votes the budget, exercises the city's borrowing power, provides the public services, and authorizes the local improvements. It becomes once more the parliament of the community, the general policy-determining authority. That is the position which it holds in English cities to-day and which it once held in this country. It is a position of which it should never have been deprived. The principle of municipal home-rule carries with it the requirement that there shall be some representative body to exercise, with due deliberation, the large measure of

[1] Sec. 3.

autonomous powers which a home-rule system confers upon the municipality. The control of these powers should be centralized, not parceled out among several organs of local authority. Here is where the city council finds its appropriate place.

Under this system the mayor ceases to be a separate organ of local government. Chosen by the council from its own membership he becomes its presiding officer, with the usual authority of a chairman but with no administrative powers except in times of public danger or emergency when he may, with the consent of the council, take temporary command of the police. He is, however, to serve as the titular head of the municipality on occasions of ceremony. His position becomes, in fact, almost identical with that of the mayor in an English borough, or, as a better analogy perhaps, with that of the American mayor before the principle of divided powers was pressed to an absurdity in our local government.

A word in summary and conclusion. The orthodox or "federal-analogy" scheme of city government provided legislative and administrative organs, a council and a mayor, quite independent of each other, the preponderance of real power resting usually with the mayor. It represented a more or less conscious attempt to reproduce in miniature the complicated machinery of the national government. The city council, usually comprising until recent years two separate chambers, possessed the right to pass the ordinances, make the appropriations and authorize borrowing on the city's credit. The mayor, on the other hand, obtained and still holds in many cities the power to make nearly all the administrative appointments, subject often to confirmation by the city council or by the upper branch of it, likewise the direction of expenditures after the appropriations have been made by the council. To assist the mayor in his formidable task of administering the business of the community there are administrative boards and officials, who are usually appointed by him for definite terms and responsible to him alone. The complications of this plan are endless; it makes a scheme of local government which, in larger municipalities, defies intelligent understanding on the part of the ordinary citizen. For nearly two generations attempts were made to simplify it, usually by defining more sharply just what functions were legislative and what were administrative. And as the latter were much the more numerous and the more important, every step in this direction made for an increase in the powers of the mayor.

Then came, with the beginning of the twentieth century, the so-termed commission plan. Hurrying to the other extreme it abolished all distinction between the two great functions of legislation and administration, making a sharp reverse upon the steady trend of the previous five decades. It ignored, not wholly, but largely, the need of an organ of deliberation. It went forward with the postulate that the business of city government is almost altogether executive and that the commission should be an executive body, first and last. Yet it did not carry this line of thought to a logical conclusion. It did not provide complete unification of administrative power and responsibility, nor did it aim to put the management of the city's business directly into trained hands.

The purpose of the present Model City Charter is to avoid the dangers and to obtain the advantages of both the foregoing plans. The city council is regarded as a necessary agency of popular municipal government, necessary as a means of protecting local autonomy against state interference, and necessary as a means of giving the citizens a body which will reflect properly the trend of electoral opinion. And if the city council is a necessary part of a well-organized municipal system, it ought to be a body of real power and dignity. Without these it will not attract the right sort of men into its ranks. It is, therefore, made the controlling organ in all branches of civic policy. On the other hand the present plan recognizes the soundness of the principle that administrative work, to be efficiently carried on, must be committed to expert hands with localized responsibility. That principle it carries to a logical conclusion, namely, the delegating of administrative power to a single, well-paid, expert administrator. To this city-manager, who has broad authority within his own sphere but who is strictly accountable for the results which he secures, the actual details of city business management are entrusted. The city-manager plan is not, therefore, a compromise between the older and the commission schemes of municipal government, but a carrying to their proper conclusion of those features which were commendable in both.

IX

THE INITIATIVE, REFERENDUM AND RECALL

With the growth of the tendency to concentrate legislative and administrative powers in the hands of a steadily diminishing number of officials, one movement for popular control (the initiative, referendum and recall) has grown with almost equal rapidity and strength. In the first Municipal Program, this idea was referred to as "direct legislation," a phrase then as now loosely used in general discussion. "Direct legislation," meaning legislation directly by the voters instead of through the medium of their elected representatives, as so used, included not only the initiative, referendum and recall, although the recall had little to do with legislation, but the methods which prevailed in New England town meetings and formerly in some of the Swiss cantons. The town meeting system was manifestly archaic and of use only in smaller communities.

"Direct legislation," however, may be expanded from small to large communities by the use of the initiative and referendum. These legislative measures may be initiated by means of written petitions, signed by a prescribed percentage of legal voters of a political district, to be referred to the decision of the entire electorate of said political unit at the next general election or at a special election. Dr. C. F. Taylor, an ardent advocate of the initiative, referendum and recall, is of the opinion, however, that "no one in this or any other country ever advocates the town meeting in large communities. Advocates of the initiative and referendum staunchly defend the representative system of legislation; but recognize that its operations, for reasons of dishonesty or lack of understanding, may not be truly representative of the sentiments, desires and welfare of the represented. Hence, they advocate the introduction of initiative and referendum powers into every municipal charter and every state constitution; so that when, in the opinion of a reasonable number of voters, any act of the legislature is unsatisfactory to the voters, this reasonable number may demand a reference of the act to the entire body of voters, usually at the next regular election; also when, in the opinion of a reasonable number of voters, the legislative body has neglected to pass a measure which this reasonable number of voters believe to be desired by a majority of the voters, this reasonable number may initiate said measure to be placed on the ballot usually at the next general election for the decision of the entire body of voters."

Obviously this is not "direct legislation" except upon those topics in regard to which the representative body has not, or is suspected not to have, been truly representative of its constituents. The initiative and referendum powers are not intended to supplant representative government, but to perfect and safeguard it; and the advocates of the initiative and referendum do not advocate "direct legislation" as a general proposition to the exclusion of representative legislation. In fact, "they consider as ridiculous any proposition to impose 'direct legislation' to the exclusion of representation upon large cities and states, where it would be absolutely unworkable. In small communities only is exclusive direct legislation applicable, as illustrated in the New England town meetings, where it is still in use."

Such advocates of the initiative and referendum insist that the term "direct legislation" shall not be used except in connection with government in small communities where government is by means of town meetings. They also recognize the fact that legislation in large communities is not practicable except through representative legislative bodies; but they also recognize that representative bodies sometimes "go wrong." In order to correct and control legislative bodies, therefore, they advocate the initiative and referendum.

The recall is sometimes linked with the initiative and referendum, but the recall is not, as already indicated, a legislative instrument. Its purpose is for the popular control of officers, not legislation. It has most frequently been applied to executive officers, although it has been applied to judicial and legislative officers. Its use is merely to remove from office an individual who has been elected to an office before the regular term of that officer has expired.

In the first Municipal Program there was no provision for recall, and the council was given power to establish a method of "direct legislation," Section 3 of Article 3 of the proposed constitutional amendment reading, "the council of any city may, with the consent of the majority of the qualified voters of the city voting thereon at the next ensuing city election taking place not less than —— days thereafter,[1] establish a method of direct legislation so that qualified voters of the city may submit and a majority thereof voting thereon may decide by direct vote propositions relative to city matters." The Municipal Corporation Act, Section II of Article V contained a provision to the same effect.

Under the strong home rule influences pervading the first Municipal Program, a city was given power to try this experiment, but the committee did not see its way clear, nor did the situation prevailing at that time justify a recommendation in favor of embodying the initiative, referendum and recall as essential, integral parts of a model city charter.

In the space of time intervening between the drafting of the first (1898-1900) and the second (1914-16) municipal programs, there had occurred several interesting and suggestive developments. In the first place there had been the introduction, growth and generally successful conduct of the commission form of government as embodied in the Des Moines Plan. This included the initiative, referendum and recall. The experience under the charters modeled on the Des Moines plan established a body of precedents of great importance. Other cities like Portland, Oregon, Los Angeles and Seattle, which were not operating under a commission form were using the initiative, referendum and recall, establishing a still further body of interesting and valuable experience. In an article published in the *National Municipal Review* [2]

[1] This, as will be recognized, constitutes a referendum.
[2] Vol. III, No. 4, page 693, 1914.

the results were given of an inquiry as to the existence and use of the initiative, referendum and recall in 279 cities then operating under a commission form of government, some of which, especially those modeled on the Galveston plan, were without provisions for them.

Of the 279 municipalities reported, eighteen seem to be entirely without the initiative, referendum or recall. Of the remaining 261 municipalities, 197 have all three; 36 have the initiative and referendum; four have the referendum and recall; four have the initiative and recall; two have the initiative only; two have the referendum only, and fourteen have the recall only. However, six, not included in the above figures as having the referendum, have a limited referendum for franchises only or bonds only, one having the obligatory referendum on franchises.

On June 30, 1914, the voters of St. Louis, Mo., adopted a new charter providing for the initiative, referendum and recall on a workable basis, the result giving St. Louis the distinction of being the largest city in the country having these instruments. Sentiment for them was increased by the successful use of the initiative under the old charter in forcing the legislature to complete the Mississippi River bridge. At that time over 50 per cent of the voters signed the initiative petition.

The Michigan home rule law of 1913 grants an interesting method of initiating charter amendments. In his "Organized Democracy," finished in May, 1913, Dr. Frederick A. Cleveland, page 355, says: "In California eleven cities which do not have the commission form of government have adopted the initiative and referendum." But the eleven cities in California referred to by Dr.

Cleveland, and the home-rule New York and Michigan cities, above mentioned, were not included in the definite figures given in the *National Municipal Review* article, owing to technical difficulties and their very recent enactment.

So much for the plain facts concerning the existence of these measures in the fundamental laws of the cities of this country. "How about their use?" the investigator asks: —

"Of the 261 municipalities that have these powers, thirty-one have used the initiative, twenty-six have used the referendum and twenty-seven have used the recall. Of the six that have the limited referendum, one has used it on franchises.

"The preceding paragraphs contain some figures that will be a surprise to those who consider the initiative, referendum and recall as radical and dangerous instruments for the voters to possess. For example, of the 197 municipalities that possess all three of these instruments, 137 have not used any of them. This, however, does not argue that these instruments are not of value. The editor of the *National Municipal Review* said in a lecture delivered at Raleigh, N. C., March 10, 1914, that these measures are 'more valuable in their existence than in their use. Their existence impresses a sterner sense of duty and keener thoughts of responsibility in the minds of officials.'"

In commenting on the data which he had gathered, Dr. Taylor made this remark: "The United States of

INITIATIVE, REFERENDUM, RECALL

America is a very large country, peopled by a citizenship which is active in many ways, so that if it were possible to have all of the facts concerning the existence and the use of the initiative, referendum and recall in the cities on a given date, another twenty-four hours would perhaps render the statement incomplete in some particular. So the above statement is as complete as it can well be made at any one writing; and so far as known to the writer, it is the first attempt to make a complete collection of these facts. The figures are corrected to September 1, 1914."

Nevertheless the results afford an excellent cross section of experience and go far toward justifying the judgment expressed in the final paragraphs: "We see in this review a safe, healthy and commendable exercise of direct powers of the voters in the public affairs of municipalities. These powers have not been abused, as is plainly seen by the large number of municipalities which have these powers, but which have never used them; and in the fact that in no place has their use been 'cranky' or excessive. These powers have been used rather freely in Portland, Oregan, and in Dallas, Texas, but we have no evidence that there is any sentiment in these places for the abolition of these powers on account of their somewhat free use. On the contrary, we may reasonably assume that the use of these powers is an evidence of their appreciation — when there is occasion for their use.

"If these powers of public control of public affairs and of officers had come sooner into the municipal life of this nation, would municipal mismanagement and corruption have become a national disgrace? I think not. I hope for and predict the continued rapid extension of the initiative, referendum and recall until they will be in the charter of every municipality under the stars and stripes. The modern American spirit demands that the public, through the electorate, shall have power to control public affairs and officers, whenever, in the judgment of the electorate, there is occasion to do so."

[1] For further information on this subject in the pages of the *National Municipal Review*, see "The Initiative, Referendum and Recall in San Francisco," by E. A. Walcott, Vol. II, page 467; "The Oregon System at Work," by Richard W. Montague, Vol. III, page 256.

Three motives unquestionably have played a part in the development of public sentiment for popular control.

First and foremost is the growth of the desire on the

[1] A more recent and more complete presentation of the actual experiences of American municipalities with the Initiative, Referendum and Recall based on original reports from officials in the cities concerned, was published in the October, 1916, issue of *Equity*. For that presentation reports had been received from 396 municipalities having one or more of these instruments of direct control. These reports contained replies to a questionnaire showing the following facts: In 258 of the municipalities heard from there had not been so far, a single instance of the use of these powers of popular control. The use of them which had occurred in the remaining 138 municipalities was thus analyzed: the Initiative was used 128 times; the Referendum 103 times (not counting compulsory referenda on franchise grants or bond issues or voluntary submissions of questions by city commissions); and the Recall 59 times.

In only seven of the reports was there express opposition to these powers. The reports from city officials, 116, definitely stated that the existence of the powers was beneficial even though they had never yet been resorted to by the voters.

part of an increasing number of people in the various communities of the United States to have a larger and more direct share in the actual government. Because of the various political ills which the American communities and particularly the cities had suffered, the voter had come to feel that he must directly bear a larger part of the burden. Hence the movements for direct primaries, direct election of United States senators, and "direct legislation."

Second: A part of this movement, although really constituting a separate motive, was the breaking down of confidence in representative government. Special interests and great political organizations had fed upon and grown powerful on the complicated machinery which had grown up, including a highly complicated system of so-called representative government. The quickest remedy for this condition seemed to be to transform the old-fashioned system of checks and balances of one department of government against another into a system of checks or control on the part of the people. In other words, to give the representatives a power of attorney revocable at the will of those whom they represent — the people — and reserving to the people the right to initiate new lines of business when they feel that the situation demands it. In the words of a well known authority:

"The old-fashioned 'checks and balances,' the divisions of powers and distribution of responsibilities do not check. They permit the intrusion of selfish interests in the government and prevent the adequate protection of the public interests. We see the need of discontinuing the 'balances,' and of concentrating the powers and responsibilities. This is the only way to increase efficiency. But concentrated powers are dangerous without the possibility of control outside the few hands into which great power has been concentrated. Where is the most rational place in which to lodge this possible control? There can be but one answer: the electorate. And the initiative, referendum and recall are the best methods yet devised in which to exercise this control." [1]

Thus the initiative, referendum and recall grew out of the failures of the old form of city government with its checks and balances and strict separation of powers. The advent of the newer type of municipal organization with its concentration of power, led to a still stronger insistence upon measures for direct popular control. Commission government appeared frankly to abandon the separation of legislative and executive powers and swept away the traditional system of checks and balances. It is true that these devices had proved to be unreliable safeguards of popular rights. Still they had been something, and when it was proposed to omit them from city charters altogether, there was a strong demand that some effective means of popular control be put in their place. Without the assurance afforded by the initiative and referendum, commission government and the manager plan would have made very slow progress.

The third motive entering into the development was the fear lest the rapid concentration of power might lead to the creation of a strong oligarchy. Given the great

[1] *National Municipal Review,* Vol. IV, page 59.

INITIATIVE, REFERENDUM, RECALL

powers of the city manager form of government under ample home rule powers, and the people might find themselves in a much worse condition than formerly. How get the best results out of concentration of legislative and administrative powers and a minimum of disadvantages — and the answer has been the initiative and referendum and recall!

When the second committee on municipal program came to consider the questions involved in the light of experience, it adopted by a majority vote the provisions that are to be found embodied in Sections 11 to 34 inclusive. This action may be regarded as fairly typical of the opinion of the students of the problem of government, among whom there is a considerable number who still regard the case of the initiative, referendum and recall as "not proven."

There are others who feel that they represent a temporary expedient to check current abuses which will pass away in time as a result of the application of the initiative, referendum and recall.

President Woodrow Wilson in an address at Kansas City, May 5, 1911, said:

"The methods of our legislatures make the operations of political machines easy, for very little of our legislation is formed and effected by open debate upon the floor. Almost all of it is framed in lawyers' offices, discussed in committee rooms, and passed without debate. Bills that the machine and its backers do not desire are smothered in committee; measures which they do desire are brought out and hurried through their passage. It happens again and again that great groups of such bills are rushed through in the hurried hours that mark the close of the legislative sessions, when every one's vigilance is weakened by fatigue and when it is possible to do secret things.

"When we stand in the presence of these things and see how complete and sinister their operation has been, we cry out with no little truth that we no longer have representative government.

"If we felt that we had genuine representative government in our state legislatures, no one would propose the initiative and referendum in America. They are being proposed now as a means of bringing our representatives back to the consciousness that what they are bound in duty and in mere policy to do is to represent the sovereign people whom they profess to serve, and not the private interests which creep into their councils by way of machine orders and committee conferences.

"It must be remembered by every candid man who discusses these matters that we are contrasting the operation of the initiative and referendum, not with the representative government which we have in theory, but with the actual state of affairs."

There are still others who maintain that these three instruments are of the essence of democracy. Judson King, the executive secretary of the National Popular Government League, is one of these and he has set forth at length his views in an article which has been published as a Senate Document.[1] Whatever the final judgment,

[1] Senate Document 736, 64th Congress, 2d session.

INITIATIVE, REFERENDUM, RECALL 171

the preponderance of sentiment at this time is certainly to the effect that the initiative, referendum and recall are mighty handy instruments of control to have nearby for use in case of necessity.[1]

That they have been so used in the main is clear from the facts which have been correlated in the *National Municipal Review* article to which I have referred, and one may say that, in examining the uses of the initiative, referendum and recall in the various cities of the country, we do not find any indication of the fact that the percentages have had much influence one way or the other.[2] In fact, many whose requirements are the lowest have not used these powers at all. Among those which have used these powers the most frequently can be found the ones which require the highest percentages. For example, Dallas, Texas, has made the most frequent and the most successful use of the recall among all the cities that have the recall, yet its recall requirement is " 35 per cent of the entire vote cast for candidates for the office of mayor on the final ballot at the last preceding general municipal election," yet not quite as high as that recommended by Professor James, as he recommends 35 per cent of the entire electorate. It would seem that when there is occasion to invoke these powers, they will be invoked even

[1] It must always be borne in mind that the referendum in one of its forms is an instrument that has been in use since the beginning of our national life, for we have from that time to the present referred to the voters for approval or disapproval, new constitutions and constitutional amendments, new charters and charter amendments (although until very recently with by no means the same frequency as the former), and grants of franchises.

[2] This refers to the percentage of voters necessary to put the initiative, referendum or recall into operation. It varies greatly in different charters.

though the conditions are difficult; and easy conditions do not cause the undue use of these powers.[1]

[1] Those who desire an extended, adequate detailed discussion of the Initiative, Referendum and Recall are recommended to consult the volume of Dr. Delos F. Wilcox (a member of the Municipal Program Committee), "Government by All the People" (Macmillan Co., 1912), which is an adequate discussion of these "instruments of democracy." He does attempt to discuss the specific forms that have been adopted in various cities and states, but rests his arguments almost entirely upon a consideration of the failures of our old system of checks, balances and upon a priori reasons for believing that the new instruments will be more effective in establishing popular self-government.

Another important volume dealing with the initiative, referendum and recall is the one edited by Prof. William Bennett Munro of Harvard University, in the *National Municipal League Series*. This volume presents both sides of the question and contains a number of interesting chapters dealing with the actual operation of these three experiments in American political life.—EDITOR.

X

THE FRANCHISE POLICY OF THE NEW MUNICIPAL PROGRAM

The National Municipal League, from the beginning, has been militantly in favor of municipal home rule. It has believed that one of the greatest obstacles to efficient, democratic government in American cities has been and is the characteristic American policy of subjecting cities, both as to their governmental forms and as to their functions, to detailed legislative limitation and regulation. It has seen that, in America at least, the die is cast for the forms of democracy. It has urged that the only possible way for a municipal democracy to keep its vitality and learn the wisdom of self-government is by being permitted to look out for its own salvation. But the League has not been content to advocate home rule merely as a vague aspiration, something that everybody favors and nobody understands; it has sought to define as well as to advocate the principle of municipal self-government.

PUBLIC UTILITIES IN ORIGINAL MUNICIPAL PROGRAM

On the general policy of municipal ownership and operation of public utilities, or of any specific class of them, the League has never taken a dogmatic stand, either for or against; but it has recognized that the right of a city to determine this issue for itself is an essential and very important element of municipal home rule. In conformity with these principles the original Municipal Program included, both in the proposed Constitutional Amendments and in the Municipal Corporations Act, provisions conferring upon cities broad powers with reference to public utilities. The Constitutional Amendments (Article Third, Section 7) provided that every city should be " vested with power to perform and render all public services, and with all powers of government," subject to legislative limitations, which could be imposed only in the manner prescribed. Moreover, these amendments (Article Third, Section 1) provided that no public utility franchise should be granted for a longer period than 21 years; that any such franchise might provide for the reversion of the property of a public utility to the city at the expiration of the grant, or for the purchase of such property by the city; that every franchise should " specify the mode of determining any valuation therein provided for," and should " make adequate provision by way of forfeiture of the grant or otherwise, to secure efficiency of public service at reasonable rates, and the maintenance of the property in good order throughout the term of the grant "; and that every grantee of a franchise should keep books and render quarterly reports to the financial department of the city showing in detail its receipts, expenditures, assets and debts, its books being open to examination by the city. The amendments also provided (Article Third, Section 2) for a general limitation upon municipal indebtedness, from which, however, were to be excluded bonds authorized by a two-thirds vote of the city council, and approved by the mayor and a majority of the qualified voters of the city, issued " for the supply of water or for other specific undertaking from which the city will derive a revenue "; provided that this exemption from the debt limit, unless the principal and interest of the bonds were payable exclusively from the receipts of the utility, should not apply to public utility bonds after the expiration of a period of not more than five years from the date of issue, if such utility failed to be self-sustaining: that is to say, if it failed to provide enough revenue to pay all costs of operation and administration, including interest and insurance against loss by fire, accident and personal injuries, together with an annual amount sufficient to pay at or before maturity all bonds issued on account of such utility.

STATUTORY GRANTS AND RESTRICTIONS

The proposed Constitutional Amendments granted to every city very large powers of home rule, as we have seen, but the exercise of these powers was subject to the constitutional limitations described and also to limitation by general legislative acts or by special legislative acts adopted in a specific manner prescribed in the amendments. The model Municipal Corporations Act represented the National Municipal League's idea of the manner in which the legislature of the state, under the constitutional provisions already described, ought to provide for, limit and regulate the powers of cities. This act provided (Article Second, Section 1) that a city might, for any purpose which it deemed necessary or expedient for the public interest, " perform and carry on any public service, and acquire property within or without the city limits by purchase, gift, devise or by condemnation proceedings, and hold, manage and control the same." The act also provided (Article Second, Section 3) that the city should have power to "construct and maintain waterworks and sewers," and (Article Second, Section 4) to "operate ferries, and charge tolls and ferriage." It also provided (Article Second, Section 10) that "the city may, if it deems proper, acquire or construct, and may also operate on its own account, and may regulate or prohibit the construction or operation of railroads and other means of transit or transportation and methods for the production or transmission of heat, light, electricity or other power in any of their forms, by pipes, wires or other means." In regard to public utility franchises (Article Second, Section 10) the act repeated the constitutional provisions limiting grants to twenty-one years and further provided that "in addition to any other form of compensation, the grantee shall pay annually a sum of money, based in amount upon its gross receipts, to the city." The constitutional provisions above described providing for the publicity of public utility accounts and for exemption of municipal utility bonds from the general debt limit were repeated in the act.

The original Municipal Program was adopted in 1900. At that time its provisions in regard to franchises and public utilities, if we consider the state of the law and the practice in most American commonwealths and cities, were comprehensive and radical. Nevertheless, the popular resentment against perpetual and long-term franchises and against the exploitation of the streets by public service corporations was becoming acute and the sentiment in favor of municipal ownership and operation of all public utilities was then coming into the ascendant. But the changes that have taken place in the public utility situation during the past eighteen years have been so rapid and so fundamental as to make the comparatively radical program of 1900 out-of-date and inadequate for the needs of 1918. These changes include an enormous expansion of public utility investments, a vast increase in municipal indebtedness for general purposes, the overflow of public utilities from strictly urban into suburban and interurban fields, and the development of the idea of the indeterminate franchise and the idea of state regulation by public service commissions. The National Municipal League is not yet committed to the policy of municipal ownership and operation of all public utilities, and is not prepared to substitute for the idea of municipal home rule in public utility matters a comprehensive and exact public utility policy to be recommended to all cities alike. Nevertheless, the League recognizes that the mere untying of the hands of a municipality so as to give it discretion to solve its utility problems in its own way, does not meet the complete requirements of a national municipal program. While many important franchise and utility questions are still mooted, even among those who look at these problems solely from the public point of view, the time is now ripe for a general declaration of principles, in accordance with which local utility policies should be worked out.

NEW PROGRAM MAKES UNIFORM GRANT INSTEAD OF
IMPOSING UNIFORM RESTRICTIONS

The new Municipal Program has been constructed upon somewhat different lines from the old. The provisions now recommended for incorporation in the fundamental law of the several states, have been drafted as a " charter of liberties " and all are brought under the general caption, " Constitutional Municipal Home Rule." The idea of uniformity in the organization of cities has been eclipsed by the idea of local freedom as to the forms of government to be adopted in any particular case, and the idea of *uniform restriction* of municipal powers has given way almost wholly to the idea of a *uniform grant* of comprehensive powers of local self-government to be exercised in the discretion of each municipality. In the statutory portions of the program, the idea of a general municipal corporations act has been replaced by that of a model city charter, to be adopted by the citizens of the city in the exercise of their free choice under constitutional guaranties.

The constitutional provisions recommended by the new program are therefore more comprehensive and less restrictive than those recommended by the old program. In so far as public utilities are concerned, the Constitutional Amendment (Section 5) provides that the general grant of powers conferred upon cities shall be deemed to include the power " to furnish all local public services; to purchase, hire, construct, own, maintain and operate or lease, public utilities; to acquire, by condemnation or otherwise, within or without the corporate limits of the

THE FRANCHISE POLICY

city, property necessary for any such purposes, subject to the restrictions imposed by general law for the protection of other communities, and to grant local public utility franchises and regulate the exercise thereof"; and "to issue and sell bonds on the security . . . of any public utility owned by the city, or of the revenues thereof, or of both, including . . . if deemed desirable by the city, a franchise stating the terms upon which, in case of foreclosure, the purchaser may operate such utility."

In the formulation of the franchise and public utility provisions of the Model Charter, the new program follows a middle course. In adopting it the League recognized the need for the establishment of certain general principles with which the franchise and public utility policy of every city should square so far as local and temporary conditions will permit. On the other hand, it was deemed inadvisable to attempt to work out in the charter itself the details of a comprehensive constructive public utility policy applicable to all utilities alike and to all cities alike. The actual provisions embodied in the Model Charter establish the following principles:

SPECIFIC PROVISIONS OF NEW PROGRAM

(1) No franchise may be granted, extended or amended except by ordinance, and no franchise ordinance may be adopted until after a printed report containing the recommendations of the city manager, or of the bureau of franchises, if there be one, has been presented, public hearings held and the ordinance itself published in its final form for at least two weeks.

(2) Every public utility franchise shall be terminable

at specified intervals of not more than five years after the beginning of operation whenever the city shall determine to acquire the property, and the method of arriving at the price paid in case of municipal purchase shall be fixed in the franchise. No maximum term limit for franchises is recommended, but it is declared in a note that if in any case a term limit is adopted, provision should be made for the amortization of the investment during the life of the franchise or for the purchase of the physical property by the city at the end of the franchise term.

(3) Under every franchise grant the right is reserved to the city to exercise regulatory powers in the matter of extensions, maintenance of the property, standards of service, quality of products, prevention of unjust discrimination, forms of accounts and reports and other regulations conducive to the safety, welfare and accommodation of the public.

(4) The consent of property owners to the construction of public utilities in the streets in front of their premises is not to be required, unless, as in New York, provision is made by which their arbitrary refusal to consent may be overcome by an appeal to the courts, but property owners are to have the right to recover from the owner of the utility the actual damages incurred by them, less the benefits received, through the construction of the utility.

(5) Revocable permits for minor or temporary privileges may be granted from time to time by the city council without restriction as to its procedure, but such permits shall be limited to classes of privileges specified in a general ordinance which may be adopted only in the

same manner and subject to the same restrictions as a franchise ordinance.

(6) Grants for extensions of plant must terminate with the original grant and be terminable as provided in paragraph (2) above.

(7) Every franchise hereafter granted shall be subject to all the specific terms and restrictions provided for in the charter, even though such terms and restrictions are not expressly set forth in the franchise grant itself.

(8) Copies of all existing franchises claimed by a public utility shall be filed with the city, and the city shall compile and maintain a public record of all franchises and of all utility fixtures in the streets.

(9) Every city shall establish by ordinance a bureau of franchises and public utilities, the head of which shall be an expert in franchise and public utility matters. It shall be the duty of this official to investigate and report on all proposed ordinances relating to public utilities, to exercise diligent oversight over the operation of privately owned public utilities, and to represent the city in all proceedings before a state utilities commission involving public utilites within the city.

(10) The accounts of every municipally owned utility shall be kept distinct from other city accounts and in such a manner as to show the true and complete financial results of city ownership, including the value of service furnished to such utility by other city departments or rendered by it to them. The accounts must also show a proper allowance for depreciation, insurance, interest on investment, and the taxes that would be chargeable against the property if it were privately owned.

It will be noted that these provisions are for the most part restrictive. They embody the rules which, in the judgment of the League, every city should impose upon itself in its charter in order that the granting of franchises, the formulation of public utility policies and the actual operation of public utilities may be done with due deliberation and full opportunity for the exercise of wisdom. The right of self-destruction is not a part of the concept of individual liberty recognized by American law and public opinion. The right of a city, by the act of officials holding a temporary mandate from their constituents or even by the act of the electors themselves who, at any given time, have the last word in the determination of municipal policies, to alienate the use of its streets for an indefinite period or forever, under terms and conditions which the inexperience, the carelessness or the temporary interest of the moment may dictate, is not regarded as an essential feature of the right of municipal home rule in any proper sense of that term. It is recommended, therefore, that the city, through its charter, impose upon its officials and its electorates certain restrictions tending to prevent hasty and ill-considered action, and to preserve the rights of future generations, which otherwise, in an unfortunate moment, might be bartered away. A model municipal charter cannot do less. The one proposed by the League does not do more.

FUNDAMENTAL AIMS OF UTILITY POLICY

However, for the guidance of individual cities in the establishment of a comprehensive and constructive franchise and public utility program, a declaration of prin-

THE FRANCHISE POLICY

ciples has been formulated by the League and incorporated in the Model Charter in the form of a note. This declaration deserves some discussion and elucidation in this chapter.

The aims of a public utility and franchise policy, as set forth in Note 20, are (1) good service, (2) municipal control of the streets, (3) removal of obstacles to municipal ownership, and (4) low rates. It is declared by way of contrast that it should *not* be the aim of such a policy to secure compensation for franchises or to supply revenues for general city purposes from an indirect tax on the patrons of public utilities.

GOOD SERVICE COMES FIRST

The order in which the constructive purposes of a correct franchise policy are stated is of very great significance. It is the opinion of the League that in many cities where the cry for low street car fares or low rates for other utilities has become a shibboleth of political reform, this particular aim of a correct franchise policy has been overemphasized. The League does not underestimate the *absolute* importance of low rates, but it believes that the *relative* importance of the other purposes enumerated as (1), (2), and (3) has been greatly neglected, to the infinite disadvantage, both present and future, of the cities and the people served by the utilities. It believes that first and foremost of the essential purposes of a correct franchise and public utility policy is good service. Clearly, *service* is the very thing for which a franchise is granted or a public utility constructed. This truth is so obvious and so inherent in the very nature of a public utility that the class of corporations operating public utility plants is known by the general title *public service corporations*. It is a curious fact, however, that the difference between good service and bad service has often been lost sight of. Perhaps there is no one factor in the recent development of public utility problems more potent for good, as well as for trouble, than the awakened demand on the part of the public for improved service in all classes of utilities. The space allotted to a single chapter is far too short to analyze and describe in detail the elements that go to make up *good service*. But it may be worth while to mention a few of them. In all utilities, adequate extensions of plant to meet the reasonable demands of a growing community are to be regarded as one of the most important elements in good service. For example, in a local transit system, it is not good service to refuse to extend a car line because the people who live beyond the end of it, after walking to the point where they can catch the car, will still be so far away from the center of the city that they will all have to ride and pay their nickels just the same as if they had been able to get on in front of their own doors. It is not good service to compel people to stand in crowded roadways without shelter from heat, cold and storm and exposed to physical danger from street traffic, while they wait five, ten or fifteen minutes to be transferred from one car line to another. It is not good service to keep the cars so cold or so poorly ventilated, or to let them get so dirty, as to endanger the health of passengers. It is not good service to have the tracks so rough, the cars so nimble and the lights so poor that patrons having a long way to go are unable to read without becoming cross-eyed or blind. It is not good service to furnish so few cars that during rush hours shop girls have to tread on each other's feet in the aisles and the workingmen have to climb on the roof or hang on the outside of the cars "by their eyebrows," as they say in Detroit. Yet all of these undesirable features of street railway transit may be realized in the highest degree in conjunction with eight-for-a-quarter tickets or straight three-cent fares. The opposites of these characteristics are desirable and, the League thinks, necessary, but they cost money and the farther service goes in the direction of these opposites, the more money it will cost. When we come to consider other utilities, good service obviously demands that light shall be light and that heat shall be hot, that communication by electricity shall be quick and that water shall run into the sewers, not sewage run into the water pipes. The League recognizes that reasonably good service under favorable conditions is not inconsistent with reasonably low rates. The League would not boost the rates for the sake of curing poor service when such service results from the operation of a public utility as a kind of ruse to conceal the exploitation of the gullible public through the manipulation of corporate securities. Where poor service has resulted from niggardly operation and maintenance, made and kept niggardly for the sole purpose of enabling real or fictitious investors to extract fabulous profits from the business and transform water into gold, an increase in the rates is certainly not the proper remedy. Nevertheless, the League insists that service is the first requisite in the operation of a public utility and that reasonably good service is essential even though it may be inconsistent with the lowest rates.

MUNICIPAL CONTROL OF THE STREETS

The purpose that is regarded as second only to good service in its importance is the continuous effective control of the streets by the people of the city. The street is the life of an urban community. It is the common property in which every citizen has a share. That this property, or special privileges in the use of it, should be conveyed in perpetuity, either by sale or by gift, to any individual or group of individuals, is directly contrary to the interests of democracy. It is an intolerable limitation of the common wealth. Therefore, perpetual franchises are not to be thought of. Franchises must be limited, but even a limitation to a period of 20 or 30 or 50 years, which would be sufficient to cover a cycle in the development of one of the great public utlities, is an inadequate limitation for the protection of the public interests. Utilities must go on, and the actual and necessary investments in utility plants must be protected without the cities being tied up by irrevocable contracts for a generation or more. Hence, the old theory of a limited-term franchise is no longer deemed sufficient, but franchises must be revocable at reasonably frequent periods, on condition that the city, when it revokes a franchise, shall purchase at its fair value the property to which the franchise gives life. Not only should the city retain the power to resume full control of its streets by the termination of franchises and the purchase of utility plants, but it is essential that such control should be continuous and vigorously effective, even during the period when franchises are held and public utilities operated by private corporations. The uses of the street are so multiplex and the development of such uses year by year is so hard to foresee, that a city cannot preserve its freedom of self-development without retaining at all times full control of the distribution of street spaces to the various necessary uses of the street. In fact, the control of the streets acquired by corporations enjoying perpetual and irrevocable franchises for the maintenance and operation of public utility fixtures, is a subtle and powerful force operating almost irresistibly to curtail liberty and strangle democracy. It is fatal to the sense of civic pride and independence without which municipal self-government is a hollow sham, and in its important practical aspects it is a stumbling block in the way of the efficient development of the city street and the complete coördination of its essential uses. But the continuous control of the public streets implies the protection of public utility investments. If the street is to be public in a continuous and real sense, then those who invest in street car tracks, gas pipes, electric conduits and pole lines, and water mains, must be regarded as creditors of the municipality, not as mere speculators in a private enterprise. It is the bane of so-called radical movements, so far as they relate to the control of public utilities, that they often refuse to recognize facts. They insist that the patrons of public utilities should be able to eat their cake and have it too. If cities are to have good service, continuous and certain control of their streets, and reasonably low rates, they must assume the essential and necessary risk in public utility investments.

REMOVAL OF OBSTACLES TO MUNICIPAL OWNERSHIP

The third purpose of a correct franchise policy is to remove the obstacles from the path of municipal ownership and make it as easy as possible for municipal ownership to succeed. In declaring and espousing this purpose, and putting it ahead of low rates in importance, the League at last expresses a theoretical and ultimate bias in favor of municipal ownership. Those who oppose this policy to the last ditch favor making it as difficult as possible for cities to undertake municipal ownership and, in some cases at least, favor making its success when undertaken as unlikely as possible. The League, in urging municipal home rule in relation to public utilities, recognizes municipal ownership as a possible and proper policy under conditions that win for it the approval of the people of a city. But the League has no use for a sham home rule that makes its promise to the ear and breaks it to the hope. When it says that it favors home rule as to municipal ownership, it does not mean the kind of home rule that would permit every cow to jump over the moon — if she can — nor even the kind that would authorize any newsboy to buy the Woolworth building — if he has the money. It means something more than technical or verbal home rule. As applied to municipal ownership, it means the removal of legal prohibitions, the inauguration of a policy of financial preparation and conservation, the development of administrative experience and the organization of special knowledge. Of the many works of old Mother Futility in connection with the reform of American city government, there is none more pathetic in its indifference to facts than the filling up of a brand-new charter with franchise restrictions applying only to the future and with big-sounding grants of power of the you-can-do-it-if-you-want-to type. Where all existing franchises are terminable or have a definite and reasonably short time limit on their lives, the problem of establishing real home rule in regard to public utilities is hard enough, but when franchises are perpetual, it is infinitely harder.

In the former case, it is a matter of getting ready. It is a common delusion that by the mere passage of time and the development of public sentiment a city may, after a while, *be* ready for municipal ownership. Far from it. Readiness means a definite purpose backed up by years of preparation. Plans must be made for fixing the purchase price and for getting the money to pay it. All franchise rights as to any one utility must be brought to expire on the same date. The whole scheme of local taxation must be adjusted to conditions that will be necessary when the utility is taken over. A thorough knowledge of the utility plant, of its operation and of the complaints and needs of the public must be got through expert study and continuous attention and control. The administrative machinery must be developed to make municipal operation a success.

When all outstanding franchises, or some of them if they are important ones, are perpetual, then the problem resolves itself into the question of how to find means to get rid of perpetuity. The city is justified in assuming an attitude of implacable hostility to a perpetual franchise, and it should use every lawful means in its power to make the holders of such a franchise so uncomfortable and their exploitation of it so unprofitable that they will be willing to surrender it for the sake of coöperation and security. Comparatively few utilities are so well intrenched that they do not need further concessions from the city from time to time. This need may be used as a leverage to pry them loose from their perpetual rights. The power of state and local taxation and the power to regulate rates and service may also be used to make perpetual franchises untenable. A city cannot effect its purpose, however, merely by oppression. It must have a constructive franchise policy, with adequate provision for the protection of legitimate investments, in order that it may be able to offer the holders of perpetual rights some inducements to give them up and come under the city's new policy.

Another necessary means of preparing for municipal ownership and of making success in municipal operation practicable, is the establishment of thorough and honest accounting methods. Every city that owns and operates a public utility should discard by charter requirement the slipshod political methods of keeping its accounts and telling its financial story which prevail so generally at the present time.

LOW RATES

Finally, it should be the purpose of a correct franchise and public utility policy to insure rates as low as can be given consistently with the rendering of good service, the retention and development of public control of the streets and the financial preparation required to make the transition to municipal ownership under promising con-

THE FRANCHISE POLICY

ditions possible. All forms of special taxes on public utilities should be sacrificed to low rates. Franchises as such, apart from the physical property to which they give life, should have no value. They should not be sold or leased for a money consideration. Utility services are so vital to the healthy development of urban communities, so public in their nature, so universal in their application that sound municipal policy forbids the adoption of any plan by which the consumers of utility services shall be taxed indirectly for the support of other governmental activities. Another reason for keeping rates as low as possible is the necessity of curbing the natural tendency to inflation of franchise values where utilities are operated as monopolies. In order to keep in control of the streets, the city has to keep its hand on the throat of the franchise holder all the time. This is a hard saying, but a true one, and one of the most effective ways of keeping a monopoly from developing arrogance is by keeping its rates pared to the quick. However, if low rates are permitted to excuse bad service, they are themselves inexcusable. It is clear that the reduction of rates, if made use of as the sole weapon of offense against the rapacity of public service corporations, will cut the hand that smites with it. It can be used with safety only as one tool of a complete kit, all of which are kept well edged and fit for constant service.

UTILITIES NOT TO BE EXPLOITED FOR RELIEF OF TAXPAYERS

The old Municipal Program required that every franchise should provide for the payment to the city of a percentage of the grantee's gross receipts. That was before the day of continuous regulation. It was thought that companies enjoying franchises for profit under fixed terms and conditions ought to share their earnings with the public. The new program contains no such provision, and moreover in its declaration of principles it states that it should be no part of a model public utility policy to secure compensation for franchises or special revenues for general city purposes by an indirect tax upon public utility consumers. This does not preclude the taxing of the physical property of public utilities at the same rate as other property; nor does it preclude a special tax on franchises or a sharing in the profits, if the city's receipts from these sources are put into a special fund for the purchase or extension of the utility itself. When the original program was formulated, the Glasgow idea was rampant in the minds of American municipal reformers. Indeed, for a time the municipal ownership movement, depending on British precedents, exploited the thrifty tax-payer's idea that with enough profit-earning utilities in operation a city might become a tax-payers' earthly paradise, if the tax-payer species did not disappear entirely, translated to another sphere by the uplift of its own happiness. The fable that Glasgow stopped paying taxes when it went into municipal ownership on an extensive scale has been relegated to its place in our municipal folk-lore. It was too good to be true, and if true would have been too undemocratic to be good. We have learned in the last fifteen years that every dollar a public utility can earn at reasonable rates is needed in rendering first-class service, keeping the plant up to the highest practicable standard of efficiency and rendering a reasonable return on the necessary investment. There may be temporary and local exceptions, but even to get a surplus for amortization it is generally necessary to lower the rate of return upon the investment by increasing its security. The actual earning power of fixed rates, such as the five-cent street car fare, has been greatly diminished since the campaign for lower rates started, a score or more of years ago. The increase in the prices of general commodities and the increase in the cost of labor and materials have reduced rates without our knowing it, and have in many cases more than offset the gains from the cheapening processes of invention, administrative progress and consolidation. Service is fed by the rates. Special taxation steals away a portion of this food.

FUNDAMENTAL RULES

In seeking to compass the larger purposes of a constructive and liberal public utility policy, every city must, in the League's opinion, conform as nearly as practicable to certain fundamental rules. Every utility serving an urban community should be recognized as a monopoly and treated accordingly, not as an obnoxious private monopoly to be harassed, and destroyed if possible, but as a public monopoly operated in the interest of the city under effective constructive control on the plan that is most economical for the rendering of a community service at the lowest practicable cost. The attempt of a city to sandbag public utilities operating in its own streets, by the granting of competing franchises, is an act of impotent hatred or greed. It is a confession of civic weakness or ignorance, or both. Where full home rule is enjoyed, so that a city is not hampered in dealing with public utilities by its lack of power, the resort to competition, either through the granting of a rival franchise to another company or by the building of a rival plant for municipal operation, is a proof of incompetence, the result of lack of experience in performing public functions and lack of appreciation of the significance of public utility service. The recognition of the monopoly principle during the continuance of private ownership involves the granting of a single comprehensive franchise for each separate utility covering the entire city, or at least the entire normal unit of operation within the city limits, with a provision for the extension of service from time to time under the terms of the general grant.

As for the duration of franchises, the purposes of the program cannot be well carried out unless every grant is revocable at reasonable intervals of time whenever the city gets ready for municipal ownership. At least in those cases where the city has already made up its mind ultimately to undertake municipal ownership, the franchise should have a maximum time limit within which it is indeterminate, and should bind the city to buy the plant at the expiration of this maximum limit, or even better, provide for the partial or complete amortization of the investment during this period so as to make purchase easy or unnecessary at a definite future date.

COÖPERATION BETWEEN STATE AND LOCAL AUTHORITIES

The vitality of local self-government could not be more seriously threatened than by the complete centralization

THE FRANCHISE POLICY

of the control of public utilities in the hands of state commissions. The League holds to this opinion in spite of its full recognition that most American cities have shown gross incompetence in dealing with public utilities and that many utilities, particularly in well-citied states such as New Jersey and Massachusetts, have overflowed the boundaries of a single municipality and in many cases have welded into a single unit of service several different municipalities. On the other hand, this declaration of opinon should not be interpreted as a sweeping condemnation of public utility laws establishing state commissions; for many of these laws make express concessions to municipal home rule, while others, including the most drastic, such as the Wisconsin law, the Washington law, and the New Jersey law, do not entirely remove the control of utilities from the municipalities. Rather, they establish a duplicate but superior jurisdiction in the state commissions. Considerable opportunity for local governmental initiative in utility matters is left even in those states where the powers of the state commissions are most sweeping. The League believes that the tendency toward state centralization has gone too far in certain cases, but mainly that public utility legislation is generally blind to the inherent necessity of active coöperation in utility matters between state and local authorities. The atrophy of such local organs of control as have been developed in the past would be a great calamity. What is needed is a broad but careful delimitation of state and local functions, coupled with the establishment of the machinery of coöperation. With these things in mind the League declares that the city should reserve to itself continuous control over the character and location of utility fixtures, and over service and rates, subject to a reasonable power of review in the state commission where one exists.

CITIES SHOULD DEVELOP THEIR OWN EXPERTS

The League recognizes that ignorance does not become inspired merely by the responsibilities of office-holding. Public utilities cannot be controlled by aldermanic eloquence or executive swaggering. There is no effective power over public utilities that is not based upon knowledge. In this field particularly the man who has the money invested and who is rendering a necessary public service, universally demanded, has an infinite advantage over the men who have merely been elected to something. He may be irritated by the mosquito bites of the pestiferous politicians, but they cannot control him. It is fundamental, therefore, that a city, if it would exercise control that is effective in any sense, must pay attention and set some one to learn the business from the public point of view and keep at learning it. In other words, the city must develop its own experts if it wishes to have any real control in public utility matters. This applies to franchise granting, to the enactment and enforcement of regulatory ordinances, to the handling of the complaints of consumers and to the representation of the city before the state commission or the courts.

LEGITIMATE INVESTMENTS MUST BE PROTECTED

Finally, cities must recognize that legitimate public utility investments constitute a trust fund. These investments are in aid of public credit. Under the old disastrous theory of public utility investments, they were private and speculative. Cities were Mexicanized by the granting of concessions. This theory lives now only in its results. American cities are now in a transition stage where new wine is being poured into old bottles that cannot hold it. The conservation of the honest and necessary investment in public utilities is not a mere cry of exploiters of the streets. The demand for it is not an earmark of conservatism and corporation sympathies. It is rather the first plank in an effective radical platform. The city can never be successful either in the control or in the operation of public utilities, except on the basis of common honesty and an intelligent recognition of facts. If the city wants good service, continuous public control, ultimate successful municipalization and low rates, it can secure these things only by throwing every safeguard around the investment necessarily devoted to the public service, thus reducing its risks to a minimum and putting it upon a basis approximating the security and the low rate of interest of municipal bonds.

Such is the League's philosophy of public utilities and the principles of franchise-granting. Necessarily, a draft of sections for a model charter cannot embody and elaborate this philosophy in full detail. Much has to be left to the wisdom of the individual city with its peculiar local conditions, which are often the outgrowth of an inescapable past. It is to be hoped, however, that every city, no matter how seriously it may be handicapped by conditions inherited from a past generation, will set its face resolutely toward the goal of complete and continuous control of its public utility functions. It is only by the achievement of such control that a city can purge itself of the poison of discord and bind up its loins for the race toward the goal of efficient municipal democracy.

XI

FINANCIAL PROVISIONS OF THE NEW MUNICIPAL PROGRAM [1]

MANY writers on municipal government in the United States have dwelt mainly or exclusively on a single phase of the problem. Some have considered the question of home rule to be, not only fundamental, but all-important; and have at least given the impression that with adequate powers of self-government cities would automatically work out their own salvation. Others have discussed the organization of municipal government, laying emphasis on various plans for securing popular control, or a system for securing responsible and expert management of municipal affairs. Still others have contended that such political questions as home rule and forms of organization were of comparatively little importance; and that the most important factors in securing good municipal government were provisions regulating the conduct of the administration so as to prevent waste, mismanagement and corruption.

The National Municipal League, both in the former and present programs, has kept in mind each of these three main phases of the general problem. In the proposed constitutional provisions, an ample measure of

[1] See Appendix A.

municipal home rule is proposed. In the earlier divisions of the model charter, a plan of municipal organization is presented, aimed at securing a responsible system of government, subject to popular control, but administered by trained and experienced officials. It remains to consider the administrative provisions, regulating the finances and other specific municipal problems.

In the proposed Constitutional Amendments and Municipal Corporations Act which formed the Municipal Program of 1900 much attention was given to the conduct of municipal finances; and standards were set up in advance of the prevailing practices of the time. But the problems of public finance had only begun to be seriously considered in the United States at that date; and enormous strides have been taken since then both in the principles of financial administration and in their practical application in American cities. On the foundations of the earlier program, committees of the National Municipal League have constructed definite systems of municipal accounting and budget making; and other organizations, both official and unofficial, have also done much in the investigation of the problems and in securing the introduction and use of new and improved methods. The financial sections of the new program, therefore, include many provisions not in the former program. For the most part, these represent a logical development from the principles of the previous program; but in some respects there is a distinct departure from the earlier views. To appreciate the changes from the Program of 1900 and the provisions now proposed, a brief analysis of the main features of the former is desirable.

THE PROGRAM OF 1900

Two sections of the constitutional amendments proposed in the program of 1900 dealt specifically with finance — section 2 of Article III on municipal indebtedness and tax rate, and section 4 of the same article on accounts and reports. In regard to both debt and taxes, the principle of a state constitutional limitation was recognized, though the exact limit was not specified; but an important extension of the scope of municipal action was made possible by providing that loans for revenue producing undertakings should (under certain restrictions) not be included within the debt limit. Provision was also made for temporary loans, and the levy of taxes was required to pay interest and principal on loans not payable from the receipts of revenue producing undertakings.

A general provision requiring the keeping of accounts was followed by more specific clauses for uniform financial reports and for state examination of municipal accounts. The reports were to show receipts, expenditures and debts; and were thus based on the cash system of accounting then in use in American cities.

Section 12 of Article II of the Municipal Corporations Act provided that cities should have the same powers of taxation as were possessed by the state; but section 14 of the same article repeated the constitutional limitations on debt and tax rates.

By section 7 of Article III, the mayor was required to submit to the council an annual budget of *current ex-*

penses, which the council had power to reduce but not to increase.

Article V provided for a city controller, to be elected by the council for an indefinite term, subject to removal by the council. This article also provided for keeping books of accounts, including separate accounts for each appropriation and a separate record for each grantee of a franchise, and for annual financial statements of receipts, expenditures and debt.

Section 10 of Article V dealt with the power of the council to provide for the assessment of property, to levy taxes and to make appropriations,— the annual tax levy and appropriations to be made not more than sixty, nor less than thirty days before the date for holding municipal elections,— though the council could also pass special appropriations and transfer unexpended balances.

These provisions recognized the importance of a general grant of financial powers to cities to make effective the powers of local self-government. At the same time they affirmed the policy of state control, by definite limitations on debts and tax-rates, and by requiring financial reports and the state examination of accounts. An important step was taken towards the establishment of a budget system for current expenses, which would give the mayor control over financial policy. But the conduct of financial administration was vested in a controller independent of the elected mayor.

THE NEW PROGRAM

In the New Municipal Program, the proposed constitutional provisions relating to finances are much shorter,

FINANCIAL PROVISIONS

and give larger powers to cities. In section 5, relating to the powers of cities, each city is authorized:

(a) To levy, assess and collect taxes and to borrow money within the limits prescribed by general law, and to levy and collect special assessments for benefits conferred;

(d) To issue and sell bonds on the security of any excess property [acquired for a local public improvement], or of any public utility owned by the city, or of the revenues thereof, or of both, including in the case of a public utility, if deemed desirable by the city, a franchise stating the terms upon which, in case of foreclosure, the purchaser may operate such utility.

Section 6 of the proposed constitutional provisions provides that:

General laws may be passed requiring reports as to their transactions and financial condition, and providing for the examination by state officials of the vouchers, books and accounts of all municipal authorities, or of public undertakings conducted by such authorities.

The powers of taxation and borrowing money are granted in general terms, and to these is specifically added the power to lay special assessments. No express constitutional limitation is provided, as in the earlier program, on the amount of municipal debt or the rate of taxation. There is, however, provision for prescribing limits by general law, which arrangement permits more flexibility to meet changing conditions, while retaining authority for such measure of state control as may be needed.

Rigid constitutional limitations on the taxing and borrowing powers of cities have often seriously hampered needed public improvements; and on the other hand have in many cases been evaded by various devices, and have proven ineffective. The widely varying limits imposed in different states show the absence of any general agreement on this question, while arbitrary limits based, as is usual, on a percentage of assessed valuation of property are of varying and uncertain application, and at the same time take no account of the different conditions which should determine the safe amount of taxation or debt.[1]

The provision for prescribing limitations by law will permit the development of a system of state regulation adapted to varying conditions; while the requirement that such limitations shall be made by general law should prevent the misuse of the power so as to hamper or to favor particular cities for partisan or other improper motives. Such methods of regulating municipal finance have long been in force in Great Britain and other European countries, and also in Canada. A similar system has recently been established in Massachusetts for borrowing money by towns in that state; and in many states a somewhat similar system of state regulation of stock and bond issues of public utilities has also been established.

In the paragraph relating to the issue of bonds secured by specific property or a public utility, authority is given to borrow money for public improvements or public utilities without adding to the burden of taxation. The Municipal Program of 1900 excepted from the debt limit loans for revenue producing undertakings under certain

[1] Horace Secrist, "An Economic Analysis of the Constitutional Restrictions upon Public Indebtedness in the United States." *Bulletin of the University of Wisconsin, Economics and Political Science Series*, Vol. 8, No. 1 (1914).

conditions. It is believed that the provision now proposed will prove more satisfactory, both as a means of enabling cities to secure funds for such improvements and utilities and also of protecting the tax payers from possible burdens. Similar provisions have been adopted in the Michigan constitution of 1908 and in the amendments to the Ohio constitution adopted in 1912. It should be noted that the provision proposed applies to excess property acquired by condemnation or otherwise in connection with public improvements, as well as to public utilities. It thus carries out the general policy of the Municipal Program to give financial power to make effective the powers of excess condemnation and of municipal ownership of public utilities.

The section providing for financial reports and state examination of accounts, while permissive and not mandatory as in the former program, should serve the same purpose of securing greater uniformity of municipal accounts, and thus making possible more publicity and more definite comparisons of financial conditions in different cities. State control of such matters does not restrict municipal home rule over questions of local policy. It is rather a means of enabling the citizens to be informed of the condition of their municipal government and of the conduct of their municipal officials. Such control over municipal accounts is also necessary as a basis for a satisfactory regulation of municipal debts.

State supervision over local accounts and financial reports has already been established in a considerable number of states. Beginning in some of the smaller states, mostly west of the Mississippi, the most comprehensive system is that established in Ohio in 1902, where the accounts of all county, municipal and local authorities are supervised and examined by state officials. The results of this system in securing more understandable and more comparable statements of local finances, and in detecting and preventing irregularities and sometimes misappropriation of funds, have clearly established its usefulness; and the far reaching municipal home rule amendment to the Ohio constitution adopted in 1912 includes a provision for continuing the state supervision of municipal accounts and financial reports. Similarly valuable results have been secured in Massachusetts by the financial reports of cities and towns in that state prepared under the state bureau of labor statistics; and progress in the same direction has been made in New York, Indiana, Iowa and other states.[1]

THE MODEL CHARTER

Department of Finance.— In the Model Charter most of the provisions relating to finances are grouped together in sections 49 to 62 inclusive. One of the important changes from the plan of organization proposed in the Municipal Corporations act of the earlier program is the provision for a comprehensive department of finance, under the supervision of a director appointed by the city manager. The former program proposed a controller, to be elected by the council and independent of the mayor; and this officer was to have charge of the financial accounts and control the disbursement of municipal funds. Under the model charter, the director

[1] *National Municipal Review*, I, 446; II, 522; IV, 696.

of finance will have charge not only of the accounts and disbursements, but will also supervise the assessment and collection of taxes and other revenues and the custody of city funds.

The former plan was based on the system which prevails in American state governments and in some municipal governments, under which an auditor or controller independent of the chief executive (usually elected by popular vote) exercises a current check on expenditures, mainly for the purpose of keeping them within the limits of the appropriations. These officials have often, however, been given other financial powers. In operation this system has divided the responsibility for financial administraton; while the auditor or controller elected on the same ticket as the chief executive has not always proved an effective check; and in most cases there has been no adequate audit of the public accounts by any one not officially connected with the accounting office.

In the national government and in some cities (as Chicago, Boston and Detroit) where auditors are appointed by the chief executive, the public accounts and the current control of expenditures have been at least as well done as under the plan of an official legally independent. The model charter follows these precedents, and applies the principle of centralizing the primary responsibility for financial administration, as for other branches of municipal government, under the city manager.

At the same time provision is made (in section 62) for a truly independent audit of municipal accounts, after the close of each fiscal year, either by state officers or by qualified public accountants selected by the council; while the council is also given power at any time to provide for an examination or audit of the accounts of any branch of the city government. It is believed that these provisions will secure more direct responsibility for financial management and also a more effective audit of the municipal accounts.

Accounts and Reports.— Section 50 provides that accounts shall be kept which shall show, not only cash receipts and disbursements, but also accrued revenues and liabilities incurred, and other transactions affecting values. Section 72 provides that separate accounts shall be kept for each public utility owned or operated by the city, so as to show the true financial results. Financial reports are required to be prepared for each quarter and also for each fiscal year.

These provisions lay the foundations for a modern system of municipal accounting with more definite requirements than in the former program. At the same time no attempt is made to prescribe in the charter a detailed system of accounts. The specific accounts to be kept should be devised with reference to each city and the provisions for uniform municipal reports; and should be amended and revised from time to time with the progress of public accounting.

In section 77 it is provided that all accounts are records of the city and shall be open to the public under reasonable regulations, except such records where the disclosure of information would tend to defeat the lawful purpose of the office or department.

The Budget.— The provisions in regard to the budget

(section 51) are much more explicit than those proposed in the program of 1900. The responsibility for preparing the annual budget is placed on the city manager, which corresponds to the duty placed on the mayor in the earlier plan. But where the former proposal only required a budget of current expenses, the Model Charter provides for an itemized statement, based on detailed estimates from the several departments, of appropriations recommended both for current expenses and for permanent improvements, and also an itemized statement of taxes required and other estimated revenues, with comparative statements for the current and next preceding fiscal years, and a statement of the financial condition of the city. This budget is to be submitted not later than one month before the end of the fiscal year; copies are to be printed and available for distribution not later than two weeks after its submission to the council; and a public hearing must be given before action by the council. These provisions call for a comprehensive financial program for each fiscal year, and for publicity and discussion before definite action is taken. It is to be expected that the director of finance will actively coöperate with the city manager in preparing the budget; but the responsibility for the recommendations will rest on the city manager.

The annual appropriation ordinance is to be passed (section 52) by the council not later than one month after the beginning of the fiscal year. This must be based on the budget submitted by the city manager; but no positive restrictions are placed on the power of the council to increase or add to the terms in the budget, as in the program of 1900, except that the total appropriations may not exceed the estimated revenues of the city. This important difference is due to the general principles of the city manager plan. Under this plan the council is the final authority in the municipal government; the city manager is the expert adviser and executive agent of the council, but is not an independent officer with legal power to interfere with the council in determining matters of municipal policy in financial or other affairs. While therefore provision is made for preparing a comprehensive executive budget, which the council is to act on as a whole, the power and responsibility of the council for the financial policy adopted are not limited. It should be noted that the former program did not in any way restrict the power of the council to initiate and pass appropriations outside of the budget for *current* expenses, and had no provisions for considering such appropriations as part of a comprehensive fiscal program.[1]

No attempt is made in the charter to define the extent of detail in which appropriations shall be made. The estimates and budget are required to be detailed and itemized. But the degree of segregation in appropriations is left to be worked out as an administrative policy.

Provisions are also made for passing temporary appropriations for current expenses, pending the passage of the annual appropriation ordinance, and for the transfer of unused balances or the appropriation of other avail-

---

[1] It is probably wiser in any plan of organization to permit the legislative body to increase appropriations proposed in the executive budget (perhaps in some cases restricted by the requirement of more than a majority vote) than to authorize it to initiate and pass special appropriations outside of the regular budget, as has been recently proposed in some states.

able revenues. Authority for these purposes is essential in the practical conduct of municpal affairs; and it is important that the charter should provide for it under suitable restrictions to prevent its abuse.

To make effective these provisions relating to the budget and appropriations, it is further definitely provided that no liabilities may be incurred except in accordance with the annual and temporary appropriations or under continuing contracts and loans authorized by the charter.

Levy and Assessment of Taxes.— Section 53 provides for an annual tax levy to meet the appropriations and amounts required on account of the city debt, less the estimated amount of other revenues, and with an allowance to meet commissions, fees and uncollected taxes.

The methods for the assessment, review and equalization of property for taxation are not prescribed by the charter; but are left to be worked out by law or ordinance. Provision is made, however, that all property subject to *ad valorem* taxation shall be valued at its fair market value, and for the separate valuation of land and improvements, the latter to be valued at the amount by which they increase the value of the land.

Special Assessments.— Several home rule charters adopted by Ohio cities have included a chapter on special assessments, prescribing a definite method of procedure. It may be questioned whether a uniform system of special assessments is advisable for all cities; and in any case the difficulties of formulating provisions adapted to the different laws and practices now in force made it impossible to propose a detailed plan in the Model Charter. In section 55, however, the council is authorized to provide by ordinance for a system of special assessments and the main principles of such a system are prescribed. Special assessments may be used for public improvements, including public utilities. For permanent works payments may be distributed over a period of not more than ten years. Provision must be made by ordinance for levying and apportioning such special assessments, for the publication of plans, for serving notice on the owners of property affected and for hearing complaints and claims before final action is taken.

Bond Issues and Other Loans.— Sections 56 to 58 deal with the subject of loans. Money may be borrowed only by the issue of bonds or temporary loans as authorized and limited by the charter; and the credit of the city may not be given or loaned to private individuals or corporations, except for the relief of the poor.

Bonds may be issued on the credit of the city up to a percentage of the assessed valuation to be prescribed in the charter, but which may also be determined by general state law. Bonds may also be issued to be secured by the property or revenues of any public utility. Public notice of at least two weeks must be given before final action on any ordinance providing for a bond issue; and such ordinance must either have the approval of two-thirds of all the members of the council, or be submitted to a referendum of the electors.

Every bond issue must be payable in equal annual serial installments, within a term of years not to exceed the estimated period of the utility of the improvement, with a maximum limit of thirty years, though it is suggested that this limit may be extended to fifty years in cities where subways and other improvements of extraordinary cost and permanency may be needed. Provision must also be made in the bond ordinance for an annual tax levy to meet the installments of interest and principal.

Temporary loans in anticipation of taxes are authorized not to exceed a definite percentage of the receipts from taxes for the preceding fiscal year, and to be repaid from the receipts of the fiscal year in which they are issued. Provision is also made for renewing outstanding floating debt incurred prior to the adoption of the charter, by loans payable with interest in not more than five years. For all temporary loans there must be public notice of at least two weeks before final action by the council, and the loan must be approved by two-thirds of all the members of the council.

These provisions, it is believed, give adequate authority to the city government to borrow funds needed for permanent improvements and also for temporary emergencies; while at the same time providing restrictions to prevent the abuse of the borrowing power. Publicity is required in all cases; and limitations are suggested both for the amount and duration of loans. The alternative of a two-thirds vote of the council or a popular referendum on bond issues seems preferable to the definite requirement of either. The use of serial bonds is prescribed in preference to the sinking fund method of payment; and a tax levy to meet the payments is definitely required. The provisions for temporary loans seem necessary to meet conditions which prevail in most cities; and the conditions imposed should keep the exercise of this power within reasonable bounds.

Custody of City Funds.— Section 59 provides that the collection of all city taxes, special assessments and license fees shall be made by the department of finance. In some states, however, exception may have to be made for taxes which by state law are collected by town, county or state officers. Minor fees for permits and privileges are not covered by the above provision; but it is definitely required that all moneys received by any city officer or employee in connection with the city's business shall be paid promptly into the city treasury. It is further provided that all city moneys shall be deposited with responsible banking institutions, furnishing security and offering the highest rate of interest, and that all such interest shall accrue to the city. These provisions are intended to prevent the holding of municipal funds as private accounts and the payment of interest to municipal officials. The council is required to provide by ordinance for the prompt and regular payment and deposit of city moneys as provided in this section.

Contracts and Purchases.[1]— Among the most important sources of waste and mismanagement in municipal administration are those connected with contracts for public works and the purchase of materials and supplies. Many city charters and state laws contain elaborate provisions on these subjects, some of which are so drastic as to hamper the public officials in securing the best results for the city, and at the same time lead to means of

[1] Nathan Mathews, "Municipal Charters," ch. 8.

evasion which destroy their effect. Difficulties in connection with contracts have caused some officials to ask for larger powers for doing public work by direct labor; and this in turn opens the door to the abuses of spoils politics.

In the Model Charter provisions are proposed for the purpose of preventing abuses without imposing burdensome restrictions. Public improvements costing more than one thousand dollars are to be executed by contract, unless a specific work is authorized by the council based on detailed estimates. All contracts for more than one thousand dollars are to be awarded to the lowest responsible bidder, after public advertisement and competition; but to avoid the danger of collusive bidding, the city manager is given power to reject all bids and readvertise.

In the case of contracts which involve payments from the appropriations of more than two years, special provisions are made. Such contracts (for water supply, street lighting, garbage collection and disposal, etc.,) may not be made for more than ten years, except public utility franchises; and are subject to some of the requirements for a public utility franchise. At least two weeks' public notice must be given before final action; and the contract must be approved by two-thirds of the council or be submitted to a referendum vote of the electors. Such contracts involving obligations for a number of years have some resemblance to public utility franchises and bond issues; and should be subject to similar restrictions.

To prevent collusion between city officials and employees and outside parties in contracts and purchases, it is provided (in section 78) that no member of the council nor any officer or employee of the city shall be financially interested, directly or indirectly, in any contract with the city, or in any sale to the city, except as a member of the city government, or as owner of a limited amount of the stock of a corporation. Any willful violation of this provision will constitute malfeasance in office and cause the office or position to be forfeited; and if done with the knowledge of the persons or corporation contracting with the city makes the contract voidable.

No definite requirement is proposed for a central purchasing system. While the advantages of a greater degree of centralized purchasing were realized, it was not considered advisable to place a general compulsory provision in the city charter; and this question has been left to be worked out by ordinance as a matter of administrative policy.

Payments.— Control over the disbursement of city funds is regulated by section 61. This places on the director of finance the duty, imposed on the controller in the former program, of examining bills and other claims against the city and of issuing warrants on the city treasury for such claims as he finds to be legally due and payable, for which an appropriation has been made and for which funds are available. The Model Charter, however, also requires vouchers to be certified by the head of the appropriate department or division of the city government, and warrants to be countersigned by the city manager. The director of finance may require

FINANCIAL PROVISIONS

a sworn statement of any claim, and may investigate any claim with power to examine witnesses under oath. These provisions should furnish security against expenditures not properly authorized or for which the city has not secured adequate returns.

The provisions of section 62 relating to the audit of accounts have been noted in connection with the general discussion of the department of finance.

XII

CITY PLANNING

When the Municipal Program of the National Municipal League was adopted in 1900 the term city planning was almost unknown in this country. The art itself was even more rare. Rarer still were legally constituted bodies with adequate control of even the street layout, much less of the city plan as a whole.

In the last ten years there has been a great awakening to the value of intelligent city planning. Lagging behind this, but still hopeful, has been a growing appreciation of the need for a city planning authority in each municipality, possessed of, or having at its command, knowledge of the principles and practice of so controlling the physical manifestations of city growth as to meet the needs of the citizens and a proper ideal for the city as a whole. To-day, a hundred cities in the United States and a goodly number in Canada have city planning boards. Most of these boards have quite limited powers and are not so keyed into the city government as to insure that their recommendations will ever be deliberated upon, adopted or rejected.

A city, as well as a house, must be built and perchance remodeled from time to time in accordance with a well conceived plan if it is to serve the manifold needs of its inhabitants in these twentieth century days. A city plan

CITY PLANNING

is far more than a surveyor's map or plat showing a gridiron of streets and the subdivision of land into the largest possible number of building lots. A real city plan meets present and foresees future needs. It is a complex of designs for big engineering and social utilities and services so worked out that each fills the particular needs it is designed to meet and all unite to form a single harmonious whole.

Although city planning is largely engineering in character, but few American engineers have yet grasped its broader aspects. This is chiefly because they have not been given the opportunity to do so. They have been employed to deal with a single element at a time, by city governing bodies themselves of limited vision and often having only piecemeal authority. The broader vision of city planning in America has come from the architects, and especially the landscape architects, rather than from the engineers. Unfortunately, embellishment, adornment, beautification, rather than fundamental knowledge of the city plan and its elements, dominated most of the architects and landscape architects who were the forerunners of city planning in the United States. The "city beautiful" was the cry and to it there was so little popular response that scores of plans and reports for "beautifying" this city and that never got beyond the paper on which they were drawn or printed.

Meanwhile, city after city has continued to grow haphazard — often not even mapped, much less planned. Such planning as has been done has been nearly all piecemeal, isolated, uncorrelated. Streets occupying 20 to 40 per cent of the area of the city, which must serve or fail to serve future generations, have been laid out to meet the real or fancied temporary need and greed of the land speculator. Water-works have been built at one time, sewers at another, with no regard for the city plan as a whole. Utility companies with an eye solely to their own gain have occupied the street surfaces, the ground beneath and the air above in accordance with their own notions of transportation, gas, electric light, telephone and telegraph service, and with utter disregard of a unified city plan. All this has resulted from a division of municipal powers between city councils, and a multitude of unrelated and uncontrolled boards, commissions, departments and bureaus on the one hand, and on the other from the turning over of public utilities to private corporations to do with as they will. Independent municipal departments have had no continuing policy as to the elements within their control. The city as a whole has not harmonized the elements; has had no fixed policy. The utility companies may have done better in working along fixed lines, but those lines have been of their own fixing and have not been under adequate, if any real, municipal control. In short, there has been no city plan, and so of course no program for its realization.

Almost side by side with the growth of interest in city planning in the United States has been the inception and spread of the commission plan of city government. The commission plan has replaced large city councils and numerous independent boards and departments and bureaus by a single small legislative and executive body. This tends towards a unification and correlation of action affecting the city plan, but in itself it has not often gone

CITY PLANNING

far towards adequate city planning. Under the straight commission plan the affairs of the city are divided more or less scientifically into five groups and a commissioner is made responsible for each. This tends towards five-headed government, which though better than having 12 or 20 or 50 heads, does not give unified results, even with the whole commission or council of five passing upon all questions of policy and all appropriations. Moreover, and a great evil, each of the five commissioners soon qualifies in his own and the official and popular mind as an "expert" by virtue of his particular commissionership. City engineers and other technically trained men are relegated to the rear under the commission plan by executive heads chosen by the chance of popular vote.

The commission-manager plan makes the commission simply a policy-determining body, substitutes a single chief executive for the five executive heads, and brings trained administrative and technical men to the front in control of executive affairs.

It might be thought that under the commission-manager plan city planning would be fully cared for by establishing a city planning office, headed by an expert under the general administrative direction of the city manager, the city planning office simply carrying out policies formulated by the commission. Ultimately this may prove to be wise for many if not most cities; for a few cities it might do even now; but as a rule there seems to be need for a city planning board even under the commission-manager plan. The reason for this conclusion is that, as matters stand to-day, city planning in the United States is too young, too much an art in the formative period, too little a science, too much a series of elements yet to be worked into a harmonious whole, too closely related with vital things in the life of the people that have not yet found full definition, to be entrusted wholly to a political body, subject to sudden changes in membership and burdened with a thousand complex problems. It is, of course, undeniable that planning involves so many questions of municipal policy and such large expenditures of money that, especially under the commission plan, the ultimate decision as to policies must rest with the commission. At the same time city planning is so technical a matter that it demands the guiding minds of those specially qualified by education, observation and experience to pass upon the many questions involved.

For the foregoing reasons, the model city charter provides for a city planning board, but one which keys into the general executive staff of the city in membership; makes the city engineer chief engineer of the board; puts all other branches of the city government at the service of the board in the way of giving desired information; compels the commission to act upon (accept or reject) all recommendations of the board, but leaves the commission supreme in the final determination of city planning as of all other policies and expenditures.

In composition, the majority of the city planning board consists of "citizen members chosen because of their knowledge of city planning," while the minority consists of the director of works and utilities, the executive sub-head under whom comes the works and services most closely related to the city plan. It may be noted that the model charter provides that the director of works must be an engineer, selected like all the directors because of " his education, training and experience in the class of work he is to administer." The city planning board, it will thus be seen, is a board of specialists or at least amateurs in city planning, with citizen members in the majority so as to keep close to the people, and with the city executive staff represented by the man in charge of public works and utilities,[1] so as to bring into the board ultimate knowledge of the affairs with which it is chiefly concerned. But, as already stated and as appears more definitely later, the city planning board has only powers of recommendation and advice, the commission being supreme in city planning as in all other matters of policy and expenditure.

The duties of the city planning board are stated in the most broad and comprehensive way. They are threefold:

(1) " To keep itself informed of the progress of city planning in this and other countries; (2) to make studies and recommendations for the improvement of the plan of the city with a view to the present and future movement of traffic, the convenience, amenity, health, recreation, general welfare and other needs of the city dependent on the city plan; and (3) to consider and report upon the designs and their relations to the city plan of all new public ways, lands, buildings, bridges, and all other public places and structures, of additions to and alterations in those already existing, and of the layout or plotting of new subdivisions of the city, or of territory adjacent to or near the city."

[1] In large cities having directors of both works and utilities, there will be three citizen members instead of two.

More briefly, the duties of the board are: (1) To keep posted on all phases of city planning; (2) to say how the city plan may be improved; (3) to pass upon everything orignating elsewhere that would affect the city plan.

Ample means for making (2) and (3) effective are provided. It is only necessary to repeat here, for the sake of emphasis, that anything and everything affecting the city plan must go to the board " for report and recommendation " and that no action by the council affecting the city plan " shall be legal or binding until it has been referred to the board and until the recommendations of the board thereon have been accepted or rejected by the council."

To keep before itself, the council and the public the recommendations which it makes, the board must summarize in each of its annual reports not only its recommendations for that year, but also the year's actions of the city council on the board's recommendations of that and of earlier years.

One of the most important and by all odds the most novel provision of the city planning section is the one which calls for a three-year program of improvements to the city plan. Each annual report of the board must outline such improvements year by year for three years to come, " with estimates of the cost thereof and recommendations as to how the cost shall be met."

This provision is designed to remove or lessen in some measure one of the greatest weaknesses in city government in the United States — the lack of a well-considered, far-seeing program of improvements, including the way of meeting the bills. Here and there a city may be found which has a program for water-works, or sewerage or some other line of improvement, but rarely does a city bring all its proposed improvements into a single program, and revise and extend the program year after year.

For effective work a city planning board must have a competent secretary. The model charter provides "that the board shall appoint as secretary a person of skill and experience in city planning." Leeway is here given as regards the time the secretary must devote to his work. This would naturally depend upon the size of the city and upon the amount of work put upon the members of the board.

Obviously, consulting service may be required at any moment. Provision is therefore made for the employment of "city planning experts as need may arise."

As has already been set forth, the board has as one of its members the director of works and utilities. This is to tie the board into the executive department of the city. It is not to be expected that the director-member (unless in the smaller cities) will perform engineering work for the board, both for lack of time and because it would be incompatible with his functions in the board and as a director. To fill such needs as may arise the model charter provides: "The city engineer shall serve as chief engineer of the city planning board, and it shall be his particular duty to make recommendations designed to bring all the engineering works of the city into harmony as parts of one comprehensive plan."

To coördinate still further all the activities of the city, the executive health officer is called upon to give the board pertinent advice as to the relation of the city plan to health, and to make this coördination complete, the board is given power to call for needed information at any time from any branch of the city government.

For the benefit of any readers who may wonder why no mention is made of the aesthetic side of city planning, it may be explained that so far as a city charter is concerned the artistic phases of city planning may safely be left to a city planning board possessed of the powers and duties for which provision has been made. In a footnote to the model charter it is suggested that in some cities it may be desirable to confer on city planning boards the powers held by art commissions in the United States. The consensus of opinion among the most experienced authorities on city planning, however, is that the two matters should be kept separate. It is a noteworthy fact that but few cities have art commissions. It has already been noted that one of the early setbacks to city planning was due to over emphasis of its relation to the "city beautiful." The beauty of a city lies chiefly in the adaptation of the design of its various elements to the ends which they are intended to serve and in making the most of the beauties nature has bestowed upon the site instead of marring them unnecessarily. Some of the elements of the city plan have aesthetic features as their chief aim, but most of the elements are primarily utilitarian.

If any object that the city planning section of the model charter is too brief, they are asked to understand that the charter itself is brief — designedly a short charter — and that the city planning section is necessarily confined to a few fundamentals, applicable to cities of diverse size and ideals.

It may not be amiss to point out that although the city planning sections of the model charter were drawn to fit into the commission-manager plan they are equally suitable for almost any type of charter. Even those who still believe that there is safety in a division of powers may readily adapt the sections to fit to that belief by going as far as they choose in giving the city planning board control over the city plan.

These sections being a part of a municipal home rule charter they contain no mention of state control of city planning. The fact is, however, that many of the states do exercise more or less control of various things entering into or affecting the city plan, although chiefly as regards quality or rates of service. The dominance of city planning by the Local Government Board of Great Britain, under the famous Town Planning and Housing Act of 1909, is worthy of mention, as is also the fact that the Canadian Government has in its employ one of the leading British authorities on city planning — Thomas Adams, who went to Canada to serve as town planning adviser, under the Conservation Commission.[1]

[1] Finally, a few references may be given. A somewhat extensive report on the organization, powers and duties of city planning boards may be found in the 1915 Proceedings of the National Conference on City Planning. The most recent American books on city planning are Shurtleff, "Carrying Out the City Plan"; Nolen, "City Planning"; and Lewis, "The Planning of the Modern City." Hundreds of references may be found in a "Classified Selected List of References on City Planning," by Theodora Kimball. A short list, also prepared by Miss Kimball, appeared in "The American City" for May, 1916. A summary of city planning accomplishments and projects in cities of the United States having 25,000 population or more and in some smaller places has been published by the Committee on Town Planning of the American Institute of Architects, with the title, "City Planning Progress, 1917." M. N. B.

XIII

BUSINESS MANAGEMENT FOR CITY COURTS [1]

A COMMITTEE of the National Municipal League was appointed in 1913 to draft a model municipal court act. The time was propitious for such work; the success of organized courts in several cities was attracting attention to something new in civic life and in the administration of justice, and there was being created at that time the American Judicature Society, a national organization devoted to efficiency in judicial administration. Harry Olson, chief justice of the Chicago Municipal Court, the pioneer organized court, was made chairman of the committee and shortly after became chairman of the board of directors of the American Judicature Society. There were appointed to serve with him: Thomas Raeburn White of Philadelphia, Judge Wilfred Bolster of Boston, A. Leo Weil of Pittsburgh, Prof. Roscoe Pound of Harvard Law School, and Hastings H. Hart, Raymond V. Ingersoll and Judge W. L. Ransom of New York; the writer became secretary of the committee as well as secretary of the society.

The first work undertaken by the judicature society was the drafting of a model act to establish a court for

[1] The following articles on this subject have appeared in the *National Municipal Review:* "The Model Municipal Court," Herbert Harley, Vol. III, p. 57; "The Municipal Court of Cleveland," Raymond Moley, Vol. V, p. 452.

a metropolitan district, because the society realized that the most insistent need with respect to court reform lies in the large cities of the country. For such work the society possessed unequaled resources. It appropriated liberally to permit of employing the most proficient draftsman. The Municipal League's committee became affiliated with the society and assisted in this phase of its work. Its formal report, comprising a legislative act with profuse commentary, is found in bulletins IV A and IV B, American Judicature Society. It is the purpose of this article to explain briefly the nature of this model act and to account for its principal features.

The act is a judicature act proper, intended to create judicial machinery suited to modern needs, and containing as little as possible of judicial procedure. The society is now engaged in drafting a schedule of procedural rules which will supplement the court act. The two phases of the work are clearly separable. The reader's attention is now called to the mechanics of judicial administration.

The act provides for the establishment of a district embracing the large city and its suburbs. In most cases the county in which the city lies would serve well as the metropolitan judicial district. Inasmuch as the difficulties of judicial administration increase with the size of the city the act is shaped to meet the needs of the largest cities, but may readily be adapted to the simpler conditions of the less populous community.

All tribunals presided over by lay judges are abolished. All other tribunals within the district, except federal and appellate courts, are consolidated to make the new court. The judges of the courts thus consolidated become the first judges of the new court. Judges formerly exercising full trial jurisdiction become senior judges and those who have served in any local or municipal court of limited jurisdiction become junior judges.

Junior judges, as well as senior judges, are given by the act complete authority to hear and determine every cause, equitable, legal or criminal. This permits of complete adjudication of every cause by the judge in whose branch it comes on for trial.

This consolidation is the necessary step preliminary to establishing a scheme of administrative authority and responsibility and providing for specialization. Before the court can become organic it must become unified.

A great variety of causes will be tried in such a court. It is possible to group them into a few broad classes. The act makes five such general divisions based upon the nature of the business to be transacted: (1) The equity division. (2) The probate and domestic relations division. To this division come also divorce and juvenile court matters. (3) The civil jury division. (4) The civil non-jury division. (5) The criminal division.

Every division must have a presiding justice whose duty it will be, besides hearing causes, to supervise calendars and assign judges of the division to particular branches within which specialization is carried out to the fullest degree. The governing body of the court will naturally comprise these five presiding justices and the chief justice. To make a judicial council of seven, one other senior judge is added. This is a simple and natural organization of administrative authority. It coördinates the entire structure; at a meeting of the council every division is represented; in every division the authority of the council is always present in the person of the presiding justice.

The judicial council is given power to regulate practice and procedure, to prescribe the duties and jurisdiction of masters, and generally to manage the business of the court and all divisions and branches. The chief justice presides over the council and is its chief executive, while the presiding justices execute its will in their respective divisions. One check is imposed upon this wide authority. It is a check of a democratic nature. A majority of the senior judges, with the concurrence of the chief justice, at a meeting for that purpose held, may exercise the powers of the council and annul or alter any of its rules. The management of the court must be in accord with the views of a majority of the senior judges.

The judges are permanently assigned to places in the various divisions and can be transferred to another division only by concurrence of the chief justice and the presiding justice of the division affected. But any judge "not for the time being occupied in the transaction of any business assigned to the division to which he may be attached" may be transferred by the chief justice to any other division for a period not exceeding six months. This protects the individual judge from too frequent shifting and still affords such flexibility that all judges may at all times be kept at work, so that there will never be congested dockets in one division and idle judges in another. It permits the court to remain always at a state of maximum efficiency despite seasonal variations in the nature of the business submitted.

Within each division there is opportunity for the highest degree of specialization. Special branches are established by administrative orders and judges best qualified for these branches are assigned by the presiding justice of the division. The right man will find the right work, not by some happy chance, but by conscious direction, and there will be specialist judges with full jurisdiction instead of special tribunals of limited capacity to adjudicate.

Of course it must be understood that the direction of the activities of judges extends only to administrative matters; in the exercise of the purely judicial function every judge is absolutely independent, answerable only to the appellate courts of the state, as at the present time. The judicial council can make rules to govern classes of causes, but can never interfere in the decision of any particular cause. The specific decison rests with the trial judge and the appellate tribunals established by the state.

The simple organization thus presented is supplemented by two related features which are necessary to responsible and intelligent operation, namely, meetings and reports. Meetings of divisions are to be held at least once a month except in August. The entire court will meet at least once every year. At these meetings there will be discussion of the operation of rules and consideration of complaints. At the annual meeting the chief justice shall present his detailed report. The meetings afford the judges opportunity to express themselves, to share in the general responsibility of management, and to receive mutual criticisms.

The chief justice will presumably receive weekly or

monthly reports from presiding justices. His annual report must contain full statistics and information concerning the state of all the branch court dockets. The data must be presented under the five following heads: (1) Litigation. (2) Efficiency of personnel. (3) Social. (4) Criminal. (5) Financial.

In certain branches a great deal of judicial time and energy can be saved by employing skilled assistants to judges. To meet this need the act provides for masters, who will relieve judges of much ministerial labor, conserving their energies for the actual trial of causes. The judges will be responsible for the work of masters. Lack of proper control has prevented the development and success of the plan in this country. Under responsible direction economy can be accomplished through masters who will become highly expert in specialized fields, and who, by reason of long tenure, can be secured for lower salaries than judges.

The act provides for a single clerk to be appointed by the judicial council and to hold at its pleasure. Branch clerks' offices are to be established by the council wherever needed. The chief justice and council are given powers as to the selection of deputy clerks and bailiffs so that they can provide an efficient staff and control their conduct. Doubtless this power would be exercised according to civil service rules to be established.

There is a provision for pensions for judges who shall have served a specified period and attained the age of seventy; also for placing them upon the retired list after they shall have become eligible if the interests of the court call for their retirement. A novel plan for grading salaries is presented: it provides that there shall be an increase of salary for each three years of service up to a certain maximum, thus recognizing the value of long experience. Other sections forbid the making or soliciting of contributions for political purposes and provide penalties.

The act clears the way for rational procedure by abolishing all existing procedure as statute law and continuing it as rules of court alterable under certain formal methods by the judicial council. This affords necessary freedom to simplify procedure without any sudden shock to established custom. Step by step, in accord with definite results, the old complexity and ambiguity of procedure can be shaped skillfully, by expert and responsible minds, to practical and economic needs. The council is of course still subject to legislative control, but experience in jurisdictions where this plan has been tried for many decades proves that the legislature acquiesces in expert control in a field in which its own work has as often been as crude as it always has been rigid.

The act as drafted is suited to the needs of a city of a million or more people. Where the entire body of judges is less than thirty there should be fewer fixed divisions to avoid the possibility of structural rigidity. With twenty judges it would probably be as well to have no fixed divisions, but to permit specialization to rest wholly upon administrative orders. If there are no more than fifteen judges the council may be dispensed with and its powers apportioned between the chief justice and the entire body of judges acting as a committee of the whole. It would be important in such case to protect the office of chief justice so that the incumbent may be a real business manager. This can be done by reserving to the head of the court the power to establish calendars of all kinds and assign individual judges. It is a comparatively easy matter to adapt the act to the needs of any community.

The act was first published in tentative form in March, 1914, as Bulletin IV, A. J. S. A report was made to the National Municipal League concerning the work at that stage.[1] The bulletin was circulated among the 300 judges, lawyers, teachers of law and political scientists who constitute the council of the American Judicature Society. An important body of criticism was received. This was published for the benefit of the directors of the society and the members of the league committee, and formed the basis for revision by the draftsman, whose work was discussed most minutely before final publication.

Concerning the organization features, divisions of business, and the distribution of administrative power appearing in Bulletin IV B we have sufficient experience to be reasonably positive. These are practical matters and there can be little fundamental disagreement concerning them. But in the political realm, comprising especially the selection and retirement of judges, there is in different sections such divergence of experience and theory that it is necessary to submit various proposals. These are found in Bulletin IV A.

In certain states the selection and tenure of judges is on a satisfactory basis. All that is needed to get the best results is a workable organization with conspicuous leadership. But in many states judges are selected by

[1] See *National Municipal Review,* Vol. IV, page 181.

hit or miss methods and the worst results are observed in large cities. What is obviously needed is the expert selection of judges and reasonable security of tenure. In view of present shortcomings it is but natural that the people should insist upon direct participation in the selection of judges. In such communities there is the greater reason for providing efficiency organization because the responsibility which must be demonstrated before the voters will consent to expert selection of judges can be attained in no other way.

Four methods of selecting judges are presented. The first is appointment by the governor with removal by the legislature, as in Massachusetts.

The second is an attempt to improve the tenure of elected judges by providing that at the end of their terms they shall stand for re-election " on their records " rather than participate in a free-for-all race, the consequence of which too frequently is the retirement of an able and experienced judge and the choice of one much inferior to him. To accomplish this, it is provided that the name of the judge, if he is willing to serve longer, is to be placed on the ballot with the query: Shall he be continued in office? Thus might be eliminated one of the obvious sources of waste and accident in the judiciary, while preserving popular election of judges.

The third plan provides for the appointment of judges by the chief justice of the metropolitan court, who is to be elected for a relatively short term and during that term fill such vacancies as may occur. Appointments are to be for a definite period, at the conclusion of which there shall be submission of the name of the judge to a referendum vote, as above explained. If approved, the judge should hold for a longer term, and a second approval should confirm him in office to the end of his judicial career.

The fourth plan provides for the appointment by the chief justice subject to removal by impeachment, by legislative vote, or by the judicial council for causes specified.

It will be observed that appointment by the chief justice conserves the principle which should govern in judicial selection, namely, that the choice should be made by an expert authority responsible for the due administration of justice. Until recently we have never had such an authority, but the chief justices of the organized courts which are being established in our cities fill such a rôle. There is every reason why such a judicial manager, for that is what he essentially is, should himself be chosen by popular vote. Since the duties of the chief justice are largely administrative there are strong reasons for expecting good results from popular choice. The voters would have the advantage of a short ballot and could pass upon the qualifications of candidates for an administrative position with far greater assurance of success than they now pass upon highly technical juristic qualifications.

There are a great number of ways of selecting judges, and many of them may be trusted to yield better results than the customary primary and election in the large city.[1] An interesting modification of two of the foregoing proposals is now before the Louisiana legislature; a draft

[1] See Bulletin VI, A. J. S., pp. 29–52; Bulletin X, A. J. S.; also "Taking Judges Out of Politics," *The Annals* of the American Academy of Political and Social Science for March, 1916, pp. 184–196.

of constitutional changes framed during a year's work by a strong committee of the Louisiana bar association provides for appointment of all judges by the governor for a definite term and submission of their names on a ballot without competition at the close of their terms of service.

As a check upon appointment by the chief justice it is proposed that choice should be made of all or part of the judges from an eligible list containing twice as many names of lawyers as there are places in the court. Names would be placed upon this list as vacancies occur by the judicial council.

Such are the salient features of the model act. Let us take a brief look at the existing situation. In no city in the entire country is there a judicial system which could conceivably be created as a matter of conscious choice. In no city is the administration of justice efficient to a degree which may reasonably be demanded. In most cities it is flagrantly wasteful; even where there are enough judges there are unconscionable delays. The time of judges is squandered and their energy dissipated. Litigants are kept waiting for months and years when they should be served in days. The supposedly inferior causes, both civil and criminal, are in hands often notoriously unfit. There is, as a rule, no unified management of the vast amount of judicial machinery which has been created in a fruitless effort to keep abreast of the growth of population, increase of business, and complexity of tribunals.

It would be as sensible to expect efficient results in a department store lacking management as in our typical congeries of city courts. At the present time we are doing our judicial business in a number of small shops.[1] We are inured to delays and costs and disappointments to such an extent that we have no conception of the benefits readily attainable from plain business management. Nobody could possibly create such a tangle. It is a heritage. Our cities have grown up like magic and the dominant force is still centripetal. One-fourth of all our people live in cities of more than 100,000 population. Many of the vestiges of outgrown village judicial machinery encumber the urban field.

The attempt to reduce delays by providing more judges is everywhere proving ineffectual. When two judges are added to a bench of four the court is given approximately fifty per cent greater capacity. Not so when ten judges are added to a bench of twenty which is lacking in concentrated and responsible direction. The law of diminished returns works inexorably. Take a typical unmanaged court of forty judges and the addition of ten more may not increase the output in any observable degree.

The attempt to get specialized effort is resulting more and more in a patchwork system of separate tribunals, which, without unified management, cannot possibly yield efficient results.

We have persistently followed a wrong policy in attempting to force tolerable results from an impossible machine. In an endeavor to force the individual judge to do the right thing in the specific case we have enacted thousands of sections of procedural law until finally the hands of the judge are so effectually tied that often he

[1] See address of Edward A. Harriman on efficiency in the administration of justice, Conn. State Bar Asso. Report 1915.

cannot do the thing required for simple justice — the thing he would like to do.

We have recognized the possibility of injury from faulty administration of rules and provided for remedy through appeal. This opens new opportunity for injury to the litigant. But nowhere in the judicial system is any provision made for removing the causes of blundering.[1] Dissatisfaction with judicial decisions is small and of little warrant compared with the dissatisfaction which should be realized over the absence of simple business management in the operation of the courts.

In the enforcement of penal laws we are a spectacle among the nations called civilized. We pile ordinance upon ordinance and statute upon statute, but power and responsibility for the enforcement of law is so scattered that the result is increase of crime and general disrespect for law and government.

The new and vital theory of court reform looks to the ultimate unification of all of the courts of a state. A start must be made somewhere in introducing order and system and the large city is the best place to begin because there the need is greatest. The larger plan, embracing all of the judges of the state, will still require special organization within metropolitan districts. If the city court is established first there will be no difficulty whatever in making it a department of the unified state court. It will still need a great deal of local autonomy with respect to administration.

The idea that courts must be charged with respon-

[1] See "Wanted a Chief Judicial Superintendent," by John H. Wigmore, *Illinois Law Review* for May, 1916, pp. 45-49.

sibility for the orderly evolution of procedure through court rules is now generally accepted after half a century of statutory regulation and varying degrees of failure in most of the states. It will not be long before the ineffectual method will be generally abandoned. As the change is made it is very important that there be provided in the large cities courts so organized that they can perform their proper rôle of developing procedure in accord with urban needs. One of the present faults arises from the fact that procedure has been enacted to fit both city and rural courts and the legislatures which frame these laws are commonly unacquainted with metropolitan needs or wholly out of sympathy with them.

The model court act recognizes the need for establishing a judicial career with provision for advancing a judge from the position of junior to that of senior judge and finally to the presidency of a division if the individual evinces talent. At the same time the practitioner of high standing, a master of some branch of substantive law, may be taken in directly as a senior judge and given an important position with appropriate salary. He can be guaranteed service in the field for which he has fitted himself by long training.

The organization as created also permits of temporary assignment of the ablest member of the court to a department which is commonly, but mistakenly, supposed to be less important, if not trivial. Investigation reveals the undoubted fact that many of the judicial functions heretofore relegated to confessedly inferior judges are of the highest concern in a social and political way. Consider the small civil causes which form the only point of contact with the court that a large majority of the population will ever experience. Because only small amounts are involved in such controversies it is economically impossible to try them with a jury and rules of evidence which require half a day or a day to ascertain whether Mary Jones is entitled to half a week's lodging or must pay half a month's rent. The employment of counsel for hundreds of these causes is a burden to the self-respecting lawyer and a mockery to his client. A capable judge can dispose of these causes to the satisfaction of litigants at the rate of four to the hour, but litigants will not accede to this idea except they have confidence in the legal ability and impartiality of the judge.

A mistaken attempt to work out economy in such causes through small salaried and palpably inferior judges defeats itself. The privilege of appeal guaranteed to the small litigant, as shown so clearly by Judge Taft, is an insult.[1] All present experience negatives the theory that economy is to be obtained by employing inferior judges for small causes. Economy lies in getting a right and lasting adjudication *in the first instance* and this requires *exceptional men* for judges.

The only light that we have in this field is afforded by efforts originated in two of the organized courts, those of Cleveland and Chicago.[2] Without the authority to segregate causes and assign judges for special work we would have gone on indefinitely breeding discontent with courts among the largest class of litigants. In the small claims branch of the Chicago municipal court three judges

[1] See "Administration of Justice," by William H. Taft, *Green Bag*, Sept., 1908, p. 444.
[2] See Bulletin VIII, A. J. S.

clear a calendar of about 13,000 cases a month, comprising all money claims under $200. In about three-fourths of these cases payment or settlement is effected before return day, so that adjudication is automatic. The deadbeat yields. The work of the conciliation branch of the Cleveland municipal court is so successful that an extension of the idea to other civil branches is certain to be made in time. In the Municipal Court of Minneapolis conciliation procedure has been extended to all causes involving $1,000 or less.

A striking instance of the flexibility of the organized court has more recently been afforded in Chicago. The Credit men's association, representing most of the important commercial concerns of the city and every line of trade, established a bureau to encourage private commercial arbitration. Investigation disclosed the fact that the weak point in arbitration in places where it is most common lies in the inability of lay arbitrators to decide mixed questions of law and fact. It is clear that there is no way of settling questions of fact so economically and correctly as by arbitrators expert in the business involved and free from the complication of court procedure. No jury can cope with the involved problems of modern business with equal prospects of success.

At this stage Chief Justice Olson was able to announce that he would create forthwith a branch court of arbitration, providing one or three judges to act promptly upon questions of law upon a case stated by lay arbitrators. This will result in a more perfect form of arbitration than has ever before been worked out. It cannot be started in a day or a year, like other branch courts, because it is dependent upon the development of a class of expert arbitrators in whom perfect confidence is reposed, but it must in time fill a great need and become a strong point of coöperation between the court and the commercial world.[1]

The arbitration court is created in accord with a well established policy of shaping procedure so that the courts can accomplish more work with a given number of judges. Many cases of the kind now tried with a jury at great expense to the public will be better tried entirely out of court. Those which involve law as well as fact will be determined by the court with a tenth of the effort now required. The court will have more time to devote to causes which necessitate formal trial with a jury.

Specialization is simply to keep the square peg and the round hole dissociated. It implies overhead unification and the expert assignment of judges. We have no idea as yet to what extent specialization may be economically utilized in city courts. But one thing we know, that the judge sitting in the specialized branch court must be empowered to try all phases of every controversy submitted to him, else specialization will merely bring about increased friction and waste as is now observable in cities which have several independent tribunals.

The criminal field presents a striking example of existing defects. We go on the theory that there are lesser and greater offenses and that for the former judges of inferior personality and experience are good enough. In

[1] Since writing the foregoing the Municipal Court of New York has established both Conciliation and Arbitration branch courts. See Journal of the American Judicature Society, Vol. I, No. 2.

these inferior criminal branches a vast number of offenses classed as legally unimportant, which are of the highest social consequence, are disposed of. If the first screening is done effectually society will have fewer notable offenses to contend with in the higher branches. At present our system is topsy-turvy. An ordinary judge can give fair results in felony trials, but first-class talent is needed to preside over a branch which takes the plea of the first offender.

The preliminary examination with trial in another branch court is probably desirable in cases of felony. The model court would undoubtedly retain this practice. But it can never make progress against the current of social offenses until it can place strong judges in the first instance branches. The city has come to grips with the slum — either city or slum must perish. Society cannot live healthfully until the canker is healed.

The ordinary lawyer is a good citizen and is disposed to see judicial procedure improved. But in his mind a court is a place in which property rights are ascertained in a meticulous manner. He scorns criminal law practice and knows nothing of the socio-criminal branches which are coming into being. He needs to enlarge his horizon and to realize that administration of justice means all of these various things and that they are inseparably related and bound together.

The ordinary lawyer and the ordinary judge shrink from accepting responsibility for the complete administration of justice. They prefer to limit their scheme to the dignified and elegant branches which they know. The remedy for this state of mind is embedded in this model act, for it makes every judge of the entire metropolitan court in a measure responsible for the working of every branch. The reputation of the single unified court will depend upon its performance in the branch courts which are down on the ground level, some of them located in the slums. Of course not every judge can be expected to participate directly in branches which are far more administrative in character than juridical — which are in fact socio-criminal clinics. But they can uphold the hands of the chief justice who is charged with the direction of the whole big field, and this they must do for their own sake, to protect the reputation of the court upon which they depend for their exalted position in civic life. When the best lawyer and judge is coupled up to the judge presiding over the most disdained tribunal he will become necessarily the most active factor in a movement to kill or cure. For these and similar reasons it is all important to have but one court in a city, however varied its operations.

The opportunity for inventing better means for administering law is boundless.[1] A few years ago Chicago was grumbling about the motor law infractions. Both state and city had enacted profusely and penalties were provided in abundance. The police worked manfully to enforce regulations. Offenders were taken to the police station nearest to the point of arrest and arraigned in a branch police court of the Municipal Court. A surprisingly large number were influential citizens or were esteemed as such by their aldermen. Many of them who

[1] See annual reports, Chicago municipal court; Address on Same, Louisiana Bar Association, Report for 1915. Published also by the American Judicature Society.

really approved of law enforcement took every available means to escape punishment. The few who were "soaked" had a sense of inequality and it rankled.

The ordinary course of events would have been to enact a lot more of penal sections, increase penalties already unrecoverable, and permit reckless driving while pretending to crush it. But Chief Justice Olson had a remedy. He ordered all offenders of the automobile laws to be taken to a special speeders' court, created by executive order, and he assigned to that court a hard-hearted and skeptical judge. Fines at once went up from $5 to $50, and from $50 to $200. In two months $10,000 was collected and vastly more was accomplished than could have been done by added legislation.

Formerly all the forces making for laxity were focussed upon an outlying member of the judicial staff and they were too strong for him. Now all the power for law enforcement, the inertia of a powerful judicial machine, is brought to bear upon the individual offender. The tables are turned. It's a mere matter of method.

We whine about disrespect of law and talk foolishly about its being a national trait. We ought to employ resources at our command to enforce existing law instead of continually clamoring for more law. Somewhere *there must be a man* or all laws break down, and that man must be part of a big, powerful and responsible machine.

And this is how responsibility works out in the organized court: by publicity and by community of interest among the judges. As to publicity: we are behind the rest of the world in not requiring full judicial statistics. It is impossible to arrive at costs, to compare results, or to frame remedial rules in the present absence of judicial data. We are blundering along in the dark. The annual report of the organized court is a document of inestimable value. It not only permits of expert criticism in lieu of guesswork and dispute, but inevitably sets a mark which the court must not fall short of in the ensuing year. Every single judge has his standard of accomplishment set out in black and white. Some judges could hardly endure the thought, but most of them would find work under such an environment highly stimulating. Nothing is so depressing as the daily and yearly grind with no prospect of being able to demonstrate good service.

It is in the judges' meetings that community of interest demonstrates its power. The judges of a unified court depend in considerable degree upon the popular appreciation of the entire court. They cannot endure to have their court depreciated by the injudicious conduct of certain members. They thus become the first and most zealous inquisitors, anxious to discipline before harm results. Such a court has been called in modern metaphor an "internal combustion court." Before the judges' meeting come the complaints of litigants, of counsel and of judges themselves. There they are threshed out. The erring judge, if one be found to err, is quietly but inexorably put upon the right path. If he is the victim of unfounded complaint he is armed to go forth and face the powers of unrighteousness.

Not the least novel and significant among the features of an organized court is this right of the citizen to enter his complaint. The right does not exist where there is no authoritative head. The individual litigant who is aggrieved or who has suffered injury which cannot be righted through any course of appeal will only bring himself into contempt if he undertakes to discuss the matter with the typical judge of an unorganized court. He must bridle his feelings even though he believes that more powerful interests have a way to exert influence upon the course of justice.

But the organized court is as democratic as it is powerful. It exists to serve the entire people and the least among them can safely register his protest. The chief justice (and, through him, the judicial council) is kept in touch with public feeling and afforded opportunity to adopt policies of administration calculated to meet the convenience of the greatest number. But if the influence exerted upon the court management is anti-social, which is quite as probable, there is in the organized court an inertia and a responsibility that enable it to pursue the right policy unflinchingly. There is assurance that no single judge is to be punished for being faithful to his trust.

The organized court is obliged to keep abreast of its work unless it can justify delays clearly. Its published reports set a standard of accomplishment. As business increases simpler and more economical methods, derived from growing expertness and having mutual confidence as a foundation, are invented. Without organization the only recourse is additional judges who increase confusion and the opportunity for shirking.

It is now ten years since the first court of this kind was established. The experiment was no timid attempt. It was a bold application to the judicial system of the principles which are universal in modern business life.

Wherever this court has been imitated there has been conspicuous success. In the entire half century during which our cities have come into being there has been no other attempt, out of hundreds, which have yielded the slightest improvement. All our other patchwork has failed even to prevent the growth of evils so that, except for this movement, the situation has become steadily worse.

These conclusions are derived from an intimate study of conditions and a careful comparison of results in cities having made some progress on the road toward unification and in those which are yet to take the first step. The measure of value is found to be precisely commensurate with the extent of jurisdiction conferred.

The movement toward unification of city courts has a close parallel in the commission government movement. Just as the Des Moines plan of government accomplished a great deal, but fell short of ideal results, so the municipal court idea has already done a world of good in the limited field in which it has been tried and points the way to ultimate success. It will reach its fullest accomplishment, supplementing and completing our magnificent program of municipal reform, when it is extended to include all the judicial agencies of a given city. The larger the city and the worse the tangle, the more striking will be the application of these simple principles of unification, specialization, administrative authority and freedom of action. For from all these results responsibility. From these results an environment which unlocks the powers of individual judges so that each strives to make his branch of the work fit to form part of an efficient whole.

XIV

MUNICIPAL DEVELOPMENT IN THE UNITED STATES SINCE 1900

AMERICAN municipal development up to 1900, when the first Municipal Program was promulgated, had been kaleidoscopic and spasmodic, and therefore well-nigh defied analysis. This was largely due to the search of the charter maker for some philosopher's stone that would take the place of the self-governing instinct; and for some form of governmental perpetual motion machine that would eliminate the necessity for the coöperation and vigilance of the citizenry. Another factor was a correlative one: the desire to avoid what had elsewhere been tried and had failed, without any effort being made to find out the cause of failure. Still another factor was the time-honored devotion to the principle, if principle it may with propriety be called, of checks and balances. This latter in turn was based on the profound distrust of the people which characterized the thinking of the nineteenth century in all governmental matters, and especially in the realm of the city.

As a consequence of these, and subsidiary factors, we find a constant shifting of emphasis, and an equally constant redistribution of powers and functions. Dr. Fairlie in his chapter on " Municipal Development in the United

States" in the first Municipal Program (Macmillan Co., 1900) describes with considerable detail the various changes which took place from generation to generation. "Thus even during the colonial period we may see the beginning of a distinctive American development differentiating the municipalities in the colonies from those in England. Close corporations were the exception; the mayor was already an active and the most important official in the city government; central control over the municipalities existed from the first in the governors' power of appointing mayors, while the way was paved for a more active control through the special legislation of the assemblies in response to the demand of the municipalities for larger powers than those conferred in their charters."

The Revolution wrought a change in the charter-granting power, although "there does not seem to have been much discussion on this change in the charter-granting power; the way had been prepared by the frequent additional grants of authority by colonial assemblies to corporations chartered by executive authority, and the tendency of the new state governments was so strongly in favor of the legislature and against the executive that the new custom was established without question."

During the first forty years after the establishment of the American Republic, the net results, according to Fairlie, were: "(1) The abolition of the close corporations and the definitive establishment of the rule that each American municipality should have a locally elected council; (2) the unmistakable legal supremacy of the state legislatures over the municipal charters and the powers of the municipalities; (3) the introduction — as yet in a very few places — of the bicameral council system and the veto power of the mayor."

From 1820 to 1850 the development consisted "(1) in the change in the manner of electing mayors, from election by the councils to election by popular vote; and (2) in the limited extension of the bicameral system of council organization. It should also be noted that by the close of this period the property qualifications for the municipal suffrage had in most cases disappeared, and the general tendency of state legislation to enter into great detail in all statutes still further tended to remove all discretionary powers from the local officials, and leave them simply administrative duties to perform. This detailed statutory regulation was, perhaps, to be expected in regard to matters of general state administration, such as poor relief, education, and taxation, which were now often under the control of the municipal authorities. Established in this sphere, it was easy to follow the same rule in legislation for purely local matters in the cities, and especially in the statutes passed without the approval of the municipal authorities in order to insure that the latter would not evade the statutes; while in the case of cities controlled by another political party than that which controlled the state legislature there was a further motive for the most strict and detailed provisions in all the legislation for such cities."

"It is not said that these results had worked themselves out on any large scale before the middle of the century. It is after, rather than before, the year 1850 that much special legislaton came to be enacted without regard to the local authorities, and hence to be considered as an interference with the local government. But even before 1850 something of this sort had been done, and the steps in the process are worth noting in the general development of municipal government."

During the next thirty years, 1850–1880, the main points to be noted are: (1) The extension of municipal functions in kind and degree; (2) the constant growth of special and partisan legislation for cities, and the first ineffective measures to prevent such legislation; (3) the steady decline of the council; (4) the tendency for the government to disintegrate into independent departments, with no unity or harmony of purpose and action; (5) the development of the mayor's authority, through the limited powers of appointment and removal and veto power.

From 1880 to 1900 there was a continual growth of urban population and municipal activity; and in the words of Dr. Fairlie " by further changes in municipal organization; by some improvement in the subordinate administrative service; and by the increasing movement against the system of partisan and legislative government of municipalities." For the period which he covered and from what I have just quoted he drew these conclusions:

" We have noted the growth of urban population and the devlopment of municipal government in the United

States from the petty colonial borough to the vast metropolitan municipality of to-day. We have seen the evolution from the simple and unorganized council government to the complicated administrative machinery of municipal departments. In the process, the central direction of municipal affairs has passed from the council, and in most American cities authority is distributed and dissipated on no fixed principle between council, mayor, and state legislature, while the influence of national and state political contests in municipal elections, and the operation of the spoils system in municipal office-holding have served to deteriorate still further municipal administration. In recent years, however, we see certain tendencies toward a more scientific distribution of authority, toward the separation of municipal from national and state elections, and toward a more permanent and efficient subordinate service; and while these tendencies have not as yet become widespread, yet it is along the lines already indicated that further advances of a permanent nature may be most rationally anticipated."

This then was the situation, in general, which prevailed when the first Municipal Program was formulated, and which it was designed to modify and mold. The tendencies referred to in the "Conclusions," however, were developing with great rapidity and assuming concrete form.

An important feature of the first Municipal Program was the emphasis placed upon the necessity for constructive reorganization of our city government and especially upon accounting as an instrument to this end.

In the words of Dr. Rowe, in discussing public accounting under the program:

"Whatever may be the influence of the Municipal Program of the National Municipal League on the administration organization and methods of our American cities, the very fact of its formulation marks a turning point in the history of modern reform movements in the United States. The most serious charge to which reform associations have been subjected has been that their efforts were confined to destructive criticism, and that they have failed to furnish a positive basis for political reorganization. Any one who has carefully observed the movement of popular opinion during recent years cannot fail to have been impressed with the danger involved in this growing distrust of the ability of reform movements to meet the practical problems of American political life.

"To make the energy, which is being lavishly expended by such large numbers of devoted citizens, really effective requires the substitution of a positive program for negative criticism. Not only are the shortcomings of our city governments to be dwelt upon, but the positive measures necessary for the improvement of existing conditions must be formulated. To do this requires the most careful consideration of the general principles as well as the technical details of every department of municipal administration."[1]

The recommendations of the Municipal Program under this head were designed to facilitate that enforcement of political responsibility which has been the end and aim

[1] See "A Municipal Program," page 88.

of all recent administrative reforms. "The close relation between public accounting and administrative efficiency is most clearly shown," Dr. Rowe maintained, "in the financiering of private corporations. It is a well-known principle of corporate management that the responsibility of president and directors is largely determined by the annual financial report. That this report should be unequivocal and readily intelligible is one of its primary requisites. Otherwise the stockholders are deprived of all means of enforcing responsibility. Whenever the system of accounting is defective, or when it has been arranged with a view to concealing the policy of the directors, all real responsibility disappears. At times, it is true, stockholders are willing to submit to such methods in order to avoid franchise taxes or other obligations.

"Although the analogy between the management of private and public corporations is often misleading, it is of value in the discussion of questions of financial responsibility. It is quite true that the standards of efficiency in the two cases are quite different. The mere fact of a large treasury balance is no necessary indication of governmental efficiency. A surplus may be due to the failure to repair the deterioration of public works, or to meet pressing obligations. While, therefore, the standards to be applied to the financial reports of private and public corporations are quite different, accuracy and intelligibility are equally necessary in both cases."

Thus it will be seen that the first Municipal Program foreshadowed that movement of the first decade of the twentieth century which has since been widely known under the caption of "municipal research" and which has had a wide and deserved vogue.

In the year following the promulgation of the Municipal Program, as a logical further step, or as some may choose to regard it, as a by-product, a movement for uniform municipal accounting and reporting was inaugurated, and early in 1901 a committee was appointed, with Dr. Edward M. Hartwell of Boston as chairman, charged with the duty of giving effect to those principles embodied in the Municipal Program which had to do with these subjects.

However, it may be noted, in passing, that it was not the purpose of this Committee to elaborate a system of municipal bookkeeping for adoption by all cities, but rather to devise a practical scheme for summarizing the accounts of any city, whatever its methods of bookkeeping might be, under the form of what was termed a "model comptroller's report." In accordance with this policy and with full recognition of the great diversity which obtains in the financial statistics and reports of American cities, the schedules recommended at the outset by this Committee were avowedly tentative and necessarily elastic in their nature. Moreover, in the words of the Committee, " we have always endeavored to determine their practicability by putting them to the test of actual use. Thus, at Rochester, in 1901, we presented, in connection with our report, the report of the auditor of the City of Newton, Massachusetts, who, with the coöperation of Mr. Chase, of this Committee, in an appendix summarized the receipts and expenditures of

MUNICIPAL DEVELOPMENT

Newton for the year 1900, in accordance with the recommendations of the Committee as embodied in its Schedule D. Similarly, as a part of the report, at Boston, in 1902, we presented in printed form, a 'Statement of the Receipts and Expenditures of the City of Boston for the fiscal year 1900–01, grouped according to the "Uniform System" of the National Municipal League,' which was prepared by the Statistics Department of Boston for the use of the Committee. That year, Mr. Chase, of the Committee, in his capacity of expert accountant and auditor, secured the adoption of some of our schedules by the city auditor of Cambridge, Massachusetts, in his report for the year ending November 30, 1902. Again, the Report of the Comptroller of the City of Baltimore, for the year 1902, was arranged throughout in accordance with our system of grouping receipts and expenditures according to the function subserved by the departments of the city government." As the scheme was in the experimental stage, and the various schedules still undergo testing and trial, it was deemed inadvisable to make final recommendations at that time. Before giving final shape to the schedules, it desired to benefit by the experience and criticism of a still larger number of comptrollers and auditors.

The most notable occurrence in the line of progress toward uniform municipal accounting in the year covered by the report was the passage by the Ohio legislature of an act to secure uniform accounts and financial reports from all cities in the state. The Ohio authorities had had the professional advice of Mr. Chase, a member of the Committee, in perfecting their organization and in shaping schedules, form of report, etc. Before their final adoption the Ohio schedules were submitted to the Committee for consideration. These schedules were in substantial accord with our tentative schedules of 1902.

At the instance of the Merchants' Association of New York, an investigation of the methods employed in keeping the accounts of the City of New York was undertaken with a view to securing simpler and more intelligible reports of the financial operations of that city. The investigation was in charge of Mr. Ford, also a member of the Committee.[1]

At first blush the connection between the municipal accounting and a municipal program may not be obvious; nor the statement that this new movement was destined to have a profound influence on the " more scientific distribution of authority." A careful study of the municipal problem in the light of Dr. Rowe's comments and of the sundry illuminating reports of Dr. Hartwell on behalf of his Committee, which contained in its membership men like Dr. Frederick A. Cleveland, who later became conspicuous as one of the chief directors of the parent bureau of municipal research, will show a close and significant connection between these several tendencies and factors. With the attempt to standardize accounts and reports, came the necessity for a more definitely scientific distribution of functions. The work of the bureaus of municipal research will show a close and significant connection between these several tendencies and factors, and has had far-reaching results. The

[1] See Proceedings of Detroit Meeting of the National Municipal League, pp. 248–249.

development is still in process; but the headway already accomplished justifies the belief that it is only a question of time, and that a relatively short time, when there will be a complete, standardized and functionalized distribution of powers and duties. In this connection reference must be made to the important and influential help rendered by the federal bureau of the Census, which early saw the significance of the National Municipal League's recommendations as to reports, and under the leadership of Dr. LeGrande Powers, adopted the schedules which had been worked out by the League's Committee.

With the development of the bureaus of municipal research, the work of the Census Bureau and of the technical bodies that had taken the subject up, the need for activity on the part of the National Municipal League diminished. Its functions in many directions is necessarily that of a pioneer, and when that work is done it is free to turn to other phases and to other spheres. This is not to be taken as an evidence of a lack or loss of interest, but merely as a recognition of its real functions in promoting movements and tendencies designed to solve American municipal problems.

Municipal research, to use the popular term which has come to cover this new movement, is something more than an organized effort to promote "righteousness via bookkeeping." In an address before the Philadelphia Bureau of Municipal Research, George Burnham, Jr., who has been actively identified with the work of the National Municipal League practically from the beginning, said:

"It is characteristic of Americans that they have always considered that any citizen was equal to any administrative position under the government if his heart was in the right place and if he was sound in the principles that underlie our political creeds.

"Hence we have taken the doctor, the lawyer, the merchant, or the blacksmith by the scruff of the neck and dumped him into the chair of the legislator, the governor of our state, the mayor of our city, and expected him to make good, whether he knew anything about the job or not. It is not my purpose to criticize . . . but to point out some results in our cities. The plan worked fairly well so long as our city governments were simple affairs, having to do with what were in reality merely outgrown villages. With the rapid growth of our cities, and the increasing complexity of city government due to such activities as electric and steam transportation, water distribution, electric and gas lighting, etc., the plan did not work so well, and the government of our cities began to fall into disrepute. Do not suppose that I think the placing of untrained officials in positions of power and responsibility the only cause of our discredited city governments, but it is certainly a strong contributing factor. In any event, we began to be dissatisfied with our municipal governments, and then began the campaign to 'turn the rascals out' and put in honest men.

"Observe that we still had the old American obsession, and demanded not qualified men so much as honest men. If a man was only honest, he would find a way to perform his job satisfactorily.

"It was soon found, however, that even honest and

well intentioned men did not necessarily make good administrators of our cities. It was then that a small group of men conceived the idea that if a thorough study were made of municipal government, not as a political theory, but as a concrete fact, and the results of such a study were brought before the administrators in being, they would be glad to avail themselves of the chance to improve their methods. This may seem unlikely — pride of office, dislike of outside interference, you may think would prevent it. But put yourself in the place of an elected official for a moment. You suddenly find yourself confronted with a concern for which you are responsible. It has a long tradition of management which may strike you as full of absurdities, but it's there; and standing before you patiently expectant are three or four clerks awaiting your action on some current matter. The immediate burden, in other words, is so heavy that you haven't time or strength to install better methods, and you probably leave the system, after your brief period of authority, as you found it.

"Now, suppose some expert in whom you have confidence steps in and says, 'We have made a careful study of this office, and find the procedure is thus and so, is this correct?' You look over the papers and find that an accurate picture of the going methods of your department has been drawn. Now, says the expert, we believe you can get far better results by doing thus and so, and here are our reasons for thinking so; further, if you find we are right we want you to get the credit for making the changes we propose, as we are not seeking any glory in the matter ourselves. Would you not be inclined to swallow your pride and accept the assistance, if the changes met with your approval."[1]

All of this has a direct and effective bearing on the question of the establishment of a "more permanent and efficient service," as well as of expert heads of departments, for these latter will not rest content with a haphazard classification, nor with the voluntary assistance of outside experts. The casual and the old-fashioned type of city official, more concerned in the holding of office than with the service he can render, may be willing to gain a passing credit by accepting outside aid; but inevitably the outside expert will be taken inside, and then his influence will be multiplied many times. In passing, I must say in duty to my own convictions, that I do not think the time will come for many years, if ever, when the need for voluntary, coöperating bodies, will cease; but the form of their coöperation will change with the times. Already within the lifetime of the National Municipal League there has been a great change in their functions. If any one had prophesied at the initial meeting that the time would come when a volunteer municipal organization would adopt the following as its program of work and methods, he would have been laughed at as a dreamer, and yet such programs are now much more frequently to be found than those which deal with "don'ts" and "we accuse":

Confer with officials responsible for the municipal department or social conditions to be studied.
Secure promise of coöperation, and instructions that di-

[1] See *National Municipal Review*, Vol. V, pp. 485-7.

rect subordinates to coöperate with the Bureau's representatives.

Ascertain how the powers and duties (and other materials of research) are distributed.

Examine records of work done and of conditions described.

Compare function with result and cost as to each responsible officer, each class of employee, each bureau or division.

Verify reports by usual accounting and research methods and by conference with department and bureau heads.

Coöperate with municipal officials in devising remedies so far as these can be effected through changes of system.

Make no recommendations as to personnel further than to present facts throwing light on the efficiency or inefficiency of employee or officer or to suggest necessary qualifications and where to find eligible candidates.

Prepare formal report to department heads, city executive officers and general public: (a) description, (b) criticism, (c) constructive suggestion.

Support press publicity by illustrations, materials for special articles, facts for city officials, editors and reporters.

Follow up until something definite is done to improve methods and correct evils disclosed.

Supply freely verifiable data to agencies organized for propaganda and for legislative, agitative, or "punitive" work.

Try to secure from other departments of the same municipality and from other municipalities the recognition and adoption of principles and methods proved by experience to promote efficiency.[1]

[1] From "Six Years of Municipal Research for New York City."

A correlative feature of the Municipal Program was the demand for publicity. If the people are to be charged with responsibility they must know the facts. Hence the demand for proper, uniform, intelligible accounts and reports. To quote Dr. Rowe again: "The numerous instances in which public opinion has been unable to reach any definite conclusions — owing to the lack of systematic presentation of financial data — would seem a sufficient reason for these provisions in the Program. One of the most striking instances is the leasing of the Philadelphia Gas Works. The conflicting statements of opposing interests were supported by data taken from the same reports. The classification of receipts and expenditures was so confusing that almost any proposition could be read into it. We cannot expect the citizen to subject every public financial statement to critical analysis. He is at the mercy of conflicting interpretations unless the official information furnished him is so clear and unequivocal as to leave no room for doubt."[1]

The old Philadelphia Gas Works affords a striking example for our purpose, because they illustrate all that was evil and detrimental in the old conditions: inadequate, indefinite, non-comparable accounts, a complete absence of publicity, accountability and responsibility. The first great step forward in Philadelphia was accomplished when the old commission was abolished, and the works placed under the control of a responsible director of public works. Another great step forward was taken when the old Public Buildings Commission was abolished and the City Hall placed under the control of an appropriate

[1] "A Municipal Program," p. 93.

bureau of the city government. Gradually these irresponsible, secretive, autocratic commissions are being displaced and the work placed in the hands of officials more directly responsible to the people, and who in time will become experts.

A striking illustration of the old and the new is afforded by contrasting the secretive methods of the Public Buildings Commission, yielding information and that most reluctantly only when forced by the strong arm of the law, and the new publicity methods of Dayton, by means of which the whole public is taken into the confidence of the commission and its city manager. Whole pages of the Dayton papers are now taken up with *advertisements* of what is being done for the city and the people, and how it is being done. Surely we are making progress!

Another illustration is to be found in the office of the Commissioner of Accounts in New York, an official investigating commission by the use of which the mayor obtains independent information as to the records and works of all departments of the city and county governments. During Mayor Gaynor's time the commissioner adopted as his motto Franklin's aphorism: "The eye of the master will do more work than both his hands." Some idea of the functions of this significant office may be gathered from a little leaflet issued several years ago entitled "The Mayor's Eye":

"The mayor of a city like Greater New York must keep his eye on thirty-four departments of the city government, employing 60,000 men and women, and spending $250,000,000 each year. As he cannot look into every detail himself, he must have records to show what these employees do, and agents who can read them in his stead and report to him what they learn.

"At present the Mayor of New York has an organization of about ninety skilled persons engaged in this work. Day in and day out this organization furnishes the mayor much of the information upon which he bases executive action. It is, in fact, 'The Mayor's Eye.' Officially, it is known as the office of Commissioner of Accounts."

Under the provisions of the Charter, Sections 119 and 195, it is empowered and required to make a detailed examination of all accounts for all moneys received into and paid out of the city treasury, in all departments, and for all purposes, and to report its findings to the mayor and aldermen.

The Charter further provides that the commissioner shall make such other examinations as the mayor may direct, or as the commissioner may deem for the best interests of the city, but he must always report his findings to the mayor and aldermen.

To enable them to ascertain the facts the commissioner is authorized to subpœna and compel the attendance of witnesses, to administer oaths, to examine such persons as they may deem necessary, and to obtain access to any records or papers having to do with the city government. The work necessarily involves the employment of accountants, engineers, lawyers, detectives, and other specialists.

It will be readily seen that with these powers and

duties, the commissioner is a most effective instrument for aiding the Mayor in securing good government.

This work, however, is by no means all of the activities of this Commission. In fact, there are a thousand and one minor things requiring study and investigation, which result in changes of policy and instructions, rather than in uncovering carelessness in the use of money or misappropriation of funds:

"Complaints, rumors, suspicions, criticisms by the press, disputes over contracts, public work in progress, delays, violations of specifications, comparison of equipment with that of other cities, chemical analyses of coal, reports on tests of materials, and so on — all these things come under the jurisdiction of this Commission."

This office has been more than an eye to the mayor; it has been the people's eye as well, giving them an insight into the operation of their affairs that has been of the greatest help in reaching and forming conclusions.

At the time of the promulgation of the first Municipal Program, the most that was then hoped for was the establishment of "a more permanent and efficient subordinate service," although there was a clear recognition of the fact that official business should be conducted in the main by "a class of public servants who by reason of experience and special training are peculiarly fitted for their official duties," meaning of course that all officials that had to do with the execution of policies should be selected without reference to politics and because of their fitness and expertness.

By 1912 interest had so far developed that the joint committee of the National Municipal League and the National Civil Service Reform League on the selection and retention of experts in municipal office called attention to a striking distinction between the administration of cities in enlightened European countries and that of the cities in the United States. Regardless of the differences in the form and organization of municipal government in European countries,

"There is always at the head of each of what may be termed the operating services of city government in European cities an expert who has won his position through his expert qualifications and experience and who holds that position during continued efficiency and good conduct. In every case he has the reasonable certainty of an honorable and permanent career in the line of his chosen calling. In the United States this essential feature of successful city government is almost wholly lacking. Corresponding positions at the head of the operating services of city government here are filled by a kaleidoscopic procession of casuals, whose appointment and tenure are usually influenced by considerations of partisan politics and no permanency of tenure or hope of a career is probable, if even possible. The application of the merit system to the operating departments thus far has been, with here and there an exception, confined to subordinate positions only. This has created the anomaly that subordinates have been withdrawn from the field of partisan politics, while their superior and directing officials are still subject to its malign influence.

MUNICIPAL DEVELOPMENT

The result upon the efficiency of the operating services of city government has been exactly what might have been expected. The absolute necessity of placing upon a permanent and independent basis the higher administrative officials who carry out, but do not create, the policies of a city government has been repeatedly emphasized by eminent earnest workers for the betterment of city government in the United States. Among them that eminent student of government here and abroad, A. Lawrence Lowell, now president of Harvard University, pointed out the need very clearly in his brief and admirable paper before the National Municipal League at its Pittsburgh meeting in 1908."

Recognition of the evil involved becoming more and more general, there has come a steadily increasing demand for some practical method of removing it. This joint committee therefore at the Los Angeles meeting of the National Municipal League (1912) submitted the following suggestions:

The operating departments of a city government should be manned by a force selected and retained solely because of competence to do the work of their positions. At the head of each such department should be an expert in the work of the department who holds his position without reference to the exigencies of partisan politics.

American political experience has proved that on the whole the most certain way of securing such a force is through what have come to be known as civil service reform methods, namely, through competitive examinations of applicants for appointment or promotion. Since 1883, when the practical application of these methods began, it has been found that such examinations need not and often should not be confined to book knowledge or to written questions and answers, and that, provided the examination be fairly conducted by competent examiners, other forms of examinations have been successful to a marked degree in filling positions requiring not only the highest expert knowledge but the highest expert administrative ability.

How shall the system which produces such examiners and such results from examinations be established and protected? The answer is through a board or commission, whose one duty it is to maintain and perfect such a system and whose members shall hold their positions independent of arbitrary removal. Whatever the particular form of municipal government may be, the members of its civil service commission should not be subject to arbitrary removal and should not, in fact, ever be removed because of any difference between the partisan political views of the members of such commission and the power that appoints them.

There should be at least three members of such a commission and the terms should be at least three years, one going out of office each year. In Illinois the civil service commissioners are considered as experts and are chosen as such. Such a commission having the authority to prescribe and enforce the conditions of appointment and promotion, but with no power itself to appoint or promote will inaugurate and, with experience, will perfect a system that will keep every position from the highest to the lowest in the operating services of a city government free from any partisan political influence.

Since the duties of such a commission are purely administrative and are not in any slightest sense of a partisan political nature, and it is important that the standard of administration in each city should be kept at the highest, we favor the administrative supervision of the city commissions by a central state board. The supervision should be administrative solely and, properly conducted, will tend to keep the level of local administration high. A local commission conscious of constant criticism from a central state board entitled to investigate and report and under proper restrictions to reprimand and punish will feel a stricter and higher responsibility to the public for the performance of its duties.

In reaching these conclusions, the committee constantly kept in mind that those officials who formulate and establish policies must be in close touch with the people, either by direct election or through appointment and removal without restraint by those who are elected by the people. On the other hand, operating officials carrying out the policies so determined should hold office during continued efficiency and good conduct, and should be experts of education, training, experience and executive ability, and selected and promoted under civil service rules of a kind to determine these qualifications.

To the objection that an incoming administration should have the power to appoint its own experts in sympathy with its proposed policies, it may be answered that experience both in public and in private work has shown that an executive does not need to change experts in order to initiate new policies. In railroading, for example, a change of administration is followed by few, if any, changes among the civil engineers and superintendents of divisions. When Mr. Harriman took charge of the Union and Southern Pacific railroads, and entirely changed their policies, he kept all the former experts, even the chief legal adviser of the road; and Mr. Hill, in his reorganization of the Northern Pacific and its branches, made only one change in its large personnel.

The Committee, which was composed of Robert Catherwood, Chicago; Richard Henry Dana, Boston; Horace E. Deming, New York; William Dudley Foulke, Richmond, Indiana; Elliott E. Goodwin, New York; Stiles P. Jones, Minneapolis; Clinton Rogers Woodruff, Philadelphia, chairman, proceeded to point out:

"To the argument that experts are likely to become bureaucratic and out of touch with the people, experience has demonstrated that they are very much alive to the needs of the people, at home and abroad, and that they often suggest improvements of which the people themselves have not thought, and which have never been made an issue. As a general proposition, neither the people nor the politicians have initiated the modern municipal improvements, but rather the experts, such as physicians, sanitary and civil engineers, architects, landscape architects, bacteriologists, philanthropists, and educators, backed up by civic leagues, boards of trade, and similar public bodies.

"It is not claimed that an ordinary academic civil service examination is a suitable method to select experts of mature experience and executive ability. The present methods employed by competent civil service commissions for such positions, however, are not such. There are two general methods employed: one selecting for the lower expert positions through very thorough technical examinations, and then promoting to the chief positions as experience becomes mature and executive ability is exhibited; the other is that of directly filling the higher positions by examinations consisting of systematic and thorough inquiry into the education and training of the candidates, their achievements, experience, success in handling men, and ability in executing large affairs, and carried on by examiners who themselves are specialists in the subjects under consideration. For example, for selecting an architect, leading architects are the examiners; for engineers, engineers.

"High-grade experts of mature experience do not like to exchange steady private employment for municipal services as conducted in the United States to-day, with short or uncertain terms during which they are subject to dictation from politicians. Where, however, positions are made practically secure, and where successors can only be chosen by a method from which favoritism is eliminated, and sufficient powers are granted them, experts do apply. This is not only true on the continent of Europe, but has proved true in Chicago, where the city engineer, the engineer in charge of bridges, the city auditor, the chief street engineer, the building inspector in chief and the chief librarian (with salaries from $3,000 to $8,000 a year) have been appointed under civil service rules. This system has also been successfully used in the appointment of the state librarian of New York State, assistants to the attorney general, and several other such officials, and, in the federal service, in the appointment of the heads of many bureaus, experts with scientific knowledge and executive ability. R. A. Widdowson, the secretary of the Chicago civil service commission, in a letter dated February 14, 1912, said: 'The higher grade examinations in the Chicago civil service, which are usually open to all qualified residents of the United States, attract men of the highest caliber where the salaries are on a commercial basis.' The same in substance is reported by the civil service commissions of Kansas City, New York City, New York State, and the United States.

" When such a system as herein recommended has been in operation for a number of years there will doubtless grow up in this country, as there has in England and in Europe, a large body of municipal experts in the various branches of municipal activity who begin their careers in cities of moderate size, or as assistants in large cities, and by promotion from one city to another or within the same city reach the highest positions.

" In the United States we have as an illustration of expert accomplishment the river and harbor work. The fact that out of the $627,000,000 actually spent for that work between 1789 and 1911 so little has gone for corrupt purposes is due to the work having been done under the detailed administration of United States army engineers, who secure their positions through strict competition at West Point and who hold their positions for life during good behavior, and who are only under about the same control as is proposed here for municipal experts. These United States army engineers have nothing to do with the initiaton of the work (except in the way of advice) or of the appropriation of the funds, and all their expenditures are carefully scrutinized by auditors and comptrollers who disallow any item not strictly within the appropriation and law.

"If by this system we should in America succeed in taking municipal contracts out of politics and putting the control of subordinate employees under persons not looking to the next election, we shall accomplish for the welfare, political morality, and reputation of our American cities a lasting good."[1]

A still further step in this direction has been taken in the organization of the "Society for the Promotion of Training for Public Service." Its program embodies: Improvement of public administration; making public service a profession; practical training for public service; harnessing civil service reform to an educational program; widest community service of our educational institutions; more agencies of accurate public information; more effective civic organizations; extension of the part-time principle in education; removing local residence requirement for public service; welfare work for public employees. Certainly an ambitious program; significant of the development of public opinion and public demands on this phase of municipal government. Another step has been taken, that is the granting of academic credit for work done in city departments and bureaus by students, and the linking up of educational institutions with city administrations, as, for instance, Columbia University and the University of the City of New York in Greater

[1] The general principles of "Expert City Government" were dealt with at length in William Dudley Foulke's presidential address of that year, which is reprinted in full in the *National Municipal Review*, Vol. I, page 549. Another article, "Civil Service Reform at Los Angeles," see *National Municipal Review*, Vol. I, page 639, further summarizes the conclusions reached and the papers read at the meeting held in that city.

New York; the University of Pennsylvania in Philadelphia; the University of Cincinnati in that city.[1] And still another is outlined in detail in a volume on "Expert City Government" edited by Major E. A. Fitzpatrick for the National Municipal League Series.

The local residence requirement for public office has long been one of the bulwarks of the existing régime. It harmonizes with the spirit of provincialism and not only makes for the *status quo,* but it helps in the maintenance of a strong political organization. Dr. Clyde L. King in an article under this title in *The Public Servant* for February, 1916, thus states the case:

"There is needed an inspector of gas in a large city at a salary of $5,000 per year. The tide of provincialism in this particular city runs strong. 'Aliens' are not wanted. Therefore, by law or by decree of the civil service commission, applicants for the position are limited to those who are residents of the city.

"The position requires integrity and willingness to put the public weal first. There are ten applicants, of whom five pass the examination. Of these five, two have been sent in by the gas company. One is a ward worker who has crammed up for the examination, and barely passes it, but passes high on 'personality and tact,' which counted 4 out of the 10 points. A fourth is a clerk in the present bureau, a man who passed low on the 'personality and tact' test, but who was sufficiently immersed in office procedure to pass his other tests with high per-

[1] See article on Municipal Universities, by Dean John L. Patterson, *National Municipal Review,* Vol. V, p. 553.

centages. A fifth is a graduate of an engineering school in a nearby university, endowments to which are being expectantly awaited. This particular graduate the faculty had not thought sufficiently capable to warrant a recommendation for private employment. Moreover, his family connections and his aspirations are such as to make him very amenable to ' social pressure ' from the gas office.

"One of the five must be chosen. What is the best choice? Is it not the hard worker?

"A similar examination is given in another city for an identical position. The examination this time is open to all without residence restrictions. Again there are five successful applicants. One is a local politician who in his oral examination assures the examiners that he can do any 'organizing' work among the voters the city administration may wish him to do. His technical qualifications are just sufficient to let him pass. A second is a resident of the city, and once an instructor in chemistry in a nearby university. His technical qualifications are high. He sends word to the appointing authority that councils are ' with him.' The character of the councils is such as to make it sure that this means inimical pressure from the gas company. A third is a highly qualified non-resident expert from a nearby gas company, who says in his written examination that utility questions are to be solved solely by conference with the president of the home gas company. A fourth is a resident graduate from a high-grade engineering school. The tests assure him to be capable and fearless. A fifth has served the public most acceptably in a similar position in a larger city at a salary of $3,500. He has excellent technical proparation, knows how to deal with the public, and his ideals as a public servant have been well tested.

"Now which of the five should be appointed? Is it not the experienced expert?

"But, you say, these are extreme cases. Quite to the contrary, they are taken almost word for word from official records and are typical of what is going on day after day in American municipalities.

"The number of qualified men free to take such a position are sufficiently limited in the United States. It stands to reason that the possibilities of a good choice are all the fewer when applicants are limited to their home towns. The residence limitation assures mediocrity in public office; the removal of the residence limitation gives opportunity for the prepared expert who wishes to be a public servant."

These contrasts bring out the situation clearly and show how students feel on the question. The fact that the newer charters are omitting the local residence clause shows how charter framers are thinking, and when administrators like Morris Llewellyn Cooke, Director of Public Works under Mayor Blankenburg, freely bring in outside experts, we see how administrators are tending. Another significant straw is to be seen in the retention of some of these outside experts under his successor, although the appointment of "aliens" had been an issue in the political campaign.

Some further idea of the tendency may be gathered from the fact that the following cities, among others, chose non-residents to serve as city managers: Dayton and Springfield, Ohio; Niagara Falls, New York; St. Augustine and Lakeland, Florida; Jackson, Michigan; San José, California; La Grande, Oregon; Webster City, Iowa; Norwood, Massachusetts; Norfolk, Virginia; Goldsboro, North Carolina; Bethlehem, Pennsylvania.

Another phase of this tendency calling for notice in this connection is the payment of adequate salaries. While we have by no means reached the foreign standards in the compensation of public service, a good start has been made in several places, and the commission form has been a very considerable lever.

So far reference has been made only to the development of the administrative side of the city government. We have seen that the development has been along sound lines, and in the direction of efficiency. Increasing emphasis is being placed upon the coördination and smooth working of departmental service; modern scientific methods are being followed in the development of each municipal function and of each part of the machinery of service; and the distribution of the funds voted for the support of each is steadily being based upon their actual relative needs and importance. The development along other lines has been equally marked and equally encouraging. The tendency has been away from complexity, toward simplicity; from irresponsibility to responsibility; from diffusion to concentration; from irresponsiveness to responsiveness. In his Yale lectures, George McAneny said: "The old-plan city charters should give way as rapidly as may be to charters that do treat cities as business and social institutions; that prevent as far as possible the intrusion of national politics in city affairs; that reduce to a minimum the number of city officers to be elected by direct vote of the people; that centralize executive responsibility; and that provide the simplest and, at the same time, the most efficient sort of working machinery for the conduct of the city's running affairs."

And this has been the undoubted tendency of the past score of years. Since the first Municipal Program the commission form of government and its modifications have embodied these ideas. The short ballot principle has gained great vogue since the Program of 1900 was published, and now we have a Short Ballot Organization which is spreading the gospel with zeal and efficiency. The idea is not new, although the happy phrase, "Short Ballot" is; but the propaganda has only taken concrete form within the past decade. Its greatest strides have been made in the field of municipal government and for some time to come are likely to be mainly confined to that field. The Short Ballot is a move in the direction of a more actual popular control on the principle that a man may manage his business more effectively through not trying to assume too large a share of the detail. In this connection it may be observed that it seems reasonable to suppose that the initiative and referendum on any extensive scale will not in the long run prove generally feasible. Representatives and executors, few in number, with large powers, and with rigid and direct responsibility to the people, may be expected to execute so satisfactorily the popular will that direct interference will be as infrequent in the world of politics as it is under similar circumstances in the world of business.

MUNICIPAL DEVELOPMENT

Some idea of the complexity and diffusion in city charters may be gathered from the diagnosis of municipal ills in Los Angeles prepared by Director Burks of the Efficiency Bureau of that city. He prepared a chart showing an outline of the city government together with an analysis which contained a number of interesting facts from which may be noted for the purposes of illustration:

Of the 72 members of the 20 boards and commissions, only 32 members had been appointed by the then mayor; 40 owing their appointment to preceding mayors;

The mayor is ex-officio member of two commissions (fire and police), but aside from this is not in a position to exercise strong authority over the administrative branches of the city government;

There is no systematic and consistent plan of government for the city;

There is confusion between the policy-making authority on the one hand and responsibility for management on the other.

The chart made it clear that there is no chief executive with definitely fixed, inclusive authority and responsibility; that there is a wide dispersion, separation, and duplication of powers instead of a classification and co-ordination of functions and personnel; that there is a multiplicity of bodies charged with legislative or policy-determining authority, instead of a single body with control over administrative officers; and that the scheme of organization is in many respects illogical and inconsistent.

Such an organization is without parallel among well

conducted, successful private enterprises, although it may be assumed that efficiency in the management of public business must be obtained by the same methods that have been found necessary in private management. The organization pictured in the chart is the logical outcome of the theory that public officials are not to be trusted and that they must be hedged about by checks and limitations that will prevent them from going too far astray. The intelligent, public-spirited, competent official is therefore compelled to work under the handicap of conditions that have been imposed by distrust and suspicion.

Contrast this arrangement with the simple, direct commission government form; or the still simpler and more direct commission manager form of government and see what has been and is being accomplished.

Another contrast is the one afforded by a comparison of the length of the old plan charters, and the new. The former went on the principle that nothing could safely be trusted to the people or their representatives. That everything had to be put down in black and white and given the binding effect of statute law. As a consequence, city charters have assumed forbidding lengths. The federal constitution and its seventeen amendments, including chapter headings and numerals, contains 5919 words. In the language of the editor of *The St. Louis Dispatch:* "Statesmen in the early days were sparing in the use of words. They aimed to say it and quit, and they did not aim to say everything; just the essential things. They knew better than to try to legislate on details for generations yet unborn. They trusted future governments to do that." So in 4476 words, the amend-

MUNICIPAL DEVELOPMENT 285

ments added 1443, making 5919 in all, the framers of the Constitution drew a charter for a great nation, declaring and defining its powers, limitations and duties, the powers, limitations and duties of the constituent states, the rights and duties of individual citizens, and set up the three coordinate branches of the government, with their subdivisions — all in 4476 words. Their successors during more than 125 years used 1443 additional words, keeping the nation's charter up to date.

The Constitution is written in simple language. Any person of average intelligence and possessing a common school education can readily understand every word of it, every statement in it. It is the world's model, among state and national charters, for its simplicity, its completeness, its efficacy, its brevity.

St. Louis' city charter is seven or eight times as long. Was it seven or eight times as hard to say, the *Dispatch* asks, "what needed to be said in the city charter as it was to say what needed to be said in the national charter? Or is the city seven or eight times as important as the nation? Or were the makers of the nation's charter seven or eight times as skillful as the city charter makers in stating essential things briefly, and omitting the nonessential? Or did the city charter makers say seven or eight times as many things as needed to be said in a city charter?

"Even the admirable charter voted on in 1910 contained more than 30,000 words — was over 26 newspaper columns in length. Its essential declarations could have been made in less than two columns."

And St. Louis is not by any means an extreme example. Prior to the adoption of its new charter, Boston's so-called charter was declared to consist of upwards of 700 separate acts of the legislature. Compare that situation, or the St. Louis charter, and these not the greatest offenders in the matter of length or complexity, with the Des Moines charter or with any of the commission type, and one can quickly gain an idea of the progress we are making in improving the popular machinery of government so that the people can really understand and run the policy-determining end of the government which is the only one with which they should be charged responsibility. If they are given actual control of that branch, then the administrative end will in time fall in line and become responsive both to the needs and aspirations of the people.

Electoral reforms have scarcely kept pace with the improvement in governmental machinery, but they are not hopeless laggards. This improvement continues steadily and in the direction of eliminating nomination monopolies, and of giving the voters a more direct actual say in the determination of their policies and the settlement of their affairs, and of helping to drive national party lines and partisanship out of municipal affairs. With only a few exceptions, every commission government represents simplified non-partisan elections. They also represent the abolition of ward politics with all their petty jealousies and rivalries, with all their dangerous log-rolling. While there is a serious appreciation of the need of keeping representatives close to the people and preserving wieldy districts, that political organizations may not be given an undue weight and influence, there has been an equally serious appreciation of the evils of the old-fashioned arbitrary ward. In the communities now under the commission government, the ward lines have gone so far as local elections are concerned, and in those cities where elections at large prevail; and in some cities, notably in Seattle, the ward lines have been legally abolished.

Municipal progress has not been confined to the improvement of governmental machinery. In two other still more important directions it has been making steady headway. I refer to the fundamental question of self-government and to the highly essential need of an adequate conception of municipal government as a factor in promoting human welfare.

Municipal home rule, as we have come to call the demand for self-government of our cities, was an academic question in 1900. To-day it is a practical political question in a majority of the states. In 1904 the people of Lynn had to go to the legislature to secure permission to change their inauguration exercises from evening to morning. In many another city charter could be found restrictions equally as unreasonable, limiting the right of the people of the city to determine purely local matters to suit themselves. Massachusetts cities are still in a large measure dependent upon their legislature; but even in that state, cities are now given an opportunity at least to write their charters, within certain narrow lines; and a series of optional charters has been passed by the legislature. These may be but slight concessions, but they are the beginning of the end, which is not far off in many other places. In 1914 I said in my annual review:

"Municipal home rule has been making great gains within the past few years. In the first place, by inserting in the state constitutions provisions giving to the cities the right to determine their own destinies, setting them free to do for their 'citizen stockholders' that which they have come to realize needs to be done, and which they cannot do so long as they are 'held under suzerainty by the rural population, expressing its will through the old-fashioned sort of legislatures.' In this class are the cities of Colorado, where the National Municipal League's constitutional amendment has been adopted in its entirety, California, Oregon, Washington, Oklahoma, Arizona, Idaho, Texas, Nebraska, Minnesota, Michigan, Ohio. The movement has made headway in those states which have given the cities the opportunity to adopt certain forms of government, as in Kansas, where the cities, can, if they wish, come under the commission form if their electors so vote. Ohio, Illinois, Wisconsin, Iowa, North Carolina, New Mexico, are in this class. There is still another form of municipal home rule, which may be said to be home rule by sufferance, in those states where the state legislatures defer to the wishes of the representatives therein from the community affected." [1]

"These three movements: Non-partisanship, the direct election of federal senators and municipal home rule all represent municipal advance of the most effective kind, in

[1] See *National Municipal Review*, Vol. III, page 5.

that they place municipal affairs clearly on their own bases, freed from outside and alien influences, and give to our cities opportunity fully to develop their resources along democratic lines."

Municipal home rule is daily gaining a firmer hold on public opinion, and in the course of the coming generation is destined to become a settled policy.

At the same time there has been an equally marked tendency toward a state supervision of municipal affairs, so that uniformity may be secured, and a wise, general policy worked out. To put the situation in another way: state legislative government of cities is gradually being replaced by a state administrative supervision and control, as advocated in the first Municipal Program.

It is in our conception of municipal government that perhaps the greatest change is to be noted. As Mayo Fesler, when a member of the Cleveland charter commission, who was also a member of the League's second Committee on Municipal Program, said: "Recognition must be given to the fact that it is the duty of the municipality to care for the welfare of its citizens fully as much as for the property and material interests of its citizens."

In a recent address Edward A. Ross defined the functions of a city in this manner:

"The starting of every young person on his or her adult life with an education and trade is a function of the community. This is not socialism, for the question in socialism is, ' Should any portion of the product go to people by virtue of their property claims or should service only participate?'

"In the city which I have in mind there will be rich and poor, there will still be plenty of competition, of success and of failure, and the individual will still have to hustle for the rent, for clothing, and for food, but health, education, culture and recreation — these will be supplied by the city."

The inspection of food and housing provision for preserving the health of its citizens, and the providing of public entertainment and recreation, as well as education, are legitimate functions of the modern city, in the view of Professor Ross. He favors central bureaus to provide work for the unemployed, industrial education to replace the apprentice system now dying out, an increase in the activities of public libraries, the suppression of vice, and the furnishing of small parks in the built-up sections of cities. He also favors municipal milk depots as a legitimate sphere of city government, and instanced Rochester, which so decreased its infant mortality by this means as to mean an annual saving of 400 babies at an expense of $2,200 a year, or $5.50 a baby. There are numerous other functions which a city is called upon to perform, and the demand seems to be daily increasing; but they are all urged that they are needed because it is the real business of the city to promote and protect the health, education, recreation, safety, convenience and prosperity of its citizens. In short, it is the function of the city to serve, as well as to govern.

In another direction the conception of the city has

developed along encouraging lines — and that is in the matter of city planning, which was regarded as a far cry in 1900, and is now a subject of vigorous discussion in sundry communities, and of settled policy in others. Nay, certain phases, like those of districting and zoning, then regarded as interesting dreams, but still dreams, are not only coming to be crystallized into municipal law, but more important still, to be upheld by the Supreme Court of the United States as a constitutional exercise of municipal authority!

The conception of the personal obligation of citizenship and that of official duty are changing for the better. As Professor Zueblin pointed out before the Association of New York State Mayors and other officials:

"A meeting of the mayors and other public officials of the cities of a great commonwealth like New York is the best possible indication that times have changed. A traditional American attitude, which has unfortunately prevailed in most cities over a century, is that of supposing that a municipal position is a thankless job in which a minimum service is exacted, and such peculiar perquisites as the official may secure from his office are tolerated. Until a decade ago municipal officials were chiefly remembered by having their names conspicuously embellishing a large tablet placed upon any building or public structure perpetrated during their incumbency. The men who gather at such conferences as this will be remembered for their services to the communities; at least their services will be remembered, what matter if they are personally forgotten! The first obligation of every public official is of course to do the work assigned to him in the organization of the city, and that is a large contract, in view of our traditions. The character of public life, however, advances so rapidly that we now expect more; and if all our public officials did their work to the complete satisfaction of their consciences there would still be a large field of possible usefulness over which, under ideal conditions, their activities might extend."

Similar associations or leagues have been organized in thirty-three other states, surely an encouraging showing, when one recalls their objects and purposes, which are well set forth in the outline of the bureau maintained by the New York Association:

1. To gather information and statistics relative to municipal problems and improvements and to distribute them among the officials of the cities of the state.

2. To keep all municipalities informed about bills introduced into the legislature and newly enacted laws affecting the cities.

3. To furnish any city upon request all available information or statistics relative to any municipal activity indicated.

4. To keep municipal officials of the state in touch with each other by distributing among them any new plans devised by an official of any department.

5. In addition, the bureau should also keep officials informed as to the progress of all municipal innovations thus reported to them, so that they might know of their success or failure.

6. To distribute such reports and other literature rela-

tive to municipal government and activities as will aid municipal officials.

Along with this satisfactory trend is to be noted the fact that public opinion gains force and effectiveness through organization rather than through disconnected action. When sufficiently aroused, citizen interest must take definite form in the organization of a citizen agency. This agency, as Mr. Burnham declared in his speech already quoted from, finds that before it may serve as a medium of communication between the citizen and his government, and before it can secure the results desired, it must have fact bases. Investigation is required to afford sound recommendations, and as a result the extensive progress being made in governmental affairs must be attributed largely to these civic agencies. It is necessary to view the work of these agencies, as well as the government itself, to find what steps have been taken to place government upon a higher plane. Their object is always a better government. They are variously known as bureaus of municipal research, institutes for public service, institutes for government research, civic or taxpayers' associations, municipal leagues, etc. The number of these agencies is increasing and their influence for good government was never greater than to-day. Logically, they give no thought to whether the administration is a party one, but instead demand that it be measured in terms of effectiveness and whether the largest possibilities are being realized through economical and efficient expenditure of public funds. Official and citizen coöperation, as it has come to be called, is really the product of the present generation. When the National Municipal

League was formed in 1894, it was an unheard of policy. Now it is a factor everywhere to be reckoned with in measuring the development of American municipal government. It is arousing the people, stimulating them and formulating their opinion in such public questions as have been considered in these chapters. Indeed the progress which has herein been recorded would have been impossible without it.

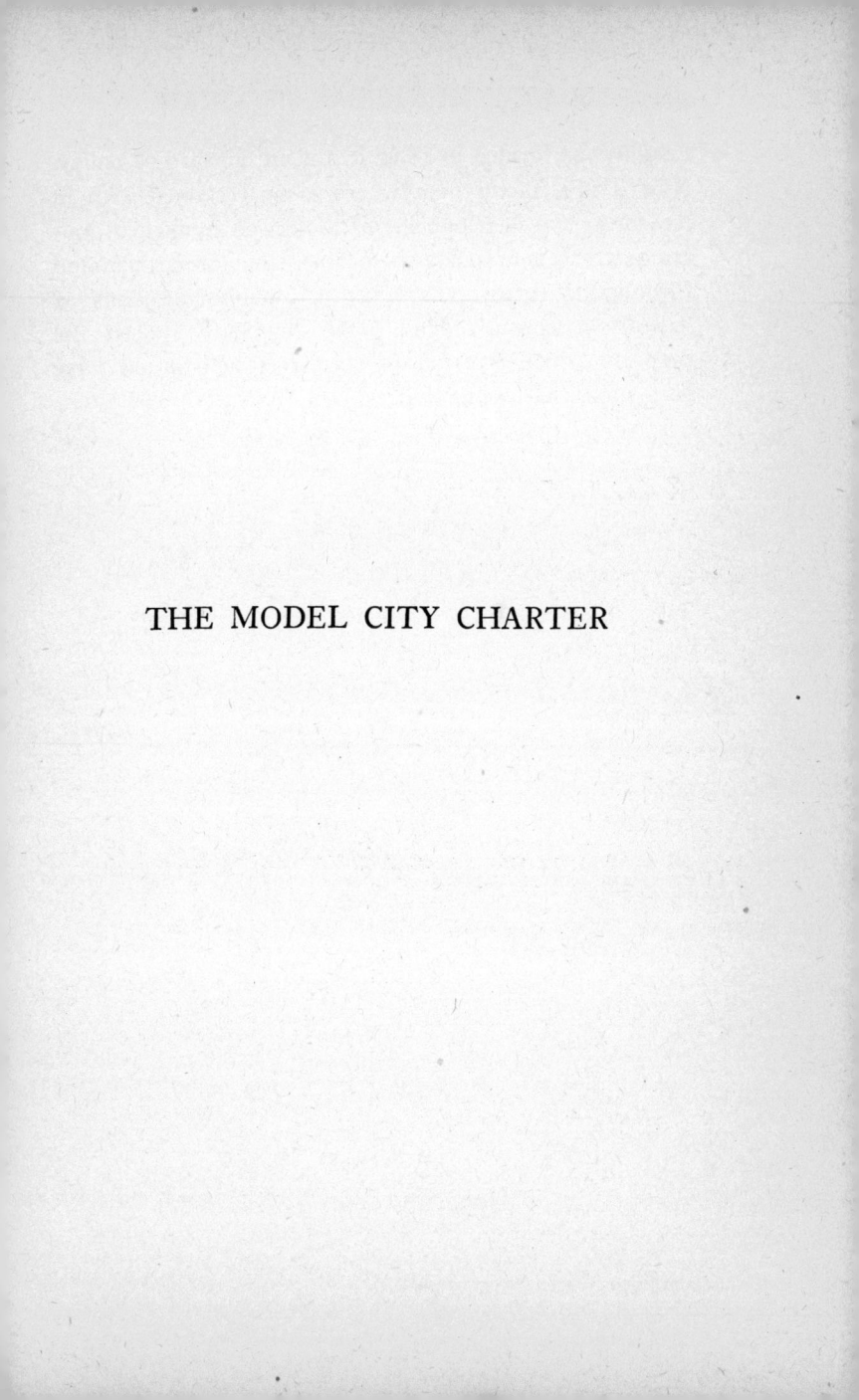

THE MODEL CITY CHARTER

TABLE OF CONTENTS

Municipal Home Rule: Constitutional Provisions

	PAGE
Section 1. Incorporation and Organization	302
Section 2. Optional Laws	302
Section 3. City Charters	303
Section 4. Amendments	304
Section 5. Powers	305
Section 6. Reports	306
Section 7. Elections	306
Section 8. Consolidation of City and County	307

The Model Charter

The Council.

Section 1. Creation of Council 307
Section 2. Composition of Council and Vacancies 308
Section 3. Powers of Council 309
Section 4. Election by Councils. Rules. Quorum.... 310
Section 5. Organization and Procedure of Council.... 310
Section 6. Powers of Mayor 311

Nominations and Elections.

Section 7. Municipal Elections 311
Section 8. Nomination by Petition 312
Section 9. Signatures to and Forms of Nomination Papers 312
Section 10. Filing Nomination Papers 313
Section 11. Regulation of Elections 314
Section 12. The Ballots and the Voting 314
Section 13. Rules for Counting the Ballots 315
Section 14. Vacancy Provisions 320

The Recall.

Section 15. Recall Provisions 321

The Initiative.

Section 16. Power to Initiate Ordinances 325
Section 17. Preparation of Initiative Petitions 325

CONTENTS

		PAGE
Section 18.	Filing of Petitions	326
Section 19.	Submission of Petition to Council	327
Section 20.	Election on Initiated Measures	327
Section 21.	Initiative Ballots	328
Section 22.	Number of Measures to be Initiated	329

THE REFERENDUM.

Section 23.	Power of Referendum	329
Section 24.	Limitations on Enforcement of Ordinances	330
Section 25.	Referendum Petition	330
Section 26.	Signatures to Petition	330
Section 27.	Certification of Petition	331
Section 28.	Referendum Election	331
Section 29.	Title of Ballot	332
Section 30.	Form of Ballot	332
Section 31.	Emergency Measures	332
Section 32.	Official Publicity Pamphlet	333
Section 33.	Conflict of Referred Measures	333

ADMINISTRATIVE SERVICE: THE CITY MANAGER.

Section 34.	The City Manager	334
Section 35.	Power and Duties of the City Manager	335
Section 36.	Annual Budget	335

ADMINISTRATIVE DEPARTMENTS.

Section 37.	Administrative Departments Created	335
Section 38.	Duties of Directors of Departments	336
Section 39.	Responsibility of Directors of Departments	337
Section 40.	Powers of Subpœna	337

CIVIL SERVICE BOARD.

Section 41.	Creation of Civil Service Board	337
Section 42.	Power to Make Rules and What the Rules Shall Provide	338
Section 43.	Supervisory Powers of Civil Service Board	341
Section 44.	Power of Removal and Suspension	342
Section 45.	Restrictions on Civil Service Appointees and Forbidden Practices	343
Section 46.	Politics and Religion Excluded	345
Section 47.	Violations of Civil Service Rules and Regulations	345
Section 48.	Power of Taxpayer to Enforce Rules	346

FINANCIAL PROVISIONS.

Section 49.	The Director of Finance	346
Section 50.	Accounts and Records	346
Section 51.	Annual Budget	347

CONTENTS

		PAGE
Section 52.	Appropriation Ordinance. Temporary Appropriations. Transfers	348
Section 53.	Tax Levy	349
Section 54.	Assessment of Property	349
Section 55.	Special Assessments	349
Section 56.	Bond Issues	350
Section 57.	Temporary Loans	351
Section 58.	Restrictions on Loans and Credit	351
Section 59.	Collection and Custody of City Moneys	352
Section 60.	Contracts and Purchases	352
Section 61.	Payment of Claims	353
Section 62.	Audit of Accounts	353

PUBLIC UTILITIES.

Section 63.	Granted by Ordinance	354
Section 64.	Term and Plan of Purchase	356
Section 65.	Right of Regulation	356
Section 66.	Consents of Property Owners	357
Section 67.	Revocable Permits	358
Section 68.	Extensions	358
Section 69.	Other Conditions	358
Section 70.	Franchise Records	359
Section 71.	Bureau of Franchises and Public Utilities	359
Section 72.	Accounts of Municipally Owned Utilities	360

CITY PLANNING.

Section 73.	Creation of a City Planning Board	360
Section 74.	Power of Board	361
Section 75.	Annual Report	362
Section 76.	Secretary of the Board	362

MISCELLANEOUS PROVISIONS.

Section 77.	Publicity of Accounts	363
Section 78.	No Personal Interest	363
Section 79.	When Charter Shall Take Effect	364

APPENDIX A. PREFERENTIAL BALLOT.

Section 1.	Preparation of Ballot	364
Section 2.	Arrangement for First, Second and Other Choices	365
Section 3.	Form of Ballot	365
Section 4.	Counting of Ballots	366

REPORT OF COMMITTEE ON MUNICIPAL PROGRAM

The Committee on Municipal Program was appointed in 1913 to consider the original "Municipal Program" adopted in 1900 and if desirable to draft a new model charter and home rule constitutional amendments embodying the result of subsequent study and developments. This committee presented a partial report to the meeting of the League in Baltimore, in November, 1914, in the form of sections dealing with the council, the city manager and the civil service board. The committee held two day sessions in New York, April 8 and 9, 1915, at which time these sections were carefully revised and sections dealing with the initiative, referendum, recall and other electoral provisions were considered and added, and a partial draft of the constitutional provisions, which had been presented at the Baltimore meeting was completed. Another meeting of the committee was held in New York, September 14, 1915, at which further revisions were made, and the financial provisions added as well as the two appendices treating of proportional representation and franchise provisions, all of which were included in the tentative draft. The Program was again submitted to the League at its annual meeting in Dayton on November 19, 1915, and the sections were approved by the members there present. The document was referred back to the Committee on Municipal Program for further amendments, and these amendments as adopted at a meeting of the committee in Philadelphia, December 27 and 28, 1915, are also contained in the following Program.

The Committee on Municipal Program consists of:

WILLIAM DUDLEY FOULKE, *Chairman*, Richmond, Ind.
M. N. BAKER, of the *Engineering News*,
RICHARD S. CHILDS, New York City,
JOHN A. FAIRLIE, University of Illinois.
MAYO FESLER, Civic League, Cleveland,
A. R. HATTON, Western Reserve University, Cleveland,
HERMAN G. JAMES, University of Texas,
A. LAWRENCE LOWELL, Harvard University,
WILLIAM BENNETT MUNRO, Harvard University,
ROBERT TREAT PAINE, Boston,
DELOS F. WILCOX, New York City,
CLINTON ROGERS WOODRUFF, Philadelphia.

MUNICIPAL HOME RULE CONSTITUTIONAL PROVISIONS

(To be adopted and incorporated in the state constitution)

SECTION 1. *Incorporation and Organization.* Provision shall be made by a general law for the incorporation of cities and villages; and by a general law for the organization and government of cities and villages which do not adopt laws or charters in accordance with the provisions of sections 2 and 3 of this article.

SEC. 2. *Optional Laws.* Laws may be enacted affecting the organization and government of cities and villages, which shall become effective in any city or village only when submitted to the electors thereof and approved by a majority of those voting thereon.

CONSTITUTIONAL PROVISIONS 303

Sec. 3. *City Charters.* Any city may frame and adopt a charter for its own government in the following manner: The legislative authority of the city may by a two-thirds vote of its members, and, upon the petition of ten per cent of the qualified electors, shall forthwith provide by ordinance for the submission to the electors of the question: "Shall a commission be chosen to frame a charter?" The ordinance shall require that the question be submitted to the electors at the next regular municipal election, if one shall occur not less than sixty nor more than one hundred and twenty days after its passage, otherwise, at a special election to be called and held within the time aforesaid; the ballot containing such question shall also contain the names of candidates for members of the proposed commission, but without party designation.

Such candidates shall be nominated by petition which shall be signed by not less than two per cent of the qualified electors, and be filed with the election authorities at least thirty days before such election; provided, that in no case shall the signatures of more than one thousand (1000) qualified electors be required for the nomination of any candidate. If a majority of the electors voting on the question of choosing a commission shall vote in the affirmative, then the fifteen candidates receiving the highest number of votes (or if the legislative authority of the state provides by general law for the election of such commissioners by means of a preferential ballot or proportional representation or both, then the fifteen chosen in the manner required by such general law) shall constitute the charter commission and shall proceed to frame a charter.

Any charter so framed shall be submitted to the qualified electors of the city at an election to be held at a time to be determined by the charter commission, which shall be at least thirty days subsequent to its completion and distribution among the electors and not more than one year from the date of the election of the charter commission. Alternative provisions may also be submitted to be voted upon separately. The commission shall make provision for the distribution of copies of the proposed charter and of any alternative provisions to the qualified electors of the city not less than thirty days before the election at which it is voted upon. Such proposed charter and such alternative provisions as are approved by a majority of the electors voting thereon shall become the organic law of such city at such time as may be fixed therein, and shall supersede any existing charter and all laws affecting the organization and government of such city which are in conflict therewith. Within thirty days after its approval the election authorities shall certify a copy of such charter to the secretary of state, who shall file the same as a public record in his office, and the same shall be published as an appendix to the session laws enacted by the legislature.

SEC. 4. *Amendments.* Amendments to any such charter may be framed and submitted by a charter commission in the same manner as provided in section 3 for framing and adopting a charter. Amendments may also be proposed by two-thirds of the legislative authority of the city, or by petition of ten per cent of the electors;

CONSTITUTIONAL PROVISIONS

and any such amendment, after due public hearing before such legislative authority, shall be submitted at a regular or special election as is provided for the submission of the question of choosing a charter commission. Copies of all proposed amendments shall be sent to the qualified electors. Any such amendment approved by a majority of the electors voting thereon shall become a part of the charter of the city at the time fixed in the amendment and shall be certified to and filed and published by the secretary of state as in the case of a charter.

SEC. 5. *Powers.* Each city shall have and is hereby granted the authority to exercise all powers relating to municipal affairs; and no enumeration of powers in this constitution or any law shall be deemed to limit or restrict the general grant of authority hereby conferred; but this grant of authority shall not be deemed to limit or restrict the power of the legislature, in matters relating to state affairs, to enact general laws applicable alike to all cities of the state.

The following shall be deemed to be a part of the powers conferred upon cities by this section:

(a) To levy, assess and collect taxes and to borrow money, within the limits prescribed by general laws; and to levy and collect special assessments for benefits conferred;

(b) To furnish all local public services; to purchase, hire, construct, own, maintain, and operate or lease local public utilities; to acquire, by condemnation or otherwise, within or without the corporate limits, property necessary for any such purposes, subject to restrictions imposed by general law for the protection of other communities; and to grant local public utility franchises and regulate the exercise thereof;

(c) To make local public improvements and to acquire, by condemnation or otherwise, property within its corporate limits necessary for such improvements; and also to acquire an excess over that needed for any such improvement, and to sell or lease such excess property with restrictions, in order to protect and preserve the improvement;

(d) To issue and sell bonds on the security of any such excess property, or of any public utility owned by the city, or of the revenues thereof, or of both, including in the case of a public utility, if deemed desirable by the city, a franchise stating the terms upon which, in case of foreclosure, the purchaser may operate such utility;

(e) To organize and administer public schools and libraries, subject to the general laws establishing a standard of education for the state;

(f) To adopt and enforce within their limits local police, sanitary and other similar regulations not in conflict with general laws.

SEC. 6. *Reports.* General laws may be passed requiring reports from cities as to their transactions and financial condition, and providing for the examination by state officials of the vouchers, books and accounts of all municipal authorities, or of public undertakings conducted by such authorities.

SEC. 7. *Elections.* All elections and submissions of questions provided for in this article or in any charter or law adopted in accordance herewith shall be conducted by the election authorities provided by general law.

SEC. 8. *Consolidation of City and County.* Any city of 100,000 population or over,[1] upon vote of the electors taken in the manner provided by general law, may be organized as a distinct county; and any such city and county may in its municipal charter provide for the consolidation of the county, city and all other local authorities in one system of municipal government, in which provision shall be made for the exercise of all powers and duties vested in the several local authorities. Any such consolidated city and county government shall also have the same powers to levy taxes and to borrow money as were vested in the several local authorities before consolidation.

THE MODEL CHARTER [1]

THE COUNCIL

SECTION 1. *Creation of Council.* There is hereby created a council which shall have full power and au-

---

[1] This number may be varied to suit local conditions in the several states.

NOTE 1. This model is assumed to be a home rule charter based upon some such provisions for constitutional municipal home rule as those suggested in this report. When this or a similar charter is made available for cities by statute it is desirable that a comprehensive grant of powers be included in the act itself. Otherwise cities securing such a charter will have only the powers enumerated in the general law of the state and be subject to all the restrictions and inconveniences arising from that method of granting powers. It is suggested, therefore, that the following grant of powers be included in any such special statutory charter or optional charter law. The changes of language necessary to adapt it to a special statutory charter readily suggest themselves:

SECTION —. Cities organized under this act shall have and are hereby granted authority to exercise all powers relating to their municipal affairs; and no enumeration of powers in any law shall be deemed to restrict the general grant of authority hereby conferred.

thority, except as herein otherwise provided, to exercise all the powers conferred upon the city.

SEC. 2. *Composition of Council.* The council shall consist of   members,[2] who shall be elected

> The following shall be deemed to be a part of the powers conferred upon cities by this section:
>
> (a) To levy, assess and collect taxes and to borrow money within the limits prescribed by general law; and to levy and collect special assessments for benefits conferred.
>
> (b) To furnish all local public services; to purchase, hire, construct, own, maintain and operate or lease local public utilities; to acquire, by condemnation or otherwise, within or without the corporate limits, property necessary for any such purposes, subject to restrictions imposed by general law for the protection of other communities; and to grant local public utility franchises and regulate the exercise thereof.
>
> (c) To make local public improvements and to acquire, by condemnation or otherwise, property within its corporate limits necessary for such improvements; and also to acquire an excess over that needed for any such improvement, and to sell or lease such excess property with restrictions, in order to protect and preserve the improvement.
>
> (d) To issue and sell bonds on the security of any such excess property, or of any public utility owned by the city, or of the revenues thereof, or of both, including in the case of a public utility, if deemed desirable by the city, a franchise stating the terms upon which, in case of foreclosure, the purchaser may operate such utility.
>
> (e) To organize and administer public schools and libraries, subject to the general laws establishing a standard of education for the state.
>
> (f) To adopt and enforce within their limits local police, sanitary and other similar regulations not in conflict with general laws.
>
> Except as otherwise provided in this act the council shall have authority to determine by whom and in what manner the powers granted by this section shall be exercised.
>
> NOTE 2. The number of members, and whether they should be chosen at large or from districts being determined by the size of the city. There should be at least 5 members, and 50 would probably suffice for cities of the largest size. Great cities may with advantage be divided into large districts, each to elect five or more members of the council. An effort should be made to keep the size of the districts down to a point where free competition for public office may prevail, the expense of a thorough canvass being not too great for an independent candidate who may lack the support of a permanent political organization.

on a general ticket from the city at large and shall serve for a term of four years from   days after their election, and shall be subject to recall as hereinafter provided.[3]

SEC. 3. *Powers of Council.* The council shall be the judge of the election and qualification of its own members, subject to review by the courts. Any member of council who shall have been convicted of a crime while in office shall thereby forfeit his office. Neither the council nor any of its committees or members shall dictate the appointment of any person to office or employment by the city manager, or in any manner interfere with the city manager or prevent him from exercising his own judgment in the appointment of officers and employees in the administrative service. Except for the purpose of inquiry the council and its members shall deal with the administrative service solely through the city manager, and neither the council nor any member thereof shall give orders to any of the subordinates of the city manager, either publicly or privately. Any such dictation, prevention, orders, or other interference on the part of a member of council with the administration of the city shall be deemed to be a misdemeanor, and upon conviction any

---

If proportional representation is not used and the number of councilmen to be elected at large, or from a single district, is more than five, provision should be made for their election — after the first time in groups. For example, if the number of councilmen to be elected were fifteen and their term were six years, five should be elected every two years.

NOTE 3. In determining whether a salary shall be paid, and if so how much, it must be borne in mind that the duties of the council are supervisory; and that it is the object of this charter to place the administrative affairs of the city in the hands of the city manager.

member so convicted shall be subject to a fine not exceeding $ or imprisonment for a term not exceeding   months, or both, and to removal from office in the discretion of the court.

SEC. 4. *Election by Councils. Rules. Quorum.* The council shall elect one of its members as chairman, who shall be entitled mayor; also a city manager, a clerk, and a civil service commission, but no member of the council shall be chosen as manager or as a member of the civil service commission. The council may determine its own rules of procedure, may punish its own members for misconduct, and may compel attendance of members. A majority of all the members of the council shall constitute a quorum to do business, but a smaller number may adjourn from time to time.

SEC. 5. *Organization and Procedure of Council.* At 8 o'clock P. M. on the first Monday in (month) following a regular municipal election, the council shall meet at the usual place for holding meetings, at which time the newly elected councilmen shall assume the duties of their office. Thereafter the council shall meet at such time and place as may be prescribed by ordinance. The meetings of the council and all sessions of committees of the council shall be public. The council shall act only by ordinance or resolution; and all ordinances and resolutions, except ordinances making appropriations, shall be confined to one subject which shall be clearly expressed in the title. The ordinances making appropriations shall be confined to the subject of appropriations. No ordinance shall be passed until it has been read on two separate days or the requirement of readings on two separate days has been dispensed with by a four-fifths vote of the members of the council. The final reading shall be in full, unless the measure shall have been printed and a copy thereof furnished to each member prior to such reading. The ayes and noes shall be taken upon the passage of all ordinances or resolutions and entered upon the journal of the proceedings of the council, and every ordinance or resolution shall require on final passage the affirmative vote of a majority of all the members. No member shall be excused from voting except on matters involving the consideration of his own official conduct, or where his financial interests are involved. Provision shall be made for the printing and publication in full of every ordinance within ten days after its final passage.

SEC. 6. *Powers of Mayor.* The mayor shall preside at meetings of the council and perform such other duties consistent with his office as may be imposed by the council. He shall be recognized as the official head of the city for all ceremonial purposes, by the courts for the purpose of serving civil processes, and by the governor for military purposes. In time of public danger or emergency he may, with the consent of the council, take command of the police and maintain order and enforce the laws. During his absence or disability his duties shall be performed by another member appointed by the council.

NOMINATIONS AND ELECTIONS

SEC. 7. *Municipal Elections.* A municipal election shall be held on the —— day of —— of the —— year [4] and of every second year thereafter, which shall be

NOTE 4. Municipal elections may be held in the odd years when there is no state or national election. If held in the same year, known as the regular municipal election. All other municipal elections that may be held shall be known as special municipal elections.

SEC. 8. *Nomination by Petition.* The mode of nomination of candidates for the council provided for by this charter shall be by petition. The name of any elector of the city shall be printed upon the ballot whenever a petition as hereinafter prescribed shall have been filed in his behalf with the election authorities. Such petition shall be signed by at least ——— electors.[5] No elector shall sign more than one such petition, and should an elector do so, his signature shall be void as to the petition or petitions last filed.[6]

SEC. 9. *Signatures to and Forms of Nomination Papers.* The signatures to the nomination petition need not all be appended to one paper, but to each separate paper there shall be attached an affidavit of the circulator thereof, stating the number of signers of such paper and that each signature appended thereto was made in his presence and is the genuine signature of the person whose name it purports to be. With each signature shall be stated the place of residence of the signer, giving the

they should be separated from the latter by at least thirty, and preferably sixty, days.

NOTE 5. If proportional representation is used, the number of names required on each petition should usually be from one-half of one per cent (in large cities) to one and one-half per cent (in the smallest cities) of the total number of voters. If proportional representation is not used, the number should be from 25 to 200.

NOTE 6. If proportional representation is not used, this sentence should be stricken out, and the following substituted: "No elector shall sign petitions for more candidates than the number of places of that particular designation to be filled at the election, and should an elector do so his signature shall be void as to the petition or petitions last filed."

street and number or other description sufficient to identify the same. The form of the nomination petition shall be substantially as follows:

We, the undersigned, electors of the city of ...., hereby nominate ...., whose residence is ......, for the office of ......, to be voted for at the election to be held in the city of ......, on the ...... day of ....., 19..; and we individually certify that we are qualified to vote for a candidate for the office named and that we have not signed any other nomination petition for that office.[7]

Name.............. Street and Number..........
(Space for signatures.)

......, being duly sworn, deposes and says that he is the circulator of the foregoing petition paper containing .... signatures, and that the signatures appended thereto were made in his presence and are the signatures of the persons whose names they purport to be.

(Signed) ....

Subscribed and sworn to before me this ...... day of ...., 19...

............, Justice of the Peace (or Notary Public).

This petition, if found insufficient by the election authorities, shall be returned to .... at No. ...... Street.

SEC. 10. *Filing Nomination Papers.* All nomination papers comprising a petition shall be assembled and filed with the election authorities, as one instrument, not earlier than thirty nor later than fifteen days before the election. Any person nominated under this charter shall file with the election authorities his written acceptance of said nomination not later than twenty days before the

---

NOTE 7. If proportional representation is not used, this clause should read as follows: "— for a candidate for the office named and that we have not signed more nomination petitions for that office than there are persons to be elected thereto."

day of the election, and in the absence of such acceptance his name shall not appear on the ballot.

SEC. 11. *Regulation of Elections.* The council shall make all needful rules and regulations, not inconsistent with this charter or with general law, for the conduct of elections, for the prevention of fraud in elections, and for the re-count of the ballots in case of doubt or fraud.

SEC. 12. *The Ballots and the Voting.* The full names of candidates nominated for the council in accordance with the provisions of this charter shall be printed on the official ballots in the alphabetical order of the surnames [8] [in rotation. There shall be printed as many sets of ballots as there are candidates. Each set of ballots shall begin with the name of a different candidate, the other names being arranged thereafter in regular alphabetical order, commencing with the name next in alphabetical order after the one that stands first on that set of ballots. When the last name is reached in alphabetical order it shall be followed by the name that begins with the first letter represented in the list of names and by the others in regular order. The ballots so printed shall then be combined in tablets so as to have the fewest possible ballots having the same order of names printed thereon together in the same tablet].

The ballots shall be marked according to the following instructions, which shall be printed at the top of each ballot under the heading of "Directions to Voters."

NOTE 8. The matter enclosed in the brackets is to be included in the charter only if rotation of the names on the ballots is desired.

Rotation should not be used if proportional representation is used, as it is inconsistent with the quickest and best methods of completing the count under the proportional system.

Put the figure 1 opposite the name of your first choice. If you want to express also second, third, and other choices, do so by putting the figure 2 opposite the name of your second choice, the figure 3 opposite the name of your third choice, and so on. You may express thus as many choices as you please. *The more choices you express, the surer you are to make your ballot count for one of the candidates you favor.*

This ballot will not be counted for your second choice unless it is found that it cannot help your first; it will not be counted for your third choice unless it is found that it cannot help either your first or your second, etc.

A ballot is spoiled if the figure 1 is put opposite more than one name. If you spoil this ballot, tear it across once, return it to the election officer in charge of the ballots, and get another from him.

SEC. 13. *Rules for Counting the Ballots.* Ballots cast for the election of members of the council shall be counted and the results determined by the election authorities according to the following rules:

(a) On all ballots a cross shall be considered equivalent to the figure 1. So far as may be consistent with the general election laws, every ballot from which the first choice of the voter can be clearly ascertained shall be considered valid.

(b) The ballots shall first be sorted and counted at the several voting precincts according to the first choices of the voters. At each voting precinct the ballots cast for each candidate as first choice shall be put up in a separate package, which shall be properly marked on the outside to show the number of ballots therein and the name of the candidate for whom they were cast. The ballots declared invalid by the precinct officials shall also be put up in a separate package, properly marked on the outside. All the packages of the precinct, together with a record of the precinct count, shall be forwarded to the central election authorities as directed by them, and the counting of the ballots shall proceed under their direction.

(c) After the review of the precinct count by the central election authorities, and the correction of any errors discovered therein, the first-choice votes for each candidate shall be added and tabulated. This completes the first count.

(d) The whole number of valid ballots shall then be divided by a number greater by one than the number of seats to be filled. The next whole number larger than the resulting quotient is the *quota* or *constituency* that suffices to elect a member.

(e) All candidates the number of whose votes on the first count is equal to or greater than the quota shall then be declared elected.

(f) All votes obtained by any candidate in excess of the quota shall be termed his surplus.

(g) The surpluses shall be transferred, the largest surplus first, then the next largest, and so on, according to the following rules.

(h)[9] Ballots capable of transfer up to the number of

NOTE 9. If it is thought worth while to eliminate the infinitesimal element of chance involved in transferring the surplus ballots according to this rule, the following alternative form of the rule may be substituted:

(h) The transferable ballots of a candidate having a surplus shall be sorted into piles according to the next choice marked on each for a continuing candidate. The non-transferable ballots shall be sorted into a separate pile. The number of ballots in each pile shall then be ascertained.

If the number of the transferable ballots is equal to or less than the surplus, they shall all be successively transferred, each votes in the surplus shall be successively transferred to the continuing candidates marked on them as next choice in accordance with rule (n). The particular ballots to be taken for transfer as the surplus of a candidate shall be obtained by taking as nearly an equal number of ballots as possible from the ballots capable of transfer that have been cast for him in each of the different precincts. All such surplus ballots shall be taken as they happen to come without selection.

(i) "Ballots capable of transfer" or "transferable ballots" means ballots from which the next choice of the voter for some continuing candidate can be clearly ascertained. A "continuing candidate" is a candidate as yet neither elected nor defeated. "Successively" means one after another separately so far as the work of one electoral official or clerk is concerned; but nothing in this

to the continuing candidate marked on it as next choice in accordance with rule (n).

If the number of the transferable ballots is greater than the surplus, such ballots to the number of the surplus shall be successively transferred, the particular ballots thus taken for transfer as the surplus being taken from the several piles proportionately according to the following directions:

(1) Multiply the number of ballots in each pile of transferable ballots by the fraction of which the numerator is the number of surplus ballots and the denominator is the total number of transferable ballots in the several piles.

(2) Of the fractions that may appear in the resulting products, as many of the largest shall be considered as having the value of one as may be necessary to make the total number of ballots transferred equal to the surplus. All other fractions shall be disregarded.

(3) The product in the case of each pile is the number of ballots to be successively transferred from the pile, each to the continuing candidate marked on it as next choice in accordance with rule (n).

The particular ballots to be taken for transfer from each pile shall be taken as they happen to come to hand without selection.

If any ballot properly reckoned as transferable at the beginning of the process prescribed in this rule (h) becomes nontransferable during the process, it shall be treated thereafter as a non-transferable ballot.

section is meant to prevent the transfer of ballots by two or more officials or clerks simultaneously, provided only that precautions are taken to avoid transferring any ballot to a candidate who has already received the quota.

(j) The transfer of each ballot shall be tallied by the tally clerk assigned to the candidate to whom the ballot is being transferred.

(k) After the transfer of all surpluses, the votes standing to the credit of each candidate shall be added up and tabulated as the second count.

(l) After the tabulation of the second count (or after that of the first count if no candidate received a surplus on the first) every candidate who has no votes to his credit shall be declared defeated. Thereupon the candidate lowest on the poll as it then stands shall be declared defeated, and all his ballots capable of transfer shall be transferred successively to continuing candidates, each ballot being transferred to the credit of that continuing candidate next preferred by the voter, in accordance with rule (n). After the transfer of these ballots a fresh tabulation of results shall be made. In this manner candidates shall be successively declared defeated, and their ballots capable of transfer transferred to continuing candidates, and fresh tabulations of results made. After any tabulation the candidate next to be declared defeated shall be the one then lowest on the poll.

(m) If after the second or any later count (or after the first count if no candidate received a surplus on the first) the total of the votes of two or more candidates lowest on the poll is less than the vote of the next higher candidate, those lowest candidates may be declared defeated simultaneously, and all their ballots capable of transfer transferred successively to continuing candidates, each ballot being transferred to the credit of that continuing candidate next preferred by the voter, in accordance with rule (n). In this operation the ballots of the lowest candidate shall be transferred first, then those of the candidate next higher, and so on. No fresh tabulation of results shall be made until the ballots of all of the candidates thus simultaneously defeated have been transferred.

(n) Whenever in the transfer of a surplus or of the ballots of a defeated candidate the votes of any candidate become equal to the quota, he shall immediately be declared elected and no further transfer to him shall be made.

(o) When candidates to the number of the seats to be filled have received a quota and have therefore been declared elected, all other candidates shall be declared defeated and the election shall be at an end; and when the number of continuing candidates is reduced to the number of seats to be filled, those candidates shall be declared elected whether they have received the full quota or not and the election shall be at an end.

(p) If at any count two or more candidates at the bottom of the poll have the same number of votes, that candidate shall first be declared defeated who was lowest at the next preceding count at which the number of their votes was different. Should it happen that the number is the same on all counts, lots shall be drawn to decide which candidate shall next be declared defeated.

(q) In the transfer of the ballots of any candidate who has received ballots by transfer, those ballots shall first be transferred upon which he was first choice, and the remaining ballots shall be transferred in the order of the counts by which they were received by him.

(r) On each tabulation a record shall be kept, under the designation "non-transferable ballots," of those ballots which have not been used in the election of any candidate and which are not capable of transfer.

(s) Every ballot that is transferred from one candidate to another shall be stamped or marked so that its entire course from candidate to candidate throughout the counting can be conveniently traced. The ballots shall be preserved by the election authorities until the end of the term for which the members of the council are being elected. In case a re-count of the ballots is made, every ballot shall be made to take in the re-count the same course that it took in the original count unless there is discovered a mistake that requires its taking a different course, in which case the mistake shall be corrected and also any further changes made in the course taken by ballots that may be required as a result of the correction. These principles shall apply also to the correction of any error that may be discovered during the original count.

(t) The candidates or their agents, representatives of the press, and, so far as may be consistent with good order and with convenience in the counting and transferring of the ballots, the public shall be afforded every facility for being present and witnessing these operations.

(u) The council shall have power to provide for the use of mechanical devices for marking and sorting the ballots and tabulating the results, and to modify the form of the ballot, the directions to voters, and the details in respect to the methods of counting and transferring ballots accordingly; provided, however, that no change shall be made in the provisions of Sections 12 and 13 of this charter which will alter in any degree the principles of the voting or of the count.

SEC. 14. *Vacancy Provisions*.[10] In the event of a vacancy occurring in the council it shall be filled for the remainder of the unexpired term by that candidate who is credited with most votes as the result of a re-count and transfer of those ballots by which the member was elected whose place is to be filled.

This re-count shall be carried out in accordance with the provisions of Section 13, the candidate lowest after each transfer being dropped out as defeated until only one is left. At the beginning of this re-count all the original candidates of the last regular election shall be considered "continuing candidates" (as defined in Section 13 (i) except those elected at or since said election, those now ineligible, and those who have withdrawn by written notice to the election authorities.

THE RECALL [11]

SEC. 15. *Recall Provisions.*[12] Any member of the council may be removed from office by recall petition.

Any elector of the city may make and file with the city

NOTE 10. If proportional representation is not used, the following form of this section should be substituted:
SEC. 14. *Vacancy Provisions.* Vacancies in the council, except as otherwise provided herein, shall be filled for the unexpired term by a majority vote of the remaining members.
NOTE 11. The original recall sections, now printed in Note 12, were inserted by a majority vote of the committee. In that form they are not applicable when proportional representation is adopted but may be used when a charter provides some other method of election.
NOTE 12. If proportional representation is not used the following section on the recall should be substituted:
SEC. 15. *Procedure for Filing Recall Petition.* Any officer or officers holding an elective office provided for in this charter may be recalled and removed therefrom by the electors of the city as herein provided.*
Any elector of the city may make and file with the city clerk

---

*Where a large city is divided into districts for electoral purposes the word "district" should be substituted for "city" in these sections.

clerk an affidavit containing the name or names of any member or members of the council whose removal is sought and a statement of the grounds for removal. The clerk shall thereupon deliver to the elector making such

an affidavit containing the name or names of the officer or officers whose removal is sought and a statement of the grounds for removal. The clerk shall thereupon deliver to the elector making such affidavit copies of petition blanks for such removal, printed forms of which he shall keep on hand. Such blanks shall be issued by the clerk with his signature and official seal thereto attached; they shall be dated and addressed to the council, shall contain the name of the person to whom issued, the number of blanks so issued, the name of the person or persons whose removal is sought and the office from which such removal is sought. A copy of the petition shall be entered in a record book to be kept in the office of the clerk. The recall petition, to be effective, must be returned and filed with the clerk within thirty days after the filing of the affidavit. The petition before being returned and filed shall be signed by electors of the city to the number of at least fifteen per cent of the number of electors who cast their votes at the last preceding regular municipal election, and to every such signature shall be added the place of residence of the signer, giving the street and number or other description sufficient to identify the place. Such signatures need not all be on one paper, but the circulator of every such paper shall make an affidavit that each signature appended to the paper is the genuine signature of the person whose name it purports to be. All such recall papers shall be filed as one instrument, with the endorsements thereon of the names and addresses of three persons designated as filing the same.

Examination and Amendment of Recall Petitions. Within ten days after the filing of the petition the clerk shall ascertain whether or not the petition is signed by the requisite number of electors and shall attach thereto his certificate showing the result of such examination. If his certificate shows the petition to be insufficient, he shall forthwith so notify in writing one or more of the persons designated on the petition as filing the same; and the petition may be amended at any time within ten days, after the giving of said notice, by the filing of a supplementary petition upon additional petition papers, issued, signed and filed as provided herein for the original petition. The clerk shall, within ten days after such amendment, make like examination of the amended petition, and attach thereto his certificate of the result. If then found to be insufficient, or if no amendment was made, he shall file the petition in his office and shall notify each of the affidavit copies of petition blanks demanding such removal, printed forms of which he shall keep on hand. Such blanks shall be issued by the clerk with his signature and official seal thereto attached; they shall be dated and addressed to the council and shall contain the name

persons designated thereon as filing it of that fact. The final finding of the insufficiency of a petition shall not prejudice the filing of a new petition for the same purpose.

Calling of Recall Election. If the petition or amended petition shall be certified by the clerk to be sufficient he shall submit the same with his certificate to the council at its next meeting and shall notify the officer or officers whose removal is sought of such action. The council shall thereupon, within ten days of the receipt of the clerk's certificate, order an election to be held not less than thirty nor more than forty-five days thereafter. *Provided,* that if any other municipal election is to occur within sixty days after the receipt of said certificate, the council may in its discretion provide for the holding of the removal election on the date of such other municipal election.

Form of Ballot to Recall Officer. Unless the officer or officers whose removal is sought shall have resigned within ten days after the receipt by the council of the clerk's certificate the form of the ballot at such election shall be as nearly as may be: " Shall A be recalled? Shall B be recalled?" etc., the name of the officer or officers whose recall is sought being inserted in place of A, B, etc., and the ballot shall also contain the names of the candidates to be elected in place of the men recalled, as follows: " Candidates for the place of A, if recalled; candidates for the place of B, if recalled," etc., but the men whose recall is sought shall not themselves be candidates upon such ballot.

In case a majority of those voting for and against the recall of any official shall vote in favor of recalling such official he shall be thereby removed, and in that event the candidate who receives the highest number of votes for his place shall be elected thereto for the balance of the unexpired term.

If the officer or officers sought to be removed shall have resigned within ten days after the receipt by the council of the clerk's certificate referred to in this section above hereof, the form of ballot at the election shall be the same, as nearly as may be, as the form in use at a regular municipal election.

Procedure on Refusal of Council. Should the council fail or refuse to order an election as herein provided within the time required, such election may be ordered by any court of general jurisdiction in the county in which said city is situated.

of the person to whom issued, the number of blanks so issued, and the name of the member whose removal is sought. A copy of the petition shall be entered in a record book to be kept in the office of the clerk. The recall petition to be effective must be returned and filed with the clerk within thirty days after the filing of the affidavit. To be effective the petition must also bear the signatures of electors of the city to the number of at least twenty-five per cent of the number of electors who cast their votes at the last preceding regular municipal election, and it must include the signatures of at least sixty per cent of the voters who signed the nomination petition of the member whose recall is demanded. To every signature on the petition shall be added the place of residence of the signer, the street and number or other description sufficient to identify the place. Such signatures need not all be on one paper, but the circulator of each such paper shall make an affidavit that each signature appended to the paper is the genuine signature of the person whose name it purports to be. The required number of signatures of electors who signed the nomination petition of the member whose recall is demanded shall be on one paper separate from those containing the other signatures. All such recall petition papers shall be filed as one instrument, with the endorsement thereon of the names and addresses of three persons designated as filing the same.

On receiving the recall petition, the city clerk shall examine it promptly. If he finds it to be sufficient according to the provisions of this section he shall certify that fact to the council, and at the expiration of thirty days from the time when the petition was filed the member whose recall is demanded shall be deemed removed from office.

Any vacancy caused by the recall of a member shall be filed in accordance with Section 14.

THE INITIATIVE [13]

SEC. 16. *Power to Initiate Ordinances.* The people shall have power at their option to propose ordinances, including ordinances granting franchises or privileges, and other measures and to adopt the same at the polls, such power being known as the initiative. A petition, meeting the requirements hereinafter provided and requesting the council to pass an ordinance, resolution, order, or vote (all of these four terms being hereinafter included in the term " measure ") therein set forth or designated, shall be termed an initiative petition and shall be acted upon as hereinafter provided.

SEC. 17. *Preparation of Initiative Petitions.* Signatures to initiative petitions need not all be on one paper, but the circulator of every such paper shall make an affidavit that each signature appended to the paper is the genuine signature of the person whose name it purports to be. With each signature shall be stated the place of residence of the signer, giving the street and number or other description sufficient to identify the place. All such papers pertaining to any one measure shall have written or printed thereon the names and

NOTE 13. The initiative sections were inserted by a majority vote of the committee.

addresses of at least five electors who shall be officially regarded as filing the petition, and shall constitute a committee of the petitioners for the purposes hereinafter named. All such papers shall be filed in the office of the city clerk as one instrument. Attached to every such instrument shall be a certificate signed by the committee of petitioners or a majority of them stating whether the petition is intended to be a " Fifteen Per Cent Petition " or a " Twenty-five Per Cent Petition."

SEC. 18. *Filing of Petitions.* Within ten days after the filing of the petition the clerk shall ascertain by examination the number of electors whose signatures are appended thereto and whether this number is at least fifteen per cent or twenty-five per cent, as the case may be, of the total number of electors who cast their votes at the last preceding regular municipal election, and he shall attach to said petition his certificate showing the result of said examination. If, by the clerk's certificate, of which notice in writing shall be given to one or more of the persons designated, the petition is shown to be insufficient it may be amended within ten days from the date of said certificate by filing supplementary petition papers with additional signatures. The clerk shall within ten days after such amendment make like examination of the amended petition, and if his certificate shall show the same to be insufficient, the clerk shall file the petition in his office and shall notify each member of the committee of that fact. The final finding of the insufficiency of a petition shall not prejudice the filing of a new petition for the same purpose.

Sec. 19. *Submission of Petition to Council.* If the petition shall be found to be sufficient, the clerk shall so certify and submit the proposed measure to the council at its next meeting, and the council shall at once read and refer the same to an appropriate committee, which may be a committee of the whole. Provision shall be made for public hearings upon the proposed measure before the committee to which it is referred. Thereafter the committee shall report the proposed measure to the council, with its recommendation thereon, not later than sixty days after the date upon which such measure was submitted to the council by the clerk. Upon receiving the proposed measure from the committee the council shall at once proceed to consider it and shall take final action thereon within thirty days from the date of such committee report.

Sec. 20. *Election on Initiated Measures.* If the council shall fail to pass the proposed measure, or shall pass it in a form different from that set forth in the petition, then if the petition was a "twenty-five per cent petition" the proposed measure shall be submitted by the council to the vote of the electors at the next election occurring not less than thirty days after the date of the final action by the council, and if no election is to be held within six months from such date, then the council shall call a special election to be held not less than thirty nor more than forty-five days from such date. But if the petition was a "fifteen per cent petition" the proposed measure shall be submitted as in the case of a "twenty-five per cent petition," except that no special election shall be called unless within thirty days after the final action by the council on the proposed measure a supplemental petition shall be filed with the clerk signed by a sufficient number of additional electors asking for the submission of the proposed measure so that the original petition when combined with such supplementary petition shall become a "twenty-five per cent petition." In case such supplementary petition is filed the council shall call a special election to be held not less than thirty nor more than forty-five days after the receipt of the clerk's certificate that a sufficient supplementary petition has been filed. The sufficiency of any such supplementary petition shall be determined, and it may be amended, in the manner provided for original petitions. When submitted the measure shall be either in its original form, or with any proposed change or addition which was presented in writing either at the public hearing before the committee to which such proposed measure was referred, or during the consideration thereof by the council; and said committee of petitioners shall certify to the clerk the requirement of submission and the proposed measure in the form desired, within ten days after the date of final action on such measure by the council. Upon receipt of the certificate and certified copy of such measure, the clerk shall certify the fact to the council at its next meeting and such measure shall be submitted by the council to the vote of the electors in a regular or special municipal election as hereinbefore provided.

SEC. 21. *Initiative Ballots.* The ballots used when voting upon any such proposed measure shall state the substance thereof, and below it the two propositions "For the measure" and "Against the measure." Immediately at the right of each proposition there shall be a square in which by making a cross (X) the voter may vote for or against the proposed measure. If a majority of the electors voting on any such measure shall vote in favor thereof, it shall thereupon become an ordinance, resolution, order or vote of the city as the case may be.

The following shall be the form of the ballot:

TITLE OF MEASURE

With general statement of substance thereof

FOR THE MEASURE	
AGAINST THE MEASURE	

SEC. 22. *Number of Measures to be Initiated.* Any number of proposed measures may be voted upon at the same election in accordance with the provisions of this charter.

THE REFERENDUM [14]

SEC. 23. *Power of Referendum.* The people shall have power at their option to approve or reject at the polls any measure passed by the council or submitted by the council to a vote of the electors, such power being known as the referendum, which power shall be invoked and exercised as herein provided. Measures submitted to the council by initiative petition and passed by the council without change, or passed in an amended form

NOTE 14. The referendum sections were inserted by a majority vote of the committee.

and not required by the committee of the petitioners to be submitted to a vote of the electors, shall be subject to the referendum in the same manner as other measures.

Sec. 24. *Limitations on Enforcement of Ordinances.* No measure shall go into effect until thirty days after its passage unless it be declared an emergency measure on the ground of urgent public need for the preservation of peace, health, safety, or property, the facts showing such urgency and need being specifically stated in the measure itself and the measure being passed by a vote of not less than four-fifths of the members of the council. But no measure granting or amending any public utility measure or amending or repealing any measure adopted by the people at the polls or by the council in compliance with an initiative petition, shall be regarded as an emergency measure.

Sec. 25. *Referendum Petition.* If within thirty days after the final passage of any measure by the council a petition signed by electors of the city to the number of at least 10 per cent of the number of electors who cast their votes at the last preceding regular municipal election, be filed with the city clerk requesting that any such measure, or any part thereof, be repealed or be submitted to a vote of the electors, it shall not, except in the case of an emergency measure, become operative until the steps indicated herein have been taken.

Sec. 26. *Signatures to Petition.* The signatures thereto need not all be on one paper, but the circulator of every such paper shall make an affidavit that each signature appended thereto is the genuine signature of the person whose name it purports to be. With each signature shall be stated the place of residence of the signer, giving the street and number or other description sufficient to identify the place. All such papers shall be filed in the office of the city clerk as one instrument. A referendum petition need not contain the text of the measure designated therein and of which the repeal is sought.

SEC. 27. *Certification of Petition.* Within ten days after the filing of the petition the clerk shall ascertain whether or not the petition is signed by the electors of the city to the number of at least 10 per cent of the number of electors who cast their votes at the last preceding regular municipal election, and he shall attach to such petition his certificate showing the result of such examination. If by the clerk's certificate the petition is shown to be insufficient, it may be amended within ten days from the date of said certificate by the filing of supplementary petition papers with additional signatures. The clerk shall within ten days after such amendment make like examination of the amended petition and certify the result thereof.

SEC. 28. *Referendum Election.* If the petition be found sufficient, the council shall proceed to reconsider such measure or such part thereof as the petition shall specify. If upon such reconsideration such measure, or such part thereof, be not repealed or amended as demanded in the petition, the council shall provide for submitting the same, by the method herein provided, to a vote of the electors at the next municipal election occurring not less than thirty days after the receipt by the council of the clerk's certificate, and such measure, or such part thereof, shall thereupon be suspended from going into effect until said election and shall then be deemed repealed unless approved by a majority of those voting thereon. Or the council by a four-fifths vote may submit such measure or part thereof with like effect to the electors at a special election to be called by said council not less than thirty days after the receipt of said clerk's certificate.

Sec. 29. *Title of Ballot.* Proposed measures and charter amendments shall be submitted by ballot title. There shall appear upon the official ballot a ballot title which may be distinct from the legal title of any such proposed measure or charter amendment and which shall be a clear, concise statement, without argument or prejudice, descriptive of the substance of such measure or charter amendment. The ballot title shall be prepared by the committee of the petitioners if for an initiated or a referendum measure, or by a committee of the council when submitted by the council.

Sec. 30. *Form of Ballot.* The ballots used when voting upon such proposed measure shall designate the same, and below it the two propositions, "For the measure" and "Against the measure."

Sec. 31. *Emergency Measures.* Measures passed as emergency measures shall be subject to referendum like other measures, except that they shall not be suspended from going into effect while referendum proceedings are pending. If, when submitted to a vote of the electors, an emergency measure be not approved by a majority of those voting thereon, it shall be considered repealed, as regards any further action thereunder and all rights and privileges conferred by it shall be null and void: *Pro-*

vided, however, that such measure so repealed shall be deemed sufficient authority for any payment made or expense incurred in accordance with the measure previous to the referendum vote thereon.

Sec. 32. *Official Publicity Pamphlet.* The city clerk, at least fifteen days before any election at which any measure or charter amendment is to be submitted, shall print and mail to each elector qualified to vote thereon an official publicity pamphlet containing the full text of every measure or charter amendment submitted, with their respective ballot titles, together with arguments, for or against such measures or charter amendments, which may have been filed with the city clerk not less than twenty days before such election. Such arguments shall be signed by the person, persons, or officers of organizations authorized to submit and sign the same, who shall deposit with the city clerk at the time of filing a sum of money sufficient to cover the proportionate cost of the printing and paper for the space taken, but no more. The text of every measure or charter amendment shall also be displayed at the polling booths in such election. *Provided,* that the validity of a measure or charter amendment approved by the electors shall not be questioned because of errors or irregularities in such mailing, distribution or display.

Sec. 33. *Conflict of Referred Measures.* If two or more measures adopted or approved at the same election conflict in respect of any of their provisions, they shall go into effect in respect of such of their provisions as are not in conflict and the one receiving the highest affirmative vote shall prevail in so far as their provisions conflict.

ADMINISTRATIVE SERVICES — THE CITY MANAGER [15]

SEC. 34. *The City Manager.* The city manager shall be the chief executive officer of the city. He shall be chosen by the council solely on the basis of his executive and administrative qualifications. The choice shall not be limited to inhabitants of the city or state.[16]

The city manager shall receive a compensation of not less than   a year.[17] He shall be appointed for an indefinite period. He shall be removable by the council. If removed at any time after six months he may demand written charges and a public hearing on the same before the council prior to the date on which his final removal shall take effect, but during such hearing the council may

NOTE 15. While the manager plan herein proposed is probably the most advanced and scientific form of municipal organization yet suggested, it is of the highest importance that any city adopting the plan should not omit any of the other principal features accompanying it in this draft. Without these provisions the manager plan, owing to its concentration of executive and administrative authority in the manager, might prove to be susceptible to perversion in the interest of a boss in cities with an undeveloped and inactive public opinion, because the members of council might then be elected upon a slate pledged beforehand to the selection of some particular candidate as manager.

It is also true that no form of government can in and of itself produce good results. The most that any plan can do is to provide an organization which lends itself to efficient action, and which at the same time places in the hands of the electorate simple and effective means for controlling their government in their own interests. The evils in city government due to defective and undemocratic organization can thus be removed; beyond that, results can only be achieved through the growth of an active and enlightened public opinion.

NOTE 16. The foreign plan of publicly advertising for a burgomeister and heads of departments and selecting the ones who show the highest qualifications has been highly successful.

NOTE 17. The minimum salary would vary according to the size of the city and the responsibilities of the office. Dayton, Ohio, a city of 117,000 inhabitants, paid its first city manager a salary of $12,500 per year.

suspend him from office. During the absence or disability of the city manager the council shall designate some properly qualified person to perform the duties of the office.

SEC. 35. *Powers and Duties of the City Manager.* The city manager shall be responsible to the council for the proper administration of all affairs of the city, and to that end shall make all appointments, except as otherwise provided in this charter. Except when the council is considering his removal, he shall be entitled to be present at all meetings of the council and of its committees and to take part in their discussion.

SEC. 36. *Annual Budget.* The city manager shall prepare and submit to the council the annual budget after receiving estimates made by the directors of the departments.

ADMINISTRATIVE DEPARTMENTS

SEC. 37. *Administrative Departments Created.* There shall be six administrative departments as follows: Law, health, works and utilities, safety and welfare, education,[18] and finance, the functions of which shall be prescribed by the council except as herein otherwise provided. The council shall fix all salaries, which in the classified service shall be uniform for each grade, as established by the civil service commission, and the council may, by a three-fourths vote of its entire membership, create new departments, combine or abolish existing depart-

NOTE 18. In places where the school system works well under a separate organization it had better not be disturbed, and in such cases the department of education will generally have to be omitted.

ments or establish temporary departments for special work.[19]

SEC. 38. *Duties of Directors of Departments.* At the head of each department there shall be a director. Each director shall be chosen on the basis of his general executive and administrative experience and ability and of his education, training, and experience in the class of work which he is to administer. The director of the department of law shall be a lawyer; of health, a sanitary engineer or a member of the medical profession; of works, an engineer; of education, a teacher by profession; of safety and welfare, a man who has had administrative experience; and of finance, a man who has had experience in banking, accounting, or other financial matters; or in

---

NOTE 19. The number of departments may be increased or diminished according to the population or other local needs of a given city. Where it is increased it will probably be desirable to divide the department of safety and welfare into two departments, and in some cases to divide the department of safety into police and fire departments. The department of utilities may be separated from department of public works when (1) the utilities are privately owned, so that their administration is chiefly regulative; and (2) in large cities where the department of works and utilities would make too large a department or where it seems desirable to put all the revenue-producing industries in one department. In reducing the number of departments, those of law, health, and finance might be cut out in the order named, either joining them with other departments (as health with welfare and safety) or making them directly subordinate to the city manager.

The number of departments can be kept down in the larger cities and reduced in the smaller ones (1) by the creation of department bureaus and (2) where so complex an organization as a bureau is not needed by having the proper official report directly to the city manager instead of to a department head.

The principle underlying the formation of departments and bureaus should be twofold: (1) functional grouping and (2) tasks which demand the time and capacity of the highest grade of administrative heads — *i. e.*, one first-class full-time man to head each department.

each case the man must have rendered active service in the same department in this or some other city.

Each director shall be appointed by the city manager and may be removed by him at any time; but in case of such removal, if the director so demands, written charges must be preferred by the city manager, and the director shall be given a public hearing before the order of removal is made final. The charges and the director's reply thereto shall be filed with the clerk of council.

SEC. 39. *Responsibility of Directors of Departments.* The directors of departments shall be immediately responsible to the city manager for the administration of their departments, and their advice in writing may be required by him on all matters affecting their departments. They shall prepare departmental estimates, which shall be open to public inspection, and they shall make all other reports and recommendations concerning their departments at stated intervals or when requested by the city manager.

SEC. 40. *Powers of Subpœna.* The council, the city manager, and any officer or board authorized by them, or either of them, shall have power to make investigations as to city affairs, to subpœna witnesses, administer oaths, and compel the production of books and papers.

CIVIL SERVICE BOARD

SEC. 41. *Creation of Civil Service Board.* A civil service board shall be appointed by the council to consist of three members. The terms of the members when the first appointments are made shall be so arranged as to expire one every two years, and each appointment made thereafter upon the expiration of any term shall be for six years. The council shall also fill any vacancy for an unexpired term. A member of the board shall be removable for neglect, incapacity, or malfeasance in office by a four-fifths vote of the council, after written charges upon at least ten days' notice and after a public hearing.

The board shall employ a secretary and a chief examiner (but the same person may perform the duties of both offices) and such further examiners and such clerical and other assistance as may be necessary, and shall determine the compensation of all persons so employed. Provision shall be made in the annual budget and appropriation bill for the expenses of the board.

SEC. 42. *Power to Make Rules and What the Rules Shall Provide.* The board shall, after public notice and hearing, make, promulgate, and, when necessary, amend rules for the appointment, promotion, transfer, lay off, reinstatement, suspension, and removal of city officials and employees, reporting its proceedings to the council and to the city manager when required. Such rules shall, among other things, provide:

(a) For the standardization and classification of all positions and employments in the civil service of the city. The classification into groups and subdivisions shall be based upon and graded according to their duties and responsibilities and so arranged as to promote the filling of the higher grades, so far as practicable, through promotion. All salaries shall be uniform for like service in each grade as the same shall be standardized and classified by the civil service board. The civil service so standardized and classified shall not include officers elected by the people, the city manager, nor the judges, and may or may not include the directors of executive departments, or the superintendents, principals, and teachers of the public schools, as may be directed by the council.

(b) For open competitive tests, to ascertain the relative fitness of all applicants for appointment to the classified civil service of said city, including mechanics and laborers — skilled and unskilled. Such tests shall be practical and shall relate to matters which will fairly measure the relative fitness of the candidates to discharge the duties of the positions to which they seek to be appointed. Notice of such tests shall be given not less than ten days in advance by public advertisement in at least one newspaper of general circulation, and by posting a notice in the city hall. The board may, by unanimous vote, provide for non-competitive tests for any position requiring peculiar and exceptional qualifications of a scientific, managerial, professional, or educational character, but all such actions of the board with the reasons therefor shall be published in its annual report.

(c) For the creation of eligible lists upon which shall be entered the names of successful candidates in the order of their standing in examination, and for the filling of places in the civil service of the city by selection from not more than the three candidates graded highest on such eligible lists. Eligible lists shall remain in force not longer than two years.

In the absence of an appropriate eligible list, any place may be filled temporarily without examination for a period limited by the rules, but not to exceed sixty days, during which time the board shall hold the necessary examination for filling the place permanently. With the consent of the board persons may be temporarily employed for transitory work without examination, but such employment shall not continue for more than sixty days, or be renewed.

No person shall be appointed or employed under any title not appropriate to the duties to be performed, and no person shall be transferred to or assigned to perform any duties of any position subject to competitive tests unless he shall have been appointed to the position from which transfer is made as the result of an open competitive test equivalent to that required for the position to be filled, or unless he shall have served with fidelity for at least two years immediately preceding in a similar position in the city. Each list of eligibles, with the respective grades, shall be open to public inspection.

Any person appointed from an eligible list and laid off for lack of work or of appropriation shall be placed at the head of the eligible list and shall be eligible for reappointment for the period of eligibility as provided by the rules of the board.

(d) For a period of probation not exceeding six months before an appointment or employment is made permanent.

(e) For reinstatement on the eligible lists of persons who without fault or delinquency are separated from the service.

(f) For promotion from the lower grades to the higher, based upon competitive records of efficiency and seniority to be furnished by the departments in which the person is employed and kept by said civil service board, or upon competitive promotion tests, or both. Appointments to such higher positions as shall be specified by the board may, if the city manager approves, be made after competitive tests in which persons not in the service of the city may also compete as well as applicants for such positions from the lower grades of the service or from other branches thereof; and the appointments shall be made to such higher positions from those standing highest as in the case of other competitive tests. An increase in compensation within a grade may be granted upon the basis of efficiency and seniority records.

SEC. 43. *Supervisory Powers of Civil Service Board.* It shall be the duty of the civil service board to supervise the execution of the civil service sections and the rules made thereunder, and it shall be the duty of all persons in the public service of said city to comply with said rules and aid in their enforcement.

The said board shall keep public records of its proceedings, of the markings and gradings upon examinations, and of all recommendations or certificates of the qualifications of applicants for office or employment; and it shall also keep a public record of the conduct and efficiency of each person in the service of the city, to be furnished by the head of the department in which such person is employed in such form and manner as the board may prescribe.

The board may make investigations concerning the facts in respect to the execution of the civil service sections and of the rules established thereunder and concerning the general condition of the civil service of the city or any branch thereof. The board shall fix standards of efficiency and recommend measures for coördinating the operation of the various departments and for increasing individual, group, and departmental efficiency. Each member of the board, or any person whom the board may appoint to make such investigations, shall have power to administer oaths, to compel the production of books and papers, and to subpœna witnesses.

The board shall keep a complete public roster of all persons in the service of the city and certify to the proper official the name and compensation of each person employed; also every change occurring in any office or employment; and no treasurer or other public disbursing officer shall pay and no controller or other auditing officer shall authorize the payment of any salary or compensation to any person holding a position in the classified service, unless the pay roll or account for such salary or compensation shall bear the certificate of the board that the person named therein has been appointed or employed and is performing services in accordance with the provisions of this charter and the rules hereby authorized. Any sums paid contrary to the provisions of this section may be recovered from any officer paying or authorizing the payment thereof and from the sureties on his official bond.

SEC. 44. *Power of Removal and Suspension.* Any officer or employee in the classified service may be removed, suspended, laid off, or reduced in grade by the city manager or by the head of the department in which he is employed, for any cause which will promote the efficiency of the service; but he must first be furnished with a written statement of the reasons therefor and be allowed a reasonable time for answering such reasons in writing, which answer, if he so request, shall (so far as the same is relevant and pertinent) be made a part of the records of the board; and he may be suspended from the date when such written statement of reasons is furnished him. No trial or examination of witnesses shall be required in such case except in the discretion of the officer making the removal. In all cases provided for in this paragraph the action of the city manager or head of the department shall be final.

The civil service board shall also have the right to remove or reduce any official or employee in the classified service upon written charges of misconduct preferred by any citizen, but only after reasonable notice to the accused and full hearing. It shall also be the duty of the board to fix a minimum standard of conduct and efficiency for each grade in the service, and whenever it shall appear from the reports of efficiency made to said board, for a period of three months, that the conduct and efficiency of any employee has fallen below this minimum, that employee shall be called before the board to show cause why he should not be removed, and if upon hearing no reason is shown satisfactory to the board he shall be removed, suspended, or reduced in grade, as the board shall determine.

SEC. 45. *Restrictions on Civil Service Appointees and Forbidden Practices.* No person shall willfully or corruptly make any false statement, certificate, mark, grading, or report in regard to any examination or appointment held or made under this article, or in any other manner attempt to commit any fraud upon the impartial execution of this article or of the civil service rules and regulations.

No person in the classified service shall directly or indirectly give, solicit, or receive or be in any manner concerned in giving, soliciting, or receiving any assessment, subscription, or contribution for any political party or purpose whatever. No person whosoever shall orally or by letter solicit or be in any manner concerned in soliciting any assessment, subscription, or contribution for any political party or purpose from any person holding a position in the classified service. No person shall use or promise to use his influence or official authority to secure any appointment or prospect of appointment to any position classified and graded under this charter as a reward or return for personal or partisan political service. No person about to be appointed to any position classified and graded under this charter shall sign or execute a resignation dated or undated in advance of such appointment. No person in the service of the city shall discharge, suspend, lay off, degrade, or promote, or in any manner change the official rank or compensation of any other person in said service, or promise or threaten to do so for withholding or neglecting to make any contribution of money or service or any other valuable thing for any political purpose.

No person shall take part in preparing any political assessment, subscription, or contribution with the intent that the same shall be sent or presented to or collected from any person in the classified service of the city; and no person shall knowingly send or present, directly or indirectly, in person or by letter, any political assessment, subscription, or contribution to, or request its payment by any person in the classified service.

No person in the service of the city shall use his official authority or influence to coerce the political action of any person or body, or to interfere with any nomination or election to public office.

No person holding office or place classified and graded under the provisions of this article shall act as an officer of a political organization or take any active part in a political campaign or serve as a member of a committee of any such organization or circulate or seek signatures to any petition provided for by any primary or election laws, other than an initiative or referendum petition, or act as a worker at the polls in favor of or opposed to any candidate for election or nomination to a public office, whether federal, state, county or municipal.

SEC. 46. *Politics and Religion Excluded.* No question in any examination held hereunder shall relate to political or religious opinions, affiliations, or service; and no appointment, transfer, lay off, promotion, reduction, suspension or removal shall be affected or influenced by such opinions, affiliations or service.

SEC. 47. *Violations of Civil Service Rules and Regulations.* Any person who shall willfully, or through culpable negligence, violate any of the civil service provisions of this charter or of the rules of the board made in pursuance thereof shall be guilty of a misdemeanor, and shall, on conviction, be punished by a fine of not less than $50 nor more than $1,000, or by imprisonment for a term not exceeding six months, or by both such fine and imprisonment. If such person be an applicant for examination he shall be excluded therefrom. If he be an eligible his name shall be removed from the eligible list, and if he be an officer or employee of the city he shall thereby be removed forthwith from the service.

Sec. 48. *Power of Taxpayer to Enforce Rules.* Any taxpayer in the city may maintain an action to recover for the city any sum of money paid in violation of the civil service provisions, or to enjoin the board from attaching its certificate to a payroll or account for services rendered in violation of this charter or the rules made thereunder; and the rules made under the foregoing provisions shall for this and all other purposes have the force of law.

FINANCIAL PROVISIONS

Sec. 49. *The Director of Finance.* The director of finance shall have direct supervision over the department of finance and the administration of the financial affairs of the city, including the keeping of accounts and financial records; the levy, assessment and collection of taxes, special assessments, and other revenues (except as otherwise provided by general law); the custody and disbursement of city funds and moneys; the control over expenditures; and such other duties as the council may, by ordinance, provide.

Sec. 50. *Accounts and Records.* Accounts shall be kept by the department of finance showing the financial transactions for all departments of the city. Forms for all such accounts shall be prescribed by the director of finance with the approval of the city manager; and shall be adequate to record all cash receipts and disbursements, all revenues accrued and liabilities incurred, and all transactions affecting the acquisition, custody, and disposition of values, and to make such reports of the financial transactions and condition of the city as may be required by law or ordinance. Financial reports shall be prepared for each quarter and each fiscal year, and for such other periods as may be required by the city manager or, the council.

SEC. 51. *Annual Budget.* Not later than one month before the end of each fiscal year the city manager shall prepare and submit to the council an annual budget for the ensuing fiscal year, based upon detailed estimates furnished by the several departments and other divisions of the city government, according to a classification as nearly uniform as possible. The budget shall present the following information:

(a) An itemized statement of the appropriations recommended by the city manager for current expenses and for permanent improvements for each department and each division thereof for the ensuing fiscal year, with comparative statements in parallel columns of the appropriations and expenditures for the current and next preceding fiscal year, and the increases or decreases in the appropriations recommended;

(b) An itemized statement of the taxes required and of the estimated revenues of the city from all other sources for the ensuing fiscal year, with comparative statements in parallel columns of the taxes and other revenues for the current and next preceding fiscal year, and of the increases or decreases estimated or proposed;

(c) A statement of the financial condition of the city; and

(d) Such other information as may be required by the council.

Copies of the budget shall be printed and available for distribution not later than two weeks after its submission to the council; and a public hearing shall be given thereon by the council or a committee thereof before action by the council.

SEC. 52. *Appropriation Ordinance. Temporary Appropriations. Transfers.* Not later than one month after the beginning of the fiscal year the council shall pass an annual appropriation ordinance, which shall be based on the budget submitted by the city manager. The total amount of appropriations shall not exceed the estimated revenues of the city.

Before the annual appropriation ordinance has been passed, the council, with the approval in writing of the city manager, may make appropriations for current department expenses, chargeable to the appropriations of the year when passed, to an amount sufficient to cover the necessary expenses of the various departments until the annual appropriation is in force. No other liabilities shall be incurred by any officer or employee of the city, except in accordance with the provisions of the annual appropriation ordinance, or under continuing contracts and loans authorized under the provisions of this charter.

At any meeting after the passage of the appropriation ordinance, and after at least one week's public notice, the council, by a three-fourths vote, may amend such ordinance, so as to authorize the transfer of unused balances appropriated for one purpose to another purpose, or to appropriate available revenues not included in the annual budget.

SEC. 53. *Tax Levy.* On or before the day of   in each year, the council shall, by ordinance, levy such tax as may be necessary to meet the appropriations made (less the estimated amount of revenue from other sources) and all sums required by law to be raised on account of the city debt, together with such addition, not exceeding five per cent, as may be necessary to meet commissions, fees, and abatements in the amount of taxes collected from the estimates.

SEC. 54. *Assessment of Property.* All property subject to *ad valorem* taxation shall be valued at its fair market value, subject to review and equalization, as provided by law or ordinance. In valuing improved real estate for taxation the market value of the land shall be valued separately; and improvements thereon shall be valued at the amount by which they increase the value of the land.

SEC. 55. *Special Assessments.* The council shall have power by ordinance to provide for the payment of all or any part of the cost of the construction, reconstruction, repair, operation, or maintenance of any structure or work in the nature of a public improvement, including a public utility, by levying and collecting special assessments upon abutting, adjacent and contiguous, or other property specially benefited. Such special assessments for works of construction or reconstruction may be payable in installments within a period of not more than ten years. The amount so assessed against any property shall not exceed the amount of benefits accruing to such property from such improvement and the operation thereof. Provision shall be made by ordinance for the method of levying and apportioning such special assessments, for the publication of plans, for serving notices on the owners of property affected, and for hearing complaints and claims before final action thereon.

SEC. 56. *Bond Issues.* Money may be borrowed by the issue and sale of bonds, pledged on the credit of the city, or on the property or revenues of any public utility owned by the city, for the purchase of land, the construction and equipment of buildings and other permanent public improvements, and for the payment or refunding of bonds previously issued. No ordinance providing for the issue of bonds shall be passed without public notice at least two weeks before final action by the council, and either the approval of two-thirds of all the members of the council or submission to the electors of the city at a regular or special election and the approval of a majority of those voting thereon. No bonds shall be issued on the credit of the city which shall increase the bonded indebtedness of the city beyond   per cent of the assessed valuation of property in the city subject to direct taxation, as shown by the last preceding valuation for city taxes.[20] Every issue of bonds shall be payable within a term of years not to exceed the estimated period of utility of the improvement for which they are issued, and in no case to exceed thirty years;[21] and shall be payable in

NOTE 20. If desired, provision may be made for the issue of bonds outside the debt limit on the credit of the city for self-sustaining utilities.

NOTE 21. In cities where subways and other improvements of extraordinary cost and permanency may be needed this period may be extended to fifty years.

equal annual serial installments, including principal and interest. Every ordinance for the issue of bonds shall provide for a tax levy for each year to meet the annual serial installments of principal and interest, and such amounts shall be included in the tax levy for each year.[22]

SEC. 57. *Temporary Loans.* Money may be borrowed, in anticipation of the receipts from taxes during any fiscal year, by the issue of notes, certificates of indebtedness, or revenue bonds; but the aggregate amount of such loans at any time outstanding shall not exceed   per cent. of the receipts from taxes during the preceding fiscal year; and all such loans shall be paid out of the receipts from taxes for the fiscal year in which they are issued. If upon the   day of   there shall be any outstanding loans or notes for money borrowed in anticipation of taxes prior to the adoption of this charter, such loans or any part thereof may be renewed or refunded by the issue of notes, certificates of indebtedness, or revenue bonds, payable in equal annual installments with interest for not more than five successive years. No temporary loans authorized by this section shall be made without public notice at least two weeks before final action by the council, and the approval of two-thirds of all the members of the council.

SEC. 58. *Restrictions on Loans and Credit.* No money shall be borrowed by the city except for the issue of bonds or temporary loans, as authorized by sections

NOTE 22. For cities having sinking funds, provision should be made for their continuation and management until maturity. The sinking fund board may consist of the mayor, the director of finance and three other members appointed by the council for a term of four years, to serve without compensation.

56 and 57 of this charter, and subject to the limitations prescribed by law and this charter. The credit of the city shall not in any manner be given or loaned to or in aid of any individual, association, or corporation, except that suitable provision may be made for the aid and support of its poor.

SEC. 59. *Collection and Custody of City Moneys.* All taxes, special assessments, and license fees accruing to the city shall be collected by officers of the department of finance. All moneys received by any officer or employee of the city for or in connection with the business of the city shall be paid promptly into the city treasury, and shall be deposited with such responsible banking institutions as furnish such security as the council may determine and shall agree to pay the highest rate of interest; and all such interest shall accrue to the benefit of the city. The council shall provide by ordinance for the prompt and regular payment and deposit of all city moneys as required by this section.

SEC. 60. *Contracts and Purchases.* No continuing contract (which involves the payment of money out of the appropriations of more than two years) except public utility franchises shall be made for a period of more than ten years; and no such contract shall be valid without public notice at least two weeks before final action of the council and the approval of two-thirds of all the members of the council, or submission to the electors of the city at a regular or special election and the approval of a majority of those voting thereon.

Any public work or improvement costing more than one thousand dollars shall be executed by contract, except where a specific work or improvement is authorized by the council based on detailed estimates submitted by the department authorized to execute such work or improvement. All contracts for more than one thousand dollars shall be awarded to the lowest responsible bidder, after public advertisement and competition, as may be prescribed by ordinance. But the city manager shall have the power to reject all the bids and to advertise again; and all advertisements shall contain a reservation of this right.

SEC. 61. *Payment of Claims.* Payments by the city shall be made only upon vouchers certified by the head of the appropriate department or other division of the city government, and by means of warrants on the city treasury issued by the director of finance and countersigned by the city manager. The director of finance shall examine all payrolls, bills and other claims and demands against the city; and shall issue no warrant for payment unless he finds that the claim is in proper form, correctly computed, and duly certified; that it is justly and legally due and payable; that an appropriation has been made therefor which has not been exhausted or that the payment has been otherwise legally authorized; and that there is money in the city treasury to make payment. He may require any claimant to make oath to the validity of a claim. He may investigate any claim, and for such purposes may examine witnesses under oath; and if he finds it is fraudulent, erroneous, or otherwise invalid, shall not issue a warrant therefor.

SEC. 62. *Audit of Accounts.* Upon the death, resignation, removal or expiration of the term of any officer of the city, other than the director of finance, the director of finance shall make an audit and investigation of the accounts of such officer, and shall report to the city manager and council.

As soon as practicable after the close of each fiscal year an annual audit shall be made of all the accounts of all city officers; and upon the death, resignation, removal or expiration of the term of the director of finance, an audit shall be made of his accounts. Such audits shall be made under the provisions of any law for the inspection and audit of municipal accounts by state officers; and if there is no such state inspection such audits shall be made by qualified public accountants, selected by the council, who have no personal interest, direct or indirect, in the financial affairs of the city or of any of its officers or employees. The council may at any time provide for an examination or audit of the accounts of any officer or department of the city government.

PUBLIC UTILITIES [23]

SEC. 63. *Granted by Ordinance.* All public utility franchises and all renewals, extensions and amendments

NOTE 23. The public utility and franchise policy embodied in a model city charter should be so formulated as to conserve and further the following purposes:

I. To secure to the people of the city the best public utility service that is practicable.

II. To secure and preserve to the city as a municipal corporation the fullest possible control of the streets and of their special uses.

III. To remove as far as practicable the obstacles in the way of the extension of municipal ownership and operation of public utilities, and to render practicable the success of such ownership and operation when undertaken.

IV. To secure for the people of the city public utility rates as thereof shall be granted or made only by ordinance; but no such proposed ordinance shall be adopted until it has been printed in full and until a printed report containing recommendations thereon shall have been made to the council by the city manager [or the bureau of franchises], until adequate public hearings have thereafter been held on such ordinance and until at least two weeks after its official publication in final form. No public utility franchise shall be transferable except with the approval of the

low as practicable, consistent with the realization of the three purposes above set forth.

It should be no part of such policy to secure compensation for franchises or special revenues for general city purposes by an indirect tax upon the consumers of public utility services.

In formulating a policy to carry out the four purposes above stated the following principles should be recognized:

1. Each utility serving an urban community should be treated as far as practicable as a monopoly with the obligations of a monopoly; and its operation within the city should be based as far as practicable upon a single comprehensive ordinance or franchise grant uniform in its application to all parts of the city and to all extensions of plant and service.

2. Every franchise should be revocable by the city upon just compensation being paid to its owners, when the city is prepared to undertake public ownership.

3. The control of the location and character of public utility fixtures, the character and amount of service rendered, and the rates charged therefor should be reserved to the city, subject to reasonable review by the courts or a state utilities commission where one exists.

4. The granting and enforcement of franchises and the regulation of utilities operating thereunder should be subject to adequate public scrutiny and discussion and should receive full consideration by an expert bureau of the city government established and maintained for that purpose, or, in case the maintenance of such bureau is impracticable, by an officer or committee designated for the purpose.

5. Private investments in public utilities should be treated as investments in aid of public credit and subject to the public control and should be safeguarded in every possible way, and the rate of return allowed thereon should be reduced to the minimum return necessary in the case of safe investments with a fixed and substantially assured fair earning power.

council expressed by ordinance; and copies of all transfers and mortgages or other documents affecting the title or use of public utilities shall be filed with the city manager within ten days after the execution thereof.

SEC. 64. *Term and Plan of Purchase.* Any public utility franchise may be terminated by ordinance at specified intervals of not more than five years after the beginning of operation, whenever the city shall determine to acquire by condemnation or otherwise the property of such utility necessarily used in or conveniently useful for the operation thereof within the city limits.[24] The method of determining the price to be paid for the public utility property shall be fixed in the ordinance granting the franchise.

SEC. 65. *Right of Regulation.* All grants, renewals, extensions, or amendments of public utility franchises, whether it be so provided in the ordinance or not, shall be subject to the right of the city:

(a) To repeal the same by ordinance at any time for misuse or non-use, or for failure to begin construction within the time prescribed, or otherwise to comply with the terms prescribed;

(b) To require proper and adequate extensions of plant and service, and the maintenance of the plant and fixtures at the highest practicable standard of efficiency;

(c) To establish reasonable standards of service and

NOTE 24. Where a term limit for the franchise is desired, provision should be made either for amortization of the investment, or at least of that portion of it within the limits of public streets and places, during the term of the grant, or for purchase of the physical property at the end of the term.

quality of products and prevent unjust discrimination in service or rates.[25]

(d) To prescribe the form of accounts and at any time to examine and audit the accounts and other records of any such utility and to require annual and other reports by each such public utility; *Provided,* that if a public service commission or any other authority shall be given the power by law to prescribe the forms of accounts for public utilities throughout the state or throughout any district of which the city is a part, the forms so prescribed shall be controlling so far as they go, but the council may prescribe more detailed forms for the utilities within its jurisdiction;

(e) To impose such other regulations as may be conducive to the safety, welfare, and accommodation of the public.

SEC. 66. *Consents of Property Owners.* The consent of abutting and adjacent property owners shall not be required for the construction, extension, maintenance or operation of any publicity utility;[26] but any property owner shall be entitled to recover from the owner of such public utility the actual amount of damages to such property on account thereof less any benefits received

NOTE 25. A franchise should include provisions for the readjustment of rates from time to time, or for the accumulation of surplus earnings for the purchase of the property in case rates are fixed for a long period in the grant.

NOTE 26. In some states there are constitutional provisions requiring the consent of adjacent property owners for the construction and operation of street railways. The constitution of New York requires such consent, or in lieu thereof approval of the proposed construction by commissioners appointed by the appellate division of the Supreme Court, and confirmed by the Court. Some such provision as the latter may be desirable.

therefrom, provided, suit is commenced within two years after the damage is begun.

Sec. 67. *Revocable Permits.* Permits revocable at the will of the council for such minor or temporary public utility privileges as may be specified by general ordinance may be granted and revoked by the council from time to time in accordance with the terms and conditions to be prescribed thereby; and such permits shall not be deemed to be franchises as the term is used in this charter. Such general ordinance, however, shall be subject to the same procedure as an ordinance granting a franchise and shall not be passed as an emergency measure.

Sec. 68. *Extensions.* All extensions of public utilities within the city limits shall become a part of the aggregate property of the public utility, shall be operated as such, and shall be subject to all the obligations and reserved rights contained in this charter and in any original grant hereafter made. The right to use and maintain any extension shall terminate with the original grant and shall be terminable as provided in section 64 hereof. In case of an extension of a public utility operated under a franchise hereafter granted, such right shall be terminable at the same times and under the same conditions as the original grant.

Sec. 69. *Other Conditions.* Every public utility franchise hereafter granted shall be held subject to all the terms and conditions contained in sections 63 to 72 hereof, whether or not such terms are specifically mentioned in the franchise. Nothing in this charter shall operate to limit in any way, except as specifically stated, the discretion of the council or the electors of the city in imposing terms and conditions in connection with any franchise grant.

SEC. 70. *Franchise Records.* Within six months after this charter takes effect every public utility and every owner of a public utility franchise shall file with the city, as may be prescribed by ordinance, certified copies of all the franchises owned or claimed, or under which any such utility is operated. The city shall compile and maintain a public record of all public utility franchises and of all public utility fixtures in the streets of the city.

SEC. 71. *Bureau of Franchises and Public Utilities.* There shall be established by ordinance a bureau of franchises and public utilities, at the head of which shall be an officer to be appointed by the city manager.[27] This officer shall be an expert in franchise and public utility matters, and he shall be provided with such expert and other assistance as is necessary to enable him to perform his duties. It shall be the duty of this officer and bureau to investigate and report on all proposed ordinances relating to public utilities, to exercise a diligent oversight over the operation of all public utilities operated under franchises, to report thereon with recommendations to the city manager, to represent the city in all, except legal, proceedings before any state public utilities commission involving the public utilities within the city, and to perform such other

NOTE 27. In the smaller cities, say those of less than 50,000 population, it may not be feasible to maintain a separate bureau of franchises and public utilities, but in every city where there is no such bureau the duties described in this section should be specifically imposed upon the city manager. The bureau, when one exists, will be a part of the department of public works and utilities; but in the large cities it may be found desirable to create a separate department of utilities as suggested in note 19.

duties under the direction of the city manager as may be prescribed by the council.

SEC. 72. *Accounts of Municipally Owned Utilities.* Accounts shall be kept for each public utility owned or operated by the city, distinct from other city accounts and in such manner as to show the true and complete financial result of such city ownership, or ownership and operation, including all assets, liabilities, revenues, and expenses. These accounts shall show the actual cost to the city of each public utility owned; the cost of all extensions, additions and improvements; all expenses of maintenance; the amounts set aside for sinking fund purposes; and, in the case of city operation, all operating expenses of every description. They shall show as nearly as possible the value of any service furnished to or rendered by any such public utility by or to any other city or governmental department. They shall also show a proper allowance for depreciation, insurance, and interest on the investment, and estimates of the amount of taxes that would be chargeable against the property if privately owned. The council shall annually cause to be made and printed for public distribution a report showing the financial results of such city ownership, or ownership and operation, which report shall give the information specified in this section and such other information as the council shall deem expedient.

CITY PLANNING

SEC. 73. *Creation of a City Planning Board.* There shall be a city planning board of three members, consisting of the director of public works and utilities and two citizen members chosen because of their knowledge of city planning.[28] It shall be the duty of the board to keep itself informed of the progress of city planning in this and other countries, to make studies and recommendations for the improvement of the plan of the city with a view to the present and future movement of traffic, the convenience, amenity, health, recreation, general welfare, and other needs of the city dependent on the city plan; to consider and report upon the designs and their relations to the city plan of all new public ways, lands, buildings, bridges, and all other public places and structures, of additions to and alterations in those already existing, and of the layout or plotting of new subdivisions of the city, or of territory adjacent to or near the city.

SEC. 74. *Power of Board.* All acts of the council or of any other branch of the city government affecting the city plan shall be submitted to the board for report and recommendations. The council may at any time call upon the board to report with recommendations, and the board of its own volition may also report to the council with recommendations on any matter which, in the opinion of either body, affects the plan of the city.

Any matter referred by the council to the board shall be acted upon by the board within thirty days of the date of reference, unless a longer or shorter period is specified. No action by the council involving any points hereinbefore set forth shall be legal or binding until it has been

NOTE 28. In larger cities having a separate director of utilities a board of five members, consisting of the director of public works, the director of utilities, and three citizen members, is recommended.

referred to the board and until the recommendations of the board thereon have been accepted or rejected by the council.

Sec. 75. *Annual Report.* The board shall submit to the council an annual report summarizing the activities of the board for the fiscal year, the recommendations made by it to the council during the year and the action of the council during the year on any and all recommendations made by the board in that or former years. The annual report of the board shall also contain a program for improvements to the city plan year by year during the three years next ensuing, with estimates of the cost thereof and recommendations as to how the cost shall be met.

..Sec. 76. *Secretary of the Board.* The board shall appoint as secretary a person of skill and experience in city planning and may employ consulting city planning experts as need may arise. The city engineer shall serve as chief engineer of the city planning board, and it shall be his particular duty to make recommendations designed to bring all the engineering works of the city into harmony as parts of one comprehensive plan. The executive health officer of the city shall advise the planning board from time to time of any municipal improvements within the scope of the board which, in his opinion, would improve the healthfulness of the city. The board shall have power to call upon any branch of the city government at any time for information and advice which in the opinion of the board will insure the efficiency of its work.[29]

Note 29. In some places it may be desirable to give the city planning board some of the powers conferred on the existing

MISCELLANEOUS PROVISIONS

SEC. 77. *Publicity of Accounts.* All accounts and the records of every office and department of the city shall be open to the public at all reasonable times under reasonable regulations, except records and documents from which might be secured information which might defeat the lawful purpose of the officer or department withholding them from access to the public.

SEC. 78. *No Personal Interest.* No member of the council nor any officer or employee of the city shall have a financial interest, direct or indirect, in any contract with the city, or be financially interested, directly or indirectly, in the sale to the city of any land, materials, supplies, or services, except on behalf of the city as a member of the council, officer, or employee; *Provided,* that the ownership of less than 5 per cent of the stock or shares of a corporation or association with which a contract may be made shall not be considered as involving an interest in the contract within the meaning of this section. No officer or employee of a public utility operating in the city shall be a member of the council. Any willful violation of this section shall constitute malfeasance in office, and any member of the council, officer, or employee found guilty thereof shall thereby forfeit his office or position.

municipal art commissions in the United States. These powers relate to the æsthetic features of public buildings, bridges, and other public structures, and embrace the acceptance or rejection of works of art or designs therefor to be placed in public buildings or in other places within the city. The section in the Cleveland charter relating to city planning commission and the ordinance based on it are commended for careful consideration, especially the method provided for the effective control of land subdivision.

Any violation of this section, with the knowledge, expressed or implied, of the person or corporation contracting with the city, shall render the contract involved voidable by the city manager or the council.

Sec. 79. *When Charter Shall Take Effect.* For the purpose of nominating and electing officers as provided herein, this charter shall take effect from and after the time of its approval by the electors of the city. For the purpose of exercising the powers of the city, establishing departments, divisions, and offices, and distributing the functions thereof, and for all other purposes, it shall take effect on the first day of

APPENDIX A

PREFERENTIAL BALLOT

(To be inserted, if desired, after section 11 of the charter)

Section 12. *Preparation of Ballot.* All ballots used in elections held under the authority of this charter shall be printed by the city and shall contain the names of the candidates without party or other designation. The order of arrangement of the names shall be alphabetical in rotation; that is, there shall be as many sets of ballots printed as there are candidates. Each set of ballots shall begin with the name of a different candidate, the other names being arranged thereafter in regular alphabetical order, commencing with the name next in alphabetical order after the one that stands first on that set of ballots. When the last name is reached in alphabetical order it shall be followed by the name that begins with the first letter represented in the list of names and by the others in regular order. The ballots so printed shall then be combined in tablets, so as to have the fewest possible ballots having the same order of names printed thereon together in the same tablet.

Arrangement for First, Second, and Other Choices. After the column containing the names of the candidates, arranged as indicated, there shall be printed three columns headed "first choice," "second choice," and "other choices" respectively. Each voter shall be entitled to place as many crosses in the column marked "first choice" as there are offices to be filled. He shall also be entitled to place as many crosses in the column marked "second choice" as there are offices to be filled, provided that he may not mark a cross in the column marked "second choice" after a name for which he has marked a cross in the first column. He may also place in the column marked "other choices" crosses after any names which he has not designated as first or second choices.

Form of Ballot. The form of the ballot with the voter's choices thereon shall be substantially the following:

REGULAR (OR SPECIAL) MUNICIPAL ELECTION

NAMES OF CANDIDATES	FIRST CHOICE	SECOND CHOICE	OTHER CHOICES
A	X		
B		X	
C			
D			X
E			X

INSTRUCTIONS

Vote your first choice in the first column. Vote your second choice in the second column. Vote in the third column for any other candidates whom you are willing to support.

Do not vote more than one first choice and one second choice for any one office.

If you wrongly mark, tear or deface this ballot, return it and obtain another.

When more than one candidate is to be chosen the foregoing instructions must be modified in accordance with the provisions of section 2.

SECTION 13. *Counting of Ballots.* The ballots shall be counted by adding up the first choices cast for each candidate. If any candidates receive a number of first choices equal to a majority of all the valid ballots cast, they shall be declared elected in the order of the votes received. As to candidates who have not received such a majority, the number of second choices cast for each candidate shall then be counted and shall be added to the number of first choices. Any candidates who have then a total of first and second choices equal to a majority of all valid ballots cast shall be declared elected in the order of the number of votes received. If a sufficient number of candidates have not yet received the required majority, the other choices cast for each candidate shall be added to his first and second choices, and candidates shall be declared elected in the order of the number of votes received. In case of a tie, the order of precedence shall be determined by the larger number of first choices in the vote.

APPENDIX B

REPORT OF NATIONAL MUNICIPAL LEAGUE COMMITTEE
ON MUNICIPAL BUDGETS AND ACCOUNTING

SPRINGFIELD, MASS., November 23, 1916

Your Committee met in April of this year, and after considerable discussion, agreed upon the requirements of the Model Budget. These requirements took the shape of proposed amendments to the financial provisions of the Model City Charter, and were presented to the Committee on Municipal Program. Since, however, this Committee had already printed its statement of the financial provisions as they should appear in the Model Charter, and it did not seem expedient to make any changes, the Committee on Budgets suggests that their report as herewith submitted, be printed separately or as an appendix to the Model City Charter, as elaborating some of its provisions, and furnishing budget forms which are not contained in the report of the Committee on City Charter.

FINANCIAL REQUIREMENTS

ACCOUNTS AND RECORDS.— Accounts shall be kept by the department of finance, which shall exhibit the financial transactions for all departments of the city. Forms for all such accounts shall be prescribed by the director of finance with the approval of the city manager, which shall be adequate for recording all cash receipts and disbursements, all revenues accrued and all liabilities incurred, as well as all transactions affecting the acquisition, custody, and disposition of municipal properties and values. Forms for reports exhibiting the financial transactions and the financial condition of the city as well as other reports which may be required by law or ordinance shall also be prescribed in the same manner. Financial reports shall be prepared for each quarter and each fiscal year, and for such other periods as may be required by the city manager, or by the council.

ANNUAL BUDGETS.— Not later than one month before the end of each fiscal year, the city manager shall prepare and submit to the council an annual budget for the ensuing fiscal year, based upon detailed estimates furnished by the several departments and other divisions of the city government. The budget shall in addition to the proposed appropriation bill and revenue measures present the following information:

(A) A brief summary showing the estimated financial requirements and the proposed methods of meeting them for the next fiscal year.

(B) An operation account to consist of a summary statement of actual revenues and expenditures for the preceding fiscal year and of the estimated revenues and expenditures for the current and for the succeeding fiscal year. This account shall be supported by (1) A detailed analysis and statement of actual and estimated expenditures classified according to departments and other organization units to which appropriations are made. (2) A detailed analysis and statement of actual and estimated expenditures classified according to functions which have been carried on and for the support of which appropriations are requested (i. e., "Work Program"), to be carried into such detail as may be required by the executive, or accounting officers of the city for the purpose of showing the unit, or other, costs to work. (3) An analysis and statement of actual and estimated expenditures classified to show amounts spent and to be spent for things bought — and to be bought — and for contractual obligations met and to be met. (4) A detailed analysis and statement of actual revenues accrued and estimated revenues to accrue under exisiting laws and conditions, classified according to sources or kinds of revenue raised (actual) and to be raised (estimated.)

(C) A statement of financial condition showing the actual current assets, liabilities, reserves and surplus (or deficit) at the end of the preceding year, also at the end of the last month, or interim statement, of the current year, and the estimated current assets and liabilities as of the beginning and end of the coming fiscal year. This statement to be supported by (1) a statement of cash receipts and disbursements showing the actual cash receipts and disbursements of the preceding fiscal year and the estimated cash requirements of the current and succeeding fiscal years classified by funds as established by law. (2) A surplus account analysis of the actual credits and debits to surplus during the preceding fiscal year, also the estimated credits and debits of the current and succeeding fiscal years.

(D) A fund statement showing the actual condition of each fund established by law at the end of the preceding fiscal year, also the estimated condition of the funds at the beginning and end of the coming fiscal year, supported by (1) A summary and detailed statement of "general fund" appropriation accounts. (2) A summary and detailed statement of special revenue appropriation accounts. (3) Trust funds. (4) Bond funds.

(E) Such other information as may be required by the council.

Copies of such budget shall be printed and available for distribution not later than two weeks after its submission to the council; and a public hearing shall be given thereon by the council or a committee thereof before action by the council.

EXHIBIT I — Summary of Estimates, showing the "Financial Plan" for the Next Fiscal Year (19)

Summary of Estimates	Totals	Expenses and Fixed Charges	Capital Outlays	Contingencies and Losses
Estimated Expenditures for 19 :				
Personal Services (estimated total of payrolls)				
Services other than personal (1)				
Materials and Supplies (estimated purchases)				
Equipments and parts (estimated purchases)				
Land and Improvements (2)				
Debt Payments and Sinking Fund Instalments				
Interests, rents, royalties and other proprietary charges				
Contributions (to institutions, etc.)				
Pensions and retirement allowances				
Judgments, mandamuses, etc.				
Other				
Total estimated requirements for next year				
Estimated funds available:				
Net expendable surplus (all funds): Cash (net)				
Resources other than cash (net)				
General fund revenues (present basis)				
Special fund revenues (present basis)				
Local improvement funds				
Loan fund accruals				
Total available for next year				
Estimated excess of expenditures over funds available				
Estimated excess of funds available over expenditures				

1 Telephones, telegraph, light, power, transportation, printing, advertising, repairs and reconstruction, etc., by contract and open-market order.
2 Docks, bridges, buildings, local improvements, etc.

EXHIBIT II — "General Operation Account," Showing Actual and Estimated Revenues for Three Years

General Classification of Revenues and Expenses	Fiscal Years			
	19.... (Actual)	19.... (Current)			19.... Estimate for Next Year
		Months (actual)	Months (estimated)	Total	
Revenues accrued (by sources):					
Real estate taxes					
Personal property taxes					
.... (1)					
Net profit or loss on municipal industries					
Miscellaneous revenues					
Total revenues					
Charges against revenues:					
Expenses (by functions):					
General and overhead					
Public service activities:					
Administration of justice					
Protection of persons and property					
Preservation of health...					
Public education and recreation					
Care of dependent, defective and delinquent.					
Providing transportation facilities					
Promoting economic interests					
Military defense (armories, etc.)					
....					
Total expenses					
Fixed charges:					
Interest					
Pensions and retirements ...					
Other					
Total fixed charges					
Total expenses and fixed charges					
Debt payments and sinking fund instalments					
Total charges against revenues					
Excess of revenues over "charges against revenues"					
Excess of "charges against revenues" over revenues..					

1 Insert other classes of revenues.

EXHIBIT III — "CURRENT BALANCE SHEET,"— SHOWING ACTUAL AND ESTIMATED CURRENT ASSETS, LIABILITIES AND RESERVES, AS OF THE RESPECTIVE DATES SHOWN BELOW

Current Assets (Available for Expenses and other Charges against Revenues)	Last Fiscal Year (19....) At Beginning (Actual)	At End (Actual)	Current Year (19....) Last Available Date (19....) (Actual)	Ensuing Year (19....) At Beginning (Estimated)	At End (Estimated)
Cash (in bank and in hand)..					
Amounts due to City:					
Uncollected real estate taxes					
Uncollected personal property taxes					
Uncollected other taxes ...					
Uncollected miscellaneous revenues					
Uncollected water rates ...					
....					
Stores on hand					
Advances:					
For rents (paid in advance)					
For insurance (paid in advance)					
....					
Other current assets					
....					
Total current assets					
Current liabilities					
Immediate demands for cash					
Mandamuses payable ..					
Vouchers audited					
Checks and warrants outstanding					
Total immediate demands					
Unaudited invoices and accounts payable					
....					
Loans against revenues ...					
Reserves:					
For expenses, etc. (unexpired months of year)...					
For uncollectible taxes					
For losses (failed banks, etc.)					
....					
Total liabilities and reserves					
Surplus (or deficit)					
Cash over "immediate demands for cash"					
Other assets over "other liabilities and reserves" ...					
Total liabilities, reserves and surplus					

EXHIBIT IV — "Surplus Account" — Showing the Credits to and Charges Against Current Surplus for Net Operating Current Year and Transactions and Losses Pertaining to Prior Periods

Items	Last Year (19) (Actual)	Current Year (19) Months Expired (Actual)	Current Year (19) Months Unexpired (Estimated)	Next Year 19.... (Estimated)
Surplus at beginning of period (see current balance sheet — Surplus Exhibit III)				
Credits to surplus:				
Excess of revenues over expenses and fixed charges (see Exhibit II)..........				
Transfers to surplus				
Additions to delinquent taxes				
Additions to inventories				
Other Credits				
Total				
Charges against surplus:				
Excess of expenses and fixed charges over revenues (see Exhibit II)..............				
Transfers from surplus				
Allowances and deductions of delinquent taxes				
Invoices audited in excess of amounts reported				
Other Charges				
Total charges				
Balance of surplus at end of period				

EXHIBIT V — "FUND STATEMENT," SHOWING THE ACTUAL AND ESTIMATED CONDITION OF FUNDS AS OF................, 19..

Funded Resources, Appropriations and Reserves	Last Fiscal Year, 191.... (Actual)					
	Funds Available for Expenses and Fixed Charges			Funds Available for Improvements and Debt Payments		
	General Fund	Special Funds	Total	Loan Funds	Improvement Funds	Sinking Funds

Funded resources:
  Unapplied (net) cash balances (1) ....
  Estimated revenues (funded for current year)...
  Net uncollected revenues and assessments (past years)....
  Loans authorized and unissued.............
  Investments ....
  Other funded resources ....
  ....

Total funded resources ....

Appropriations and encumbrances:
  Unexpended balance of appropriations ....
  Encumbrances of appropriations (contracts, etc.)....
  Unencumbered balance of appropriations ....
  Fund reserves ....
  Total appropriations and reserves ....
  Unappropriated balances — surplus ....

Total appropriations, reserves and surplus ....

[1] Total cash in hand and in bank, less audited vouchers, outstanding checks and other immediate demands (See Exhibits III and VI).

EXHIBIT V.—"FUND STATEMENT," SHOWING THE ACTUAL AND ESTIMATED CONDITION OF FUNDS AS OF................ 19.. (*Continued*)

Funded Resources, Appropriations and Reserves	Current Fiscal Year, 191..... (Actual) to Last Available Date							Next Fiscal Year, 191..... (Estimated)						
	Funds Available for Expenses and Fixed Charges			Funds Available for Improvements and Debt Payments				Funds Available for Expenses and Fixed Charges			Funds Available for Improvements and Debt Payments		
	General Fund	Special Funds	Total	Loan Funds	Improvement Funds	Sinking Funds		General Fund	Special Funds	Total	Loan Funds	Improvement Funds	Sinking Funds
Funded resources:													
Unapplied (net) cash balances (1)													
Estimated revenues (funded for current year)													
Net uncollected revenues and assessments (past years)													
Loans authorized and unissued													
Investments													
Other funded resources													
....													
....													
Total funded resources													
Appropriations and encumbrances:													
Unexpended balance of appropriations													
Encumbrances of appropriations (contracts, etc.)													
Unencumbered balance of appropriations													
Fund reserves													
Total appropriations and reserves													
Unappropriated balances — surplus													
Total appropriations, reserves and surplus													

[1] Total cash in hand and in bank, less audited vouchers, outstanding checks and other immediate demands (See Exhibits III and VI).

EXHIBIT VI.—"Cash Receipts and Disbursements,"— Summary Showing Cash Received and Disbursed, Classified by Funds for the Period ———— to ———— 19—

| | Last Fiscal Year, 191.... (Actual) ||||||
| | Funds Available for Expenses and Fixed Charges ||| Funds Available for Improvements and Debt Payments |||
Items	General Fund	Special Funds	Total	Loan Funds	Improvement Funds	Sinking Funds
Unapplied (net) cash balance at beginning of year (see Exhibit V)						
Plus amount set aside to meet immediate demands for cash at beginning of period						
Total cash on hand and in bank (see Exhibit III beginning dates)						
Cash receipts:						
Revenues — taxes						
Revenues — miscellaneous						
Assessments						
Loans						
Sales						
Other						
Transfers to funds						
..Total receipts						
Total receipts plus cash balance						
Cash Disbursements:						
Vouchers for						
Expenses and fixed charges						
Improvements						
Debt payments						
Mandamuses						
Transfers from funds						
Total disbursements ...."immediate demands for cash"						
Amount required to meet "immediate demands for cash"						
Unapplied (net) cash balance, available at end of period						

EXHIBIT VI.—"Cash Receipts and Disbursements," — Summary Showing Cash Received and Disbursed, Classified by Funds for the Period ———— to ———— 19—(Continued)

Items	Current Fiscal Year, 191..... (Actual) to Last Available Date							Next Fiscal Year, 191..... (Estimated)						
	Funds Available for Expenses and Fixed Charges			Funds Available for Improvements and Debt Payments			Sinking Funds	Funds Available for Expenses and Fixed Charges			Funds Available for Improvements and Debt Payments			Sinking Funds
	General Fund	Special Funds	Total	Loan Funds	Improvement Funds	Sinking Funds		General Funds	Special Funds	Total	Loan Funds	Improvement Funds	
Unapplied (net) cash Balance at beginning of year (see Exhibit V)........													
Plus amount set aside to meet immediate demands for cash at beginning of period													
Total cash on hand and in bank (see Exhibit III beginning dates)............													
Cash receipts:													
Revenues — Taxes													
Revenues — Miscellaneous ..													
Assessments													
Loans													
Sales													
Other													
Transfers to funds													
...Total receipts													
Total													
Cash disbursements:													
Vouchers for													
Expenses and fixed charges..													
Improvements													
Debt payments													
Mandamuses													
Transfers from funds													
...Total disbursements													
Amount required to meet immediate demands for cash ...													
Unapplied (net) cash balance available at end of period...													

INDEX

Accounting and reporting, connection of, with municipal development, 260; development of, 258.

Accounts, auditing of, in Model City Charter, 207, 208, 353; Commissioner of, in New York City, value of office of, 247; keeping of, in Model Charter, 208; keeping of, in Municipal Program of 1900, 201, 202; keeping of, in new Municipal Program, 203, 205; of municipally owned utilities in Model City Charter, 360; publicity of, in Model City Charter, 363.

Accounts and records in Model City Charter, 346; National Municipal League on, 367.

Administration, city, in European countries, 148.

Administration organization, 119; summary of, 143, 144; city manager or chief executive in, 119; annual budget of, 129; appointive power of, 126; appointive power of, limitations upon, 127; appointment of, by council, 120; appointment of, not limited by local residence, 121; appointment of, on basis of qualifications, 120; civil service board under, status of, 126; disciplinary and removal powers of, 128; participation of, in council meetings, 128; powers and duties of, 126; removal of, by council, 124; removal of, written charges and public hearing necessary for, 125; salary of, 22; term of, 123.

Administrative departments, 130; awarding of posts in, as political rewards, 132; creation of new, 135; functions of, 133; number of, 130; reduction in number of, 136; school system in, independence of, 136; directors of, advice of, to city manager, 142; appointment of, by city manager, 138, 139; information of, to city manager, 143; qualifications of, 139; removal by city manager, 141; responsible to city manager, 142; in Model City Charter, 335; creation of, 335; duties of directors of, 336; powers of subpœna regarding, 337; responsibility of directors of, 337.

Administrative power of council, 146; loss of, 147; necessity of, 149; of commissions, 147, 148.

Alternative methods of electing council, 103.

Amendments to city charters, constitutional provisions for, 304.

American Judicature Society, 228; founding of, 228; judicature act drafted by, 228.

American Judicature Society, court projected by, 228; cases tried in, 230; clerk in, 233; expert "masters" in, 233; judicial officers of, 229, 230, 231, 232; judicial officers in, number of, 234; meetings and

INDEX

reports of, 232; pensions for judges of, 233; procedure rules in, 229, 231; procedure rules in, changes in, 234; salaries of judges of, 234.

Appropriation ordinance in Model City Charter, 210, 348.

Arbitration, commercial court of, 243.

Assessment of property in Model City Charter, 349.

Assessments, special, under Model Charter, 211.

Assessments and taxes, provision for, under municipal home rule charter, 26.

Balance sheet, current, exhibit, 373.

Ballot, discussion of, 14; preferential, in Model City Charter, 364; counting of, 366; form of, 365.

Ballot, short, 13, 14, 282; principle in Model City Charter, 109–114; application of, 114; application of, in the unwieldy district, 115; application of, in the wieldy district, 117.

Ballots in initiative elections, 328; in Model City Charter, 314; in referendum measures, 332.

Baltimore, annual National Municipal League conference at, Nov., 1914, 22.

Beard, Charles A., on commission government, 12; on commission-manager plan, 17.

Bond issues in Model City Charter, 212, 350; in municipal home rule charters, 26, 92.

Bonds, issue and sale of, in New Municipal Program, 203, 204.

Boston city charter, 286; working of short ballot principle in, 116.

Bradford, Ernest S., on city manager plan, 17; on commission government, 12.

Budget, annual, in Model City Charter, 208, 347; in Program of 1900, 201; National Municipal League on, 368; of city manager, 129, 335.

Burnham, George, Jr., on value of municipal research to elected officials, 261.

Cabinets, national, awarding of posts by, as rewards to political leaders, 132.

California, municipal home rule provision of, 80.

Cash and receipts disbursements, exhibit, 377–378.

Census, reporting reform in, 261.

Charter, Model City, 206. See also Model City Charter.

Charter directors and city manager, inter-relation of, under Model City Charter, 43, 44; provisions for selection and duties of, in Model City Charter, 43.

Charters, city, amendments to, constitutional provisions for, 304; complexity and diffusion in, 283; constitutional provisions for, 303; length of, 284; of Missouri Constitution of 1875, 78; simplicity of, 281.

"Checks and balances," system of, 167.

Chicago, advantages of law regarding "removals" in, 66; court of commercial arbitration in, 243; enforcement of motor speeding law in, 246; short ballot principle in, working of, 117; small claims court of, work of, 242.

Childs, Richard S., on commission government, 12; on commission-manager plan, 17.

Cities, home rule for. *See* Home rule; legislative control of, 73; abuses of, 75; constitutional restriction of state legislatures in regard to, 75, 76; history of, 74; politics in, 75; special legislation by states over, 75, 76; specific prohibitions against passage of specified laws respecting, 76.

City and county consolidation, constitutional provisions for, 307.

City, powers of, constitutional provisions for, 305.

City charters, amendments to, constitutional provisions for, 304; constitutional provisions for, 303; of Missouri Constitution of 1875, 78.

City Club of New York, work for the Philadelphia Conference for good city government by, 1.

City control of local elections boards, 93; local police, 92.

City courts, management of, 228. *See also under* Courts.

City engineer on city planning board in Model Charter, 225.

City experts, and municipal development, 269; civil service examinations for, 271; for public utilities problems, 196; keeping in touch with people, 273, 274; need of, 28; recommendation of, by civic bodies, 270, 271.

City health officer, on city planning board, in Model Charter, 225.

City manager in Model City Charter, 119, 334; and charter directors, 43, 44; annual budget of, 129, 335; appointive power of, 41, 42, 126; appointive power of, limitations upon, 127; appointment of, by council, 120; appointment of, not limited to local residence, 121; appointment of, on basis of qualifications, 120; civil service board under, status of, 126; disciplinary and removal powers of, 128; efficiency records and, 58; participation of, in council meetings, 42, 128; powers and duties of, 40, 41, 126, 335; provisions for, 39; removal of, by council, 124; removal of, written charges and public hearing necessary, for, 125; salary of, 122; term of, 40, 123.

City-manager plan, advantages of, 17; in report of Second Committee on Municipal Reform, 22; opening-up of profession through, 18.

City planning, 218, 291; æsthetic side of, 226; history of, 218; need of, 218; state control of, 227; under commission form of government, 220, 221.

City planning in Model Charter, 222, 360; consulting experts in, 225; three-year program of improvements in, 224.

City planning board in Model Charter, 222, 225; annual report of, 362; creation of, 360; duties of, 223, 224; power of board of, 361; secretary of board of, 362.

City's public property, need of safeguarding of, 10.

Civil service, discussion of differences in first and second Municipal Program on, 69; examinations for expert city officials, 271; in Model City Charter, 44; provisions for, in the Municipal Program of 1900, 69.

Civil service board in Model City Charter, 337; appointment of, 48, 50; creation of, 337; investigations conducted by, 62, 63; politics and religion excluded from, 345; power of, to make rules, 338; power of taxpayer to enforce rules, 346; removal and suspension powers of, 68, 342; restriction on appointees of, and forbidden practices, 343; supervisory powers of, 341; violation of rules and regulations of, 345.

Civil service board, in report of service committee on Municipal Program, 22; need of freedom of, from political control, 48, 49; status of, under city manager, 126.

Claims, payment of, in Model City Charter, 353.

Claims court, small, work of reform in, 242.

Cleveland, Dr. Frederick A., on growth of referendum and recall, 163.

Cleveland, municipal conference at (1895), 4.

Columbus, municipal conference at (1900), 8.

Commercial arbitration, court of, 243.

Commission government, city planning under, 220, 221; first trial of, 10; development of, 162; growth of, 220; history of, in American cities, 11; lasting effects of, 21; legislative and administrative powers combined in, 150; report on, by committee of National Municipal League, 12.

Commission-manager plan, report on, 16.

Commissions, special administrative power transferred to, 147, 148.

Committee of Five, report of, on commission government, 12-16; report of, on commission-manager plan, 16.

Committee of Seven, objectives sought by, 3; proposal for appointment of, 3.

Committee on Municipal Program, second, appointment of, 1913, 21; digest of, 22; personnel of, 22; purpose of, 21; reading of partial report of, 22.

Competitive system, as a substitute for the employment bureau, 47; bearing of upon public school system, 51; in England, 60; in Model City Charter, 48; in various municipalities, 53; need of an independent civil service board under, 48; necessity for, 47; popularity of, among better classes, 52; promotions under, 56; tests and promotions, under, in Model City Charter, 62; publication of eligible lists in, 54, 55; realization of value of, by second Committee for Municipal Program, 47; "removals" and, 64; requirements of, 61; Ridley investigation and, 61; suggestion for scope of, 57; universal desirability of, 68; value of, to the lower grades of service, 59.

Constitution of the United States, length of, 284.

Constitutional amendments National Municipal League adoption of (1900), 8.

Contracts and purchases in Model City Charter, 214, 215, 352.

INDEX

Controller, responsibilities of, under Model Charter, 207.

Council, administrative power of, loss of, 147; alternative methods of electing, 103; appointment of city manager by, 120; as administrative body, 146; as administrative body, necessity of, 149; composition of, 152; election of, 154; legislative and administrative powers confined in, 150; loss of appeal of, 149; meetings of, participation of city manager in, 128; nomination of, 154; powers of, 154; powers of mayor in, 156; principle of, 146: removal of city manager by, 124; report of second Committee on Municipal Program on, 22; size of, 150; summary of provisions for, 156.

Council in Model City Charter, 39, 307; composition of, 308; creation of, 307; elections by, 310; mayor's power in, 311; organization and procedure in, powers of, 309.

Courts, municipal, existing conditions in, 238; for commercial arbitration, 243; for criminal cases, defects and needs of, 244; for small claims, work of reform in, 242; management of, 228; reform in system of, by model court act, results of, 240; judges of, selection of, 235; by appointment by the chief justice, 236, 237; by appointment by the governor, 238; by reëlection on their record, 236.

Courts, municipal, organized or unified, responsibility fostered in, 247; by community of interest among judges, 248; by publicity, 247; by right of citizen to complain, 248; success of, 249.

Court, municipal, projected by the American Judicature Society, 228; cases tried in, 230; clerk in, 233; expert "masters" in, 233; judicial officers of, 229, 231; judicial officers in, number of, 234; meetings and reports of, 232; pensions for judges in, 233; procedure rules in, 229, 231; procedure rules in, changes in, 234; salaries of judges in, 233, 234.

Criminal courts, defects and needs of, 244.

Curtis, George William, on "removals," 64.

Custody of funds, in Model Municipal Charter, 214.

Dayton, annual National Municipal League Conference at (Nov. 19, 1915), 22, 23.

Departments, administrative. *See* Administrative departments.

Des Moines, commission government plan in, 19, 20.

"Direct legislation," 161; in Municipal Program of 1900, 161.

Director of finance in Model City Charter, 346; duties of, 216.

Education experts, growth of importance of, 32.

Education, public provision regarding, under municipal home rule charter, 27.

Efficiency records, difficulties inherent to general use of, 57, 58.

Elections, as a popular function, 19; constitutional provisions for, 306; local, city control of, 93; municipal, holding of, provisions for, in

INDEX

Model City Charter, 311; ballots and voting in, 314; ballots in, counting of, 315; nomination papers in, filing of, 313; nomination papers in, signatures to and forms of, 312; nominations in, by petition, 312; regulation of elections in, 314; vacancy provisions in, 320; ward, value of, 20.

Electoral provisions in New Municipal Program, 95; alternative methods of electing council in, 103; elimination primary system with majority, election at large, 103; Hare system of proportional representation in, 96; methods of election in, 96; nominations by petition in, 96; non-partisanship in local elections in, 95; preferential voting system, 104; voters' responsibility in, 108.

Electoral reforms, 286.

Eligible list in competitive service, 54, 55; necessity of publicity for, 55.

Elimination primary system with majority election at large, 103.

England, experience with competitive system and promotion in, 60; method of procedure in municipal government in, 31.

European countries, municipal administration in, 147, 148.

Excess condemnation in home rule charters, 92.

Expert administration and democracy, discussion of, 32.

Expert public service, duties of the expert in, functioning in a two-fold capacity, 37; duties of the layman in, 37; independence of political change of, condition of, 34, 35; need of proper promotion and recognition for services for, 36; permanence as a condition of, 33; recruiting and training for, 35; relation between expert and layman in, 37.

Experts, city, and municipal development, 269; civil service examinations for, 271; for public utilities problems, 196; keeping in touch with people, 273, 274; recommendation of, by civic bodies, 270, 271; value of, 28.

Federal competitive service, positions filled through, 52.

Federal removal rules, operation of, 65, 66.

Finance, director of, in Model City Charter, 346; duties of, in Model Charter, 216.

Financial estimates plan, exhibit, 371.

Financial provisions in Model City Charter, 206, 346; accounts and records in, 346; annual budget in, 347; appropriation ordinance in, 348; assessment of property in, 349; audit of accounts in, 353; bond issues in, 350; collection and custody of city moneys in, 352; contracts and purchases in, 352; department of finance in, 206; director of finance in, 346; payment of claims in, 353; restrictions on loans and credit in, 351; tax levy in, 349; temporary loans in, 351.

Financial provisions in New Municipal Program, 202; state regulation of, 204.

Financial provisions in Municipal Program of 1900, 201.

Financial provisions, municipal, 199.

Financial responsibility, 257.

Finances, state regulation of,

in Municipal Program of 1900, 202.

Franchise provisions, in report of second Committee on Municipal Programs, 22.

Franchises, provisions for public utilities, 173, 176; grants and restrictions in, 175; records of grants, in Model City Charter, 359; uniform grants in, 178; specific provisions for, 179.

Franchises and public utilities, bureau of, in Model City Charter, 359.

Fund statement, exhibit, 375-376.

Funds, custody of, in Model Municipal Charter, 214.

Galveston, commission government in, 10, 11.

Germany, municipal government in, 30.

Hare method of proportional representation, 96; advantages of, 99; arguments against, 101.

Home rule, municipal, 287; advantages of, 82, 83; bond issues in, 92; conditions of, in America, 73; conditions of, in England, 74; conditions of, in Europe, 74; contributions to betterment of municipal government by charters of cities having, 84-86; control of local elections boards in, 93; control of local police in, 93; development of, 77; excess condemnation in, 92; history of inception of, 23; in St. Louis, 78; now inclusive of, in commmission government, 15; provision of the California constitution on, 80; provision of the Missouri constitution of 1875 on, 78; scope of municipal power under, 26; suggestion for optional charter law for, 25; value of, 73.

Home rule, municipal, constitutional provisions of, 302; on amendments to city charters, 304; on city charters, 303; on consolidation of city and county, 307; on elections, 306; on incorporation and organization, 302; on option laws, 302; on powers of cities, 305; on reports, 306.

Home rule, municipal, provisions for, in Municipal Program of 1900, 86; authorization to cities to frame and amend charters, 86, 89; enumeration of more important powers to cities, 91; general grant of full power to cities over municipal affairs, 86, 90; legislature to organize broad system of home rule based on statutes, 86, 87-89.

Incorporation and organization of cities, constitutional provisions for, 302.

Indebtedness in Model City Charter, 212, 350, 351; in Municipal Program of 1900, 201, 202; in new Municipal Program, 203, 204.

Indianapolis, municipal conference at, Nov., 1898, 6; action of, on preliminary report of the Municipal Program Committee, 8.

Initiative provisions in Model City Charter, 325; ballots, 328; elections on initiative measures, 327; number of measures to be initiated, 329; petitions, filing of, 326; petitions, preparation of, 325; petitions, submission of, to

INDEX

council, 327; power to initiate ordinances, 325.
Initiative, referendum and recall, development of, 163; in commission and manager forms of government, 168; reasons for growth of, 166; report of second Committee on Municipal Program on, 22; use of, 164; working out of, 14.
Initiative, system of, 160; value of, 159, 161.
"Internal Combustion Court," 248.

Judges in court projected by American Judicature Society, 229, 230, 231, 232; number of, 234; pensions for, 233; salaries of, 233, 234.
Judicature act of American Judicature Society. *See under* American Judicature Society.

King, Dr. Clyde L., on local residence requirement for expert officials, 278.

Legislation, "direct," 159, 161; representative system of, advantages and disadvantages of, 160; town meeting system of, 159.
Loans and credit in Model City Charter, restrictions on, 351.
Loans, temporary, in Model City Charter, 351.
Local residence, appointment of city manager not limited by, 121; requirement for expert officials, 278.
Los Angeles, analysis of government organization of, 283.
Louisville, Municipal Conference at, platform construction by, 4.

Mayor, duties of, under Model City Charter, 39; power of, in council, 156; power of, in council, in Model City Charter, 311.
Mayor-and-council plan, disadvantages of, compared with city-manager plan, 18.
"Mayor's Eye, The," 267.
Milk depots, municipal, 290.
Minneapolis, municipal conference at (1894), 4.
Missouri, municipal home rule provision of, 78.
Model City Charter, 206.
Model City Charter, Administrative departments in, 335; creation of, 335; duties of directors of, 336; powers of subpœna regarding, 337; responsibility of directors of, 337; adoption of, 24; bond issues in, 212; charter directors under, duties and functions of, 43.
Model City Charter, city manager in, 41, 334; annual budget of, 335; duties of, 39, 40; powers and duties of, 335; selection of, 39; term of office of, 40.
Model Charter, city planning in, 222, 360; æsthetic side of, 226; consulting experts in, 225; state control of, 227; three-year program of improvements in, 224.
Model City Charter, city planning board in, 222, 225; annual report of, 362; city engineer on, 225; city health officer on, 225; creation of, 360; duties of, 223, 224; power of, 361; secretary of, 362.
Model City Charter, civil service appointments under, 44.
Model City Charter, civil service board in, 50, 51, 337; creation of, 337; politics and religion excluded from, 345;

INDEX

power of, to make rules, 338; removal and suspension powers of, 342; restriction on appointees of, and forbidden practices, 343; supervisory powers of, 341; power of taxpayer to enforce rules of, 346; violation of rules and regulations of, 345.

Model City Charter, competitive service and, 48, 50, 51, 52, 53; competitive tests and promotions under, 62; contracts and purchasing in, 214, 215; coördinate and group efficiency under, 58.

Model City Charter, council in, 39, 307; composition of, 152, 308; creation of, 307; elections by, 310; mayor's power in, 311; organization and procedure of, 310; powers of, 309; size of, 152.

Model City Charter, custody of funds in, 214.

Model City Charter, elections in, municipal holding of, 311; ballots and voting in, 314; ballots in, counting of, 315; nomination papers in, filing of, 313; nomination papers in, signatures to and forms of, 312; nominations in, by petition, 312; regulation of elections in, 314; vacancy provisions in, 320.

Model City Charter, eligible lists in, 55.

Model City Charter, financial provisions in, 346; accounts and records in, 346; annual budget in, 347; appropriation ordinance in, 348; assessment of property in, 349; audit of accounts in, 353; bond issues in, 350; collection and custody of city moneys in, 352; contracts and purchases in, 352; director of finance in, 216, 346; payment of claims in, 353; restrictions on loans and credit in, 351; tax levy in, 349; temporary loans in, 351.

Model City Charter, history of inception of, 23; indebtedness in, 212.

Model City Charter, initiative provisions in, 325; ballots in, 328; election on initiated measures in, 327; number of measures to be initiated, 329; petitions in, filing of, 326; petitions in, preparation of, 325; petitions in, submission of, to council, 327; power to initiate ordinances in, 325.

Model City Charter, mayor under, 39; need of public support for, 45; no personal interest in, 363.

Model City Charter, non-competitive places under, 53; payments in, 216.

Model City Charter, preferential ballot in, 364; arrangement of choices in, 365; counting of, 366; form of, 365.

Model City Charter, promotions under, 57.

Model City Charter, public utilities in, 354; accounts of municipally owned utilities in, 360; bureau of franchises and public utilities in, 359; consents of property owners in, 357; extensions in, 358; franchise records in, 359; grants by public ordinance, 354; other conditions in, 358; revokable permits in, 358; right of regulation in, 356; term and plan of purchase in, 356.

Model City Charter, publicity of accounts in, 363.

Model City Charter, recall provisions in, 321.

Model City Charter, referendum measures in, 329; ballot in, form of, 332; ballot in, title of, 332; conflict of referred measures in, 333; election in, 331; emergency measures in, 332; limitation on enforcement of ordinances in, 330; official publicity pamphlet in, 333; petition for, 330; petition for, certification of, 331; petition for, signatures to, 330; power of, 329.

Model City Charter, relation of city manager and charter directors, 43, 44; relation of experts and public representatives under, 39.

Model City Charter, "removals" in, 66; responsibility under, concentration of, 46.

Model City Charter, short ballot principle in, 109-114; application of, 114; application of, in unwieldy district, 115; application of, in the wieldy district, 117.

Model City Charter, simplicity of, 281; table of contents of, 297-299; when charter shall take effect in, 364.

Municipal administration, complexity of, 29; European countries, 147, 148.

Municipal conference, need for, 2.

Municipal Corporations Act, adoption of (1900), 8; on public utilities, 175.

Municipal courts, management of, 228. See also under Courts.

Municipal development, accomplishments in, 281; accounting in, 267; accounting and reporting in, 258, 260; city charters in, complexity and diffusion in, 283; city charters in, length of, 284; city charters in, simplicity of new, 281; city planning in, 291; electoral reforms in, 286; expert officials in, 269; financial responsibility and, 257; local residence requirement in, 278; municipal home rule in, 287; municipal research in, value of, 261; National Municipal League in, value of, 261, 264; need of constructive reorganization for, 255; personal obligation of citizenship and official duty in, 291, 293; political responsibility and, 256; publicity in, 266; salaries in, 281; short ballot in, 282; since the Revolution, 252-255; since 1900, 255; social welfare in, 289; state supervision of municipal affairs in, 289; tendency toward, 281; training for public service in, 277.

"Municipal Development in the United States," publication of, 8.

Municipal expert in England, 31; in Germany, 30.

Municipal government, appointment to office as political reward in, 38; efficiency in, 12; in England, 31; in Germany, 20; short ballot in, 13; unification of powers through, 13.

Municipal home rule. See under Home rule.

Municipal League of Philadelphia, work for the Philadelphia Conference for Good City Government by, 1.

Municipal indebtedness in Municipal Program of 1900, 201, 202; operation of public utilities, 175, 176; ownership of public utilities, 177, 188;

INDEX 389

platform, first steps in formulation of, 4.

"Municipal Program, A," publication of, 9; influence of, 9.

Municipal Program of 1900, adoption of, 8; civil service procedure in, 69; "direct legislation" in, 161; discussion of feasibility of, 6, 7; municipal home rule in, 86; proposal for, 1; public utilities provisions in, 173.

Municipal Program Committee, first, appointment of, 5; preliminary report of, 6; personnel of, 5; report of, 301.

Municipal reform, necessity for exchange of views as to, 2.

Municipal research, value of, in municipal development, 261.

Municipal training, value of, to public servants, 10.

Munro, William Bennett, on commission government, 12; on commission-manager plan, 17.

National Civil Service Reform League, on civil service board appointment, 49; on "removals," 64.

National Municipal League, conferences brought about by, 4.

National Municipal League Committee on Municipal Budgets and Accounting, 367; on accounts and records, 367; on annual budgets, 368; on municipal ownership of public utilities, 177; organization of, May, 1894, 4; program of work and methods of, 264; National Municipal League, on Galveston's Commission Government, 10; value of, in municipal development, 261, 264.

National Municipal League and National Civil Service Reform League, joint commission of, on city experts keeping in touch with people, 273, 274; on selection of expert city officials, 270, 271.

New Municipal Program, electoral provisions in, 95; alternative methods of electing council in, 103; elimination primary system with majority election at large, 103; Hare system of proportional representation in, 96; methods of election in, 96; nominations by petition in, 96; non-partisanship in local elections in, 95; preferential voting system in, 104; voters' responsibility in, 108.

New Municipal Program, public utilities provisions in: city experts for utilities problems, 196; coöperation between state and local authorities, 194; franchise grants and restrictions, 175; fundamental rules, 193; legitimate investments in utilities, a city trust, 197; specific franchise provisions, 179; uniform franchise grants, 178; utilities not to be exploited for relief of taxpayers, 191.

New York City, office of commissioner of accounts in, value of, 267.

New York State Mayors, Association of, 291.

Nominations by petition, in Model City Charter, 312; filing of papers in, 313; signatures to and forms of nomination papers in, 312.

INDEX

Nominations by petition in New Municipal Program, 96.

Non-competitive places, provision for, under Model City Charter, 53, 54.

Norfolk Charter, discussion of operation of regarding "removals," 67.

Official responsibility, lodgment of, 10.

Ohio, accounting and reporting legislation in, 259; system of supervising local accounts, 206.

Operation account, general exhibit, 372.

Option laws, constitutional provisions for, 302.

Payments, in Model Charter, 216.

Personal interest in Model City Charter, 364.

Pensions for judges, 233.

Permanence, as a condition of expert public service, 33, 34.

Personal obligation of citizenship and official duty, 291.

Philadelphia Gas Works, 266.

Police, local, city control of, 92.

Popular election, discussion of, as a popular function, 19.

Political privilege, surrender of, as a condition of expert public service, 35.

Popular will, right to self-expression of, 10.

Preferential ballot in Model City Charter, 364; arrangement of choices in, 365; counting of, 366; form of, 365.

Preferential voting system, 104; advantages of, 105; objections to, 106.

Promotions, as a problem of municipal administration, 56; determination of, by efficiency records and competitive examinations, 59.

Proportional representation, in report of second Committee on Municipal Program, 22.

Public experts, functions of, 38, 39.

Public improvements, provision regarding, under municipal home rule charter, 26.

Public office, as political reward, danger of, 38.

Public school system, relation of, to competitive service, 51.

Public service training, 277.

Public utilities, constitutional amendments on, 174; franchises for, granting of, 176.

Public utilities, fundamental aims of National Municipal League regarding, 182; good service, 183; low rates, 190; municipal control of streets, 186; removal of obstacles to municipal ownership, 188.

Public utilities in Model Charter, 354; accounts of municipally owned utilities in, 360; bureau of franchises and public utilities in, 359; consents of property owners in, 357; extensions in, 358; franchise records in, 359; granted by public ordinance, 354; other conditions in, 358; right of regulation in, 356; term and plan of purchase in, 356.

Public utilities in Municipal home rule charter, 26.

Public utilities in Municipal Program of 1900, 173.

Public utilities in New Municipal Program: city expert for problems of, 196; cooperation between state and local authorities on, 194; franchise grants and restrictions in, 175; fundamental

INDEX

rules for, 193; legitimate investments in, a city trust, 197; specific franchise provisions for public utilities in, 179; uniform franchise grants for public utilities in, 178; utilities not to be exploited for relief of taxpayers, 191.

Public utilities, Municipal Corporations Act on, 175; municipal operation of, 175, 176; municipal ownership of, 177; situation, changes in, 177.

Publicity in municipal courts, 247; in municipal affairs, 266.

Purchasing, contracts and, 214; in Model Charter, 215.

Recall in Model City Charter, 321; percentage of requirement in, 171; purpose of, 161.

Records, franchise, in Model City Charter, 359; National Municipal League on, 367.

Referendum measures in Model City Charter, 329; ballot in, form of, 332; ballot in, title of, 332; conflict of referred measures in, 333; election in, 331; emergency measures in, 332; limitation on enforcement of ordinances in, 330; official publicity pamphlet in, 333; petition for, 330; petition for, certification of, 331; petition for, signatures to, 330; power of, 329.

Referendum, system of, 160.

"Removals," Chicago civil service law regarding, 66; federal civil service commission rule on, 65; in competitive service, 63, 64; in Model City Charter, 66; power of civil service board regarding, 68.

Referendum, value of, 159, 161.

Reporting, financial, constitutional provisions for, 306; in Model City Charter, 208; in New Municipal Program, 203, 205; in Municipal Program of 1900, 201, 202.

Representative system of legislation, advantages and disadvantages of, 160.

Residence, local, requirement, for expert officials, 278.

Responsibility, direct, in city-manager plan, 19; financial, 257; official, 256; official, in Model City Charter, 46; official, lodgment of, 10.

Richmond, municipal conference at (1911), 12.

Ridley investigation, in competitive system, 61.

River and harbor improvements, work of U. S. Army on, 276.

Rochester, municipal milk depots of, 290.

Rowe, Dr., on publicity in municipal affairs, 266.

Salaries in public office, 281.

San Francisco, consolidation of city and county government in, 81; constitutional home rule for, 80.

Sanitation, public provision regarding, under municipal home rule charter, 27.

Schurz, Carl, on "removals," 65.

Self-government, right to, 10.

Shaw, Lieut. C. P., on provisions for group efficiency in proposed Model City, Charter, 58; on "removals," 66, 67.

Short ballot, 13, 14, 282; commission government, 13, 14; in commission-manager plan, 17.

INDEX

Short ballot principle in Model Charter, 109-114; application of, 114; application of, in the unwieldy district, 115; application of, in the wieldy district, 117.

Small claims court, reform in, work of, 242.

Social welfare, 289.

St. Louis City Charter, 285; initiative, referendum and recall in, 163.

St. Louis, municipal home rule in, 78.

State control of cities, 73; abuses of, 75; constitutional restrictions against, 75, 76; history of, 74; politics in, 75; special legislation regarding, 75, 76; specific prohibitions against, 76.

State supervision of municipal affairs, 289.

Staunton, trial of commission-manager plan by, 16.

Surplus account, exhibit, 374.

Tax levy in Model City Charter, 349.

Tax rate, municipal, in Program of 1900, 201, 202.

Taxation in Model City Charter, 211; in New Municipal Program, 203.

Taylor, Dr., on growth of initiative, referendum and recall, 164.

Toronto, municipal conference at (1913), 16.

Town meeting system of legislation, 159.

Voters' responsibility, 108.

Ward elections, value of, 20.
Ward lines, abolition of, 15.
Welfare, social, 289.

Wilcox, Dr. Delos F., on "A Municipal Program," 9; on fundamental principles of Municipal Program of 1900, 10.

Wilson, President Woodrow, on initiative and referendum, 170.

Woodruff, Clinton Rogers, examination of municipal government by, 12; on commission-manager plan, 17; on selection of city experts by civil service examinations, 274.

Zueblin, Prof., on personal obligation of citizenship and official duty, 291.

(1)

DARTMOUTH COLLEGE
3 3311 01991 3419

THE CIVIL WAR

in

FAUQUIER COUNTY

Virginia

Eugene M. Scheel

The Fauquier National Bank
—Fauquier's Bank

Warrenton • View Tree • The Plains
New Baltimore • Catlett
347-2700

The Civil War in Fauquier County, Virginia © 1985 by Eugene M. Scheel. Printed in the United States of America. No part of this book may be used or reproduced in any manner without written permission except for brief quotations embodied in critical articles and reviews. For information address Eugene M. Scheel, Rt. 1, Box 119, Waterford, Virginia 22190.

FIRST EDITION
JUNE, 1985

Library of Congress Catalog Card Number 85-80333

DEDICATION

To the People of Fauquier County
And Especially the Many Who Gave Their Lives
To Preserve Freedom

FOREWORD

This history presents the war in a chronological format, adding the background of how the county appeared and acted, both in the war years, and the times preceding and following the conflict. In her foreward to *The Years of Anguish*, Clara McCarty noted that book was to "be regarded as a part of a progressive project." This book continues that project.

The Fauquier National Bank, in its care to preserve the heritage of this area, has sponsored both the book and the accompanying Map of Fauquier County. My special thanks to C. Hunton Tiffany, president, the officers and staff of the bank, and Diane G. Granger, director of marketing, for their encouragement and helpful ideas.

Thank you's also go to the hundreds of persons who helped me in regard to the book and map, and in addition to those cited on the map, area Civil War historian John E. Divine thoroughly read the final draft and offered many suggestions; Harper's Ferry National Historical Park historian Dennis E. Frye garnered materials on Fauquier units at The Ferry in 1859; Alan Poe of the *Fauquier Democrat* read the printed copy and provided valued thoughts on design and production; Al Schmitz of Williams & Heintz, printers of the map, did yeoman work to insure its excellence; Edie Fishback and Alice Moriarty typed the manuscript with fewer errors than I could have imagined; and Gertrude Trumbo proofread the printed pages and saw to it that such spellings as 'comradery' never made it past my typewriter.

Libraries were most resourceful in their loan of books and research materials. Besides the top-notch staff at the Fauquier County Library, Warrenton, the repositories of Alexandria, Culpeper, Fairfax, Leesburg, Purcellville, and Winchester deserve citations. The Huntington Library, San Marino, California; Library of Congress; National Archives; U.S. Army Military History Institute, Carlisle Barracks, Pennsylvania; Virginia Historical Society; and Virginia State Library allowed me to probe through their holdings.

And I must not forget the many writers, editors, and compilers of previous materials, published and unpublished, who contributed unknowingly to this project. For this century, Nancy Chappelear Baird, B. Curtis Chappenlear, Marvin D. Gore, Frances G. Foster, John K. Gott, Fairfax Harrison, Emily G. Ramey, and William Wallace Phillips especially come to mind.

CONTENTS

Dedication
Foreward

1	Profile	1
2	Preparing For War	10
3	The Front Draws Close	19
4	Invasion And Repulse	26
5	Fall And Winter Raids	40
6	The Debatable Land	54
7	Meade's Army	61
8	Guerillas and Bushwackers	71
9	The Rebuilding	88
	Sources For Fauquier, 1856-1870	100
	Where To Find The Rosters	107
	Index	110

Photographic Plates

I	Three Black Horse Privates	18
II	Warrenton, The Alexandria Pike	between 18-19
III	Warrenton, Courthouse Square	18-19
IV	Rappahannock Station	25-26
V	Catlett	25-26
VI	Warrenton, Station Area	25-26
VII	The Springs Hotel	25-26
VIII	The Springs Bridge	39-40
IX	Fugitives Fording Rappahannock	39-40
X	An 1862 Map of Fauquier	52-53
XI	The Officers And The Lady	52-53
XII	Infantry Pose At Bealeton	60-61
XIII	Fife and Drum Corps At Bealeton	60-61
XIV	The Camp At Castle Murray	60-61
XV	Officers Dine At Bealeton	60-61
XVI	The War Correspondents	70-71
XVII	Repairing After Stuart's Raid	70-71
XVIII	Warrenton Junction	70-71
XIX	The Camps At Rappahannock Station	70-71
XX	Mosby's Men	87-88

1. PROFILE

*A suspected slave revolt — The county in 1860 —
In the slaves' words*

1856-1860

Fauquier's war comes to most of us through stories growing better with passing years: trusted servants carrying and hiding people and food; attractive women defying the enemy with bold looks and strong words, goods and even men tucked underneath their skirts; hiding places always under threat of burning; stragglers demanding food and valuables, encountering women alone; nip-and-tuck visits of Rebs and Yanks, sometimes exchanging shots, but more often missing each other by a cloud of dust. And then there were the diarists, notably Eliza Dulany, Amanda Edmonds, Catherine Hopley, and Edward Carter Turner — mixing the everyday with the suddenness — their jottings complementing and contradicting a host of Northern chroniclers.

The untold unrest began as the county prepared for Christmas, in the year 1856. By early December rumors had also surfaced in Culpeper, Orange, and Rappahannock. Slaves were gathering arms, and at an appointed time, rumored to be Christmas Day, they would revolt. John G. Beckham, a prominent Warrenton merchant, asked the town council on December 13th to do something, and with the council's words, "in view of the uneasiness existing with regard to the Negro population," they divided the town into nine sections, each under direction of a councilman, and asked citizens to serve on neighborhood night watches. The council also appointed a four-man police force. William Johnson, John W. Parkinson, Thomas B. Fisk, and Sergeant Edgar N. Cologne, and placed a heavy fine, $100 to $500, on persons selling firearms or weapons to slaves and free Negroes.

Warrenton's Richards Payne, a wealthy lawyer, presided over the county court. Three days before Christmas he and his fellow justices, Silas B. Hunton, William J. Morgan, and Henry F. Kemper, heard similar requests to sound an alert, but the foursome refused to appoint a patrol, an action readily taken by the Culpeper County Court a week before. The Fauquier Court did, however, forward copies of their action to the various local justices, and if these justices saw fit, they could appoint a patrol to keep order. The occasion never arose, for Christmas and New Year's passed without incident. On January 7th, 1857, the Town of Warrenton, some ninety dollars poorer — four dollars a day paid to the four-man police team — abandoned its new lawkeepers and night watch.

Less than three years to John Brown, but they were years disturbed only by the pre-Christmas do you remember's.

Many 19th-century writers imply in their descriptions of Fauquier that the county today looks nearly the same as it looked one hundred or more years ago. And as the following statistics indicate, they were correct.

Census-taker Robert Henry Downman counted 21,706 people living in Fauquier County when he made his rounds in the fall of 1860. The county's population had been nearly the same for a generation. Fifty-two percent of the population were black, and 821 of the 11,276 blacks were free. One hundred ninety-eight persons or nearly two percent of the 10,430 white citizens were born in another country — Ireland was the most common answer. Of free families, white and black, there were 2,111 — an average family size of about five. For comparisons, Fauquier today has 38,000 persons, and an average family size of 2.9. The county's rural population has not changed appreciably since 1860, and in 1960, before the advent of subdivisions, the county had 24,000 persons. About ten percent of 1860's population lived in towns, six in all: Warrenton, Upperville, Salem, Paris, Rectortown, and New Baltimore.

The ninety percent were farmers, who, with the aid of slave labor, cultivated some 269,000 acres of the county's total 422,400. Today there are 248,000 acres of farm land. 'Cultivated' land sold for $16-$22 an acre, and included the 'Old Field' — land improved in the last half-decade or so, but currently not used. When 'New Field' fertility waned, the Old Field would become the New — typical of the Southern system of crop rotation. On this land grew 717,450 bushels of corn, 280,300 bushels of wheat, 178,900 bushels of oats, and other crops, including 271,230 pounds of tobacco, once a staple. To an experienced eye the crops would have looked mighty thin; yields, twenty or so bushels of corn an acre, and half that for wheat, were a quarter of today's average. Today's viniculturists might note that Fauquier grapes produced 383 gallons for the commercial market.

In 1860 there were 6,721 horses, 5,489 milk cows, 23,192 head of cattle, 24,754 sheep, and 26,912 swine. Today there are half as many horses and less than a fifth of the sheep and swine. The cattle and cow population remains stable.

In all, perhaps the biggest difference an observant person would have noticed concerned the stone and rail fences. Animals were fenced out, not in.

As with all Piedmont counties the main industry was the blacksmith shop; scores stood by strategic corners and crossroads. According to the census, however, the county had seventeen; undoubtedly many smiths told the census-taker that their shop was for private use — a way to avoid taxes.

At least twenty-eight water-powered mills punctuated stream bottoms. And as with the smiths, several millers claimed their manufactures were for plantation use only; they, too, were not counted. Isham Keith's and John Ambler's woolen mills at Waterloo were the county's largest employers with twenty-six hands between them (ten women). Each mill was valued at $32,000, some five times the cost of a typical mill. To give an idea of wage scales, the mill paid its workers an average salary of $210 a year. A dollar a day — in general the cost of growing a bushel of wheat and corn for sale — was considered a good daily wage.

Eleven lumber mills, nine wagon and cart makers, and seven land-plaster and lime kilns were the other main manufactures. The census also reported five shoemakers, five tanners, five saddlery and harness shops, and four carriage makers.

The total real estate of the county was worth $13,308,772, or about $31.25 an acre. Personal property was valued at $14,052,831. Thus the average free family had assets of land and property worth $12,960. Little wonder that Fauquier was so high in the pecking order of Virginia counties. Only Loudoun, its neighbor to the north, sported that type of wealth.

Today's newspapers gleefully announce the county's wealthiest; yesteryear's were more discreet. But if not they would have featured Upperville's Robert B. Bolling, of Bollingbrook, with land worth $315,830 and personal property worth $591,846; then, he had nine children. Fauquier's second wealthiest man was John Augustine Washington of Waveland, near Salem, soon to be slain in battle. A collateral descendent of George, his lands were worth $212,000, his personal property $125,000. William H. Gaines, Sr., a retired Warrenton merchant, had personal property valued at $189,875, and land at $97,700. Others whose wealth came to about $200,000 were Bealeton's John G. Beale, Sr., for whom the village was named; Richard H. Foote of Loretto, near Warrenton; R. C. Ambler, a physician living near Linden, and Eliza L. Marshall, living near Waterloo, wealthiest of the Marshalls. Four other Marshalls, all living near Markham, had assets of more than $160,000. Most of the wealthy were, in today's terminology, gentlemen farmers.

An anomaly was John W. Kincheloe, Fauquier's delegate to the General Assembly. He rented out quarters and had personal property assets of only $6,400. But even so, he was wealthier than the county's most prosperous blacks, Warrenton-area farmer Daniel Warner and Warrenton butcher Thomas Hudnal. Each owned land and house worth $1,000, and had personal property worth, respectively, $75 and $50.

Schooling was a subject untouched in the 1860 census, but a decade before — and statistics would have been about the same — 554 children attended twenty-five 'public' schools taught by twenty-seven teachers. One puts quotes around public because attendance was not compulsory, and mostly poor children went to these schools. The more affluent, numbering 350, attended sixteen academies taught by twenty-four 'professors' and misses. Five hundred and twenty-six adults, or about ten percent of the free population eighteen or over, admitted they could not read or write.

Fauquier was certainly a church-going county in the prewar decade. There were forty-three houses of worship with congregations of 11,400 — a number equal to the free population. Baptists had fourteen churches and 4,200 members, Methodists had seventeen churches and 4,050 members, Episcopalians six and 1,575, and Presbyterians three and 1,025. Three Union churches had 550 members. Union had nothing to do with politics, but designated a church for non-denominational Christians.

Most churches had slave members, usually house servants and trusted field hands. The Baptists proselytized widely, and their Potomac Association Minutes for 1856, the only year a designation between white and black members appears, indicate that about forty percent of their membership was black. Their largest church, Long Branch at Halfway, had 105 blacks among its 215 members, their second largest, Broad Run, had 75 blacks among 198 members, and their third largest, Liberty, had 116 blacks among its 165 members. Congregations west of Warrenton and in Upper Fauquier had few blacks. An unsigned editorial in a March, 1858, Warrenton *Flag of '98* called for a church for the town's slaves, but the plea went unheeded. The only known place of worship specifically for Negroes was the Thompson bush-meeting grounds, north of Goldvein and the site of today's Clever's Oak Church.

Twenty-seven county post offices — twenty today — bore some unfamiliar names. Today's Remington was officially Mill View, but everyone called the village Rappahannock Station. Similarly, there was a nearby New Brighton Post Office, but then as today, people called the hamlet Fayettesville. Delaplane was Piedmont Station or just Piedmont, described as "a brick depot, a brick house, and a brick store — all new and substantial." One had to specify Salem Fauquier on their letters, or the missive was likely to end up at Salem, Roanoke County; hence the 1881 change to Marshall. The Plains, though a name penned on letters since 1831, persisted as White Plains. Calverton was officially Owl Run, but all called the railroad junction Warrenton Junction. Warrenton Springs, a summer resort of note, also known by the unwieldy title of Warrenton or Fauquier White Sulphur Springs, locally went by The Springs. Goldvein was called Grove Church, even though there were two churches named Grove. Three other unfamiliar huddles of buildings occasionally turning up in war documents are Rector's Cross Roads, now Atoka, where Mosby organized; Barbee's Cross Roads, now Hume; and Three-Mile Switch or Three-Mile Junction, now Casanova. One village has changed its location. Somerville was at today's Ensor's Shop, and today's Somerville was called White Ridge.

Post office villages usually contained a store, blacksmith shop, a few houses, makeshift pens and outbuildings, and if on a stream of some formidability, a mill. Muddier-than-usual streets and dirtier-than-usual surroundings were the norm. One is not surprised that in such a milieu churches chose the countryside. Of the six towns, census-taker Downman thought it necessary to list only two, Upperville and Warrenton, as distinct settlements. The others blended in and out of the woods and fields.

But Salem, listed as a town in 1850, deserves some note. Some forty houses, five stores, three churches, an academy, a physician, and 300 people lined a wide, half-mile-long stretch of the Manassas Gap or Thoroughfare Gap Road, depending on which way you were headed. Paris, described by a

Southerner as "a very forlorn village," and by a Northerner as a "dirty little village," had three stores, Ben Adams' hotel, two churches, and some twenty homes. Its population was about 200, most living along the somewhat-less-dusty Main Street as the Ashby Gap Turnpike occasionally received a load of rock. Rectortown, buoyed by merchant Alfred Rector's insistence that the Manassas Gap Railroad (he was a large stockholder) loop past his store and warehouse, was about the size of Paris. New Baltimore, home of the noted academy for boys and Ball's Tavern, where Lafayette and Andrew Jackson stopped, had two stores, some twenty-five homes, and 150 people. And lest one think that six or seven crowded into a house, populations given in gazetteers included slaves, but excluded their dwellings, considered outbuildings.

Upperville, called "a very odd looking place," was Fauquier's second largest town with 239 whites, 10 free blacks, and 149 slaves. In addition to four churches, three stores, two taverns, a hotel, and an academy, the community boasted of tanners, cabinet-makers, a smattering of lawyers and doctors, and a dental surgeon. Several Irishmen, builders of the turnpike road to Piedmont Station in 1854-1855, added spark. Its sixty-four "houses are scattering," noted a contemporary.

Warrenton, with a population of about 1,200, including 564 whites and 40 free blacks, could not best the number of Upperville's houses of worship, but there were fifteen laywers, five physicians, five academies, and a 600-volume subscription library. Businesses included fifteen stores, three bakeries, three tailors, two boot makers, druggists, and jewelers, and two coach and carriage makers, George F. Booth and Charles Bragg, the wartime mayor. Antoine Manyett operated an iron foundry. There were two established newspapers, one Democratic in politics, the other, Whig. Three hostelries beckoned the traveler, the Warren Green, Warrenton House, and Farmers' Hotel. Wags said let the horse do the choosing; his feed and board ran $1.20 a day, the rider's ran a dollar.

Several gave their occupations unusual twists. Samuel Phillips listed himself as a "Daguerrean Artist" — we would say photographer. Richard Shirley called himself a "Negro trader" — and indeed his ads, "I will pay the highest cash prices . . .," appeared weekly in Warrenton and Alexandria newspapers. John Scott, Jr., proudly told census-taker Downman he was a Captain in the "Black Horse."

Then as today the main roads to Washington, Winchester, Fredericksburg, and The Springs converged at the courthouse. But then, the square was larger and amorphous, and in every direction brick and frame buildings packed in on each other. It was a Warrenton visible until the fire of 1909. Six compact blocks from Main to Lee, and from Ashby to Sixth, held most of the town. Residences were spreading outward along Winchester, Culpeper, and Lee Streets. Board sidewalks lined Main Street, and so pedestrians could avoid mud, stepping stones jutted out at corners and marked a path down to the railroad. There, an open wooden platform served as a station, and about stood several new stores and warehouses.

Writer Alexander Hunter, in remembrances fifty years later, pictured Warrenton as "a rushing, thriving trade center. Huge wagons and vans came over the mountains from the rich counties, loaded with wheat, corn, and oats; the housewife sent her poultry and dried fruit; great herds of cattle wended their way to this town . . . astute merchants . . . the richest town, per capita, in the whole South."

Connecting these communities, and the corners and crossroads, was a transportation network similar to today's, except roads were narrower, and, in season, dustier or muddier. Complainers in Fauquier, and their counterparts in adjacent counties, took pride in calling their roads the worst in Virginia. One described a road to Warrenton as the "worst to be found within the metes and boundaries of the Western World." Four toll roads, the Warrenton Pike — called the Alexandria Pike in Fauquier — the Waterloo Turnpike, Ashby Gap Turnpike, and the Piedmont-to-Upperville Turnpike, sometimes got loads of stone dumped on them, courtesy of the tolls, from three cents a horse to ten cents a cart and twenty-four cents a wagon — vehicles paying half price on the return trip. A toll-gate stood every six miles or so. Over the Halfway Road bumped the county's last stage, a link between The Plains railroad depot and Middleburg, where the stage line still plied to Alexandria.

As today, there were two railroads, then called the Manassas Gap and Orange and Alexandria. The O & A had its Warrenton Branch, leaving the main line at Warrenton Junction. Edward C. Marshall, president of the Manassas Gap, did not let his trains run on Sunday. Aside the single track of each line ran the county's only overhead wires — the telegraph.

Some words should be said about the black population. In years past Fielding Lewis Marshall and Alexander Hunter had been their spokesmen, for they were Fauquier's leading chroniclers of the mid 19th century. In 1912 Hunter wrote: "The farmers of Fauquier held their slaves by love rather than fear. They had steady but easy work; there was no driving; none of the brutality portrayed in Uncle Tom's Cabin. Their food was abundant, every family having their own garden, chickens, and hogs. Their holidays were many. They were well-clothed and had not a care on their minds."

Here, in the slaves' words, is ante-bellum Fauquier. William Brown looked eighty when he was interviewed in 1856; nearly bald, what little hair he had was gray. His countenance was pleasant but subdued. "I am not eighty — only sixty-three — but I am worked down, and worn out with hard work. When I began work in the morning I could usually see a little red in the east, and I worked 'till ten before eating. At two I would eat again, and then work, at some seasons, until ten at night. Then I would have a pint of meal and a roasted herring. Tired and hungry, the slaves are obliged to steal; they are so hungry they will steal whatever they can find to eat.

"I could generally find the tobacco worms by a hole through the leaf. But in the heat of the day they get under a leaf and do not eat; and the hands passing along, breaking off suckers, don't always see them. Then the overseer follows along behind, looking, and if he finds the worm the man is called back to kill it, and he gets five or six blows from the hickory or cowhide.

"In hoeing corn the overseer will perhaps stand in the shade of a tree, where he can see the slaves; if they slacken work he calls out to hurry them up, but he don't like to leave the shade of the tree, it is so hot. But sometimes, if a man drops behind, the overseer comes up, gives him some lashes, and then goes back to his tree."

Silas Jackson remembered his birthdate as 1846 or 1847 when he was interviewed in 1937. He was born near Ashby Gap, and his grandfather had run away to Philadelphia, saved $350, and purchased his grandmother.

"Where I was they raised tobacco, wheat, and corn. I have had a taste of all the work, besides of digging and clearing up new ground to increase the acreage. We began work on Monday and worked until Saturday. That day we were allowed to work for ourselves and to garden or to do extra work. When we could get work, or work on someone else's place, we got a pass from the overseer to go off the plantation, but to be back by nine o'clock on Saturday night or when cabin inspection was made. Sometime we could earn as much as fifty cents a day, which we used to buy cakes, candies, or clothes.

"On Saturday each slave was given ten pounds corn meal, a quart of black strap, six pounds of fat back, three pounds of flour and vegetables, all raised on the farm. All of the slaves hunted, or those who wanted, hunted rabbits, opossums, or fished. These were our choice food as we did not get anything special from the overseer. Our food was cooked by our mothers or sisters, and for those who were not married by the old women and men assigned for that work. Each family was given three acres to raise their chickens or vegetables, and if a man raised his own food he was given ten dollars at Christmas time extra, besides his presents.

"When warm weather came each slave was given something, the women, linsey goods or gingham clothes, the men, overalls, muslin shirts, top, and underclothes, two pair of shoes, and a straw hat to work in. In the cold weather we wore woolen clothes, all made at the sewing table.

"My master was named Tom A____ — a meaner man was never born in Virginia — brutal, wicked, and hard. He always carried a cowhide with him. If he saw anyone doing something that did not suit his taste, he would have the slave tied to a tree, man or woman, and then would cowhide the victim until he got tired; or sometimes the slave would faint.

"The A____'s home was a large stone mansion, with a porch on three sides. Wide halls in the center, up-and-down stairs, numerous rooms, and a stone kitchen built on the back connected with dining room.

"Mrs. A ____ was kind and lovely to her slaves when Mr. A____ was out. They did not have any children of their own, but they had boys and girls of his own sister, and they were much like him. They had maids or private waiters for the young men if they wanted them.

"Tom A____ was a large slave owner having more than 100 slaves on his farm. They were awakened by blowing of the horn before sunrise by the overseer, started work at sunrise and worked all day to sundown, with not time to go to the cabin for dinner; you carried your dinner with you. The slaves were driven at top speed and whipped at the snap of the finger, by the overseer. We had four overseers on the farm, all hired white men. I have seen men beaten until they dropped in their tracks or knocked over by clubs, women stripped down to their waist and cowhided.

"I have heard it said that Tom A____'s father went to one of the cabins late at night; the slaves were having a secret prayer meeting. He heard one slave ask God to change the heart of his master and deliver him from slavery so that he may enjoy freedom. Before the next day the man disappeared, no one ever seeing him again; but after that down in the swamp at certain times of the moon, you could hear the man who prayed in the cabin praying. When the old man A____ died, just before he died he told the white Baptist minister that he had killed Zeke for praying, and that he was going to Hell.

"There was a stone building on the farm; I saw it this summer while visiting in Virginia. The old jail, it is now used as a garage. Downstairs there were two rooms, one where the whipping was done, and the other used by the overseer. Upstairs was used for women and girls. The iron bars have corroded, but you can see where they were. I have never seen slaves sold on the farm, but I have seen them taken away, and brought there. Several times I have seen slaves chained taken away and chained when they came.

"No one was taught to read or write. On Sunday the slaves who wanted to worship would gather at one of the large cabins with one of the overseers present and have their church. After which the overseer would talk. When communion was given the overseer was paid for staying there with half of the collection taken up; sometimes he would get twenty-five cents. No one could read the Bible. Sandy Jasper, Mr. A____'s coachman, was the preacher. He would go to the white Baptist church on Sunday with family and would be better informed because he heard the white preacher.

"Twice each year, after harvest and after New Year's, the slaves would have their protracted meeting or their revival, and after each closing they would baptize in the creek. Sometimes in the winter they would break the ice singing 'Going To The Water,' or some other hymn of that nature. And at each funeral, the A____'s would attend the service conducted in the cabin where the deceased was, from there taken to the slave graveyard, a lot dedicated for that purpose, situated about three-quarters of a mile from the cabins near a hill.

"There were a number of slaves on our plantation who ran away. Some were captured and sold to a Georgia trader; others were never captured. To intimidate the slaves, the overseers were connected with the patrollers, not only to watch our slaves, but sometimes for the rewards for other slaves who had run away from other plantations. This feature caused a great deal of trouble between whites and blacks. In 1858, two white men were murdered near Warrenton on the road by colored people. It was never known whether by free people or slaves.

"When work was done the slaves retired to their cabins; others cooked or rested or did what they wanted. We did not work on Saturdays unless harvest times, then Saturdays were days of work. On Christmas day Mr. A⸺ would call all the slaves together, give them presents, money, after which they spent the day as they liked. On New Year's Day we were all scared; that was the time for selling, buying, and trading slaves. We did not know who was to go or come.

"I do not remember playing any particular game; my sport was fishing. You see, I did not believe in ghost stories nor voodooism. We boys used to take the horns of a dead cow or bull, cut the end off of it; we could blow it, some having different notes. We could tell who was blowing, and from what plantation.

"When a slave took sick, she or he would have to depend on herbs, salves, or other remedies prepared by someone who knew the medicinal value. When a valuable hand took sick, one of the overseers would go to Upperville for a doctor."

A score of years ago, old-timers in the Hopewell area could still recite a song slaves sang going to work: "Cold frosty morning, nigger feel good. Axe on his shoulder, going to the wood. Little to eat, 'cept corn cake and fat. And the white folks grumble, if you eat much of that."

2. PREPARING FOR WAR

The march to Harper's Ferry — Breckinridge wins in Fauquier; Lincoln gets one vote — Secession Resolutions — Scott and Marr elected — War preparations

OCTOBER, 1859-MAY 23, 1861

Turbulence came again with the October-to-November 1859 days of John Brown's raid, trial, and execution. Newspaper accounts following the October 16th Harper's Ferry raid placed the number of invaders at more than 250 (there were twenty-two), and it became the thing to do for bands of armed men to ride as quickly as possible into Jefferson and Clarke Counties, where rumors of slave revolts and attempts to rescue Brown were rampant, and where impromptu camps of itchy-fingered irregulars lined roads and railsides.

On official duty in Jefferson County were three Fauquier units, the Mountain Rangers, Black Horse Troop, and the 85th Regiment Militia. The Mountain Rangers had organized in 1852 to protect northern Fauquier from Manassas Gap Railroad workers—those Irishmen again—who might have gotten out of line. Thomas L. Settle, the venerable Paris physician who became a surgeon in Ashby's Cavalry, in 1907 wrote Clarence Thomas, first biographer of Turner Ashby, and told how it all started: "The employees raised a racket in the shape of a riot. Ashby promptly gathered together a few brave and courageous spirits, marched to the scene of trouble and speedily restored peace and order." After the incident, railroad president Edward C. Marshall, who had just purchased Rose Bank, the Ashby homeplace, from the debt-ridden family, paid Ashby to organize some friends to patrol the railroad. The men stayed together, and when hostilities broke out were mustered into the Virginia Militia. Col. Robert E. Lee, commander of the relief force at Harper's Ferry, assigned Captain Ashby's forty-five men to guard the railroad bridge. Newspapers sometimes referred to the unit as the Upper Fauquier Cavalry or Black Hawk Rangers.

The Black Horse Troop, sometimes called the Lower Fauquier Cavalry or Black Horse Rangers, were at Charles Town, guarding the prison where John Brown was confined. N. M. Green once said that Brown, breaking a long silence, told him: "You Virginians are a remarkable people. I know you feel a bitter hostility toward me, and regard me as the worst of your enemies and desire my death. I have been for weeks entirely at your mercy and have yet to hear an insulting word or receive any unkind treatment at your hands."

The idea for a military company from Lower Fauquier was brought up at a dinner party hosted by William H. Payne. John Scott, Jr., a guest and fellow Warrenton lawyer, said he would volunteer as leader. Only recently had he become a convert to slavery, his mind changed by Georgia Senator John MacPherson Berrien. After one of the 1859 spring court days, Payne and Scott addressed an assemblage and several men enlisted. They elected Scott captain, and Robert Randolph and Charles Gordon lieutenants. Scott chose the name, a play on the White Horse, reputed emblem of the Anglo-Saxons when they invaded Britain in the fifth and sixth centuries. Former cavalry captain H. H. Jones put the men through their first paces on June 18th, and many wore the required black plume and had black mounts. Katherine Isham Keith, who collected reminiscences about the troop in 1923, wrote that early joiners were often sons of planters who would inherit land and follow in the stead of forefathers. Others were young, foot-loose, and fancy-free. But in all "the love of soil and of State beat in their blood as a natural inheritance."

As rumors of attempts to save Brown increased, two days before his scheduled execution, a portion of three companies of Fauquier's 85th Regiment Militia under Col. John Emmett Scruggs arrived in Jefferson County. Some weeks later an oyster and champagne supper ended the adventure, and the December 22nd Charles Town *Virginia Free Press* noted: "The military companies which have been here for the last fortnight have left us." The ladies of Warrenton fêted their return with a Black Horse Ball.

One disappointed group of young men were the Warrenton Rifles, hurriedly organized that November by Capt. John Quincy Marr, ex-Fauquier sheriff and former instructor of military tactics at VMI. His riflemen never made it to 'Jeff'son,' possibly because of their perceived immaturity. Marr was the type of man to whom a mother could entrust her eighteen-year-old, and Warrenton ladies had dubbed his recruits "The Warrenton Babies."

Eighteen-sixty came without incident. The companies trained periodically, their meetings more for camaraderie than for purpose. But without doubt they questioned the identity of free Negroes and checked the passes of slaves. Beaver Dam Creek, the unofficial boundary between the abolitionist Quakers of Loudoun and the proslavery people to the south, meandered just a few miles north of the Fauquier-Loudoun line, and the main escape route led under the shadow of the Blue Ridge, and wound among its sparsely populated foothills.

On June 24th the county court set its annual budget — $35,340.78, with $20,000 of that levy allotted to "volunteer military companies." Their first court-appointed duty, authorized December 24th, was to set up a system of patrols. Turner Ashby's Mountain Rangers were responsible for the region west of Carter's Run and north of the Manassas Gap Railroad, the suspect area of slave escapes; Marr's Warrenton Rifles and George W. Deatherage's Warrenton Home Guard were to cover the area in and about town; and John Scott, Jr.'s Black Horse Troop was to guard the rest of the county. The court reminded the patrollers "to use the utmost prudence and humanity in the discharge of their duties," and to allow subordinate patrols "only when and where necessary."

Barbarossa was introduced to the county in 1860. The learned Professor

Bacon at the Fauquier Seminary would have known that the strange name was Arabic, and meant Red Beard, a pseudonym for the author of *The Lost Principle of The Federal Government or The Sectional Equilibrium*, a work as complex as its title. Those in the know correctly surmised that Barbarossa was John Scott, Jr., the Black Horse leader. His book, a defense of slavery addressed to the young men of the slaveholding section, was more talked about than read, but as knowledge of authorship spread, its message — the U.S. Constitution upheld a compact among free and slave states and territories — strengthened the county's sentiment for state's rights. Scott gave the county another surprise that fall when he announced he would relinquish command of the Black Horse and offer his services to the governor of South Carolina.

On election day that November a record number of Fauquier men cast ballots for president, nearly all voting for two middle-of-the-roaders who had left the Democratic Party. Forty-seven votes separated Kentuckian John Cabell Breckinridge, the victor, and Tennesseean John Bell, the winner in Virginia. Breckinridge's strong showings in the small-farm precincts of New Baltimore and Liberty, and Bell's large margins in the large-plantation precincts of Upperville, Paris, Salem, and Landmark, indicate that voters perceived Bell — owner of many slaves — as the man who, while having no love for abolitionists, had no sympathy for extremists who might topple the status quo. Democrat Stephen A. Douglas, perceived as anti-slave, garnered a smattering of twenty-nine votes to Breckinridge's 1,035. The Alexandria *Gazette* did not bother to mention that Abraham Lincoln received one vote, cast at Salem by Henry Dixon, pistol in hand. Later it was no surprise that this testy militia colonel, a born Virginia aristocrat from the foot of Big Cobbler, went north to be a colonel in the Federal Army. Many said the retribution was just when Dixon was killed in an Alexandria street duel after the war.

In the words of South Carolina's state convention president, Abraham Lincoln's election proved "there is no common bond of sympathy or intent between the North and the South and all efforts to preserve this Union will be not only fruitless but fatal to the less-numerous section." The state seceded December 20th, 1860.

Within a month six states had left the Union and the Virginia Legislature had passed two significant actions. They approved of Gov. John Letcher's call for a February 4th national peace convention in Washington to work out Constitutional differences, and against Governor Letcher's wishes they voted to convene a February 13th state convention to consider seceding from the Union.

On January 17th, at Orlean, Jaquelin Ambler Marshall, son of the Chief Justice, organized a meeting and proposed two candidates for the secession convention, John Quincy Marr and Robert Eden Scott. Though absent, both were chosen. Hearing of the honor, next day Marr prepared a speech; Scott soon followed suit. Both declined to take a specific position due to the changing political situation, and if they differed their parting was noticeable only in language, Marr's forceful and stentorian, Scott's calmer and diplomatic — befitting a man to whom Lincoln had offered the post of Secretary of the Navy.

Captain Marr's sister, Fannie, particularly liked this paragraph: "As for myself, whether in a representative capacity or as a private citizen, my fortunes are indissolubly connected with Virginia, the land of my birth, and by whom I have been nurtured with more than a parent's care, and on whose bosom I shall repose when time with me shall be no more. 'She shall know no peril but that it shall be my peril, no conflict but that it shall be my conflict, and there is no abyss or ruin to which she may sink, so low, but that I shall share her fall.'"

At Warrenton on January 28th, hundreds packed the courthouse and others milled about in the cold. They had assembled to choose candidates for the state convention. Mayor John Emmett Scruggs opened with some words, and then County Court Justice Silas B. Hunton appeared at the podium, flanked by Scruggs, Col. Winter Payne, and C. McLean Johnson. Scruggs and Johnson, appointed to take down the minutes, were combining politics and business; they were, respectively, editors of the rival Warrenton *Weekly Whig* and *The Flag of '98*. Payne began to speak, and said he would propose six resolutions — after the candidates had their say.

Robert Eden Scott stepped to the podium and for thirty-five minutes spoke about preserving the Union, peaceable solutions, and the need "to save my own and my neighbor's hearth-stones from the bloody horrors of Civil War." However, he said that if a state tolerates slavery, so be it. The federal government must respect diversity and should not forcibly coerce any state. William H. Payne of the Black Horse then gave another lengthy address, and John Quincy Marr spoke briefly. Each faction loudly applauded their man.

Finally, Winter Payne read his resolutions. The first and second referred to Article 4, Section 2, of the United States Constitution, and stated that since northern states refused to return escaped slaves, the Constitution had been violated and the Union thereby dissolved. The third resolution, in Payne's words, said, "Withdrawal of the Southern States from the Union, now existing, is neither revolution, treason, or secession from a constitutional Union, but simply an act declaring a forfeiture of the Union, under the broken convenant." The fourth resolution restated the South's right to resist "coercion, direct or indirect," and the fifth asserted that Virginia should remain a slave state.

Colonel Payne's sixth resolution, though, spoke to bringing together the factions of dissent, a close most unlike the warlike Culpeper County Resolutions adopted the day after Christmas. "We cherish undiminished attachment for the constitutional Union created by our fathers," Payne intoned. "And we hereby pledge ourselves, each to the other, to use all fair and honorable means, with due diligence to construct the same, with such additional guarantees as will place the rights and institutions of the South beyond the reach of future molestation."

Those used to listening to protracted sermons at all-day revivals were not prone to go home after a mere two hours, and in response to loud and repeated calls, James Vass Brooke spoke for a half-hour, and B. Howard Shackelford took the podium and had his say. Then, Winter Payne, in a delivery the secretaries described as "animated and stirring," nominated Shackelford as a Fauquier delegate to the state convention. After the nomination was ratified by a unanimous vote, Shackelford declared himself a candidate. Throughout January similar meetings enlivened the squares of Virginia communities.

On February 4th John Quincy Marr, now strongly for secession — if we can believe the Alexandria *Gazette* — and Robert Eden Scott, the moderate, won handily, garnering 1,443 and 1,318 votes, respectively. William H. Payne received 654 tallies and Shackelford, 409. The latter two were strongest in the Catlett, Morrisville, and New Baltimore precincts, and ran poorly in the Farrowsville, Paris, and Salem precincts — an election pattern similar to that of 1860, and an indication that Payne and Shackelford were more extreme in secessionist views. Also on the ballot: Should the secession question be brought to popular vote? 954 agreed, 922 did not. The New Baltimore precinct that had given Shackelford his strongest majority voted 86-5 against popular referendum.

As Richmond church bells rang in the noon hour of February 13th, Robert Eden Scott called to order the convention that was to decide secession. A fellow moderate — indeed as it turned out a strong preservationist — John Janney of Leesburg, Loudoun County, was elected president of the convention. Initially, Marr and Scott believed that secession was to be only a last resort, and moderates such as they dominated the two months of procedural issues and resolutions.

On the home front John Scott, Jr., still made the news. For the while, at least, his South Carolina plans had been forestalled, and in February the Black Horse unanimously elected him captain; his militia rank was now major. Noted the Alexandria *Gazette*, "The Company seemed loth to part with their old commander." The men also elected Alexander Dixon Payne third lieutenant.

Despite the Richmond convention's conservative course, a martial air pervaded Fauquier. Newspaper ads announcing the musters sported cartoons of toy soldiers, and "Attention Black Horse" ads pictured a man on a horse with bugle and plumed hat. Some Black Horsers drilled at Warrenton on first Saturdays, others at Waterloo and Bealeton on second Saturdays, and others at New Baltimore on third Saturdays. The full company drilled at Warrenton on the last Saturday of the month. At Salem on April 1st, physician John A. Adams organized the Wise Dragoons, officially Company H, 6th Regiment, Virginia Cavalry. Also on the 1st, at Warrenton, Robert Eden Scott's son, Robert Taylor Scott, organized the Beauregard Rifles (one of three Virginia military companies to have that name), Company K, 8th Regiment, Virginia Volunteers. On April 6th all commissioned officers of the

44th Regiment Militia were to meet at Salem — "in full uniform," added Col. Gibson J. Howard.

April 4th saw the convention put the matter of secession to a vote; 88-45 the delegates said no, Marr and Scott voting with the majority.

But a week later the South's guns and mortars were goaded into bombarding Fort Sumter, and on April 14th, a Sunday, Lincoln declared war. The president's call for 75,000 militiamen to suppress the insurrection meant that states remaining in the Union, Virginia being one, were to provide their quota. On Monday, former governor Henry Wise, Turner and Richard Ashby, and others, secretly met in Richmond to plan the capture of the U.S. armory and arsenal at Harper's Ferry. On Tuesday, Governor Letcher sent Lincoln a reply to his request for troops: "You have chosen to inaugurate civil war, and having done so, we will meet it in a spirit as determined as the Administration has exhibited toward the South." The same day, at Warrenton, James Vass Brooke organized Company A (1st) of the 12th Battalion, Virginia Light Artillery, also known as Brooke's Battery.

On Wednesday, April 17th, 1861, delegates to the Richmond convention voted to secede from the Union by a vote of 88-55. Scott voted with the majority. Marr was absent, "called home by circumstances of an imperative and controlling character." In late April he returned and belatedly voted 'for.' Most of the pro-Union vote came from delegates of counties soon to be in West Virginia, though both Frederick County delegates voted 'against.' Other surprises in the minority column were Hugh Mortimer Nelson of Clarke, John Armistead Carter of Loudoun, and William Henry Dulany of the Welbourne Dulanys, a delegate from Fairfax. Fauquier-born Eppa Hunton, a delegate from Prince William, voted 'for.' Convention president John Janney's 'no' vote was expected; his subsequent signing of the secession resolution was not.

After the vote Governor Letcher decided to call out Virginia's militia, 18,300 in number, though 11,800 'strong,' if that adjective were to mean 'armed.' However, Letcher would keep the order a secret for three days to allow for the capture of the armory and arsenal at Harper's Ferry and the nation's largest navy yard at Norfolk. Marching to the Ferry on the 17th were combined units of the Mountain Rangers and Black Horse Troop, commanded by Capt. Turner Ashby. Second in command were Black Horse Captains John Scott, Jr., and Welby Carter. But they arrived after retreating Federals had set fire to the works, and again it was picket duty.

One can indeed sense the frustration of these military companies from some notes about the Black Horse, found on the back of an April 28th, 1861, muster roll. The notes explain that forty-six men had been to Harper's Ferry, were there five days, and then were ordered back the 55 miles to Warrenton Springs on April 25th. Immediately they were to march to Dumfries, but after reaching Brentsville, a 20-mile trek, were told to retrace their steps to The Springs, a 14-mile hike. The notes said the men were all uniformed, and reasserted that they were feeling fine. By May they were scattered along the

Orange and Alexandria Railway, guarding bridges. They also had a new leader, Capt. William H. Payne. Captain Scott, weary of forced marches and guard duty, had left for Confederate service in Alabama.

Organization of additional volunteer companies from Fauquier followed Governor Letcher's May 3rd call for more volunteers. The northern Piedmont's recruiter was Brig. Gen. Philip St. George Cocke, a man of journalistic bent. His May 5th notice, shortly affixed to courthouse and tavern doors, read, in part: "Men of the Potomac border, men of the Potomac Military Department, to arms! Your country calls you to her defense. Already you have in spirit responded. You await but the order to march, to rendezvous, to organize, to defend your State, your liberties, and your homes.

"Women of Virginia! Cast from your arms all cowards, and breathe the pure and holy, the high and glowing, inspirations of your nature into the hearts and souls of lover, husband, brother, father, friend!"

"The military spirit in old Fauquier continues high," gushed *The Flag of '98*. The May 9th newspaper spoke of Captain Winfield's Company at Orlean, "ready to march at a moment's notice," Captain Murray's Company, ex-governor Billy Smith's mounted "Silver Greys," a volunteer company being organized at Morrisville, and two reserve corps of Warrenton citizens, The Rev. J.W. Pugh's Lee Guard, and the Home Guard. And as Federal troops were expected to occupy Alexandria, several military companies from that city trained for two-week stints in Warrenton.

Official records note the birth of the following military companies from Fauquier during those turbulent months:

From Orlean, Company B of the 7th Regiment, Virginia Cavalry, Capt. John Q. Winfield's Company, enlisted under Winfield, a Rockingham County boy, some time in April.

From Rectortown, Company B, 8th Regiment, Virginia Volunteers, known as the Rectortown Company or Piedmont Rifles, and organized by their captain, Richard H. Carter, on May 17th. The company also elected Henry Clay Bowie captain, and James W. Pierce and John T. Ashby lieutenants.

From Morrisville, Company I of the 11th Regiment, Virginia Volunteers, known as the Rough and Ready Rifles or Morrisville Company, organized by Andrew Jackson Jones, later a captain, and enlisted under Culpeper's Capt. James Henry Jameson, May 25th.

From Warrenton, Company C, the Fauquier Guards or Captain Edward Murray's Company, 49th Virginia Infantry, organized by Murray and Capt. Buckner M. Randolph, May 28th.

From Farrowsville and Markham, Company G, first known as the Markham Guards, then the Fauquier Artillery or Stribling's Battery, of the 49th Virginia, organized by Capt. Robert M. Stribling, June 22nd.

Fauquier men also served with companies from other counties, especially Company C, the Bull Run Rangers, later the Evergreen Guards, 8th

Regiment, enlisted under Capts. Edmund Berkeley and Robert H. Tyler near Haymarket, May 8th; and the Loudoun Dragoons, the Dulany Troop, Company A, 6th Regiment, Virginia Cavalry, enlisted under their captain, Richard Henry Dulany, at Unison, in June.

As each of the eleven Fauquier companies garnered the fifty men required by law, the captain reported to John M. Forbes, Rice W. Payne, or James Vass Brooke, appointed April 22nd by the county court to distribute funds to arm and equip the military companies. The money came from $20,000 in issued bonds — the amount requested by the court the previous June.

Seven hundred to eight hundred men, paying three dollars for the privilege, had joined these military companies and had elected their officers. But the bulk of Fauquier's 2,400 eligibles for the military — those between eighteen and forty-five — remained in two militia units, the 85th and 44th Regiments, 2nd Division, Virginia Militia. Former Warrenton Mayor and newspaperman Col. John Emmett Scruggs still commanded the 85th, and Col. Gibson Howard, the 44th. Militiamen didn't enjoy the elite status of those in military companies. Militias mustered only three times a year, and one could skip musters by paying a two-dollar fine — seventy-five cents before May, 1860.

Governor Letcher appointed six from Fauquier as officers in the provisional Virginia forces during May, four of whom accepted: On the first, G. B. Horner, First Lieutenant, and Thomas G. Hart, Second Lieutenant. Hart declined, but soon joined the 17th Virginia Infantry and was named Sergeant Major. On the second, Warrenton's J. L. Henderson, Commander in the Virginia Navy, and John Quincy Marr, Lieutenant Colonel, 17th Regiment, Virginia Volunteers. Marr declined, preferring to remain Captain of his Warrenton Rifles. On the sixteenth, Warrenton's Samuel B. Fisher, Surgeon of Volunteer Forces; on the twenty-second, F. M. Sudduth, Second Lieutenant. Three of the six, Hart, Marr, and Sudduth, did not survive the war.

At home the woolen mills were hiring new help. Uniforms were in demand, and Isham Keith's and John Ambler's factories at Waterloo, and the nearby Glen Mills in Culpeper, turned full time for the Confederacy. And as in more recent wars, women and girls met in homes and sewed incessantly, fashioning clothes, bandages, and banners.

Presentations of the colors were special. On April 6th the ladies of town gave the Warrenton Rifles their company flag, received by Captain Marr, and on July 4th Rectortown's James W. Kincheloe, orderly sergeant of the Fauquier Guards, accepted their colors. On receiving the flag he told the throng: "When we return to tell the story of victory, grant us this last boon: Decorate the graves of our slain with the flowers of spring, and their monuments with the mottoes of liberty." Lieutenant Kincheloe was mortally wounded near Smithfield, Jefferson County, and died July 29, 1864.

On May 23rd, for the last time under an old regime, Fauquier voters went to the polls. The action was a formality, and 827 votes affirmed the Virginia Convention's decision to withdraw from the Union. No secret ballot then; the Richmond *Enquirer* reported that one of the four men declining to vote was Elias Edmonds, Fauquier's General Assembly delegate in the 1830s and '40s; the others, "men without property, information, or influence."

PLATE I

Fauquier Historical Society Bulletin   Photographer unknown, ca. 1861
I, 1 (June, 1923)

Warrenton's "Daguerrean Artist," Samuel Phillips, possibly posed these Black Horse privates. Flanking Erasmus Helm, killed in 1862, James Keith (left), later Adjutant of the 4th Virginia Cavalry, long-term circuit-court judge, and President of the Virginia Supreme Court of Appeals; and fellow lawyer Alexander D. Payne, who shortly became 3rd lieutenant, and then captained the troop in October, 1863.

Library of Congress   PLATE II   Timothy H. O'Sullivan, August, 1862

Warrenton, "Quiet, healthful, and the populace civil," remarked Brig. Gen. Rufus King. His troops had occupied town for more than two months when this photograph was taken at the corner of the Alexandria Pike and Diagonal Street. Of the buildings, only the courthouse, declaiming the beginning of the pike, stands today. Mayor Charles Bragg's carriage works can be glimpsed midway up the pike, through the trees at left.

Library of Congress   Timothy H. O'Sullivan, August, 1862

U.S. Army Military History Institute   PLATE III   Timothy H. O'Sullivan, August, 1862

Covered wagons round courthouse square, heading toward the Farmers' Hotel, burned in the 1909 fire. East of the courthouse a brick building occupies the site of the 1928 County Office Building. The brick building at left of inset now houses the Fauquier Pharmacy, and several background buildings stand. The 1854 courthouse façade has not changed, but one wonders why no flag flew that sunny August day.

3. THE FRONT DRAWS CLOSE

*Marr, Tyler, Ashby die — Readying for First Manassas —
A Britisher describes Warrenton*

MAY 24, 1861-MARCH, 1862

Next morning Federal troops crossed the Potomac and seized Alexandria and Arlington Heights. Anticipating the event, many Alexandrians had been staying at Warrenton and The Springs. Shortly after the invasion, Myrta Lockett Avary, a Virginia girl who stopped at Robert Bolling's plantation near Upperville, had this to say of the master of Bollingbrook. One notes Bolling's words because he was, by far, the county's wealthiest planter, and second, because at fifty-six (he appeared old and gray-haired to Miss Avary) he was too old for military duty. And lastly, because when speaking to the younger generation — remember he had nine children — he chose language with care. "I am a believer in state's rights, and I am a Secessionist, I suppose. But I hate to fight the old flag. I hate that." When Miss Avary innocently replied that it was then a good thing that he was exempt from service, Bolling countered: "Ah, no, my dear! Since fighting there is, I wish I could be in it. If I were young enough and strong enough I'd take that sword down and follow Robert Lee. Virginia is invaded."

The May 27th county court, first to meet under the Stars and Bars, ordered the Lee and Home Guards to patrol Warrenton and vicinity. The court also sanctioned a "special police," captained by Hamden A. White, county school superintendent. On White's staff were Thomas E. Saunders, Robert E. Newby, former Mayor William H. Gaines, Alfred Gaskins, John A. Chilton, and briefly, James Vass Brooke. The policemen's role might have been to maintain a semblance of order in an area now traversed by thousands of strangers, and to provide means of communication between the Orange and Alexandria and Manassas Gap Railroad corridors, the two avenues of main travel and telegraph.

Other than these actions there were no written flourishes of rhetoric, and no indications that, indeed, the court now functioned under a new government. Richards Payne, presiding justice of the 1850s, was still at the helm, but joining him were new associates: Isham Keith, Landon Allen, William P. Ficklin, and Staunton G. Embrey.

Most of Fauquier heard the news before the Thursday newspaper arrived. Escorted by somber citizens and the Lee Guard, the body of Capt. John Quincy Marr came home June 1st, early Saturday evening — shot through the heart, people said. Col. John Emmett Scruggs called a meeting and named Marr the "first great martyr in defense of Southern rights." On

Sunday at five, 1,500 attended his funeral. Within two weeks eulogies appeared in the Richmond *Whig* and *Dispatch*, and in the Nashville (Tennessee) *Union and American*, edited by Marr's brother, Thomas S. Marr. He noted that his sibling was the first to "baptize the soil of the Old Dominion with his Patriotic Blood." In the June 13th *Flag* a plaintive poem, "The First To Fall," appeared on page one. The poetess signed her name "Gertie." Historians now qualify the words "first to fall," saying that John Quincy Marr was the first Confederate officer to die in the war.

Of the June 1st, 1861, fight at Fairfax Court House, *The Flag* noted the Warrenton Riflemen were outnumbered eighty to forty: "This was the first fight with the enemy, and Fauquier's men having had the honor of the first to meet them, have most nobly borne aloft the flag of their country and come out of the conflict crowned with victory." The newspaper also mentioned that after Marr's death, former Governor 'Extra Billy' Smith, age sixty-five, took charge of the Riflemen before transferring the command to Col. Richard Ewell. By June 6th Smith announced he would run for Marr's seat on the Virginia Convention. B. Howard Shackelford, the lost leader's former political adversary, became captain of the Riflemen.

On June 19th Fauquier voters again trekked to the polls and handed Smith, a U.S. Congressman until Virginia's secession, a surprising defeat. *The Flag* said Smith refused to campaign, remaining at his military post at Manassas. Underdog James Vass Brooke, meanwhile, diligently convassed the lower end of the county. Brooke's margin was 598-506, with most of his strength in Upper Fauquier. Smith was hardly ready to retire, soon becoming a colonel at First Manassas, Confederate Congressman, brigadier general, and Virginia Governor for the second time.

Home-front newspaper articles, and even ads, now became markedly war-oriented. Merchant John H. Price enticed customers with "Fort Sumter Taken, 75,000 Soldiers In The Field, Marching Directly to Warrenton to lay in a stock of goods. . . ." On June 8th Colonel Scruggs placed a rental ad in *The Flag*, leasing his house, furniture, and meadow, for "three or more months." He warned Lee Guarders and Home Guarders that they, too, were to report for militia duty, and two weeks after Marr's death announced three-day drills June 20-22, at Warrenton and Elk Run. Those not showing up would be considered deserters. By June 27th John M. Martin's Germantown Company trained every Saturday.

And since most Fauquier military companies were now stationed at Manassas, the ladies were busy sending packages. A letter from Capt. J. S. Richardson of the Sumter Volunteers publicly thanked Mrs. Robert C. Newby, Mr. and Mrs. Joseph Settle, Lucy E. Settle, J. W. Settle, Cynthia and Sallie Armstrong, and W. A. Parr for their gifts and concerns of the "wants and comforts of the soldiers amid the toils and hardships of camp life."

In early June Upper Fauquier turned out for the unusual sight of an Alexandria, Loudoun, and Hampshire Railroad locomotive being pulled by twelve yoked oxen along the dusty Manassas Gap Road. General Lee had ordered Eppa Hunton's command to destroy bridges and rolling stock of the Alexandria-to-Leesburg rail line, or remove the stock to the Manassas Gap Railroad. Since the tracks of these railroads did not connect, Hunton had the engine partly dismantled and moved to the Manassas Gap tracks at Alexandria. But they couldn't reassemble the engine properly, and so parts and locomotive began a seventy-mile journey to Piedmont Station, where, we assume, it was placed in working order, along with another A. L. & H. locomotive and cars, pulled by oxen and mules down the Old Carolina Road from Leesburg, and west along the Little River and Ashby Gap Turnpikes. On August 8th the entourage turned the corner at Number Six Road and made its way toward Piedmont.

Saturday, June 16th, marked the first of ten days of wartime fasting and prayer proposed by President Jefferson Davis. He wrote the following words on the 13th, and perhaps the message reached some of the Fauquier churches in time. "With one accord, join in humble and reverential approach to Him in whose hands we are, invoking Him to inspire us with a proper spirit and temper of heart and mind to bear our evils, to bless us with His favor and protection, and to bestow His gracious benediction upon our government and country."

The prayer hit home when people read the June 27th *Flag*. On June 3rd, two miles west of Falls Church, two of the Black Horse Troop were killed, Samuel Gordon and Madison Tyler, son of Circuit Court Judge John Webb Tyler. The July 11th *Flag* reported at length on the deaths in western Virginia of two Mountain Rangers, Oswald Foley and Capt. Richard Ashby. Ashby, according to eyewitnesses, "received a blow from an unseen hand that felled him to the earth," and when found had fourteen distinct wounds besides the blow.

The season of The White Sulphur Springs had commenced as usual. Tidewater ladies with their children and house servants had arrived, fresh from the annual spring shopping trip to Richmond. Only the railroad cars, jammed with soldiers, most polite and considerate, were reminders of an unusual summer. Proprietor Robert Hudgin had not raised rates, and m'lady boarded at $10 a week or $30 a month. White servants stayed for three-quarters the price, black servants and children ten and under for half-price. A New York physician, William Burke, had disseminated The Springs' charms, calling its waters good for dyspepsia and light and comforting to the stomach. But one drank the water 'straight'; mixed with bourbon it ruined the whiskey. The Virginia Legislature had met there in 1849, but not to give the impression that Fauquier Springs was a Greenbrier, Turner Ashby climbed the main ballroom stairs on his horse and drew but the slightest rebuke. All in all a comfortable bathing establishment, similar to today's spas at Capon or Bath.

Diary in hand, Mary Boykin Chestnut arrived July 6th. Her pen tells us that rumors and war talk filled the air: Beauregard could stop 60,000; Lincoln wants $400 million and men in proportion. Joe Johnston was in full retreat.

The Southern girls wore palmetto cockades, honoring the Palmetto Sharpshooters. Northern ladies were suspect. One, she wrote, "exhibited unholy joy as she reported seven hundred sick soldiers in the hospital at Culpeper — and that Beauregard has sent a flag of truce to Washington." On the night of the 9th cannon fire could be heard. On the 11th one could hear it during the day.

July 19th, 1861: The first of the tired, drawn-out lines of men that were to cross Fauquier for another four years emerged in the night at Ashby Gap. Brig. Gen. Thomas Jackson (not yet Stonewall) and his 4,300 men were the first to cross — in route to First Manassas. The twenty-mile forced march from Winchester began at dawn, and by 2 a.m. the First Brigade halted on the slope above Paris. Many had fallen, exhausted, when an officer reminded Jackson that no sentries had been posted. "Let the poor fellows sleep, I will guard the camp." At dawn, after a cat-nap, Jackson roused his men for the six-mile hike to Piedmont Station, where trains for Manassas were waiting. Some 6,000 men, the remainder of Brig. Gen. Joseph E. Johnston's Armies of the Shenandoah, followed Jackson. Overloaded trains delayed boardings, and so did railroad personnel, who insisted on getting a good night's sleep. Had it not been for the efforts of Col. E. F. Fisher, former President of the North Carolina Railroad, Johnston's rear brigade, which entrained at 2 a.m. July 21st, wouldn't have reached Manassas in time.

How could the trains not slow down? At every station people held out baskets full of provisions and luxuries. Just past the waving handkerchiefs and loud huzzahs at one station, a woman stood with hands uplifted and eyes upturned to heaven — Miriam the prophetess, one hand lifted in praise, the other in prayer.

In Lower Fauquier — and lest one think the term derogatory, it and Upper Fauquier were in constant use in decades past — some troops moving through stopped at Kitty Shacklett's White Ridge Tavern. When refreshed they offered Miss Kitty gold in payment; she replied, "Go fight, I won't have your gold." Many handed out dinners to the marchers, sang "Dixie" and "Dissolution Wagon" with them, and exchanged buttons for bouquets. Cheers sent them on their way.

"We have won a glorious though dear-bought victory," wrote President Jefferson Davis on the 21st. To view the action people climbed the Bull Run Mountain and its southward ridges. With telescopes fixed on puffs of smoke they spied the proceedings, ten miles away in the lowlands of Bull Run.

Now the war came home. Trains loaded with wounded puffed along the Orange and Alexandria, south to the Culpeper hospital. It filled, and they were brought to homes of proper ambience and with servants. They filled. On August 2nd the Warrenton Town Council asked J. C. Lindsay to turn his schoolroom into a hospital, John R. Spilman to make mattress frames, John G. Beckham to get hay for the mattresses, and James Vass Brooke and John R. Tongue to procure more mattresses. There was uncertainty as to who was to pay the bill, but nurses were hired, males at $20 a month, females at $10.

Attending to burial services were Tongue, James H. Stephens, and William H. Gaines. They selected the Warrenton Graveyard, and asked girls of the Fauquier Female Seminary to mark the graves. Within two years some 600 crosses and pine stakes were to fill that green.

By August 22nd the wounded overflowed Mr. Lindsay's schoolroom, and the town council ordered Tongue, Brooke, and John L. Fant to look for a larger hospital. Mrs. James Vass (Mary E.) Brooke, Margaret A. Combs, Roberta Phillips, and a Miss Allen helped to equip the facility. By winter the churches, public buildings, and homes were hospitals. Families boarded grateful relatives of the sick and dying. Visitors to town that fall told of six to seven deaths a day. By late winter the overcrowding, the filth, the dying, led the town council to ask James Vass Brooke to petition Confederate authorities to remove the hospital from Warrenton.

Catherine Cooper Hopley, a British schoolteacher in a blockaded Virginia, provided the most vivid reminiscences of a county so close to war. At the first touch of autumn she had taken the train from Richmond, and at Warrenton Junction changed for Warrenton. North of Gordonsville crowded Orange and Alexandria trains gave space first to soldiers joining regiments. No porters, a scarcity of passenger cars, Negroes handing travelers trays of refreshments "enough to take away whatever inclination for food one might have felt": everywhere was confusion. Whenever a train started off the cry was "Manassas! Manassas!"

Arriving at her destination she saw a Negro turn the corner of a storehouse. She called, asking the way to Warrenton.

"Dis heah's Warrenton, mistus."

"But where is the town? And which is the way to go to it?"

"Dis heah's deepo; ther's the courthouse up yon."

Finding out that the ladies' college was "a mile" away, Miss Hopley persuaded the man to transport her and baggage for a half-dollar. Then, thinking better of the idea, she decided to walk the stepping-stone path and let the baggage ride. Reaching the seminary she viewed Warrenton: houses interspersed with thick groves of trees, two pretty church spires arising from the midst, and all enveloped by a setting sun and far-off spurs of the Blue Ridge.

As a teacher of music she found her pupils would learn nothing but songs, marches, and dances composed for the Confederacy: "Dixie," "The Jeff Davis Waltz," "Beauregard's March," and "Palmetto Waltzes." Some of her pupils were from Culpeper, Fairfax, and Loudoun Counties, and to her, "scarcely six girls could be selected among the three dozen whose names did not end in 'ie'." Nearly all had brothers or relatives in the army, and an evening seldom passed without a guest to keep the ladies posted on the annals of the camps.

Warrentonians constantly spoke of the Manassas battle, and complained that because of all the soldiers about, they did not have enough to eat. The schoolgirls had honey and jelly, but wanted butter, too. They told Miss

Hopley that as the black horses had been killed, and had become difficult to replace, the Black Horse title died with the devoted steeds. She also heard that John Quincy Marr was the first victim of a battle on Virginia soil, and that his Warrenton Rifles alone held Fairfax Court House against the June 1st attack.

Alexander Hunter's more generalized recollections of this autumnal Warrenton are colored by such nostalgia as will arise in a half-century: The barns were rich, the provisions plentiful, and the land flowing with milk and honey. For the soldier on leave, courting and making love were weekday diversions. On weekends, parties, balls, and impromptu dances were in style, and on Sundays, "devotional exercizes." Famous for its lovely women and unstinted hospitality, Warrenton was, indeed, "a hasheesh dream."

With winter coming, and goods becoming scarce due to blocked travel to Alexandria and Baltimore, the main shopping centers for Fauquier, some tried blockade-running. One man bought a great quantity of shoelaces for twenty-five cents a pound in Baltimore and sold them for four dollars a pound in Richmond. But he paid in gold, and he was paid in Confederate money. Many nonchalantly walked past Federal lines, but that had its risks; a Miss Buckner from the Salem neighborhood was captured, her petticoat thickly quilted with quinine.

Articles were grabbed up by hospitals or by soldiers paying exorbitant prices. Matches, soap, candles, starch, and glue were scarce, and though all these staples could be made at home, Miss Hopley felt that Southern "extravagance and affluence" precluded their production. Because of a shortage of oil and wicks, shops closed at sunset and evening church services were suspended. Coffee had risen in price from ten to seventy-five cents a pound. She observed that rye whiskey was mixed with coffee, but did not say which beverage the combination was to improve. Tea at $3.50 a pound — a dollar before the war — was a treat. Milk was always plentiful. Salt, given out only to good customers, was $3.50 a sack — $2.50 prewar — but then it sold for $28 a sack in Lynchburg. Once, when a clothier received a supply, the seminarians wrote to their parents for funds. But by the time the money arrived a Richmond merchant bought the entire stock. Overshoes, which Miss Hopley had previously sought for in Richmond, were available, and she attributed their existence to the mud of Warrenton — "surpassed all other mud, in quality and quantity, that I ever saw."

Country people learned that soldiers were good customers. If paid in Confederate money they charged high prices; currency exchangers were giving less that ninety cents on the dollar. But, the government's appropriation of wagons and animals had increased prices of gear and stock. Butter, usually 12 to 15 cents a pound, brought 40 to 60 cents. Eggs, usually 30 cents a dozen, were 40 to 60 cents. Turkeys went from a dollar to $2.50, chickens from 30 cents to $1.50 a pair. Townspeople were accorded somewhat better deals.

Coal furnaces had made their way into Warrenton in the 1850's, but now, with no coal available, perhaps a dozen homes had been abandoned for the winter. The seminary, upon opening in 1857, had one coal stove in each girl's room. But finally a wood-burner surfaced, and at a cost of ten dollars a cord — the price had been three — the college drawing-room became "the crowded resort of all those shivering daughters of Virginia."

General Joseph Johnston's haphazard withdrawal from the Manassas line began March 6 1862, and for a week men and supplies traversed Fauquier. Most soldiers crossed the Rappahannock over a "weak and shaky bridge" at The Springs, and by the railroad bridge, converted to foot and wagon traffic. Retreating Confederates then burned all the Orange and Alexandria Railway bridges, tore up ties, and carried rails off. Civilians and soldiers plundered supplies left behind.

One million pounds of salted meat packed Chapman's Mill at Thoroughfare Gap, and lay about a slaughterhouse just to the east. As wagons and railway cars were full, leftovers would be burned. But until evacuation the meat was for the taking. The fire set at the six-story stone mill was a half-hearted attempt; the burners could not miss the etched stone, "Rebuilt by John Chapman, 1858." Miller Chapman soon extinguished the blaze and gave thanks; he had at least received compensation. The Confederates had given him $1,300 in rent for his property.

Library of Congress

PLATE IV

Attributed to Timothy H. O'Sullivan, August, 1862

A federal detachment guards the telegraph house at Rappahannock Station, now Remington. Slave quarters flank the farmhouse at left. Flowers line the Orange and Alexandria Railway tracks.

Library of Congress

PLATE V

Attributed to Mathew B. Brady, August, 1862

Catlett, in one of its last serene days before Jeb Stuart's August 22nd, 1862, raid. Soldiers sunbathe atop box cars of the U.S. Military Railroads — in peace time the Orange and Alexandria Railway. The combined station, post office, and store of the Catlett family stands at right, a warehouse at left. The pole supports telegraph wires.

U.S. Military History Institute

PLATE VI

Timothy H. O'Sullivan, August, 1862

Last stop on the Warrenton Branch — two platforms at center. Surrounding storehouses — all new within the decade — and older dwellings no longer stand. Note the stock yards at right. Photographer O'Sullivan set his camera at the present Fifth Street overpass, and took care to include the courthouse spire and St. James' steeple in his lens.

PLATE VII
U.S. Army Military Timothy H. O'Sullivan,
History Institute August, 1862

The guests had departed, no longer to promenade the 188-foot long three-story portico of The Springs' main hotel, built 1835, destroyed in late August, 1862. Locals contend that Union artillery fired the salvos in order to dislodge Georgia Sharpshooters.

brary of Congress   Attributed to Mathew B. Brady,
October, 1863

4. INVASION AND REPULSE

Two months of Geary - Pope's armies in Warrenton — Stuart's Catlett raid — Jackson outflanks Pope

MARCH 15, 1862-SEPTEMBER 2, 1862

Colonel John W. Geary's infantrymen were the first Northern troops to enter Fauquier soil, reaching Upperville at 4 p.m., March 15, 1862. The 1,500 Pennsylvanians had spent three weeks occupying Loudoun, a county familiar to Geary as a landowner and President of the Potomac Iron Company, one of the state's largest furnaces. For nine days his men scouted about, taking possession of Paris and Ashby Gap, and capturing an officer and some privates of the 6th Virginia Cavalry, 8th Infantry, and Ashby's Cavalry. Reconnoitering south on the 19th, about 125 Confederate cavalry fled north of Piedmont. The invaders noted Manassas Gap Railroad bridges had been burned. On the 21st Geary heard that formidable Southern commands had grouped at Warrenton and Salem, and on the 23rd Geary's men left for Snickers Gap via Aldie.

Next day the Fauquier County Court met, but there was not a word said about a war.

The morning of March 27th Geary's men marched from Philomont to Middleburg, and were met by 300 of Jeb Stuart's cavalry and infantry, just arrived from Upperville. In Geary's words — the only surviving account of Fauquier's first skirmish — "We opened a well-directed fire upon them, and they retreated in disorder to the mountains." According to Geary, Middleburg was the only Loudoun town to "manifest violent secession feeling." Yet, he reported that militia generals Asa Rogers, Robert Wright, and Col. A. Chancellor promised not to take up arms against the Union. Rogers had been Loudoun's staunchest secessionist during the campaign to elect delegates to the Richmond Convention.

At 2 p.m. on the 29th Geary's marauders left Middleburg and at 7 o'clock reached The Plains. Fog enveloped the village, and half an inch of ice and snow covered the ground. No Confederates were seen. Elijah V. White's cavalry had been in the area, but rumor had it they were now at The Springs. In this area the Manassas Gap Railroad had not been disturbed. Telegraph wires were down, but poles stood. The Broad Run road bridge had been burned, but the stone piers and bolts were fine. From Thoroughfare Gap a stench arose; meat still smoldered.

In Lower Fauquier, Brig. Gen. Oliver O. Howard's force of some 3,500 followed the Orange and Alexandria tracks into Fauquier in late morning, March 28th. Encountering resistance at Cedar Run, the advancing force was consistently flayed by Col. W. E. "Grumble" Jones's sharpshooters at the front and flanks. At Bealeton the last remnant of Dick Ewell's troops ran for a train of cars, in Howard's words, "nearer to me than themselves." But Ewell's men hopped aboard, and then the supply train puffed up the drawn-out grade of Lucky Hill and crossed the Rappahannock. As soon as the train reached safety in Culpeper, the bridge, wired with explosives, was blown up. Reaching the river, Howard's men were met by fire from Parrott guns, and immediately countered. Through to nightfall the across-river cannonade continued. General Howard reported four wounded, three prisoners taken, and booty of 230 head of cattle, sixty claimed by farmer William Bowen. In order to obtain a receipt for the cattle and some forage, Bowen said he had taken an oath of allegiance to the Union.

Now that was the Northern version. Brig. Gen. Jeb Stuart's more precise report differed by mentioning the enemy stopped for a day before crossing Cedar Run. The report did not speak of prisoners. Furthermore, Stuart said that on March 30th Grumble Jones's cavalry recrossed the Rappahannock, pursued the enemy with vigor, and attacked their encampment near Warrenton Junction, Howard's headquarters. Several Federals were wounded and fifty prisoners taken. Stuart, always gracious in his citations, detailed the exploits of sixteen, among then Musician David Drake and Adjutant John Singleton Mosby, both of whom "volunteered to perform the most hazardous service." Mosby and three companions had skirted Howard's columns to determine his force was not in the van of McClellan's main army.

Fighting was nearly continuous near the Rappahannock rail bridge until April 16th, but of the skirmishes only Federal reports survive. On April 2nd a reconnaissance force of Col. John F. Farnsworth's 8th Illinois Cavalry encountered skirmishers along the Carolina Road, a mile from the river, and he chased them across Norman's Ford. Other troops of his command met skirmishers near Beverley's Ford.

A third Federal recon force set out April 15th to observe Confederate strength in Culpeper. On their way from Warrenton Junction an Irishman living along the railroad told them the river was two miles away when it was really a third that distance. Near the destroyed railroad bridge a hidden battery opened fire upon them and they retreated. A short distance from Bealeton two black women turned informer and said the Confederates often met Robert Willis at Liberty Church — the same Robert Willis who often came to the Federal camp to shoe horses. The reconnoiters also visited Eastern View, the Randolph plantation. Mary Randolph told them nothing, and was in no mood to mention that at her home young Robert E. Lee received an education.

Next day blacksmith Willis was in custody, and the battalion picking him up exchanged shots with pickets at the railroad bridge. Another squadron absconded with one of the Eastern View field hands, who said that Mr. Olinger and Dr. John Gordon Beale had helped Southern forces. They, too, were arrested.

Inside Lincoln's army, Provost Marshal Marsena Rudolph Patrick wrote in his diary that on the 16th whiskey and water flowed freely at his Catlett headquarters. He visited the Quesenberry farm and the overseer told how Union officers refused to give his boss receipts for more than 600 butchered animals, mostly sheep. He also chatted with the Stephen McCormicks at Auburn. All told Patrick they were good Union folk.

Not until May 4th did the Northerners cross the Rappahannock, at Beverley's, the only passable ford. Almost empty of Confederate troops, a lush Culpeper awaited bleeding.

The "sad fate of Warrenton," as Miss Hopley phrased it, is hinted at through snippets of Union correspondence. At Warrenton Junction on March 29th, Brig. Gen. Edwin Voss Sumner asked, "Shall I take Warrenton tomorrow? There is much forage in our vicinity. I will send organized parties to collect; certificates will be furnished the owners, specifying they will be paid fair prices for property on presentation of certificates to the proper officer, on condition they take at time of presentation the oath of allegiance to the United States." A McClellan adjutant, Seth Williams, okayed the proposed movement for April 3rd. At The Plains, Colonel Geary heard rumors that Confederate forces had left Warrenton on that day.

Occupation forces did not interfere with the May 1st town council meeting, but Federal officers were undoubtedly present; the minutes might have been written on any normal spring day. The council would not meet again until September, 1864.

The first known casualties of the invasion were civilians, John Matthews and Robert Eden Scott, killed on May 3rd. Five days later the U. S. House of Representatives passed a resolution calling for information relative to the homicides, and these events surfaced. Scott, age fifty-four, had led a party of mostly middle-aged non-combatants to capture two marauders accused of rape and stealing. They had been staying at the home of G. W. Franklin Smith near Meadowville. Scott's men came upon the pair, and in the melee they shot Scott, then Matthews. One of the murderers was then killed; the other escaped, but was apprehended by Union forces. At a court of inquiry, Brig. Gen. Herman Haupt testified that Scott's death evoked indignation throughout the community, and thereafter was frequently referred to as evidence of the character of Union forces.

By May 5th Geary's men had occupied the twenty-five-mile-long Manassas Gap Railroad corridor from The Plains to near Front Royal. His headquarters were at Triplett's Goose Creek Mill, with other companies stationed at nearby Rectortown, Salem, Piedmont, and Markham. Guerillas, he said, kept his troops in readiness, but there were no attacks. On the 10th, scouting the Blue Ridge from Paris to Manassas Gap, they found only abandoned campsites. Geary then told Secretary of War Edwin Stanton that he had driven the guerillas south of the gap, and that "their force partakes of the nature of bandits."

The same day Federal forces in Lower Fauquier sent another message to Stanton: "Very few white men at home, and women all secessionists; some of them bitterly so, treated soldiers very coldly. Roads below Elk Run good, and some planting going on."

On May 15th Confederates attacked Geary's drawn-out forces. Five hundred cavalrymen led by Col. Thomas T. Munford suddenly descended from the hills and captured a supply train a mile from Linden. They killed one and took fifteen prisoners. In retaliation the Yanks searched the village "in a thorough, yet respectful manner," and arrested every man there. The prisoners put on an act, condemning Munford's men for shooting at men who had surrendered, and said the raiders were ashamed of the incident. Munford's report added that the Federals were "elegantly armed," and that nine horses and two wagons added luster. Geary then complained to Secretary Stanton that his command of 1,400 was in peril, especially since he heard that Stonewall Jackson's cavalrymen in the Valley were disbanding to form guerilla bands east of the Blue Ridge.

Through the 23rd Geary's reports spoke of threatening guerillas to the south and west. That day Jackson's entire force levelled Geary's westernmost command at Front Royal. Next day, after hearing that Confederate cavalry, infantry, and artillery were advancing up the Blue Ridge from Front Royal, Geary pulled back his headquarters to The Plains. Next day two slaves warned him that Jackson with 10,000 men was on his way to Markham, and another force of 10,000 was moving north from Orlean. When Geary tried to straighten out the reported troop movements — at the request of President Lincoln — his sentries atop the Blue Ridge told another story. Jackson was to cross into Loudoun at Snickers Gap, ten miles north of the Fauquier line. And next day two reports from Geary again told of Jackson's purported advance, this time through Ashby Gap.

Jackson, meanwhile, was marching north to Winchester and Harper's Ferry to draw forces from McClellan, advancing on Richmond. And one imagines that Geary's three-week fear of guerillas, coupled with the mystique of Jackson, introduced paranoia into Stanton's reports and letters. "The enemy in great force are marching on Washington," he wrote Massachusetts Governor John Andrew.

By May 26th Geary had withdrawn his headquarters to Broad Run Station — a two-day retreat of ten miles. His perimeter troops roamed about The Plains — "I am holding the town with cavalry," he said — and other peaceful areas near New Baltimore. His scouts reported roads blocked with brush, and Confederate pickets at Piedmont and north of Warrenton. In the only bit of verifiable truth about Confederate movements that month, Geary noted with an "I give you this for what it is worth" clause that staunch secessionist Asa Rogers said Jackson was marching toward Harper's Ferry. But two hours later, having received Stanton's "if threatened — fall back to Manassas" telegram, Geary dutifully obeyed, noting "Hopeless circumstances surrounding us." That same day Stanton ordered Maj. Gen.

James Shields' troops to fall back from Catlett to Manassas. So by the 27th, solely on the strength of Geary's summaries and Jackson's repute, the occupying armies — except for one company at Catlett — left Fauquier.

Shields thought "the whole, a disgraceful panic," but Geary talked from fear. "My cavalry still hold Aldie," he wistfully told Stanton, and again there were tales of large bodies of troops advancing from the Blue Ridge gaps. Geary said his scouts had been fired upon at Thoroughfare Gap and they had seen the enemy in the Pond Mountains. He also wrote of seeing plenty of smiles on the faces of Fauquier. Shields again decried the stampede, and wrote both his commander, Maj. Gen. Irvin McDowell, and Secretary of War Stanton, to tell them so. Without naming Geary, he called for his replacement.

Upper Fauquier residents would have seconded the idea. Fanny Carter Scott, living at Glen Welby, told in her diaries of his men stealing cattle, corn, and fowl, taking off with women servants, taking possession of kitchens and ordering dinner, and addressing ladies with insolence and profanity. She couldn't understand how Geary ever could have been mistaken for a gentleman, but then she had her own image of officers, being the daughter of Capt. Richard H. Carter of the Rectortown Company and wife of Capt. Robert Taylor Scott of the Beauregard Rifles. Of lasting import, her description of the countryside in early April was one that would hold for three more years: "Scarcely anyone ploughing, fences pulled down, fields many of them in commons, stores closed, no one traveling about, the public roads deserted; a few travelers on old, broken-down steeds that no one would care to possess himself of."

James Shields would now take charge of operations in Fauquier, and again push to beyond Warrenton and reoccupy the railroad corridors. To him the Confederates Geary spoke of were "rabble cavalry." Within a day, with McDowell now sending the dispatches to Stanton, no Confederates were to be seen in Fauquier County. President Lincoln, finding such a turn-around hard to believe, telegraphed McDowell: "You say General Geary's scouts report that they find no enemy this side of the Blue Ridge. Neither do I. Have *they* been *to* the Blue Ridge looking for them?"

Smoldering gear and goods and a charred Broad Run Station greeted General Shields as the train made its way to Rectortown on the 28th. Scavengers were picking over the mess, set afire by Geary's retreating men. Writing to Edmund Schriver, his chief of staff, Shields trusted that the "shameful effects of the shameful panic" would be repaired or obliterated. As for Geary, Schriver admonished him to stay in Aldie and frequently report to headquarters or Shields, and to nobody else.

Fauquier again had become a thoroughfare for supplies, sent to the Valley and to the south. General McDowell described Catlett as full of stragglers and broken-down men from every brigade. In June, after a heavy rain, Provost Marshal Patrick called the village vile and wretched — "The stench is insupportable."

Partisans, supported by some Confederate regulars, still controlled the hinterlands. In late May Union troops marching from Catlett to Thoroughfare Gap were repeatedly harassed by sniper fire, some of it from houses. Herds of cattle and officers' horses followed, all to battle Jackson in the Valley. Physician Edward P. Clarke often told how he sat on his front porch at The Plains and whittled, cutting a notch for every cannon that passed. Then by courier via Middleburg, Clarke sent Jackson the count.

On June 2nd Brig. Gen. Rufus King made Warrenton his headquarters, describing the town as quiet, healthful, and the populace civil. Wood and water were plentiful. No partisans were about, but King heard stories of mounted parties carrying off slaves to the south. Patrick found King at a hotel, living in fine style. The citizens Patrick found to be not as spiteful as Fredericksburg's, but still not pleased to see streets full of Yankee soldiers.

Provost Marshal Patrick's job was to keep order among Union troops, and especially to prevent stealing. Many bivouacked at Elk Run and at Tuloss's Mill near Town Run. Patrick sensed their indifference to the war, hence the pilfering and destroying of fruit. He also blamed officers; most thought rebel property fair game. In early June twenty-one were arrested for taking sheep and killing hogs. Seventeen agreed to pay the five-dollar fine; four elected to stand trial. King had offered Fauquier homeowners a personal guard until discipline improved, and Patrick visited several homes; he recalled Major Saunders', and Mrs. Campbell's and her aunt, Mrs. Horner's; they gave him strawberries and ice cream. A young widow, Mrs. Carter, told Patrick she was disappointed; the Yankees appeared so handsome and behaved so well. As he prepared to mount she took his hands and said, "I cannot wish you success, but I do hope that no evil will befall you." When the home guards were recalled, Patrick remarked that some did not return to their commands.

A Marylander from the Eastern Shore gave us the best glimpse of a bustling occupied Warrenton. Charles Townsend, twenty-one and reporting for the New York *Herald*, roomed at the Warren Green, managed by James 'Jemmy' DeShields, frank and fair — unusual qualities, thought Townsend, for an American innkeeper. A bare hotel lobby held creaking benches, whittled chairs with broken arms, a high desk on which were kept a row of numbered bells to call rooms. Hand bills, mostly dated, announced William Higgins was paying top prices for field hands, Timothy Ingersoll's stock of dry goods was the finest in the Piedmont, and James Mason's mulatto woman had decamped Whitsuntide eve and $100 would be paid for her return. More recent bills were labeled "Ho! for winter-quarters in Washington," "Sons of the South arise!" and "Liberty, glory, and no Yankeedom!"

Three bells, their purpose explained by a servant, announced dinner. "De fust bell, suh, is to prepah to prepah for de table; de second bell, suh, is to prepah for de table; de last bell, to come to de table." Nine dollars a week for room and board did not bring beef or butter, and if a guest requested such delicacies the servants stared at him as if he had eaten an entire cow. A bar, opened stealthily, offered hard cider (called champagne) at three dollars an hour; a dollar tip could procure a week's supply of ice.

Warrenton's pretty women occupied much of Townsend's prose. They stepped into the gutter to avoid walking under the flag — even regimental flags — and stopped their ears when bands played patriotic music. The *New York Ninth,* a regimental newspaper published in town, quipped that the "She-cesh" gathered together singing Southern songs and "vaunting superior beauty, gallantry, bravery, and all that sort of thing of the F. F. V.'s." And while the *Ninth* said the women turned up their noses at officers, Townsend said that in the evenings they promenaded with them — arm and arm.

The old-timers met late every morning beside the Warrenton House, and one man read aloud from borrowed New York newspapers. They laughed when he read an ad in the *Ninth* offering a fifteen-dollar reward for a saddled horse, "strayed or stolen" from in front of the Warrenton House. The men had drafted a petition to General Pope, commander of the occupying army, asking his forbearance and charity; Pope had threatened to transport them well within Union lines. Many blacks were in town, and when bands played in the evening they held carnivals. The *Ninth,* trying to print kind words about Fauquier, decried the disorderly actions of Negroes "treated so kindly and who love their masters so dearly." The occupiers did warn citizens about selling too much liquor to soldiers, and about an illegal mail network.

With the arrival of Maj. Gen. John Pope, and his army's imminent removal from two weeks of bliss, Townsend decided he should buy a horse. For $130 he could get one from the Federal pound, but being in horse country, decided, upon advice, to approach Mayor Bragg. His Negro, Jeems, trotted out two colts, both black, and the second, a four-year-old who would not bolt in the face of gunfire, appealed to Townsend. After the usual bargaining, initiated with the traditional drink of whiskey, the $190 price came down to $125, a harness thrown in. For payment, Mayor Bragg would only take Yankee greenbacks.

One evening the Federals held an impromptu outdoor theatre, replete with candles for footlights and a stage festooned with U.S. flags. In deference to the audience the performers sang no Union airs. As Townsend listened, and heard the Negroes guffaw from their perches in the trees, "the war lost half its bitterness, but I thought with a shudder of Stuart's thundering horsemen, charging into the village, and chasing the night's mimicry with a horrible tragedy."

But when Stuart's horsemen came, the Federals had gone. Lt. Col. Thomas L. Kane's report to his commander began "I am sorry," and when those words appear you can tell disaster had struck. Jeb Stuart's lengthy resume began "I have the honor," and thus began the saga of the first major engagement in Fauquier, one that still beckons to writers' fancies.

The prelude took place at daylight on August 21st, when Col. Thomas Rosser's advance guard recrossed the Rappahannock, attacked, and for nearly a day held the Fauquier side of Beverley's Ford. That same day other Confederate raiders probed left-bank entrenchments at Freeman's and Kelly's Fords. Rosser said he captured and killed several Federals, with one of his men captured. The Washington *Chronicle* reported nine prisoners taken, one an "intelligent-looking and determined negro" who fought desperately.

Next day Capt. John Pelham's artillery pounded the enemy at Freeman's, while eleven and thirteen river miles north, Stuart crossed at Hart's Mill and Waterloo bridge. Taking the pike to Warrenton, his 1,000 men and two cannon halted for a half-hour to get information and graze horses. The New York *Times* reported that some of Stuart's men stopped to sign the Warren Green's guest register and to have a spot of tea. No Yankees had been seen in town for two days.

Stuart's objective was to burn the Cedar Run railroad bridge and cut the telegraph line, but when one of those thunderstorms broke he got lost in a very dark night. Pushing on by Auburn, and led by Rosser's command, the intruders found themselves amid encampments near Catlett. As one raider, Lt. Col. Richard Lee Beale, said in classic 19th-century prose, "The Storm King dwarfed to stillness the tramp of our horses." Serendipitously, Stuart's men captured a Negro whom Stuart had known in Berkeley County. The contraband told Stuart how to reach Bailey Shumate's, where a parked wagon train stood — a train believed to be none other than that of John Pope. Quickly, as a swollen Rappahannock could cut off escape, Brig. Gen. Fitz Lee selected cousin William H. Fitzhugh 'Rooney' Lee to swoop in.

A captured officer later said they had been sitting around drinking some toddy when someone said, "Now this is something like comfort. I hope Jeb Stuart won't disturb us tonight." Just then the Rebel Yell broke and the speaker, recognizing Stuart from U.S. Army days, said "There he is, by God!" Correspondents from the *Times* and Philadelphia *Enquirer* said in their reports that the raiders charged with the yell "Surrender or Die!" Flashes of lightning highlighted a melee of slashing sabres and men running about in their underwear. Tents and wagons burned, and the raiders herded together hundreds of prisoners and thousands of horses and mules. In the rain and confusion many escaped, Lieutenant Kane among them. The raiders' casualties were slight.

At Catlett, Fitz Lee's men came upon a seven-car train being oiled. The engineer and guard fled, and while Lee was trying to smoke out Yankees who had crawled under the station platform, he yelled out to Mrs. Catlett, "Tell my family all is well." Aboard the train a New York *Herald* reporter said Lee's men yelled "Fire The Train! Fire The Train!" A conductor and some passengers bolted, but the remainder fell to the floor. Then brakeman Jack Wistner ran a gauntlet of bullets, opened the throttle, and lying flat on the engine-cabin floor he steered the train through its pursuers and to safety.

Meanwhile, Colonels Rosser and L. T. Brien attacked a second camp, destroyed it, and then rode to the Cedar Run bridge, which they tried to chop down. But with wet wood, rising water, and fire from Federals positioned on the high east bluff, they abandoned the raid's initial purpose. At about 3 a.m. they began the return to Warrenton, laden with prisoners and paraphernalia, among the items, Pope's dispatch book. Much of the booty was distributed to townspeople. When the raiders reached safety in Culpeper they had 300 prisoners, among them a woman in uniform.

Herald staffers, beavering down details five days after the raid, mentioned that Stuart's men captured 220 horses, burned six wagons, two filled with supplies, and got $6,000 in cash from Pope's wagon train. And, quipped the *Herald*, "Not a staff officer was left with a clean shirt." From McDowell's safe they absconded with a few thousand dollars and a quantity of liquor. The New York *Times* reported that a concealed bluecoat at McDowell's baggage train overheard Stuart say, "Damn it! This is McDowell's baggage. He is a gentleman. Let it alone." They left — after downing two bottles of liquor.

Attackers Heros von Borcke and William Willis Blackford both wrote in their memoirs how they heard that half a million in greenbacks and $20,000 in gold had been taken. With differing nuances, they told of a leisurely breakfast in Warrenton after the raid, and of delicious coffee served by one of those charming Warrenton girls. After hearing of the take, she told von Borcke that one prize, Pope's quartermaster, Maj. Charles Goulding, stopped at her house a day before and declared his intention of entering Richmond before the month was out. She bet him a bottle of champagne he would not. Would somebody give her the bottle? Blackford did, and with a smile she paid the quartermaster her debt. Blackford said that Stuart sent Pope's broadcloth, brass-buttoned uniform on to Richmond, where it was exhibited in a Main Street bookstore with a card labeled "Headquarters in the saddle," a play on Pope's assertion that that's where his headquarters would be. Richmond newspapers said the uniform wound up in the loft of the State Capitol, on exhibition with other war trophies. Blackford also mentioned that the plunder, including field glasses, watches, jewelry, many pistols, and "excellent underclothing," was just compensation for Stuart's loss of hat and cloak at Verdiersville in Orange County.

A clever *Herald* reporter — Townsend? — had the last word. "The rebel cavalry are smart fellows — great on the dash — here to-day and there to-morrow." He told readers he had visited remnants of Pope's wagon train and determined that the following personal effects had been saved: a ridge pole of his tent, two dozen paper collars, a liquor case (only), spectacles, three spoiled socks, one piece of spoiled linen, a brush broom, and a bottle of hair tonic. He said Pope had selflessly divided the collars with his aide, James Selfridge. He also said Stuart had found a darkey in camp, dressed in Pope's best, and rode him through Warrenton on a mule labeled "No Retreat" and "Onward to Richmond." No wonder that after the raid Henry Halleck, Lincoln's military observer, forbade correspondents to visit the camps.

The Washington *Star* said kinder things, calling Pope's retreat but a detour, and at that brilliant and successful. The vitriolic *Herald*, noting a scarcity of hard tack, said, "We shall make a desperate stand, and write another tribute to Northern valor on the guidebook to Richmond." Their August 26th article closed: "Our retreat from Culpeper was a masterly thing, and is not believed to be marked by the loss of so much as an old boot or a haversack. When shall we learn the masterly art of advancing as well?"

Herman Haupt, Pope's chief of construction and transportation, could not believe that Stuart could pull off such a move. A day after the attack he sent his theory to Halleck: The teamsters panicked and shot it out among themselves. Pope told Halleck the damage was "trifling, nothing but some officers' baggage destroyed."

There was also a good deal of action up-river. Brig. Gen. Jube Early, writing six months after the event, told Lee of his August 23rd crossing at The Springs and at the Sandy Ford Dam of the old Rappahannock Navigation, and of Brig. Gen. Alexander Lawton's previous crossing two miles south near Foxville. As Lawton's men could not be found, Early sent an aide, Maj. A. L. Pitzer, to look for them. Some hours later, as the soaking party waited, Pitzer returned with six surprised prisoners, all armed. Riding near The Springs, Pitzer had been captured by the six, but as they rode on he told the Federals they were now surrounded and if they tried escape would be fired upon.

Federal troops near The Springs, though, meant that Early would have to stay put, and by morning the raging river had cut him off from Jackson in Culpeper. Jackson suggested recrossing at the intact Waterloo bridge; meanwhile he would try to rebuild The Springs bridge. From the Culpeper bank Jackson's scouts then guided Early's men and prisoners up-river seven winding miles. As cautious Federals followed the movement, Brig. Gen. Beverly Robertson's raiders, held in reserve during the Catlett take, rode up. Robertson had spied an enemy wagon train near The Springs, and near the hotel his cannon opened up on the train, closely guarded by a six-gun battery. George Neese, Robertson's gunner, said the Federals "scattered their shell all over the adjacent fields, ranging in altitude from the earth to the moon." The *Times* and *Star* had other stories, the *Star* saying that eight invalid soldiers guarding the wagon train drove off the attackers. The *Times*, implying a Confederate victory, said the attackers yelled "Surrender or die!" as they charged. Neither newspaper told of any artillery.

Evening again fell for Early's men, who now heard a volley in the woods followed by three cheers and "a tiger" — cited by one Confederate general as "the purest delirium of New York militia achievement." Early fired at the cheerers, and they did not fire back. Encounters with so many Federals so far up river meant that Pope's armies were converging on The Springs, and Early was relieved when General Ewell ordered all commands back to the Culpeper side; they crossed a temporary span at The Springs. There was not one Confederate casualty during the two-day sojourn.

Another engagement in Fauquier might have taken place on August 23rd. Stuart, in his report to Lee, mentioned his sending signal officer Capt. J. Hardeman Stuart, to capture the signal station at View Tree, an oak atop the

Watery Mountains. But Stuart's writing then took a different bent, and he never mentioned the outcome, concluding his report by mourning the death of Hardeman Stuart a week later at Groveton Heights.

If View Tree Mountain were captured, it would have been retaken quickly. The evening of the 23rd McDowell's force entered Warrenton, and next morning, under heavy fire, Maj. Gen. Franz Sigel's troops crossed Great Run, occupied the Sulphur Springs resort, and destroyed the bridge that Jackson had personally tried to repair a day before. On Sunday, the 24th, and on Monday, at nearly every ford between Kelly's and Waterloo, each side's river-bluff artillery kept up constant fire. One casualty was Fauquier's grandest building, the seventy-five-room, four-story stuccoed-stone hotel at The Springs. No side's reports mentioned the destruction, and some years later the Washington *Capitol* summarized the event: "Whether the fire was kindled by Jackson shooting at Pope or the hero of the saddle firing, is a question that never will be solved."

"All Eyes are directed to the Rappahannock," read Monday morning's lead sentence of the New York *Herald's* "The Situation" column, and from the Culpeper side William Dorsey Pender correctly surmised that situation: "I can form no idea of what we are to do but suppose to advance."

Early Sunday afternoon Lee had visited Jackson's headquarters at Jeffersonton and had told Jackson of his plan to outflank Pope's forces and drive them back to Washington. Stuart's minor outflanking movement to Catlett had worked perfectly, and there was good reason to believe a large-scale turn would work. Despite Lee's army being outnumbered, 75,000 to 55,000, Pope was a weak general in unfamiliar country, and when confronted with a force in his midst he would fumble. Success in turning Pope's army north and west of The Springs, then cutting it in two, would depend on speed; and so, Jackson's troops were to be the forced marchers. Map-maker J. K. Boswell plotted the route: from Amissville — far enough from the Rappahannock to be out of sight — to Hinson's Ford, five river miles above the northernmost Union detachment at Waterloo; then via Orlean and Thumb Run Church to Salem, and east along the Thoroughfare Gap Road to strike the Orange and Alexandria Railway near Gainesville. Maj. Gen. James Longstreet would play decoy, and that afternoon rode around and openly repeated that he would cross at The Springs and drive off the enemy. On Monday morning Pope wrote Lincoln, telling him he thought Jackson was marching to Thornton Gap — probably because Jackson's initial march to Amissville was in a westerly direction, and because his dust-kicking wagons were at Gaines Cross Roads, even farther west.

Twenty-four thousand men, already having marched some eight miles, crossed into Fauquier by the mill at Hinson's. They had been told to prepare three days' rations, but some didn't get the word and some didn't have time. Captain Boswell guided the lead force, Ewell's division, and when a road right-angled a field he cut across it. Jackson rode among the commands, exhorting "Close up! Close up!" Men seeing him wasted strength and cheered; then the word "no cheering" was passed down the column. Onlookers handed them food, urged them on, or stared in amazement. Marcher J. F. J. Caldwell, a South Carolinian, said, "This was then a land of plenty; but we made sad havoc in the great cornfields, for we subsisted almost entirely on roasting-ears."

At Salem, the first day's objective, the marchers halted, some reaching the town at four, others after midnight. In ten hours they had trekked some twenty-three miles. Asked about the march many years later, Salem storekeeper Philip Augustus Klipstein remembered that Jackson wore a black hat and black plume. At Salem, Stuart's cavalry, having taken the same route, joined forces. But finding the main road blocked by baggage trains and artillery, the newcomers, aided by scouts, rode through the Free State hills, crossed the Pond Mountains south of Thoroughfare Gap, and once more met Jackson near Gainesville.

At dawn the march resumed, and at Kinloch, east of The Plains, Edward Carter Turner described the men: "hungry, thirsty, barefooted, and some of them almost naked, but bright and buoyant asking only a mouthful to eat and to be led against the enemy." Next day, August 27th, the last of Jackson's army passed through Fauquier, and Federal cavalry, "all light-hearted and hopeful," appeared at The Plains, picking up many stragglers. Reports that Jackson had taken Manassas placed the country in great commotion — "people nearly wild with excitement."

Meanwhile, on the Rappahannock, Longstreet had been feinting crossings at various fords, but the evening of the 26th, with Jackson's army at The Plains, still eighteen miles from their destination, Pope finally realized what Jackson was up to. He withdrew from the Rappahannock and evacuated Warrenton and Warrenton Junction. Of interest, that morning the Richmond *Enquirer* blundered and announced Jackson's advance toward Manassas.

General Longstreet's men left their positions on the 26th, and followed by General Robert E. Lee and staff, bivouacked near Orlean that night. As Col. Charles Marshall was Lee's aide-de-camp, propriety dictated that the generals should be invited to a Marshall home for dinner. They accepted, and they and their staffs ate two of those grand meals of ante bellum Virginia before departing at dawn. Riding briskly onward in the fresh morning air, Lee's party were some distance in advance of the column when a quartermaster, still farther in the van, dashed back, calling, "The Federal cavalry are upon you." Forming a skirmish line across the road, the staff told Lee to skedaddle. But the Federals, seeing the line of horsemen, presumed it to be the head of many others, and rode off in the opposite direction.

Near Salem, Lee noticed an abandoned family carriage, and close by, taking refuge in a house, was the lady who owned it. She had wanted to meet Lee, and with her daughter had driven out to the road. But the Federals got there first and stole the team. Lee was sympathetic, but explained he could not replace the steeds. The lady was pleased at having seen and spoken to Lee, but wondered if a pair of her best bays were worth the encounter.

At Bunker Hill, Lee learned that Jackson's two-day, forty-seven-mile march had been a success. His army had cut off Pope from Washington, had captured two trains and torn up track at Bristoe Station, and had taken Manassas Junction, meeting place of the Orange and Alexandria and Manassas Gap Railroads. As Jackson's dispatch indicated slight resistance, Lee, not wanting to overtax his men, camped near The Plains. Lee stayed at Glenville, home of James William Foster, and again was invited to dinner, this time at the T. Bolling Robertsons, who lived near Broad Run Station. Brig. Gen. Armistead L. Long, Lee's Secretary, and a man who remembered gastronomic delights, recalled that good appetites and genial manners prevailed "as if the occasion was an ordinary one, not a moment in which victory or ruin hung trembling in the balance."

An incident of war took place at a corner near The Plains. In the van of Longstreet's troops, Lt. Gen. John B. Hood came across a scout pointing north. "This way general," he said, motioning the troops toward Middleburg. The scout explained that as Thoroughfare Gap had been too heavily fortified, Jackson had turned north to Aldie. Hood and Longstreet were to follow. Hood, suspicious, asked probing questions, had the man searched, and after many minutes had elapsed declared the man a spy. A drum-head court martial of three brigadiers imposed the death sentence. As the man was placed on a horse, the noose attached to a tree, his last words announced his identity: "I am Jack Sterry, a Jessie Scout from Loudoun County. I palavered with you for a good half hour while General Pope was battering in your precious old Stonewall." Sterry folded his arms, and as the horse was led from him, General Hood turned aside and in a subdued voice gave the order — March. The column moved on.

To the east lay the even crest of the Bull Run Mountains, broken by Thoroughfare Gap, a 500-foot-deep abyss of rocks scattered in wild confusion. In June, the popular magazine, *Frank Leslie's Illustrated Weekly*, featured a drawing of the gap and labeled it "The Virginia Thermopylae since a few determined men might hold it against thousands." The Federals had blocked the gap road by felling trees and rolling boulders down the cleft's sheer south face. Sharpshooters peered from the barricade and from cliffside rocks and trees. Lee asked Eppa Hunton, who knew the area from boyhood, if there were another way across, and Hunton recommended Hopewell Gap, three miles north.

Longstreet's army now split into three groups, one trying Hopewell Gap; another, Col. Evander M. Law's brigade, a trail up from Broad Run Station. The third, under Maj. Gen. David R. Jones, would assault Thoroughfare. Law's men crept over the top of Old Mother Leathercoat the night of the 28th, and when the enemy again saw the beginnings of a flanking movement they planned a withdrawal. Next morning Jones's Georgians broke through limited resistance, the advance described by gunner George Neese, who drew his allusion from swift-flowing Broad Run in the gap's north face: "a storm-driven wave . . . sweeping everything before it like a flood of rushing water."

A major battle had been avoided, and Jackson was reinforced in time.

By the Kinloch gate troops still passed on the 29th and 30th. Diarist Turner called many of them able-bodied, lingering to avoid battle. He felt almost 20,000 were skulking from duty, and perceived the shirkers to be mostly South Carolinians and Georgians. "Our yards are crowded with them all day and the barn and stable lofts at night. They are begging for food of people who have none to give and are insolent and revengeful when disappointed." At the gap he came across some twenty unburied Federal dead. At Stover's Mill lay the Confederate wounded; six had died on the 29th and others would follow.

Major Sam H. Hairston, asked by Lee to scout about Warrenton on the 29th, continually came upon stragglers, and also picked up forty-six Federal prisoners, a deserter from Stuart's horse artillery, and a sutler wagon. Wounded from Bristoe, Second Manassas, and the others, continued to give Warrenton the look of a vast hospital. "A veritable charnel house," wrote Alexander Hunter. "The wounded died off like flies." But with the 600 reported buried by August, 1862, 104 had been nursed back to health. How Hunter arrived at such an exact figure will not be known, but with the aid of Bettie Miller Blackwell of Oak Spring, he cited the women responsible: Janet and Meta Weaver, Mamie Mason, Fannie Horner, Sue Scott, Mrs. Richards Payne, Harriet Ward, Mary Amelia Smith, the Misses Annie, Fanny, and Elizabeth Lucas, and Mary C. Brooks, Frances Caldwell, Ann McIlhaney, and Rebecca B. Shackelford. To Mrs. Johnzie Tongue, Hunter gave a special designation — The Florence Nightingale of Mosby's Confederacy.

Jackson's turning movement had worked, and while Lee had failed to destroy Pope's army, by September 1st it had withdrawn into the defenses around Washington. On the 2nd Lincoln relieved Pope of his command. The general returned west, fought Indians in Minnesota, and lost no time in writing an apologia for his actions, published in Milwaukee in 1863.

5. FALL AND WINTER RAIDS

*Stuart counters at Upperville; is routed at Barbee's —
Northern depredations — McClellan relieved of command —
Warrenton expected to starve — Mosby goes out on his own —
Lower Fauquier's winter raiders*

SEPTEMBER 21, 1862-MARCH, 1863

Eight hundred Pennsylvania cavalrymen under Col. Richard Butler Price initiated autumn's hostilities by attacking 130 Confederate wagon-train guards west of Aldie on September 21st. As the train set off west the force protecting its rear was chased to within a half-mile of Paris. One wagon was burned, but Federal reports noted four Confederate dead, fourteen prisoners, and 140 sick and wounded, including at least twenty from the chase, at Aldie and Middleburg hospitals. Price paroled all of the infirm. Edward Carter Turner's diary reads: "The Feds have passed up the Little River Turnpike in force. Skirmishing occurred to Upperville in which they were twice driven back. Some think their object is to get possession of about three thousand army cattle grazing in that neighborhood; others think it is a movement towards Winchester to get in the rear of Lee's army."

On the 25th, thirty Ohio cavalrymen set out from Centreville and at Catlett observed an estimated 300 Confederates and a train on the Orange and Alexandria. They had set the Cedar Run bridge on fire, but the Union raiders put out the blaze. Halting that night, the raiding party then rode to Warrenton Junction, and noted that the train had left for the Rappahannock.

Union probers now grew bolder, and on the 29th, 500 cavalrymen under Lt. Col. Joseph Kargé, riding from Centreville, entered New Baltimore with outriders flanking the Warrenton Turnpike at a distance of one to two miles. At 2:30 p.m. an advance guard charged through a Warrenton crowded with convalescents and stragglers. Townspeople told the invaders that thirty cavalry had been on guard, and Kargé described the people as "very friendly." Physician Samuel B. Fisher told Kargé that every house was crowded with wounded and sick, and Kargé reported sufferers lying on floors, wrapped in blankets, "with seldom a straw pillow under their heads." Others were decaying in their own filth. Fisher said that despite a staff of forty "surgeons," there were fifty deaths a day, some from malnutrition. "Ladies of high respectability" certainly hoped the U.S. authorities could do something. Continuing in this exaggerated stance, Fisher assured the colonel that the sick would rather rot than take up arms. So after two hours, Kargé paroled the 1,300 to 1,400 wounded. He and his aides left, with the colonel concluding in his dispatch that the county was bare of sustenance and "starvation stares the people in the face."

Library of Congress   **PLATE VIII**   Timothy H. O'Sullivan, August, 1863

Major General Irvin McDowell's engineer corps re-lay The Springs Bridge. Looking into Fauquier, the riverside building, once a cheese factory, then a brewery, was swept away by an early-20th-century flood. Only the far bank's stonework remains.

U. S. Army Military History Institute   PLATE IX   Timothy H. O'Sullivan, August, 1862

Library of Congress   Timothy H. O'Sullivan, August, 1862

Nineteen-eleven captions entitle these two photographs "Fugitive Negroes Crossing The Rappahannock Following The Retreat of Pope's Army." They are fleeing Culpeper south of a temporary Orange and Alexandria Railway bridge. George Martin's flour and grist mill, a landmark until it burned about 1915, stands north of the bridge.

Forage and livestock were the goals of many Union forays. On October 17th and 18th the *Official Records* mention, without amplification, an expedition to Thoroughfare Gap and a skirmish there. On the same dates the entries in Turner's diary read: "Feds arrive at The Plains at night . . . [at Kinloch] early this morning for corn. They take a small quantity for which they pay nothing. They are polite. Two soldiers visited Avenel to get corn and finding a horse in the stable branded U. S. proceeded to halter and lead him off. . . . St. Louis Tom [Turner] ran down to the stable and fired on them with his pistol and put them to flight." An October 19th skirmish between Catlett and Warrenton Junction remains unamplified.

On Saturday, October 25th, the one troop of decimated Confederates from Antietam entered the county when Brig. Gen. John G. Walker's division, up from the Valley, camped at Ashby Gap; within a few days they had traversed the county and were in Culpeper. A few days later Mary Eliza 'Ida' Powell Dulany wrote in her diary: "On two occasions we have had the mortification of seeing our cavalry retreat before equal or inferior force." Turner's diary comments: "We occupy the skirmishing ground and are liable to daily visitations from scouting parties of both armies."

For the first time since March the county court met on October 27th. Commonwealth's Attorney and Black Horse Captain William H. Payne brought up the following motion: "To consider the propriety of removing the records of the Fauquier County Court to a place of safety in consequence of an invasion of said County by the Public Enemy." Loudoun County had moved its records to far-off Rockbridge County, and Culpeper had carted theirs to Rappahannock County. But the Fauquier records remained at the clerk's office, and through the diligence of those now unknown, remained intact.

By November 2nd Federal cavalry under Brig. Gen. Julius Stahel had established westerly outposts at Greenwich and Catlett. Next day cavalry reinforced by pickets moved toward Aldie and Hopewell, and cavalry advanced to New Baltimore and then north to Little Georgetown. Reports cited Confederate infantry and artillery at Thoroughfare Gap, cavalry about Buckland and New Baltimore, and some 7,000 infantry and cavalry near Warrenton Junction. In the only action of these early November days, Stahel's men encountered opposition in taking Thoroughfare Gap on the 3rd.

Belatedly pushing south from Antietam, Union forces, now termed Hessians by many locals, began their reoccupation of Upper Fauquier on November 2nd. For two days, at Aldie, Mountville, Philomont, and Unison, they had battled Stuart's cavalry, and on fording Panther Skin Creek on The Trappe Road that morning, they again spied their adversary on the high ground at Upperville. Wrote Ida Dulany: "Stuart's cavalry fell back slowly, disputing every inch of the way, the enemy occupying the ground as he retreated." The 3rd she called "a day of days," as she watched the battle taking place in the fields about her home, Oakley. From the high ground, known as Vineyard Hill, Union forces moved east and south through Number Six, Oakley, and Rokeby, and Mrs. Dulany's writings preserve the event: "The soldiers here and Hal [Dulany] with them rode at this time away — suddenly I saw them start their horses in a gallop and from the right I saw our videttes coming in more rapidly. Then looking at the hills beyond Number Six I saw them covered with Yankees, and soon the field in front of our house was filled with sharp-shooters. Soon we saw a battery on Cousin Robert Carter's hill just in front of Oakley, which began to play on our men and then there were no more southerners in sight. The house was surrounded by Yankees. For an hour I watched the battery pouring out shells against our battery which was planted in the Vineyard."

Stuart's report of the action, written a year and a half later, said little save for telling how successive shots from Capt. Robert Hardaway's twelve-pound rifled Whitworth Gun, considered the world's finest, and parked near Ashby Gap, drove off the enemy at a range of three or four miles. Other reports told of repeated attacks and retreats and mentioned that Capt. John Pelham's battery on Vineyard Hill killed at least four. Heros von Borcke, the Prussian who had a tendency to exaggerate, wrote in his 1867 memoirs that he and Stuart were the last to ride through the village at the first attack, and despite flying bullets, young ladies appeared at Main Street doorways, waving farewells with cambric handkerchiefs. Von Borcke's writings also tell of many Confederate wounded, lying in agony in the dusty street, a "fatal carbine fire" at 200 yards directed against Pelham's battery, and an unsuccessful charge at the murderous volleyers. With field glasses, an observant New York *Times* reporter spied Pelham's battery, "admirably placed on high ground," and then saw "Stuart, mounted on his gray horse, here waved his hat; his men responded in a lusty cheer, and the three thousand redoubtable horsemen charged down the hill." Faced with "round after round" of rifle fire, Stuart retired, "illustrating his fine horsemanship by dashing off with his followers after him, at the top of their speed." Even in retreat Stuart was a northern hero.

At the close-by Joshua Fletcher place, The Maples, Mrs. Fletcher's sumptuous dinner awaited Stuart, but when his men took shelter behind the house she fled to the basement. Good thing, too, for one shell exploded in my lady's boudoir. The repast, though cold, "was diverted to more loyal digestion," said the New York *Herald*. A Union general then proceeded to make the house home, bringing with him a lady friend who Ida Dulany names "Miss Chaste." When they took off together, gone were brushes, combs, bed linens, towels, and Mrs. Fletcher's side-saddle.

On the evening of November 3rd, Union troops cut south, and Stuart, wary that a flanking maneuver could isolate him from the rest of his force guarding wagon trains near Piedmont, withdrew to south of the Manassas Gap Railroad. By next morning Piedmont, that important rail station, was in Federal hands, and by day's end Salem, Paris, and Ashby Gap had been captured. A second force striking south from Middleburg occupied The Plains on the 6th. On the 4th, Gen. George Brinton McClellan, the Union commander, had spent most of the day at the gap, observing the Shenandoah

Valley. To feed his Army of the Potomac he ordered 360,000 rations to Thoroughfare Gap. According to the several diarists of Upper Fauquier they were sorely needed; the troops were taking every animal in sight, some killed before the owners' eyes. Federal guards posted at homes had to shoot at marauders to keep them away.

And should one think the diarists biased, Union Provost Marshal Marsena Patrick, encamped near Rectortown, penned this entry in his diary, November 6th: "As soon as breakfast was over I started out to put a stop to depredations — I know not how many men I have had arrested today. . . . I have got a number of horse thieves in Custody & have handled some marauders very severely." Next day Patrick noted, "The Brandy . . . which I have kept so carefully, was stolen out of my tent Yesterday, just when I most needed it." The New York *Times* also spoke of the pillage: "Pigs, poultry, sheep and calves have been swept remorselessly into the insatiate maw of the army; orchards have been cleaned out, and cabbage gardens ransacked for choice morsels to season the pork. Some of the more conscientious offer pay for what they want or take."

In at least one instance there was a difference of opinion. On the 6th, Susan Q. Curlette, of Waverley, near Piedmont, wrote a Union quartermaster and called his attention to at least eight killed sheep and twenty stacks of grain stolen — "which renders me nearly destitute of provisions." Her letter elicited comment in the *Times*, whose reporter acknowledged the theft of grain, but added this description: "A Mrs. Curlette, a widow, but wealthy lady, who owns two hundred and forty acres of fine land, with ample barns and a kitchen, gardens containing a handsome variety of vegetables which no one had disturbed. Her house is one of the best in that region, and will compare favorably with the best residences in New York, being furnished in elegant style. Four or five servants, male and female, remained to do her farm and housework. Her fat pigs were counted almost by the score, which the guard had protected from seizure, and a flock of fine sheep broused undisturbed around her quiet premises; notwithstanding Mrs. Curlette persisted in the assertion that she 'had been reduced to beggary by the troops, and would starve to death before Spring.'"

Several soldiers' joittings, Northern and Southern, also told of an idyllic Upper Fauquier. Such abundance, when placed in contact with McClellan's army in need, was bound to create havoc. The army's Col. Philippe Regis de Trobriand recalled shoeless and poorly clad soldiers laboriously marching from Antietam over horrible roads and in unseasonable piercingly cold weather. Heros von Borcke, the Prussian tactician traveling with Stuart, felt that if the Southern armies could have bought from these locals the war would have been prolonged. The standard procedure was to draw supplies from Richmond, send them to Staunton, then to Winchester, and then to the troops.

The *Times* thought it fit to print a comparison between Upper Fauquier folk and the Loudoun County Quakers: "Most of these confessors evidently hide their light under a bushel while their rebel neighbors are bold and outspoken in their treason." Lt. Tully McRea, a Connecticut Yankee leading horse-drawn batteries from Ashby Gap to Rectortown, came across an old farmer, "the coolest specimen of Secesh that I have yet seen." He had eight horses, but they were too lame to pull. "He did not try to conceal that he was a Rebel, and said he had let *his army* have nice horses, all that was fit for anything. Oh, how I did want to take some of his horses!"

At Farrowsville the old Leeds Manor Road turns south, and there, under Col. Thomas L. Rosser, the leader of Stuart's Catlett raid, the Confederates prepared for battle, placing two cannon at the corner. It was early afternoon on November 4th when Brig. Gen. William Averell's forces overran the emplacement on their second charge. But then the Confederates attacked and retook the position. Once more the Union charged, recaptured the cannon, and once more they lost the booty. Their dispatches noted that by 3:45 Averell was in trouble, and an hour later he needed reinforcements. Two hours later Averell's superior, Brig. Gen. Alfred Pleasanton, wrote: "[Averell] does not give me his killed and wounded, but tells me one of his squadrons was overwhelmed by superior numbers."

Coming upon the scene the next day, a *Times* reporter saw several fresh graves of Confederate soldiers, one a captain, by the roadside. Nine or so compatriots lay unburied, by a stone fence they had charged. Hearing that the home of Turner Ashby — killed that June and already a legend — was close-by, the correspondent paid homage. He noted a "small, poor log house, plastered without," occupied by an innkeeper.

At Woodside, correspondent "E. S." and twelve officers dined with Anne Lewis Jones, granddaughter of Chief Justice John Marshall. "The good lady entertained us in a style of hospitality once so characteristic of the old families of Virginia. She seemed quite free from the whine and cant quite common among the first families, about the losses and vexations of the war." Her husband had held out against conscription until the servants absconded, and she told the sad story of how her older brother, Col. Lewis Marshall, had freed his thirty slaves, and had given them the farm and stock — on the condition they would care for two old Negro women, one of whom had nursed the master in his infancy. The slaves had remained faithful to the trust, and had twenty or so cows. Colonel Marshall had left for South Carolina.

Stuart, meanwhile, was fortifying the Leeds Manor Road approaches at Barbee's Cross Roads, where the main road from Warrenton to Chester Gap crossed, and where the Leeds Manor Road led south to easy-to-ford upper Rappahannock River crossings. So Rosser withdrew, leaving Maj. Beverley Douglas and seven men to guard the rear and delay any advance. On the morning of the 5th, as Douglas's command rode south, sharpshooters placed about Mountain View, the Robert Stribling place, flayed the eight. The Federals were driven off, but then the eight were attacked by cavalry riding through Stribling's barnyard. They too were repulsed, but then sharpshooters opened up from west of the Leeds Manor Road. Finally, twenty of Stuart's cavalry came to the rescue. Stuart later called Douglas's men "My Regiment of Eight."

South of Thumb Run the Leeds Manor Road ascends a grade, and Stuart placed Fitz Lee's men on the crest's east and Maj. Gen. Wade Hampton's men on the west. In between ran the road, and at the cross roads Stuart positioned his reserve strength. General Pleasanton, leader of the attackers, spoke of Stuart driving his men in confusion from their fortified positions with a severe loss. Pleasanton had attacked all three points with 1,500 men, half the size of Stuart's force, and reported thirty-seven Confederate dead, more than that number captured, and his own loss at five killed and eight wounded. Col. James B. Gordon, whose North Carolina cavalry suffered the most losses, blamed Wade Hampton, saying that he ordered Gordon's men to charge a stone fence that wasn't there. Heros von Borcke remembered hand-to-hand combat as his men were pursued toward Orlean.

Little wonder that Stuart gave short shrift to the action, saying that while he was in "complete control," the "lack of vigor" in the Union attack made him believe that their action was a tactic to divert attention from the main Union force moving on Warrenton. Accordingly he had Hampton withdraw by the Fiery Run Road to Flint Hill, and the remainder of his command, including Rosser's brigade, retreated to Orlean. One notes that neither of these roads leads to Warrenton. By November 7th Pleasanton's troops had crossed the Rappahannock and captured Amissville and Jeffersonton.

On the eastern front, Union clearing operations encountered their first snag the afternoon of November 4th. Several hundred 4th Virginia cavalrymen, including Col. William H. Payne's Black Horse, attacked an advance guard of 150 near New Baltimore. "It was really amusing," began the words of the New York *Times* reporter at the scene. "Men had their little pots of coffee on the fires, roasting pork, and a few were indulging the hope of eating roast turkey." Fourteen ranks deep, the Virginians charged east on the Warrenton Pike, and by nightfall they had pushed the attackers into Prince William County. But retreat was inevitable, and next day "flying artillery" pursued the 4th Virginia Toward Warrenton.

Riding from Orlean, Colonel Rosser's troops reached Warrenton the morning of November 6th. They found the enemy in town, and retreated to south of the Rappahannock. At noon a heavy snow began to fall. "Our forces in Possession of Warrenton," read the *Times* headline, for at 3 p.m. on the 5th, a Colonel Payne's brigade of 400 and two howitzers had entered without a fight. Residents told the invaders that Col. William Payne's Black Horse had left that morning and had postponed an earlier capture by shifting howitzers to confuse scouts. They said Stuart had told him to hold Warrenton at all hazards. The *Times* noted that 275 rebels were still in hospitals, an interesting comment since little more than a month before there were 1,300. Surgeon Samuel Fisher probably had half the Black Horse in bed. The *Times* also paraphrased Kargé: "Great distress prevails among the citizens hereabouts for the necessities of life. All the stores are exhausted of supplies and are closed up."

The sudden influx of tens of thousands of soldiers was taking effect. The New Hampshire 12th, stationed near Orlean at a place they nicknamed Starvation Hollow, told how they persuaded farmers, "all of whom claimed to be good Union men, to contribute a little to the commissary department." They reminded the farmer that if he were good Union he certainly wouldn't object to assisting the cause by donating a few sheep — and a few horses, to be exchanged for a receipt that would be fully payable, with interest, at the war's end. The 12th's historian remarked that the disappearance of miles of rail fence demonstrated that it was nearly as expensive to warm an army as to feed it.

Four days the Army of the Potomac had been in Fauquier, fighting their way through more than twenty miles of up-and-down countryside. But, it had taken them seven weeks to get there. Since the tarnished victory at Antietam, the army's commander-in-chief, Maj. Gen. George Brinton McClellan, had languished in Maryland for five weeks. To one of McClellan's many pleas for shoes and steeds, Lincoln answered: "I have just read your dispatch about sore-tongued and fatigued horses. Will you pardon me for asking what the horses of your army have done since the battle of Antietam that fatigues anything?"

McClellan had established headquarters near the Rectortown railroad station on November 5th, the day Lincoln wrote the order relieving the general of command. Two days later, with the order in hand, Brig. Gen. C. P. Buckingham got off the train at Rectortown. Through falling snow he was directed to the tent of Maj. Gen. Ambrose Everett Burnside, Lincoln's choice for new commander. If Burnside declined — his poor leadership at Antietam had helped Lee escape annihilation — Buckingham was to return to Washington without breaking the news to McClellan. Lincoln did not want a leaderless army.

But Burnside accepted the challenge, and he and Buckingham entered McClellan's tent late at night. The general was penning a letter to his mother. The trio exchanged pleasantries, and then Buckingham handed over the order. "Alas for my poor country!" said McClellan, and then, smiling, he said to Burnside, "I turn the command over to you." Alone, McClellan continued the letter, repeating the phrase "Alas for my poor country!" and adding, "No cause is given." No reason was ever given.

A score of memoirs, of officers and enlisted men, tell of universal sadness. But, then, who would not love a general who kept the troops out of battle and in one place. A patriotic New York *Times* reporter, standing by the depot next morning, told another story: The news was received by soldiers "as the harbinger of victory." One exclaimed "That's good news"; a second, "I am mighty glad to hear that"; another, "This war will soon be ended."

Partings began Sunday evening, the 9th: first the officers in full-dress and the clinking of wine glasses; on Monday the enlisted men, whipped into impassioned demonstrations by the officers — many of whom threatened to resign. It was all "Mac" and "Burn," hail and farewell. Tuesday morning the whole was repeated for townspeople in front of the Warren Green, and again at Warrenton Junction, where his last words were: "Stand by Burnside as you have stood by me. Good-bye." The train would finally stop at Trenton, New Jersey. McClellan had received his last military order.

Burnside had time to hear out McClellan's strategy — move south along the Orange and Alexandria Railway. But Herman Haupt, the chief of transportation and construction on military railroads, warned Burnside that the single-track O & A — if in prime condition, and it was not — could handle 900 tons a day. The 70,000-man Army of the Potomac needed 1,500 tons. So Burnside chose another direction, to Fredericksburg.

As leaders and orders changed, Union troopers mopped up south and west of Warrenton, securing the railway and occupying Rappahannock Station and Waterloo on the 8th. Next evening Confederate cannon opened up from the Culpeper side of Beverley's Ford and above the railroad bridge — half a dozen shots at each site. Federals moving toward the fords were continually harassed from the rear, especially in the Fayettesville neighborhood, where citizens were peaceful and unarmed one minute, and hovering guerillas the next. From the 13th through 15th, across-river artillery fire and Southern probes at The Springs kept Burnside guessing. At Warrenton, surgeon Sam Fisher said that Jackson with 70,000 men was ten miles from town. That one they had heard before.

Northern sources printed rather pithy comments about leading Fauquier citizens. An almost premature obituary of Maj. Gen. 'Extra Billy' Smith appeared in the *Times:* "[He] boastingly sought a traitor's doom. To-day he is a ruined man, prostrated upon a bed of sickness from which he will rise, if at all, a mere wreck of his former self." Smith had lost two sons in the war, but perhaps was feigning his sorry state; he was paroled.

Of other Warrentonians the New York *Herald* reported, "All the accomodations furnished were given grudgingly, and at exhorbitant prices ... Coffee, tea, sugar, salt, are matters connected with the past history of this place, and remembered only by the 'oldest inhabitants.'" Coffee consisted of water flavored with burnt rye, corn cake, and bacon. However, provisions were distributed to several "Union families." The widowed Mrs. Robert Eden Scott had to ask Burnside for food. He replied that starvation was a consequence of civil war, but ordered some stores left for her use. The *Herald's* New Baltimore correspondent called Warrenton a "hotbed of disloyalty. The churches and the hotels are filled to overflowing, with secesh sick and wounded." He noted that nearly every single girl was dressed in mourning habiliments, and doubted whether people could make it through the winter. Of Rectortowners: "hostile and treat our army with derision." They, too, sold to the army, but being patriots, preferred Confederate notes.

New Englanders camping near Warrenton said the Novembers back home were not nearly as frigid. By the 10th water had frozen in canteens, and an inch of ice covered running streams. Two had died of exposure. Green cedar smoked up the camps so that eyes smarted, and there were the standard complaints of wormy hardtack. Whiskey and quinine rations were given out. A *Herald* reporter called Warrenton "neat" and "attractive," but admitted, "the presence of our armies is not improving it at all."

Lower Fauquier left no diarists, or else their writings do not survive. But we have this fragment from alien private William Hamilton, stationed three miles from Rappahannock Station. "Neither dwellings nor people of any account near us, nor any sign of civilization except a negro village called Tuipan." On the march he ate salt pork, but mentioned that beans, potatoes, and onions could be bought for a few cents from roadside Negroes. And the *Times* did have a kind word for Weaversville, "a village of some six families . . . enjoying life as well as they could."

Four days after McClellan's departure, Burnside broke camp at the Warren Green, and by November 16th his army had evacuated Warrenton and moved to Catlett. The largest army ever to trek across the county passed by Bristersburg and White Ridge, and flankers guarding the west took the Marsh Road. By the 18th they had left Fauquier. Their scouting parties remained active, however, countered by the Black Horse Troop in the central and lower county. Veteran Hugh Hamilton, writing about the winter in 1902, recalled that duty was hardly strenuous. The Black Horsers would sometimes chase foxes, or stake their best riders and swiftest horses against each other in match races.

As the New Year approached, slaveowners waited to see what would happen. Lincoln had announced his intent to free Southern slaves in July, but waited until a major military victory — Antietam. The September 22nd Emancipation Proclamation was to take effect January 1st. Ida Dulany's November diary entries note a marked difference in servants' conduct during the invasion: "Their indignation equals ours . . . [they] make way with *their* chickens and other goods unscrupulously as if they had been the original secessionists." In early December, Edward Carter Turner remarked that the proclamation would not change things as the Northern armies always enticed slaves to abscond. On Christmas Day he wrote that most local slaves looked forward to receiving their freedom. The minority, Carter contended, were spoken of in dialogues such as this: "When 'The Emancipation Proclamation' was issued, my father told him of it and that he was a free man, and he was not able to pay wages. 'Well,' said the faithful old servant, 'I promised Mars Richard [Horner] to stay 'til he come and I'm going to do it and take care of things.' "

Ever the suspicious journalist, Douglas Southall Freeman surmised that Stuart's four early-winter raids through Lower Fauquier were prompted more by a desire to keep in readiness by capturing sutlers' wagons than for tactical purpose. Wade Hampton's 208 men were the first to cross, at Kelly's Ford, on November 27th. Passing Morrisville, and taking the back road by the Franklin Gold Mine and to Somerville, they learned that the enemy guarded White

Ridge and Deep Run. Avoiding the pickets, next day Hampton's force attacked west of Hartwood Church, capturing about ninety men and 100 horses, and returned safely into Culpeper at Barnett's Ford.

Federal troops also ventured forth, but with less style and, usually, fewer men. On December 1st, having heard of incursions near Grove Church and Deep Run, two detachments cautiously made their way up the Rappahannock. Fording Deep Run on the back road by Cropp's Mill, twenty-one cavalry encountered three at the church; they captured one, a Mr. Stone. If Brig. Gen. William W. Averell's report was correct, Stone said entirely too much, mentioning that south of Kelly's Ford such small scouting parties maintained a system of signals to forward information rapidly. The Union horsemen then approached Morrisville, took a look at the risky crossing at Barnett's Ford, and returned to base at Hartwood Church. Stone said that the ford at Kelly's was a good one; Averell would remember that.

Three days later scouts from Stafford Court House came along back roads to within three miles of Catlett. People along the way had told them about rebel forces numbering in the thousands, riding about Warrenton and Catlett. Little wonder they about-faced before reaching the village.

Wade Hampton's next raid began December 10th, through Fauquier, but of route unknown, to Dumfries and Occoquan, where his 520 men captured fifty and took seventeen wagons. By the night of the 12th, after a forty-mile jaunt that snowy day, they emerged at Morrisville, and next morning forded the Rappahannock at Kelly's.

Hampton's adventurers started out again on December 17th at the railroad bridge, and east along roads paralleling the Orange and Alexandria Railway, into Prince William County, and to Occoquan. Two day later they returned without losses and with 150 prisoners and twenty wagons laden with 300 pairs of pants and all the ingredients for a hefty wine-and-cheese party.

With Hampton safely across the river the Federals' turn came, and on the 21st a scouting party spied stragglers near Zoar Church at Bristersburg, and followed them toward Warrenton Junction. The scouts then observed a peaceful Catlett and made their way to a quiet Greenwich. Two days before Christmas that force encountered Confederate horsemen west of Morrisville, on the road to Mt. Holly Church. The Union party fled back to the village and brought forward the main force. Now they could only find non-combatants, but as some wore gray caps and tunics, they were arrested. At the canal bridge just east of Kelly's Ford, and to the north at Wheatley, strong rifle fire from Culpeper harassed the intruders. They returned to Stafford via Morrisville.

Two days before Christmas one of Averell's most observant foot scouts reconnoitered the Rappahannock from United States Ford in Stafford County, to Kelly's, some eighteen miles. He told of pickets guarding each river crossing, and of scouting parties sent into Fauquier every few hours. Averell also sent scouts to Warrenton that day and the next. The first party was followed and had to return, but the second got to within four miles of Warrenton on Christmas. On the road north from Warrenton Junction they met a man who showed them his oath of allegiance papers and said two companies of the Black Horse Troop under Lt. William R. Smith held Warrenton. At Turkey Run, Confederate pickets attacked and drove the scouts back to Three-Mile Switch. There, sixty Southerners joined the fray and captured five invaders. Christmas Day on the Rappahannock was even noisier. Union reports told of Stuart's men celebrating by running races, firing cannon, and "whooping and yelling."

Averell's raiders missed by a day the 1,800 Dumfries raiders of Stuart and Hampton, and Fitz and Rooney Lee. Crossing at Kelly's the night of the 26th, they split at Morrisville, Fitz Lee taking the back roads to Hartwood Church, and the others, unfrequented routes past Somerville and White Ridge. Surprising outposts in Stafford, Prince William, and Fairfax Counties, Stuart's raiders returned by a northerly route with 200 prisoners, as many horses, twenty wagons, arms, and other loot. From Middleburg they re-entered Fauquier on the 30th, and traveled past The Plains. At Kinloch, Edward Carter Turner sold them corn for $7.50 a bushel barrel and hay at $150 for a hundred pounds. The prices were four times the normal rate but the money was Confederate. On past Warrenton, and by New Year's Eve they were at Culpeper Court House. Contents of the wagons may have been emptied along the way, for Maj. Henry B. McClellan, who rode with Stuart, mused that the wagons could inflict almost as much damage as the enemy's rifles.

One would not normally mention that on December 29th the raiders stopped west of Dover, at Oakham, the Hamilton Rogers place, except that John Singleton Mosby mentioned the stopover. On the morning of the 30th, Lieutenant Mosby went to Stuart's room and asked if he could stay behind for a few days with a squad. Stuart agreed, and gave Mosby nine men, including Fountain Beattie, who volunteered. Remembering the event in 1887, Mosby wrote, "This was the beginning of my career as a partisan."

The last action of 1862 in Fauquier took place the day before New Year's at Barnett's (Ellis's) Ford. Federal outriders, coming in from Grove Church, encountered a cavalry detachment north of the ford, and drove them off. To Averell the crux of the matter was the height of the Rappahannock: passable now, but in the spring?

Nine days into January a Union offensive to harass Lower Fauquier with New Yorkers began. From Hartwood Church, Maj. Samuel E. Chamberlain's 100 mounted scouts set out to destroy the Rappahannock railroad bridge, but they were only able to cut the telegraph wires. On their return they scattered some of Wade Hampton's men near Elk Run. A second party, of seventy, under Lt. Leicester Walker, was not as fortunate. Returning from Brentsville and Catlett, and after a brisk fire fight with forty Confederates at Grove Church, Walker's entire rear guard was captured near Deep Run. Commanding general Averell docked the raiders a month's pay and relieved them from scouting duty. Chamberlain's report rephrased words of the previous fall: "Many young rebels assemble, mount, and form scouting parties at the shortest moment." When superior forces approached they became "idle, loitering, and ignorant citizens without arms." He asked for, but did not receive, Averell's okay to arrest all men between Brentsville and the Rappahannock River.

On the 26th of January, a Federal scouting party sent toward the river fords and Elk Run was attacked at Grove Church and suffered seven killed and wounded. The Union report stated that word of daily foraging parties was reaching the Confederate commands, and that's why the invaders were intercepted.

But Union raids persisted. On February 2nd a recon force rode north along the Marsh Road, divided at Morrisville, reunited at Mt. Holly Church, and then probed Kelly's Ford and Rappahannock Station. Near the railroad bridge they observed Fitz Lee's men completing a large pontoon bridge, and only at the riverside were they fired upon.

Three days later a party set out from Hartwood Church to destroy the railroad bridge. On the 6th they secured Grove Church, Ellis's Ford, and a cross roads near Morrisville. Opposing sides' reports differ, the Union dispatch saying that despite a violent snowstorm the bridge was destroyed and the party returned safely the next day. Wade Hampton's communique mentioned a few cut timbers and other timbers set on fire, and the burners being driven off after an hour's fighting. They were not pursued because of the condition of Hampton's horses. Hampton said his scouts had captured twenty-five and killed six in the last few days.

The last winter raid of record took place February 9th. Hearing rumors of the Black Horse at Morrisville, Union cavalry entered the village. Finding it empty, they rode north to Somerville, and there charged troops concealed in a wood, scattering them completely. No Confederate report countered that assertion.

In central Fauquier, Col. Sir Percy Wyndham, the proper Englishman, recovered some laurels from an ignominious Middleburg street battle with Mosby, when his cavalry surprised Warrenton on February 2nd, and destroyed eighty stand of arms. He then sent out strong patrols to Rappahannock Station, The Springs, and Waterloo, and, unmolested, returned to his base at Fairfax Court House.

From Upper Fauquier all reports concern Mosby. His February 4th letter to Stuart said he arrived in "Fauquier County" about a week ago. No location was given, but he was bothering the enemy about Middleburg, and had captured twenty-eight cavalrymen.

The same day Mosby received a letter from Middleburg Town Councilmen, asking him to discontinue his warfare as Percy Wyndham threatened to burn the town and destroy property in retaliation for the running cavalry chase down Washington Street. Mosby refused to comply, calling the council's suggestion "a degrading compromise." His attacks on scouts, patrols, and pickets — "provoked threats," he called them — were sanctioned by "customs of war & the practice of the enemy." But Mosby had heard the townsmen's message, and thereafter refrained from attacks close to his operational base.

A month later Mosby's band numbered seventeen, including such future stalwarts as Walter Frankland, George Whitescarver, Joe Nelson, and James F. 'Big Yankee' Ames, a New York deserter who didn't want to fight to free the slaves. And by mid-March, Mosby felt comfortable enough to ask Pauline, his wife, to meet him at Western View, the James Hathaway home, on a back road three miles east of Rectortown. He had sent Pauline two newspaper clippings of his exploits; she was with him at the Hathaways when Lee forwarded his promotion to captain.

Now came the tiff. In a March 25th letter from Stuart to Mosby, the mentor urged the pupil to use "Mosby's Regulars," not "Partizan Ranger" — a term Stuart thought in bad repute. Mosby disagreed. After all, in April, 1862, the Confederate Congress had sanctioned partisan rangers — they could keep the spoils; the regular army had to turn them over. And Mosby knew that the promise of booty was the way to attract enough men to carry through his uncertain missions. Lee sided with Stuart, but the thirty-year-old captain took the matter to Secretary of War James Seddon, and Seddon ruled for Mosby.

William Woods Averell never admitted to a connection between his St. Patrick's Day attack and the name Kelly. He said he chose Kelly's Ford because he knew the Culpeper terrain across the river from it, and because if the ford were captured, five miles of nearly flat fields lay between the ford and the Orange and Alexandria Railway. He also might have known that across-river Kellysville, the manufacturing complex of John P. and Granville Kelly, was the largest river-mill village west of Fredericksburg. Before dawn Averell's cavalry secured the road to Kelly's Ford from Rappahannock Station, and sent outriders to command Elk Run, Morrisville, and Bealeton. A command center at Morgansburg monitored the three perimeter posts. Starting from Morrisville, at 5 a.m., they crossed, and within two hours an army of 2,100 and six cannon were in Culpeper. Overrunning Kellysville, Averell found the mill works dismantled — sent to Lynchburg the previous summer. By afternoon Averell failed to press his front, only two miles from the railroad, and by nightfall, Fitz Lee, his old West Point classmate, had pushed him back into Fauquier. At Mt. Holly Church lay many of the wounded, and on the other side, the South had lost "The Gallant Pelham."

THE CAMPAIGN OF THE MOUNTAINS.

Map Showing the Blue Ridge Region, the various Mountain Gaps Recently Occupied by Our Troops, their Relations with the Rebel Army at Winchester and with its Line of Retreat into Eastern Virginia.

PLATE X

his page-one, top-center ngraving in the November h, 1862, New York *Times*, troduced Fauquier County many readers. Such pellings as "Hopeville" and Elk Town" had been andard on Virginia maps nce 1827.

Mr. and Mrs. Harold D. Kube   PLATE XI   Mike Hickey, February, 1985

Widow Elizabeth Hunton enters her own Fairview parlor, then the headquarters of Union officers, to plead for her last old gray mare. So impressed was an aide, that when Mrs. Hunton swept from the room, he penciled the scene for posterity on the wall.

6. THE DEBATABLE LAND

Living with Mosby — Upperville again; Stuart vs. Gregg — The troops leave for Gettysburg; some too late

MARCH, 1863-JUNE, 1863

Through spring Lower Fauquier remained a no man's land, with the only continual Federal presence at the stations and bridges of the Orange and Alexandria, the supply line for guarders of the fords, strategic corners and cross roads, and Warrenton.

Burnside had been battered at Fredericksburg, and 'Fighting Joe' Hooker was now commander of the Army of the Potomac. As Lee's Army of Northern Virginia had reinforced their Fredericksburg defenses, Hooker sent about a third of his army, some 40,000 men, north along the Marsh Road, past Hartwood and Grove Churches, and to Kelly's Ford. The marchers were soft from their long rest in camp, and along the eighteen miles from Hartwood to the ford, cast-off clothing and stragglers littered the roadside. At Kelly's on a hot 29th of April, the army drove pickets from the Culpeper side and turned south along the south side of the Rappahannock to strike the rear of Lee's army at The Wilderness.

Mosby was at Warrenton on May 2nd and heard of Hooker's wide envelopment. Bostered by some Black Horsers and a North Carolina troop, his command of 125 planned to strike Hooker at United States Ford in Stafford County. But at Warrenton Junction they came across some fifty lounging West Virginians, many of whom dashed into a close-by home and opened fire. Mosby's men charged the home, set it afire, and about forty prisoners emerged. The victors then went about picking up stray horses, and in such disorganization that usually follows a win were in no condition to take on seventy mounted New Yorkers who charged at 200 yards. They had been camping by Cedar Run bridge, two miles away, and had heard firing.

Colonel Othneil DeForest, their commander, spoke of "complete annihilation of Mosby's command," and a five-mile running fight in all directions, "their killed being strewed along the road from Warrenton Junction to Warrenton." DeForest's men captured 23 prisoners, 17 badly wounded, and 30 horses. A Mr. Templeton — "the notorious spy" said De Forest, "one of Jackson's best scouts" said a Mosby biographer — was killed on his first raid. No one remembers his first name. The Federals lost two and had fifteen wounded. Mosby admitted he should have avoided the temptation. He had given up a fifth of his force. For DeForest, a week's looking had paid off; he had sought his adversary at Upperville, Salem, The Plains, Aldie, and Middleburg.

This spring of 1863 saw the beginnings of "The Debatable Land," a term, incidentally, coined by Edgeworth's 'Navy John' Marshall, and forwarded to the Richmond *Enquirer*. For nearly two years there would be a repeated pattern of two- or three-day Union raids, searching, and destroying or foraging when necessary. The guardians of the county were to be mainly Mosby's men, or the Black Horse, often riding in concert. But if one read the newspapers, or the official reports, Mosby got the press.

On May 6th there was a skirmish at Warrenton, but no reports survive. On May 13th, at Upperville, 200 New York cavalrymen under Capt. William H. Boyd, heading from Middleburg, encountered forty of Mosby's band and killed one and wounded several. The cavalry's spokesman said, "Mosby's men don't wear uniforms, but appear like citizens." A day later a Federal party came across some Confederates at the Marsteller place near Warrenton Junction. Homeowner Marsteller was killed, and there were at least three wounded on each side.

On the 16th a forty-five-man Federal raiding party from Charles Town rode south and at Piedmont 120 Confederate cavalry charged. One surviving report — Union — stated that the opposing captain and other Southerners were killed. The raiders had five wounded, three captured, and abandoned 56 prisoners and 75 horses taken earlier. From Belle Grove, two miles south of Paris, diarist Amanda Virginia Edmonds saw the raiders, "a hundred or two," firing on some of their own men, dressed in gray, wounding two — "The best of it," wrote Miss Edmonds.

How did the Union enlisted men view life with Mosby? Walter Carter, an observant Bay Stater encamped near Morrisville — a village described by his brother Bob as "two or three old shanties" — spoke of a blissful Lower Fauquier: "a vast stretch of open fields, sloping to the river, surrounded by groves of fragrant spruce, cedar, and other evergreens. Our camp was ornamented with shades over our shelter tents; company streets were laid out and springy bunks made, the whole enclosed by leafy arbors, and during our leisure moments we enjoyed the *dolce far niente* [it is sweet to do nothing] of our army life." But the sharp voice would ring out and "air castles were shattered." Walter Carter said that on the night of May 30th "our favorite little chaplain was ruthlessly murdered by the guerillas and freebooters of Stuart's and Moseby's Cavalry, that infested all the wood paths and trails leading to the fords of the river." Brother Bob always expected "the Johnnies to gobble us" at night.

And how did the gentry view life with Mosby? Ida Dulany's May diaries mention that the partisan and his 125 rangers occupied the country around Upperville and used the town as a rendezvous point for raids. "The men live upon the citizens and consequently there is not a house where they are not quartered, and as a change of residence takes place after every raid, we have strangers every few days, and the house always full to overflowing. The impression seems to be that we are protected by them from the Yankees, but I fear it is just the reverse for after every raid by Mosby's men there is retaliation by the enemy, in which the citizens suffer severely." Mrs. Dulany said the broken stone turnpike bridge across Goose Creek gave some protection from Union avengers, "but the people of Middleburg and vicinity have suffered severely."

Late that month Union Maj. Gen. David Gregg, whose troops patrolled Fauquier, wrote "depredations of guerillas and bushwhackers are continued," and soldiers are shot daily. Joe Boteler and Dallas Gordon, who lost an arm at First Manassas, killed two for stealing meat. On their trail, 500 Federals from the vast camp at Elk Run searched the woods by the Gordon place at Somerville, and came back waving two hats and shouting "We got 'em! They're lying down in the pines." But the Federals were doing the lying; they merely found their hats.

Michael Graham, a U.S. secret service man in Winchester, wrote a May 28th memo on the lurking places of rebel cavalry and guerila bands. First, Graham said, look along the Ashby Gap Turnpike, all seventeen miles of it from Berry's Ferry on the Shenandoah to Middleburg. Then search the roads from Middleburg to Rectortown and look along the Halfway Road to The Plains. Then try the road to Thoroughfare Gap, and from the gap to New Baltimore. Then the roads from New Baltimore to Orlean, and from Orlean to the Cobbler Mountains. Next try the roads from the Cobblers to Piedmont, from Piedmont to Springfield, and finally, from Springfield to Linden. And to think, Graham was paid for that information.

His memo notwithstanding, Mosby had been concentrating southward, on the Orange and Alexandria, tearing up rails and burning the Cedar Run bridge. He asked Stuart for a howitzer to bombard supply trains, and on the 29th of May his command met at a place called Patterson's and looked over the Richmond-made piece, captured at Ball's Bluff. John Munson recalled in 1906 that Sam Chapman, a former gunner with the Dixie Battery, knew the difference between a howitzer and a saw-log, and so Sam showed the men the difference between the muzzle and touch-hole.

Next morning, east of Catlett, the howitzer peered from a woods by a section of torn track and downed telegraph wires, freshly mangled by the partisans. As the Bealeton-bound train stopped, Chapman sent one shell into the engine boiler and a second into the middle of the ten cars. The guard scattered to the opposite side, thinking they were raided by Stuart — Mosby wasn't thought to have artillery — and forty-eight plundered, taking barrels of fresh shad, oranges and lemons, and bundles of shoe leather. When Union cavalry finally converged from both directions of track, the attackers fled on the Burwell Road toward Greenwich. Near Kettle Run they were enountered by 170 New York cavalry, riding cross-country from near Nokesville. Mosby didn't want to lose the gun on its first mission, so at Grapewood Farm, just inside Prince William, he made a stand. The New Yorkers were to his north, and following the trail of dropped shad, other Federals were at his rear. Sam Chapman again set up his cannon in the middle of Fitzhugh's narrow lane. The first shot killed three of Lt. Elmer Barker's New Yorkers and wounded seven, and then Mosby's men counterattacked and hand-to-hand fought the 5th New York. Col. Simon Preston's 1st Vermonters then charged, and despite a second discharge from the howitzer they made headway in hand-to-hand combat. Abandoning the gun, Mosby's men scattered.

"An extremely hot affair for a small one," wrote Col. William D. Mann, commander of the railroad guard. There were four Union dead and fifteen wounded, and Mosby lost six, including Capt. Bradford Smith Hoskins, an Englishman who had fought in Crimea, and had twenty wounded, among them gunner Chapman, and Fount Beattie and R. P. Mountjoy, who stood by the gun. The Federals also took ten prisoners. Stuart, when he heard the news, said that Mosby could sell a gun for such a high price any time. A train had been destroyed; Mosby had lost one-third of his command in the action.

June 3rd initiated the Gettysburg campaign; Lee's troops began their move from Fredericksburg to Culpeper. At The Springs, a smaller Southern force crossed the Rappahannock and advanced to near Fayettesville, where four men were killed by Union forces under Lt. Daniel H. C. Gleason, himself severely wounded. After a few hours the Southerners retired, their move the first of some feints eastward.

On June 10th, at Clinton Caleb Rector's stone house by Rector's Cross Roads, Mosby met with four men, telling them that they were to be officers in his newly formed Company A, 43rd Battalion Partisan Rangers. The five then rode south to the woods by Lakeland School and met an awaiting group. Mosby told them they were now partisan rangers, and also told them to vote for his slate: Capt. James William 'Willie' Foster, 1st Lt. Thomas Turner, 2nd Lt. William L. Hunter, and 3rd Lt. George H. Whitescarver — killed the next day at Seneca, Maryland.

Ewell's corps had left Culpeper June 10th, via Gaines Cross Roads and Chester Gap, and on the 11th Lee again feinted an attack east. A small force of cavalry forded the Rappahannock at The Springs, and for a short while drove back Union forces. By midnight Hooker's forces were reinforced and were to hold the river from Kelly's to Beverley's Fords, the area of expected crossing, and, incidentally, the places where Union troops had crossed on the 9th en route to Brandy Station.

Next day a most unexpected set of dispatchers passed between Federal hands. Brig. Gen. Alfred Pleasonton, whose cavalry would soon spar consistently with Stuart's along the Ashby Gap Pike, wrote his chief quartermaster, Brig. Gen. Rufus Ingalls, and asked, "How much of a bribe he [Ingalls] can stand to get Mosby's services." Ingalls wired back, "If you think your scheme can succeed in regard to Mosby, do not hesitate as to the matter of money." Nothing more of the matter ever appears.

Because Lee's army was quite a way up-river, Joe Hooker, in his last days as commander of the Army of the Potomac, expected his adversary to move north via the Shenandoah Valley. But headquarters at Washington said no: Hooker's job was to stay between Lee and the capital. President Lincoln reminded him: "I think *Lee's* Army, and not *Richmond* is your true objective point." So on the 12th Hooker told Maj. Gen. Julius Stahel to thoroughly scout and search "the country beyond [west of] Bull Run Mountains, and towards New Baltimore, Salem, &c."

Lee, undoubtedly remembering the capital city's fear of a Stonewall Jackson attack through Fauquier in May, 1862, would again play to such apprehensions. On June 15th he massed a heavy force at Beverley's Ford, at the same time sending Lt. Gen. James Longstreet with the divisions of Hood, McLaws, and Pickett — some 25,000 men — north by Hinson's Ford, Orlean, and Barbee's Cross Roads, to the road junction at Farrowsville. Taking the same route, Lee arrived at Farrowsville on the 17th. Two days later Lee traveled up the Crooked Run valley, over Ashby Gap, and to Berryville. Longstreet's divisions remained in camp in the Farrowsville-Markham area, and Maj. Gen. George Pickett's troops bivouacked at Cool Spring Church. Stuart, his tent pitched in Kitty Shacklett's front yard at Yew Hill, would stay east of the Blue Ridge to prevent Pleasonton's cavalry from ascertaining the routes of Lee's army.

Hooker, meanwhile, obeyed Lincoln, and on June 16th the bulk of his Fauquier army left their Rappahannock defenses and moved northeast along the Orange and Alexandria rail corridor. Near Warrenton on the 18th and 19th his westernmost forces, ever seeking to observe Lee, skirmished and were driven back by Wade Hampton.

Frequent and furious clashes had commenced along the Ashby Gap Turnpike corridor on the 17th, and for four days the cavalries of Pleasonton and Gregg proved that the coming of age of the Federal mounted at Brandy Station was not a mere flash. Stuart and Gregg had met near Mountville in the hardest-fought small cavalry battle of the war, and on the 19th they mixed at Mount Defiance, a mile west of Middleburg.

While in the midst of charges and counter-charges to hold the hill, Maj. Heros von Borcke fell with a bullet through the neck. He was moved to Dr. Talcott Eliason's at Upperville, and Dr. Eliason said the wound was mortal. But the burly six-foot-four Prussian's health improved, and he was moved to secluded Bollingbrook. From Mount Defiance, Stuart's men withdrew to the west of Crummey's Run and forced another stand. Union Col. Strong Vincent, soon to die at Gettysburg, called his men's charges across the run "truly inspiring," accomplished to "the triumphant strains of bands." On the west bank they overran one of Capt. James F. Hart's rifled Blakey guns, an 1862 model, abandoned because of a broken axle. It was the first cannon ever captured from Stuart's horse artillery.

On the 20th, in a continuous rain, the running battle moved west of Goose Creek, where, near the stone turnpike bridge, Col. Thomas Rosser's brigade drove the Federals from the bridgehead west of the creek. By 8 a.m. next morning an artillery barrage showed that Gregg was not going to observe the sabbath. Under cover of the salvos his 7,000 men recrossed the creek and marshland. As the beautiful day dawned, one Union combatant looked at the country to be contested: "The mountains sharply defined against the blue sky, seemed to look down upon this varied, undulating battleground like a gigantic empire chosen by the Great Unknown for the occasion."

On the high ground west of the bridge Stuart's forces held behind a stone wall, but then fell back one mile to another stone wall. Then it was another wall and another mile, and finally it was the heights of Vineyard Hill, just east of Upperville. As the dismounted cavalry and infantry advanced along the turnpike, one Bay Stater discovered an amputated arm, hand and fingers outstretched, near a house where some surgeon had carelessly thrown it. The temptation proved too much; he gave it a slight kick, and soon the arm became a football for everyone, running the gauntlet from the head of the brigade to the rear.

Two-or-so miles north of the pike, on the parallel Millville Road, Maj. Gen. John Buford's division of some 6,000 pursued Col. John Chambliss Jr.'s and Grumble Jones's brigades of some 3,500. Stuart, wary of a split force, called these northern forces in by The Trappe Road. On their heels, Buford's intrepid cavalry were distracted, first by trying to aid an outnumbered force, and second by spying a wagon train trotting toward Ashby Gap. Ditches and stone walls stopped their first effort, and a rallied Chambliss and Jones, supported by Capt. Robert P. Chew's four-gun Laurel Brigade battery, ended Buford's idea of capturing the wagons. He later wrote that the battery "made some excellent practice on the head of my regiments." His men did finally drive the gunners from their positions east of The Trappe Road, but stone fences prevented capturing the artillery. A charge south on The Trappe Road by Col. Charles Marshall's 7th Virginia — "in magnificent style," said Buford — ended the threat, but superior numbers eventually forced the Confederates back to Paris.

During an advance through a fence gap at Ayrshire, bullets felled Capt. Charles T. O'Ferrall of the 12th Virginia. While being nursed back to health by Paris physician Thomas Settle, O'Ferrall claimed he could distinctly hear the roar of cannon at Gettysburg, seventy miles away. The same Dr. Settle had felt the lifeless pulse of John Brown after the hanging. O'Ferrall achieved fame as U.S. Congressman and Governor of Virginia, and Settle continued a practice that lasted sixty-two years.

Meanwhile, along the pike east of Upperville, Union Brig. Gens. Hugh Judson Kilpatrick and Wesley Merritt led their brigades by the stone fences, barns, and outbuildings of Number Six, Oakley, and Vineyard Hill, toward town. At Oakley, Eliza Dulany stood on the balcony, transfixed, watching the armies charge and counter-charge through her grounds; it was nearly an exact replay of what had happened six months before.

Because of the women and children in Upperville, Stuart wanted to avoid a conflict there, but the enemy, he said, "true to those reckless and inhuman instincts, sought to take advantage of this disinclination on our part." And by 3 p.m. the forces clashed on Vineyard Hill, the Confederate lines broke, and Union troops supported by artillery on the hill overran the town an hour later.

Search parties began to look for a prominent rebel, rumored to be severely wounded. Townspeople said he had died and been buried, and in Northern newspapers appeared this story: "The big Prussian rebel who was Stuart's right arm, had been killed at last, and his body buried at Upperville." But the searchers had missed Bollingbrook, off the road and two miles from town, and Heros von Borcke lived to old age.

Probers behaved in their usual manner. At Oakley "they poured in in such numbers that everything in the place was soon eaten up and still they came." Ida Dulany was particularly miffed because during the early hours of fighting, neighbor Robert Gray and some two companies of men had come to the house and were told to leave by Mrs. Dulany's mother; she was afraid Oakley would be shelled. A Union leader demanded the keys to the cellar and meathouse, and to one profane threat Mrs. Dulany responded: "He had better reflect before he disgraced himself by offering violence to a lady."

West of town Gregg's stubborn troops pursued the Confederates two miles to the heights of Lost Mountain. There, three charges led by Wade Hampton drove the invaders back to Panther Skin Creek. Evening fell, Gregg withdrew, and Hampton retired in a walk to Paris. Stuart called his maneuvering "brilliant."

As four batteries of Stuart's horse artillery and Maj. Gen. Lafayette McLaws' division of 6,000 guarded Ashby Gap, with Brig. Gen. Joseph Kershaw's brigade holding Paris, Pleasonton remained in Upperville for the evening and withdrew toward Aldie the next day, his rear guard harassed at Goose Creek and east to Middleburg. To the north, Buford's scouts had reached the Blue Ridge crest and had returned with vital information: Longstreet was in the Shenandoah Valley, marching toward the Potomac.

Because of the geographical spread of the actions from the 17th through 21st, casualty reports vary. Union totals for June 21st note 18 killed, 179 wounded, and 114 missing. Confederate losses for that day, probably not complete, read 26 killed, 83 wounded, and eight missing. Stuart's four-day losses were 65 killed, 279 wounded, and 166 missing. Total Confederate casualties for the four days, 660; Union, 827.

To the south, other Fauquier-based forces harassed the tail of the Pennsylvania-bound legions. To thwart any rear-guard or flanking actions, Maj. Gen. Winfield S. Hancock's cavalry guarded Thoroughfare Gap and the Warrenton Pike. At 1 p.m. on the 22nd, an unknown Confederate force ambushed one of Hancock's squadrons just east of New Baltimore, and drove it five miles east on the pike, almost to Gainesville. A Union dispatch reported a loss of thirty men.

The county court continued to meet on a "court in course" schedule, the phrase signifying a session whenever expedient — meaning when the Federals were not in town. On June 23rd one of the few war-related items — and the only item recorded that day — came to the docket when Justices Richards Payne, William H. Gaines, and Isham Keith appointed Anderson D.

Smith "Salt agent" for the county. The May court had recommended to the governor that The Plains's Thomas R. Foster hold the position, but something changed their minds. Salt, selling at seventy-five dollars a sack, was rare, and priced beyond the average family's means; the agent's job was to buy it in bulk. Justice Keith, his woolen mills burned, sold the land, and when court adjourned, in a true act of patriotism he journeyed to Richmond, partly on foot, to put the proceeds in Confederate bonds he must have known were worthless, for the Confederate dollar was now worth a quarter.

Before the Upperville battle, Lee had tentatively agreed to Jeb Stuart's plan to take some brigades east of the Bull Run Mountains and keep an eye on Joe Hooker's progress northward. On the 23rd, with Stuart at Rector's Cross Roads, Lee approved the plan, and at 1 a.m. on the 25th, Stuart's three brigades, Chambliss's, Hampton's, and Fitz Lee's, rendezvoused near Salem station and rode over the little-used Biscuit Mountain Road through unguarded Glascock Gap. Hours before, Stuart had sent Mosby toward Dranesville to scout the Potomac fords for a place of crossing. Staying behind to guard Ashby Gap were the brigades of Grumble Jones, who did not get along with Stuart, and Bev Robertson, hardly a strong leader. Once east of the mountains Stuart found Hooker's force so strung out that his mission was negated, and because he forded the Potomac behind schedule he was unable to advise Lee about Union movements at Gettysburg. As for the brigades at Ashby's, Lee kept wondering why they had not advanced, and finally, on the 28th of June he sent a messenger ordering Jones and Robertson to Gettysburg.

Occasionally a diary still turns up some answers to important military questions, and on the 29th, Mrs. Dulany tells us, she was breakfasting with none other than Brig. Gen. Beverly Robertson, whose whereabouts had been unknown to history. He and Jones, his junior officer, did not reach Gettysburg until July 3rd, two days after the fighting started.

Stuart had arrived July 2nd, and had he been on schedule, the battle would not have been fought at that location — nearby, or perhaps in Maryland, but on terrain familiar to Lee, and scouted out and hand-picked for the occasion by Stuart.

7. MEADE'S ARMY

Union troops settle in — Executions and burn-and-destroy orders — The Bristoe Campaign — Lee's worst defeat, the tête de pont

JULY, 1863-NOVEMBER 7, 1863

Beginning the second week in July, 1863, and through the month, Union troops returning from Pennsylvania maneuvered through Fauquier. They were now led by Brig. Gen. George Gordon Meade, who had succeeded Hooker as commander of the Army of the Potomac two days before Gettysburg. From Loudoun they rumbled south on the Halfway Road and on the roads leading south from Rector's Cross Roads and Upperville. The View Tree signalers guided their final maneuverings, and by late July most encamped at the old grounds, south of Warrenton, along the Orange and Alexandria Railway, and about Morrisville. The vanquished Confederates had trekked south via the Shenandoah Valley.

Northern diaries provide vignettes. On July 22nd Col. Charles S. Wainwright reached The Plains, a "little, intensely 'secesh' village," and as his superior, Brig. Gen. John Newton, loved the comforts of life — "baked beans and cayenne pepper never satisfied him" — they ate supper "at the house of the principal inhabitant. The lady's good husband is in the rebel army, but she was none the less willing to do the best she could for the general commanding, and gave us the best meal I have had in a long time. The corn bread surpassed any I have ever seen, being light and delicate as any sponge cake."

Provost Marshal Marsena Rudolph Patrick took another perspective. On the 23rd, at Markham, he wrote, "Officers & men are turned thieves & robbers — The whole country is full of Stragglers & the Officers all permit it and say nothing —" Next day, from Salem, "The Whole Valley was alive with Troops, pouring down through, to get on the lines to White Plains, Warrenton etc. where they can get something to eat. Some of them have not a cracker left —" On the 27th, at camp by The Springs Road near Warrenton: "An Officer belonging to the Cavalry with the Cattle Herd, was shot dead at the door of Mrs. Campbell's house, by half a dozen of Mosby's men, dressed in the federal Uniform — . . . The Country seems to be swarming with them & we have lost a number of our Officers & men in that way." On August 1st at Germantown: "There is a very good feeling existing in regard to our Troops in *town*, where they have been kept close, tho' their outrages in the *Country* have been perfectly infamous." On the 4th, near Germantown: "My scouting party succeeded in capturing ten men of the 6' Cavy. out on a robbing expedition & representing themselves as belonging to a patrol from me."

Library of Congress

PLATE XII

Timothy H. O'Sullivan, August, 1863

At rest, at Bealeton, each company of the 93rd New York Infantry posed for O'Sullivan's camera. Here, a toughened Company E, its ranks diminished after Gettysburg. The minimum strength for an initial Union company was 83, for a Confederate company, 50. Confederate units could not afford the luxury of photographers.

Library of Congress

PLATE XIII

Timothy H. O'Sullivan, August, 1863

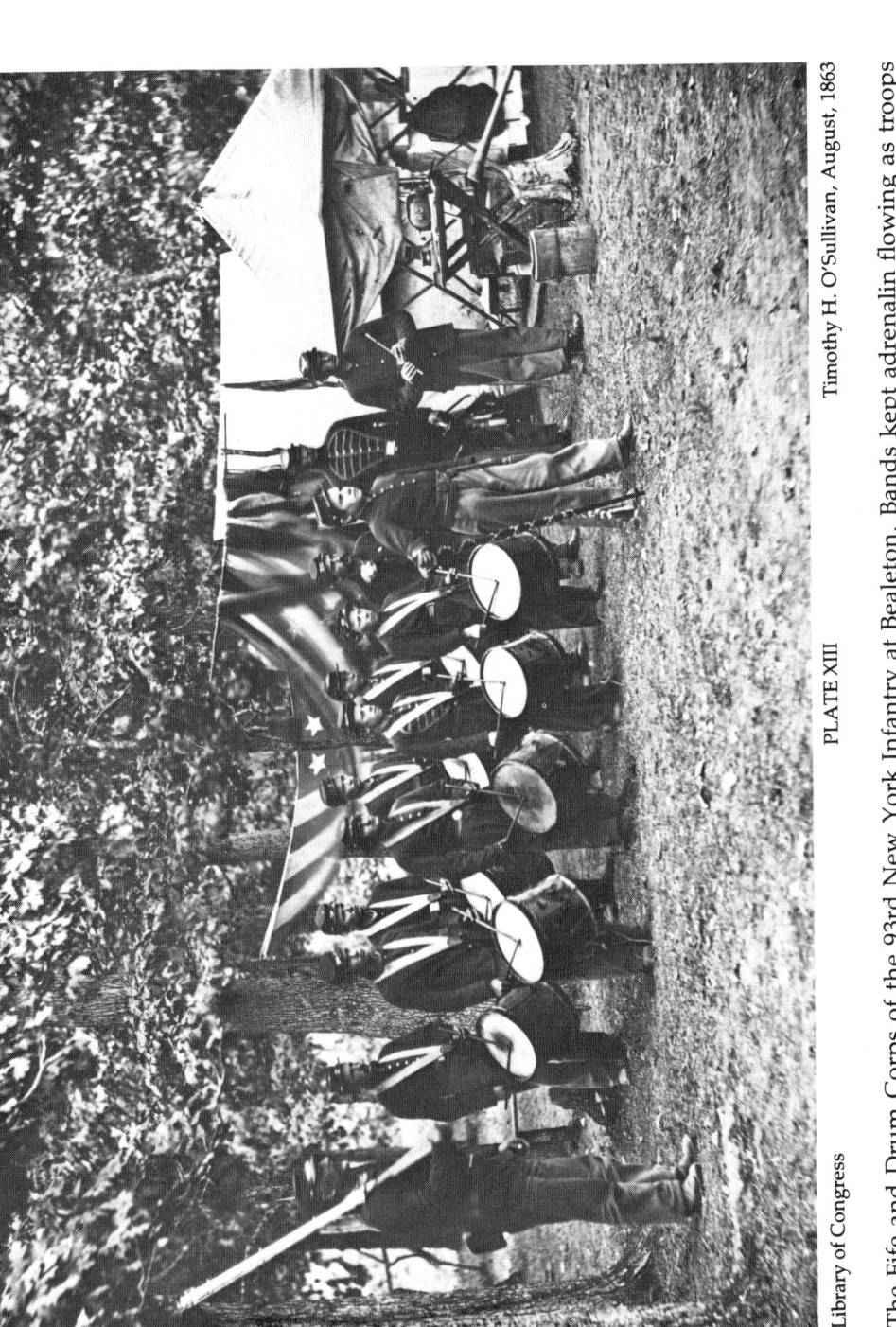

The Fife and Drum Corps of the 93rd New York Infantry at Bealeton. Bands kept adrenalin flowing as troops went to battle, and in slack times kept up morale. During the occupation, courthouse concerts were a fixture. After the Union armies had left for their final time, one Warrenton maiden said wistfully that she would never again hear that air from *Trovatore*.

Library of Congress   PLATE XIV   Timothy H. O'Sullivan, November, 1863

A temporary Union camp in front of Melrose, Dr. James Murray's 1849 home, north of Three-Mile Switch, now Casanova. Soldiers dubbed the edifice "Castle Murray." Officers often quartered themselves in the finer homes, welcomed by residents as protection against thievery. The castle's grand circular staircase inspired guest Mary Roberts Rinehart to write her first mystery in 1908.

Library of Congress   PLATE XV   Timothy H. O'Sullivan, August, 1863

Officers dine in style, lacking only table cloth and wine glasses. This Company F quintet of the 93rd New York Infantry sit at Bealeton, backed by their waiter boys and cook, who deferentially doff hats — or are they fanning the officers? Other less-respectful messmen join the act. The proposed toast hardly looks civil.

New York City-born photographer Timothy H. O'Sullivan worked with Mathew Brady before and during the war. Twice shell fragments hit his camera. His late 1860's and 1870's photographs of the American West are as memorable as those of Fauquier.

From Warrenton, Maj. Gen. John Sedgwick wrote his sister on July 26th: "This is a beautiful country, but has not been cultivated this year; fences all down, houses deserted, and everything denoting the presence of both armies last fall, and the fear of both coming again; there are no such articles as vegetables or groceries to be had. We captured twelve thousand head of cattle and eight thousand head of sheep that the enemy had driven from Pennsylvania."

To give the home-county perspective, at Glen Welby on July 28th, Fanny Carter Scott wrote: "The incessant streams to and from the house . . . I fear our sheep are all gone . . . All our meal was taken . . . some of our hogs were killed . . . one colt . . . perhaps some of the young cattle . . . We are thankful and consider ourselves fortunate and are thankful to have a house left and to have suffered no personal violence. Some have lost all, a few I've heard from had their houses burned."

A proclamation greeted citizens in early August. Issued by General Meade on July 30th, and to affect all living within ten miles of the Orange and Alexandria Railway (in Fauquier everywhere southward from an arc drawn through Orlean, Salem, and The Plains), the decree warned people in this region that if the railroad were damaged in any way "they will be impressed as laborers to repair all damages." And if that did not stop depredations, all inhabitants "along the railroad" would be relocated behind Union lines "and their property taken for Government uses." The first dictum was imposed, to a degree, by using black and poor-white labor; the second was not.

Brigadier General Herman Haupt, in charge of construction and operation of U.S. military railroads, undoubtedly urged issuance of the decree. A few days later he wrote Maj. Gen. Henry Halleck, Lincoln's military advisor, and explained the typical manner of rail destruction. Cross-ties and fence rails were set on fire and the rails placed atop the blaze. Haupt, however, found that he could straighten three-fourths of the bent rails without heating, and the rest could be restored by heating — all in a shorter time than it took to create the damage. Haupt, who offered to work without pay, resigned in September due to interference and restrictions placed on his work and suggestions.

Confederate Col. A. R. Boteler suggested an intriguing plan concerning the O & A on August 25th. Why not place some of Rains's "subterra torpedoes" under the tracks? Stuart and Mosby agreed. Brig. Gen. Gabriel James Rains had developed the first land mines and booby traps, then looked upon in the same manner as poison gas. The plan was not approved, but Rains's land torpedoes were laid at the approaches to Richmond and along the James in June, 1864.

As usual the Union pickets and scouts kept to the main roads. In late August and early September, New York cavalry hunted Lije White and Mosby on the roads from Weaversville to New Baltimore and The Plains, and north to Middleburg. By late July these partisans had tolled twelve wagons, 123 horses and mules, and 141 prisoners — all taken in Fauquier from

Gettysburg veterans. As Union armies now blocked the routes to Libby Prison, Mosby had set up his own p.o.w. camp, its camouflaged pup tents nestled in the Bull Run Mountains a short distance south of Hopewell Gap.

Private William Hamilton wrote in his diary on August 25th that deserters were pouring into his camp at Rappahannock Station daily; 300 had come one Sunday evening. With scarcely an exception, he said, they said they were from South Carolina. A New York *Times* article datelined September 1 reported that groups of "deserters" joined the Union army, stole horses and goods, and then rejoined old comrades.

Private Hamilton continued his observations of Lower Fauquier: "This is a funny looking country. It has all the appearance of never having been cultivated. The land looks and I guess is good. It will take a man some time after the war is over to hunt up his possessions if he has been absent from them." Catching Hamilton's eye was a two-mile road lined with cedars; but first the fences went, then, two weeks later, the cedars — cut down for shade. New soldiers, he said, were more destructive than old ones.

Newcomers were mainly conscripts, and Andrew Ford, historian for the 15th Massachusetts Volunteers, stationed at Morrisville, stated that nearly half of the 200 conscripts added to the regiment in mid-August deserted daily or found their way to hospitals. At least eight executions for desertion took place near Morrisville that summer, five from the 118th Pennsylvania on August 29th. The guard, ten to a prisoner, led the funereal column to a square formed by soldiers. A band played "The Dead March in Saul," and as clergy whispered words of consolation and prayer, the victims, preceded by their coffins, walked slowly to the square. Seated on the head of their coffins, beside their dug graves, they bade each other good-bye with embraces. They were blindfolded, and balls soon riddled their bodies. Instant death. And to the strains of "The Girl I Left Behind Me," the columns were marched past the bodies. Wrote an onlooker, "Poor privates must suffer for their crimes, but officers for the same offense are dismissed, or imprisoned for a few months."

Not until late August did Confederates begin their harassment in earnest. At Weaversville on the 27th, a scouting party under Hogan captured the entire mail train of Judson Kilpatrick's division, bound from Catlett to Hartwood Church.

On September 1st, after Maj. Samuel Chamberlain's Bay State cavalry pursued some 200 horsemen west into the woods at Manassas Gap, Col. Horace B. Sargent, whose Massachusetts cavalry guarded these remote locations, wrote his formula to rid the area of "soldiers to-day, farmers to-morrow." Each house needs to be destroyed, every tree girdled and set afire. "Attila, King of the Huns, adopted the only method that can exterminate these citizen soldiers, no mortal can do it any other way. The attempt to discriminate nicely between the just and the unjust is fatal to our safety; every house is a vedette post, and every hill a picket and signal section. The prisoner Rector is a case in point. I believe him to be a dangerous spy. He is a cripple and probably exempt [from service], but all his sympathies and family ties are rebel, and he is a dangerous neighbor."

One Federal contingent, encamped at Orlean, daily patrolled the Leeds Manor Road to Barbee's Cross Roads. Learning of the procedure, on September 1st Elijah V. White's 35th Virginia Cavalry waited in the thick bushes on both sides of the road a mile and a half south of the cross roads. Then, true to their nickname, "The Comanches," they swooped in and cut down or captured all but seven of Maj. J. H. Cryer's fifty-man 6th Ohio Cavalry patrol. White's men killed six, wounded ten, including Cryer, and took thirty horses. The remnant they pursued nearly all the way to a Union camp at Manassas Gap.

Other ambushes followed. Shortly after midnight, on September 6th, Lt. William T. Turner and forty of Mosby's Rangers charged a Federal camp at Gaskins' Mill on Carter's Run, killing three, wounding a number, and bringing out seven prisoners and twenty-five horses. Turner lost one man who wandered off in the darkness and got captured. On the 12th his men encountered a scouting party at The Plains and wounded one, and four days later they captured four sutlers' wagons and twelve horses at Fayettesville.

With success came recruits, and at a company meeting at Scuffleburg on October 1st, a second company of sixty rangers yea'd Mosby's selection of Lt. William R. Smith, of the Black Horse Troop, as Company B captain. The same day an unknown force attacked Union scouts at Auburn, with the assailants wounding two before retiring on the Carolina Road toward Greenwich.

Brigadier General John Geary, whose promotion signified improvement since his spring, 1862, tenure in Fauquier, received a surprise telegram from President Lincoln on September 12th. Geary, at Kelly's Ford, was asked to comment on the "conduct and disposition" of Edward Jacquelin Smith of Ellerslie, near Salem, and since that spring a resident of Old Capitol Prison. The exchange of correspondence on this matter showed how testimonies differed, memories faded, and the quickness of the president's concern when friends wrote of Southerners' hardships.

Lincoln's request came a day after U.S. Postmaster General Montgomery Blair sent him a letter from Mrs. Smith and a covering note: "The bearer of this Mrs. E. J. Smith is a relative of mine . . . Her husband is confined in the old Capitol for no offense save that he lives in the 'belt of desolation' & refuses to take the oath of allegiance, and his only reason for this refusal is that the Govt has not heretofore protected the people of his neighborhood. He has been a consistent Union man . . . Was an intimate friend of [Robert Eden] Scott & is well known to Geary."

Geary replied to Lincoln a day later, stating Smith "was a warm secessionist disposed to aid the rebel cause to the extent of his ability. He plotting and his son William T. Smith executing. This son was arrested by me May 28th. 1862. and sent to Washington . . . as a noted spy and bearer of dispatches for rebels." On September 15th Geary sent a second dispatch to Lincoln: "I have a telegram from Mrs. E. J. Smith relative to her husband. My telegraph of Sept. 12th referred to E. Jacquline [sic] Smith of Fauquier County. E. Jacqulin Smith of Clark[e] County is also a warm secessionist & abettor of the rebel cause. His son William gave (8) horses to the rebel cavalry early in the war. Both families were similarly disposed." So much for the ubiquitous Smiths.

Uncooperative natives were sometimes handled in other ways. On September 17th, near Buckland, an officer asked a lean unkempt, "Where does this road go to, my good man?"

"It stays right here where it is, and don't go anywhere," came the quick and crisp reply.

Then came the male chorus, organized for such occasions: "Beware! old man, beware! There are Massachusetts men behind us; an answer like that to them will bring down upon your hoary head the dire vengeance of all New England."

Events leading to the last maneuverings of the great armies through Fauquier began September 28th, 1863, when Lee learned that two corps, some 16,300 men, of Meade's Army of the Potomac had been withdrawn to reinforce Chattanooga. Even though Lee's armies were quite outnumbered, 80,700 to 50,000 at best, it was time for another offensive, again an outflanking maneuver, similar in its geography to Stuart's Catlett raid of August, 1862, but on a much larger scale.

The campaign to be known as Bristoe commenced about 4 a.m. on a chilly October 12th when Fitz Lee's forces drove in Gregg at Fox's Mill and Stuart's cavalry, supported by salvos from Armistead Long's eight-gun artillery, crossed at The Springs. There, under heavy fire from snipers, Lt. George Baylor's 12th Virginia led the charge across the wooden bridge, only to find the planks torn up. Falling back they plunged in at the ford and waded waist-deep through the Rappahannock. A Union report said, "losing many gallant officers and men, and 170 horses." Another specified seventy killed, wounded, and missing, and blamed the weak defense on a lack of ammunition due to a detained courier who could not produce the proper credentials. Ewell's following troops crossed a relaid bridge.

Meade's retreat followed two main routes, along the railway, where his men were unopposed, and from Foxville and various fords north to The Springs, to Fayettesville, Three-Mile Switch, Auburn, and then along the railroad. The main body proceeded unmolested, but the rear-guard 2nd Corps met continued resistance beginning at Cedar Run ford at Auburn.

Through the night of the 13th, Stuart's cavalry patiently waited in the hills east of the ford, trying to come up with a plan against a larger force. No less than six messengers had been sent to Lee, at Warrenton; perhaps he could attack from the Dumfries Road. As the Union troopers and wagon train lumbered by, Stuart's men could discern the conversations. But still no Lee.

Seven thousand wagons lined the road at daylight, and as they joggled across the ford and up the hill toward Auburn, Stuart ordered Maj. Gen. Robert Rodes' division to open up from the hillside. But his cavalry, ready to charge the train, were held back by the Auburn Mill pond, marshy ground, and fire from the Irish Brigade deployed on a hill west of the ford. Meanwhile, Jubal Early's troops crossed Cedar Run below the mill and attempted to cut off the front end of the wagon train. They could not. Rodes' cavalry dismounted, kept up carbine fire, and with a supportive seven-gun artillery battered the train. For a mile south of the ford, recalled an advancing Ohioan, "we had to pass under a galling fire." But when relief still did not come the gray began to retreat east. Union reports noted their casualties as twenty-four, with twenty-eight prisoners taken from Rodes' dismounted cavalry. At least eight of Rodes' men died after a "Come on boys, go into them!" charge of Maj. Gen. David Bell Birney.

"Before us lay a very picturesque valley full of farmhouses and barns," wrote Ohioan Thomas Galwey, and as day broke the train and troops moved south on the old Dumfries Road down the Cedar Run valley. Maj. Henry Brainard McClellan, Stuart's adjutant, described Auburn village as consisting of the residence of Stephen McCormick, a post office, and a blacksmith shop.

Three miles south, at St. Stephen's Church and Post Office, the Federal force split, the wagon train rumbling toward Catlett, contested all the way, Gregg's forces heading north on the Greenwich Road. Confederate batteries on Auburn heights had been moved to the wooded hills north of St. Stephen's, and again bombarded the 2nd Corps. But the Federals moved east of Prospect Hill, skirting the guns, and were on the way to a decisive victory at Bristoe Station later that day.

Unable to cut Meade's army in two, Lee's forces began their return to the Culpeper side of the Rappahannock on October 18th. Their main success was the destruction of the Orange and Alexandria, using a technique not mentioned by Herman Haupt. When the center of the rail was red hot, soldiers would carry the rail on a litter to the nearest tree or post. Then they would quickly wind the rail around the wood in an "iron necktie." Rail sections in good condition were hauled across the Rappahannock. On the 15th and 16th the Confederates once more destroyed the Broad Run, Cedar Run, and Licking Run bridges — the Union army already having blown up a pier of the Rappahannock River span.

Cavalry guarded Lee's retreat, and on October 19th Stuart's and Fitz Lee's horsemen joined to repulse the Federals in a running action known in Southern circles as "Buckland Races." Stuart, on picket duty near Bull Run, had fallen back along the Warrenton Pike, and Fitz Lee, scouting the Auburn-Catlett-Bristoe triangle, was at Auburn. At dawn Stuart's forces massed on the lower slopes of Saint's Hill by Broad Run, and held ground south to the Buckland turnpike bridge and ford, the two safe crossing places. Fitz Lee's courier then rode up with promise of reinforcements and his commander's suggestion that Stuart withdraw to New Baltimore and then counterattack when Fitz Lee charged the enemy's rear left flank. Stuart agreed.

The 7th Michigan Cavalry of George Armstrong Custer, a brigadier general at age twenty-three, had, after two hours, driven Stuart's men away from the bridge, ford, and hill slopes. The New York *Herald* cited Col. Russell Alger's 6th Michigan, dismounted, deployed, and using the celebrated Spencer Repeating Carbine. On orders from Brig. Gen. Hugh Judson Kilpatrick, Brig. Gen. Henry E. Davies, Jr.'s cavalry advanced west to New Baltimore. Kilpatrick then ordered Davies to hold the village and challenge Stuart, whose troops had taken a stand three miles west, on the heights at Chestnut Forks.

When Stuart heard Fitz Lee's guns, Hampton's brigade whirled about and Brig. Gen. Pierce M. B. Young's and Thomas Rosser's troops charged Davies' flanks. Sensing a trap, Davies about-faced and commenced the race for Buckland, six miles distant. At the bridge the stubborn "yellow hair," whose cavalry sustained the highest losses of any Federal mounted unit, refused to retreat. Only when Custer saw the oncoming dust cloud along the pike did his men recross the bridge. Davies recrossed upstream. Not until they rode another four miles, to Haymarket and to Gainesville, did the routed rest. Union reports spoke of 150 killed, wounded, or missing. Stuart reported 250 prisoners taken along with much booty, and wanted to follow up the offensive with a raid to the Potomac. Lee said no.

Stuart withdrew to the north side of Beverley's Ford on October 20th, and when Meade's armies, to quote Marsena Patrick, were "pretty sure" their adversaries were south of the Rappahannock they began reoccupying Fauquier County. On the 21st cavalry skirmished and artillery dueled at The Springs, and Warrenton fell without opposition. The victors then proceeded to mollify the townspeople with a series of band concerts.

On the 24th the New York *Times* told readers that Fauquier citizens "bordered on starvation," and that passing Southern armies took every bit of forage and subsistence. At Warrenton, Stuart was invited to dine, but sent back word that he would accept only if the hosts fed his entire command. Divine services were held at Christ Episcopal Church, the one open house of worship. The *Times* correspondent attended, remarking, "the sound of the bells made the town seem quite homelike." The preacher omitted politics, "No doubt out of respect to the large number of Union officers present."

Meade soon realized that Lee had not recrossed into Culpeper, but was busy fortifying the north as well as the opposite bank of the Rappahannock. For more than two weeks some ten miles of flat wood and farm land separated the forces of Meade — his headquarters first at Mecca on the Culpeper Road, then Auburn, then Rock Hill — from Southern troops hovering about the Fayettesville-Bealeton region.

Near Fayettesville on the 22nd, Maj. C. F. Taggart, called by the *Times* the best swordsman in the Union army, died while fighting with Gregg's cavalry, driven back to Liberty. On the 27th a brisk counterattack drove Union troops to within a mile of Germantown, described by the perceptive Colonel Wainwright as "so-called: there is no town, but there may have been a post office somewhere around." The *Times* noted that bold bushwhackers and guerilas made it unsafe to venture from camp at night, and several citizens along the Orange and Alexandria Railway had been arrested for harboring guerillas.

Protesting the arrests of innocents, Kinloch's Edward Carter Turner had written his brother, Union Maj. H. S. Turner of Philadelphia, and Turner asked Lincoln's military advisor, Henry Halleck, what he could do to remedy the situation. Halleck's October 28th reply placed the blame on "pretended non-combatants," aiding and sheltering "guerilla and robber bands. . . . Men who act in this manner, in disguise, and within our lines, have, under the laws of civilized war, forfeited their lives."

On the 28th Provost Marshal Patrick wrote about his general: "He acts strangely, keeping up no continuous picket line towards the enemy, who are, as guerillas all around us, stampeding our horses & running them off every night. Lee's Army is, a large portion of it, on this side the Rappahannock, throwing up Rifle pits & making himself very strong, generally— Meade is doing nothing & appears indifferent— If he would attack Lee now he could nearly Annihilate his Army."

The night before, fifty of Mosby's men had crept up on the middle of a Warrenton-bound wagon train on the pike near Chestnut Forks, unhitched some forty wagons, and took off with 120 horses and mules and thirty-three prisoners. Only when the raiders were about to burn the wagons did the guards at the front and rear of the train appear. The raiders rode off without a shot being fired. "Hurrah for Mosby!" exclaimed Stuart. "This is a good haul. Mules! and fat, too!" On the 30th Mosby reminded Stuart that his "species of warfare" could not be measured by numbers of prisoners or war matériel, but by increased guards on enemy communications lines — "to that extent diminishing his aggressiveness."

Late Saturday evening, the 31st, Mosby captured two New York *Herald* reporters at Stephen McCormick's, Auburn, and in a beautiful public-relations ploy allowed the prisoners, L. A. Hendricks and George Hart, to write home. The *Herald*, of course, reprinted the letters, full of praise and compliments to "a perfect gentleman" and his men, "intelligent beyond the average," and reverent toward their leader, "who, to use their own words, can wear out any four of them by his labors." A November 27th *Herald* editorial called Mosby "A Modern Rob Roy."

Sudden night attacks by Mosby in Fauquier took place about twice a week during the fall of 1863. Later he wrote, "No human being knows how sweet sleep is but a soldier." In late October, Lt. Theodore Sage, quartermaster of Brig. Gen. Wesley Merritt's cavalry, on his way to get forage, was shot dead between Morrisville and Warrenton Junction, and the same day several pot shots sent Merritt for cover. Most of Mosby's raids continued to bring in animals and supplies for a hungry and weary Army of Northern Virginia. And to scout out spots for ambush, Mosby and lieutenants rode out in small groups. On November 3rd, near the large Federal camp at Weaversville, Mosby, Capt. William R. Smith, and two men were surprised and forced to shoot a way to safety. Doing so they wounded one, captured five, and took six horses.

As for the stripped civilians, Provost Marshal Patrick told of their recourse: *"they* ask permission to purchase from the Commissary, a few articles, which can be given on oath of allegiance."

Meade's advance on the Rappahannock began the morning of November 7th, 1863. A Bay Stater, passing through Bealeton, a familiar haunt, found it "to have entirely disappeared; its buildings burned, railroad track, ties and telegraph poles destroyed." Two pincer columns reached the river about noon, one at the now-infamous *tête de pont* (bridgehead), a quarter-mile north of the destroyed railroad bridge, the other at Kelly's Ford. The wood and earthen bridgehead had originally been built by Union forces to guard the railroad. But the Confederates turned its banks around, and at the north end of the extensive fortification that stretched up-river for another quarter-mile, laid a pontoon bridge across the river. The Culpeper bank had been too steep at the main redoubt.

As Brig. Gen. William Henry French's troops crossed at Kelly's, its defenses softened by batteries near Mt. Holly Church, Maj. Gen. John Sedgwick's infantry inched toward the heavily fortified bridgehead. Finding the seven-regiment opposition too formidable, they could do little but enfilade the position with a cross-fire from fourteen guns set up on hills less than three-quarters of a mile away. Southern gunners on the Culpeper bluffs found these emplacements beyond their range. At Kelly's, French's men encountered across-river rifle fire, but pontoons were laid and the left wing marched into Culpeper. There they halted, waiting to hear from the right at the *tête de pont*.

Dusk fell, and the guns ceased their barrage. Lee thought the attack just a cover for the advance at Kelly's, and, if not, the Federals had never attacked a fortified position of the Army of Northern Virginia at night. But Sedgwick had other thoughts, and his men stealthily approached the works' north side — close to the pontoon bridge. The 5th Wisconsin and 6th Maine scaled the parapets, grabbed bayonets, grappled, and used clubs and fists in a twenty-minute free-for-all. They lost half their number, but overran the fortification and hemmed in more than 1,500 of Jube Early's men and four cannon. Only some 600, swimming the river or running the gauntlet of fire across the pontoon bridge, escaped. To prevent an advance, Early set the span on fire, losing the five pontoons.

Major Walter Taylor, of Lee's headquarters staff, stated that *L'Affaire tête de pont* was "the saddest chapter in the history of this army," and evinced "miserable, miserable management." While Early lost six and had 39 wounded, 1,629 of his men were captured or missing. At Kelly's, Maj. Gen. Robert Rodes' forces in Culpeper lost five, had 59 wounded, and 287 missing. Several men deliberately broke ranks and fled to the vacant Kelly house and mill. The November 10th New York *Herald* reported 140 Union dead and 260 wounded.

James Stine, historian of the Army of the Potomac, called the isolation of a division exposed to attack "certainly a very peculiar idea of Lee's." To Maj. Samuel Hale, Jr., one of Early's staff officers, went some of the blame. Early had sent Hale to check the situation after dusk, and when Hale saw men running across the pontoon bridge, yelling that their line had broken, he thought them liars. Early himself had thought the works badly located — lower than the railroad right-of-way and hills to the north, and with no moat; a defect he had pointed out to engineers.

Meade did not, however, follow up the victory, and on the 10th Lee withdrew from the hurriedly drawn Brandy Station-Stevensburg line south to the Orange County side of the Rapidan. One month and one day before he had been in the same position — heading north to Bristoe.

Liberty of Congress PLATE XVI Attributed to Timothy H. O'Sullivan, August, 1863

New York *Times* and *Herald* reporters followed the Union armies, and from 1862 to 1864 wrote a great deal about Fauquier. Two months after this picture was snapped at Bealeton, Mosby's men captured two *Herald* staffers and allowed them to write home. They dutifully called their captor "a perfect gentleman who could wear out any four of his men by his labors." The *Herald* noted that while they missed the reporters, they also missed the wagon and six horses lost that month.

Repairing Orange and Alexandria Railroad near Catletts Station, after its destruction by the Confederates October 1863.

PLATE XVII

Library of Congress Attributed to Mathew B. Brady, October, 1863

When this photograph first appeared in the 1911 *Photographic History of the Civil War*, its caption read: "Repairing After Stuart's Raid" — part of Lee's Bristoe Campaign to cut off Meade's withdrawal from the Rappahannock line. Note the rails, twisted by fire; it took a month to repair the damage. And while Lee did not entrap Meade, he forced a forty-mile withdrawal.

National Archives

PLATE XVIII

Attributed to Mathew B. Brady, ca. 1864

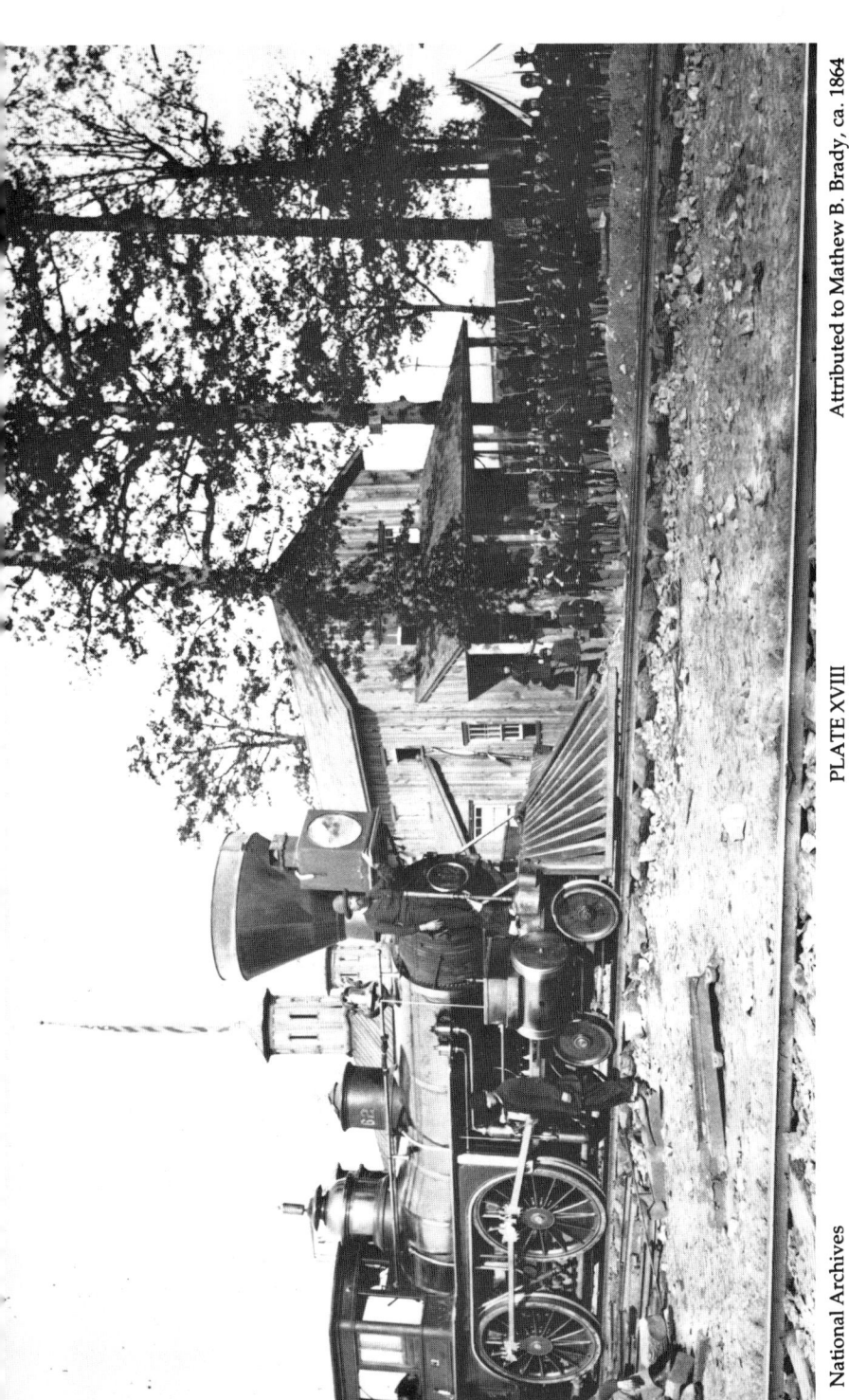

Old captions title this photograph "McClellan's Troops Awaiting Transport to Alexandria." But, Baldwin built Engine 162 in 1864, well after 'Mac' had been retired. The location, Warrenton Junction, now Calverton, with the combined station, store, and Owl Run Post Office in the background.

Library of Congress   Timothy H. O'Sullivan, March, 1864

The precisioned camp of the 50th New York Engineers at Rappahannock Station, today's Remington. Scores of similar camps, used for two and three winters, extended south from Warrenton. Note the stumps in the foreground. Two months later the pontoon boats at left were hitched, and U. S. Grant's armies began their final campaign of attrition.

PLATE XIX

Library of Congress   Timothy H. O'Sullivan, March, 1864

Officers of the 50th New York Engineers lived in style, and only makeshift log chimneys belie permanence. Note the board walks — and, to provide that homey touch, some trees were left standing.

8. GUERILLAS AND BUSHWHACKERS

Mosby gets the press — The grandest ball ever held in Warrenton — Petite guerre — Hangings — The Burning Raid — Surrender

NOVEMBER 8, 1863-APRIL 21, 1865

The armies of note had left, and with them ended a myriad of reports and dispatches recorded in the *Official Records*. The war correspondents stayed about a month more — Mosby was always good press. Fauquier's record from that decisive November day now becomes one of Mosbyana spiced with Alexander Hunter, guerillas and bushwhackers, and diary entries backed up by vivid and vague reminiscences faithfully jotted down by The Plains's Frances B. Foster and Sumerduck's Marvin D. Gore in the 1930's.

No let-up followed the bridgehead battle. On November 8th there was a skirmish at The Springs, but details do not survive. The New York *Herald* reported a dozen officers and enlisted men captured between the 8th and 10th by a band of rangers roaming the Catlett area. The band had picked up some trackmen working on the Orange and Alexandria, put them through a mock trial at Auburn, threatened them with death, and then sent them walking back to Catlett in their underwear. Little wonder that Hezekiah Shacklett, Kitty's brother, received a similar mock trial which ended with a rope around 'Kiah's neck and a shock from which he never rallied.

On November 21st Capt. William Smith's and Lt. Thomas Turner's companies, decked out in Union tunics, stopped a wagon train near Liberty. They killed about eight, captured a number, and rode off with three wagons and two ambulances, as well as 12 prisoners, 10 horses, and 17 mules. Northern reports said the wagoneers mistook the attackers for friends, and said there were five Confederate wounded.

Meanwhile, Col. Charles R. Lowell, Jr.'s 250-man cavalry had been combing Upper Fauquier for three days, their sortie piloted by Alexander F. 'Yankee' Davis, a Union sympathizer who lived close to Mt. Zion Church east of Aldie, and Charles Binns, a Mosby deserter — found drunk, he feared reprisals. In The Plains-Hopewell neighborhood they killed two, captured eighteen uniformed soldiers claiming to be Mosby's men, seven "smugglers & horse-thieves," and thirty-five horses. Binns knew where his former compatriots stayed, and several were caught asleep.

By November 23rd the 572-foot-long Rappahannock rail bridge had been repaired, and the O & A was again navigable through Fauquier; the repairs had taken seven days. Two days later Mosby told Stuart that railway guards now stood in sight of each other, and intimated that attacks on that line were not advisable. Since the 5th his men had captured seventy-five, taken more than 100 horses and mules, and six wagons — all without the loss of a man.

According to the *Herald,* Mosby's stock was reduced considerably the night of the 23rd, when 200 head of cattle, sheep, and mules were led by Federal forces into Bristoe Station. The newspaper did not reveal the place of capture. Mosby's December accounting mentioned only that during the month he had captured 100 horses and mules, the same number of men, and killed and wounded a "considerable number."

An unknown force of Confederate raiders captured one-third of a twenty-one man guard near Fayetteville on November 30th, and telling of the event, Col. Chapman Biddle warned that the small group invited attack. James Williamson, one of Mosby's men, observed that during that winter Union troops bivouacked in large camps, too strong to be attacked, and dispensed with multiple pickets. Of the 30th, the New York *Times* reported from Bealeton: heavy and continuous firing from early dawn to 3 p.m. From the *O. R.'s,* only a December 3rd skirmish at Ellis's Ford, with no circumstantial reports, emerged from a very cold early winter. And from Upper Fauquier the picture was the same, Amanda Edmonds writing from Belle Grove near Paris on the 18th, "The Yanks have recently paid several visits to this section — raiding without accomplishing much, and making the Rebels skedaddle to the mountains."

Christmas was observed by "the grandest ball ever given in Warrenton." Describing the festivity many years later, Bettie Miller Blackwell gave Alexander Hunter fifteen pages of facts and innuendo. The Warren Green had been transformed into a mass of color: holly and berries, costly hothouse roses, and the red, white, and blue, festooned and furled on every wall. The 8th Illinois, garrisoned in town, had decorated, and to join them were Merritt's brigade at Three-Mile Switch and Kilpatrick's cavalry at Warrenton Junction. Officers only, of course, unlike the Confederate variety where "the gray jacket of the private and the gold-laced coat of the officer rubbed elbows in perfect equality."

The officers had invited all the society girls of Warrenton, and as some courteously replied "they had nothing to wear," a fashionable Washington dressmaker was summoned to order gowns of the ladies' choosing. Annie Lucas, turned twenty and affianced to R. P. Mountjoy, wrote down the details, sent them to her lover, and through the underground mail received word that Monty would be there. Warrenton had never been attacked, but a veteran Union officer took no chances and had the streets leading to the Warren Green closed by two telegraph wires, stretched curb to curb. The lower wire would trip the horse; the upper would fell the rider. Annie, seeing the wires, acted. She handed an officer a blue veil, and asked him to send it to a lady friend who was to attend the ball. And when the veil made its way to the unsuspecting friend, she, perceiving it to be an omen, closely examined it and in the fabric's hem found a snip of tissue: "Town wired, tell Monty not to come." And if the story had an unhappy ending it did not come until eleven months later when the handsome Mississippian died in a fire fight with the

Loudoun Rangers near Leesburg.

Eighteen sixty-three also had its functions of state, carried forth unrecorded to history except in result. Fauquier citizens elected Benjamin Howard Shackelford and James Vass Brooke to the House of Delegates, but did they run against their predecessors, merchant John M. Forbes and Judge Richards Payne, or did Forbes and Payne merely relinquish positions that had become mostly honorary? In the Senate, Alexander J. Marshall had won a second term; he had previously succeeded kin James Keith Marshall. Perhaps the former Clerk of the Court of the 1830s and '40s was buoyed to victory by the release of his book, a just-as-wordy successor to John Scott, Jr.'s *The Lost Principle*. Alex's *Book For The Times*, to give part of its thirty-five-word title, took a fight-to-the-end theme. And one would be remiss not to mention Maj. Gen. William 'Extra Billy' Smith, elected governor in May, but who fought at Gettysburg, and would not take office until the first of 1864. Compatriots in arms joked that Smith, age sixty-eight, received the heaviest vote from his troops because . . . well, soldiering was not Smith's forte.

Alexander Hunter, his Alexandria command decimated, began a half-century love affair with Fauquier when he joined the Black Horse Troop on the 1st of January. Swashbuckling and opinionated, his 1905 and 1912 books certainly riled the county gentry. He wrote that Capt. Robert Randolph's attempt to swell the fifty-man troop in 1863 only led to the addition of "trifling, scary, no-account men that ever propagated a free-born race." Specifically, he called a third of the troop undisciplined, untruthful, and cowardly — in those phrases that make Hunter so readable: "A good half dozen would valiantly rush upon a blood-thirsty Yankee all unarmed, in the desperate act of carrying a half dozen canteens of milk purchased from some neighboring farmer. He would suddenly find himself confronted by these Black Horsemen and ordered to surrender. Of course he would yield himself and all portable possessions, his boots, his hat, his watch, &c., not forgetting the milk; and thus despoiled he would be permitted to go. His captors would re-enter the thicket and proceed 'to cast lot for the raiment,' and then they would present themselves before Captain Randolph and lie worse than old Ananias himself." Hearsay, though, as Captain Randolph had resigned in October to become a lieutenant-colonel, a promotion that later cost him his life.

Hunter's words for Randolph: "born soldier . . . absolutely fearless . . . in times of danger as cool as an iceburg." But for his successor, Warrenton's Alexander D. Payne: "a village attorney. Utterly deficient in military qualifications, under his leadership the Black Horse steadily declined." Private Bob Martin should have been their captain: "That such a born soldier should have gone through the war in the ranks is but one of the numberless cases of the incompetency of the Confederate Government." And of Warrenton's Charles Bragg: "The worthy Mayor always met the visiting military with a bow and a smile, and offered them the keys and the freedom of the town."

Women of the Debatable Land, those "Circes," as Hunter delighted in calling them, received the greatest accolades, and one wonders how the near-emanicpated 1912 Fauquier lady perceived such glorious predecessors as the near-six-foot-tall Miss Sue Gutheridge, "like Madame Du Farge in the days of the Terror: cold, calm, and resolute," and Miss Hallie Hume, "called Lady Di Vernon, after Scott's heroine, because of her splendid horsemanship and her dexterity with firearms." They, ever as much as Mosby, were the reigning monarchs of Fauquier.

"The New Year opens quiet upon all the armies. From none of them do we even get a paragraph of news. Winter quarters and holiday amusements are the chief features of present campaigns." The *Times* might have printed that paragraph on the 2nd as well, for no news of the New Year's Day Five Points skirmish leaked northward.

Risk of defeat was slight, but risk of retaliation to citizens was great. Then, again, it was a severe mid-winter, and Mosby decided to risk a battle in the land that kept his men alive.

One of Capt. A. N. Hunter's Maryland cavalry detail had been killed by a sniper at Upperville, but taking such events in stride, the troopers rode on as scheduled to Rectortown. There Mosby's men had been called to muster, but now rode about the hills, observing the interlopers. As Hunter's detail of seventy-eight set out toward Middleburg, Capt. William Smith's thirty-two mounted men appeared on their right flank just south of Five Points, where five stone-wall-lined lanes met, while R. P. Mountjoy, Henry Ashby, and John Edmonds fired pistols at the cavalry's rear. Hunter's horse was shot out from under him at first fire and was captured. His men, strongly positioned behind a stone wall, fled toward Middleburg. Twenty-one escaped. Four had been killed, ten or so wounded, and fifty horses taken.

Lieutenant Thomas Turner's last raid took place the snowy sub-zero night of January 7th. On Lee's Ridge he captured a picket, who, at pistol point, told Turner that forty held the main post on The Springs Road. Turner, with thirty-two, attacked, wounded 10 and took 20 prisoners and 46 horses. Several of the raiders were frostbitten, and three were captured when a close-by force of 100 pursued. Two days later, at Loudoun Heights, Turner and Captain Smith died. Of Mosby's formidable raiding team, Stuart said: "Both had inscribed their fame in old Fauquier imperishably in the blood of her enemies." Of Mosby, "His exploits are not surpassed in daring and enterprise by those of *petite guerre* [a minor war] in any age."

January jottings from the New York *Herald* tell of continuing anonymous guerilla raids, mainly in the Warrenton area — where the correspondents were billeted. Deserters continued to come in, many expressing "disaffection, destitution, and discouragement," others as a result of President Lincoln's "amnesty proclamation." The document was the president's December 8th reconstruction plan for the South: When ten percent of a seceded state's voters in 1860 agreed to freeing slaves and taking oaths of allegiance, the state would be readmitted to the Union. The January 13th *Herald* reported deserters coming in with less frequency.

Two days later the newspaper said that Fauquier citizens appreciated Provost Marshal Marsena Patrick's doling out food to the people, and that this deed atoned for that perennial winter offence, "the mustering of several acres of fence rails out of service."

The largest concerted party to search for Mosby's men set out from Warrenton on the coldest night of that severe winter, February 17th. Their guide, wagoneer John Cornwell, had gone to Charlottesville and back, bringing ammunition, and Mosby's quartermaster, Capt. Walter E. Frankland, had disallowed some of Cornwell's expenses. When Mosby sided with Frankland, Cornwell went to Gregg's camp and volunteered his services to capture the command. The 350-man search party split at Rectortown, and Capt. James H. Hart and 150 New Jerseyans headed west to Markham and north on the Leeds Manor Road toward Paris. Near morning, Capt. William Chapman and R. P. Mountjoy rode south from the village to check on Hart's party. Amanda Edmonds, awakened at Belle Grove with "mortification" that February 18th, wrote in her diary that Hart's men captured three, but let two others, teenagers, go. Then they only searched the house — sassed from attic to cellar by Miss Edmonds — and even left behind horses. "Lenient for Yankees," concluded Miss Edmonds.

Just south from Paris, Hart's men ambushed Chapman's twenty-five, while a second Federal force, under Lt. Col. John W. Kester, having taken the Leeds Manor Road north from Markham, joined the fray. Chapman retreated to Paris, but then reorganized, added a century of men, and harassed Kester's rear guard as they rode down the Crooked Run valley. Union reports tell of one wounded, Hart, four Confederate wounded, and twenty-eight captured. James Williamson footnotes the latter figure with "included a number of citizens." Turkey and chickens were also among the loot, and in accord with Provost Marshal Patrick's policy of feeding the needy, Warrentonians had fowl for a week.

Ranger J. Marshall Crawford, writing about the raid in 1867, said its aftermath changed a fundamental policy: Instead of boarding at homes, Mosby's men constructed huts in the hills or retired to overhangs and caves. Lieutenant Colonel Mosby, alone or with one or two of his staff, would rest at a friend's house near enemy lines — the safest place.

Several biographers touch upon Mosby's February 21st victory and chase at Blakeley's Grove School, in Loudoun, three miles northeast of Upperville, but few mention events of the previous day. Williamson tells of five captured, and of Maj. Henry Cole's Maryland scouts reaching Piedmont. The New York *Times*, though, mentions a sharp skirmish, with seventeen of Mosby's men captured, including three officers in dress uniform. At Piedmont, the rangers were celebrating Mosby's promotion to lieutenant-colonel — to quote the *Times*, "having a jollification spree over the good luck they believed would attend the promotion." Then came the surprise, Cole's contested retreat toward Upperville, a charge into his resting column — two killed and two wounded — and his final flight to Blakeley's Grove.

March's breaking weather brought out Federal raiders on the 9th, when Maj. George F. McCabe's Pennsylvania cavalry charged forty of "Mosby's men" at Buckland, chased them along the east slope of the Pond Mountains, through Thoroughfare Gap, and to their camp at The Plains. McCabe estimated 100 in the camp, but as they formed behind a stone wall he was unable to press an attack. On the 19th a scouting party of Gregg's captured a lieutenant at Salem and a sergeant of "Gilmor's band" at Orlean. Another detachment of Gregg's commandoes returned from Hartwood Church and Lower Fauquier with "Mrs. Monroe brought in as a prisoner, and her house burned. No rebels seen." Her domicile's destruction was the first in the area to be documented.

Two aging veterans had memories published of the snowy March 25th when Mosby and six men, returning from the Valley with four prisoners and their horses, stopped at Benjamin Triplett's Hill-and-Dale, two miles south of Paris, and left Sgt. James W. Wrenn in charge of the captives. A Corporal Simpson of the 21st New York, pretending to tether his horse to a stile, put his foot in the stirrup, swung himself upon Mosby's steed, and drawing a pistol from the saddle holster, fired at Wrenn. In similar manner another prisoner followed. And as they galloped off to Paris, limited visibility precluding a chase, one eyewitness said Simpson yelled out, "Mosby, how do you like our style of fighting?" Williamson recalled that Mosby regretted the loss of the gray mount more than the loss of the men. Amanda Edmonds, after hearing what had happened next door, wrote: "I enjoy a hearty laugh over it . . . from the scene pictured in my imagination — seeing the flight of the two and the Rebels awe struck and Mosby's utter surprise and his blood boiling."

April's news focused on two murderous attacks by Black Horse scouts. On the 11th, near Greenwich, Richard Lewis and A. A. Marsteller killed Capt. Samuel A. McKee, a.w.o.l. with three other officers at a house between the Balch and Marsteller places. Maj. Gen. Gouverneur K. Warren, the officers' superior, reacted strangely to the incident, restating General Meade's proclamation of the previous July: Clear out all residents within fifteen to twenty miles of the Orange and Alexandria Railway. The d.m.z. would have included all but Fauquier's northwest corner. On the 16th, Lewis, Channing M. Smith, and James M. Love attacked five and killed four near Catlett.

Buoyed by success in two Fairfax and Loudoun County April raids against Mosby, Col. Charles R. Lowell, Jr.'s 2nd Massachusetts Cavalry stopped in Leesburg, Bloomfield, and Unison in Loudoun, and Paris, Upperville, and Rectortown. Searching homes designated by commanding officer Maj. Gen. Christopher Colin Augur, they took twenty-three captives, twenty horses, and a great deal of wool stored at John Holland's Blooming Dale woolen mill. Lowell's report did not state where the action was, but his losses were three killed and two wounded, and Confederate losses were two killed and four wounded. Fauquier's war had indeed become *petite guerre.*

Ulysses Simpson Grant had taken over the war's strategic direction on March 12th, and on May 4th his armies evacuated Culpeper and Fauquier and began their final campaign of attrition: through The Wilderness, Cold Harbor, Petersburg, and the road to Appomattox. No more would John Wesley Dodd hear "the prettiest music and beating of drums" at White Ridge, and no longer would an air from *Trovatore* waft a Warrenton girl to heaven.

On May 27th Grant told Halleck that 2,000, supplied with thirty days' rations, and quartered in blockhouses built in a week at each railroad bridge and junction, would hold the O & A between Bull Run and the Rappahannock River. "When we get established on the James River, there would be no further need of occupying the [rail]road South of Bull Run." Grant's timetable was accurate within two weeks; his troops crossed the James on June 14th. On May 28th Meade's telegraph to Grant read: "There are no troops now at Warrenton." Gregg's command had moved south to Three-Mile Switch, and would cross the Rappahannock within two days. Meade saw no need for soldiers at the court house, "except to keep at Mosby's men. This can be done by Scouting parties from the junction."

Halleck wrote Grant on May 12th, a week after the last of his troops left Fauquier: "A considerable number of our deserters are said to be on the Rappahannock, robbing for subsistence, and waiting to get through our lines or to be picked up by rebel cavalry. Some are said to have reached the Potomac." Marvin Gore's vignettes of Lower Fauquier during this period name White Ridge as the dangerous area, partially because of two bushwhackers, Bill Ennis and Ben West, who would lie in waiting for stray Federals and strangers. When a Union patrol captured young William L. Royall, they accused him of sniping and were ready to hang him on the big oak by Grove Baptist Church. But, say Goldvein old-timers, Royall's last words went so eloquent that they brought tears to the officer's eyes and he spared Royall — who later was famous for his deliveries in court. One of the nervier home folk, Billy Herndon of Black Jack Hill, had some words for soldiers killing fowl. "Are these secesh chickens?" they laughed, lopping off heads. "Yes," shot back Herndon, "and if you cut my head off it will still be secesh." The Black Horse Troop, unofficial guardians of lands south of Warrenton, were not in control, and if not quite the equal of the violent Valley of Virginia, memorialized in *Shenandoah*, Lower Fauquier, was indeed "The Debatable Land."

As for the oft-quoted phrase "King of The Debatable Land," Navy John Marshall's letter to the Richmond *Enquirer* referred explicitly to Upper Fauquier: "Old Fauquier was now under the reign of a king, who heard petitions, settled disputes, and by his justice and legal knowledge gained universal approbation, and that the section of the county had never during the memory of man been so cheaply and ably governed." Marshall could have said all that in four words: Upper Fauquier feared Mosby. He, alone, brought the unexpected raids, and had his rangers not boarded and foraged in the countryside there would have been few Union forays. The romance was not there then.

For Alexander Hunter there were no sacred cows, and while admitting the partisan ranger was the greatest leader of irregular warfare, other choice words flowed: "To shake hands with him was like having the first symptoms of a congestive chill." Hunter called Mosby "utterly self-centered" and without human sympathy. "He would have been a Stoic had he lived in Athens in the days of Pericles." Many Free Staters agreed, for Mosby was a teetotaler, and their living came from bootleg. On one still-destroying foray the rangers killed Sandy Jeffries, self-styled 'King of The Free State,' and a good fiddler to boot. Mountain men said the rangers destroyed the liquor by absorbing it.

"Mosby's Confederacy" was not totally in Fauquier, and the often misused phrase did not refer, as John Marshall implied, to an autonomous state. The name took its derivation from a June 22nd, 1864, order from Mosby, setting the limits within which his men were to remain when not on duty: From Linden, east on the Thoroughfare Gap Road (roughly the northern boundary of the Free State) to the gap; north along the Bull Run Mountains to Aldie; northwest along the Snickersville Pike to Snickers Gap; then south along the Blue Ridge to Linden.

Avenel, Ayrshire, Brookside, Glen Welby, Hathaway, Heartland, Lakeland, Waveland, Western View: all still evince the ambience that made them the colonel's favorite haunts. He seemed to be particularly fond of the views from Ayrshire and Glen Welby. At Rawlingsdale, near Heartland, he tested captured horses by racing them against John Douglas Rawlings' colts and fillies, reportedly the swiftest in Upper Fauquier. In the last year of the war Mosby frequently visited Waveland, tenanted to an attractive woman whose husband was off panning gold in California. His men liked to congregate at Scuffleburg; "The enemy imagined it a second Gibraltar," wrote biographer Crawford.

Eleven months to the day since the last county "court in course," a three-man court, William H. Gaines, Anderson D. Smith, and William J. Morgan, decided on May 23rd to resume monthly sessions as a step toward normalcy. And on June 27th Richards Payne was back as presiding justice — with ten associates. Amidst the lengthy agenda was a proposal to appoint agents "with the power of impressment" under an October, 1863, General Assembly act to provide funds for indigent soldiers and their families. But who and what was to be impressed? And the item was postponed to July, then September.

At the July 25th court a felony trial was postponed "until after a ratification of a treaty of peace between the United States and Confederate States of America" — the one and only time either country was mentioned in wartime court minutes.

Judge William Henry Fitzhugh Payne, the former Black Horse captain, in four days to become a brigadier general, chaired a twelve-man court on September 26th. The large turnout was due to the impressment question, tabled in the first item of business in favor of purchasing necessities. The justices authorized Sampson P. Bayly to buy, within six months of October 13th, 300 barrels of flour and 300 barrels of corn at market prices. At more than twelve dollars a barrel for flour, and eight for corn, prices had about doubled since prewar days. The court also ordered Sheriff William M. Hume to prepare a list of those eligible for aid: disabled soldiers and sailors, their widows and children, and needy families of those in military service.

Four days later the Warrenton Town Council met for the first time since May, 1862, and authorized unspecified payments to Thomas B. Finks and others for "night service" and "night duty," and gave five dollars to Jim Evans for digging graves on December 28th, 1863. A duo named Webster & Perry had repaired the town pump "for 4 pieces Confederate Bonds."

Searches for Mosby in Fauquier began September 24th, five days before he returned from a Petersburg meeting with Lee. Five hundred men, led by Col. Henry S. Gansevoort, left Centreville and followed the Manassas Gap Railroad to Piedmont. They were looking for the home of Joseph Blackwell, for informers had told of it being "Mosby's Headquarters." Once found, Gansevoort's men burnt the home, barns, and outbuildings — "as directed," noted the dispatch. They also discovered a supply of pistols and carbines. Mosby's men had often met at Blackwell's, and without forethought began to call the place by its fatal phrase, "Mosby's Headquarters."

Grant, on September 22nd, had decided to repair the railroad to supply Phil Sheridan in the Valley, and on the 28th Gansevoort described the line east of Piedmont as passable except for grass growing on the tracks. A few days later a work party moved through Fauquier, checking the road bed.

On October 5th, south of Salem, atop 751-foot-high Stephenson's Hill, but nearly a mile from the tracks and station, Mosby's two mountain howitzers opened up on the work party and guards at the station area while some 200 of his cavalry charged "the British," Sam Alexander's pet name for the Federals. One errant ball fell through Emily Fry's ceiling and bounced on the floor between her two grandchildren. She calmly picked it up and heaved it toward the Federal picket outside. Another ball destroyed the brick railroad station. The work party retreated toward Rectortown, but not before Mosby's men "killed and wounded a considerable number," captured about forty, and helped themselves and the Salemites to the usual run of equipage. Phil Klipstein remembered the brand-new tents, tin cups, plates, and cutlery. The tents were used to drag the loot home. Lee wrote Mosby: "Your success at Salem gives great satisfaction. Do all in your power to prevent reconstruction of the road."

Next day the band tore up track north of Salem and moved the howitzers to Negro Mountain south of Rectortown. Their fire was not effective, however, and they were too outnumbered to advance upon the more than 1,000 troops and two long trains. At Salem that day Mosby's men were tearing up track, and two miles to the north the 8th Illinois was re-laying track.

By mid-morning a relief train tried to make it through from The Plains, but was turned back by guerilla fire. Then, Alfred Glascock's company pried loose a rail just west of The Plains, and it threw a second relief train, killing M. J. McCrickett, the railroad's assistant superintendent. For a third day the relaying and demolishing of track continued, and now it was the Northerners turn to occupy Stephenson's Hill, a vantage point that gained them a victory in the track war on October 8th. But west of Piedmont the Goose Creek bridge was still down, and west to Front Royal the tracks would not be reliable until 1867.

Halleck's October 4th assessment: a three-week repair job from Piedmont to Strasburg — if entrenched garrisons and cavalry pickets guarded the crews, and if inhabitants along the railroad were relocated. By October 12th Halleck was more specific, and he ordered every alien house within five miles of the railroad destroyed, all forage and animals in that areas confiscated, and all brush and trees within musket fire of the railroad cut down and burnt. Men suspected of involvement with Mosby were to be sent to Old Capitol Prison, and all citizens found within the ten-mile d.m.z. were to be taken prisoner. The incapable-of-being-carried-out order added that if those steps did not work, an additional ten-mile strip on each side of the railroad would be "laid waste, and that section of the country entirely depopulated."

An isolated shooting provoked the Chancellor's Mill raid of the same day. A spy, sent to scout out locations of cattle and horses, had been telling farmers he was a Confederate soldier. Mosby's men encountered the spy at Chancellor's, on the Rappahannock River, and shot him. Col. William H. Powell then sent a West Virginia detachment under Capt. Shesh Howe, and they burned the mill, house, barn, and outbuildings. The partisans chased the burners six miles to the Rixey farms by the foot of Big Cobbler, but as other enemy forces were to the north they stopped pursuit. A day later, at the site of today's Willis Chapel, in Rappahannock County five miles from Chancellor's, Powell's men hung Absalom C. Willis of Mosby's command. A note pinned to Willis's clothes noted, "in retaliation for the murder of a U.S. Soldier by Messrs. Chancellor and Myers."

Three days later, Colonal Gansevoort, tipped off as to the whereabouts of Mosby's howitzers, led two squadrons from Piedmont and began ascending one of the Cobblers at a spot called Emory's. Guards opened fire, were repulsed, and a captured driver of the artillery, "by intimidation," said the report, disclosed the guns' trail. At the summit, hidden in a thicket, stood three mountain howitzers and a three-inch ordnance gun. The pieces and seven prisoners were taken to General Augur at Rectortown, and as Gansevoort took a fancy to one of the howitzers he was allowed to keep it.

On October 29th, Capt. Walter E. Frankland's newly formed Company F of Mosby's Rangers trailed an 8th Illinois cavalry party from Rectortown to Hatcher's Mill, and on the return, at Hal Dulany's Number Six plantation, Frankland's 100 decided to ambush the somewhat larger force. But a ditch and high rail fence confused one squadron, and at the mansion the Lincoln men bore into the confusion, with two volleys from their Spencer rifles bringing down five. Frankland's men fled. Both sides' reports noted eight killed, nine captured, and "a few" Union dead and wounded. The affair was the last to be fought in Old Fauquier, and took place on the same ground as the county's first recorded skirmish, of March 27th, 1862.

Two letters, their writers not known, present a picture of fall life. From Wyanoke, a home three miles from Rappahannock Station, a young girl wrote on November 1st: "Our life . . . the abomination of desolation. Grandpa, ma and Lucy and Jane and I, exist; I don't call it living. It seems as if we were on a little island in the middle of the ocean, for not a soul do we see; . . . We haven't laid eyes on a Confederate soldier since last spring. Most all of our neighbors left last spring, and we would have gone, too, but we had no place to go. As our place sits well back from the main road, we are spared the raiding parties, . . . Ma is listless and indifferent to everything since pa was killed at Gettysburg. . . . We live on corn and bread; no butter since last spring. We have sassafras root for tea, sweetened with sorghum, and we have learned to eat to live. . . . Ma and I took the last of our sheets and dyed them with butternut bark and made ourselves dresses, now in tatters. . . . We found a leather valise in the attic and ripped it up and made moccasins. They are really fine, and as we never expect to travel again, we do not regret the valise."

Another, affianced to a soldier, answered her love: "I would feel ashamed shall I marry: a bride among the sick, wounded and dying, and instead of the music of marriage bells I would hear only the groans, the cries and the death rattle."

Not to leave the impression that at least some Federals were concerned, even at that late date, for the well-being of Fauquier citizens, a November 5th affidavit noted that three portraits in oil, rendered by Charles Willson Peale, and stolen by a Union soldier from Edward Carter Turner at Kinloch, were "bought." On orders of Maj. Gen. John Sedgwick, they were "to be returned to the family at the first opportunity." The miniatures, of George Parke Custis, John Parke Custis, and Martha Parke Custis, were later exhibited at the National Gallery and at Mount Vernon.

Sunday was not a day for men to draw lots to see who was to be hanged, but the last of twenty-seven prisoners, all belonging to Custer's cavalry, had come to Rectortown that November 6th. At Front Royal, on September 23rd and 24th, Custer's men had executed six of Mosby's Rangers, four shot and two hanged, and Private Ab Willis had been hanged October 13th. Custer would have said he was following orders, for on August 16th Grant had written to Sheridan, Custer's commander: "Where any of Mosby's men are caught, hang them without trial." Mosby had asked Lee if he could hang an equal number of Custer's men, and Lee assented.

Twenty-seven pieces of paper, seven numbered, were put into a cap, and the seven were sent off to the scheduled place of execution, on the Valley Pike near Winchester — as close to Sheridan's headquarters as possible. As the party passed through Ashby Gap they encountered Captain Mountjoy, returning from the Shenandoah Valley with some prisoners. One of the doomed, a lieutenant, noticed that Mountjoy wore a Masonic emblem, and he gave the Mason's sign of distress. The lieutenant then pointed out another Mason, and Mountjoy, being senior officer, substituted two of his prisoners. When he heard of the switch, Mosby, whose wife Pauline was Catholic, was offended. He reminded Mountjoy that his command was not a Masonic Lodge.

The story's end takes place in Clarke County, for when a prisoner escaped into the darkness near Berryville, the sentences, in part, were carried out there. After hanging three, a slow task, they decided to shoot the remainder and botched the job; all three lived. Pinned to the clothing of one of the hanged was Mosby's note, a near copy of the "hung in retaliation" note found on Private Willis. Mosby's epistle ended in "Measure for Measure." Eight days after the executions the Confederate War Department approved of the hangings.

Eighteen years later, poet Walt Whitman, who had been in the area as a war correspondent, had the autumn executions published as "Glimpses of War's Hell-Scenes" in *Specimen Days*. Whitman, though, indulged in a bit of composite journalism, changing the scenes to a gory Confederate attack on a wagon train of wounded, and a mass shooting of seventeen captured in the attack. But Whitman made his point: "Multiply the above by scores, aye hundreds — verify it in all the forms that different circumstances, individuals, places, could afford — light it with every lurid passion, the wolf's, the lion's lapping thirst for blood — the passionate, boiling volcanoes of human revenge for comrades, brothers slain — with the light of burning farms, and heaps of smutting, smoldering black embers — and in the human heart everywhere black, worse embers — & you have an inkling of this war."

March to September's marauding, of late more prevalent in the Valley, had netted Mosby 1,600 horses and mules, 230 beef cattle, and 85 wagons and ambulances — as well as 1,200 killed, captured, and wounded. Grant, while not privy to the figures, knew that Mosby's suppliers had to be cowed. On August 16th Grant had suggested carrying off crops, animals, and men of military age in Loudoun County — a suggestion Sheridan did not follow. On November 9th Grant again questioned Sheridan: "Do you not think it advisable to notify all citizens east of the Blue Ridge to move out north of the Potomac all their stock, grain, and provisions? There is no doubt about the necessity of clearing out that country so that it will not support Mosby's gang ... they must be prevented from raising another crop."

Major General Philip Henry Sheridan had been busy devastating Jubal Early's armies in the Valley, and when the October 19th Battle of Cedar Creek nearly ended Confederate resistance he could effectively concentrate on Mosby's Confederacy. Sheridan wrote Halleck on November 26th, "I will soon commence work on Mosby [and on] Loudoun County, and let them know there is a God in Israel."

Why Loudoun, when more of the Partisan Rangers stayed in Fauquier? Perhaps because of Grant's omission of Fauquier in his August 16th dispatch, perhaps because the Loudoun Valley was the main bread-basket. Whatever the reason, the omission spared most of Upper Fauquier and did little to hurt Mosby. The greatest havoc was wreaked upon the Loudoun Valley Quakers, neutral or sympathetic toward the Union.

Brigadier General Wesley Merritt's two brigades came through Ashby Gap the morning of November 28th, the 1st brigade turning south at Paris, the 2nd north along The Trappe Road and into Loudoun County. That evening they were to meet at Upperville. The 1st brigade headed down the Crooked Run valley to Grigsby, then "west of Piedmont," quite possibly Scuffleburg. By nightfall they were in Upperville, a twenty-mile trip through rough country. They may have spent more time hiking than following Sheridan's orders: destroy all forage and subsistence, burn barns and mills, and drive off stock. Next morning the 1st brigade left for Rectortown, with "strong columns" sent to Salem and The Plains. The same day, taking separate routes, the columns met the main brigade at Middleburg; at least twenty-five miles in less than a day. A communique that evening placed Mosby's command in the Hamilton-Waterford area of northern Loudoun, and thus the enusing quick march north.

Yet, James Williamson and others of the Partisan Rangers, after eating dinner that evening at Ayrshire, north of Upperville, rode out and "saw flames bursting out in the direction of town, from burning hay-stacks, barns, and stables." At the Widow Mrs. Joshua Fletcher's, soldiers destroyed her winter's supply of pork by placing the hogs on a burning pile of rails. At least one mill, Hatcher's, on Crummey's Run, was set fire. Near Halfway, at Long Branch Female Seminary, headmaster John Sanford Pickett had the girls go to the barns, fill their aprons with wheat, and carry it to the lofts above the slave quarters. Amanda Edmonds wrote one brief entry: "The Yankees burned our barn!" The burners left no résumé of deeds.

Preparations for the coming season began November 11th, when Warrenton's Town Council arranged "for the Relief of the suffering poor of the Town during the ensuing winter." James S. Rogers would distribute supplies to destitute families, and to ensure there were enough goods to go around, the council issued $1,500 in bonds, "payable in gold or silver or its equivalent in current funds bearing interest." The first recorded purchase authorization came December 5th, when John A. Spilman was told to buy 150 barrels of corn, an expense that nearly ate up the amount of the bond issue.

Unaware of the Burning Raid, the November 28th county court's first item of business was salt — selling at $90 a barrel. Samuel W. Skinker, one of twelve justices present, motioned, and the court ordered, that Anderson D. Smith, "Cotton and Salt Agent for Fauquier County," appear before the December court to show why he should not be fired. Rumors were flying that Smith was either keeping some funds or was not properly doling out the rations. The court ordered him to get a receipt from each person receiving salt. Flour was next on the agenda, and Sampson P. Bayly, county agent to supply the needy, said it was nowhere to be found. But, he would try for wheat instead. Noting Smith's difficulties, Bayly reminded the justices that he was bonded. The court then announced that to buy wheat and corn it would sell $10,000 in bonds at auction in Warrenton. The "highest bidder" would be paid that amount within twenty years.

Closing the agenda was an item of "surprise and regret" in regard to a new government tax, and in one lengthy argument the court said 'how could you?' "In consequence of the invasion and occupancy of it [Fauquier County] by the public enemy since the withdrawal of the Confederate forces from Manassas Junction the extent to which the property of the people has been despoiled can only be approximated by an inspection of the face of the county, and where the devastated homesteads, the burnt mansions, fields once blooming with crops and alive with lowing herds now coated with violence, the woodlands stripped of their trees present an inadequate idea of the consequences to the proprietors of the real damage done them. All these ill effects great and grievous as they are, together with the loss of labor. They have been borne by our citizens and they unmurmuringly remain as loyal to the Confederate Government and the cause of the South as the people of any portion of the Confederate States. But now while the gross products . . . are barely, if indeed they be sufficient for the sustenance of its population to have the tax collector draw the last shilling to be raised by the sale of their capital is a blow they but little expected and against which they most earnestly protest." The court prayed that the government abondon its effort to collect taxes, but with so many counties in similar or worse straits the poignant request could not be heeded.

On the 21st of December, Mosby and Thomas Love, after observing a Federal scouting party near Rectortown, dined at nearby Lakeland, and this time Mosby's theory of safety near the opposing forces failed. Cavalrymen appeared at the front and back doors, fired, and brought the man down. "I am shot," he cried, and in the melee pulled off his coat with colonel's stars, hid it, and fell to the floor. An officer entered, struck a light, and asked Ludwell Lake's daughter who the man was. She did not know, so he bent over the blood-stained body and repeated the question. "Lieutenant Johnson of the 6th Virginia," came the gasp. After a Union physician said the stomach wound was mortal, Maj. Douglas Frazar — slightly inebriated, said the Union report — gave the eulogy: "Have him decently buried; he seems to be a brave soldier." While Frazar intoned, his men stripped off boots, pants, and overcoat — containing damning personal papers. Williamson then tells us that after the Federals left Mosby walked into the room where the Lakes were sitting. But everyone agrees Mosby was carted three miles to out-of-the-way Rockburn, abode of the Widow Mrs. Aquila Glascock.

Frazar's raiders, on the prowl for four days, had wounded one and taken five prisoners, Love included. And at Oakham, where Mosby had begun his career as a partisan just about two years before, they stopped. Examining the papers they realized who 'Lieutenant Johnson' was. Through to the New Year search parties combed homes, barnyards, and chicken coops for the wounded Mosby, and by the 29th they discovered he was at Rockburn. But by then Mosby had been taken south, eventually to a home near Lynchburg. Sheridan's year-end comment: "I have no news to-day, except the death of Mosby. He died from his wounds at Charlottesville." With those words the search ended.

Christmas 1864. Salem's Amanda Klipstein wrote her husband, Phil, up in his fifties and just conscripted into service. She had flour and bran to make cakes, and pumpkin for pies, and if the stockings were not full with sweets and trinkets, they bulged as invitingly with apples. It might have been another Christmas, but "how the children wished Poppy could help to eat their good things."

A number of the Black Horse took the holiday at John Martin's, a familiar haunt west of Three-Mile Switch. Riding into Warrenton to see what was up, they were greeted by "speculators and extortioners," Alexander Hunter tells us, who filled their canteens with the best of blockade whiskey, "a piece of generosity they were never known to repeat."

Christmas evening a picked group of two cavalry divisions under Maj. Gen. Alfred T. A. Torbert rode from the Valley via The Springs into Warrenton. Next morning one of Hunter's circes, Roberta Pollock, noticed a stranger walk into the provost marshal's office and overheard the conversation. For a fee he would point the way to the whereabouts of Mosby's Rangers. Miss Pollock demurred, commandeered a horse, and set out to find a Confederate — no easy task. Torbert described the weather as "it either rained, hailed, or snowed, and sometimes all three," and through it the intrepid Roberta made her way to Salem. Meanwhile Torbert's men dispersed, one division riding off to New Baltimore, Little Georgetown, The Plains, and Middleburg, the other directly to Middleburg, then west on the pike to Ashby Gap. The Washington *Chronicle* told of the outcome: "The officers, it is said, had certain information of Mosby's whereabouts, but if they had *the secret was betrayed*, for not a Rebel was captured, through many houses were searched. . . . The troopers suffered greatly, and they were in anything but a joyous mood on their return from the goose-chasing expedition." Torbert reported that "the country through which we passed was thoroughly cleaned of stock and forage."

The same day, from Fairfax Court House, a second raiding party, of 400 8th Illinoisians under Capt. John Sargent, reached Thoroughfare Gap, and south of Little Georgetown searched the home of Mrs. Lewis, picking up two Black Horse cavalrymen. Next day, as they returned through Hopewell Gap, both prisoners escaped. The forays had ended.

Court and council minutes provide glimpses into the late winter. With Brig. Gen. William H. F. Payne in the field, J. M. Spilman presided over the January 23rd, 1865, county court. Spilman, who pastored Warrenton, Carter's Run, and Mt. Holly Baptist Churches, told an amusing story. People usually addressed him as 'Colonel,' his militia rank before the war, and a Union patrol overheard the salutation. Gleeful that they had captured an officer, it took a bit of explaining on Spilman's part to put that rank to rest. Salt agent Anderson D. Smith was back in good standing, but no one had offered a fair amount for the $10,000 bond, and so a new approach was taken; $8,000 worth of $500 notes and $2,000 in $100 notes would be offered by Sheriff William Hume. The twenty-year notes were to bear six percent interest annually.

February's court was the last, for a while, to hold sessions in the court house — "in consequence of ill condition occasioned by the public enemy." They would now meet in the Clerk's Office. There still were no takers for the bonds, and Sampson P. Bayly was told to offer them to people from whom he had bought corn and grain. The staples had come down in price a bit, corn at six dollars a barrel, wheat at two dollars a bushel. And in the only such case since the war began, the court approved Francis B. Gibson's emancipation of slave William Chinn.

Judging from disbursements of supplies, the winter was not a hard one. In late March 200 pounds of salt were still on hand, and the court ordered Smith to sell it. James S. Rogers, supply agent for Warrenton, told the Town Council on April 4th that there was "considerable" surplus corn. The council told him to sell it "for not less than Five Dollars in Gold, ten in Greenbacks and thirty in Virginia State Money" — a bargain if one paid with the Confederate dollar; its real exchange value was less than two cents. Two days later Mayor Bragg had received $36 in silver and gold, $116.50 in Federal greenbacks, and $30 in Virginia funds for some twelve bushels.

Slowly, and without fanfare or a parade down Main Street, the men came home. There was time for at least a late spring planting. Maj. Gen. Winfield S. Hancock's office in Winchester handled most of the paroles, and as the old soldiers retired with their slips of paper they were thankful for being allowed to keep their horses. Many had come to town on their feeblest nag, thinking the steed might be confiscated.

Only with Mosby were there difficulties. On April 10th, a day after Lee's surrender at Appomattox, a broadside announcing terms noted: "The guerilla chief Mosby is not included in the parole." General Grant then approved Mosby's parole, but the damage had been done, and by the 13th Mosby still had not surrendered, and Hancock threatened a raid east of the Blue Ridge to destroy the rangers. Then the shooting of Lincoln intervened, and eight and a half hours after the president's death, Grant wrote on April 15th at 4 p.m.: "Assassination remains the order of the day with the rebels." All paroled officers were to be arrested unless they took the oath of allegiance.

Mosby, apparently not aware of the event, communicated with Major General Hancock on the 16th and agreed to suspend hostile operations; Hancock, in turn, would not march against Mosby. Hours later Hancock received a dispatch from Secretary of War Edwin M. Stanton: "If Mosby is sincere he might do much toward detecting and apprehending the murderers of the President."

At a meeting of Mosby's men at Salem on the 17th, scout Channing Smith told Mosby of Robert E. Lee's reaction to their leader's fight-or-surrender dilemma. Lee said he was under parole and could not therefore give any advice.

On the 18th some fifteen officers of Mosby's command expressed their regrets to Hancock at the death of Lincoln. Mosby was not among them, and was not ready to surrender. On the 19th he asked Hancock for ten days' time to decide. Mosby wanted to find out if Joseph Johnston's army in North Carolina had been beaten or had surrendered. Hancock complied. Not known to Mosby, Johnston had signed an armistace with General Sherman on the 14th. On the morning of the 19th Stanton again wrote Hancock and said there was evidence that Mosby knew of John Wilkes Booth's plan and had even met with Booth in Winchester. Grant, without alluding to the rumor, had no time for bargainers, and late that afternoon telegraphed Hancock: "If Mosby does not avail himself of the present truce end it and hunt him and his men down." Then came a tacit admission: "Guerillas, after beating the armies of the enemy, will not be entitled to quarter."

Hancock informed Mosby the truce would end at noon the 20th, at Millwood, Clarke County. It did, though the partisan announced he still would not surrender, and after a huff brought about because of a suspected Union ambush, he rode off to Ashby Gap with his men. Hancock was satisfied, though, and notified his chief of staff that be believed most of the rangers' command had disbanded. That came the next day, in a field at the north end of present Frost Street in Salem.

Rain fell on the 21st. Perhaps a quarter of Mosby's 800-man command was there, but by that date it was hard to tell who was a member; some had ridden with the rangers for a day. They gathered in town and by noon mounted and proceeded to the field where they formed by companies in line. The rain had stopped. Company adjutant, Mosby's brother, William, read the short farewell address. Its words made clear that Mosby chose to disband the organization rather than surrender it, and there were the usual parting phrases that covered pride of achievement and recollections of kindness towards its leaders. Afterwards, Thomas Richards, Captain of Company G, read a lengthier and more high-flown expression of praise.

All such messages have eloquence, but few could match the postscript of Lt. Col. Robert M. Stribling, head of the Fauquier Artillery: "In this War, all reward a Confederate Soldier expected was that his manhood would be recognized, for love of home and of Country was his inspiration. Though he marched and fought with bare feet and tattered clothes, and with nothing but a small ration of corn meal and coarse pork for his diet, and with worthless money for his scant pay, he wrote, in the record of his acts, with what bravery and fortitude it is possible for manhood to assert itself."

National Archives

PLATE XX

Photographer unknown, ca. 1864

Mosby's men strike fraternal poses against a tent-like backdrop. (*Front, l to r:* Walter W. Gosden (father of Freeman Gosden, the Amos of "Amos 'n' Andy"), Harry T. Sinnott, O. L. Butler, I. A. Gentry. *Middle, l to r:* Robert B. Parrott, Thomas Throop, John W. Munson, Col. John S. Mosby, ——— Newell, ——— Quarles. *Top, l to r:* Lee Howison, W. Ben Palmer, John W. Puryear, Thomas Booker, A. G. Babcock, Norman V. Randolph, Frank H. Rehm.

9. THE REBUILDING

The suffering land — Living with the Bureau and 96th New York — Black people organize and attend school — Nostalgia, tournaments, and literary pursuits

APRIL, 1865-1867

A war had ended, but rumors of resistance were fueled by Joseph Johnston's North Carolina armies; they did not give up until April 26th. Mosby, too, was a fugitive. After his rangers disbanded at Salem, many rode to Winchester to sign their paroles — Mosby not among them. Hancock offered a $2,000 reward for his capture, upped to $5,000 on May 3rd. Ten days later, when Mosby paid a fleeting visit to his parents near Lynchburg, his last words to his father were: "I am an outlaw, and self-preservation is the first law of nature." On June 12th, Mosby and his brother rode armed, with Mosby in full Confederate regalia, into Lynchburg. They had expected a parole, but something went amiss, and the overture ended in a near fight, and flight. Five days later, after Grant reiterated his orders for protection and parole, Mosby became the last Confederate officer to surrender.

Virginia's head of state, seventy years old, commanded higher stakes. On May 18th occupation troops tacked the following notice on the closed courthouse door and in public places: "$25,000 REWARD. By Direction of the Secretary of War a reward of $25,000 is hereby offered for the arrest and delivery for trial of William Smith, rebel governor of Virginia." The bounty went uncollected, and Smith, in Richmond on June 8th, turned himself in to Marsena Rudolph Patrick, the provost marshal Smith had met in wartime Warrenton. Smith was paroled, but was to be confined to Monte Rosa, his home outside town.

The farmers had returned to a county devastated in parts. By far the hardest-hit areas were along the Orange and Alexandria Railway and its Warrenton Branch, the Marsh Road, the stretch from Catlett south to Weaversville and Elk Run, and around Warrenton. Since the winter of 1862-1863, hundreds of thousands of Union troops had encamped in these regions. Fences were non-existent, and any out-of-way outbuilding had been fair game for clapboards used to build winter quarters for troops. Because there was not a stand within three miles of town, in December, 1865, wood sold for five dollars a cord in Warrenton.

Nearly every church had been defaced, and at least four, Broad Run, Carter's Run, and Mt. Holly Baptist, and St. Stephen's Episcopal, had been pulled down or gutted. When speaking of church damage, the typical local words were, 'The Confederates used them for hospitals, the Yankees for stables.'

Fauquier suffered far less damage than Culpeper or Prince William, and as was the case with Loudoun, rich soils deemed that prosperous years were not far off. But the first postwar harvest was not bountiful. On October 23rd presiding county court justice William H. Gaines penned the following words to none other than "His Excellency, the Hon. Andrew Johnson, President of the United States. Four years of war have so empoverished the people of this County, that much suffering for the necessaries of life has occurred, and that much more must occur the coming winter, that the crops of 1862, 63 & 64 were generally used or destroyed by the passing armies, that the crops of the present year are very inadequate to the wants of the people, that the live stock has nearly disappeared, and that there is no prospect for amelioration in the condition of the people before the end of the next year. In the midst of such destitution with many dwelling houses and farm buildings destroyed or in ruins, with more than half the arable land of the County turned into common for want of fences, and no adequate force of horses, oxen & labor, to cultivate the enclosed land, the tax gatherer has appeared amongst us, demanding . . . twenty seven cents upon each one hundred dollars of land of the valuation of 1860 — which in the aggregate amounts to a very large sum of money, greatly more than is believed to be possessed by the entire population of the County."

It was worth a try, even though the court remembered well that a similar appeal to the Confederate government had failed a year before. After all, local newspapers had just reported that 1,228 of the county's some 2,500 white males had taken oaths of allegiance to the United States. However, if the letter did reach the president, it was not accorded the courtesy of a reply.

Statistics tell their story, though they are tempered by the five seasons that passed before the first postwar agricultural census. Tilled land that had measured 269,000 acres in 1860 measured nearly 289,000 acres in 1870, evidence that some of the derelict 'Old Fields' were now being farmed. Corn, the money crop, harvested out to nearly 824,950 bushels, a better per-acre ratio than the 717,450 bushels harvested in 1860. But wheat production was down some three percent, to 269,950 bushels. Oats, at 180,590 bushels, remained stable. Only a pittance of tobacco was grown, but commercial production of wine had nearly doubled since 1860. Another decade would pass before herds built up to prewar levels. In 1870 there were half as many cattle, sheep, and swine as there were in 1860, dairy cows were down three percent, and horses, fourteen percent.

Warrenton newspapers reported many horse thefts during the postwar years, and even Mosby had a steed stolen from him in the fall of '65. With indignation, *The True Index* upbraided a December, 1865, Federal proclamation ordering all horses and mules branded "U.S." turned over to government authorities. The newspaper argued that at least the beasts were getting "paternal care," and otherwise would have been relegated to the bone yards.

As in the old days, two newspapers vied for readers. James G. Cannon's

Virginia Sentinel came out October 28th, and Lycurgus W. Caldwell and John W. Finks had their first *True Index* off the press on November 11th. At first, people felt Caldwell in the correct spot. He was pointed to as the man who had ticked off "What hath God wrought," the first telegraph message, and he had been a former editor of the town's first newspaper, *Palladium of Liberty*, founded by his father, James, in 1817.

But, after reading the close of Caldwell's editorial message, a recalcitrant Warrenton was not too sure. "It is part of folly," he wrote, "to ignore undoubted facts and rebel against inevitable destiny . . . *universal freedom* and a *restored Union* are facts which must be recognized and accepted." As any good editor, Caldwell prefaced his point with more soothing words: "Through the smoke of deadly strife, our eyes were ever strained to catch a glimpse of her proud standard, borne aloft by the hands of her heroic sons. We mourned to see it so often baptized in the blood — and when it went down before the shock of irresistible numbers, we grieved over its fall with an honest and heart-felt sorrow. We shall therefore indulge in no vapid boastings of uninter-rupted devotion of the Union, nor in abuse of leaders upon whom but recently all profused to look upon with pride and admiration."

The *Virginia Sentinel* took a harder line, opposing the occupation in strong, sarcastic words. But Caldwell had a deft way with words, and he and his partner had home-town seniority. By 1872 the *Sentinel* was a memory. *The True Index* became the county newspaper, in 1905 changing its name to *The Fauquier Democrat*.

About 100 men of the 96th New York Volunteers still guarded Warrenton, and the government's chief agent was Capt. M. E. Orr, who headed the local Freedmen's Bureau, officially the Bureau of Refugees, Freedmen, and Abandoned Lands. Congress had authorized the Bureau in March to see that ex-slaves received a fair deal, and in *The True Index*, a Bureau circular reminded blacks that the two essential conditions to maintain "a state of freedmen" were visible means of support and fidelity to contracts.

The Freedmen's Bureau guidelines for wages to be paid black field hands were equivalent to those paid any laborer: $12 to $15 monthly with board, including clothes and medical attention, or $20 to $23 without board. Women field hands were to receive $5 to $8 with board, or $13 to $16 without. Women cooks and house servants between $6 and $10 with board, or $14 to $18 without. Commented the *Index*: "There is little difficulty in obtaining colored cooks and field hands for a day, a week or a month; but the vast majority domiciled here prefer to lead the life of vagrants."

Several enterprising freedmen leased farms for one-third to one-half the profits. Blacksmithing continued as a popular vocation. The *Index* applauded John G. Beckham when he sold two town blacksmith shops to Beverly Howard and Minor Grayson, "colored men and good mechanics."

Otherwise, the "old regime," as it was called by Lt. William McNulty, the next town Bureau agent, tried to adhere to old laws. In January, 1866, the county court granted Eliza Pleasants permission to open a restaurant, but refused her request to serve liquor based on a prewar law forbidding "free persons of color" to serve drinks. McNulty, on record as a teetotaler, told his superior that Mrs. Pleasants needed the license to support her family. But his letter never received an answer, and the court did not rescind its order.

Ex-slaves in the Foxville area were better off than most. Upon John Fox's death in 1858 his 193 slaves were freed in accord with his 1839 will. His 335-acre Great Run tract was divided into thirty-three equal lots given to the freedmen. A legal battle followed, and at the urging of Eli Tackett, representative of the legatees, the Freedmen's Bureau in October, 1865, asked executor Charles P. Chilton to settle accounts. Chilton, writing to McNulty the following February, pointed out in a lengthy, deferential letter, that claims were not settled, and besides, scores of displaced blacks were living on the property, and many were blighting it. The Bureau did not evict the alleged squatters, but allowed the case to have its turn in court.

Some whites who helped freedmen feared reprisals. John R. Holland, owner of the Blooming Dale Woolen Factory, adjacent to Brookside, one of Mosby's old haunts, in September wrote to Brig. Gen. Oliver Howard, a state Freedmen's Bureau commissioner, stating "I want protection." A neighboring lady had threatened to burn down his mill because he rented a room in the mill to a black man. Holland said that "there has been some houses burned down about here just because the men rented to blacks," and added that people in the Upperville area tried to make blacks feel "that freedom is worse than slavery [and] it is a general remark with the Secesh here (and there is very few of anything else) that the blacks may live in with the whites but the people shall not rent them houses." Despite Holland's references, Maj. Gen. Colin Augur, head Mosby hunter late in the war, and noted Loudoun Quakers, educator and historian Samuel Janney and mapmaker Yardley Taylor, no troops were dispatched. And, Holland's mill was not burned.

By the first of September Orange and Alexandria trains were running. As they puffed through "places of imperishable interest in the public mind," stated the railroad advertisements — in Fauquier naming Catlett and Rappahannock Station — the throttles were eased to slow. Weakened tracks also necessitated a leisurely two-hour ride from Alexandria to Warrenton Junction, and in late November a caved-in embankment a half-mile east of the junction threw the Brentsville train. The mishap killed the brakeman, and killed two and injured twenty-eight of the New York occupation force.

As the village of Rappahannock Station — its name now changed from Mill View to Bowenville — had been destroyed, Culpeper interests felt the new rail stop should be on their side of the Rappahannock. O & A president John Barbour, a Culpeper man, gave his county a chance, and for a month trains stopped on both sides of the river to see how many passengers got off on each side. Elkwood's Richard Hoope Cunningham and Fauquier's William A. Bowen both thought up enticing ideas, but Bowen won handily by sponsoring excursions to The Springs. Thus his post office of Bowenville, today's Remington, remained in Fauquier.

The Manassas Gap Railroad would not run again under its old name. When its right-of-way was at last clear, in the spring of 1867, it had merged with the Orange and Alexandria under the name Orange, Alexandria and Manassas Railroad.

Road bridges across the Rappahannock at Waterloo and The Springs were not repaired until 1867, with the Waterloo span given priority because of an attempt to revive the prewar Warrenton-to-Sperryville turnpikes. Warrenton citizenry subscribed some $500 toward the bridge's rebuilding. The Kelly's Ford bridge, originally built by 1848, was not rebuilt until 1885, and the same year a second iron truss spanned the heights at Rappahannock Station. Three prewar spans, at Beverley's and Wheatley's Fords, and at Carter's Mill, would remain only in memories.

With the first postwar winter approaching, *The True Index* printed several articles about the plight of the county's ex-slaves. A mid-November issue noted the unloading of "negroes and their boxes" from wagons in front of the Freedmen's Bureau headquarters in Warrenton. "These unfortunate people, to our knowledge, had recently the best of homes; but by idleness became so great a tax on their late owners as to render it obligatory to send them off." That month the newspaper also noted many blacks "afflicted with consumption," attributing the outbreak to lack of "that kind of care which ownership formerly exercised." There had been talk of a freedmen's church, but in mid-November, Captain Orr's superior, Capt. Daniel W. Bohanon, advised Orr not to take any active steps in the matter.

The True Index's infrequent references to everyday county life indicate a quick return to normalcy for the white populace, now a majority since many blacks had left for the cities. Business taxes were back by September — at the prewar rate of $10 on each Warrenton enterprise. That month the county court authorized a bond issue of not more than $5,000 "to repair and improve the court house, jail, and Public Lot" of the county, with some of that money going "to the support and maintenance of the poor."

November 21st's edition proudly announced that Fauquier land was assessed at $16.50 an acre, while Culpeper land was assessed at $13 and Stafford land at $9. But then more than today, official land values were below the market price, and when famous plantations changed hands the prices ranged from an inflated $32.50 to $55 an acre. At least three farms between Warrenton and The Springs were sold that first postwar year: St. Leonard's, Waverley, and the Thomas Saunders place—bought by Maj. Gen. Lunsford Lindsay Lomax, the prominent Virginia soldier, later to become president of V.P.I. Which spread commanded the $55? The John M. Patterson farm north of Halfway.

The same issue noted that the ladies of town were "called in" to sign a petition to pardon Jeff Davis, and that "only two withheld their signatures." And by the first of November, a familiar figure had hung up his shingle outside the California Building, and had placed his notice alongside the first-page ads of such fellow luminaries as William H. Payne and Eppa Hunton. "John S. Mosby, Attorney at Law of Warrenton, Fauquier County, Virginia, Practices in the Courts of Fauquier and adjacent counties." Mosby and his family had rented Road Island, north of town, and in an airy letter to his wartime surgeon, Aristides Monteiro, he mentioned that the county had been "quite gay" that first summer, with "tournaments . . . the order of the day."

Eppa Hunton was the only Fauquier native to write of postwar politics, and he charged Lt. William McNulty with changing the gay atmosphere. A Down-Easter from Portland, William Augustus McNulty served as a cannoneer at Fredericksburg, his gallantry earning a promotion to first lieutenant and the loss of a right arm. He could have resigned, but elected to stay in the service. In early December, McNulty set up office in the California Building, and inserted an ad in *The True Index* stating that any planter entering into a contract with a freed black had to come to his office so he could witness and sign all agreements. For many that meant an all-day forty-mile round-trip.

Knowing that the traditional verbal contract meant more than a written one, the Freedmen's Bureau dictum was breached more than observed; just another bit of harassment to be overlooked. And so in the country, the old paternal relationships continued, changing only in regard to compensation, often paid in rentals of dwellings, animals, and equipment.

In Lower Fauquier there were rumors of a Christmas uprising by blacks — shades of '56; and why, no one knows. Instead, the fracas took place in Warrenton. Christmas Day started off with good cheer: "Egg-nogg, apple toddy, and plain liquors were freely imbibed," said *The True Index*, "but peace and good order were maintained until 9 or 10 o'clock at night, when several of our arms-bearing citizens and a squad of Federal soldiers got up a free fight. Several pistol shots were fired, two or three of which took effect." Andrew Withers and a Federal soldier were slightly wounded, but a little drinking will do that. Additional troops were not called out. In fact, by mid-January, all Northern soldiers were withdrawn from Warrenton.

On a more somber note, six lengthy resolutions occupy a December 25th entry in the county court minutes. They had been drawn up twelve days before by the circuit court to honor five fallen members of the bar: Judge John Webb Tyler and his son, Madison Tyler, Robert Eden Scott, James W. Kincheloe of the Fauquier Guards, and Robert Randolph, the Black Horse leader. The court also included John Quincy Marr.

In *The True Index* appeared excerpts from a New York *News* series on Mosby's exploits. And reciprocating, the *Index* allowed the *News* to advertise for subscribers. The elusive partisan ranger succumbed to an interview in January, stating in the *Index* that "The life of me, advertised by somebody in Urbanna, Ohio, is a pure fiction — a mere romance, concocted for sensation purposes. The author has neither my countenance or sanction." Mosby then let out that John Scott, Jr., "has in possession, and will publish during the spring, an authentic history of our command." In April, Scott advertised a pre-publication price of $3.50 for the book, issued in 1867.

Through the first two mild months of 1866, local newspaper articles were brief and chatty. Townsmen were reminded that snow on sidewalks in front of homes had to be removed within twenty-four hours or else risk a $2.50 fine. A masked ball at Mrs. Judge Tyler's didn't end until 7 a.m. Warrentonians were asked to raise $500 for the widow and infant "of the only world-renowned chieftan who died in our defence" — Stonewall Jackson. And, because of opposition from Lower Fauquier, by a 17-13 vote, county court justices rejected a new state law making every man's boundary a legal fence. Three more years would pass before animals would have to be fenced in.

Meanwhile the black population organized. Freedmen's Bureau records indicate that local freedmen had been campaigning for a school since October. On January 24th, 1866, the head of the regional Freedmen's Bureau in Fredericksburg, Maj. James Johnson, wrote to his superior: "I have the honor to state that the Colored People at Warrenton desire the establishment of a school at that place." Lieutenant McNulty had learned that seventy-five children wanted to attend, but he could only find a room big enough for forty "scholars." He also couldn't find a teacher, but noted in a February 14th letter to Major Johnson his "determination to establish a freedman School at Warrenton."

Three days later *The True Index* noticed that A. Rindsburg's frame building at the corner of Lee and Fourth Streets was being converted into a school with the teacher a Miss Wood from Middleboro, Massachusetts. A month earlier the Richmond *Times* had aptly remarked: "Pretty Yankee girls, with the smallest of hands and feet, have flocked to the South as a missionary ground, and are communicating a healthy moral tone to the 'colored folks,' besides instructing them in chemistry, botany, and natural philosophy, teaching them to speak French, sing Italian, and talk Spanish, so that in time we are bound to have intelligent, and probably, intellectual labor."

Miss S. Fannie Wood had her expenses and salary paid by The New England Freedmen's Aid Society of Boston. She boarded at the Misses Cox, and on the first day of school an anonymous letter was placed under the door. It read: "Head Quarters, Negroeville Va. Feb. 19, 1866. Mrs. Fannie Wood, We the young men of this town think you are a disgrace to decent society and therefore wish you to leave this town before the first of March and if you don't there will be violence used to make you comply to this request." The next paragraph got nastier, with the letter's closing salutation in French.

Next week's *True Index* reported that Miss Wood had been "serenaded" by "songs and expressions not intended for ears polite," and the newspaper warned that such an "unpopular performance" could bring back a Federal garrison. It did, in the last days of February. On March 15th, with the cavalry withdrawn, stones pelted Miss Wood's schoolroom. Next day seven pleaded guilty to writing the letter, among them Alexander Hunter, who undoubtedly added the touch of French. Mayor Charles Bragg and Lieutenant McNulty offered the young lady protection. On behalf of the town, Mayor Bragg apologized for the incidents. In that day's town council minutes, Recorder Lycurgus W. Caldwell, the newspaper editor, penned a wonderful double entendre: "Conducting the school for freedmen — which conduct deserves and has received the condemnation of all good citizens." Next day Miss Wood — unaware of Caldwell's words — wrote the mayor and thanked him for his kind words, closing with an understatement: "My mission is of a character which may be somewhat at variance with your views."

A month later Miss Wood filled out a school report as detailed as any today. She had named her institution "The Whittier School" in honor of the Massachusetts Quaker poet and abolitionist, John Greenleaf Whittier. The average daily daytime attendance was 55, and an average of 110 attended a night session taught by John W. Pratt. Of the 110, 90 were sixteen and over, and 50 of the 110 could read and spell — the main subjects taught. Miss Wood's later school reports note Mary J. Keyes helped teach in April, and Abbie McNulty, the lieutenant's wife and an experienced teacher, became a third instructor in May. Her husband taught at night. In May the schoolroom shifted from the loft to a lower room, the pupils "indulging now in the luxury of *three* windows instead of *two*."

Lieutenant McNulty had other troubles. On February 10th he had John Martin, the wartime protector of the Black Horse, arrested for fighting with a Negro hunting on Martin's property. The arbitrary arrest shocked locals, and was exacerbated by Martin's returning from a few days' detention in Richmond a sick man. On February 14th, McNulty asked for, but did not receive, a bodyguard of two enlisted men.

As spring broke, Warrenton turned to its number-one concern: the town graveyard: Cows grazed among the wooden markers denoting war dead, and the *Index* called the special section enclosing a slew of unidentified men "The dreary plat." By the close of March the young people of town had raised $230; a March 26th concert had netted $120, and Jennie Day, a leader of the drive, had received $50 from a New York merchant to erect "a handsome monument in Warrenton graveyard to the memory of Confederate dead." The Old Dominion Minstrels concert brought $30 to erect an iron railing around John Quincy Marr's headstone. In early May the town fathers persuaded Mrs. James Vass Brooke to sell two-plus acres to enlarge the graveyard, and by mid-June the town began to fence in the graveyard, iron on the front side, plank on the rear. The town council also appropriated $300 of its available $780 for "filling, marking, and somewhat adorning the graves of the Confederate dead." At The Plains, a mid-September tournament raised added funds.

Through late winter and spring *The True Index* devoted a fair amount of space to politics. Not local politics. Not even Virginia politics. But Pennsylvania politics. That old familar nemesis of Upper Fauquier, John W. Geary, was running for governor. In March the newspaper warned

Keystaters that Geary "united rapacity and cruelty to a sheepish timidity, which made him the butt and by-word of every negro in the county, [and] there exists such a feeling of contempt and scorn which no other General in the Federal service, unless it be Beast Butler, could possibly excite." The *Index* repeated its editorials with the hope that an issue would find its way up north to be copied. If they did they were to no avail, for Geary became Republican Governor of Pennsylvania, a post he held until his death in 1873.

There were the beginnings of nostalgia. John Henry drew a Saturday evening crowd paying twenty-five cents a head at the "old Episcopal Church" on March 3rd when he lectured on the First Battle of Bull Run. And when Martha Braddox died in June, *The True Index* mourned "this good old colored woman" with an obituary that was to become nearly standard. "She appeared to sympathize wholly with the South in the late struggle, . . . With marked pleasure she contributed unmasked her mite towards feeding the Confederate soldiers whenever they passed through town on their weary marches; and without fee or reward she nursed the sick and wounded."

And the military spirit had not died. On June 16th the 85th Regiment militia held its elections at the Germantown muster grounds. Elected captains were veterans John M. Porter of the Warrenton Company, R. C. Florence of the New Baltimore Company, H. L. Willis of the Germantown Company, and Hugh Hamilton of the Mill View Company. Hamilton took his honorary rank seriously, and soon received ninety dollars for apprehending three Union deserters. The newspaper omitted the captain of the Morrisville Company. Upper Fauquier was not ready for militiamen.

To keep in shape, several old soldiers entered the many tournaments held that summer. The riders were colorfully decked out as knights, their names drawn from *King Arthur* and Sir Walter Scott, and with a bowed lance to that special lady, one at a time they galloped off and attempted to spear three suspended rings on one turn. The July 24th tournament, held somewhere by The Springs Road, was special. *The True Index* called it "The grand Tourney, so long contemplated by our chivalry," and it was followed by a coronation ball held at Washington's Hall in Warrenton, lasting 'till the "shrill-toned trumpeter of the morn." The winning knights received no press, but their queens of love and beauty did: Lizzie Robertson, and her maids of honor: Lizzie Lucas, Mattie Byrne, and a Miss Tiernan. The *Index* also reported that the Black Horse Troop had demonstrated their horsemanship at Herring Run, in the first purported tournament ever held in Baltimore. The newspaper concluded: "We wish for our young people many a return of such happy and innocent recreation."

Literary pursuits were not forgotten, and dentist William N. Bispham took the lead in reorganizing the Warrenton library. Early in the war, the hundreds of books, plus magazines and newspapers, had been packed in boxes and sent to homes for safekeeping. They all had been returned, but the borrowers' cards had been left in a desk, and the furniture could not be found. Who had books out? Could they please be returned? There would be no fines.

Late summer meant school, and as in prewar years the private academies flourished. Schools for blacks opened a bit late that year, with S. Fannie Wood beginning her second year October 1st. With her came a second teacher, a Miss Kempton of New Bedford, and they again hoped to board at the Misses Cox. "We will look out for ourselves," she wrote in a breezy letter to Lt. W. S. Chase, the new Warrenton Freedmen's Bureau head. She sent special regards to Aunt Carrie, a freed black.

Lieutenant Chase had come up from Culpeper in August, exchanging duty stations with the controversial Lieutenant McNulty. And by mid-November the Misses Wood and Kempton were teaching black children at Culpeper Court House, and George M. Morse, a former soldier in the Army of the Potomac and another Bay Stater, had taken their place. As with his predecessors and successors, the New England Freedmen's Aid Society paid all bills through 1869.

Enrollment at The Whittier School equalled that of the previous term, and on November 19th the regional Freedmen's Bureau headquarters, now at Gordonsville, Orange County, wrote Lieutenant Chase with these words: "It is contemplated to erect a school house at Warrenton for the freed people." Could Chase supply an estimate of lumber needed? The building would have two classrooms, a teachers' room, kitchen, and bedroom, and was to be seventy-five by twenty-two feet.

As was typical with the bygone written record, the question as to whether the school was actually built was not answered, but Lieutenant Chase, in a July 31st, 1867, letter, implied that it was yet in the planning stages. Chase also provided the first overall picture of public education in Fauquier County: "The Freedmen have all done remarkably well . . . the feeling against them by the Whites has been very bitter but I begin to see a change brought about by the political change of the country. . . . The desire of the grown people for Education has been greatly stimulated by reason of their rights given them . . . I have 4 School Houses . . . built of Logs and answer for Church Service as well. . . . Upon the whole I am very much gratified with the progress that the Freedmen have made in the past two months and also the Whites who are beginning to see matters in proper light." Chase also mentioned that there were few cases of freedmen leaving employers or employers discharging freedmen.

School reports provide specifics. At Professor Morse's Whittier School, in December, 1867, enrollment was 110, with an average attendance of about 50, and with an average of 15 in night school. Of the 110, 48 could read and spell quite well, 50 not as well. Twenty-four pupils were more than sixteen years of age. There was no Sunday School, and in a somewhat confused sentence further marred by a tear, Morse noted, "While some people are friendly, the community would not all[owe?] them. . . ." Later reports assess the whites' attitude as "Hostile." By September, 1868, Morse implied that a new school was to be built, or was built, on E. T. Low's land in Warrenton.

At Piedmont, Helen Jewel Warren taught at Howard School, with a surviving report dated January, 1868. The school, as the more illustrious university of slightly later date, was named for Brig. Gen. Oliver Otis Howard, Commissioner of the Virginia Freedmen's Bureau. Cook Shacklett rented out the eleven-by-twenty-foot building for five dollars a month; it's not known who paid this bill or the others. Average daily attendance was 18, with 14 who could spell and read easy lessons. Three were over sixteen, and all had been slaves. Thirteen attended Sunday School and seven were in a Bible class. Miss Warren noted that all the students traveled a great distance to school, and that public sentiment toward the school had "much improved."

No reports survive for the other two schools mentioned in Lieutenant Chase's March, 1867, letter, but one may have been at Boxwood Farm north of Halfway. Neighbors of the 1930's recalled that Elias Smith, nicknamed 'Yankee' by locals, taught a school which they believed to be the first for Negro children in the county. "He made a great impression on native Virginians," one old-timer remarked pensively.

Lyttleton A. Jackson opened a school at Clift Mills on Carter's Run in August, 1867. Local blacks paid his salary and board, and Jackson, himself black, noted that "The Colored People" owned the building, which stood on Alfred Meyer's land. In February, 1868, average daily attendance was 46, with 16 who could spell and read easy lessons. Twelve were advanced readers. Twenty scholars were more than sixteen years of age, and 13 were free before the war. No Sunday School was taught, but a church had been established the previous August. After the notation "attitude of Whites," Jackson wrote: "they are bearely tolerated."

Two other Fauquier schools for blacks were planned, but they evidently did not receive enough funds from the Freedmen's Bureau. In July, 1867, missionary Leland Warring organized a Foxville Church, and next month tried to begin classes. That December, Horner Frederick received $125 from the Bureau for a school at Salem. Both enterprises receive no further mention.

With a host of alien institutions open or envisaged, and with few sympathetic locals to oversee their operation and safety, Brig. Gen. Orlando Brown, Assistant Freedmen's Bureau Commissioner for Virginia, asked Lieutenant Chase to provide him with the names of "loyal persons" in Fauquier County. In mid-March, 1867, Chase sent in his findings. Heading the list was Piedmont's Cook Shacklett, "true as steel"; followed by John Holland, the nervous mill owner; William Blackman; C. G. Foster of Owl Run; and James Rogers of the Landmark area. Lieutenant Chase regretted that no loyal Warrenton citizens could be found: "I find them *bitterly opposed* to anything that looks like reconstruction or true loyalty."

Six black men made the list, headed by teacher Lyttleton Jackson: Wesley Cephus, John Jordan, Beverly Thornton, Samuel Morgan, and William Howard, a blacksmith. Lieutenant Chase added the information that four could read and write; Cephus and Morgan could read.

If the eleven were of any help to the Freedmen's Bureau and its schools, their role never surfaces among the copious papers that contain much of Fauquier's postwar record. And through 1869 the Bureau tells the official story, Warrenton newspapers relate the gripes, and county court and town council minutes record the return to normalcy. The march to war, the conflict, the aftermath: in time less than one-thirtieth of the county's written history, in interest a far weightier portion. Scholars may decry the emphasis and gear into the next decade: the end of the gentlemen justices of the court and the beginning of an elected board of supervisors, public schools for all, and taxes levied by the new magisterial districts. But they have not seen the names and dates etched on mill and church walls, nor have they had a gentleman point out Shooters' Hill, where his father lay for hours, waiting for a dust cloud on the road. While memories and places remain — a cannon ball wedged between rocks at a Rappahannock rapids, a cache of arms sunk in the Elk Run Copper Mine — the war cannot be forgotten.

>Eugene M. Scheel
>Orchardcroft,
>near Waterford, Virginia
>December 11th, 1984

SOURCES FOR FAUQUIER, 1856-1870

Hundreds of books, and as many manuscripts and letters, speak for the men who trod through wartime Fauquier, but the works listed here add something special. I have not mentioned the stand-bys, hence the bypassing of such familiar authors as Blackford, Casler, Douglas, McClellan, and even Catton and Freeman. Their primary concern was with the movement of troops and biography, my concern: Do words create a picture of the land and its people.

BOOKS

Andrews, Marietta Minnigerode. *Scraps of Paper.* New York: E.P. Dutton, 1929.
A most treasured scrap is a good part of Ida Dulany's diaries, later copied in *Years of Anguish.* The originals are at the Virginia Historical Society, and Leesburg's John Divine has a copy of the many unpublished sections.

Carter, Robert Goldthwaite. *Four Brothers in Blue.* Austin: University of Texas Press, 1978.
Camp life, mainly in Lower Fauquier, with some of the countryside thrown in. Don't try to figure out which Carter is writing, but when the book was first published (1913), such niceties weren't a bother.

Divine, John, and others. *Loudoun County and The Civil War.* [Leesburg], Va.: Civil War Centennial Commission, County of Loudoun, 1961.
Tells the story in Fauquier's northern neighbor.

Edmonds, Amanda Virginia. *Journals of Amanda Virginia Edmonds . . . 1859-1867.* Ed. Nancy Chappelear Baird. Stephen's City, Va.: Commercial Press, 1984.
What a pleasure to have the full say of this testy gal from Belle Grove. The originals are at the Virginia Historical Society.

Hale, Laura Virginia. *Four Valiant Years In The Lower Shenandoah Valley, 1861-1865.* Strasburg, Va.: Shenandoah Publishing House, 1968.
Covers events across the mountain and occasionally ventures east of the Blue Ridge.

Haupt, Herman. *Reminiscences of General Herman Haupt.* Milwaukee: Wright & Joys, 1901.
The orders and narratives of this railroading genius contain much pertinent information about the wartime transportation network, especially the Orange and Alexandria Railway.

[Hopley, Catherine Cooper]. *Life in the South From The Commencement of the War by a Blockaded British Subject.* Vol. II. London: Chapman & Hall, 1863. Reprinted, New York: Augustus M. Kelley, 1971.
Miss Hopley taught music, but had a distinct talent for prose. Her details of Warrenton ready for the taking are unsurpassed.

Hunter, Alexander. *Johnny Reb and Billy Yank.* New York: Neale Publishing, 1905.
With the uncanny ability to write a war story as if he were there, Hunter zestfully looks at the conflict's human side; a pioneer work in this genre. Tells a good bit about the Black Horse Troop.

Hunter, Alexander. *The Women of The Debatable Land.* Washington: Corden, 1912.
Hunter had the good sense to comb Oak Spring's Bettie Miller Blackwell for material, and though he had a tendency toward overstatement, his amplifications are drawn from fact.

Marshall, Fielding Lewis. *Recollections and Reflections of Fielding Lewis Marshall.* Comp. Maria Newton Marshall. [Orange?], Va.: Privately Printed, [1911?].

Patrick, Marsena Rudolph. *Inside Lincoln's Army.* Ed. David S. Sparks. New York: Thomas Yoseloff, 1964.
Terse and blunt diaries from the Army of The Potomac's Provost Marshal General. He tells of the interaction between friend and foe, giving the 'who, when, where,' — but not the 'why.'

Pope, Maj. Gen. John. *The Campaigns in Virginia of July and August 1862.* Milwaukee: Jermain & Brightman, 1863.
From the pen of the man Jackson marched around: Pope's "retire," written in retirement.

Scheel, Eugene M. *Culpeper: A Virginia County's History Through 1920.* Culpeper: The Culpeper Historical Society, 1982.
Relates the action between the Rappahannock and Rapidan.

Stine, James Henry. *History of the Army of the Potomac.* Philadelphia: J. B. Rodgers, 1892.
With frequent referrals to other works, always agreeing or disagreeing, the 1st Corps' historian tells, without spice, and with many commas, the before-and-after Gettysburg ventures.

Townsend, George Alfred. *Rustics in Rebellion.* Chapel Hill: The University of North Carolina Press, 1950.
Written on the spot and first published in 1866, Townsend's picture of Warrenton under Pope vies with Miss Hopley's descriptions of the previous months.

Von Borcke, Heros. *Memoirs of the Confederate War for Independence.* Philadelphia: J. B. Lippincott, 1867.
The title page notes the author "Chief of Staff" to Jeb Stuart, a non-existent position; he was an aide. The error prefaces what is to come: braggadocio, but with color to spare.

Wainwright, Charles S. *The Personal Journals of Colonel Charles S. Wainwright, 1861-1865.* Ed. Allen Nevins. New York: Harcourt, Brace & World, 1962.
An observant writer and a clear one.

The Years of Anguish: Fauquier County, Virginia, 1861-1865. Eds. Emily G. Ramey and John K. Gott. [Warrenton]: The Fauquier County Civil War Centennial Committee, 1965.

This "commemoration of the valor and sacrifices of those troublous years" contains a smidgeon of everything. Especially valuable for its diarists and several rosters.

MOSBYANA

Alexander, John H. *Mosby's Men.* New York: Neale Publishing, 1907.

Loudoun's Alexander joined the rangers in spring, 1864, and there he begins, writing in a personal vein, with clarity and reliability.

Crawford, J. Marshall. *Mosby and His Men.* New York: G. W. Carleton, 1867.

Mosby contended that the book "contains about as much truth as the Arabian Nights' Entertainment or Gulliver's Travels," perhaps because it scooped Scott by a few months. But, Crawford's first-hand account contains much veracity, and is clearer than his rival's work.

Daniels, Jonathan. *Mosby: Gray Ghost of the Confederacy.* New York: J. B. Lippincott, 1959.

For readers in their teens or pre-teens. Daniels' simple though lively presentation could serve as a model for budding war writers — you always can comprehend the overall picture.

Guy, Anne Welsh. *John Mosby: Rebel Raider of the Civil War.* New York: Abelard-Schuman, 1965.

An attempt to tell the story to youngsters. Better to have Dad read Daniels than to begin here.

Jones, Virgil Carrington. *Ranger Mosby.* Chapel Hill: The University of North Carolina Press, 1944.

The standard, now in its umptieth printing. Jones, a journalist by trade, occasionally lets breathless prose and exaggerations hold sway when background material is skimpy.

Monteiro, Aristides. *War Reminiscences by the Surgeon of Mosby's Command.* Richmond: Privately Printed, 1890. Reprinted, Gaithersburg, Md.: Butternut Press, [1983?].

Monteiro joined Mosby in late summer, 1864. His flowery style is suited to gossip, of which there is plenty, but not to action.

Mosby, John S. *The Memoirs of Colonel John S. Mosby.* Ed. Charles W. Russell. Boston: Little, 1917. Reprinted, Bloomington: Indiana University Press, 1959.

The pen is now leaden, whether it be the thoughts of brother-in-law Russell, or those of Mosby's twilight years.

Mosby, John S. *Mosby's War Reminiscences: Stuart's Cavalry Campaigns.* Boston: George A. Jones, 1887. Reprinted, New York: Pageant Book, 1958.

Told simply and without bravado. The biography leans more toward the style of Crawford than Scott. The second section attempts to justify Stuart's pre-Gettysburg maneuverings.

Munson, John W. *Reminiscences of a Mosby Guerilla.* New York: Moffat, Yard, 1906.

As with Alexander, you feel that Munson writes the way he speaks. There are many personal touches, and Munson contacted Union veterans to present their side.

Scott, John. *Partisan Life With Col. John S. Mosby.* New York: Harper & Brothers, 1867.

The first "authorized" history of the command, written in a "Dear Percy" format — a play on Union Col. Percy Wyndham, who Mosby disdained for calling him "a horse thief." Scott put the 492 pages together in a year — quite a feat.

Siepel, Kevin H. *Rebel: The Life and Times of John Singleton Mosby.* New York: St. Martin's Press, 1983.

The first comprehensive biography of Mosby; half the book focuses on postwar years. Historian Siepel avoids some linguistic excesses practised by his predecessors.

Williamson, James J. *Mosby's Rangers: A Record of The Operations . . .* New York: Ralph B. Kenyon, 1896. 2nd Ed., Rev. New York: Sturgis & Walton, 1909.

Still the complete wartime Mosby, all 511 pages of it — in small print; the revised edition runs to 554 pages. A fine writer, Williamson presents the *Official Records'* text along with his own. Contains an almost complete roster.

SERIALS AND MANUSCRIPTS

Ambler, Mrs. Richard Cary (Susan). Diaries. Privately owned. Appeared in *The Fauquier Democrat,* September 20, 1962-January 17, 1963. Typescript in the newspaper's morgue.

Usually brief, but sometimes pithy. Jotted down by the mistress of The Dell, west of Hume.

Confederate Veteran.

I found nine volumes with pertinent material, much of it about Mosby: VII, 389, 510; VIII, 74; XII, 286, 538; XIII, 211, 511; XVIII, 201, 429; XXVII, 330; XXXII, 18; XXXI, 356-357; XL, 100.

Dulany, Mary Eliza (Ida) Powell. Diaries.
See Andrews, *Scraps of Paper.*

Edmonds, Amanda Virginia. Diaries.
See Edmonds, *Journals.*

Fauquier County, Censuses of Agriculture, 1860 and 1870.

If it is individuals and farms you're after you must risk a headache reading the National Archives' microfilm. Compendiums were issued as *Agriculture of the United States in 1860.* Washington: U. S. Government Printing

Office, 1864; and *Statistics of Agriclture.* Washington: U.S.G.P.O., 1870.

Fauquier County, Censuses of Population, 1860 and 1870.
   If your eyes can take it, much can be read into its figures. The Fauquier County Library and Fairfax County Library, Main Branch, have the rolls on microfilm.

Fauquier County Court Minute Books.
   The originals are at the county clerk's office, available for viewing with special permission. The Fauquier County Library has the prewar and wartime minutes on microfilm.

Fauquier County, Slave Schedules, 1850 and 1860.
   Gives the names of slave owners, number of slaves, their age, sex, and other statistics. The Fauquier County Library has both schedules on microfilm.

Freedmen's Bureau records. The National Archives, Record Group 105.
   Box 57 houses the bulk of materials, with others on Microcopy Roll 10, M-253, Records of the Superintendent of Education in Virginia.

Hamilton, William. Papers. Library of Congress, Accession No. 79-24646.
   Albeit a Yankee, thanks to Private Hamilton some glimpses of Lower Fauquier survive.

[Jackson, Silas]. *Slave Narratives.* Vol. 15, *Maryland Narratives.* St. Clair
   Shores, Mich.: Scholarly Press, 1976. 29-33
   The Reverend Jackson's stirring portrayal at age ninety-one balances the ante bellum dabblings of Hunter, James, and Marshall.

James, G. P. R. "Life in Virginia." *Knickerbocker Magazine.* September, 1858.
   269-282.
   An on-the-mark vignette of the upper crust. James's focus is on The Springs.

Keith, Katherine Isham. "The Record of The Black Horse Troop." *Fauquier Historical Society Bulletin.* I, 1 (June, 1923). 434-460.
   Based on reminiscences from children of the Black Horsers. Gives a roster, "including all of its officers and men throughout the war."

Southern Historical Society Papers.
   At least nine volumes contain pertinent and often overlooked material: 10, 377-378; 14, 179-181; 21, 224-226; 24, 108-109, 218-225; 25, 154, 239-244; 27, 303-307; 30, 142-146; 32, 143; 36, 213-214.

Turner, Edward Carter. Diaries. Owned by J. Page Turner, The Plains.
   Abridged in *The Years of Anguish;* excerpted with comment in *Northern Virginia Heritage,* I, 2 (June, 1979).
   The master of Kinloch tells with expressive sensitivity of his waverings, anger, and final sorrow.

*The War of the Rebellion: A Compilation of the Official Records of the Union and
   Confederate Armies.* Washington: U.S.G.P.O., 1880-1901. 70 Vols.

Affectionately known in the trade as 'the O. R.'s,' volumes 12, 19, 21, 25, 27, 29 and 33 cover most of the action in Fauquier.

Warrenton Town Council Minutes.
In perfect condition at the Town Office.

Works Progress Administration of Virginia. Historical Inventory for Fauquier County. 1936-1937.
The county was blessed, indeed, to have The Plains's Frances B. Foster and Sumerduck's Marvin D. Gore as beavers. Their work surpasses that in most counties.

NEWSPAPERS

Alexandria *Gazette*.
Provides some snippets of prewar assemblies, elections, and martial preparations. On microfilm.

[Warrenton] *The Flag of '98*.
Democratic in politics, as was prewar Fauquier — thus *The Flag's* access to the inside track. The Fauquier County Library, Warrenton, has several copies on microfilm.

The New York *Herald*.
The *Herald's* behind-the-scenes dispatches more than made up for the management's assertion that the newspaper 'lost' six horses and a wagon a month in Fauquier. On microfilm.

The New York Ninth.
Even then New Yorkers were known for their public relations, and the *Ninth's* two issues of July 31st and August 7th, 1862, are as breezy as hometown sheets. The American Antiquarian Society, Worcester, has the first issue, the Library of Congress the second.

The New York *Times*.
Newspapermen say the *Times's* coverage of the sinking of the *Titanic* established its reputation for accuracy, but their Fauquier-based reporters were no slouches. On microfilm.

[Warrenton] *The True Index*.
Postwar Fauquier's newspaper of record. The Fauquier County Library has several issues on microfilm.

[Warrenton] *Virginia Sentinel*
Despite an occasional scoop, the *Sentinel* presents less news in a less interesting manner than its rival. The Fauquier County Library has some issues on microfilm.

[Warrenton] *Weekly Whig*.
Not as lively as *The Flag*, but two fine descriptions of town appear in the May 26th, 1860, issue. The Fauquier County Library has some copies on microfilm.

MAPS AND PHOTOGRAPHS

Boswell, J. K., and Jed Hotchkiss, *A Map of Fauquier Co. Virginia* . . . 2 miles equals one inch. 1863. Gilmer Collection, United States Military Academy.

As with all war maps, this one evinces artistry. Field surveyed by Hotchkiss. The first detailed map of the county.

Dwight, C. S. Two maps covering Upper Fauquier, and the area west and north of Warrenton. 1:4,000. 1863. Gilmer Collection, United States Military Academy.

Unsurpassed workmanship. Names most of the large land holders.

Gardner, H. D. *Map of Fauquier County, Virginia* . . . 1 mile equals one inch. 1876.

Crudely drawn. Shows the names of most landowners. The copy I have seen circulated in the last decade omits the legend and several landowners.

Gardner, Alexander. *Gardner's Photographic Sketchbook of The Civil War.* New York: Dover Publications, 1959. First published 1866 as *Gardner's Photographic Sketch Book of The War.* 2 Vols.

The original plates were at the U.S. Military History Institute, and evidently were more numerous than those published. The collection, however, has been lost (purportedly stolen).

Gilmer Collections. At the United States Military Academy and Virginia Historical Society.

Maj. Gen. Jeremy Francis Gilmer was Chief of the Engineer Bureau of the C.S.A. Each collection has maps the other does not.

Hotchkiss Collection. At the Library of Congress.

Maj. Jedediah Hotchkiss was the foremost of Civil War map-makers. When Gilmer and Hotchkiss differ, I would usually side with Hotchkiss, the better field-checker.

Miller, Francis Trevelyan. Ed. *The Photographic History of the Civil War.* New York: Review of Reviews, 1911. Reprinted, New York: T. Yoseloff [1957]. 10 Vols.

Contains many of the photographs taken in the county. The captions are often misleading. The three best archival sources are the Library of Congress; U.S. Army Military History Institute, Carlisle Barracks, Pa.; and the National Archives. There is no comparable published collection of prints. Many unpublished prints are at the above repositories.

The Official Atlas of the Civil War. New York: Arno Press, 1978. First published as: *Atlas to Accompany The Official Records of the Union and Confederate Armies.* Washington: U.S.G.P.O., 1891-1895. 3 Vols.

Plates most pertinent: 7, 8, 21, 22, 45, 100, 137.

Scheel, Eugene M. *Fauquier County: Commonwealth of Virginia.* 1 inch equals one mile. Rev. Ed. Warrenton, Va.: Fauquier National Bank, 1985.

Shows place names, sites of actions, and other historic detail not appearing on the 1:24,000 Geological Survey maps. Field checked. Hundreds supplied names and locations.

WHERE TO FIND THE ROSTERS

For units, organization dates, and officers, see Wallace, Lee A., Jr., Comp. *A Guide to Virginia Military Organizations, 1861-1865*, Richmond: Virginia Civil War Commission, 1964. This yeoman job is admittedly deficient because many records were lost before 1913, when much of the data was first compiled.

Mountain Rangers (organized 1852), later Co. A, 7th Reg. Va. Cav.
> Names with ranks in *The Years of Anguish*. Names "Furnished by Joshua C. Fletcher" in McDonald, William N., *A History of The Laurel Brigade, Originally The Ashby Cavalry* . . . Ed. Bushrod C. Washington. Baltimore: Kate S. McDonald, 1907. Reprinted, Arlington, Va.: R. W. Beatty, 1969

The Black Horse Troop (Spring 1859) later Co. H, 4th Reg. Va. Cav.
> Names and ranks in *The Years of Anguish; Fauquier Historical Society* throughout the war"; and Microfilm 69 at the Fauquier County Library, Warrenton, compiled from the roll book of Sgt. Robert Martin "as it stood when the war closed." Also on Microfilm 69, rolls of May 7th, 18th, 1861. Roster in the Memorandum Book of Alexander Dixon Payne, Virginia Historical Society.

Warrenton Rifles (November, 1859) later Co. K, 17th Reg. Va. Vols.
> Names and ranks in *The Years of Anguish*. Names, ranks, and data on roll dated September 1st, 1861, in Wise, George, *History of the Seventeenth Virginia Infantry*. Baltimore: Kelly, Piet, 1870. This apparent roll, without ranks and data, was sent by the Virginia Division of Confederate Veterans to the Fauquier Clerk of the Court in 1932, on Microfilm 69.

44th Reg. 2nd Div. Va. Militia (Before 1860; called out July 13th, 1861)
> No roster available.

85th Reg. 2nd Div. Va. Militia (Before 1860; called out July 13th, 1861)
> No roster available.

Warrenton Home Guard (1859 or 1860)
> No roster available

Lee Guard (Spring, 1861)
> No roster available

Wise Dragoons, Co. H., 6th Reg. Va. Cav. (April 1st, 1861)
>   Names, ranks, and data in Gott, John K. *A History of Marshall . . . Fauquier County, Virginia*. [Middleburg], Va.: Denlinger's, 1959.

Beauregard Rifles or Scott's Co., Co. K, 8th Reg. Va. Vols. (April 1st, 1861)
>   Names, ranks, and data in Divine, John E. *8th Virginia Infantry*. Lynchburg: H. E. Howard, 1983. Names and ranks in *The Years of Anguish*.

Brooke's Battery, Co. A (1st), 12th Bat. Va. Light Arty. (April 16th, 1861)
>   Names and ranks in *The Years of Anguish*.

Winfield's Co., Co. B, 7th Reg. Va. Cav. (April, 1861)
>   Names "furnished by Cyrus Fitzer" in McDonald, *The Laurel Brigade*.

Bull Run Rangers or Evergreen Guards, Co. C, 8th Reg. Va. Vols. (May 8th, 1861)
>   Names, ranks, and data in Divine, *8th Virginia Infantry*.

Piedmont Rifles or Rectortown Co., Co. B, 8th Reg. Va. Vols. (May 17th, 1861)
>   Names, ranks, and data in Divine, *8th Virginia Infantry*. Names and ranks in *The Years of Anguish*.

Rough and Ready Rifles or Morrisville Co., Co. I, 11th Reg. Va. Vols. (May 25th, 1861)
>   Names and ranks in *The Years of Anguish*.

Fauquier Guards or Murray's Co., Co. C, 49th Va. Inf. (May 28th, 1861)
>   Names, ranks, and data compiled by W. B. Tompkins in 1903, "partially from an old muster roll dated October, 1863, and from recollections," in Hale, Laura Virginia, and Stanley S. Phillips, *History of the Forty-Ninth Virginia Infantry, C. S. A. . . .* Lanham, Md.: S. S. Phillips, 1981

Markham Guards, Fauquier Artillery or Stribling's Battery, Co. G, 49th Va. Inf. (June 22nd, 1861)
>   Names and ranks in *The Years of Anguish*. Another roll will appear in a book about the unit being written by John Hennesey, historian at Manassas National Battlefield Park.

Loudoun Dragoons or Dulany Troop, Co. A, 6th Reg. Va. Cav. (June, 1861)
>   Names, ranks, and data in Gott, *History of Marshall*.

Mosby's Rangers (December 30th, 1862), later 43rd Bat. Va. Cav. Partisan Rangers, later Mosby's Reg.

> Substantially the same rolls in Williamson, *Mosby's Rangers;* and typed (by Byrd M. Smith), and given to the Fauquier County Clerk's Office in 1921, following the unveiling of the Mosby Monument in Marshall, on Microfilm 69. Units and officers in *The Years of Anguish* and Wallace, *Virginia Military Organizations.*

A plaque in the Virginia Room, Fauquier County Library, Warrenton, titled "Confederate Soldiers Buried in Warrenton Cemetery," undated, lists 193 dead.

INDEX

Roman numerals refer to photographic plates. For numbered military units see *Military units*. Map names are not indexed.

Adams, Ben 5
Adams, John 14
Alabama 16
Aldie 26, 30, 38, 53, 59, 71, 78; actions near 40-41
Alexander, Samuel 79, 102
Alexandria 5-6, 12, 16, 19, 21, 24, XVIII
Alexandria, Loudoun and Hampshire Railroad 20-21
Alexandria Turnpike 6, II
Alger, Russell 67
Allen, Miss ___ 23
Allen, Landon 19
Ambler, John 2, 17
Ambler, R. C. 3
Ambler, Susan 103
Ames, James 52
Amissville 36, 45
Andrew, John 29
Antietam battle 41, 43, 46, 48
Appomattox 77, 86
Arlington Heights 19
Armstrong, Cynthia 20
Armstrong, Sallie 20
Army of Northern Virginia 53, 68-69
Army of The Potomac 43, 46-47, 53, 56, 61, 65, 101
Ashby Gap 7, 22, 26, 29, 41-42, 44, 57-60, 82-83, 87
Ashby Gap Turnpike 5-6, 21, 55-58
Ashby, Henry 74
Ashby, John 16
Ashby, Richard 15, 21
Ashby, Turner 10-11, 15, 21, 44
Ashby's Cavalry 10, 26 (see Mountain Rangers)
Atoka 4 (see Rector's Cross Roads)
Auburn 28, 33, 65-68, 71; described 66; actions at or near 64-66
Auburn Mill 66
Augur, Christopher 76, 80, 91
Avary, Myrta 19
Avenel 41, 78
Averell, William 44, 49-52
Ayrshire 78, 83; action at 58

Babcock, A. G. XX
Bacon, Professor 11-12
Balch Place 76
Ball's Bluff battle 55
Ball's Tavern 5
Baltimore 24, 96
Barbee's Cross Roads 4, 44, 57; actions near 45, 64
Barbour, John 91
Barker, Elmer 55
Barnett's (Ellis's) Ford 49, 51; actions at 50, 72
Bath 21
Baylor, George 65
Bayly, Sampson 79, 84, 86
Beale, John 3, 27
Beale, Richard 33
Bealeton 3, 14, 27, 52, 55, 67, XII-XIII, XV-XVI; described 69; actions at or near 26, 72
Beattie, Fountain 50, 56
Beauregard, Pierre 21-22
Beauregard Rifles 30; organized 14; roster information 108
Beaver Dam Creek 11
Beckham, John 1, 22, 90
Bell, John 12
Belle Grove 54, 72, 75, 100
Berkeley County 33
Berkeley, Edmund 17
Berrien, John 11
Berry's Ferry 55
Berryville 57, 82
Beverley's Ford 28, 56-57, 67; actions at 27, 33, 47; bridge 92
Biddle, Chapman 72
Big Cobbler Mountain 12, 80
Binns, Charles 71
Birney, David 66
Biscuit Mountain Road 60
Bispham, William 96
Black Hawk Rangers 10
Black Horse Rangers 10
Black Horse Troop 5, 11-15, 21, 41, 45, 48, 50-51, 53-54, 64, 73, 76-78, 85, 93,

95-96, 101, 104, I; organized 10-11; name origin 11; roster information 107
Blackford, William 34
Black Jack Hill 77
Blackman, William 98
Blackwell, Bettie 39, 72, 101
Blackwell, Joseph 70
Blair, Montgomery 64
Blakeley's Grove School action 75-76
Bloomfield 76
Blooming Dale Mill 76, 91
Blue Ridge 11, 28-30, 57, 59, 78, 82, 100
Bohanon, Daniel 92
Bolling, Robert 3, 19
Bollingbrook 3, 19, 57, 59
Booker, Thomas XX
Booth, George 5
Booth, John 87
Boston, Massachusetts 94
Boswell, J. K. 36, 106
Boteler, A. R. 62
Boteler, Joe 55
Bowen, William 27, 91
Bowenville 91-92 (see Rappahannock Station)
Bowie, Henry 16
Boxwood Farm 98
Boyd, William 54
Braddox, Martha 96
Brady, Mathew XV
Bragg, Charles 5, 32, 73, 86,95, II
Brandy Station battle 56-57, 70
Breckinridge, James 12
Brentsville 15, 50-51
Brien, L. T. 33
Bristersburg 48-49
Bristoe action 39
Bristoe Campaign 65-67, 70, XVII
Bristoe Station 38, 66, 72; battle 66
Broad Run 38, 66
Broad Run bridge (O & A Ry) 66
Broad Run bridge (Thoroughfare Gap) 26
Broad Run Church 4, 88
Broad Run Station 29-30, 38
Brooke, James 14-15, 17, 19-20, 22-23, 73
Brooke, Mary 23, 95
Brooke's Battery organized, 15; roster information 108
Brooks, Mary 39
Brookside 78, 91
Brown, John 1, 10, 58
Brown, Orlando 98
Brown, William 6

Buckingham, C. P. 46
Buckland 41, 65; actions at or near 66-67, 76
Buckland Races 66-67
Buckner, Miss _____ 24
Buford, John 58
Bull Run 22, 66, 77
Bull Run battle (see Manassas, First Battle of)
Bull Run Mountain 22, 38, 57, 60, 63, 78
Bull Run Rangers organized 16; roster information 108
Bunker Hill 38
Burke, William 21
Burnside, Ambrose 46-48, 53
Burwell, Road 55
Butler, Benjamin 96
Butler, O. L. XX
Byrne, Mattie 96
Caldwell, Frances 39
Caldwell, J. F. 37
Caldwell, James 90
Caldwell, Lycurgus 90, 95
California 78
California Building 93
Calverton 4 (see Warrenton Junction)
Campbell, Mrs. _____ 31, 61
Cannon, James 89
Capon Springs 21
Carter, Mrs. _____ 31
Carter, Bob 54
Carter, John 15
Carter, Richard 16, 30
Carter, Robert 42
Carter, Walter 54
Carter, Welby 15
Carter's Mill bridge 92
Carter's Run 11, 64, 98
Carter's Run Church 85, 88
Casanova 4, XIV (see Three Mile Switch)
Castle Murray XIV
Catlett 28, 31, 33, 40-41, 48-50, 63, 66, 88, 91; described 30, V; Stuart's raid on 33-36, 44, 65
Catlett, Mrs. _____ 33
Catlett family V
Catlett Voting Precinct 14
Cedar Creek battle 82
Cedar Run 27, 66; actions at 26, 65-66
Cedar Run railroad bridge 33, 53, 66; actions at 33, 40, 55
Centreville 40, 79
Cephus, Wesley 98

Chamberlain, Samuel   50, 63
Chambliss, John   58, 60
Chancellor, Mr. _____   80
Chancellor, A.   26
Chancellor's Mill   80; action at 80
Chapman, John   25
Chapman, Samuel   55-56
Chapman, William   75
Chapman's Mill   25
Charles Town   10, 54
Charlottesville   75, 85
Chase, W. S.   97-98
Chattanooga   65
Chester Cap   44, 56
Chestnut Forks, actions at   67-78
Chestnut, Mary   21
Chew, Robert   58
Chilton, Charles   91
Chilton John   19
Chinn, William   86
Christ Church   67, 96
Clarke County   10, 15, 65, 82, 87
Clarke, Edward   31
Clever's Oak Church   4
Clift Mills   98
Cobbler Mountains   55, 80
Cocke, Philip   16
Coid Harbor   77
Cole, Henry   75
Cologne, Edgar   1
Comanches, The   64
Combs, Margaret   23
Connecticut   44
Cool Spring Church   57
Cornwell, John   75
Cox, Misses _____   94, 97
Crawford, J. Marshall   75, 78, 102-103
Crooked Run   57, 75
Cropp's Mill   49
Crummey's Run   57, 83
Cryer, J. H.   64
Culpeper County   1, 13, 16-17, 23, 27-28, 34-35, 41, 49, 52-53, 56, 66-67, 69, 77, 91; compared with Fauquier 89, 92
Culpeper Court House   22, 50, 97
Culpeper Road   67
Cunningham, Richard   92
Curlette, Susan   43
Custer, George   66-67, 81
Custis, George   81
Custis, John   81
Custis, Martha   81
Davies, Henry   67
Davis, Alexander   71

Davis, Jefferson   21-22, 92
Day, Jennie   95
Deatherage, George   11
Deep Run   49; action at 50
DeForest, Othneil   53
Delaplane   4 (see Piedmont)
DeShields, James   31
DeTrobriand, Philippe   43
Dixie Battery   55
Dixon, Henry   12
Dodd, John   77
Douglas, Beverley   44
Douglas, Stephen   12
Dover   50
Downman, Robert   2, 4-5
Drake, David   27
Dranesville   60
Dulany, Eliza (Ida)   1, 41-42, 48, 54-55, 58-60, 100
Dulany, Hal   42, 80
Dulany Troop   organized, 17; roster information 108
Dulany, William   15
Dumfries   15, 49-50
Dumfries Road   65-66
Dwight, C. S.   106
Early, Jubal   35, 66, 69-70, 82
Eastern Shore   31
Eastern View   27
Edgeworth   54
Edmonds, Amanda   1, 54, 72, 75-76, 83, 100
Edmonds, Elias   18
Edmonds, John   74
Eliason, Talcott   57
Elk Run (village)   20, 29, 31, 51-52, 55, 88, X; action near 50
Elk Run Copper Mine   99
Elkwood   91
Ellerslie   64
Ellis's (Barnett's) Ford   49, 51; actions at 50, 72
Emancipation Proclamation   48
Embrey, Staunton   19
Emory's, action near   80
Ennis, Bill   77
Ensor's Shop   4
Evans, Jim   79
Evergreen Guards   organized 16; roster information 108
Ewell, Richard   20, 27, 35-36, 56, 65
Fairfax County   15, 23, 50, 76
Fairfax Court House   51, 85; actions at 19, 24

Fairview XI
Falls Church 21
Fant, John 23
Farmers' Hotel 5, III
Farnsworth, John 27
Farrowsville 16, 57; action at 44
Farrowsville Voting Precinct 14
Fauquier Artillery 87; organized 16; roster information 108
Fauquier County agricultural statistics 2, 89, 103-104; church-going in 3-4, 8; compared with Culpeper 80, 92; Loudoun 43-44, 89; Prince William 89; Stafford 92; courthouse 13, 86, 88, 92, III, XIII; court meetings 1, 11, 17, 19, 26, 41, 59-60, 78-79, 83-86, 89-91, 93-94, 99, 104; described 2-4, 30, 62-63, 84, 89; education in 3, 94-95, 97, 104; elections, presidential 12; for secession convention delegates 14, 20; withdrawal from Union 15, 17-18; personal property 3; population 2
Fauquier Female Seminary 12, 23, 25
Fauquier Guards 17, 93; organized 16; roster information 108
Fauquier White Sulphur Springs 4, 21 (see The Springs)
Fayettesville 4, 64-65, 67; actions at or near 47, 56, 67, 72
Ficklin, William 19
Fiery Run Road 45
Finks, John 90
Finks, Thomas 79
Fisher, E. F. 22
Fisher, Samuel 17, 40, 45, 47
Fisk, Thomas 1
Fitzer, Cyrus 108
Fitzhugh's Lane 55
Five Points, action at 74
Fletcher, Joshua 42
Fletchers, Mrs. Joshua 42, 83
Flint Hill 45
Florence, R. C. 96
Foley, Oswald 21
Foote, Richard 3
Forbes, John 17, 73
Ford, Andrew 63
Fort Sumter, South Carolina 15, 20
Foster, C. G. 98
Foster, Frances 71, 105
Foster, James 38, 56
Foster, Thomas 60
Fox, John 91
Fox's Mill, action at 65

Foxville 35, 65, 91
Foxville Church 98
Frankland, Walter 52, 75, 80-81
Franklin Gold Mine 48
Frazer, Douglas 84
Frederick County 15
Frederick, Horner 98
Fredericksburg 5, 31, 47, 52-53, 56, 94; battle of 53, 93
Free State 37, 78
Freedmen's Bureau 90-94, 97-99, 104
Freeman, Douglas 48
Freeman's Ford, action at 33
French, William 69
Front Royal 28-29, 80-81; action at 29
Fry, Emily 79
Gaines, Cross Roads 36, 56
Gaines, William H. 19, 23, 59, 78, 89
Gaines, William H., Sr. 3
Gainesville 36-37, 59, 67
Galwey, Thomas 66
Ganesvoort, Henry 79-80
Gardner, Alexander 106
Gardner, H. D. 106
Gaskins, Alfred 19
Gaskins' Mill, action at 64
Geary, John 26, 28-29, 64, 95-96
Gentry, I. A. XX
Georgetown 41, 85
Georgia 8, 11; troops from 38-39, VII
Germantown 61, 96; action near 67; described 67
Germantown Company 20, 96
Gettysburg battle 57-58, 60-61, 63, 73, 81, 101, 103, XII
Gettysburg Campaign 56
Gibson, Francis 86
Gilmer, Jeremy 106
Gilmor's Band 76
Glascock, Alfred 80
Glascock, Mrs. Aquila 84
Glascock Gap 60
Gleason, Daniel 56
Glen Mills 17
Glenville 38
Glen Welby 30, 62, 78
Goldvein 4, 77 (see Grove Church)
Goose Creek 28, 55, 57; actions at 59; bridge (near Piedmont) 80; bridge (near Upperville) 57
Gordon, Charles 11
Gordon, Dallas 55
Gordon, James 45
Gordon, Samuel 21

Gordonsville 23, 97
Gore, Marvin 71, 77, 106
Gosden, Freeman XX
Gosden, Walter XX
Goulding, Charles 34
Graham, Michael 55
Grant, Ulysses 77, 81-82, 86-88, XIX
Grapewood Farm, action at 55
Gray, Robert 59
Grayson, Minor 90
Great Run 36, 91
Green, N. M. 10
Greenbrier 21
Greenwich 41, 49, 64; actions near 55, 76
Greenwich Road 66
Gregg, David 55, 57, 59, 65-66, 75-77
Grigsby 83
Grove Church 4, 49, 51, 53; actions at 50-51
Grove Church, Baptist 4, 77
Grove Church, Presbyterian 4
Groveton Heights, action at 36
Gutheridge, Sue 74
Hairston, Sam 39
Hale, Samuel 70
Halfway 4, 83, 92, 98
Halfway Road 6, 55, 61
Halleck, Henry 34-35, 62, 68, 77, 80
Hamilton 83
Hamilton, Hugh 48, 96
Hamilton, William 48, 63, 104
Hampton, Wade 45, 48-51, 57, 59-60, 67
Hancock, Winfield 59, 86-88
Hardaway, Robert 42
Harper's Ferry 10, 15, 29
Hart, George 68
Hart, James F. 57
Hart, James H. 75
Hart, Thomas 17
Hart's Mill 33
Hartwood Church 49-51, 53, 63, 76
Hatcher's Mill 80, 83
Hathaway 78
Hathaway, James 52
Haupt, Herman 28, 35, 47, 62, 66, 100
Haymarket 17, 67
Heartland 78
Helm, Erasmus I
Henderson, J. L. 17
Hendricks, L. A. 68
Henry, John 96
Herndon, Billy 77
Herring Run, Maryland 96

Higgins, William 31
Hill-and-Dale 76
Hinson's Ford 36, 57
Hinson's Mill 36
Holland, John 76, 91, 98
Holland's Mill 76, 91
Home Guard 11, 16, 19-20; roster information 107
Hood, John 38, 57
Hooker, Joseph 53, 56-57, 60-61
Hopewell 9, 41, 71, X
Hopewell Gap 38, 63, 85
Hopley, Catherine 1, 23-24, 28, 100-101
Horner, Mrs. _____ 31
Horner, Fannie 39
Horner, G. B. 17
Horner, Richard 48
Hoskins, Bradford 56
Hotchikiss, Jedediah 106
Howard, Beverly 90
Howard, Gibson 15, 17
Howard, Oliver 26-27, 91, 98
Howard School 98
Howard University 98
Howard, William 98
Howe, Shesh 80
Howison, Lee XX
Hudnal, Thomas 3
Hudgin, Robert 21
Hume 4, 103 (see Barbee's Cross Roads)
Hume, Hallie 74
Hume, William 79, 86
Hunter, Alexander 6, 24, 39, 71-74, 78, 85, 94, 101
Hunter, A. N. 74
Hunter, William 56
Hunton, Elizabeth XI
Hunton, Eppa 15, 21, 38, 93
Hunton, Silas 1, 13
Illinois, troops from 27, 72, 79-80, 85
Ingalls, Rufus 56
Ingersoll, Timothy 31
Jackson, Andrew 5
Jackson, Lyttleton 98
Jackson, Silas 7-9, 104
Jackson, Stonewall 22, 29-31, 35, 47, 53, 57, 94, 101; march around Pope 36-39
James, J. P. R. 104
James River 62, 77
Jameson, James 16
Janney, John 14-15
Janney, Samuel 91
Jasper, Sandy 8
Jefferson County 10-11, 17

Jeffersonton   36, 45
Jeffries, Sandy   78
Johnson, Andrew   89
Johnson, C. McLean   13
Johnson, James   94
Johnson, William   1
Johnston, Joseph   21-22, 25, 87-88
Jones, Andrew   16
Jones, Anne   44
Jones, David   38
Jones, W. E.   27, 58, 60
Jordan, John   98
Kane, Thomas   32-33
Kargé, Joseph   40, 45
Keith, Isham   2, 17, 19, 59-60
Keith, James   I
Keith, Katherine   11, 104
Kelly, Granville   52
Kelly, John   52
Kelly's Ford   48-51, 56, 64; actions at 33, 36, 49, 52-53, 69; bridge 92
Kellysville   52
Kemper, Henry   1
Kempton, Miss ___   97
Kentucky   12
Kershaw, Joseph   59
Kester, John   75
Kettle Run, action at   55
Kilpatrick, Hugh   58, 63, 67, 72
Kincheloe, James   17, 93
Kincheloe, John   3
Kinloch   37, 39, 41, 50, 68, 81, 104
King, Rufus   31, II
Klipstein, Amanda   85
Klipstein, Philip   37, 79, 85
Lafayette, Marquis de   4
Lake, Ludwell   84
Lakeland   78, 84
Lakeland School   56
Landmark   98
Landmark Voting Precinct   12
Law, Evander   38
Lawton, Alexander   35
Lee, Fitzhugh   33, 45, 50-52, 60, 65-67
Lee Guard   16, 19-20; roster information 107
Lee, Robert E.   10, 19-20, 27, 35-39, 52-53, 56-57, 60, 65-68, 79, 81, 86, XVII
Lee, Rooney   33, 50
Leeds Manor Road   44-45, 64, 75
Leesburg   21, 73, 76
Lee's Ridge   74
Letcher, John   12, 15-17
Lewis, Mrs. ___   85

Lewis, Richard   76
Libby Prison   63
Liberty   67; action near 71
Liberty Church   4, 27
Liberty Voting Precinct   12
Licking Run bridge   12
Lincoln, Abraham   12-13, 15, 21, 29-30, 34, 36, 39, 46, 48, 56-57, 62, 64, 68, 74, 86-87
Linden   3, 29, 55, 78; action near 29
Lindsay, J. C.   22-23
Little Georgetown   41, 85
Little River Turnpike   21, 40
Lomax, Lunsford   92
Long, Armistead   38, 65
Long Branch Church   4
Long Branch Female Seminary   83
Longstreet, James   36-38, 57, 59
Loretto   3
Lost Mountain, action at   59
Loudoun County   11, 14-15, 23, 26, 29, 38, 41, 61, 75-76, 82-83, 91; compared with Fauquier 43-44, 89
Loudoun Dragoons   organized 17; roster information 108
Loudoun Heights   74
Loudoun Rangers   73
Loudoun Valley   83
Love, James   76
Love, Thomas   84
Low, E. T.   97
Lowell, Charles   71, 76
Lower Fauquier   10, 22, 26, 29, 48, 50, 53, 76-77, 93-94, 100; described 54, 63
Lower Fauquier Cavalry   10
Lucas, Annie   39, 72
Lucas, Elizabeth   39, 96
Lucas, Fanny   39
Lucky Hill   27
Lynchburg   24, 52, 85, 88
Maine   93; troops from 69
Manassas   20, 22-23, 25, 29-30, 37
Manassas, First Battle of   22-23, 55, 96
Manassas Gap   28, 63-64
Manassas Gap Railroad   5-6, 10-11, 19, 26, 28, 38, 42, 79-80, 92
Manassas Gap Road   4, 20
Manassas Junction   38, 84
Manassas, Second Battle of   39
Mann, William   56
Manyett, Antoine   5
Markham   3, 16, 28-29, 57, 61, 75; action near 44
Markham Guards   organized 16; roster

information 108
Marr, Fannie 13
Marr, John 11-15, 17, 19-20, 24, 93, 95
Marr, Thomas 20
Marsh Road 48, 51, 53, 88
Marshall 4 (see Salem)
Marshall, Alexander 73
Marshall, Charles 37, 58
Marshall, Edward 6, 10
Marshall, Eliza 3
Marshall family 3
Marshall, Fielding 6, 101
Marshall, Jaquelin 12
Marshall, James 73
Marshall, John 12, 44
Marshall, 'Navy' John 54, 77-78
Marshall, Lewis 44
Marsteller, Mr. _____ 54
Marsteller, A. A. 76
Marsteller Place, actions at 54, 76
Martin, George IX
Martin, John 20, 85, 95
Martin, Robert 73, 107
Martin's Mill IX
Maryland 31, 46, 56, 60; troops from 75
Mason, James 31
Mason, Mamie 39
Massachusetts 29, 54, 58, 69, 74, 76, 94, 97; troops from 63, 65
Matthews, John 28
McCabe, George 76
McClellan, George 27-28, 42, 46; relieved of command 46-48, XVIII
McClellan, Henry 50, 66
McCormick, Stephen 28, 66, 68
McCrickett, M. J. 80
McDowell, Irvin 30, 34, 36, VIII
McIlhaney, Ann 39
McKee, Samuel-76
McLaws, Lafayette 57, 59
McNulty, Abbie 95
McNulty, William 90-91, 93-95
McRea, Tully 44
Meade, George 61-62, 65, 67-70, 76-77, XVII
Meadowville 28
Mecca 67
Melrose XIV
Merritt, Wesley 58, 68, 72, 83
Meyer, Alfred 98
Michigan, troops from 66-67
Middleboro, Massachusetts 94
Middleburg 6, 26, 31, 38, 40, 42, 50-51, 53, 55, 57, 74, 83, 85; actions at 51, 59, 62

Military Units, numerical by state (also see state names, troops from, and names of individual units)
8th Illinois Cavalry 27, 72, 79-80, 85
6th Maine 69
15th Massachusetts Volunteers 63
2nd Massachusetts Cavalry 76
6th Michigan Cavalry 66
7th Michigan Cavalry 67
12th New Hampshire 46
5th New York 56
50th New York Engineers XIX
96th New York Volunteers 90
93rd New York Infantry XII, XIII, XV
6th Ohio Cavalry 64
118th Pennsylvania 63
1st Vermont 56
Co. A, 6th Regiment Virginia Cavalry organized 17; roster information 108
Co. H., 6th Regiment Virginia Cavalry organized 14; roster information 108
Co. A, 7th Regiment Virginia Cavalry roster information 107
Co. B, 7th Regiment Virginia Cavalry organized 16; roster information 108
Co. B, 8th Regiment Virginia Volunteers organized 16; roster information 108
Co. C, 8th Regiment Virginia Volunteers organized 16-17; roster information 108
Co. K, 8th Regiment Virginia Volunteers organized 14; roster information 108
Co. I, 11th Regiment Virginia Volunteers organized 16; roster information 108
Co. A (1st), 12th Battalion, Virginia Light Artillery organized 15; roster information 108
Co. C, 49th Virginia Infantry organized 16; roster information 108
Co. G, 49th Virginia Infantry organized 16; roster information 108
4th Virginia Cavalry 45, 107, I
6th Virginia Cavalry 26, 61, 84
7th Regiment Virginia Cavalry 58, 107
8th Virginia Infantry 26

17th Virginia Infantry 17
17th Regiment Virginia Volunteers 17, 107
43rd Battalion Partisan Rangers organized 56; roster information 109
44th Regiment Militia 15, 17; roster information 107
85th Regiment Militia 10-11, 17; roster information 107
5th Wisconsin 69
Mill View 4, 91 (see Rappahannock Station)
Mill View Comany 96
Millville Road 58
Millwood 87
Milwaukee 39
Minnesota 39
Mississippi 72
Monroe, Mrs. _____ 76
Monte Rosa 88
Monteiro, Aristides 93, 102
Morgan, Samuel 98
Morgan, William 1, 78
Morgansburg 52
Morrisville 16, 48-52, 61, 63, 68; described 54
Morrisville Company 96; organized 16; roster information 108
Morrisville Voting Precinct 14
Morse, George 97
Mosby, John 4, 27, 51-56, 60-64, 68, 71-72, 74-87, 91-93, 102-103, XVI, XX; begins partisan career 50; organizes rangers 56; burning raid against 82-83; disbands command 87
Mosby, Pauline 52, 82
Mosby, William 87
Mosby's Confederacy 39; defined 78
Mount Defiance, action at 57
Mount Holly Church 49, 52, 69, 85, 88
Mount Vernon 81
Mount Zion Church 71
Mountain Rangers (Ashby's Cavalry) 11, 15, 21; organized 10; roster information 107
Mountain View, action at 44
Mountjoy, R. P. 56, 72, 74-75, 82
Mountville, actions at or near 41, 57
Munford, Thomas 29
Munson, John 55, 103, XX
Murray, Edward 16
Murray, James XIV
Murray's Company organized 16; roster information 108
Myers, Mr. _____ 80

National Gallery of Art 81
Neese, George 35, 38
Negro Mountain 79
Nelson, Hugh 15
Nelson, Joe 52
New Baltimore 2, 14, 29, 40-41, 47, 55, 57, 62, 66; actions near 45, 59, 67; described 5
New Baltimore Company 96
New Baltimore Voting Precinct 12, 14
New Bedford, Massachusetts 97
New Brighton 4 (see Fayettesville)
Newby, Robert 19
Newby, Mrs. Robert 20
Newell, Mr. _____ XX
New England 65
New England, troops from 47
New England Freedmen's Aid Society 94, 97
New Hampshire, troops from 46
New Jersey 47; troops from 75
Newton, John 61
New York 21, 52, 95; troops from 35, 50, 53-56, 62, 76, 90-91, XII-XIII, XV, XIX
New York City 32, 43, XV
Nightingale, Florence 39
Nokesville 55
Norfolk 15
Norman's Ford, action at 27
North Carolina 87-88; troops from 45, 53
North Carolina Railroad 22
Number Six actions at 41-42, 58, 80
Number Six Road 21
Oakham 50, 84
Oakley, actions at 41-42, 58-59
Oak Spring 39, 101
Occoquan 49
O'Ferrall, Charles 58
Ohio 66, 93; troops from 40, 64
Old Capitol Prison 64, 80
Old Carolina Road 21, 27, 64
Old Dominon Minstrels 95
Old Mother Leathercoat 38
Olinger, Mr. _____ 27
Orange, Alexandria and Manassas Railroad 92
Orange and Alexandria Railway 6, 16, 19, 22-23, 26-27, 36, 38, 49, 52-53, 55, 57, 61-62, 65-66, 68, 71, 76-77, 88, 91-92, 100, IV-V, XVII-IX; capacity 47
Orange County 1, 34, 70, 97
Orlean 12, 16, 29, 36-37, 45-46, 55, 57, 62, 64, 76
Orr, M. E. 90, 92
O'Sullivan, Timothy VI, XII, XV

Owl Run 4, 98, XVIII (see Warrenton Junction)
Palmer, W. Ben XX
Palmetto Sharpshooters 22
Panther Skin Creek 41, 59
Paris 1, 10, 22, 26, 28, 40, 42, 54, 58-59, 72, 75-76, 83; action near 75; described 4-5
Paris Voting Precinct 12, 14
Parkinson, John 1
Parr, W. A. 20
Parrott, Robert XX
Patterson, John 92
Patterson's 55
Patrick, Marsena 28, 30-31, 43, 61, 67-69, 75, 88, 101
Patrols 1, 8
Payne, Col. ____ 45
Payne, Alexander 14, 73, 107, I
Payne, Rice 17
Payne, Richards 1, 19, 59, 73, 78
Payne, Mrs. Richards 39
Payne, William 10-11, 13-14, 16, 41, 45, 78, 85, 93
Payne, Winter 13-14
Peale, Charles 81
Pelham, John 33, 42, 52
Pender, William 36
Pennsylvania 59, 61, 95-96; troops from 26, 40, 63, 76
Perry, Mr. ____ 79
Petersburg 77, 79
Philadelphia 7
Phillips, Roberta 23
Phillips, Samuel 5, I
Philomont 26; action near 41
Pickett, George 57
Pickett, Sanford 83
Piedmont (Piedmont Station) 5, 21-22, 26, 28-29, 42-43, 55, 75, 79-80, 83, 98; actions at or near 54, 75; described 4
Piedmont Rifles organized 16, roster information 108
Piedmont-to-Upperville Turnpike 5-6
Pierce, James 16
Pitzer, A. L. 35
Pleasants, Eliza 91
Pleasonton, Alfred 44-45, 56-57, 59
Pollock, Roberta 85
Pond Mountains 30, 37, 76
Pope, John 32-39, 101, IX
Porter, John 96
Portland, Maine 93
Potomac Baptist Association 4

Potomac Iron Company 26
Potomac Military Department 16
Potomac River 16, 26, 60, 67, 77
Powell, William 80
Pratt, John 95
Price, John 20
Price, Richard 40
Prince William County 15, 45, 49-50, 51; compared with Fauquier 89
Prospect Hill 66
Pugh, J. W. 16
Puryear, John XX
Quarles, Mr. ____ XX
Quesenberry Farm 28
Rains, Gabriel 62
Randolph, Buckner 16
Randolph family 27
Randolph, Mary 27
Randolph, Norman XX
Randolph, Robert 11, 73, 93
Rapidan River 70, 101
Rappahannock County 1, 41, 80
Rappahannock Navigation 35, 49
Rappahannock railroad bridge 25, 66, 71, IX; actions at 27, 47, 50-51, 69-70
Rappahannock River 25, 27-28, 32-33, 36-37, 40, 44-45, 49-51, 53, 56-57, 65-69, 77, 80, 91-92, 101, XVII, IX
Rappahannock Station 4, 47-48, 51-52, 63, 81, 91-92, XIX; actions at or near 27, 47, 50-51, 69-70; described IV
Rawlings, John 78
Rawlingsdale 78
Rector, Alfred 5
Rector, Clinton 56
Rector's Cross Roads 4, 56, 60-61
Rectortown 1, 4-5, 16-17, 28, 30, 43-44, 47, 52, 55, 74, 76, 80-81, 83; action near 79; McClellan at 46
Rectortown Company 30; organized 16; roster information 108
Rehm, Frank XX
Remington 4, 92, IV, XIX (see Rappahannock Station)
Richards, Thomas 87
Richardson, J. S. 20
Richmond 14-15, 21, 23-24, 29, 34-35, 43, 55-56, 60, 62, 88, 95
Richmond Convention 14-15, 20, 26
Rindsburg, A. 94
Rinehart, Mary XIV
Rixey farms 80
Road Island 93
Roanoke County 4

Robertson, Beverly 35, 60
Robertson, Lizzie 96
Robertson, T. Bolling 38
Rockbridge County 41
Rockburn 84-85
Rockingham County 16
Rock Hill 67
Rodes, Robert 65-66, 69
Rogers, Asa 26, 29
Rogers, Hamilton 50
Rogers, James 98
Rogers, James S. 83, 86
Rokeby, action at 41
Rose Bank 10
Rosser, Thomas 32-33, 44-45, 57, 67
Rough and Ready Rifles organized 16; roster information 108
Royall, William 77
Russell, Charles 102
Sage, Theodore 68
St. James' Church VI
St. Leonard's 92
St. Stephen's 66
St. Stephen's Church 66, 83
Saint's Hill 66
Salem 2-4, 12, 14, 24, 26, 28, 36-37, 42, 53, 57, 60-62, 64, 76, 83, 85, 98; actions at or near 79-80; described 4; Mosby's men disband at 87-88
Salem, Roanoke County 4
Salem Voting Precinct 12, 14
Sandy Ford Dam 35
Sargent, Horace 63
Sargent, John 85
Saunders, Maj. ____ 31
Saunders, Thomas 19, 92
Schriver, Edmund 30
Scott, Fanny 30, 62
Scott, John, Jr., 5, 10-12, 14-16, 73, 93-94, 102-103
Scott, Robert E. 12-15, 28, 64, 93
Scott, Mrs. Robert E. 47
Scott, Robert T. 14, 30
Scott, Sue 39
Scott, Walter 74, 96
Scruggs, John 11, 13, 17, 19-20
Scuffleburg 64, 78, 83
Seddon, James 52
Sedgwick, John 62, 69, 81
Selfridge, James 34
Seneca, Maryland, action at 56
Settle, Lucy 20
Settle, J. W. 20
Settle, Mr. and Mrs. Joseph 20

Settle, Thomas 10, 58
Shackelford, Benjamin 14, 20, 73
Shackelford, Rebecca 39
Shacklett, Cook 98
Shacklett, Hezekiah 71
Shacklett, Kitty 22, 57, 71
Shenandoah River 55
Shenandoah Valley 29-31, 41-43, 56, 59 61, 76-77, 79, 82
Sheridan, Philip 79, 81-82, 85
Sherman, William 87
Shields, James 29-30
Shirley, Richard 5
Shooters' Hill 99
Shumate, Bailey 33
Sigel, Franz 36
Silver Greys 16
Simpson, Cpl. ____ 76
Sinnott, Henry XX
Skinker, Samuel 83
Slaves 6-9, 32, 104, IV, IX; emancipation of 48, 52, 86, 91; revolts 1, 10; worship 4, 8-9
Smith, Anderson 59-60, 78, 83-84, 86
Smith, Channing 76, 87
Smith, Edward 64-65
Smith, Mrs. Edward 64
Smith, Elias 98
Smith, Mary 39
Smith, William 16, 19, 47, 73, 88
Smith William R. 50, 64, 68, 71, 74
Smith William T. 64-65
Smithfield, Jefferson County 17
Snickers Gap 29, 78
Snickersville Pike 78
Somerville 4, 48, 50, 55; action at 51
South Carolina 12, 14, 37, 44; troops from 39, 63
Sperryville 92
Spilman, J. M. 85-86
Spilman, John A. 83
Spilman, John R. 22
Springfield 55
Stafford County 49-50, 53; compared with Fauquier 92
Stafford Court House 49
Stahel, Julius 41, 57
Stanton, Edwin 28-30, 86, 88
Starvation Hollow 46
Staunton 43
Stephens, James 23
Stephenson's Hill 79-80
Sterry, Jack 38
Stevensburg 70

Stine, James 69
Stone, Mr. ____ 49
Stover's Mill 39
Strasburg 80
Stribling, Robert 16, 44, 87
Stribling's Battery organized 16; roster information 108
Stuart, J. Hardeman 35-36
Stuart, Jeb 26, 32, 37, 39, 45, 50, 52, 54-57, 60, 62, 68, 71, 74, 103; at Catlett 33-36, 44, 65, V; at Upperville 41-42, 57-60; winter raids 48-51; Bristoe Campaign 65-67, XVII
Sudduth, F. M. 17
Sumerduck 71, 105
Sumner, Edwin 28
Sumter Volunteers 20
Tackett, Eli 91
Taylor, Walter 69
Taylor, Yardley 91
Templeton, Mr. ____ 53
Tennessee 12
Tete de pont 69-70
The Dell 103
The Maples 42
The Plains 4, 26, 28-29, 31, 37-38, 41-42, 50, 53, 55, 60-62, 64, 71, 83, 85, 95, 105; actions at or near 76, 80
The Springs 4-5, 15, 19, 26, 35, 51, 56, 65, 85, 92, 104; actions at or near 35-36, 47, 56, 65, 67, 71; hotel destroyed 36, VII; described 21, VII; bridge at 25, 35, 92, VIII
The Springs Road 61, 74, 96
The Trappe Road 41, 58, 83
The Wilderness 53, 77
Thomas, Clarence 10
Thompson's Bush Meeting 4
Thornton, Beverly 98
Thornton Gap 36
Thoroughfare Gap 25-26, 30-31, 37, 41, 43, 55, 59, 78, 85; actions at or near 38, 41, 76; described 38
Thoroughfare Gap Road 4, 36, 55, 78
Three Mile Junction 4
Three Mile Switch 4, 50, 65, 72, 77, 85, XIV
Throop, Thomas XX
Thumb Run 45
Thumb Run Church 36
Tiernan, Miss ____ 96
Tompkins, W. B. 108
Tongue, John R. 22-23
Tongue, Mrs. Johnzie 39

Torbert, T. A. 85
Town Run 31
Townsend, Charles 31-32, 34, 101
Trenton, New Jersey 47
Triplett, Benjamin 76
Triplett's Mill 28
Tuipan 48
Tuloss's Mill 31
Turkey Run, action at 50
Turner, Edward 1, 37, 39-41, 48, 50, 68, 81, 104
Turner, H. S. 68
Turner, Thomas 56, 71, 74
Turner, Tom 41
Turner, William 64
Tyler, John Webb 21, 93
Tyler, Mrs. John Webb 94
Tyler, Madison 21, 93
Tyler, Robert 17
Unison 76; action near 41
United States Ford 49, 53
Upper Fauquier 4, 20, 22, 41, 43, 51, 72, 78, 83, 95-96, 106; described 30, 77
Upper Fauquier Cavalry 10
Upperville 2, 4, 9, 19, 26, 53-54, 57, 61, 74-76, 83, 91; actions at or near 26, 40-42, 54, 57-60; described 5
Upperville Voting Precinct 12
Urbanna, Ohio 93
Valley Pike 81
Verdiersville 34
Vermont, troops from 56
View Tree 35, 61
View Tree Mountain 36
Vincent, Strong 57
Vineyard Hill, actions at 41-42, 58
Virginia Military Institute 11
Von Borcke, Heros 34, 42-43, 45, 57, 59, 101
Wainwright, Charles 61, 101
Walker, John 41
Walker, Leicester 50
Ward, Harriet 39
Warner, Daniel 3
Warren, Gouverneur 76
Warren Green Hotel 5, 31, 33, 47-48, 72
Warren, Helen 98
Warrenton 1-4, 8, 10-11, 13-17, 19-20, 23-24, 26, 29-30, 33-34, 37, 39-40, 44-45, 47-50, 53, 61-62, 72-75, 77, 84-85, 89, 92-101, 106, XIII; actions at or near 51, 54, 57, 74; described 5-6, 23-24, 31-32, 45-48, II-III, VI; courthouse at 13, 86, 88, 92, II-III, VI, XIII; hospitals at 22-

23, 39-40, 45; library at 5, 96-97; newspapers 5, 13, 32, 89-90, 105; occupations of 28, 36, 45, 67; town council meetings 1, 22-23, 28, 79, 83, 86, 95, 99, 105
Warrenton Babies   11
Warrenton Baptist Church   85
Warrenton Branch Railroad   5-6, 88, VI
Warrenton Company   96
Warrenton Home Guard   11, 16, 19-20; roster information 107
Warrenton House   5, 32
Warrenton Junction   4, 6, 23, 28-29, 37, 40, 47, 49-50, 68, 72; actions at or near 41, 53-54; described XVIII
Warrenton Rifles   17, 19, 24; organized 11; roster information 107
Warrenton White Sulphur Springs   4, 15, 36 (see The Springs)
Warrenton Turnpike   6, 40, 45, 59, 66
Warring, Leland   98
Washington, George   3
Washington, John   3
Washington, D. C.   5, 22, 29, 31, 35, 38-39, 46, 56-57, 64, 72
Washington's Hall   96
Waterford   83
Waterloo   2-3, 14, 17, 47, 51; action at 36; bridge at 33, 35, 92
Waterloo Turnpike   6, 33
Watery Mountains   36
Waveland   3, 78
Waverley   43, 92
Weaver, Janet   39
Weaver, Meta   39
Weaversville   62, 88; actions at 63, 68; described 48
Webster, Mr. _____   79
Welbourne   15

West, Ben   77
Western View   52, 78
West Virginia 15; troops from 53, 80
Wheatley, action at   49
Wheatley's Ford bridge   92
White, Elijah   26, 62
White, Hamden   19
White Plains   4, 61 (see The Plains)
White Ridge   4, 48-50, 77
White Ridge Tavern   22
Whitescarver, George   52, 56
Whitman, Walt   82
Whittier, John   95
Whittier School   95, 97
Wilderness, The   53, 77
Williams, Seth   28
Williamson, James   72, 75-76, 83-84, 103
Willis, Absalom   80-82
Willis Chapel   80
Willis, H. L.   96
Willis, Robert   27
Winchester   5, 22, 43, 55, 81, 86, 88
Winfield, John   16
Winfield's Company   organized 16; roster information 108
Wisconsin, troops from   69
Wise Dragoons   organized 14; roster information 108
Wise, Henry   15
Withers, Andrew   93
Wood, S. Fannie   94-95
Woodside   44
Wrenn, James   76
Wright, Robert   26
Wyanoke   81
Wyndham, Percy   51, 103
Yew Hill   57
Young, Pierce   67
Zoar Church   49

Joe
from
Beverly

The
Saturday Evening
POST
Reader of
Sea Stories

The Saturday Evening POST Reader of Sea Stories

Edited by
DAY EDGAR

Doubleday & Company, Inc.
Garden City, New York
1962

All of the characters in this book are fictitious, and any resemblance to actual persons, living or dead, is purely coincidental.

Library of Congress Catalog Card Number 62-15885
Copyright © 1910, 1934, 1936, 1940, 1947, 1948,
1951, 1953, 1955, 1957, 1959, 1960, 1961, 1962
by The Curtis Publishing Company
All Rights Reserved
Printed in the United States of America
First Edition

Preface

The stories in this volume are, in one man's opinion, the best twenty of the thousand sea stories published by *The Saturday Evening Post* since the short story emerged as a recognized literary form.

There is one way in which these and all sea stories differ from others—in the eternal, unchangeable nature of their background. To illustrate by contrast, consider the background of such familiar American fiction as tales of the early explorers, the fur trappers, the colonial wars, the Indian scouts, the cowpunchers. Suppose the characters from those early chronicles were to return, today, to their former stamping grounds.

To be specific, suppose Fenimore Cooper's Natty Bumppo has come back from Valhalla and is seeking out a remembered spot in a hushed forest where, through parted foliage, he once watched hostile Iroquois file past. Even if Bumppo happened to locate and stand on the very spot, he'd never know it—he would probably be standing in a supermarket.

Other characters would be similarly bewildered by the change in their once familiar background. A professional hunter would wait in vain for the buffalo herds which, in dust clouds spreading from horizon to horizon, used to rumble past like migratory earthquakes. And those endless miles of towering, primeval forests? Could anything so vast, so inseparably a part of the fact of a continent, simply disappear? Grassy range that was once silent save for the bawling of longhorns bristles today with oil derricks. And where are the hordes of pigeons that used to dim the sun for days in passing? A fur trapper's Paradise, formerly teeming with profitable pelts, today lies somewhere on the bottom of a man-made lake reaching farther than the eye can see.

No such changes would baffle the sea rovers if they returned to their old haunts. No matter what century they came from—the Phoenicians rowing their triremes, the Vikings in their dragon boats, the sailors aboard the Spanish caravels, the canvas-clawing crews of the East Indiamen—they would find their background just as they left it. Every aspect and mood of the sea would be just as it was in their memory—all the menace and mystery, all the glamour and monotony and lure that have made the sea the setting for so much of the world's great literature, and that helps explain why mankind has always found a special fascination in the adventures of the men who spend their lives on salt water.

> Day Edgar,
> Assistant to the Editor of
> *The Saturday Evening Post*

Contents

Preface BY DAY EDGAR	v
Under the Deck-Awnings BY JACK LONDON	1
The Beast from 20,000 Fathoms BY RAY BRADBURY	9
Vengeance Reef BY DON WATERS	17
The Snowflake and the Starfish BY ROBERT NATHAN	29
Hornblower and the Man Who Felt Queer BY C. S. FORESTER	40
The Capture of the Swordray BY CLAY BLAIR, JR.	56
Jarge Makes In BY CHARLES RAWLINGS	75
The Living Torpedo BY TOM YATES	94
A Sailor to the Wheel BY BILL ADAMS	113
Cargo of Gold BY CHARLES RAWLINGS	127
The Ransom of Peter Drake BY JACLAND MARMUR	141
Port of Call BY BUD HUTTON	156
The Sea Devil BY ARTHUR GORDON	162
The Kid in Command BY JACLAND MARMUR	172
Troubled Voyage BY WILLIAM HOLDER	187
Captive Captain BY JOHN PAUL HEFFERNAN	203
Without Warning BY ROBERT MURPHY	216
Treachery's Wake BY OLAF RUHEN	229

NOVELETTES

Dr. Blanke's First Command BY C. S. FORESTER	243
The Cruise of the Breadwinner BY H. E. BATES	274

The
Saturday Evening
POST
Reader of
Sea Stories

Under the Deck-Awnings

Jack London

"Can any man—a gentleman, I mean—call a woman a pig?" The little man flung this challenge forth to the whole group, then leaned back in his deckchair, sipping lemonade with an air commingled of certitude and watchful belligerence. Nobody made answer. They were used to the little man and his sudden passions and high elevations.

"I repeat, it was in my presence that he said a certain lady, whom none of you knows, was a pig. He did not say swine. He grossly said that she was a pig. And I hold that no man who is a man could possibly make such a remark about any woman."

Doctor Dawson puffed stolidly at his black pipe. Matthews, with knees hunched up and clasped by his arms, was absorbed in the flight of a guny. Sweet, finishing his Scotch and soda, was questing about with his eyes for a deck-steward.

"I ask you, Mr. Treloar, can any man call any woman a pig?"

Treloar, who happened to be sitting next to him, was startled by the abruptness of the attack, and wondered what grounds he had ever given the little man to believe that he could call a woman a pig.

"I should say," he began his hesitant answer, "that it—er—depends on the—er—the lady."

The little man was aghast.

"You mean——" he quavered.

"That I have seen female humans who were as bad as pigs—and worse."

There was a long, painful silence. The little man seemed withered by the coarse brutality of the reply. In his face was unutterable hurt and woe.

"You have told of a man who made a not nice remark, and you have classified him," Treloar said in cold, even tones. "I shall now tell you about a woman—I beg your pardon—a lady—and when I have finished I shall ask you to classify her. Miss Caruthers I shall call her, principally for the reason that it is not her name. It was on a P. & O. boat, and it occurred several years ago.

"Miss Caruthers was charming. No; that is not the word. She was amazing. She was a young woman and a lady. Her father was a certain high official whose name, if I mentioned it, would be immediately recognized by all of you. She was with her mother and two maids at the time, going out to join the old gentleman wherever you like to wish in the East.

"She—and pardon me for repeating—was amazing. It is the one adequate word. Even the most minor adjectives applicable to her are bound to be sheer superlatives. There was nothing she could not do better than any woman and than most men. Sing, play—bah!—as some rhetorician once said of old Nap, competition fled from her. Swim! She could have made a fortune and a name as a public performer. She was one of those rare women who can strip off all the frills of dress and in a simple swimming suit be more satisfyingly beautiful. Dress! She was an artist. Her taste was unerring.

"But her swimming. Physically, she was the perfect woman—you know what I mean; not in the gross, muscular way of acrobats, but in all the delicacy of line and fragility of frame and texture; and combined with this, strength. How she could do it was the marvel. You know the wonder of a woman's arm—the forearm, I mean; the sweet fading away from rounded biceps and hint of muscle, down through small elbow and firm, soft swell to the wrist, small—unthinkably small and round and strong? This was hers. And yet, to see her swimming the sharp, quick English overhand stroke, and getting somewhere with it too, was—well, I understand anatomy and athletics and such things, and yet it was a mystery to me how she could do it.

"She could stay under water for two minutes. I have timed her. No man on board, except Dennitson, could capture as many coins as she with a single dive. On the forward main deck was a big canvas tank with six feet of sea-water. We used to toss small coins into it. I have seen her dive from the bridge deck—no mean feat in itself—into that six feet of water and fetch up no less than forty-seven coins, scattered at random over the whole bottom of the tank. Dennitson, a quiet young Englishman, never exceeded her in this, though he made it a point always to tie her score.

"She was a sea-woman, true. But she was a land-woman, a horsewoman—a—she was the universal woman. To see her, all softness of flowing dress, surrounded by half a dozen eager men, languidly careless of them, or flashing brightness and wit on them and at them and through them, one would fancy she was good for nothing else in the world. At such moments I have compelled myself to remember her score of forty-seven coins from the bottom of the swimming tank. But that was she—the everlasting wonder of a woman who did all things well.

"She fascinated every betrousered human around her. She had me—and I don't mind confessing it—she had me to heel along with the rest. Young puppies and old gray dogs who ought to have known better—oh, they all came up and crawled round her skirts and whined and fawned when she whistled. They were all guilty, from young Ardmore, a pink cherub of nineteen, outward bound for some clerkship in the consular service, to old Captain Bentley, grizzled and seaworn, and as emotional, to look at, as a Chinese joss. There was a nice middle-aged chap, Perkins, I believe, who forgot his wife was on board until Miss Caruthers sent him to the right-about and back where he belonged.

"Men were wax in her hands. She melted them, or softly molded them, or incinerated them, as she pleased. There wasn't a steward, even, grand and remote as she was, who at her bidding would have hesitated to souse the Old Man himself with a plate of soup. You have all seen such women—a sort of world's desire to all men. As a man-conqueror she was supreme. She was a whiplash, a sting and a flame, an electric spark. Oh, believe me, at times there were flashes of will that scorched through her beauty and seduction and smote a victim into blank and shivering idiocy and fear!

"And don't fail to mark, in the light of what is to come, that she was a prideful woman: pride of race, pride of caste, pride of sex, pride of power—she had it all, a pride strange and willful and terrible.

"She ran the ship, she ran the voyage, she ran everything—and she ran Dennitson. That he had outdistanced the pack even the least wise of us admitted. That she liked him, and that this feeling was growing, there was not a doubt. I am certain that she looked on him with kinder eyes than she had ever looked with on man before. We still worshiped and were always hanging about waiting to be whistled up, though we knew that Dennitson was laps and laps ahead of us. What might have happened we shall never know, for we came to Colombo and something else happened.

"You know Colombo, and how the native boys dive for coins in the shark-infested bay? Of course it is only among the ground sharks and fish sharks that they venture. It is almost uncanny the way they know sharks and can sense the presence of a real killer —a tiger shark, for instance, or a gray nurse strayed up from Australian waters. But let such a shark appear and, long before the passengers can guess, every mother's son of them is out of the water in a wild scramble for safety.

"It was just after tiffin and Miss Caruthers was holding her usual court under the deck-awnings. Old Captain Bentley had just been whistled up and had granted her what he had never granted before—nor since—permission for the boys to come up on the promenade deck. You see, Miss Caruthers was a swimmer and she was interested. She took up a collection of all our small change and herself tossed it overside, singly and in handfuls, arranging the terms of the contests, chiding a miss, giving extra rewards to clever wins; in short, managing the whole exhibition.

"She was especially keen on their jumping. You know, jumping feet-first from a height, it is very difficult to hold the body perpendicularly while in the air. The center of gravity of the human body is high, and the tendency is to overtopple, but the little beggars employed a method new to her, which she desired to learn. Leaping from the davits of the boat deck above, they plunged downward, their faces and shoulders bowed forward, looking at the water; and only at the last moment did they abruptly straighten up and enter the water erect and true.

"It was a pretty sight. Their diving was not so good, though there was one of them who was excellent at it, as he was at all the other stunts. Some white man must have taught him, for he made the proper swan dive and did it as beautifully as I have ever seen it done. You know, it is head-first into the water; and from a great height the problem is to enter the water at the perfect angle. Miss the angle and it means at the least a twisted back and injury for life. Also, it has meant death for many a bungler. This boy could do it—seventy feet I know he cleared in one dive from the rigging—clenched hands on chest, head thrown back, sailing more like a bird, upward and out, and out and down, body flat on the air, so that if it struck the surface in that position it would be split in half like a herring. But the moment before the water is reached the head drops forward, the hands go out and lock the arms in an arch in advance of the head, and the body curves gracefully downward and enters the water just right.

"This the boy did again and again to the delight of all of us, but particularly of Miss Caruthers. He could not have been a moment over twelve or thirteen, yet he was by far the cleverest of the gang. He was the favorite of his crowd and its leader. Though there were many older than he, they acknowledged his chieftaincy. He was a beautiful boy, a lithe young god in breathing bronze, eyes wide apart, intelligent and daring—a bubble, a mote, a beautiful flash and sparkle of life. You have seen wonderfully glorious creatures—animals, anything, a leopard, a horse—restless, eager, too much alive ever to be still, silken of muscle, each slightest movement a benediction of grace, every action wild, untrammeled, and over all spilling out that intense vitality, that sheen and luster of living light. The boy had it. Life poured out of him almost in an effulgence. His skin glowed with it. It burned in his eyes. I swear I could almost hear it crackle from him. Looking at him, it was as if a whiff of ozone came to one's nostrils—so fresh and young was he, so resplendent with health, so wildly wild.

"This was the boy, and it was he who gave the alarm in the midst of the sport. The boys made a dash of it for the gangway platform, swimming the fastest strokes they knew, pell-mell, floundering and splashing, fright in their faces, clambering out with jumps and surges, any way to get out, lending one another a hand to safety, till all were strung along the gangway and peering down into the water.

"'What is the matter?' asked Miss Caruthers.

"'A shark, I fancy,' Captain Bentley answered. 'Lucky little beggars that he didn't get one of them.'

"'Are they afraid of sharks?' she asked.

"'Aren't you?' he asked back.

"She shuddered, looked overside at the water and made a *moue*.

"'Not for the world would I venture where a shark might be,' she said, and shuddered again. 'They are horrible! Horrible!'

"The boys came up on the promenade deck, clustering close to the rail and worshiping Miss Caruthers, who had flung them such a wealth of bakshish. The performance being over, Captain Bentley motioned to them to clear out; but she stopped him.

"'One moment, please, Captain. I have always understood that the natives are not afraid of sharks.'

"She beckoned the boy of the swan dive nearer to her and signed to him to dive over again. He shook his head and, along with all his crew behind him, laughed as if it were a good joke.

"'Shark,' he volunteered, pointing to the water.

"'No!' she said. 'There is no shark.'

"But he nodded his head positively and the boys behind him nodded with equal positiveness.

"'No, no, no!' she cried. And then to us: 'Who'll lend me a half-crown and a sovereign?'

"Immediately the half-dozen of us were presenting her with half-crowns and sovereigns, and she accepted the two coins from young Ardmore.

"She held up the half-crown for the boys to see, but there was no eager rush to the rail preparatory to leaping. They stood there grinning sheepishly. She offered the coin to each one individually, and each, as his turn came, rubbed his foot against his calf, shook his head and grinned. Then she tossed the half-crown overboard. With wistful, regretful faces they watched its silver flight through the air, but not one moved to follow it.

"'Don't do it with the sovereign,' Dennitson said to her in a low voice.

"She took no notice, but held up the gold coin before the eyes of the boy of the swan dive.

"'Don't!' said Captain Bentley. 'I wouldn't throw a sick cat overside with a shark around.'

"But she laughed, bent on her purpose, and continued to dazzle the boy.

"'Don't tempt him,' Dennitson urged. 'It is a fortune to him and he might go over after it.'

"'Wouldn't you?' she flared at him. 'If I threw it?' This last more softly.

"Dennitson shook his head.

"'Your price is high,' she said. 'For how many sovereigns would you go?'

"'There are not enough coined to get me overside,' was his answer.

"She debated a moment, the boy forgotten in her tilt with Dennitson.

"'For me?' she said very softly.

"'To save your life—yes; but not otherwise.'

"She turned back to the boy. Again she held the coin before his eyes, dazzling him with the vastness of its value. Then she made as if to toss it out, and involuntarily he made a half movement toward the rail, but was checked by sharp cries of reproof from his companions. There was anger in their voices as well.

"'I know it is only fooling,' Dennitson said. 'Carry it as far as you like, but for Heaven's sake don't throw it.'

"Whether it was that strange willfulness of hers, or whether she doubted the boy could be persuaded, there is no telling. It was unexpected to all of us. Out from the shade of the awning the coin flashed golden in the blaze of sunshine and fell toward the sea in a glittering arch. Before a hand could stay him the boy was over the rail and curving beautifully downward after the coin. Both were in the air at the same time. It was a pretty sight. The sovereign cut the water sharply, and at the very spot, almost at the same instant with scarcely a splash, the boy entered.

"From the quicker-eyed black boys watching came an exclamation. We were all at the rail. Don't tell me it is necessary for a shark to turn on its back. That one didn't. In the clear water, from the height we were above it, we saw everything. The shark was a big brute and with one drive he cut the boy squarely in half.

"There was a murmur or something from among us—who made it I did not know; it might have been I. And then there was silence. Miss Caruthers was the first to speak. Her face was deathly white.

" 'I—I never dreamed!' she said, and laughed a short, hysterical laugh.

"All her pride was at work to give her control. She turned weakly toward Dennitson, and then on from one to another of us. In her eyes was a terrible sickness and her lips were trembling. We were brutes—oh, I know it, now that I look back upon it; but we did nothing!

" 'Mr. Dennitson,' she said—'Tom, won't you take me below?'

"He never changed the direction of his gaze, which was the bleakest I have ever seen in a man's face; nor did he move an eyelid. He took a cigarette from his case and lighted it. Captain Bentley made a nasty sound in his throat and spat overboard. That was all—that and the silence.

"She turned away and started to walk firmly down the deck. Twenty feet away she swayed and thrust a hand against the wall to save herself; and so she went on, supporting herself against the cabins and walking very slowly."

Treloar ceased. He turned his head and favored the little man with a look of cold inquiry. "Well?" he said finally. "Classify her."

The little man gulped and swallowed.

"I have nothing to say," he said. "Nothing whatever to say."

The Beast from 20,000 Fathoms

Ray Bradbury

Out there in the cold water, far from land, we waited every night for the coming of the fog, and it came, and we oiled the brass machinery and lit the fog light up in the stone tower. Feeling like two birds in the gray sky, McDunn and I sent the light touching out—red, then white, then red again—to eye the lonely ships. And if they did not see our light, then there was always our voice, the great deep cry of our foghorn shuddering through the rags of mist to startle the gulls away like decks of scattered cards, and make the waves foam. "It's a lonely life, but you're used to it now, aren't you?" asked McDunn.

"Yes," I said. "You're a good talker, thank the Lord."

"Well, it's your turn on land tomorrow," he said, smiling, "to dance the ladies and drink gin."

"What do you think, McDunn, when I leave you out here alone?"

"On the mysteries of the sea." McDunn lit his pipe. It was a quarter past seven of a cold November evening, the heat on, the light switching its tail in two hundred directions, the foghorn bumbling in the high throat of the tower. There wasn't a town for a hundred miles down the coast, just a road which came lonely through dead country to the sea, with few cars on it, a stretch of two miles of cold water out to our rock, and rare few ships.

"The mysteries of the sea," said McDunn thoughtfully. "You know, the ocean's the biggest damned snowflake ever? It rolls and swells a thousand shapes and colors, no two alike. Strange.

One night, years ago, I was here alone, when all the fish of the sea surfaced out there. Something made them swim in and lie in the bay, sort of trembling and staring up at the tower light going red, white, red, white, across them, so I could see their funny eyes. I turned cold. They were like a big peacock's tail, moving out there until midnight. Then, without so much as a sound, they slipped away, the million of them was gone. I kind of think maybe, in some sort of way, they came all those miles to worship. Strange. But think how the tower must look to them, standing seventy feet above the water, the God-light flashing out from it, and the tower declaring itself with a monster voice. They never came back, those fish, but don't you think for a while they thought they were in the Presence?"

I shivered. I looked out at the long gray lawn of the sea, stretching away into nothing and nowhere.

"Oh, the sea's full." McDunn smoked his pipe nervously, blinking. He had been nervous all day and hadn't said why. "For all our engines and so-called submarines, it'll be ten thousand centuries before we set foot on the real bottom of the sunken lands, in the fairy kingdoms there, and know real terror. Think of it, it's still the year 300,000 Before Christ down under there. While we've paraded around with trumpets, lopping off one another's countries and heads, they've been living miles deep, beneath the sea, and cold in a time as old as the beard of a comet."

"Yes, it's an old world."

"Come on. I got something special I've been saving up to tell you."

We ascended the eighty steps, talking and taking our time. At the top, McDunn switched off the room lights, so that there'd be no reflection in the plate glass. The great eye of the light was humming, turning easily in its oiled socket. The foghorn was blowing steadily, once every fifteen seconds.

"Sounds like an animal, doesn't it?" McDunn nodded to himself. "A big lonely animal crying in the night. Sitting here on the edge of ten billion years calling out to the deeps, 'I'm here, I'm here, I'm here.'

"And the deeps do answer; yes, they do. You been here now for three months, Johnny, so I better prepare you. About this time of year," he said, studying the murk and fog, "something comes to visit the lighthouse."

"The swarms of fish, like you said?"

"No, this is something else. I've put off telling you because you might think I'm daft. But tonight's the latest I can put it off, for if my calendar's marked right from last year, tonight's the night it comes. I won't go into detail; you'll have to see it yourself. Just sit down there. If you want, tomorrow you can pack your duffel and take the motorboat into land and get your car parked there at the dinghy pier on the cape and drive on back to some little inland town and keep your lights burning nights; I won't question or blame you. It's happened three years now, and this is the only time anyone's been here with me to verify it. You wait and watch."

Half an hour passed with only a few whispers between us. When we grew tired waiting, McDunn began describing some of his ideas to me. He had some theories about the foghorn itself.

"One day many years ago a man walked along and stood in the sound of the ocean on a cold, sunless shore and said, 'We need a voice to call across the water to warn ships. I'll make one. I'll make a voice like all of time and all of the fog that ever was. I'll make a voice that is like an empty bed beside you all night long, and like an empty house when you open the door, and like trees in autumn with no leaves. A sound like the birds flying south, crying, and a sound like November wind and the sea on the hard cold shore. I'll make a sound that's so alone that no one can miss it, that whoever hears it will weep in his soul, and hearths will seem warmer and being inside will seem better to all who hear it in the distant towns. I'll make me a sound and an apparatus, and they'll call it a foghorn, and whoever hears it will know the sadness of eternity and the briefness of life.'"

The foghorn blew.

"I made up that story," said McDunn quietly, "to try to explain why this thing keeps coming back to the lighthouse every year. The foghorn calls it, I think, and it comes."

"But——" I said.

"S's's'st!" said McDunn. "There." He nodded out to the deeps. Something was swimming toward the lighthouse tower.

It was a cold night, as I have said, the high tower cold, the light coming and going and the foghorn calling and calling through the raveling mist. You couldn't see far and you couldn't see plain, but there was the deep sea moving on its way about the night earth, flat and quiet, the color of gray mud, and here were the two of us alone in the high tower, and there, far out at first, was a ripple, followed by a wave, a rising, a bubble, a bit of froth. And then, from the surface of the cold sea came a head, a large head, dark-colored, with immense eyes and then a neck. And then—not a body, but more neck and more! The head rose a full forty feet above the water on a slender and beautiful dark neck. Only then did the body, like a little island of black coral and shells and crayfish, drip up from the subterranean. There was a flicker of tail. In all, from head to tip of tail, I estimated the monster at ninety or a hundred feet.

I don't know what I said. I said something.

"Steady, boy, steady," whispered McDunn.

"It's impossible!" I said.

"No, Johnny; we're impossible. It's like it always was ten million years ago. It hasn't changed. It's us and the land that've changed, become impossible."

It swam slowly and with a great dark majesty out in the icy waters, far away. The fog came and went about it, momentarily erasing its shape. One of the monster eyes caught and held and flashed back our immense light, red, white, red, white, like a disk held high and sending a message in primeval code. It was as silent as the fog through which it swam.

"It's a dinosaur of some sort!" I crouched down, holding to the stair rail.

"Yes, one of the tribe."

"But they died out!"

"No, only hid away in the deeps. Deep, deep down in the deepest deeps. Isn't that a word now, Johnny, a real word; it says so much: the deeps. There's all the coldness and darkness and deepness in the world in a word like that."

"What'll we do?"

"Do? We got our job; we can't leave. Besides, we're safer than in any boat trying for land. That thing's as big as a yacht and almost as swift."

"But here, why does it come here?"

The next moment I had my answer.

The foghorn blew.

And the monster answered. A cry came across a million years of water and mist. A cry so anguished and alone that it shuddered in my head and my body. The monster cried out at the tower. The foghorn blew. The monster roared again. The foghorn blew. The monster opened its great toothed mouth, and the sound that came from it was the sound of the foghorn itself.

"Now," whispered McDunn, "do you know why it comes here?"

I nodded.

"All year long, Johnny, that poor monster there lying far out, a thousand miles at sea and six miles deep maybe, waiting, biding its time. Perhaps it's a million years old, this one creature; think of it, waiting a million years. Could you wait that long? Maybe it's the last of its kind; I sort of think that's true. Anyway, here come men on land and build this lighthouse, five years ago. And set up their foghorn and sound it and sound it out toward the place where you bury yourself in sleep and sea memories of a world where there were thousands like yourself, but now you're alone, all alone in a world not made for you, a world where you have to hide.

"But the sound of the foghorn comes and goes, comes and goes, and you stir from the muddy bottom of the deeps, and your eyes open like the lenses of two-foot cameras and you move, slow, slow, for you have the ocean sea on your shoulders, heavy. But that foghorn comes through a thousand miles of water, faint and familiar, and the furnace in your belly stokes up, and you begin to rise, slow . . . slow. You feed yourself on great slakes of cod and minnow, on rivers of jellyfish, and you rise slow through the autumn months, through September, when the fogs started; through October, with more fog and the horn still calling you on, and then, late in November, after depressurizing yourself day by day, a few feet higher every hour, you are near the surface and still alive. You've got to go slow; if you surfaced all at once, you'd explode. So it takes you all of three months to surface, and then a number of days to swim through the cold waters to the lighthouse. And there you are, out there in the night, Johnny, the biggest damn monster in creation. And here's the lighthouse calling to you, with a long neck like your neck sticking way up out of the water, and a body like your body and, most important of all, a voice like your voice. Do you understand now, Johnny; do you understand?"

I saw it all; I knew it all; the million years of waiting alone for someone to come back who never came back. The million years of isolation at the bottom of the sea, the insanity of time there.

The foghorn blew.

"Last year," said McDunn, "that creature swam round and round, round and round, all night. Not coming too near—puzzled, I'd say. Afraid, maybe. And a bit angry after coming all this way. But the next day, unexpectedly, the fog lifted, the sun came out fresh and the sky was as blue as a painting. And the monster swam off away from the heat and the silence and didn't come back. I suppose it's been brooding over it for a year now, thinking it over from every which way."

The monster was rushing at the lighthouse now.

The foghorn blew.

"Let's see what happens," said McDunn. He switched the foghorn off.

The monster stopped and froze. Its great lantern eyes blinked. Its mouth gaped. It gave a sort of rumble, like a volcano. It twitched its head this way and that, as if to seek the sounds now dwindled off into the fog. It peered at the lighthouse. It rumbled again. Then its eyes caught fire. It reared up, thrashed the water and rushed at the tower, its eyes filled with angry torment.

"McDunn!" I cried. "Switch on the horn!"

McDunn fumbled with the switch. But even as he flicked it on, the monster was rearing up. I had a glimpse of its gigantic paws, fish skin glittering in webs between the fingerlike projections, clawing at the tower. The huge eye on the right side of its anguished head glittered before me like a caldron into which I might drop, screaming. The tower shook. The foghorn cried; the monster cried. It seized the tower and gnashed at the glass, which shattered in upon us.

McDunn seized my arm. "Downstairs!"

The tower rocked, trembled and started to give. The foghorn

and the monster roared. We stumbled and half fell down the stairs. "Quick!"

We reached bottom as the tower buckled down toward us. We ducked under the stairs and into the small stone cellar. There were a thousand concussions as the rocks rained down. The foghorn stopped abruptly. The monster crashed upon the tower. The tower fell. We knelt together, holding tight, while our world exploded.

Then it was over, and there was nothing but darkness and the wash of the sea on the raw stones. That and the other sound.

"Listen," said McDunn quietly. "Listen."

We waited a moment. And then I began to hear it. First, a great vacuumed sucking of air, and then the lament, the bewilderment, the loneliness of the great monster, folded over and upon us, above us, so that the sickening reek of its body filled the air, a stone's thickness away from our cellar. The monster gasped and cried. The tower was gone. The light was gone. The thing that had called to it across a million years was gone. And the monster was opening its mouth and sending out great sounds. The sounds of a foghorn, again and again. And ships far at sea, not seeing the light, not seeing anything, but passing and hearing late that night, must've thought: *There it is, the lonely sound, the Lonesome Bay horn. All's well. We've rounded the cape.*

And so it went for the rest of that night.

The sun was hot and yellow the next afternoon when the rescuers came out to dig us from our stoned-under cellar.

"It fell apart, is all," said Mr. McDunn gravely. "We had a few bad knocks from the waves, and it just crumbled." He pinched my arm.

There was nothing to see. The ocean was calm, the sky blue. The only thing was a great algal stink from the green matter that covered the fallen tower stones and the shore rocks. Flies buzzed about. The ocean washed emptily on the shore.

The next year they built a new lighthouse, but by that time I had a job and a wife and a good small warm house that glowed yellow on autumn nights, the doors locked, the chimney puffing smoke. As for McDunn, he was master of the new lighthouse, built to his own specifications, out of steel-reinforced concrete. "Just in case," he said.

The new lighthouse was ready in November. I drove down alone one evening late and parked my car and looked across the gray waters and listened to the new horn sounding, once, twice, three, four times a minute far out there by itself.

The monster? It never came back.

"It's gone away," said McDunn. "It's gone back to the deeps. It's learned you can't love anything too much in this world. It's gone into the deepest deeps to wait another million years. Ah, the poor thing. Waiting out there, and waiting out there, while man comes and goes on this pitiful little planet. Waiting and waiting."

I sat in my car, listening. I couldn't see the lighthouse or the light standing out in Lonesome Bay. I could only hear the horn, the horn, the horn. It sounded like the monster calling. I sat there wishing there was something I could say.

Vengeance Reef

Don Waters

WITH A HISS OF FLYING SPRAY as her forefoot trod the waves under the rumble of the sea slushing along her bilges, wing and wing, the little schooner Tiburon boomed over the blue water before a stiff southeaster. To the westward scarcely a mile away, the high, rounded outline of an island was silhouetted in the rays of the setting sun. The white strip of beach shadowed by the fringe of coco palms that lined the shore, the dark green of the bushes that ran up to the top of a steep conical hill, the surf breaking on the reef that surrounded Saxons Cay, were plainly in sight.

John Pindar squatted on the deck, his back against the cabin side, splicing a rope, a steel marlinespike dangling from his wrist by a lanyard. He glanced ahead as his vessel approached the cay, and noted that a couple of gray, tide-washed rocks just to the northward were awash. The tide was still flooding, coming in strong. Astern, a thick bank of thunderheads was piling up in the east. It would squall on the turn of the tide tonight, he was certain. The storm was traveling toward them. He knew they'd be in, though, and snugged down before it hit. It was dangerous for a sailing vessel to be struck in the narrow reaches of Saxons Pass by a sudden squall.

It had been several years since his last visit here. His glance rested on the top of Saxons Hill. It seemed as though a small space on the crest had been cleared of bushes. Curious, that. He gazed intently at the bald spot above. A casual sponging vessel coming in for shelter or firewood, a sloop loaded with mangoes and cassava from Haiti, a fishing smack from Abaco out of drinking water—these might have run in behind the island for a mooring, but their crews would have no reason to clear off the very summit of Saxons Hill. He fancied he saw a figure move up there. Then he shook his head. Probably that was but a shadow of the branches of the big mastic tree on the hilltop, swaying in the stiff wind. The schooner drove ahead and the bushy-headed crowns of a clump of tall, leaning coco palms came between him and the hilltop.

Over the bowsprit end, the rollers climbing the reef were close enough now so that the rumbling as they charged up on the coral came plainly to his ears against the wind. Each deep-sea surge, as though resentful at meeting the first obstruction to its passage across the whole width of the Atlantic Ocean, growled heavily as it struck, mounted high and then exploded with flying spray that threw a running strip of creaming foam into the quiet lagoon beyond.

The man aft, steering, stood up, the better to see ahead. One bare foot was on the cabin top, the other on the tiller. He pulled his palm-plait hat down to shade his eyes. Straight for the break in the reef the Tiburon drove. It required a steady helm here. If a ship struck on the edge of the pass, it wouldn't last long. Close to on either side, the charging white horses of the sea dashed in a welter of tumbling water.

The Tiburon crossed the bar. A high wave ranged up under her. She lifted, and as though some mighty hand had her in its grip, she was pitched ahead for fifty feet. The small boat trailing astern, like a flung spear, followed in her wake. Down the center of the channel the little white schooner rolled and swung with the green-gray rocks baring their sharp fangs less than a cable's length away to port and starboard. The water smoothed out. Behind them the might of the ocean raged and grumbled, as though growling in anger at being balked of its prey.

The channel turned to the right. In a wide sweeping curve as graceful as a gliding gull, the Tiburon followed the blue water of the passage. Her mainsail swung over with a clatter of blocks in the traveler. Up forward, one of the crew hauled down the fluttering headsails. Under fore and main sail, she pointed for the opening between two rocky cliffs that led into the harbor beyond.

The little basin, entered through the narrow cut surrounded by the steep hills, was a secure haven even during a hurricane. Isolated, the nearest settlement more than thirty miles away, Saxons Pond was seldom visited. But in times past many a ship had sought shelter here.

A short while ago there had been a half-dozen families living along the beach in palmetto-thatched huts. They had worked a salt pond, evaporated the sea water, piled the glistening crystals in heaps on the shore. Then schooners from Jamaica and from Boston, smart fishing smacks from Nova Scotia and Newfoundland, came here to load.

But since the war had started across the Atlantic, vessels had ceased to moor at Saxons Pond. There was more money to be made running the submarine blockade, carrying guns and ammunition, food and supplies to Europe, than in loads of rough sea salt. It had been years since the pond was flooded. John Pindar saw that the palmetto shacks along the beach had fallen into ruin. The jungle had taken the little gardens on the hillside where once cassava and sweet potatoes had been planted. But the orange and lime trees, sapodillas and papayas grew rank and wild, with few hands to pick them.

The horseshoe-shaped island that encircled the tranquil basin rarely was disturbed now, save for the sea birds which soared overhead by day, and the loggerhead turtles that crawled up on the beach to lay their eggs by moonlight.

The schooner cleared the entrance, swung up to the north. Once through the opening, the wind was cut off, the canvas fluttered limply, the booms swung idly from side to side. Coasting on her momentum, the Tiburon lost way. Two of the crew were at the halyards, ready to lower the sails. The third man stood at the tiller. John Pindar quickly tucked his knife back into the sheath on his belt. As they passed through the gap, his eyes narrowed. Streaked along the cliff a foot above the surface of the water, the high-tide mark showed plainly, too plainly.

A little thing, that—just a level, glistening line where the gray of the rocks was marked by a black stripe. Sometime, and not long ago, a film of oil had floated up there. The receding tide had left a thin streak. He raised a cautious head above the level of the cabin top. In the little gap below the main boom he saw it. A long black hull was moored right in the center of the pond, a long black steel hull, low-lying, with the slim muzzle of a gun pointed right at them. Behind that gun a couple of men stood.

At that sight, John Pindar crouched and sprang overside. The water closed over him, cut off his yell of warning. So quickly had he moved that the iron marlinespike with which he had been working was still fastened by the lanyard around his wrist. His crew were frozen immovable in surprise. A loud, ear-splitting crash sounded. A streak of fire flared out. The surface of the pond between the schooner and the submarine was riffled into a lather of foam by the muzzle blast. The Tiburon disintegrated in the din that seemed to follow almost instantly behind the ripping smash of the gunfire. The explosion of the five-inch shell was so terrific that the dinghy trailing astern flew up in the air, turned end over end and burst into splinters before it hit the water. John Pindar was deep under water when the concussion of the double explosion drove the air from his lungs. He came up right in the path of the sun, which streaked a narrow band of shimmering light across the harbor. A big geyser was splashing down. Pieces of plank, the frayed ends of rope, chunks of timber showered around him. He caught his breath, dove again. The schooner and her crew were gone. He wondered how long it would be before he, too, would be no more. He'd been opposite the gun crew, concealed behind the cabin side. They had not noticed him when his schooner came in.

Swimming under water, he made for the deep shadow of the western shore a scant hundred feet away. Here the waves had undercut the beach, forming a little cavern. Numbed by the impact when that shell had struck his vessel, his ears ringing, he crouched under the overhanging rocks. The last of the flood tide was coming in. The long shadows of the setting sun slowly spread over Saxons Pond. With the sunset, the wind died. The palms on the shore line that all day had rustled and clashed their fronds became silent, like long-legged birds with drooping plumes. A hush fell, a hush broken only by the low murmur from out on the reef. There the sound of the sullen deep-sea surges, regular and unvarying, rose and fell like some monster breathing.

John Pindar watched a small boat put out from the island. There were a half-dozen men in it. He hefted the marlinespike, felt around in the back of his belt. His sheath knife was still there. If they found him, he'd put up what fight he could.

Tensely, he waited. Evidently, the crew in the small boat were convinced that there were no survivors from the schooner. They prodded with their oars among the scattered wreckage for a few minutes, and then went back toward shore. He heard their guarded talk, saw them tie their boat up and join the group gathered on the bank opposite. His head gradually cleared. The ringing left his ears. He began to figure out this thing that had come on him so suddenly.

The lookout on the hill above had undoubtedly watched the Tiburon, anchored off the reef just a mile or so to the southward. For the schooner's crew had spent the afternoon setting a long, deep shark net in the channel that ran through the shoals to the westward there. They had intended to lift that net in the morning. Many sharks used that passage across the banks that led off toward Cuba. Perhaps the raiders camped on the shore opposite cruised through that channel themselves. Perhaps they thought the shark net had been set to entrap them. From a distance they could not see that the big mesh was but cotton line. They may have imagined it to be flexible steel wire. They may have thought the round glass floats were bombs set in its mesh.

This was their hidden base, where they went ashore to rest between raids. Here was where they brought the stuff they looted from ships before they sank them. They could not have found a better place. The hilltop formed a good lookout. Any vessel sailing down the coast on one side, over the banks on the other, could be seen for miles. They had taken this way of keeping their hide-out a secret. "Dead men tell no tales," was just as true now as it was back in the days when the sinister banner bearing the skull and crossbones fluttered over these seas.

As the shadows lengthened and the haze of twilight fell over the quietness, John Pindar cautiously worked his way up from in under the rocks. The afterglow faded from the sky above. A thick bank of clouds rolled up from the eastward. The damp, cool scent of rain was in the air. Ashore on the other side of the pond, in the twinkling light of a campfire, the shadows of many men could be seen crossing back and forth in front of it. A puff of wind brought to John Pindar the odor of cooking food. The small boat put out from shore again. He heard the clump of oars when it made the short trip out to that black hull and back to the camp. He tried to penetrate the darkness, for the night was very black. But he could only vaguely make out the outlines of the boat.

A thin drizzle started to fall. He might be able to slip along the shore, cut the small boat moored in front of the camp loose and, unseen, get away with it. Then he thought of his crew, of his schooner. He remembered how, just a few years ago, he had felled a big pine tree, hewed it into shape for a keel. He recalled how, with the three men who were no more, they had searched the woods for natural crooks for her frames and knees. Mastic and madeira, horseflesh and dogwood, hard tropical timbers, they had been difficult to drag out of the Abaco jungle, tough to hew and adz to shape. There was many a hard-struck hammer blow, many a saw cut before the schooner was planked and decked. The yellow-pine boards for planking, the hardware for fastenings—he'd made several trips to the States, to Miami and Palm Beach, to buy those.

He thought of the four, himself and his crew, sitting crosslegged under the shade of the tamarind trees, stitch by stitch sewing canvas for her sails. Those white wings were now sodden shreds, spread over the bottom of the harbor. They never again would rustle to the soft warm breath of a southeaster. That trim hull would never again, like a living thing, run free and fast over the indigo seas of the Caribbean. Of the four men who had built the Tiburon and watched her slide down the skids into the gin-clear water off Conch Cay a hundred miles to the northward, he was the only one left.

A cold calculating rage spread over him. His head was clear, his eyes blazed with anger. They had sunk his ship, sunk it without warning, without giving anyone aboard a chance for life. He thought of other ships bound down the Old Bahama Channel or plugging their way over the violet waters of the Gulf Stream, that, all unsuspecting, were sailing these seas; of other men engaged in peaceful commerce. That low slimy hull was a menace to them; a sinister, skulking menace that must be destroyed. But how? What could one man do against at least two score? A marlinespike and a sheath knife were poor weapons to contend with rattling machine guns and high explosives.

As he looked over toward the dull red glow of the fire blinking through the rain on the shore opposite, suddenly a thought startling in its possibilities swept over him. That long narrow hull out there, with its wedge-shaped tower amidships, its deck barely five feet above the water, was filled with intricate machinery. There were ponderous Diesels in it that spun whirling generators, complicated valves and tanks that allowed it to submerge and rise at the touch of a hand. The periscope on the conning tower could lift its single eye above the sea and bring below the reflection of whatever showed all the way around the horizon. Up forward were torpedoes, titans of destruction, each loaded with the ultimate in man's power to kill and destroy. And yet all that mechanism of death was only as effective as the men who operated it were. They had sunk his ship, but they had better guard their own closely.

On board their vessel they were supreme. But in Saxons Pond, John Pindar was in his own environment. Among the long-dead pirates and buccaneers, blockade runners and wreckers who had come in here for shelter in the roistering days of long ago were many of his fathers' fathers. For a full five minutes he stood barefooted and bareheaded in the waist-deep water, unmoving as the rain grew heavier. Then he waded out up to his shoulders. He was swimming with scarce a ripple to betray his progress, swimming out to where that black shadow lay over the gray surface of the water. He touched the cold wet side of the steel hull, felt the slimy growth of moss along the water line, the sharp, rough clusters of barnacles. It had been months since this ship was in a dry dock, and her bottom was foul.

Even while he floated alongside, the rain had become a heavy downpour. Cautiously he worked his way along. Amidships near the conning tower he made out the blurred figure of a man whose back was turned to him. In the old days when the wreckers worked along this reef, the lookout on board a moored vessel always kept a wary eye on the anchor line. But this fellow huddled amidships probably never had heard of the ways of wreckers.

In the sudden glare as the fire ashore spurted up in flame, John Pindar could dimly see the rifle he carried, the glistening sheen of his wet black slicker. It was almost three hundred feet along the hull of the cruising undersea raider from its bow to the stern. He made his way aft. He eased himself out of the water onto the propeller guards that extended out like flat fins over the stern. As quietly as a seal crawling up onto a wet rock, he slid up onto the deck. The noise of the rain drummed hollowly on the steel plates, hissed in the water around him.

He crept up toward the conning tower. He was but four feet away from that figure which stood hunched over in the lee of the amidships structure when he straightened up. His arm swung in a swift short arc. The marlinespike landed with a dull thud. The man on guard fell backward. John Pindar tried to catch him, but the limp figure slithered across the slippery deck and, like a half filled sack, slid overside into the water. That fellow at least would give him no trouble. There might be others aboard, probably were. They were just part of the long chance he was taking. Perhaps they would not come above for a few minutes.

His bare feet making little sucking sounds on the deck, he hurried forward, leaned over, grasped the anchor chain, slid down it link by link. He took a deep breath when he hit the water and, hand over hand, went down the chain to where the anchor lay on the bottom twenty feet below, its flukes buried deep in the sand. Squatting on the bottom, he hooked an arm around the shank to hold himself down. He felt the shackle that fastened the chain to the anchor, found the pin that ran through the shackle. The tapered key which held the pin in place was locked with a ring. He sprang the soft iron ring open with his marlinespike, worked it out. For a full two minutes he twisted at the shackle. His head was throbbing, his ears were beginning to crack when he came up to the surface.

It was slack water now. The tide would soon turn and begin ebbing out through the pass like a millrace. He'd have to work fast before the current put a strain on the anchor chain. He caught two or three swift, full breaths, and down he went again. His groping hands found the big three-inch shackle that fastened the chain to the anchor ring. Using his marlinespike for a lever, he pried out the tapered key. The pin was loose in the shackle, for it came out easily. He floated upward. The tide had turned and had begun to run out. He was halfway back the length of the boat when his head broke above the surface.

Astern, a ten-inch Manila hawser was cleated. They'd run that line to a tree on the bank to keep their ship from swinging. There was no room for a long scope of mooring chain in Saxons Pond. To the pull of the tide, the submarine was slowly angling out from shore, held by the hawser aft. John Pindar swam back to where the bight of the mooring cable was beginning to lift from the increasing strain of the pull of the tide. It did not take many cuts with his knife before the heavy rope parted. He held on to the shore end to keep it from splashing loudly when it fell.

As the last strand parted, he was dragged under water for ten feet by the weight of the wet cable. Little that mattered. The submarine was adrift. An old wrecker's trick, that. More than one ship along this reef in times past had been cut loose from her anchor in the night by a diver working under water. Many things could happen in the next few minutes. If there were men aboard, they might start the engines and maneuver back into place. The crew ashore, should they notice the empty pond, the slack cable——

Tense, scarcely breathing, John Pindar floated silently as a bobbing coconut. The long black shadow of the undersea raider had swung. Tide borne, faster and faster, it moved, dragging its futile anchor chain over the white corals and on the bottom. Heading toward the opening, it merged into the darkness of the night.

He swam ashore fifty yards below the camp. Down behind the shelter of a bunch of sea-grape bushes, he waited while the tropical downpour hissed on the water in front and pattered heavily on the rocks around him. He could see the camp through the bushes. They had rigged a big tarpaulin over the fire to protect it from the rain. They were grouped around that fire. Occasionally he could hear the sound of loud talk and laughter. John Pindar gritted his teeth, cursed them under his breath. Unless some diversion occurred to distract their attention, it would be difficult for him to get to the small boat without being noticed.

Ten long slow minutes passed while he crouched under the sea grapes with the rain beating upon him. Then, with startling abruptness, from the hill above, a rifle shot reverberated. There were yells and shouts. Above the noise of the rain, he could hear the bushes crashing, feet clattering up the rocky path on the hillside. Din and confusion, the sound of many frantic voices rose.

Suddenly a flare lit up the rain-filled night with a hard white glare, showing the little circular basin empty, the surface of the water patterned with splashing sheets of rain. Again a shot crashed hollowly from the hilltop. The flare died; the darkness that followed seemed blacker than before. John Pindar flattened himself out and crawled toward the camp. In the glare from the fire, he saw that the place was deserted.

As he started to move toward the small boat, a couple of figures appeared. In a hard run, they stumbled over the rocks. One leaned over and began to untie the line from the trunk of the tree to which it was fastened. They stood poised on the bank, ready to haul the boat in. John Pindar leaped out and up. He struck between them, locked an arm around each, caught a full, deep breath. With a splash, all three tumbled into the water. There was a silent struggle for the next few minutes beneath the velvet, rain-dappled surface of Saxons Pond. But few men could live under water as long as John Pindar.

Down at the other end of the basin was a shoal slough that led out over the abandoned salt flats through the island. It was dry at low water, but it was high tide now. Using one of the oars for a push pole, John Pindar set the small boat over the shoals. Out from the lee of the island, the rising night breeze caught him, shoved him to the northward. He leaned his whole weight into each lunge. The dinghy surged along, its bow rising at every stroke, a wake raveling aft. The island was a quarter of a mile astern when a red streak of fire shot upward.

A light pop sounded high above. Then a parachute flare burst into incandescence with a brilliant, blue-white calcium light. In a series of sharp, abrupt crashes, the rattle of rifle fire ripped red spurts of flame in the darkness. Little geysers jumped off the waves around him. Bullets whined spitefully overhead like angry bees or ricocheted, whirring, off the water. One struck the boat. A couple of feet of the gunwale splintered into slivers.

He stood up erect in the bobbing dinghy, shook his fist and cursed the men who fired at him. The break of luck had put him far from shore before he had been sighted. A small boat, lifting and falling on the waves at that distance, makes a very uncertain target. In this pelting rain there was no chance for accurate shooting. The flare slowly floated down, struck the sea off to one side and sputtered out. His oar plunged down, found no bottom. He was past the shoals now, out in deep water. He stuck the oar over the stern and, with a practiced lunge and swing, began sculling, helped by the tide.

The heavy squall that had filled the last hour with rain had swept off to the westward. Through a rift in the clouds, the waning moon flooded the sea with a soft, silvery glow. Each lifting surge that struck the reef turned to quicksilver and broke like a shower of platinum drops, tinged with the blue-green sheen of phosphorescence. Wind borne, down to him came the heavy, hollow exhaust of a Diesel engine. He listened for a few minutes and speculated on what had happened. There had been men aboard and they had started the engines. They were not aware their craft was adrift as it was swept down the sheltered reach of Saxons Pass on the swift ebb of the tide. Not till the deep-sea surge at the bar had lifted and swung the submarine had they noticed anything wrong.

With a loud, coughing chatter, the noise of the exhaust stopped abruptly. To the southward, out on the reef, came sounds as though a battery of sledge hammers were beating on the hollow, reverberating steel shell of a boiler. A flare sailed up. In its light, a mile away a black lump on the reef was afoam where the sea rose high and burst like exploding bombs.

A grim smile of satisfaction crossed John Pindar's face. They had struck at high water. Full moon was past three nights ago. Each tide would come in lower from now on. The reef had the vessel in its grip. Each lifting surge was setting the hull higher up on the rocks. Receding, it dropped it with a clattering clang. The coral was doing its work. That ship was holed now. The rising water inside had flooded the motors.

He sat down on the stern seat of the dinghy and listened to

the steady, monotonous, dull roar of the reef as each heavy deep-sea surge rose and fell on the quietness of the night. Alien and harsh, another sound beat between the moans of the sea—the sound of steel shearing and ripping against rock. They had destroyed his ship. The score was even. Their vessel was on the reef to stay.

John Pindar began sculling again. It was a long way to the nearest settlement and a wireless station.

The Snowflake and the Starfish

Robert Nathan

The sea witch came in on the tide, riding on the waves like foam, and her hair floated out behind her like seaweed. She came to the beach and lay there breathing slightly, and her eyes searched everywhere like a hungry gull. And Michael Doyle's little daughter, Vicky, walking along the beach in search of colored shells, turned to her brother, Little Thomas, and said, "It's time we went home to supper."

"I think I saw something behind those rocks," said Little Thomas.

"All right," said Vicky, "do you want to go and look?"

"No," said Little Thomas.

The two children turned and started home down the beach; and the sea witch lowered herself gently into the water and swam quietly along the shore, halfway out, keeping an eye on them, and now and then diving through the waves like a porpoise. She was lonely; she had no children of her own to play with.

Vicky and her brother, Little Thomas, lived in a house close to the water with their father Michael Doyle, the professor, and his wife Helen. It was a good place for playing or looking for shells, except in winter, when the fogs came in or when it rained. Then they stayed indoors or walked on the hills above the sea in the weedy grass and looked down at the ocean, gray and cold and lonely everywhere.

But now it was summer, and they went almost every day to the beach. They knew that there were many strange things in the sea, some of which they wouldn't like; but they were mostly far out where they would never bother ordinary people, like the giant octopus that lived far down in the deep dark bottom of the ocean somewhere on the way to China.

But the things that were nearer at hand they knew very well. They knew the sea gulls and the little sand crabs who lived there, and the hermit crabs in their shells, and the quick, darting sandpipers; and they knew the fishermen who came there to spin their lines out over the surf and stand patient and still until it was time to reel their lines in again. Or sometimes a skin diver would clump down to the water in his big rubber fins and put on his mask and go sliding out to sea like a seal, pushing a blown-up rubber tube in front of him.

Their mother was very kind to them and sewed Little Thomas' buttons on when they came off, and often gave Vicky pennies to put in her hope chest, which was an earthenware bank in the shape of a pig. Vicky loved to hear it jingle when she shook it. She thought that someday when she was grown up she would be able to buy anything she wanted in the world for three or four dollars. She didn't know exactly what it would be. Mrs. Doyle thought that with a hope chest it would be nice to buy silver spoons or linen pillowcases, but that wasn't what Vicky wanted at all. What she wanted was——

And there she stopped, because she wasn't sure what it was she wanted.

"Why," asked her father, who was a professor at the university, "don't you buy yourself a nice dictionary, or a small encyclopedia?" And he wrinkled up his nose and nodded his head and knocked the ashes out of his pipe. "A little learning never did anybody any harm."

But Vicky shook her head; that wasn't what she wanted either. What she wanted was something beautiful and strange, not everyday. Something different—something that nobody else had.

That night as they were getting ready for bed she said to her brother Little Thomas, "What do you want most in all the world?"

Little Thomas bounced up and down in his bed once or twice

before settling down for the night. "I guess I got everything I want," he said, "or almost. What I want is a private snake."

Vicky lay back with a sigh and looked up at the ceiling. Her brother's answer was no help to her. Little boys always seemed satisfied with something ordinary, whereas little girls always had to look for something curious and rare. A secret treasure that nobody else knew about, a strangeness, a difference—a little moon to wear in her hair, a star of her own, a personal snowflake. They were such lovely dreams. That was what a hope chest was for: to hold dreams. That was why boys didn't have them.

Outside in the dim blue night the sea witch lay on the sand near the Doyle house and sang a sad sea song and wept a little. Neither of the children heard her.

A secret treasure, thought Vicky drowsily. *A star of my own, a snowflake for my cheek.*

"Empty is the sea," sang the sea witch, "and the shore empty——"

The children slept, and the sea witch stirred a little and began to weave her spell. "Sea porcupine," she whispered, "sea anemone; crab, oyster, kelp, plankton, barnacle, clam, abalone—like a snail, quiet, blind, creep into a girl's mind. Find among her little pleasures what she treasures here below. Herring, sturgeon, pompano, little octopus and squid, creep along, safely hid; where a child lies asleep, creep, creep. Halibut and sea trout, what do children dream about?"

But the spell missed Vicky, for whom it was intended and crept like a little gray fog around Little Thomas' bed instead. And the sea witch drew back in surprise. "A private snake?" she exclaimed. "How odd."

She thought for a moment. "Something has gone wrong," she declared. "There has been some mistake. Abalone! Pompano! Try again."

This time the spell worked properly, and then the sea witch knew what she wanted to know.

Next morning when the children woke up there was a tiny, silvery starfish lying at the foot of Vicky's bed, and on Little Thomas' counterpane a small stuffed eel.

"I declare," said Mrs. Doyle, sweeping them out-of-doors, "how a person is to keep her house in order, I don't know."

Vicky and Little Thomas looked at each other. "But mother," said Vicky, "it wasn't us."

"I suppose they walked in by themselves," said Mrs. Doyle.

"Leptocephalus conger," said Michael Doyle, the professor, "minor; and Asterias Rubens. They couldn't have walked in by themselves, my dear. Besides, they were quite dead."

"See," said Little Thomas. "I told you."

"Woman's work is never done," said Mrs. Doyle with a sigh.

Because it was a lovely warm day, the two children went down to play on the beach, and as they were playing there in the bright sunny foam, the sea witch looked out of a wave and saw them.

Her feelings had been hurt at seeing her gifts swept out with scraps of paper, old bottle caps, bits of string and a stocking with a hole in it; and it was some time before she could bring herself to speak to them. At last, however, when it was almost time for lunch, she took a deep breath and came out of the water onto the sand, dressed in striped bombazine like somebody's nurse.

"Well," she said, "hello, there."

Vicky looked at her in surprise. What a strange thing for somebody's nurse to say, she thought: "Hello, there." They usually said things like, "How do you do, little children?" or, "Har-rum." Come to think of it, she didn't look very much like a nurse, either—with her sad face and her sea-colored eyes and her long hair with seaweed in it.

As a matter of fact, the sea witch didn't know how to talk to children at all. "I know a secret," she said. "Do you?"

"No," said Little Thomas. "And if I did," he added, "I wouldn't tell you."

The sea witch drew back with a hurt look. "Sticks and stones can break my bones," she said, "but words can never hurt me."

"That isn't true," she said a moment later, because she was honest; "words are full of power to harm and to heal. Like 'hateful,' which is like a stick for beating; and 'lovely,' which melts in your mouth like oysters."

"Oysters don't melt in your mouth," said Vicky. "They just sit there till you swallow them."

"What I really meant," said the sea witch in a faraway voice, "was marzipan."

"Marzipan is what witches eat," said Vicky and, rising to her feet, she said to Little Thomas, "I think I hear our mother calling us. She wants us to come home for lunch."

Little Thomas obediently rose, and the two children went back to their house, not looking over their shoulders, holding their breath and being very careful to walk withershins around the piles of seaweed lying on the sand.

Nevertheless, Little Thomas had forgotten his pail and shovel; and these, with a sly smile, the sea witch took back with her to her cave in the rocks. It was very important for her to have something belonging to one of the children if she ever hoped to gain power over them.

And besides, the pail smelled of little boys playing in the sand in the sun, and that was a comfort to her.

That afternoon Vicky and Little Thomas stayed home and played quietly in their room. It puzzled Mrs. Doyle that they didn't seem to want to go out. "It's such a lovely day," she said. "Don't you want to go down and play on the beach some more?"

"No," said Vicky.

When their mother had left the room, Vicky said to Little Thomas, "Do you think she was a witch?"

"Who?" asked Little Thomas.

"The lady on the beach."

"Yes," said Little Thomas. "On account of the marzipan."

"Well," said Vicky, "we must be very careful."

They decided not to tell anybody, but they thought it would be all right to ask questions. That night at supper, with her mouth full of peanut butter, Vicky asked her father, "Did you ever see a witch?"

Michael Doyle gave his wife a twinkling, shining sort of look. "I suppose," he said, "you don't mean your mother?"

"No," said Vicky.

"In that case," said her father, "I have nothing further to say."

Even Little Thomas could see that his father wasn't much help to them. And that night when the children were in bed the sea witch came to the house again, clutching the pail and the shovel, and sang a song and wove a spell.

> *Pompano and grampus,*
> *Sea horse (Hippocampus),*
> *Barracuda, sea trout,*
> *Bring Tom and Vicky out.*

And she added as an afterthought:

> *Sea mice (Aphrodites)—*
> *In their nighties!"*

This time Little Thomas heard her. "Vicky!" he cried, shaking his sister by the shoulder. "Wake up! She's after us!"

"What?" mumbled Vicky sleepily. "Who? What's the matter?" And she tried to snuggle down and go back to sleep again.

"Vicky! Wake up! The witch is after us!"

Vicky sat up very suddenly, the sleep all gone from her head. "How do you know?" she demanded.

"I heard her singing," said Little Thomas. "I heard her ordering them to bring us out in our nighties." And he added in a trembling voice, "I haven't got my nightie on. Only my shirt."

"Well," said Vicky, "what we've got to do is hide."

"It's no use," said Little Thomas. "She knows we're here." And he added halfheartedly, "We could tell mother."

"She'd only say, 'Go back to sleep,'" said Vicky. "What we've got to do is to get out of here." She thought for a moment. "We'll go somewhere up the hill," she said, "where she won't find us."

"There's snakes on the hill in summer," said Little Thomas. "Public snakes."

"That's right," said Vicky. "I forgot. Well then," she said after a while, "we'll go way down on the beach somewhere, and she'll have to look for us so long she'll get tired. Put your space suit on; and I'll take my hope chest in case we need it."

The two children silently put on their warm wrappers, and Little Thomas put on his space suit over it because he was shivering; and Vicky took her hope chest, which already had forty-seven cents in it; and they tiptoed out of the room, making sure that the door didn't squeak behind them. They shuffled in the dark down the hall to the French windows, which opened onto the porch, and peeked out. "You go first," said Vicky.

"You go," said Little Thomas. "You're the oldest."

"But you're a boy," said Vicky.

"Well," said Little Thomas, "you're a bold girl and unafraid of mice."

So Vicky slipped out of doors into the gray, misty night, followed by Little Thomas. Right away they began to run as hard as they could, which was a great mistake, because the minute they started to run the piggy bank began to jingle, and the witch heard them and was up and after them like a shot; whereas if they had gone very quietly she might never have known they were there.

They ran faster than they had ever run before in their lives, taking great leaps and hops, while their throats grew dry with fear and their breath came in gasps and their legs hurt. They fled like shadows through the dark, and the cold, wet sticky fingers of the fog brushed their faces and clutched at them and let them go; and all the time the witch followed them like a black wind, like the night itself, sniffing the air for their scent.

"Vicky," she cried, and her voice was like the edge of a breaking wave. "Little Thomas! Wait!"

"Oh, never!" sobbed Vicky, feeling the strength ooze out of her; and collapsed at last behind a pile of seaweed that made a deep black shadow all around her. A moment later Little Thomas sank to the ground beside her; and the two children crouched there together, shivering, holding their breath, listening like hunted rabbits to the sounds of the sea witch, rustling and snuffling in the sand.

Clutched to Vicky's soft little stomach, the hope chest made no noise; and the sea witch, momentarily baffled, stopped and peered through the darkness with her sad, nearsighted eyes, listening for the sound of heartbeats, her thin, beautiful nostrils flaring this way and that to catch the little-boy-and-girl smell, the bread-and-butter fragrance of children, among the iodine odors of the kelp.

When at last she realized that she had lost them, she sat down in the sand and began to weep.

Back of their dark shadowy pile of seaweed Little Thomas and his sister looked at each other in consternation. "She's crying," said Little Thomas. "She is sad."

"It isn't like what I expected," said Vicky.

"Do you think," asked Little Thomas, "that maybe we ought to go out and pat her on the head?"

"I don't know," said Vicky. "I never heard a witch cry before." And she added uncertainly, "Maybe she's lonesome."

"Maybe she only wanted to play with us or something," said Little Thomas.

"Why don't you go and ask her," said Vicky, clutching her hope chest firmly to her.

"I would," said Little Thomas doubtfully, "only—maybe she's crying because she's hungry."

"Hush," said Vicky; "she'll hear you."

Nevertheless, when the sea witch's sobbing had died down after a while to a mere foamy sniffle, the two children crept out of their hiding place, and with Vicky in the lead went slowly and with some misgivings toward where the sea witch lay like a shadow on the sand. "Don't cry," said Vicky in a small, scared voice; and Little Thomas said, "There, there," and gave her a timid pat on the head.

The sea witch started up in surprise. "Why," she cried, "how nice of you! I thought I had lost you, and I did so want to take you home with me."

"To eat?" asked Little Thomas, backing away and dropping his space helmet in the sand, so that he had to bend down to look for it. But the sea witch gave a silvery laugh that sounded the way a school of minnows looks when it flashes by this way and that in the clear water. "Whatever gave you that idea?" she cried. "I only want to play with you."

"Oh," said Little Thomas, "in *that* case——"

"We'd like that very much," said Vicky politely.

The sea witch jumped to her feet and at once began calling in her spells from up and down the beach. "Pompano," she called. "Amber jack! Come back! Sea bass, Sea rover—give over! And all you currents, tides and courses—the lost are found! Trumpet fish, sound! Hitch up my twelve sea horses! . . .

"We're going to have so much fun," she told the children. "Wait till you see the Grand Banks, and Fujiyama. Wait till you see Capri! And think of all the treasures: pearls and corals, grottoes and caves, the banquet halls of lobsters—necklaces of amethyst, minuets of angel fish——"

"Haven't you got any pirate ships?" asked Little Thomas.

"Dozens of them," said the sea witch happily, "all sunk in fathoms five and full of skeletons."

She put her arms around the children and led them gently down to the water. It was a curiously light feeling, they thought, almost as though they were being held up by water wings. Little Thomas kept thinking of the skeletons he was going to see, maybe with their heads chopped off or an arm or a leg missing; and Vicky felt a little afraid, as though what she was doing was very dangerous, and if she took a wrong step, who could tell—she might never come back.

"And so," said the sea witch under her breath to a barracuda that was swimming past, "she won't if I have anything to do with it!"

Not that she was really wicked—as she explained to Little Thomas later on, somewhere off Tierra del Fuego: she never ate meat, only vegetables, and fish on Fridays. The thing was, she was lonely, and tired of swimming about with only anchovies for company.

"If I can coax her into letting me have the hope chest," she thought; "if I can tempt her to spend her red real copper pennies for dreams, she'll never get away from me—never! I shall have her forever."

She felt happy because she didn't think that any little girl would be able to resist the marvelous treasures she meant to show her.

Drawn by twelve magnificent sea horses, shaking the foam from their shoulders, and preceded by a band of trumpet fish scattering notes like drops of water, the sea witch and her two little companions swept through the clear, luminous sea, up and down the great green currents which ran like roads across the ocean floor. Past lost galleons they galloped, across mountains of coral glowing like sunsets, over the meadows of the sea, down into caves as blue as moonlight, past schools of sheepshead, croakers, minnows, mackerel, bass, zebra fish, goldfish—fish of every size, color and shape; past squid and octopuses waving their weedlike arms, whales going by like battleships, tiny shrimp bobbing about in country dances. And every once in a while the sea witch would point to a great heap of pearls or a big lump of amethyst, or to piles and piles of golden doubloons, and ask hopefully, "Is this what you want? Will you buy it?" And every time, with a little gasp, Vicky would say, "No, thank you," and clutch her hope chest tighter.

They galloped up under the North Pole, and Vicky had a snowflake on her cheek, but when they got as far south as Oregon it melted. And in the coral seas there were a million golden stars reflected in the water, but when she reached for them they rippled away into nothing. "Will you buy? Will you buy?" cried the sea witch, but Vicky still said, "No."

She saw mermaids with little moons in their hair; they looked rare and curious, but they looked lonely, too, without any fathers and mothers. "Stay here with us," they cried and held out their arms to her; but Vicky only said, "Thank you, but I don't think I want to."

She saw many things that were curious and rare—secret treasures that nobody knew about. They looked like her dreams—except that there was something the matter with them. They should have made her feel happy and beautiful, but they didn't; on the contrary, they made her feel sad and they gave her a lost, lonesome feeling. Was it because she was really seeing them at last? She didn't know.

All she knew was that there wasn't anything she wanted to give up her hope chest for. And the strange part of it was that the more she saw of these wonderful things that didn't belong to her, the more she longed for the little, unwonderful things of her own: her father and mother around the breakfast table, her own cup of milk, the warm, cozy supper of bread and butter and rice pudding and Brussels sprouts, and her mother's good-night kiss.

"I do think," she said to herself in surprise, as they were rounding the Cape of Good Hope, "I do think that what I really want is just to be me—without any difference!"

When the sea witch saw that Vicky wouldn't part with her hope chest for any of the things she'd shown her, she grew very sad and silent and a little older, and drove them home by way of Catalina, Santa Monica and Malibu. "Good-by, Vicky," she said gently. "I thought I could get you to exchange the things you really need for things that are no use to you, but you were too wise for me. I don't hold it against you, because that's the way you are. You will grow up to be a lovely young woman, and marry and have little children of your own; and maybe someday I'll come back again when they're as old as you are now and see if they are all as wise as you."

She leaned down to Vicky and touched her hair. "I should like to give you a kiss," she said. "Just one, if you don't mind. May I?"

"Of course," said Vicky politely, holding up her face. The sea witch stooped to kiss it and dropped a single tear on Vicky's cheek.

As for Little Thomas, the sea witch shook him heartily by the hand. After that she gave a little cry and went into the sea in a long, beautiful arc and swam out on the tide, with her hair floating out behind her like seaweed.

Vicky and Little Thomas went home to bed. The morning star was in the sky, but it was still far from dawn.

Next morning, with the sun shining so bright, and a mockingbird singing outside the window, and the breakfast smell of coffee for the professor and cocoa for the children and bacon for everybody in the air, it was hard to believe that it had all happened. Except that Little Thomas' hand was stained with a greenish color, like kelp, for several days, and on Vicky's cheek there was a little pattern like a snowflake. "You probably slept on it," said Mrs. Doyle, "and got a crease."

But that didn't explain why, ever afterward, whenever Vicky kissed anyone, she was told it was like being kissed by a breath from the sea.

Or why, when the hope chest was opened at last to buy a silver spoon and two linen pillowcases for Vicky's wedding, a little piece of dried seaweed fell out.

Hornblower and the Man Who Felt Queer
C. S. FORESTER

THIS TIME THE WOLF was prowling round outside the sheepfold. H.M. frigate Indefatigable had chased the French corvette Papillon into the mouth of the Gironde, and was seeking a way of attacking her where she lay anchored in the stream under the protection of the batteries at the mouth. Captain Pellew took his ship into shoal water as far as he dared, until, in fact, the batteries fired warning shots to make him keep his distance, and he stared long and keenly through his glass at the corvette. Then he shut his telescope and turned on his heel to give the order that worked the Indefatigable away from the dangerous lee shore—out of sight of land, in fact.

His departure might lull the French into a sense of security which, he hoped, would prove unjustified. For he had no intention of leaving them undisturbed. If the corvette could be captured or sunk, not only would she be unavailable for raids on British commerce but also the French would be forced to increase their coastal defenses at this point and lessen the effort that could be put out elsewhere. War is a matter of savage blow and counterblow, and even a forty-gun frigate could strike shrewd blows if shrewdly handled.

Midshipman Hornblower was walking the lee side of the quarter-deck, as became his lowly station as the junior officer of the watch, in the afternoon, when Midshipman Kennedy approached him. Kennedy took off his hat with a flourish and bowed low, as his dancing master had once taught him, left foot advanced, hat down by the right knee. Hornblower entered into the spirit of the game, laid his hat against his stomach and bent himself in the middle three times in quick succession. Thanks to his physical awkwardness, he could parody ceremonial solemnity almost without trying.

"Most grave and reverend signior," said Kennedy, "I bear the compliments of Captain Sir Ed'ard Pellew, who humbly solicits Your Gravity's attendance at dinner at eight bells in the afternoon watch."

"My respects to Sir Edward," replied Hornblower, bowing to his knees at the mention of the name, "and I shall condescend to make a brief appearance."

"I am sure the captain will be both relieved and delighted," said Kennedy. "I will convey him my felicitations along with your most flattering acceptance."

Both hats flourished with even greater elaboration than before, but at that moment both young men noticed Mr. Bolton, the officer of the watch, looking at them from the windward side, and they hurriedly put their hats on and assumed attitudes more consonant with the dignity of officers holding their warrants from King George.

"What's in the captain's mind?" asked Hornblower.

Kennedy laid one finger alongside his nose. "If I knew that, I should rate a couple of epaulets," he said. "Something's brewing, and I suppose one of these days we shall know what it is. Until then, all that we little victims can do is to play, unconscious of our doom. Meanwhile, be careful not to let the ship fall overboard."

There was no sign of anything brewing while dinner was being eaten in the great cabin of the Indefatigable. Pellew was a courtly host at the head of the table. Conversation flowed freely and along indifferent channels among the senior officers present—the two lieutenants, Eccles and Chadd, and the sailing master, Soames. Hornblower and the other junior officer—Mallory, a midshipman of more than two years' seniority—kept silent, as midshipmen should, thereby being able to devote their undivided attention to the food, so vastly superior to what was served in the midshipmen's berth.

"A glass of wine with you, Mr. Hornblower," said Pellew, raising his glass.

Hornblower tried to bow gracefully in his seat while raising his glass. He sipped cautiously, for he had early found that he had a weak head and he disliked feeling drunk.

The table was cleared and there was a brief moment of expectancy as the company awaited Pellew's next move.

"Now, Mr. Soames," said Pellew, "let us have that chart."

It was a map of the mouth of the Gironde with the soundings; somebody had penciled in the positions of the shore batteries.

"The Papillon," said Sir Edward—he did not condescend to pronounce it French-fashion—"lies just here. Mr. Soames took the bearings." He indicated a penciled cross on the chart, far up the channel.

"You gentlemen," went on Pellew, "are going in with the boats to fetch her out."

So that was it. A cutting-out expedition.

"Mr. Eccles will be in general command. I will ask him to tell you his plan."

The gray-haired first lieutenant with the surprisingly young blue eyes looked round at the others.

"I shall have the launch," he said, "and Mr. Soames the cutter. Mr. Chadd and Mr. Mallory will command the first and second gigs. And Mr. Hornblower will command the jolly boat. Each of the boats except Mr. Hornblower's will have a junior officer second in command."

That would not be necessary for the jolly boat with its crew of seven. The launch and cutter would carry from thirty to forty men each, and the gigs twenty each; it was a large force that was being dispatched—nearly half the ship's company.

"She's a ship of war," explained Eccles, reading their thoughts. "No merchantman. Ten guns a side, and full of men."

Nearer two hundred men than a hundred, certainly—plentiful opposition for a hundred and twenty British seamen.

"But we will be attacking her by night and taking her by surprise," said Eccles, reading their thoughts again.

"Surprise," put in Pellew, "is more than half the battle, as you know, gentlemen. . . . Please pardon the interruption, Mr. Eccles."

"At the moment," went on Eccles, "we are out of sight of land. We are about to stand in again. We have never hung about this part of the coast, and the Frogs'll think we've gone for good. We'll make the land after nightfall, stand in as far as possible, and then the boats will go in. High water tomorrow morning is at four-fifty; dawn is at five-thirty. The attack will be delivered at four-thirty, so that the watch below will have had time to get to sleep. The launch will attack on the starboard quarter, and the cutter on the larboard quarter. Mr. Mallory's gig will attack on the larboard bow, and Mr. Chadd's on the starboard bow. Mr. Chadd will be responsible for cutting the corvette's cable as soon as he has mastered the forecastle and the other boats' crews have at least reached the quarter-deck."

Eccles looked round at the three other commanders of the large boats, and they nodded understanding. Then he went on, "Mr. Hornblower with the jolly boat will wait until the attack has gained a foothold on the deck. He will then board at the main chains, either to starboard or larboard, as he sees fit, and he will at once ascend the main rigging, paying no attention to whatever fighting is going on on deck. He will see to it that the main topsail is loosed, and he will sheet it home on receipt of further orders. I, myself, or Mr. Soames in the event of my being killed or wounded, will send two hands to the wheel and will attend to steering the corvette as soon as she is under way. The tide will take us out, and the Indefatigable will be awaiting us just out of gunshot from the shore batteries."

"Any comments, gentlemen?" asked Pellew.

That was the moment when Hornblower should have spoken up—the only moment when he could. Eccles' orders had set in motion sick feelings of apprehension in his stomach. Hornblower was no maintopman, and Hornblower knew it. He hated heights, and he hated going aloft. He knew he had none of the monkey-like agility and self-confidence of the good seaman. He was unsure of himself aloft in the dark even in the Indefatigable, and he was utterly appalled at the thought of going aloft in an entirely strange ship and finding his way amid strange rigging. He felt himself quite unfitted for the duty assigned to him, and he should have raised a protest at once, on account of his unfitness. But he let the opportunity pass, for he was overcome by the matter-of-fact way in which the other officers accepted the plan. He looked round at the unmoved faces; nobody was paying any attention to him, and he jibbed at making himself conspicuous. He swallowed; he even got as far as opening his mouth, but still no one looked at him and his protest died.

"Very well, then, gentlemen," said Pellew. . . . "I think you had better go into the details, Mr. Eccles."

Then it was too late. Eccles, with the chart before him, was pointing out the course to be taken through the shoals and mudbanks of the Gironde, and expatiating on the position of the shore batteries and on the influence of the lighthouse of Cordouan upon the distance to which the Indefatigable could approach in daylight. Hornblower listened, trying to concentrate despite his apprehensions.

Eccles finished his remarks and Pellew closed the meeting, "Since you all know your duties, gentlemen, I think you should start your preparations. The sun is about to set and you will find you have plenty to do."

The boats' crews had to be told off; it was necessary to see that the men were armed and that the boats were provisioned in case of emergency. Every man had to be instructed in the duties expected of him. And Hornblower had to rehearse himself in ascending the main shrouds and laying out along the main-topsail yard. He did it twice, forcing himself to make the difficult climb up the futtock shrouds, which, projecting outward from the mainmast, made it necessary to climb several feet while hanging back downward, locking fingers and toes into the ratlines.

He could just manage it, moving slowly and carefully, although clumsily. He stood on the foot rope and worked his way out to the yardarm—the foot rope was attached along the yard so as to hang nearly four feet below it. The principle was to set his feet on the rope with his arms over the yard, then, holding the yard in his armpits, to shuffle sideways along the foot rope to cast off the gaskets and loosen the sail.

Twice Hornblower made the whole journey, battling with the disquiet of his stomach at the thought of the hundred-foot drop below him. Finally, gulping with nervousness, he transferred his grip to the brace and forced himself to slide down it to the deck—that would be his best route when the time came to sheet the topsail home. It was a long, perilous descent; Hornblower told himself—as indeed he had said to himself when he had first seen men go aloft—that similar feats in a circus at home would be received with "Oh's" and "Ah's" of appreciation.

He was by no means satisfied with himself even when he reached the deck, and at the back of his mind was a vivid picture of his missing his hold, when the time came for him to repeat the performance in the Papillon, and falling headlong to the deck—a second or two of frightful fear while rushing through the air, and then a shattering crash. And the success of the attack hinged on him as much as on anyone—if the topsail were not promptly set to give the corvette steerageway, she would run aground on one of the shoals in the river mouth, to be ignominiously recaptured, and half the crew of the Indefatigable would be dead or prisoners.

In the waist, the jolly boat's crew was formed up for his inspection. He saw to it that the oars were properly muffled, that each man had pistol and cutlass, and made sure that every pistol was at half cock, so that there was no fear of a premature shot giving warning of the attack. He allocated duties to each man in the loosing of the topsail, laying stress on the possibility that casualties might necessitate unrehearsed changes in the scheme.

"I will mount the rigging first," said Hornblower.

That had to be the case. He had to lead—it was expected of him. More than that; if he had given any other order, it would have excited comment . . . and contempt.

"Jackson," went on Hornblower, addressing the coxswain, "you will quit the boat last and take command if I fall."

"Aye, aye, sir."

It was usual to use the poetic expression "fall" for "die," and it was only after Hornblower had uttered the word that he thought about its horrible real meaning in the present circumstances.

"Is that all understood?" asked Hornblower harshly; it was his mental stress that made his voice grate so.

Everyone nodded except one man. "Begging your pardon, sir," said Hales, the young man who pulled stroke oar, "I'm feeling a bit queerlike."

Hales was a lightly built young fellow of swarthy countenance. He put his hand to his forehead with a vague gesture as he spoke.

"You're not the only one to feel queer," snapped Hornblower.

The other men chuckled. The thought of running the gantlet of the shore batteries, of boarding an armed corvette in the teeth of opposition, might well raise apprehension in the breast of any of them. Most of the men detailed for the expedition must have felt qualms to some extent.

"I don't mean that, sir," said Hales indignantly. "'Course I don't."

But Hornblower and the others paid him no attention.

"You just keep your mouth shut," growled Jackson.

There could be nothing but contempt for a man who announced himself sick after being told off on a dangerous duty. Hornblower felt sympathy as well as contempt. He himself had been too much of a coward even to give voice to his apprehensions—too much afraid of what people would say about him.

"Dismiss," said Hornblower. "I'll pass the word for all of you when you are wanted."

There were some hours yet to wait while the Indefatigable crept inshore, with the lead going steadily and Pellew himself attending to the course of the frigate. Hornblower, despite his nervousness and his miserable apprehensions, yet found time to appreciate the superb seamanship displayed as Pellew brought the big frigate in through these tricky waters on that dark night. His interest was so caught by the procedure that the little tremblings which had been assailing him ceased to manifest themselves; Hornblower was of the type that would continue to observe and to learn on his deathbed.

By the time the Indefatigable had reached the point off the mouth of the river where it was desirable to launch the boats, Hornblower had learned a good deal about the practical application of the principles of coastwise navigation and a good deal about the organization of a cutting-out expedition, and by self-analysis he had learned even more about the psychology of a raiding party before a raid.

He had mastered himself, to all outside appearance, by the time he went down into the jolly boat as she heaved on the inky-black water, and he gave the command to shove off in a quiet, steady voice. Hornblower took the tiller—the feel of that solid bar of wood was reassuring, and it was old habit now to sit in the stern sheets with hand and elbow upon it—and the men began to pull slowly after the dark shapes of the four big boats. There was plenty of time, and the flowing tide would take them up the estuary. That was just as well, for on one side of them lay the batteries of St. Dyé, and inside the estuary on the other side was the fortress of Blaye; forty big guns trained to sweep the channel, and none of the five boats could withstand a single shot from one of them.

He kept his eyes attentively on the cutter ahead of him. Soames had the dreadful responsibility of taking the boats up the channel, while all he had to do was to follow in her wake—all, except to loose that main topsail. Hornblower found himself shivering again.

Hales, the man who had said he felt queer, was pulling stroke oar; Hornblower could just see his dark form moving rhythmically back and forward at each slow stroke. After a single glance, Hornblower paid him no more attention, and was staring after the cutter when a sudden commotion brought his mind back into the boat. Someone had missed his stroke; someone had thrown all six oars into confusion as a result.

"Mind what you're doing, blast you, Hales," whispered Jackson, the coxswain, with desperate urgency.

For answer there was a sudden cry from Hales, loud, but fortunately not too loud, and Hales pitched forward against Hornblower's and Jackson's legs, kicking and writhing.

"The swine's having a fit," growled Jackson.

The kicking and writhing went on. Across the water through the darkness came a sharp, scornful whisper. "Mr. Hornblower," said the voice—it was Eccles putting a world of exasperation into his sotto voce question, "cannot you keep your men quiet?"

Eccles had brought the launch round almost alongside the jolly boat to say this to him, and the desperate need for silence was dramatically demonstrated by the absence of any of the usual blasphemy. Hornblower opened his mouth to make an explanation, but he fortunately realized that raiders in open boats did not make explanations when under the guns of the fortress of Blaye.

"Aye, aye, sir," was all he whispered back, and the launch continued on its mission of shepherding the flotilla in the tracks of the cutter.

"Take his oar, Jackson," he whispered furiously to the coxswain, and he stooped and with his own hands dragged the writhing figure toward him and out of Jackson's way.

"You might try pouring water on 'im, sir," suggested Jackson hoarsely as he moved to the after thwart. "There's the bailer 'andy."

Sea water was the seaman's cure for every ill, his panacea. But Hornblower let the sick man lie. His struggles were coming to an end, and Hornblower wished to make no noise with the bailer. The lives of more than a hundred men depended on silence. Now that they were well into the actual estuary they were within easy reach of cannon shot from the shore, and a single cannon shot would rouse the crew of the Papillon, ready to man the bulwarks to beat off the attack, ready to drop cannon balls into the boats alongside, ready to shatter approaching boats with a tempest of grape.

Silently the boats glided up the estuary; Soames in the cutter was setting a slow pace, with only an occasional stroke at the oars to maintain steerageway. Presumably he knew very well what he was doing; the channel he had selected was an obscure one between mudbanks, impracticable for anything except small boats, and he had a twenty-foot pole with him with which to take the soundings—quicker and much more silent than using the lead. Minutes were passing fast, and yet the night was still utterly dark, with no hint of approaching dawn. Strain his eyes as he would, Hornblower could not be sure that he could see the flat shores on either side of him. It would call for sharp eyes on the land to detect the little boats being carried up by the tide.

Hales at his feet stirred and then stirred again. His hand, feeling around in the darkness, found Hornblower's ankle and apparently examined it with curiosity. He muttered something, the words dragging out into a moan.

"Shut up," whispered Hornblower, trying, like the saint of

old, to make a tongue of his whole body, so that he might express the urgency of the occasion without making a sound audible at any distance. Hales set his elbow on Hornblower's knee and levered himself up into a sitting position, and then levered himself farther until he was standing, swaying with bent knees and supporting himself against Hornblower.

"Sit down, damn you," whispered Hornblower, shaking with fury and anxiety.

"Where's Mary?" asked Hales in a conversational tone.

"Shut up!"

"Mary!" said Hales, lurching against him. "Mary!"

Each successive word was louder. Hornblower felt instinctively that Hales would soon be speaking in a loud voice, that he might even soon be shouting. Old recollections of conversations with his doctor further stirred at the back of his mind; he remembered that persons emerging from epileptic fits were not responsible for their actions, and might be, and often were, dangerous.

"Mary!" said Hales again.

Victory and the lives of a hundred men depended on silencing Hales, and silencing him instantly. Hornblower thought of the pistol in his belt, and of using the butt, but there was another weapon more conveniently to his hand. He unshipped the tiller, a three-foot bar of solid oak, and he swung it with all the venom and fury of despair. The tiller crashed down on Hales' head, and Hales, an unuttered word cut short in his throat, fell silent in the bottom of the boat.

There was no sound from the boat's crew, save for something like a sigh from Jackson, whether approving or disapproving, Hornblower neither knew nor cared. He had done his duty, and he was certain of it. He had struck down a helpless idiot, most probably he had killed him, but the surprise upon which the success of the expedition depended had not been imperiled. He reshipped the tiller and resumed the silent task of keeping in the wake of the gigs.

Far away ahead—in the darkness it was impossible to estimate the distance—there was a nucleus of greater darkness, close on the surface of the black water. It might be the corvette. A dozen more silent strokes, and Hornblower was sure of it. Soames had done a magnificent job of pilotage, leading the boats straight to that objective. The cutter and launch were diverging now from the two gigs. The four boats were separating in readiness to launch their simultaneous converging attack.

"Easy," whispered Hornblower, and the jolly boat's crew ceased to pull.

Hornblower had his orders. He had to wait until the attack had gained a foothold on the deck. His hand clenched convulsively on the tiller; the excitement of dealing with Hales had driven the thought of having to ascend strange rigging in the darkness clear out of his head, and now it recurred with redoubled urgency. Hornblower was afraid.

Although he could see the corvette, the boats had vanished from his sight, had passed out of his field of vision. The corvette rode to her anchor, her spars just visible against the night sky—that was where he had to climb! She seemed to tower up hugely. Close by the corvette he saw a splash in the dark water—the boats were closing in fast and someone's stroke had been a little careless. At that same moment came a shout from the corvette's deck, and when the shout was repeated, it was echoed a hundredfold from the boats rushing alongside. The yelling was lusty and prolonged, of set purpose. A sleeping enemy would be bewildered by the din, and the progress of the shouting would tell each boat's crew of the extent of the success of the others. The British seamen were yelling like madmen. A flash and a bang from the corvette's deck told of the firing of the first shot; soon pistols were popping and muskets banging from several points of the deck.

"Give way!" said Hornblower. He uttered the order as if it had been torn from him by the rack.

The jolly boat moved forward while Hornblower fought down his feelings and tried to make out what was going on on board. He could see no reason for choosing one side of the corvette in preference to the other, and the larboard side was the nearer, and so he steered the boat to the larboard main chains. So interested was he in what he was doing that he remembered only in the nick of time to give the order, "In oars." He put the tiller over and the boat swirled round and the bowman hooked on.

From the deck just above came a noise exactly like a tinker hammering on a cooking pot; Hornblower noted the curious noise as he stood up in the stern sheets. He felt the cutlass at his side and the pistol in his belt, and then he sprang for the chains. With a mad leap he reached them and hauled himself up. The shrouds came into his hands, his feet found the ratlines beneath them, and he began to climb. As his head cleared the bulwark and he could see the deck, the flash of a pistol shot illuminated the scene momentarily, fixing the struggle on the deck in a static moment, like a picture. Before and below him a British seaman was fighting a furious cutlass duel with a French officer, and he realized with vague astonishment that the kettlemending noise he had heard was the sound of cutlass against cutlass—that clash of steel against steel that poets wrote about. So much for romance.

The realization carried him far up the shrouds. At his elbow he felt the futtock shrouds, and he transferred himself to them, hanging back downward with his toes hooked into the ratlines and his hands clinging like death. That lasted for only two or three desperate seconds, and then he hauled himself onto the topmast shrouds and began the final ascent, his lungs bursting with the effort. Here was the topsail yard, and Hornblower flung himself across it and felt with his feet for the foot rope. Merciful God! There was no foot rope—his feet searching in the darkness met only unresisting air. A hundred feet above the deck he hung, squirming and kicking like a baby held up at arm's length in his father's hands. There was no foot rope; it may have been with this very situation in mind that the Frenchmen had removed it. There was no foot rope, so that he could not make his way out to the yardarm. Yet the gaskets must be cast off and the sail loosed—everything depended on that. Hornblower had seen daredevil seamen run out along the yards, standing upright, as though walking a tightrope. That was the only way to reach the yardarm now.

For a moment he could not breathe as his weak flesh revolted against the thought of walking along that yard above the black abyss. This was fear, the fear that stripped a man of his manhood, turning his bowels to water and his limbs to paper. Yet his furiously active mind continued to work. He had been resolute enough in dealing with Hales. Where he personally was not involved he had been brave enough; he had not hesitated to strike down the wretched epileptic with all the strength of his arm. That was the poor sort of courage he was capable of displaying. In the simple vulgar matter of physical bravery he was utterly wanting. This was cowardice, the sort of thing that men spoke about behind their hands to other men. He could not bear the thought of that in himself; it was worse—awful though the alternative might be—than the thought of falling through the night to the deck. With a gasp, he brought his knee up onto the yard, heaving himself up until he stood upright. He felt the rounded, canvas-covered timber under his feet, and his instincts told him not to dally there for a moment.

"Come on, men!" he yelled, and he dashed out along the yard.

It was twenty feet to the yardarm, and he covered the distance in a few frantic strides. Utterly reckless by now, he put his hands down on the yard, clasped it and laid his body across it again, his hands seeking the gaskets. A thump on the yard told him that Oldroyd, who had been detailed to come after him, had followed him out along the yard—he had six feet less to go. There could be no doubt that the other members of the jolly boat's crew were on the yard, and that Clough had led the way to the starboard yardarm. It was obvious from the rapidity with which the sail came loose. Here was the brace beside him. Without any thought of danger now, for he was delirious with excitement and triumph, he grasped it with both hands and jerked himself off the yard. His waving legs found the rope and twined about it, and he let himself slide down it.

Fool that he was! Would he never learn sense and prudence? Would he never remember that vigilance and precaution must never be relaxed? He had allowed himself to slide so fast that the rope seared his hands, and when he tried to tighten his grip so as to slow down his progress, it caused him such agony that he had to relax it again and slide on down with the rope stripping the skin from his hands as though peeling off a glove. His feet reached the deck and he momentarily forgot the pain as he looked round him.

There was the faintest gray light beginning to show now, and there were no sounds of battle. It had been a well-worked surprise—a hundred men flung suddenly on the deck of the corvette had swept away the anchor watch and mastered the vessel in a single rush before the watch below could come up to offer any resistance.

Chadd's stentorian voice came pealing from the forecastle, "Cable's cut, sir!"

Then Eccles bellowed from aft, "Mr. Hornblower!"

"Sir!" yelled Hornblower.

"Sheet that topsail home!"

A rush of men came to help—not only his own boat's crew but every man of initiative and spirit. Halyards, sheets and braces; the sail was trimmed round and was drawing full in the light southerly air, and the Papillon swung round to go down with the first of the ebb. Dawn was coming up fast, with a trifle of mist on the surface of the water.

Over the starboard quarter came a sullen, bellowing roar, and then the misty air was torn by a series of infernal screams, supernaturally loud. The first cannon balls Hornblower had ever heard were passing him by.

"Mr. Chadd! Set the headsails! Loose the fore-tops'l! Get aloft, some of you, and set the mizzen tops'l."

From the port bow came another salvo—Blaye was firing at them from one side, St. Dyé from the other, now that they could guess what had happened on board the Papillon. But the corvette was moving fast with wind and tide, and it would be no easy matter to cripple her in the half-light. It had been a very near-run thing; a few seconds' delay could have been fatal. Only one shot from the next salvo passed within hearing, and its passage was marked by a loud snap overhead.

"Mr. Mallory, get that forestay spliced!"

"Aye, aye, sir!"

It was light enough to look round the deck now; he could see Eccles at the break of the poop, directing the handling of the corvette, and Soames beside the wheel, conning her down the channel. Two groups of red-coated marines, with bayonets fixed, stood guard over the hatchways. There were four or five men lying on the deck in curiously abandoned attitudes. Dead men; Hornblower could look at them with the callousness of youth. But there was a wounded man, too, crouched groaning over his shattered thigh. Hornblower could not look at him as disinterestedly, and he was glad, maybe only for his own sake, when at that moment a seaman asked for and received permission from Mallory to leave his duties and attend to him.

"Stand by to go about!" shouted Eccles from the poop; the corvette had reached the tip of the middle-ground shoal and was about to make the turn that would carry her into the open sea.

The men came running to the braces, and Hornblower tailed on along with them. But the first contact with the harsh rope gave him such pain that he almost cried out. His hands were like raw meat, and fresh-killed at that, for blood was running from them. Now that his attention was called to them, they smarted unbearably.

The headsail sheets came over, and the corvette went handily about.

"There's the old Indy!" shouted somebody.

The Indefatigable was plainly visible now, lying to just out of shot from the shore batteries, ready to rendezvous with her prize. Somebody cheered, and the cheering was taken up by everyone, even while the last shots from St. Dyé, fired at extreme range, pitched sullenly into the water alongside. Hornblower had gingerly extracted his handkerchief from his pocket and was trying to wrap it round his hand.

"Can I help you with that, sir?" asked Jackson. Jackson shook his head as he looked at the raw surface. "You was careless, sir. You ought to 'a' gone down 'and over 'and," he said, when Hornblower explained to him how the injury had been caused. "Very careless, you was, beggin' your pardon for saying so, sir. But you young gennelmen often is. You don't 'ave no thought for your necks nor your 'ides, sir."

Hornblower looked up at the main-topsail yard high above his head, and remembered how he had walked along that slender stick of timber out to the yardarm in the dark. At the recollection of it, even here with the solid deck under his feet, he shuddered a little.

"Sorry, sir. Didn't mean to 'urt you," said Jackson, tying the knot. "There, that's done, as good as I can do it, sir."

"Thank you, Jackson," said Hornblower.

"We got to report the jolly boat as lost, sir," went on Jackson.

"Lost?"

"She ain't towing alongside, sir. You see, we didn't leave no boat keeper in 'er. Wells, 'e was to be boat keeper, you remember, sir. But I sent 'im up the riggin a'ead o' me, seeing that 'Ales couldn't go. We wasn't too many for the job. So the jolly boat must 'a' come adrift, sir, when the ship went about."

"What about Hales, then?" asked Hornblower.

" 'E was still in the boat, sir."

Hornblower looked back up the estuary of the Gironde. Somewhere up there the jolly boat was drifting about, and lying in it was Hales, probably dead, possibly alive. In either case, the French would find him surely enough, but a cold wave of regret extinguished the warm feeling of triumph in Hornblower's bosom when he thought about Hales back there. If it had not been for Hales, he would never have nerved himself—so, at least, he thought—to run out to the main-topsail yardarm; he would at this moment be ruined and branded as a coward instead of basking in the satisfaction of having capably done his duty.

Jackson saw the bleak look in his face. "Don't you take on so, sir," he said. "They won't 'old the loss of the jolly boat agin you, not the captain and Mr. Eccles, they won't."

"I wasn't thinking about the jolly boat," said Hornblower. "I was thinking about Hales."

"Oh, 'im?" said Jackson. "Don't you fret about 'im, sir. 'E wouldn't never 'ave made no seaman, not no 'ow."

The Capture of the Swordray

CLAY BLAIR, JR.

SHORTLY BEFORE MIDNIGHT, a dank fog had rolled upriver and settled over the long rows of finger piers at the United States Submarine Base in New London, Connecticut. When Lt. Edward F. Coxe, Jr., USN, opened the forward hatch of the new nuclear-powered submarine Swordray, moored in Slip 10, and climbed out onto the slippery steel deck, he could not suppress a sneeze. *Damn*, he thought as he wiped his nose with a handkerchief. *What a hell of a way to spend Christmas Eve.* Coxe, as the .45-caliber pistol on his hip signified, was watch officer aboard the Swordray. There were twenty enlisted men below decks. The remainder of the crew were either on leave or liberty.

He slammed the hatch shut, blinked his eyes several times in a futile attempt to adjust them to the dark; then half felt his way aft to conduct a routine inspection of the mooring lines. Coxe was casual in his inspection. For one thing, he knew that conditions would not have changed since his last inspection shortly after 2200. For another, it was his last week aboard the Swordray—in fact, his last week in submarines—and Coxe had lost all enthusiasm.

He leaned on the after end of the conning tower and stared blankly at the fog-shrouded fantail light. In his mind he was for the one-hundredth time reliving a scene which had occurred in the captain's stateroom a week earlier, when Swordray had completed her shakedown cruise and had put into port for traditional Christmas leave.

The captain, Comdr. Martin H. White, USN, had been sitting at his folding desk when Coxe knocked on the stainless-steel bulkhead and snapped, "Coxe reporting, sir."

"Come in, Ed," Commander White said.

He put down a sheaf of ship's dispatches and waved toward a chair. White's square-jawed face was well tanned, evidence of much time spent on Swordray's bridge, steaming in and out of Key West. At thirty-eight, White was senior submarine skipper in the fleet, with additional duty as commander of the nuclear-powered-submarine Division Six, consisting of the Nautilus and the Swordray.

Lieutenant Coxe sat down uneasily. He tipped his chair slightly until the back of his head rested against the lower outside edge of the compartment's upper bunk. Commander White eyed the junior officer meditatively. Though Coxe was unusually tall—six feet five according to his jacket—White nevertheless considered the maneuver with the chair perilous. Certainly it lacked dignity. But then, White thought, Ed Coxe had been brought up in submarines. *Why did it fall to me to have to tell him, of all people, he isn't a submariner?*

"Ed," White said softly, getting to the point, "I don't have to tell you your old man was the greatest submariner we ever had. I was just your age when I reported aboard his boat in 1943, and he taught me everything I know. Before he went down, he took seventeen Jap ships with him—nearly five hundred thousand tons. His Medal of Honor was well deserved." White could hear his own voice as if from a distance and he wondered, *Is this the way to do it?*

It mattered little to Ed Coxe how he did it. He knew what was coming. He had endured these scenes many times before, and they traditionally began with a reference to his father. First had been the turn-down for being too tall when he applied for the academy, but the Secretary of the Navy had waived the requirements after no fewer than twenty-five captains wrote letters on his behalf. Then came the rejection from the Navy Crew, and the question of his graduating from the academy because of low grades. After that it was the application for Nuclear-Power School and duty on the Nautilus, both of which were rigged for him by his father's submarine friends, now in positions of influence in the submarine force.

Suddenly Ed Coxe blurted out untypically, "Why don't you get to the point, sir? You feel it is your unpleasant duty to tell me that I have failed in qualification for submarine duty and that I must be transferred elsewhere."

Commander White fumbled for words. "Ed, son, I don't know what to say. I know you've tried very hard. I know how much this means to you and to your mother, and I know— Well, I want you to know this is the toughest thing I have ever had to do in my life. And I mean it." White could feel himself trembling inside, and he wished it were done with. Further, at that moment he wished he had never heard of Ed Coxe, or Commander Coxe, or the Nautilus, or the Navy.

Lieutenant Coxe was now on his feet. Awkwardly he stuck out his long, bony hand, and as Commander White grasped it firmly, he said, "Thanks, commander. Thanks for trying so hard for me—and for my father and all. I guess I should have stayed out of the Navy, but I——"

His voice trailed off and he turned, bent his neck and left the captain's cabin.

White stared after him for a moment thinking, *How could Mary and Ed Coxe ever have such a nonnautical misfit?* Then he took out a sheet of ruled paper and a pencil and began scribbling:

To: ComSubLant,
From: ComDivSix,
Subject: Disqualification From Submarines, Lieutenant Edward Fausten Coxe, Jr., USN——

Now on his last duty watch, Ed Coxe ambled slowly aft toward the fantail light on the Swordray, thinking. The question was: Should he leave the Navy, or should he struggle on bearing the cross of his illustrious father until someday he might retire, undistinguished, as a captain? The lure of the outside was inviting. Having studied and had practical experience with nuclear engines, especially as assistant reactor officer of the Swordray, his services were very much in demand by the electrical companies who were beginning to build nuclear generating plants.

Coxe had stopped halfway down the afterdeck and was staring blankly into the fog. Suddenly he realized that the white sheen cutting through the swirling moistness had disappeared. The fantail light had gone out. *This we will have to fix immediately,* he thought. Swordray's stern stuck well out into the channel, and while there was little likelihood of traffic that time of night, it was a ComSubLant regulation to keep a fantail light burning.

Coxe felt his way aft through the utter darkness until his big field shoe struck the coaming of the after hatch. He undogged the hatch wheel, lifted it and yelled, "Hey, below! Below!"

A sleepy-eyed face appeared, wreathed in a blinding shaft of light. It was Torpedoman's Mate Second Class Welch.

"Pass me up a light bulb. The stern light's out," Coxe said. Then he added, "And a three-sixteenths wrench."

Coxe squatted by the hatch while waiting for Welch to fetch the bulb and wrench, staring into darkness, deliberately keeping his eyes turned from the hatch, so that he would not be blinded. He thought he heard a scraping noise near the stern. He looked aft and fancied he saw several dark forms bobbing around the light post. But believing that the bright light of the hatch had temporarily distorted his vision, he did not give it a second thought.

Torpedoman's Mate Welch passed the bulb and wrench up, and Coxe, after carefully dogging the hatch shut, crawled aft along the narrow, tapering superstructure of the submarine. His right hand found the lower shaft of the light post, and he was inching it upwards toward the bulb enclosure when suddenly a blinding sheet of fire dazzled his eyes. For a split second he believed that somehow the light had gone back on, right in his face. But when he became aware of the pain on the back of his head and the fact that he was slipping rapidly into unconsciousness, he knew he had been struck.

One of the dark forms that Coxe had seen a few minutes earlier emerged from his hiding place behind the after-line chock. He dragged Coxe up the deck toward the conning tower. A second, then a third, dark form appeared.

One of the men whispered into the fog, "All right. Come aboard and sink the rubber boat."

Had Coxe been conscious he would not have understood the language, for the man was speaking Russian.

Within thirty seconds several more men clambered aboard. One said, "The rubber boat has been sunk."

The Russians gathered in a knot on the afterdeck of the Swordray. Coxe, still unconscious, lay at their feet.

One of the Russians—obviously the leader of the group—spoke softly. "All right. This will be Coxe, here on the deck. He is the assistant reactor officer and we'll need him. There should be twenty men sleeping below decks. Dispose of them as planned. Remember, do not use your guns. Knives will suffice. I will remain topside to meet the midnight base-security check. Now hurry!"

The leader was Comdr. Ivan Ilychev, Soviet submarine service. His mission: to steal the U.S.S. Swordray, so that Soviet nuclear engineers, who had been unsuccessful in creating a nuclear-powered submarine of their own, could copy her. Among the men under his command were two other Soviet submarine officers and two Soviet physicists. The mission, code-named Lotus, had been planned and studied for more than a year. A sizable Soviet spy net had been especially created to gather information about the operating schedule and crew of the Swordray and the operation of the United States submarine base. A Soviet submarine had brought the party to Long Island Sound, where they had launched into the fog a rubber boat powered by a specially built silent outboard motor. They were working on a precise time schedule—one that would permit them to get Swordray under way, steam downriver and disappear beneath the sea before daybreak.

Commander Ilychev, as calm as the river water lapping against Swordray's pudgy hull, dragged Coxe forward on the starboard side of the deck until his body was hidden behind the conning tower. Then he removed Coxe's jacket, pistol, belt and battered cap, and donned them himself. Lastly, he scrubbed the lampblack off his face and hands and walked around the conning tower. Ilychev was confident that his mission would succeed. He knew that if it did he would be a hero of the Soviet Union, and would surely be promoted to admiral, if not put in command of the entire Soviet submarine force.

He could still hear the stern words of the Defense Minister: "Commander Ilychev, I cannot overemphasize the importance of this mission to the Soviet and to the party. An entire shipyard and a great laboratory of nuclear physicists are standing by, waiting for your successful return. Within a year they will duplicate the Swordray. Within two years they will have a fleet ready for action. It will be a fleet composed of nuclear-powered submarines capable of destroying all the NATO navies."

Commander Ilychev had tried to picture in his mind how Soviet historians would treat his adventure and ultimate promotions. "I will be the greatest Soviet naval hero since Marakov or perhaps even Peter the Great."

Now aboard the Swordray, Ilychev, disguised in Coxe's uniform, took up a stance near the gangway leading from the deck of the Swordray to the finger pier. There was no gangway watch—he had died as Coxe felt for the broken stern light. The pier, like the rest of the submarine base, was dark and deserted. But Commander Ilychev knew that at exactly midnight the base-security guard would drive out onto the pier in a jeep and make a routine check. He glanced at his watch: 2355. He wondered how his comrades were making out below decks.

They were doing very well indeed. Four men had entered the Swordray through the forward hatch, which let down into the chrome-plated officers' wardroom. They crawled down through a second hatch into the crew's mess, just below the wardroom. As expected, it was deserted. Just off the crew's mess to port was the chief's quarters, a special sleeping compartment. They found Chief Electrician's Mate James Dorsey asleep. By prearranged agreement, one of the two Soviet naval officers slipped into the bunkroom and slit Dorsey's throat. Then the four men climbed through a hatch into the forward torpedo room, where they found several more Swordray sailors in their bunks, including Welch, who was not yet asleep. All were murdered by the Soviet officers. Another Russian party entered the after sleeping compartment.

It was now midnight. Precisely on schedule, the headlights of the security jeep swung out onto the pier. Commander Ilychev, who had stuck a clip into Coxe's .45, made one final check to see that the holster was unsnapped. The jeep ground to a halt on the pier opposite Ilychev.

The driver of the jeep, a shore patrolman, opened a flap in the plastic side and shouted, "O.K.?"

In perfect English, Commander Ilychev responded, "All O.K. here! Merry Christmas!"

The jeep driver shouted back, "Merry Christmas!" swung the vehicle hard around and roared off the pier.

Meantime, the comrades below were working swiftly. They had rendezvoused in the control room. Now they were gathered around the foot of the ladder which led up to the fire-control compartment, where they knew they would find the one remaining United States sailor on the Swordray, the below-decks watch. The Soviet naval officer who had killed Chief Dorsey mounted the steps carefully, then disappeared into the compartment above. He was back at the top of the ladder two minutes later and waved his comrades up. The body of Quartermaster Walker lay in one corner in a pool of blood.

A detail of four men scrambled up a long, stainless-steel tube which led to the deck. Quickly they dragged Coxe's still-unconscious body to the forward hatch and lowered it into the officers' wardroom, where it was laid on the leather sofa along the rear bulkhead. The officers hurried back on deck and singled up Swordray's mooring lines. It was now 0005. In twenty minutes ten Russians had gained complete command of the Swordray and were almost ready to get under way. According to the sunrise tables, exactly seven hours remained before daylight.

The two Soviet physicists had obtained from Coxe's pocket the keys to the reactor and maneuvering rooms of the Swordray—always kept locked in port. Now they were gently bathing his face and neck with cold water. Coxe came to slowly, aware only of a tremendous stabbing pain in the back of his head and of a contrasting coolness on his face. Soon he blinked his eyes open. When he saw two strange men, dressed in black trousers and turtle-neck sweaters, faces darkened with lampblack, leaning over him, he believed he was having a nightmare.

Suddenly he remembered, and sat bolt upright, shouting, "What kind of joke is this?"

One of the physicists replied, "This is no joke. If you do not want to die like your shipmates, then you will do what we say. Try to stand on your feet."

Coxe stared at the two men unbelievingly; then he swung his long legs onto the floor, and, steadying himself with one hand on the wardroom table and the other against the shelf library, he stood up shakily. For the first time he noticed that one of the men held a pistol leveled at his chest. Coxe felt faint.

The physicist with the pistol said, "All right. We go aft to the maneuvering room."

Coxe responded automatically, as though spouting a Navy regulation, "No one is allowed in the reactor or maneuvering room without a Q clearance."

The man with the gun moved in closer. "Get moving," he said.

Coxe did as ordered. The three men, with Coxe in the middle, walked aft and climbed through the hatch into the fire-control room. Coxe noticed a huddle in one corner, and he peered for a better look.

"Walker!" he shouted, kneeling beside the dead below-decks watch. Then he turned to the two men in black. "What have you done to him?" he asked.

"We have killed him, and we will kill you if you do not keep moving," the man with the pistol said.

Coxe stared in bewilderment at the two men. A shudder swept through his body. Then, without further comment, he turned and walked to the locked hatch leading to the reactor compartment. He felt in his pocket for the key.

One of the men in black handed him the key ring and said, "We already have the keys. Open the door, fast."

Coxe unlocked the door and swung it open. The three men stepped into a compartment cluttered with dials and dominated by a large, stainless-steel cylinder which reached from the deck to the overhead.

The man with the gun pointed to the cylinder and asked, "What's that?"

Coxe looked the Russian directly in the eye. By now, his head had cleared appreciably, and he thought, *What is going on here? Who are these men? What do they want? Where is the crew? All murdered too?* Then he remembered the midnight security patrol. *If I am not up topside to report, they will come aboard to investigate,* he thought. Slowly he turned his head toward the clock on the bulkhead: 0010. With a sinking feeling, he realized that the men, whoever they were, had probably taken care of the patrol too. He was alone and alive, and presumably they wanted to keep him that way—at least until they obtained what they were after. *Very well,* Coxe thought, *I will play their game until I can find a way out.*

He responded aloud, "That is the housing for the reactor-control rods." It was a true statement.

One of the Soviet physicists said, "Take us to the maneuvering room and show us how to start the reactor."

"O.K.," Coxe said, and he moved aft through a large room—the steam room—jammed with pipes, boilers, turbines, valves and gauges. At length the three men entered a small compartment which contained a large board filled with dials and meters, blinking red, green and yellow lights, and levers that were obviously the reactor controls.

The man with the pistol jammed it into Coxe's side and said, "Start the reactor."

Coxe, committed to stalling tactics, flicked several switches, changing the order of the blinking lights.

As though conducting a tour for CNO, he said, "We have a small heating unit like an electrical stove which we must turn on first to heat the water in the primary water system." Coxe then stood mutely before the board, intently watching the dial needles and the order of the blinking lights. Three minutes later he said, "Now I will remove the hafnium control rods from the reactor core. Hafnium absorbs neutrons, and, of course, stops the nuclear fission. When I pull these out, the fission process will begin. Now, as you can see by the order of these lights, the water in the primary system is already moving through the reactor. Very soon the water will be hot enough to transfer heat to the secondary steam system."

The two Soviet physicists were watching Coxe's every move. Though the mechanical operating parts were strange to them, they more than grasped the fundamental working principles of the reactor. Very quickly, they understood which lever controlled which system, and it was difficult for them to hide their astonishment at how simply and how efficiently the reactor performed. Steam began to build up in the boilers.

The man with the gun said, "How do you connect the electrical generators to the motors and shaft?"

"Very simple," Coxe said, swinging around to another control panel. "Once steam is up, the bridge gives traditional signals on these engine-order telegraphs. You answer by turning this knob; then, to give the desired RPM's, you simply twist this dial. One man can operate the entire system, if necessary."

The physicist with the gun was so impressed with this statement that he could not hold back a Russian exclamation of admiration.

Coxe, recognizing the foreign dialect, spun around and asked, "Are you Russian?"

The man with the gun snapped, "Never mind who we are. Keep on with the lecture."

At that instant a noise like the sharp bark of a dog filled the compartment. The two Russians looked around, startled. Coxe waved his hand toward the bulkhead. "It's the phone," he said. Then he wondered who could be calling. Could it be the security patrol? He reached for the telephone, but the physicist with the gun brushed his arm away and answered himself.

It was Commander Ilychev, calling from the fire-control room. All lines had been cast off and he was eager to get under way. He had started up the radar set and would use it to navigate downriver through the fog. Twenty times in Russia he had maneuvered a Soviet submarine by radar down a river with almost the same topography. Two other Russians were manning the rudder and the engine telegraph.

The physicist spoke Russian into the phone. With the discovery that there were more Russians aboard—he had no way of knowing how many—Coxe then realized what they were after. *Incredible,* he thought. *Steal the Swordray.*

But, as he pondered the scheme, he concluded that it was not so fantastic as it first appeared. Most of the men on the submarines and the base were away on leave or liberty. Few men, if any, would be walking about on the base this time of night on Christmas Eve. In the darkness and in the fog, Swordray, only one of a hundred submarines moored in the slips, would probably not be missed. *The only real problems are the midnight security check, which they have taken care of someway, and starting the reactor, which I have already done for them,* he thought. Then a painful realization swept over him: *I am the only one left who can stop them. But how?* There was one way. If he was lucky.

With a smile, Coxe turned to the physicist with the gun. "Do you wish to get under way?" he asked.

"Yes," the Russian said.

"Very well. You may tell your friends we are ready to answer bells."

The physicist with the gun relayed this word to Ilychev by phone, and soon the engine-order telegraph on the starboard shaft flicked to "Back 2/3."

Coxe answered the bell and spun the valve which would make the shaft turn. The three men could both hear and feel the great propeller churning water as the Swordray slowly backed out into the river. Coxe could imagine that whoever was in the control room had put the rudder hard to port and that the ship was now backing her stern around upriver. Two minutes later, the engine-order telegraph registered "All stop." Then, in a moment, it went to "All ahead 2/3." Coxe answered, winding up two-thirds speed on both shafts. Swordray, with her blunt nose rolling back an enormous bow wave, disappeared into the fog. When Swordray reached the railroad bridge at Groton, the draw was open, the operator dead at the controls. A Soviet agent closed the draw, then leaped onto the stern of Swordray.

Coxe sat in the maneuvering room for three hours, staring blankly at the shaft-turn indicator while the Soviet physicists familiarized themselves with the reactor controls. Soon he could feel the ship rolling gently. The Soviets would probably submerge as soon as possible in order to avoid radar detection, but the Sound was too shallow. His thoughts were interrupted by the sharp bark of the phone. It was Commander Ilychev again.

"Can you operate the reactor controls now?" he inquired of the physicist with the pistol.

"Yes," the physicist replied.

"Very well," Ilychev replied. "We will dive shortly. Have Petrov bring Coxe to the control room."

By the time Coxe and his escort reached the control room, Commander Ilychev had removed Coxe's jacket and hat; although, Coxe noted, he was wearing the .45. He was hunched over the radar screen, and occasionally barked an order in Russian to the two Soviet naval officers who were manning the helm and engine controls in the compartment below. Coxe's eye wandered from Ilychev's face, eerily lighted by the reflection of the green radar screen, to Quartermaster Walker's body, still slumped in the corner.

Ilychev glanced up. "Well, well," he said in English. "Lieutenant Coxe? I am Commander Ilychev, Soviet Navy."

Coxe was at a loss for words.

Ilychev swept his stocky arm toward the radar set. "Well, we're out in open water. I can relax. Why don't we go back to the captain's cabin?" Commander Ilychev turned to the physicist, Petrov, who had escorted Coxe forward, and told him to put his gun away and return to the reactor compartment. A Soviet officer was stationed at the radar to maneuver Swordray past Montauk Point to the open Atlantic. Then Ilychev walked forward into the officers' wardroom and ducked off the passageway into Commander White's compartment. Coxe followed.

"Well," said Ilychev, settling down on the edge of the lower bunk and motioning Coxe into a chair. "This is a very fine ship. I notice that the diving controls are standard submarine equipment, and I feel that my men and I should have no trouble. But is there anything special we should know?"

"Only the operation of the diving and stern planes, which can be operated by one man, like the controls of an airplane," Coxe answered. It was true.

"Yes, we know about that," Ilychev said. "We have already rigged the planes and made a few test operations. The controls are very remarkable indeed. In fact, the entire ship is remarkable."

"Yes," Coxe said. "There is no need to make adjustments when diving. The ship is in trim." This was correct.

"Good," Ilychev said. "You want to be sure of that, I suppose, because if anything happens, you will go down with us."

"Yes, I know," Coxe said.

"We will remain submerged for about three hours. Then we will surface and rendezvous with the submarine that brought us in. We will transfer a larger crew aboard, so that the trip home will not be too strenuous."

"Yes," Coxe said.

"Coxe," Ilychev said, "you have been very helpful to us. I can assure you that if you continue to be, it could go very well for you in the Soviet Union. We intend to nuclearize the entire Soviet submarine fleet and, needless to say, your services could be invaluable, if you want to co-operate. Your father was a very famous submariner. You could become equally famous in the Soviet Union, working for me."

Coxe thought to himself, *This man is really incredible.*

Ilychev had stuck a cigarette between his yellowed front teeth, and was now searching through the drawers of the desk for a match, scattering the papers on the deck. "You seem to have as much paper work in the United States Navy as we have," he grunted. But Coxe had not heard the last statement. His eyes had fastened on one of the papers. It was the typed-up draft of Commander White's message to ComSubLant disqualifying him from submarines. In the rush to get home for Christmas, the ship's yeoman had failed to send it through. Coxe picked up the paper and handed it to Ilychev.

"You see, I may not be of much use to you. I am not a very good submariner," Coxe said.

Pursing his lips around the unlighted cigarette, Ilychev read the draft. At length he turned to Coxe and said, "Well, we'll see about this," then he tore the paper into shreds and dumped the remains into the chrome wastepaper basket beneath the desk. He turned to Coxe and held out his hand. "O.K.?"

Coxe shook his hand and replied, "O.K." The two men chatted for a long while. Finally, Ilychev, glancing at a clock, said: "Well, it is almost time. Let's go."

When they entered the control room, Coxe could see in an instant that the two Soviet naval officers on the controls knew what they were about. One of them had already closed the ballast-tank vents and checked the hatches shut. The Christmas-tree board showed "Straight," which meant Swordray was ready for diving.

Coxe turned to Ilychev: "On the dive, watch your angle. The blunt bow gives her a tendency to dive rather slowly. She likes to cling to the surface. You have to give her plenty of down angle. I recommend that you take her under at about fifteen knots on the first try; keep your diving angle at about twenty-five degrees." This was a flat lie. Swordray's blunt bow gave her a tendency to plunge underwater, and Coxe knew that with a twenty-five-degree down angle she would go down like a rock.

Ilychev nodded thoughtfully. "Very well." Then he turned to the Soviet officers at the controls and said in Russian, "Take her down."

The Red officer standing at the main-ballast-tank blow-and-vent manifold pulled four levers in quick succession, opening the ballast tanks. The other officer put the diving planes on full dive, and Swordray at once nosed under steeply. Quickly the angle on Swordray became acute—past thirty degrees.

Out of the corner of his eye, Coxe could see that Ilychev was beginning to pale. In the crew's mess, coffee cups fell out of their racks and clattered across the deck. Coxe knew that he had only a few seconds to act, because Ilychev would order the officer on the diving planes to pull back on the stick. Swordray would come out of the dive quickly, then nose up steeply.

Commander Ilychev and his two assistants were now so engrossed in maneuvering the Swordray that they momentarily neglected their lanky hostage. It was the moment of distraction Coxe had been waiting for. He had never swung on another man in anger, and the blow he delivered against Commander Ilychev's jaw was at best a glancing one. But, combined with

Swordray's steep down angle, it was enough to knock Ilychev off balance and send him reeling forward against the diving controls.

Coxe spun on his heel and leaped up the ladder, two steps at a time. On reaching the level of the fire-control room, he raced aft to a small door, opened it, jumped inside the sonar room, slammed the door shut and slid the heavy lock bolt in place.

Ilychev was wildly angry. He shouted to the two men on the controls, "Level her off at a hundred feet! I'll get Coxe!" Then, as Swordray nosed up steeply, he lurched up the ladder to the fire-control room, waving Coxe's .45. But Coxe was already out of sight. Ilychev reached for a telephone and called his physicists in the maneuvering room.

"Petrov? Coxe has escaped! He's probably coming aft! One of you stick by the reactor controls, and one of you come forward! He can't go anyplace else! We'll trap him between us!" Ilychev slammed the phone into its cradle and started moving aft slowly.

Locked in the sonar room, Coxe was working at a frantic rate. First he lowered the long-range, hydraulically operated, high-frequency sonar head. He turned on the equipment and broke out the telegraph key. Hoping that Ilychev would not discover that the sound head could be raised in the forward torpedo room, he slowly tapped out in Morse code: "Mother Goose. Mother Goose. Emergency. Emergency. Swordray."

Mother Goose was a call sign for one of the Navy's best-kept secrets: a vast and effective, shore-based, underwater sonar system, which guarded the coastline of the United States for hundreds of miles out, like a huge underwater radar-warning net. Almost immediately Coxe received a response in his earphones, the metallic, wavy sound of Morse code being transmitted underwater: "Swordray. Mother Goose. Go ahead."

Coxe tapped out: "Mother Goose. Soviet agents steal Swordray. I am prisoner on board. Locked in sonar room. Lieutenant Coxe."

In the busy central-control room of Mother Goose, located on the tip of Cape Cod, a sonarman first class stared incredulously at the words he was spelling out on the white message form on his desk. He jerked off his earphones and called for the watch officer, Ensign McVey. The latter took one look at the message and grabbed the earphones. He called Swordray and asked Coxe to repeat the message.

In the sonar room of Swordray now steaming at 100 feet, Coxe slowly repeated his message. This time he added: "Steaming 100 feet. Course 090. Speed 15 knots." The sonar room was equipped with a compass repeater, pit log and depth gauge.

Ensign McVey took down the message, then raced to peer into a huge sonarscope which presented an image much the same as that of radar. He spun the knobs, cursing the fact that the machine had not been working properly all evening. He was looking for a blip which would confirm Swordray's presence. At length a dim spot of light appeared on the scope. Swordray. Then he ran to an electronic console and picked up a red telephone: "ComSubLant? This is Mother Goose. We have message from Coxe on board Swordray——"

Ilychev opened the watertight door into the reactor compartment. He glanced cautiously around the room, then slammed the door shut. He met Petrov on the other side of the stainless-steel, reactor-control-rod housing.

Petrov said, "I am sure that he is not back here."

Ilychev answered, "Then he must have gone forward. Let's go."

The two men turned and ran forward into the fire-control room.

They stopped alongside the door to the sonar room, and Ilychev said, "He could be in here."

At ComSubLant headquarters, the duty officer had already called the admiral and the base security patrol. With unchecked amazement, the latter had confirmed that Swordray was indeed missing from her slip. The admiral called Comdr. Martin White, who was in New London asleep, after a late evening go at decorating the Christmas tree. Together they determined that the best course of action open was to send another nuclear-powered submarine, the Nautilus, which was at sea on sonar patrol, in pursuit. Arrangements were made to put White on board Nautilus via helicopter, and within twenty-five minutes he was airborne. ComSubLant had notified the Navy Department in Washington, and Mother Goose had alerted Navy patrol bombers and anti-submarine killer planes. When Commander White boarded Nautilus, he ordered her skipper to make flank speed.

Meantime Coxe was still slowly tapping out messages to Mother Goose: "Reactor-control rods on Swordray locked at two-thirds maximum. Unknown to Soviet agents. Believe Nautilus could overtake."

Mother Goose replied: "Nautilus in pursuit. Please send constant signal in order to fix position continually. We getting extremely weak and intermittent presentation on sonarscope."

Coxe replied: "Roger," and screwed down the telegraph key until it transmitted a steady signal. There was nothing to do now but wait.

Holding the .45 at the ready, Ilychev put his hand on the doorknob of the sonar room and turned slowly.

"It's locked," he whispered to Petrov. Then Ilychev gave a mighty heave with his shoulder. But still the door did not budge.

Petrov pressed his ear against the door. "He is using the sonar," he said.

A frown crossed Ilychev's brow. This could mean real trouble. But he knew only one way to prevent it.

"Stand back!" Ilychev shouted. Savagely he swung the .45 toward the door lock and fired. The bullet ricocheted off the hard, stainless steel and twanged dangerously around the compartment. Then Ilychev screamed, "We'll deal with him later! Cancel the rendezvous! We'll have to make a run for it at full speed! Go aft and make sure we're getting all the turns the reactor will put out!"

As Petrov ran aft, Ilychev scampered down the ladder to the control room. Glancing at the fathometer, which was now indicating 500 feet under the keel, he shouted to the officers on the controls, "Take her down to five hundred feet! Ring up flank speed!" The physicists in the maneuvering room, unaware that Coxe had set a special control which would limit the reactor output to two-thirds of capacity, turned the generators and motors up to maximum speed. Swordray moved ahead—and down—at seventeen knots.

Nautilus, guided toward Swordray by sonar signals from

Mother Goose, quickly began to close the lead. Comdr. Martin White was in constant sonar communication with the admiral.

The last message from the admiral stated: "Nautilus. Navy Department orders follow. Quote. Destroy Swordray unquote. This headquarters concurs. COMSUBLANT."

When he received the message, White recoiled, but nevertheless ordered all of Nautilus' forward torpedo tubes made ready and armed with long-range homing torpedoes.

Now Mother Goose had a message for Coxe on board the Swordray: "Coxe. Nautilus' position twenty-five miles due west, closing rapidly. What is status on board? Can you take over? Mother Goose."

Coxe tapped back: "Status follows. At least ten maybe more armed agents on board under command of Commander Ilychev, Soviet Navy. Two physicists. Walker dead. Believe Dorsey, Welch, Pleve and rest of crew same. If I leave sonar room may be overpowered. Do not want to take chance and have you lose contact. Over. Coxe."

Mother Goose replied: "Roger. Will relay to Nautilus."

Coxe knew what action he must now take. But he was too busy to think about its consequences. He lowered a second sonar head—the special one that would permit talk between submerged submarines at a distance up to seven miles. Later he advised Mother Goose: "Please have Nautilus man underwater telephone." Then he waited. Every ten minutes he spoke into the telephone: "Hello, Nautilus. Swordray calling."

One hour later, Coxe heard a faint but recognizable voice come in over the underwater phone, "Hello, Swordray. Go ahead." It was Commander White.

Coxe responded, "On course zero-four-five, speed seventeen knots, depth five hundred feet. Sonar room secure in my hands. Do not believe Soviets capable of manning torpedoes. Over."

White replied, "Roger." His voice was becoming more distinct as the distance between the two submerged submarines narrowed.

Coxe now secured contact with Mother Goose and switched

his high-frequency sonar to "Attack," which gave him a visual presentation of Nautilus.

Then he got back on the underwater telephone: "Nautilus. I see you clearly. True bearing from me, two-two-seven. Range nine thousand yards. Zero-four-five T. You are dead astern. Over."

"Ed"—it was Commander White—"we have you on sonar now. Our TDC checks perfectly with your estimate. Good setup. Damned good setup. Ed, is there anything we can do?"

Coxe snapped back, "Just one thing. Fire when you have a solution light on TDC. Over."

"I mean—is there anything else we can do for——"

Coxe broke in, "Fire when you have solution light. I must go off the air now. Have local calls to make." Coxe put down the underwater telephone, picked up the local ship's phone, set the call button on "Control Room," and turned the crank.

Ilychev answered instantly.

Coxe said, "It's me, commander. I wanted to tell you that we'll be down a lot longer than you think!"

Ilychev's response was drowned out by the whine of the six homing torpedoes as they bore down on Swordray.

After giving the order to fire and hearing the subsequent explosion on sonar, followed by the breaking-up noises of Swordray as she plunged down for the last time, Commander White had left the fire-control room of Nautilus and gone to the captain's cabin. Now he was sitting at the folding desk, writing out a dispatch on ruled paper:

To: Secretary of the Navy.
Via: ComSubLant.
Subject: Medal of Honor, Recommendation
       For Edward Fausten Coxe, Jr.

Jarge Makes In

Charles Rawlings

The pink cliffs of Newfoundland brood immovable, gigantic, adamant against the North Atlantic that beats upon their feet in ceaseless rhythm. The waves cream slowly into foam that holds for the moment frozen as you come in from far off and are still too far away to see the surge and hear the roar. It is a land of great rocky valleys, of crevasse and gorge and cliff; a theater for giant men, or a haunt for gnomes.

Jarge was one of the gnomes. He was a little Newfoundlander with faded blue eyes and a south-of-Ireland mug of a face. As the cod move following the feed and the currents, he drifted, an unmoored, sad-eyed sea waif. A toss of his sea bag and a pierhead jump, and he was to the northward or the southward; fishing, a fleet flunky with the yachts at Halifax, a rigger, a painter, whatever the northern sea had for him. This particular winter he was back at the fishing. He was a bow doryman in the Helen, Marty Zimmerman's big power banker, one of the highliners of the Lunenburg winter fleet.

His small round chest, hard as a chunk-stove butt, creaked the suspender straps of his oilskin pants as he threw back against the oars. He had to trim down the top of his dory boots so his bandy legs could break at the knees and not chafe. There was no command in him, no fire in his eyes. Even an eighteen-foot banks dory has its master and its man, and Jarge had always been the man. He had a bow-hand look about him.

"Dere's two t'ings big about Jarge," Marty Zimmerman said.

"His chewin' teeth and his cud a tobacca. We keeps him for luck, like de cat."

But Marty was joking. Jarge was a good fisherman, steady and quiet; and when the Helen was ready that February to cast off on her second winter cruise, he was sitting on a trawl tub, his duffel stowed below in his bunk, reading a letter.

It had started out a wicked winter. There had been early gales. Three dories had already been lost from the fleet, astray in the cold and snow, their men frozen or drowned. Fish were scarce. So scarce that the story was about that the Helen was going foraging. Marty verified the rumor to the dockside idlers and the tall lady reporter from the Malagash News, Lunenburg's evening newspaper. She had asked him for an interview.

"Let those farmer skippers piddle and tickle those little scrod on Liscomb's and Emerald and all those small shoals close in, if dey wants," he said. "We're bound up to Burgeo. We're after those Grand Bank lads. Dat's where dey spends the winter. Dere's codfish and haddocks winters up dere as big as fat schoolpoys. Burgeo Bank, up in the Newfie country, is where we're bound."

Jarge lifted his eyes from the letter. It was on crisp white paper, with the *l*'s and the *t*'s of its bold, scholarly handwriting standing up like stern, dark prelates. Its envelope was covered with addresses crossed out and new ones added. His mouth gaped at Marty, then incredulously down at the letter, as if the news from both sources were, in some mysterious way, connected. The surprise slowly drained from his face, and a sadness possessed it. He stared, looking at once toward the Helen's destination and the origin of the long wandering letter in his hand, up over Marty's head, up over Lunenburg hill into the northeastern sky, as if he could see the clouds that floated high over the green cold swell of that lonely bank, clouds that caught their skirts on those high pink cliffs of Newfoundland. He sat for a time lost in the sky, his face slowly darkening with anguish, then, folding the letter, he walked up the deck to the forecastle and climbed down into its gloom. He slipped his boots and slid into his bunk.

The forecastle was as full of tense excitement and talk as it was of smell. Marty's men, save Jarge, were all Lunenburgers whose ancestors from Lüneburg in Hanover had given them big

German bone and strength of body. Marty could not go too far nor through too hard a chance to daunt them; not if there were fish at the end. They swung down the ladder, shouting not about the danger and the hardships but the more important things. They threatened the cook about enough stores. They opened their chests and rechecked their plugs of tobacco. They wondered where Burgeo was exactly on the chart. What the weather would be like up there for setting out the gear? How many fathoms deep and what kind of bottom? Would there be a chance ashore for a swing with—what kind of girls? Indians, no doubt. They sat on their chests, which served as seats for the forecastle table, leaning forward as the mate drew coast lines with his thumbnail on the red tablecloth. The cook, in his white apron, came from his galley behind the foremast butt, his dough pan embraced in his arm, stirring and peering down into the crowded circle of disheveled heads.

Jarge lay silent, staring at the deck beams close above his eyes. Silence was not unusual in him, for he existed almost wordless in that world of bigger, louder men who grinned at his Irish brogue; but the look on his face caught the eye of the mate. The mate was a heavily shouldered, bald haddocker, the biggest and kindest man on the ship. Angus Oxner, Jarge's dory mate, was the only man anywhere near him in size.

"What's the matter, Newfie?" the mate called. "Burgeo too far away for you?"

Jarge's eyes jumped back from far away, and he turned as if frightened at the intrusion.

"No, sor-r-r," he said. "Oi—Oi likes it fine."

He tried to smile, and automatically fished in his pocket for his pipe. He held the pipe unfilled in his hand and turned his head back to stare at the deck beams again when their eyes left him. After a moment he pulled the green curtains of his bunk and lay in the heavy reeking darkness.

The Helen's big Diesel engine cleared its throat. It found its voice, rumbled a low growl and a "ru-u-u-up" of glee as it shifted from reverse to full ahead. The long voyage began. The crew took the galley fire away from the cook and stoked it so hot it scorched the top of his pies. They left its warmth only to stand their watches. Marty roared good-naturedly up and down the wet decks. Jarge's white mittens held the big wheel spokes every four hours, and his eyes bore steadily on the compass card's letter E as he held it true against the lubber line. The Helen drove her heavy black bows steadily into a long green head swell, and the snow-covered hills of Nova Scotia, heliotrope and purple in the distance, slowly slid by the port rail.

At supper the second night out, Angus Oxner, Jarge's dory mate, peered down the table through the fog of steam from heaped-up pans of hash and fish and brewis and baked beans. "Ain't we," he called, "bound where you lives handy, Jarge? You lives somewhere up on dat Newfie coast?"

"Jarge lives more to the eastward, over by the Bay of Bulls," the mate said. He grinned at Jarge, trying to cheer him up. "It's near de Bay of Bulls where Jarge was made. Look at the size of him."

"No, 'tis Witless Bay," someone suggested. "De wit's out of him."

Jarge tried again to grin. The wit indeed was out of him. He cast his eyes down at his plate and the table silenced.

"Somethin' ails the little man," the mate announced. "Jarge," he called kindly, "what's wrong, lad? You feel sick?"

"Dere's only three kinds," Angus said. "Lovesick! Seasick! Homesick! A Newfie ain't got one of dem."

"Shut your face, Angus," the mate commanded. . . . "Jarge, is it bad news now?"

"No, sor-r-r." Jarge's watery eyes looked about, hunted, desperate. "'Tis naught, sor-r-r. Oi'll be all right in the marnin'."

"If dere is, now"—there was a worried mate's tone in his voice—"tell Marty now. When the fish start comin' in, dere's little time for feelin' bad."

And Jarge closed the door of the tiny master's cabin the next morning and waited for Marty to look up from his bunk.

"Please, sor-r-r," he said, "could I speak to ye, sor-r-r? Right handy to Burgeo, sor-r-r, is that Frinch island, St. Pierre. After we're full now, could ye be puttin' me ashore on the beach while ye runs back?"

"Ashore, lad? Why?"

"Oi has an engagement, sor-r-r."

Jarge Makes In

"A vat?"

"An engagement, sor-r-r."

"So?"

"An engagement and a duty, sor-r-r."

"I don't know where you learned words like dat, but engagement or whatever it is, dere's no landin' men on foreign ground."

"Please, sor-r-r, Oi'd be waitin' for ye next toime up. 'Tis a pressin' engagement, sor-r-r. Not with the Frinch. I wants to get to me own land, a little away over the water. Oi knows de trails, sor-r-r."

"Lad," Marty shook his head with unquestionable finality, "it's against the law."

"De law!" He looked down at his boots. "Thin ye can't. Oi has to stay, may God forgive me." He said it softly and closed the door without meeting Marty's quizzical eyes.

The Helen's ice-coated bow slowly settled as her engines slowed and the sounding lead went down and came up. The crew's breath, as they waited about Marty, wreathed into the gray air under the gray winter sky. Marty upended the lead and peered at the pad of yellow soap on its bottom.

"Look at dat," he shouted. "Green rocks! Little pimply pebbles and shells. Dere's fish bottom like pasture land. Bait!" He waved the lead like a scepter. "Bait all five tubs!"

The tubs of coiled gear, heavy with the frozen mackerel bait, waited on deck. The first five clumped into the top dory. Her men clambered in, the master astern, the bow hand forward. The hands at the falls lowered away. The dory drifted down the Helen's side, swirled astern and started down the valleys of the seas. The next dory followed, a hundred yards distant. Each bow man rowed from the forward thwart. The stern man stood rolling on his sea legs as the dory pitched and lifted. He payed out the trawl, flicking it up from the tub with a smooth sapling wand. The coils and the baited hooks flew out and settled into the sea.

Jarge held his oars. His mittens curled over the oar stocks like dingy white kittens thick with hair.

"Angus," he said, "dere's snow comin'."

"Well, what of dat?" said Angus.

"Angus, Oi'm afeared."

That night at supper the dorymen's faces were as red as radishes in the heat of the forecastle. The laundry smell of the steaming wool mittens drying behind the stove mingled with the steam of the onions in the hash, the reek of fish blood, and strong pipe tobacco. It was a happy meal, for twenty thousand pounds of codfish, each one a Grand Bank lad as big as a schoolboy, were gutted and stiff in the ice bins in the hold.

"Jarge, dere," Angus announced, "smells snow." He drooped his lips to imitate Jarge's south-of-Ireland mouth. "'Oi'm afeared,' dat's what he says before de first tub was out. 'Oi'm afeared dere's snow handy,' he says."

"Out of de bay now," Jarge tried to make himself heard, "it can come up quick, Oi tells ye. Shockin' quick. Out of de bay now."

"G'wan," Angus glared at him, towering alongside the foremast butt that made a central pillar in the room. He knocked the heel of his pipe out irritably against the mast. "We'll eat any snow dis little bay country flies. Why, dis is half fresh water. 'Out of de bay!' Dat Gulf of St. Lawrence! Why, dis is damn near river moorin'."

"It comes up shockin' quick, Oi tells ye. Thim Yankees up after de herrin' in the Bay o' Islands in de old days—thim vessels could tell ye. Dey died frozen stiff in de ice and squalls."

"Listen to dat!" Angus cast his eyes in disgust over the forecastle. "Dere's me dory mate for you. Ain't dat cheerful? . . . Newfie, what de hell's de matter with you? Scared of snow! Scared of dyin'! Dyin'!"

Jarge gaped about the suddenly silent table. He dropped his knife with a clatter.

"Oi can't be dyin'," he said, and swallowed, terror on his face. "Oi can't be now."

"Dere was a Newfie in dat dory of de Mary Newcomb's was lost on Sable Bank last month," someone said. "He got you thinkin'? Did you know him maybe?"

"Oi was close friends to him," he said in a frightened, hoarse whisper. "'Twas Tim O'Shane."

"Means nothin' about you, save ye feelin' sad for him," the mate said. "Ye knows dat."

"Oi knows," Jarge said, and stared into the ring of waiting

faces. "But 'tis that he's gone. Oi can't be goin' too. Not now. Oi's afeared terrible."

He licked his lips and suddenly buried his head in his arms. The mate shoved back his plate and walked down the top of the chests and stood over him. His hand reached down under Jarge's chin and heaved. Jarge came up dangling from his arm, his face tipped up helplessly, quivering and blanched.

"We've teased because you is a Newfie and a runt," the mate said, "but we're baitin' with the same herrin' for all of dat. Somethin' ails. Just dat Tim bucko lost ain't all of it. If it's shipmates ye needs, we're comin' wit'. What's the matter, little man?"

He studied Jarge's eyes.

"Ah! Ah!" he said softly.

He slowly moved until Jarge was beside his bunk. Gently he shoved him in and pulled the curtains.

"Leave him be. 'Tis deep in his belly," he commanded the room. "You, Angus, carry him along in de runs tomorrow. Den we'll see."

But Jarge needed no carrying. Angus' dory was top of the starboard nest and Jarge, his eyes bloodshot, a tight white ring about his lips, was standing ready when the mate called, "Top dory's in de air!" to send them away. The Helen deposited them upon the sea and went on. She slowed again in a hundred yards and dropped her next boat, and the next and the next, until all eleven were afloat. When she squared away with clear decks, Angus and Jarge were two miles away from her two spike masts and her foresail's peak when she slid off into the trough.

They worked without a word. Angus hauled the trawl over the bow and slung the fish off the hooks over his shoulder. Jarge, his head bent, his hands bare, coiled the icy line in the tubs.

"Well," Angus said, "here comes your snow."

Jarge lifted his face, and the first flake brushed his cheek. He looked instinctively to the northwestward, although there was not a breath of wind. The snow was like a gauze backdrop of opal and French gray, delicate against the leaden sky. It had no jagged wraiths like fog, no groping fingers. It moved down on them boldly until it was all about them. Then it was no longer opal and gray, but light and white. As white as Jarge's face, as he stared up over Angus' head into the air that was dark with the tumbling, hissing flakes.

"Take your last sight on de schooner," Angus said.

Jarge followed his nod. The Helen was washing out. Her black hull as she came up on a sea was faded to gray. Her yellow masts and rigging were invisible.

"Well," Angus taunted him, "you're just right for prayin', kneelin' as ye coils down. Coil on."

He hauled sturdily on the trawl.

"Dere ain't nothin' to snow," he said. "We hangs to the gear. Marty knows where we are like we lived on a street."

The fish, chuckle-headed cod with round, amazed eyes, thumped into the dory's midship. Jarge placed the two midship thwarts on edge and made the section a deeper bin. The fish filled it level with the dory's gunwales.

"Plenty!" Angus studied the load. "We'll not put her too down in de water. Dere's wind comin'."

Jarge already had his head cocked, listening. The northwester made a moan, far off. It was muted by the falling snow until it sounded like some unhappy giant in anguish leagues away in Cabot Strait. Jarge's head sank on his chest and Angus' eyes watched him while his hands threw a bight in the trawl and made fast the dory's painter. Slowly the dory swung and lay pointing the sound.

The softness left the snow as the first squall drove in. It hurled in swooping clouds that stung their cheeks and reached up under their sou'westers and laid cold clammy fingers on their necks. Angus' jet eyebrows, arched as he studied Jarge, changed from black to white as if they had been dusted with flour.

"Come on, Marty; any time now!" he called out into the wind. "We lives on No. 1 Burgeo Street! In de little yella house! Come on, Marty!"

They waited an hour. Angus, crouched on the after thwart, looked like Jarge save that he was twice as big. Both their heads were sunk out of the wind, their rubber-jacketed backs were humped up to it. In the lulls, Angus stood and tried to see. The resuming howl and sweep of wind and the stinging snow made him cower on the thwart again and hump his back.

"My Gott," he shouted, "where is dat fella Marty, now? Here's dories out in de blizzard and he don't come!"

Jarge made no answer. He had his hands between his knees, his sou'wester's brim almost flat on his chest.

"Listen for de horn, Jarge," Angus said. "Do you hear me? Talk to me, Jarge. Listen for dat horn. He'll be blowin' the foghorn. Where is he, Jarge?"

He stumbled forward and poked Jarge's shoulder.

"Yes, Angus," Jarge said.

He slowly turned his face. It was gray with hopelessness under its white, snow-caked brows.

"Marty won't come, Angus," he said.

"Marty won't come? Marty always comes. Listen! He's shoutin' now. He's shoutin' to de cook. 'Put dat poker in de stove, cook,' Marty's shoutin'. 'Put dat poker in de stove.' Marty's riggin' the schwivvle gun. He's hanging it in de starboard riggin'. He stands wid his hat over the fuse. 'Come on, cook; run, cook, run wid de poker.' Listen, Jarge! Listen!"

There was but the howl of wind, the steady drumming of snow against their hard sou'westers, the snarl of passing seas.

"Dere!" Angus snatched off his hat. "Dere! I heard it. Yonder!" He burst into a roar of laughter. "Dere's Marty up t' windward. We're all right, Newfie."

His fingers shook as he snatched at the painter's hitch. The dory swung beam to wind. Angus stumbled aft and clumped out his oars.

"Row, Newfie, row," he commanded.

He dug his blades into the water and Jarge, turning slowly, reached out his hand for his oars. They pulled in doubles, the oars thumping together.

"Jarge," Angus pleaded, "where is he?"

"Oi never heard de gun," Jarge said, gray-lipped.

"Marty shot! Marty shot! I heard him. Marty! Marty! Shoot dat schwivvle one more time. . . . Hark! Dere! Dere it is. Hear it, Newfie? Dere!"

He flung his arm, pointing down wind, where they had been.

"Hear, Newfie, hear?"

"'Tis no gun," Jarge said softly. "'Tis no gun, Angus"—he

lifted to his feet slowly, as if a demon had him by the hair—"Angus, we're—astray!"

His legs rode the dory's long pitching, his hands limp, his face mirroring the horror of the word to the sky. To men on the winter banks there is no further word to express despair. Too often it is but another way of saying "death." His lips formed it again.

"Astray!" His eyes squeezed shut. "Mary, don't make Oi die, alone."

The dory pitched him, a pitiful waif of a little man, afraid—stark afraid. Suddenly he opened his eyes and blinked as if he had seen something in the close dark sky. His back straightened and he sucked a fill of air.

"Angus!" he shouted. "Angus!"

He darted his head, looking for Angus. The big Lunenburger was huddled in the stern. He looked as if the certainty of their plight had drugged him, dulled his senses as a blow dulls an ox. "Angus, Oi sees. Oi sees plain, Angus. Oi sails her to de coast."

He dug madly in the gear and found the wooden bailing bucket. From it he snatched the small box compass and set it on the thwart.

"Nor'wist, she be!" he shouted. "Yonder"—he pointed to the northeast—"lies Newfoundland! We stands it reachin'!"

He held his hand across the wind, pointing the course. "We lays for White Bear Bay. Angus, it's me road, plain!" His shout was shrill, almost exultant. "It's me way, plain from hivin! Oi sails her into White Bear Bay!"

His mittens grasped a codfish by the jaw and ripped its stiff form from the frozen pile and hurled it overboard. He dug madly at the rest, casting them into the water as fast as he could tear them free. Angus sat up drunkenly.

"Newfie," he shouted, "you trows away de fish?"

"We gets her down to sailin' trim. Oi sails her, Angus."

"We waits for Marty. Stop wastin' fish."

"Angus"—he scrambled aft—"we's got to go. If we stays we dies. Soon's gettin' bitter cold. Dis"—he threw his arm out at the sea and wind—"is me way, me very road. Oi got to git on de coast. Dis is me way. God in hivin sent it."

"We stays here, Newfie."

Angus threw out his fist and knocked the little man back across the thwart. Jarge's mitten grasped an oar as he struggled to rise. With both hands he lifted it and brought it down with all his strength over Angus' head.

"Oi's got to go!" he shouted.

He turned again to the fish and cast them away, stopping when the pile was down to the level of the thwarts. He felt the dory's ballasting with his legs. The sail was lashed about the spar and stowed with the oars. It was a tiny thing, made of light canvas, stained dark brown. He unfurled the jib and tied its upper cloth in a knot. The mast upended and dropped into its step in the forward thwart. The mainsail flapped about his face. He grabbed the gaff and brought it to the spar on the leeward side and lashed it tight with the halyard, goosewinging it. Quickly he snapped the jib's tack into its ring on the dory's bow, made its sheet fast and crawled aft. There were two iron oarlocks hanging in the stern sheets, and he fitted the port one in its place and shipped the steering oar. He leaned down at last to peer in Angus' face. There was a slow trickle of blood running down the temple, but inside the jacket his bare hand felt the big man's heart beating strong and warm.

"We goes, Angus," he said.

The two tiny triangles of canvas filled as he dug the stern oar into the sea. The dory heeled far down, then came up again as she gathered way, and she darted, a tiny, frail shell of hopelessness, off into the immensity of snow and sea and wind and bitter cold.

To have looked down at him from the sky would be to cover your eyes in despair. A dory has an aspect of diminutiveness abroad on the sea. It casts off from its mother, the big schooner, and moves out alone like a seagull chick trying its strokes. There is a tenderness and a fragility about the little things floating off alone on the broad expanse of open sea that makes your heart catch in your throat even in bright clear weather. In a hard chance, with the snow swirling and the seas snarling like a pack of wolves, to picture one of them alone is to feel as you did when a child and thought of the hundredth lamb in the hymn where the ninety and nine are safe.

But a dory is a good boat. The one Jarge sailed was new and

sound. She had no name. On both her yellow bows was a number "10" painted in black. She was eighteen feet long. She had three thwarts, two pairs of oars, a bucket, two bailers shaped like dustpans, a tin of hardtack, a jug of water, the small box compass. She also had those lovely dory lines that have been shaped not as art, whole out of one man's mind, but curve by curve, streak by streak, laid by experience in decades of use; in reality shaped by the sea itself. She could ride the swell of seas with the bosomy, feathery lift of a water bird and slide down into the trough as easily as a swimming gull.

The log of her journey is something Jarge could not have written. He could not have even told it intelligently. "Shockin' bad, sor-r-r. 'Twas that, no mistake." One wave is very like another wave. Ahead of him were all waves of seven hours or, if not seven, the number it would take to reach across thirty-five miles of snow-swept, snarling ocean. About him were the sounds—the howl of air, the hiss of snow, the boil of seas. He was in a little world even while daylight lasted and he could still watch the compass. The snow narrowed the horizon to a tiny circle.

All he thought about was the next wave, the next lurch, racing like mad down into the trough, backing of sail with the speed, then climbing slowly up the watery hill again, the canvas filling hard as steel, tugging like some strong hand, driving him forward, trying to upset him. The kicking oar under his left arm, its live quiver under his mittens, its responsiveness to his push and pull, the answer of the dory—these things were all he thought of.

Save what was in his own secret heart, that rode with him and the Newfoundland coast, bursting with surf; that was a picture in his mind, flashing on and off like a nightmare's scene. White Bear Bay with its broad mouth, its shelter, he saw. The cliffs on either side of the harbor opening. They were sheer cliffs, dropping straight down into deep water, and they stretched for miles east and west of the harbor mouth.

He would have to hit the opening, be close enough to see the light, and that was very close if the snow did not stop. The way to do it was to be high when he found the coast. Be to the westward, to the windward. If you are high, you can always drop down, slide off on the wind. If you are low, sometimes you cannot climb back up. It is a rule of the sea and wind, a rule of life. Every chance he had, he yanked the steering oar toward him, laid its stock against his ribs, close to his heart. The dory's nose, answering, ate up, up, a little more up.

He would not remember, if he sat down to tell you, how the snow caked under his sou'wester up against his neck, so that he had to dig it out, or how his eyelashes, wet with wind tears, became caked with ice, and he had to hold the heel of his hand against them one at a time to thaw them free. Or how his mittens took a layer of spray, then a layer of snow, then more spray, until they were five inches thick and he had to beat them against the dory's side to loosen the ice. Or how the lop from waves, blown inboard, made a slush out of the snow in the dory's bottom and he despaired that the real cold he knew was coming would catch it and freeze it before Angus could come to and bail it out.

"Angus," he shouted, "wake up and bail! We's heavy wid water, Angus!" He splashed the slush with his boot so it struck Angus on the face and he opened his eyes and felt his head.

"Where vere we?" he asked.

"Bail," Jarge commanded. "Git de sea out of her."

"Oh-h-h, me head!"

" 'Twill pass. Bail! De life is out of de dory for water."

"Where vere we?" Angus came to his knees and picked up the bailer.

"We goes to White Bear Bay, nord, nordeast. Oi figures foive more hours."

Angus started to his feet, then dropped back to his knees again and bailed madly.

"We makes it in, b'y!" Jarge shouted. "Don't be afeared!"

And Angus, without further questions, for he was, dull or no, a seaman, scooped at the water, tossing it out for the wind to tear to splatters.

Angus lost a mitten.

"Jarge," he said, staring over the side, "dere it goes. It blew off de thwart."

"Take mine," Jarge said. "Come and sail her."

Jarge stumbled forward, stiff and numb, and beat his arms about his chest and thumped his legs. He took a drink of water from the jug, then started to undress. He peeled down his rubber fishing pants, then his heavy Bannockburn-tweed trousers, then three pairs of woolen underdrawers. With the dory's rusty fish knife, he sawed at the seat of the inner drawers and cut out a patch two feet wide. He twisted his neck about to see, and the snow dusted his small buttocks, shining white and bare. Quickly he hoisted the many layers back in place and rubbed his hands over the chilled portions. The swatch of woolen drawers, thick as a mackinaw, he placed over his hand and lashed it into a tight bag at his wrist.

"Oi sits on de naked place," he said. "Oi sails her now."

For a time he was almost gay. They munched on the emergency hardtack and took a chew of tobacco for dessert. The dory was making beautiful weather of it. The miles were slipping by astern. Then came the darkness and, with it, the real cold. Before, there had been a dampness in the air that chilled to the bone, but hands and feet and face, hardened in both of them by the winter fishing, reached a state of numbness they understood, then stayed that way. It was no worse than baiting, or coiling down, or dressing fish on the schooner's deck at night. But the new, dryer, true northwest cold struck in. Their feet were the worst. They could not move them or beat them as they could their hands and cheeks.

"De swoilers, whin dey's huntin' de harp swoiles and the hood swoiles on de ice," Jarge shouted, "gits sore, cold feet. Dey gets two swoiles and splits he up de belly wid deyre knoives. Den dey pulls off de boots and socks, and shoves deyre feet up inside de swoiles. De swoiles' blood is so hot now, it fair steams in de cold, and dey has warm feet."

"We's got no seals," said Angus. "I believe me feet are goin' to freeze."

" 'Tis warmin' to think on, swoile's blood, steamin'."

But Angus slumped in dejection on the middle thwart. Finally he slid to the dory's bottom and curled up beside Jarge.

"We makes in, b'y," Jarge said.

With the darkness, he had only the wind to steer by. It blew its icy breath against his left cheek. The coast, near now, was constantly before his mind's eye. He could visualize its wicked surf. Sometimes he thought he could hear it. He snugged the oar against his ribs. Up! Hold high! The action became automatic. He jabbered to Angus, who did not answer. He tried to sing. His feet were like stiff clubs that hurt, when he clumped them together, almost more than he could bear. A sleepiness was coming over him.

"Angus!" he shouted. "Wake up, Angus!"

"I'm wit'," Angus said. "I'm wit' ye. When I don't move I get warm."

"No! No!" Jarge strained down in the darkness to shrill the ominous warning. "Ye feels de like of dat whin the cold is strikin' in. Wake up, Angus! Wake up!"

Suddenly through the murk he saw a light. It was a weak gleam, but large in size. Shining through the snow, it looked pink and it wore, like the beaming face of a saint, a halo caused by the snow.

Jarge strained forward, trying to see it clearer. As suddenly as it had appeared, it went out. He rubbed his stiff left cheek and blinked his eyes. Then he heard the sound of surf.

"Mother of God," he cried, "where is we? Oi'm on de sunkers. Angus! Angus!"

His shout dwindled to a whimper as the light flashed on again. He could see the white gleam of breaking water under it. The light was on a tall tower. Quickly he shot the dory into the wind, and her sail, flapping madly, showered him with ice from the leech.

"One chimpanseses, two chimpanseses——" He counted the seaman's way of measuring seconds. The light was dark for "five chimpanseses." It flashed on again while he counted ten.

"Tin on, foive off. Not tin? Angus, we's weathered White Bear Bay. We's in Wake Bay. Mother o' God, 'tis the very place! Oi's come to de very place, Angus! Hivin itself was steerin' this night. Oi! Oi!" He whimpered feebly in wonder. He let the dory fill again and passed the light. The water quieted. In the darkness he could see the looming cliffs on either hand. The entrance swung to the westward and the sail flapped idly.

"Come and row!" Jarge cried in Angus' ear. "We's in Wake Bay!"

But Angus was drugged with the cold. He pushed Jarge away and would not move. Jarge shipped the oars and pulled the dory alone toward the western cliff. He listened for the lap of water on a beach. There was only the sob and groan of swell against the sheer walls with their caves and suck holes. Then he heard the "shissh" of wave on shingle. He pointed the dory's nose at the sound and pulled madly. The bow grated on sand. He jumped over the rail and ran in with the dory beside him. He ran as far up as he could. Then he waited for the next wave to lift her and heave her in again.

"Angus," he shouted, "get out and feel the land!"

He dragged the drooping form of the big man over the dory's rail and dumped him on the shingle. The fall roused him and he staggered up on legs that clumped like wooden stumps.

"Pull, Angus!" Jarge commanded. "Pull her up and we tips her over for a shelter. Oi makes a fire. Den we sleeps."

"Gott, like broken bones is me legs," Angus said. "Aye, haul her up. Den we sleeps."

Together they pulled the dory a length on the sand and tipped her bottom side up. Jarge put a trawl tub under the leeward rail so they could crawl in. Angus started on his hands and knees.

"No! Angus, run wid me. Chase me, Angus! Look!" He pulled at the big man's shoulder and sprawled him on the sand. "Look! Oi can slap big Angus' Dutch face! Ho! Ho! Ho! Look, little Jarge is de better man! Look! If Marty could see!"

He wormed on top of Angus' chest and pulled off his mittens. Right and left hand he slapped the big man's blinking face. Angus tossed and bellowed, and threw him off. He tried to rise, and Jarge gave him a hand, then darted away, dancing before him, reaching in like a boxer, slapping the swinging, lowered head as he willed. Angus, like a bear, lumbered after him faster, faster, until Jarge had to turn and run forward. A cliff appeared. He tried to sidestep, but Angus caught him. Jarge kicked and stomped with his boots, but the big fist pommeled about his head until he reeled.

"Gott"—Angus fell back on the sand—"de pain in me feet is terrible."

Jarge darted in again and kicked at the big boots.

" 'Tis the frost goin' out," he yelled, "de hot blood comin' in! Keep dem hurtin'! Jump on dem! Up and dance, ye big soft Dutchy! Takes Oi to keep ye from dyin'!"

Jarge Makes In

"Newfie," Angus shouted, "I catches you——"

Jarge tripped him and pulled on the boot that waved before his face. It came off in his hands. Beyond the sand which had been cleared by the tide was a white bank of snow. Far up into it Jarge galloped and dropped the boot. He ran back and grabbed the other.

Angus kicked at him, but he fell back with it in his hand and ran to leave it with its mate.

"Now," he shouted, "go git thim! When ye gets back, Oi'll have shavin's for a fire!"

The soft pine thwart gave off shavings sodden at first, but white and dry underneath. He made a pile of them and fished under his oilskins for his match box. The tiny flame bore against the shavings, flickered, then caught. Yellow and warm, the blaze burned.

Jarge sank on his back under the dory.

"Sweet Mary," he said, "we makes in. 'Twas a hard bit of travel. Bring the marnin'."

Angus hobbled up in his boots and peered under the dory. He crawled up close beside Jarge and, sitting with his legs stretched out toward the warmth, slowly broke the thwarts into small pieces of fuel and piled them slowly and neatly.

The village was deserted as they paddled to the dock. The sun was breaking the clear horizon. Virgin snow lay on the winding street, thick on the housetops. The sun burned it purple and pink. There were no trees. They stood and watched the smoke drifting from the chimneys for a moment, then made the dory fast and broke the first trail up the street. A Newfoundland dog as large as a pony barked at them, then followed silently at their heels, his breath steaming. His black coat was as jet as their rubber suits. They passed the church, alone and omnipotent in its drifted, fenced yard. The path of the parish house had been freshly swept.

Jarge opened the gate and walked steadily toward the door. Angus, looking about, hesitated, then followed. A woman with a white cap and an apron opened the door, and they moved into a large room where a fire crackled in the grate.

The room was full of the smell of heat to their fresh noses.

There was the smell of bacon frying. They both breathed deeply to get enough air, relishing the bacon.

A door opened and the priest appeared. He was tall and white-skinned above his black robe. His hawklike face was set with intense black eyes. The eyes regarded Jarge calmly.

"So," he said, "you have come."

"Yis, father."

"You got my letter?"

"Yis. It said regardin' that Oi had an engagement wid ye. A duty ye said, Oi had."

"Yes, you have. Where is Tim? Tim O'Shane?"

"He's gone. On Sable Bank. He was astray and gone."

"He's dead?"

"Yis, father."

"Which one of you—you or Tim"—the priest's black eyes were steady as balls of jet—"is the one?"

Jarge trembled in his neck as he swallowed.

"Oi," he said, white-faced, his eyes held by the steady jet eyes of the priest. Their blackness became gentle. So did the voice:

"How did you come?"

"We comes from Burgeo Bank. We sails in de dory."

"Last night?"

"Yis. We was astray. 'Twas hivin planned it, father."

"Yes," the priest said slowly. "Yes."

His hand reached for a bell pull, and the bell jangled in the back of the house.

"You are all right?" he asked. "You have no frozen places?"

"Angus, dere, had swold feet. Oi's foine. Me blood was warm all de way."

"Some breakfast for these men," the priest told the white-capped woman who answered the bell, "and a basin and some water. Hot and cold water to bathe that man's feet. They are not frozen," he told Angus, "or you would be in agony. I must go say mass. Have your breakfast and wait for me. I want to go with you. I want to see her eyes."

The three, the priest in a fur coat and sealskin boots, turned in at the small, unpainted cottage. There was a curl of smoke from its rock chimney, drifting away into the blue, clear air.

The priest opened the door and held it while Jarge and Angus filed inside. A stove was in the center of the single room. Rocking beside it, a hooked rug under her feet, was an old, wrinkled woman with white hair. Beside the window, with the sunlight streaming across its patchwork quilt, was a bed, and on its pillow a girl's face. It was young and of a singular peasant beauty; pale and eager and lonely. Brown eyes dominated it, possessed it utterly, for she could neither speak nor hear. They filled with question as Jarge moved forward on his boots. Question that leaped into panic and terror as he walked forward slowly. For Jarge's eyes, watery and blue, were filled with an ecstasy as if the room were echoing with hosannas and peals of organ.

"Tim's dead," his lips formed the words without sound. They said it over again, shaping the words so she could read his lips. "Oi's come—to take his place."

She shook her head at him wildly, tossing her hair. Her hand reached up and brushed it from the baby's face on her shoulder. It was a knob of tiny skull, fuzz-covered, asleep. Jarge sank on his knees and his black heavy-coated arms enfolded them both. Her arms were white as gull breast against the black. Her fingers plucked at his rubber-coated back.

The priest stood above them, writing a note. He held it before her eyes. Jarge read it with her.

"Tim O'Shane is dead," it read. "George, here, has told me he is the father of the child. Is this so?"

Jarge pushed the priest's hand away.

"Oh, father, don't shame her wid the question," he pleaded. "'Tis Oi. Oi comes in wid hivin steerin'. Oi loves her dear. Say us de mass. Say it quick and give de brat a name. 'Tis mine."

The priest watched her eyes for verity. Their panic drained away and gratitude, breathless as worship, glowed and enveloped Jarge with its warmth. It was a warmth beyond the smoking blood of seals, beyond the glow of the fire on the shingle. The priest nodded gravely in judgment. He did not stop when her head—so slowly it barely seemed to move—made the "No" that was the unimportant truth.

"Bow your heads," the priest said.

He began the simple wedding ceremony:

"*Ego conjungo vos*——"

The Living Torpedo

Tom Yates

THE SUBMARINE TRICORN was fifty hours out, and two degrees south of the Arctic Circle at noon that day. She was at a depth of two hundred feet, traveling on a course taking her steadily in toward the Norwegian coast, when Rogers called Harris and Ryan to the wardroom and opened their orders.

He began reading aloud, "'You will attack and destroy the German battleship Prinz Wilhelm now lying in Nordkyn Fiord—'"

He read slowly on through three closely typed pages of instruction and information, and there was a long silence when he had finished. Ryan and Harris were trembling very slightly, and Rogers felt himself sweating in spite of the dank chill of the oil-tainted air.

"It won't be very comfortable," said Rogers at last.

"Nothing's comfortable in this water," said Ryan. He eased his stocky body away from the bulkhead and sat on the forward bunk next to Harris. "Thirty-two degrees is just on freezing point," he said.

Rogers got up from the narrow bench and peeled off his dirty jacket with the stripes of a commander on the sleeves. He tossed the jacket into a corner and pulled out a bottle of gin from the bottom drawer of the tiny sideboard built against the curving plates of the pressure hull.

"I don't envy you," said Rogers. "The Germans have been hiding the Prinz Wilhelm in this fiord for over a month now, and they're bound to be expecting trouble." He placed three cracked glasses on the table, picked up the orders and studied them again. "The Norwegians who sent us the dope about the defense nets report that explosive charges are being dropped all round the ship if the kraut submarine detectors pick up as much as a shoal of fish. They must be pretty jittery." Rogers pulled the empty water carafe from its socket on top of the sideboard, stared at it, then pushed it across the table. "Harris," he said, "nip along to the messroom and get some water, will you?"

Harris stood up—a slight, almost delicate-looking figure in soiled dungaree trousers and a thick, white diver's sweater. His dirty, laceless sneakers slopped on the threadbare carpet as he made for the curtain dividing the wardroom from the alleyway.

"Get some out of the galley, Bogey," said Ryan. "It's quicker."

Harris nodded, and they heard the hurried slip-slop of his shoes receding.

"A man of few words, our Harris," said Rogers.

"He can be loquacious at times," grinned Ryan. "When I

The mission of destruction described in this story will no doubt seem as incredible to many readers as it did to the Post editors when they first read it. As fiction it is, however, no more fantastic—perhaps even less so—than the similar missions on which author Yates himself served as a real-life human torpedo in World War II. In 1941, when he was twenty-five years old, Tom Yates had been a soldier of fortune, a professional welterweight boxer, a seaman on the China coast, and a deep-sea diver. This last experience led to his serving for thirteen months in one of the war's most nearly suicidal jobs—torpedo driver. In that duty the casualties were, of course, enormous. As to the accomplishments of the living torpedoes, it can only be said they were so extensive that the British Admiralty still classifies the names of the ships they sank and the ports they attacked as Top Secret. —*The Editors.*

started off training—in ordinary diving dress—I had to attend him while he did an emergency job on some ship's screw. I let him fall ten feet, and what he told me when I got him up and got his helmet off was an education."

"I can quite imagine," said Rogers dryly.

Ryan chuckled. "I was green to this human-torpedo game, then. I told him that that was no way for a seaman to talk to a lieutenant."

"What did friend Harris have to say to that?"

"He pointed out that being killed underwater by me wouldn't be any more pleasant for him if I were an admiral, let alone a lieutenant. And a reserve lieutenant at that. And, as he was a qualified diver and I wasn't, he was the best judge of the capabilities of whoever was attending him." Ryan smiled. "I had to admit the justice of his argument. And after that we decided to team up together on the Jeeps."

"He's a good boy," said Rogers.

"We're all good boys . . . or we'd better be," replied Ryan, as Harris returned.

Rogers poured a stiff tot for each, and they showed the glasses to the water carafe.

"Here's luck," said Rogers, and emptied his glass. He set it down with a sigh.

"Do you think you've got everything taped?" he said.

Ryan put his drink down and leaned back on the bunk with his eyes half closed. "You launch us three miles off the mouth of the fiord at eleven o'clock tonight," he said in a flat monotone. "We run in those three miles, course about east-nor'east, and another two and a half up the fiord until we come to the antisubmarine boom. This should take about two hours. Right?"

Rogers nodded. "Your part now, Harris," he said.

"Boom consists of three nets. Antisubmarine net with a wide mesh—we'll get her through that, Alan . . . sir. Then two antitorpedo nets made of small, intermeshed rings. We'll have to get under them, unless we can find a gap somewhere. Nets are about two hundred yards apart."

"Yes. There's a point there," said Rogers. "The German nets are sixty feet deep from top to bottom, and, according to what charts we've got, even at high tide there is only about sixty feet of water in that stretch of the fiord where they're laid. You might have trouble getting under."

"No chance of going round the end, sir?"

"Not a hope," replied Rogers. "They're carried right up the beach."

"As usual," said Ryan. "Right! Then we've got about a quarter of a mile to go before the next lot."

"That's it," said Rogers. "About five minutes' run. . . . Harris?"

"Two more intermeshed antitorpedo nets enclosing the Prinz Wilhelm in the form of a rectangle. Nets are about twenty yards apart, and a hundred and fifty yards from the ship's hull at the nearest point."

"Yes." Rogers poured out another tot for each, but left the glasses on the table. He put the bottle back in the bottom drawer and kicked it shut. "Just how you are going to get through those two, I wouldn't know," he said. "They're also sixty-foot nets, and apparently there is only fifty feet of water where Prinz Willie is lying. Your best proposition would be to tackle one of the corners, I think. There's bound to be a small gap somewhere."

Harris tugged gently at his right ear. "The only other thing is the submarine detectors," he said.

"You'll just have to be damn careful, that's all." Rogers grinned at him, but his eyes were doubtful. "If it's any comfort to you, what German gear we have captured isn't as good as ours; and, as you know, even ours doesn't always pick you up."

"Fair enough," said Harris.

"Well, that's that," said Ryan. "Apart from a head wind and sea, and freezing water, the run in is a piece of cake."

"Um-m," said Rogers. "You'll set the fuse for five o'clock, Harris, eh?"

"Yes, sir. Head to be attached to the keel plate under the engine or boiler room."

"That's the ticket. The whole job should take about five hours. Two hours in, an hour for the nets and placing the head, and two hours to get out again. That'll leave you one hour's spare oxygen in your breathing sets in case of accidents."

There was a short silence.

"I mean——" began Rogers.

"Quite, sir," said Ryan. He spoke rapidly, "The rendezvous with Tricorn is at the spot where you launch us. You'll surface at three-thirty A.M., and dive again at four-thirty, whether we're there or not."

"That's it, I'm afraid. I can't leave it any later. We'll flash a masked green light in the direction of the fiord while we're waiting, but it will be visible at one mile only. So don't panic if you don't pick it up first shot." He handed the drinks around. "I think that's about all," he said. "What torpedo are you riding?"

Harris smiled faintly. "Number Six, sir. Lucretia," he said.

"Lucretia?"

"She took us down to a hundred and twenty feet the first time we rode her, and we both had a bad go of oxygen poisoning before we could get her up again," explained Harris.

"I see. Well, here's luck," said Rogers. He drained his glass again, and then, for the first time, showed signs of awkwardness. "I know, of course, that—— Look, I don't need to impress on you guys the importance of sinking this battle wagon," he said at last. "If you bring it off—— Well, damn it all, you know what I mean. Morale back home, and freeing some of our ships from watching for her, and one thing and another." He looked vaguely at the empty glasses. "But I certainly don't envy you," he said again.

"It'll be all right, sir," said Ryan.

"No trouble at all," affirmed Harris.

"I hope so," said Commander Rogers. "Well, I'm going to take her up to periscope depth and have a squint round. You fellers had better get some sleep. I'll see you are shaken in plenty of time."

Harris woke slowly. He felt sluggish, and there was an unpleasant taste in his mouth. The submarine, submerged since she had surfaced to charge batteries at midnight the night before, was very cold; the air, damp from the sweating hull, was dead and badly vitiated. There was an electric silence, intensified rather than broken by the almost inaudible hum of the motors as they crept in toward the enemy coast at a depth of ninety feet.

Ryan appeared through the tiny doorway in the watertight bulkhead. He, too, had been sleeping. He looked drawn and nervy. Harris could understand it. There was a void where his own stomach should have been.

They knew fear. All the Jeepmen did. There were so many things that could go wrong, even before they got near the enemy. A breakdown in the breathing apparatus in deep water. The constant risk of being trapped in the toxic zone below thirty-three feet, where oxygen poisoning crept on you. First one's lips quivering, then twitching spasmodically, so that one could not grip the mouthpiece and suck in the essential but deadly oxygen. Then the whole body shaking, shuddering violently, until it went into convulsions, and one died a dreadful death alone in the cold, hostile depths. There were isolated fresh-water patches from mountain torrents that sent the Jeep plunging toward the bottom while they struggled madly to adjust oxygen supplies and to clear their ears against the tremendous, rapidly increasing pressure of the water. A breathing bag, torn on the barnacle-encrusted nets, injecting a rush of icy water, instead of warm oxygen, full into the lungs with a blinding shock.

And always the persistent fear that perhaps, when real danger came, their courage would fail, and they would succumb to that lurking panic that constantly sought to master them.

Down in the submarine they thrust these thoughts aside. It was always like this before a dive, and nothing ever happened. But it might. Jimmy Spears had blown his lungs to shreds, and Ted Winship had drowned in training. And this time it was the real thing. If they got into trouble below, there could be no help, no hope for them. And if they were detected they would be showered with depth charges, and met with a hail of bullets if they surfaced. And they had no defense.

Ryan cleared his throat. "Half past ten, Bogey," he croaked. "Won't be long now."

Harris grunted, and forced a smile. Together they bent to examine their gear for the last time. The one-piece suits with the skirted opening in the belly where they struggled in. They were of light rubberized fabric, with a heavy, sponge-rubber headpiece or hood with a black rubber gas-mask facepiece cemented on the front. There was no air in the suits when they dived. A tube ran from the mask to the breathing bag, and connected to a rubber mouthpiece that projected inside the dress. This was gripped between the teeth, with a shield between lips and gums making an airtight joint through which to suck the oxygen. The suits were dry and freshly chalked along the seams where extra solution had been rubbed in, and they stank of rubber and disinfectant.

They went over the webbing harnesses that fitted over their shoulders and belted round their waists. They each carried a weighted, rectangular, black rubber breathing bag, or lung, high up on the chest; and a cage containing two alloy bottles of oxygen at high pressure that rested low on the back. The lung and the bottles were connected by a flexible tube, and a by-pass valve was fitted to enable a burst of high-pressure oxygen to be injected into the bag at will. One liter of oxygen per minute flowed constantly into the bag.

They examined the rope laces of the weighted canvas boots. The long knives were greased. Everything was ready, and, as they completed their inspection, they heard quiet orders being given in the control room:

"Break down. . . . Dead slow. . . . Up to periscope depth."

They felt the boat tilt slightly; then came the gentle upward pressure of the deck as she lifted. She straighted on to even keel again.

"Up periscope!"

They looked at each other. Ryan took a little phial of tablets from his pocket, and they swallowed three each. Harris gave Ryan a cigarette, and put one in his own mouth. The match burned feebly in the stale air. Their tension mounted in the long silence.

Rogers came as the boat dived again. "We are on the spot, men," he said, "and there's a gale blowing up top." He hesitated for a moment, then held out a signal form. "I've got some bad news, I'm afraid," he went on. "While you were sleeping I received a retransmitted message from a recco plane. It warns us that the Germans are sweeping the nets around the ship with a searchlight."

"A searchlight!" ejaculated Harris.

Ryan sat down heavily and drew hard on his cigarette. Harris gazed blankly at Rogers.

"Things look a bit doubtful," said Rogers. "They've got their boats patrolling their nets, too, and a launch on the center net of the boom defense."

"It seems almost as though something has leaked out in Norway," said Ryan thoughtfully.

"It's possible that they have been tipped off," Rogers agreed, "but they can't know exactly what they are looking for." He avoided their eyes carefully. "The question is: Are you going to chance having a stab at it?"

Ryan frowned down at the steel deck, then looked at Harris. Harris smiled faintly back at him.

"Nearly time we got dressed, isn't it, Alan?" he said evenly.

Ryan nodded.

Rogers opened his mouth to speak, then closed it again. He gestured toward the suits.

"O.K. Hurry," he said.

They stripped, and the two dressers took their clothes, their paybooks and their identity disks. They pulled on union suits of pure, heavy silk, and silk socks. Similar suits of soft, closely woven wool, and woolen socks. Then two heavy white sweaters, two pairs of long underpants, and two pairs of thigh-length stockings of the same heavy white wool.

They sat down, opened the skirts of the suits and forced their legs in, pulled the suits over their shoulders and thrust their arms down the sleeves, hands through the tight rubber cuffs. Wrist bands adjusted, they ducked their heads inside and forced them up through the narrow necks into the rubber helmets.

The attendants folded the skirts and clamped them, making a watertight joint which they tucked away, buckling the folds of the suit over all. The high boots were laced tight, a long sharp knife in a metal sheath tucked into each one. Nose clips were fixed tightly over the nostrils, and when mouthpieces were comfortably adjusted, the helmet straps were pulled tight. Finally, the visors, heavily coated inside with an antidimming compound, were closed down and clamped tight. They were ready as far as they could be.

The boat slanted suddenly, and they felt her rising again. There came a noise of rushing water and the sound of waves slapping against the outside of the thin hull. She leveled and began to roll slowly.

The attendants picked up the harnesses, and the divers clumped in their heavy boots along to the control room. As they arrived, the order, "Divers and dressers on the bridge!" came down the voice pipe. The attendants started up the steel ladder. Ryan and Harris took one last look round the control room, dim in the red night light, and followed. They were both sweating profusely now, and as he struggled through the lower hatch into the conning tower, and clambered up toward the bridge hatch, Harris reflected grimly that they would pay for it later.

On the bridge the gale hit them. The night was black. The wind, howling out of the east, whipped the sea into sharp, choppy waves which were flattened almost as soon as they were formed. Ryan saw, and cursed softly into his mask.

The Jeep was being dragged out of its cylinder as they shrugged into their harnesses. The breathing tubes were connected to the facepieces, the bottles opened and the soft hiss of oxygen started. They closed the exhaust valves at the bottom of the bags and sucked them empty of air, coughing slightly from the fine dust off the carbon-dioxide absorbent canister, expelling the air by switching the mouthpiece cocks alternately from air to oxygen. Then they cracked their by-pass valves until they were breathing pure oxygen.

Down on the casing they were alone with the Jeep. Harris waved a hand when they were ready, and saw the head on the bridge duck toward the voice pipe.

For a moment nothing happened. Then there was a roar of escaping air. Fountains of spray leaped high from the vents, and they felt a wave of unreasoning panic as the casing deck sank beneath them. The suits contracted and gripped as the water swirled about their knees, then their waists. The long torpedo with the detachable head bobbed free of the cradle, the top of the body just above the racing waves.

They scrambled astride it, crouching behind their rounded shields; Ryan at the controls and Harris behind. Ryan flicked the throttle and they moved slowly away from the submarine. Fifty yards off they stopped, and, opening the sea cock, Ryan started the pump. Slowly they sank into the black water. Harris threw the lever that opened the main ballast tank in front of him, and they dropped a foot, suddenly.

Carefully Ryan judged his time until, with their eyes just level with the surface, and the machine weighted with water until it would lie motionless, neither rising nor sinking, he switched off the pump and closed the sea cock.

Harris twisted to face the submarine and gave a momentary blink of the underwater flashlight. The figure on the bridge disappeared.

The dim black bulk surged slowly forward. Great gouts of water and compressed air spurted from the tanks, and the sea boiled white as the last of the deck submerged. The conning tower tilted, diminished slowly, vanished. The periscope standard left a streak of white water, then was gone. There was a smooth, swirling patch in the broken seas.

The gale whistled in their helmet exhaust valves, and the icy waves battered at them. The Jeep rolled wildly. Oxygen hissed sibilantly into their breathing bags. They were alone, and each began the long, lonely battle against his own fear.

They were cruising with their eyes just above surface, the wind-blown waves smacking full into their faces. They were well up the fiord, and they could see, dimly, the hills on either side, looming an intenser black against the blackness of the sky.

The luminous dial of the clock on the instrument panel showed one o'clock. They had been away two hours now, and already their hands were numb and swelling, their feet and legs dead and cramped. The clothing under their suits, dampened when they had sweated in the heat of the Tricorn's belly, had long ago chilled through; the penetrating cold creeping through the woolens, slowly freezing and numbing. Only two hours gone.

Ryan crouched over the controls, concentrating on keeping a steady course, wondering and worrying how much farther they had to go before they reached the boom. Harris, while his eyes kept ceaseless vigil, had blanked off half his brain and was thinking of Janet and his next leave. He had found this the only way of enduring the long run-in before he did his part on the nets and the ship's bottom. It kept his mind off things that might go wrong, off the cruel cold, and stifled the ever-present thought that the slightest false move would bring the shattering depth charges to crush them to pulp in their suits below. Just keep on thinking of Janet.

Faintly, borne on the wings of the gale, they caught the restless, eternal clanging of the net buoys as they jostled and bobbed against one another on the hurrying waves.

There was a sudden blinding flash up the fiord, and the Prinz Wilhelm's searchlight swept deliberately along the nets hemming her in. The glare reflected momentarily on the buoys of the boom nets two hundred yards ahead. Then the light died, leaving a denser blackness.

Ryan sighted his compass, waved his hand and pushed forward on the joy stick. The Jeep tilted, and the roar of the wind was shut off abruptly as she slid below in a long, steep glide. They dived deep, charging their bags with short blasts from the by-passes; blowing their noses hard against the nose clips to relieve the agony of uncleared ears; letting quick spurts of oxygen past their lips into the helmets to keep the masks from crushing in on their faces.

At sixty feet they leveled out in a cold black world that pressed in on them fiercely. They moved in a cloud of phosphorescent sparks, leaving a comet tail behind them. For some minutes Ryan kept her at full speed, then throttled down to half. Seconds later they felt the cushioned bump as they met the first net. Ryan switched off, and they clambered stiffly along the head to the net, and hung there like two grotesque spiders while they struggled to force the Jeep through the mesh. After what seemed an age, they succeeded, and the machine lay there, still, with just the slightest tendency to rise. They climbed aboard again, and dived toward bottom. It was nearer than Ryan thought, and they bumped badly at sixty-eight feet.

They skimmed along, barely clear of the rocky bottom. They went on and on across the two hundred yards between the nets. Then startlingly, ghostly, phosphorescent and weed-grown, the second net swept out of the blackness over their heads, clear by a foot. Somewhere, nearly seventy feet above them in the clean cold gale, a boat was floating; German seamen huddled together for warmth, watching for a vague menace.

Ryan looked again at the clock. One-eighteen. They had been nearly seventy feet down for seventeen minutes. His breathing was shortening, and he prayed silently that they would not be held up too long on the last net. He could not stay much longer at this depth.

Harris, in the rear seat, lay over the ballast tank, alternately swearing and praying into his mouthpiece. The cold had crept up his thin, wiry body until it had reached his waist. Icy daggers of pain stabbed through the small of his back, his kidneys aching until he could have wept with the pain. Confined in his suit, alone in the vast blackness, he struggled desperately with the almost-overwhelming temptation to charge his emergency buoyancy bag, shoot to the surface and flash the torch until a patrol boat came and picked him up. To risk the prison camp . . . or a bullet. Anything was better than this.

They struck the third net hard. Harris pulled himself off and reeled along the ocean bed like a man in drink. Ryan, although more fleshy than Harris, was also feeling the chill beginning to creep up his spine, and he was thankful for the break from sitting still in the frigid water.

Until they got forward and examined the net. Five rows of rings rested on the bottom in a tangled heap. The rest of the net vanished upward in the darkness, a rigid steel wall.

Somehow those five rows of foot-wide steel rings, inert there on the bottom, had to be lifted clear while the Jeep was passed underneath. Somehow they had to support a weight of some hundred and fifty pounds each, four feet off the bottom, and move the Jeep at the same time. In pitch blackness, hampered by the constricting but vulnerable dress and breathing apparatus, they had to struggle with a mass of heavy, hopelessly entangled steel rings and the twenty-seven-foot length of the torpedo.

They went in opposite directions along the net, searching for a gap or gully in the sea bed where there would not be such a great mass of net. They returned knowing that there was not a foot of difference in depth all the way across that deeper section of the fiord.

They wept tears of rage and exhaustion. The net slipped and tore from their hands. Isolated rings hung down, and as fast as they gathered one up, two more would fall in its place. They snagged on the breakwaters, they caught on the controls and jammed there. The whole weight fell across Harris' saddle, and they had to rest before they could start to raise it again. They labored and strained and sweated in the darkness, heaving and tugging like madmen. They ran insane risks of tearing the lungs on the clustered barnacles, of being trapped under the net. Their numbed hands were torn to ribbons, lacerated until they felt the pain even through the numbness. They got the Jeep through, but they were in a bad way.

They had been almost seventy feet under water for three quarters of an hour. Their jaws were shuddering, their quivering lips letting go oxygen that their heaving lungs demanded.

They fell rather than climbed aboard the Jeep, and, fighting off oblivion, Ryan sent her reaching full speed for the surface in a steep climb. For ten minutes they lay there, heads just above water, until their lips steadied, the panting stopped and the poisoning oxygen began to work out of bloodstream and tissue. Until the cold began to creep on them again.

They waited for the searchlight to sweep round, and Ryan lined his compass on the nearest corner of the antitorpedo nets in the flash. Then they forged ahead once more, with a quarter of a mile to go to the last barrier.

They were a bare two hundred yards from the nets when the searchlight flashed again. A cutter, the crew pulling silently and slowly, was silhouetted before the light died. They dived to fifteen feet at half speed, down into the dead silence below. They hit the net, and Ryan held on while Harris worked along the rings and located the corner. As he fumbled in the darkness, the black water glowed into a deep emerald as the enemy search-light passed over the surface. In the dim light Harris saw the corner. Where the joint of the net came there was a gap a foot wide that extended down to his level at fifteen feet.

He thought, *O God, we'll never get out of this,* and there came the rush of desire for the clean air above; the surging, fear-driven instinct that fought against putting any more obstacles between himself and safety. The words "Attack and destroy . . . attack and destroy," began running through his mind, over and over in crazy repetition, and the saliva began dribbling and bubbling in his mouthpiece. He gripped desperately at the cold steel of the net, and fought to regain his failing courage.

At last he went slowly back to the Jeep, and together he and Ryan dragged the machine to the gap and forced it through. The net's own weight, stretching to the bottom, kept it rigid, and they had to lever and strain before it gave way to them.

A wire rope, part of the moorings, ran between the outer and inner nets, and they pulled themselves and the Jeep across the intervening space on this. The corner of the inner net had a corresponding gap that was, if anything, slightly larger. They struggled again, cursing the total blackout that followed each flash of the lights, venting that fierce nervous rage that seizes the diver when the slightest thing goes wrong.

At two-fifteen they were through. Ryan steered about twenty feet away from the inner net and parallel to it. The Prinz Wilhelm was a hundred and forty yards or so to their left. They ran for a few minutes, then Ryan eased down to dead slow and brought their heads to within two feet of the surface. He waited until the light swept over them again, then poked his head above water for a split second. The massive hulk loomed up, blotting out the frosty brilliance of the stars. They were amidships, abreast the towering funnel. Ryan ducked back and sent the Jeep into a steep dive, turning in toward the ship.

They hit the side glancingly at twenty-five feet. As they touched, Ryan switched off, and Harris, a flat multiple magnet in each hand, gripped the torpedo with his legs and began pulling the machine down the hull.

At thirty-three feet the side began to sheer in to form the bottom. They worked in under the bilge keel, which projected a yard or more. Then, with the depth gauge showing forty feet, they were right under in the suffocating blackness, clinging with the magnets to the vast, almost-flat bottom.

Harris, holding on to both magnet lanyards with one hand, felt around above his head until he found a double row of rivets. They would be holding a small rib inside the hull. He started again with his magnets, placing them as gently as he could, hand over hand, following the rivet line. He had no other means of sensing direction in this unfamiliar territory, and they were in such blackness that they could not even see the inside of their masks. Without a lead to the center line of the ship, they would wander, possibly for hours, before finding the vital keel.

Harris went slowly on until, beginning to think that he had missed it, he felt the thick, heavily riveted keel plate above his head. He plugged the two magnets against the plate and lashed the lanyards to the rail across the ballast tank, anchoring the Jeep firmly. They were right where the charge would break the ship's back and flood the machinery compartments above them. They could hear the boiler-room noises clearly. The slow, soft hiss and click of a pump. An occasional clang or clatter that brought their hearts to their mouths. They were preparing to blast the men that made those sounds into eternity, and the thought brought to their minds the measure of the mercy they could expect if they were discovered.

In spite of their exertions on the nets, the cold had gripped them again. Harris turned around with difficulty, his frozen lower body obeying his will only with immense effort. His brain, beginning to be affected by the cold and the oxygen, worked slowly. He had to think hard before he knew what he wanted to do, then force himself, step by step, to do it. There were more magnets in the locker behind him, and he lifted them out, all clinging together in a tight bunch. Painfully he detached the two spares, replaced them, and twisted the lanyards of the other two round his left wrist.

Then he slid out of his seat and pulled himself forward. When he reached the head he paused for a moment and checked, once again, the position of the keel above the Jeep. Satisfied that the head was directly below the plate, he clamped on the magnets and lashed the lanyards to the securing rail along the top of the head. Again he had to pause, to stretch his cracking muscles against a cramp that had suddenly seized his loins. To fight a dread, a violent spasm of fear that swept him, bidding him, while he could still move, to get out from under the huge mass above him. To get to where he could surface quickly in case of trouble. He had to hang there in the thick darkness for seconds that felt like hours until, having checked the blast of his by-pass valve and made sure that his deadened hands could still work the tap, he was able to conquer that piercing stab of fear.

Slowly he worked his way along the head. He found the fuse switch and removed the protective cover, which he tucked into his left boot. Each movement took an age, his senseless fingers feeling again and again before he could be sure that he was doing what he wished. His thumbs would not stay rigid, and he had to clasp his fist around the switch before he could move it. He counted the clicks. Half an hour, an hour, an hour and a half, two hours, two and a half. Set for five o'clock. He could not feel the raised figures on the fuse face, and he had to risk flicking the torch on the dial. Two and a half hours.

He made his way back to the joint between the head and the body, and hung on Ryan's leg shield. Then he pulled the securing pin out, lifted the lever and detached the head. It floated gently upward until it nudged the keel plate.

Deprived of the slight buoyancy of the head, the Jeep body tilted forward a little. As Harris worked aft toward his seat, Ryan opened the seacock with trembling, fumbling hands, and pumped enough water out of the foremost tank to compensate for the loss.

As he settled himself, Harris removed one of the two magnets supporting the body, and banged Ryan on the shoulder. He felt the slight vibration as the motor started, and wrenched the other magnet free. They dropped, leveled; then, as they cleared the ship's sphere of magnetic influence, and the compass steadied, they steered for the net.

They missed the corner, and it took Harris seven precious minutes to find the gaps. They carried a coil of light rope in the locker, and he climbed up and along the net with the end made fast to his belt while Ryan kept the slack in hand. By the time they had once again forced the Jeep through, both men were exhausted. It would be nerve only from then on. Frozen, physically almost finished, minds numbed with cold and oxygen, they were as good as beaten.

As they cleared the antitorpedo nets, Ryan sent the torpedo down to thirty. He timed the dive by the clock, and did not surface until they were four hundred yards away—within easy distance of the inner boom net.

There seemed to be a lull in the gale when they surfaced, and the waves were now beating on their backs. Ryan looked again at the clock; 2:47.

He had to force his sluggish brain to think. They had been two hours running in, and three quarters of an hour getting through the three boom nets. It was thirteen minutes to three now, and Tricorn would dive at four-thirty sharp. They had a following wind and sea which would cut their cruising time down the fiord considerably, but even then the most that they could allow for clearing the boom was twenty minutes.

It was impossible. Apart from the time factor, Ryan knew—they both knew—that they could never survive another breakthrough on the inner net. When they had tackled it before, they had been comparatively fresh. Now they were dead tired, and, furthermore, the tide was ebbing and had probably dropped about two feet already. The mass of netting on the bottom would be even greater now. The only hope was to risk going over the top. That or give the game up.

Ryan steered for the shore. The buoys took the weight of the nets, and in shoal water the greater part of the net rested on the bottom, rendering it easier to force a passage between the buoys. The great danger lay in being sighted while the Jeep was showing above surface, half over the net. But the chance had to be taken.

He crept in at seven feet below the hissing waves. When they hit the steep beach he came up, bringing their heads above water, and turned down the fiord until they came to the buoys. He stayed with the machine while Harris went exploring along the net. He was back in a matter of minutes, and hung on alongside the body, steering. They struck the wire jackstay supporting the net between the sixth and seventh buoys. It was sagging almost two feet in the center, and it would be necessary to blow the main ballast tank and pump the internal tanks dry to get her over.

Harris maneuvered the nose of the body onto the jackstay while Ryan lay in the water working the pump controls. The Jeep rose out of the water, higher and higher. They could hear, plainly, the engine of the German boom-patrol boat on the center net.

They timed their effort with the intermittently flashing lights of the Prinz Wilhelm and, as one glare died, Ryan blew the main tank. The Jeep heaved out of the water and floated like a duck on the surface. With frantic haste they dragged her over the wire. It seemed impossible that they could escape detection. But they had vented the main tank and were pumping in again before the next flash came from up the fiord.

As the Jeep sank into the water they climbed aboard again, and Ryan made another laborious calculation. The center net had been about six feet off the bottom when they had come through. There would still be a space of some four feet if they were lucky. If they turned her on her side—

They cruised to the center of the fiord, eyes just showing. Ryan delayed the dive as long as possible, then, as the buoys came in sight, pushed her nose down and dropped almost vertically. He pulled her out at sixty, and they went down the last few feet on the net itself. It was a tight squeeze, and although they took only ten minutes to get her through, their depleted reserves were already fighting a losing battle against a recurrence of oxygen poisoning. They rose swiftly to ten feet and, despite his swimming head, Ryan kept her there until they came to rest on the last net.

Easily as they had cleared the antisubmarine net on the way in, it nearly broke them going out. Their limbs and the lower part of their bodies were practically useless, their muscles ineffectual, their heads aching to bursting point. But to give up at this stage was unthinkable, and in spite of their exhaustion they finally thrust the Jeep out to the safe side.

They kept at ten feet for five minutes, and surfaced some four hundred yards clear. They blew the main tanks and pumped out every ounce of interior water ballast, bringing themselves high out of the water and presenting a greater area to the following wind.

Harris looked back. The searchlights were still sweeping the nets around the Prinz Wilhelm, and down the wind came the faint chugging of the motorboat, still watching the boom nets.

Their bodies were finished. The nose clips pressed intolerably on nostrils worn raw, and their jaws were aching from the continual grip on the mouthpieces. The rubber cuffs of the suits bit into their swollen wrists, inflicting further agony on their already tortured arms.

Tricorn was somewhere in the blackness, six weary miles

away, but they were singing to themselves inside their masks as they set off down the fiord.

At four twenty-five that morning, the signalman of the Tricorn stopped flashing his shaded light and reported a white light appearing off the port beam. Rogers steadied himself against the periscope standard and trained his night glasses. . . .

They had to lift them aboard. They hoisted them up onto the bridge and lowered them gently down, through the conning tower, into the control room.

As they came out of the water, their torn hands streamed blood, and in the comparatively warm air of the hull the pain of returning circulation broke through their stupor, making them groan in agony.

The attendants stripped off their suits, cutting away the cuffs to get the sleeves over their distorted hands. They sat shuddering in a pool of water, propped up on the steel deck plates, while the coxswain trickled fiery neat rum between their locked jaws.

They were both beyond speech. Rogers questioned them gently, and Ryan managed to hold his thumbs up. Harris pointed weakly to the fuse cover that had fallen from his boot, and held up the finger and thumb of one hand. Then they both went suddenly and solidly to sleep where they sat.

Tricorn dived at 4:30 A.M., precisely. Commander Rogers sat motionless in the cramped wardroom, scarcely breathing. He had his wrist watch on the table before him, and he watched the second hand on its tedious journey round and round the dial. Slowly the minute hand crawled up to the hour, and the lines on Rogers' face deepened.

Even at the distance of ten miles they felt the tremendous concussion of the half-ton torpedo war head that shattered the mighty Prinz Wilhelm into a flaming ruin.

Rogers exhaled gustily, and his eyes closed for a moment. Then he methodically strapped his watch back on his wrist. The Jeepmen, bandaged and blanketed, were dead asleep in the two lower bunks, and Rogers' eyes softened as he looked at them. Then he picked up his cap and went back to the control room.

A Sailor to the Wheel

Bill Adams

THE SHIP had been three days at sea when the mate came up from the sail locker, dragging a stowaway by one ear. Maybe he'd brought a bite of something to eat with him when he came aboard and hid down there. Maybe he'd not. He looked starved, whether or no. You never saw such a package of skin and bone. You could see his ribs plainly through the rags of his tattered shirt. Barefoot he was, and without any hat. His ragged trousers were tied to his middle by a bit of frayed string. His hair was sandy and scant. His cheek bones stuck out. He was colorless quite; not a trace of pink in his face. A lad of maybe nineteen or twenty or so. But the queer thing was that he didn't look scared. Not a bit scared, with all the crew staring at him. He'd the most patient look you ever saw in his blue eyes. And not patient only. He actually wore something of a look of content!

The mate took him along to the skipper on the poop, of course. An old hard-case, the skipper was. Been skipper for twenty years or so. No sort of skipper to fool with, or try it. You could tell that by the sharky look in his gray eyes, by the way his lips set; and by his bony finger knuckles too.

Well, you can't turn a ship back when she's three days out, just to put a stowaway ashore. The mate shoved him in front of the skipper, and said, "Found him in the sail locker, sir."

The skipper gave the mate a look that would have frozen tropic water; looked at him for half a second, and turned away with a grunt, as much as to say, "What the devil d'ye mean by letting a stowaway get into her? And what the devil d'ye mean by bringing him to me, now you've found him?"

It was a cracking fine crew the ship had. Picked men, every one, barring the big Finn. The skipper'd picked them himself. He'd been round the Horn in midwinter plenty often, and was going round in midwinter again now. You don't want a crew of no-goods down there. One'd be too many altogether. It takes strong hands, and skilled, to pick up storm canvas in a hurricane in Latitude 56 south. And among all those dozen leathery, hard-case, able-bodied seamen, the kid looked—losh, I don't know what he looked like! Like a little lost cur pup among a pack of mastiffs maybe.

Same as it was with the skipper, the mate was no man to fool with. He wasn't exactly a bully bucko, but he'd been a lot too long at sea to have any exterior signs of any gentleness left to him. Maybe he wasn't as rough as he looked. But anyway he gave the kid a kick that sent him flying down the poop ladder and landed him sprawling on the quarter-deck below.

The kid got to his feet instantly, and stood looking at the mate, who was taking his time coming down the poop ladder after him. And the kid's expression seemed to say, "Anything you say, sir. I'm asking no favors."

"Get a holystone and a bucket of water. Start in and holystone the decks," said the mate.

"A holystone, sir?" asked the kid wonderingly. He'd never heard of a holystone, of course. So the mate called the big Finn, who was tucking an eye splice close by, and said to him, "Take him along and get him a holystone and a bucket of water."

The Finn looked at the mate from big, round, stolid eyes, and didn't move. That was the way with him. You had to tell him everything twice always, before he'd get it. If an order was given to all hands, or to two or three men together, he'd catch on right away by watching the others. But if he got an order direct, all to himself, it had to be repeated. Sort of slow, he was. Dumb, as you might say, but a cracking good hand despite it; for once he did catch on to an order he'd carry it out, hell, Hull or Halifax. Strong as an ox he was too. The skipper'd taken him because there had been no other hand around the shipping office near as husky. He wanted big, husky men as well as cracking good ones, the skipper did. And having taken eleven cracking good ones, he guessed maybe it'd be all right to take this dumb Finn fellow. Beef's what tells in a southern hurricane sometimes. Sometimes beef's as valuable as, sometimes more valuable than, sailorly skill and smartness down there.

The mate swore at the Finn and repeated the order; and then away rolled the Finn, with the stowaway tagging along at his heels. Looked like a starved Shetland pony at the heels of a dray horse. The Finn could have lifted him with one hand easily.

Back to the quarter-deck, with a holystone in one hand and a bucket of water in the other, came the stowaway kid.

"Yes, sir?" said he to the mate. "What do I do now, sir?"

"Get down on your knees and start scrubbing the planks with that stone," said the mate. The kid looked a bit puzzled, but got down on his knees and went to work. It was a bit after eight o'clock in the morning, just after breakfast. But no one had as much as asked him if he'd eaten, or wanted to eat.

Well, you know how it was in a ship at sea. She'd get her decks holystoned from end to end every year, at any rate. All hands were put to the job, usually in rainy weather when it wasn't too cold or too steamy hot. It'd take all hands a good many days to holystone her from forecastle head to the end of her poop. The most deadly, dull, monotonous job there is in a ship, just about. A sort of housemaid's job. No skill whatever needed. It'd take a whole crew a couple of weeks to get the entire deck holystoned, and maybe longer if the planks were pretty grimy.

Well, her decks were grimy all right. She was loaded with coal for Vallapo. It takes a lot of holystoning to clear pine planks of coal grime. By noon the kid hadn't got more than a few feet cleaned up. The mate came along and said, "All right. Go get your scoff now." And off to the forecastle went the kid, to get his scoff. He looked mighty tired and weak. The men were already scoffing when he got there, swigging down pea soup and munching salt pork. They'd emptied the mess tins and there wasn't a scrap of anything left. One of them glanced up and said, "Ye'll have to make out wi' hard-tack. Can ye make out wi' hard-tack, d'ye reckon?"

"What's hard-tack, sir?" asked the stowaway, and there was a guffaw all around at that. One of them picked a bit of hard-tack from the bread barge and held it up for the kid to see. "That's hard-tack," said he. "We've ate everything else. It's hard-tack or nuthin' for ye."

Well, you should have seen the shine in the kid's eyes! Pretty nigh starved he was, no doubt. "Thank you, sir," he said, and sat down and munched the flinty sea biscuit for all the world as though it were the finest scoff on earth. He ate three of them, one after another; just big, dry, flinty, ship biscuits, without so much as a smear of margarine on them. He started on a fourth, but gave out when half done. Hard-tack's made of pea meal and meat scraps; and it's mighty filling, even if it isn't very palatable.

Having been on duty all morning, the mate's watch turned into their bunks to sleep till four of the afternoon. The kid could have slept, too, but didn't. He went back to work, supposing he had to; and the second mate, supposing the mate had told him to, didn't say a word, but let him holystone all through the afternoon. When the mate came back on duty at four, he didn't notice the kid for a while; and then, when he did see him, supposed that he'd slept since noon. And he left him go on holystoning till six o'clock, when the day's work ended. Sort of a long day for the kid, eh?

When the mate's watch went below for supper, they sat down to hard-tack and margarine, with skilly to wash it down. "Skilly's" ship's name for tea. It's just a hot, thin, brown drink and tastes of nothing at all. But it's sort of comforting in a way, just as most any hot drink is when a man's cold and weary. The kid didn't have any margarine, of course, because the weekly allowance was always served out on Monday evening and it wasn't till Tuesday morning that the mate had found him. And he had no pannikin to drink skilly from. So he ate three and a half hard-tack plain again, and got some cooled-off skilly after the men were done with their pannikins.

The kid was dog tired, of course, but there wasn't a spare bunk he could lie down to sleep in till the mate's watch went back on duty at eight o'clock. So, while they sat yarning in the forecastle, he went out and lay down on the hard, bare planks and went dead-oh asleep in half a tick. But he didn't sleep long, for a bit of a squall blew up and the wind shifted; and running to haul a sail down, one of the second mate's men stumbled over him in the gloom. The man cussed, and the kid jumped up. It was dim starlight and he saw the second mate's men hauling on the ropes and went and joined them, not knowing enough to know that he didn't need to do so. It took the second mate's watch till eight o'clock to get sail off her and trim the yards for the shifted wind, and the kid worked among them till they were done; no one paying any attention to him at all. He was so thin they likely didn't even see him in the gloom. At eight it was time for the mate's watch to return to duty till midnight. The mate asked, "Where's that stowaway?" And he told the kid to get up to the forecastle head and keep lookout. "You can keep lookout till midnight," he said. A watch always takes it in turn to keep lookout, of course; each man keeping it for two hours. But the mate thought, "I'll have that kid keep lookout for the full four-hour watch every night. It'll give me all the men when there's any sail to be taken in or when the yards need trimming." The kid went up to keep lookout, and he was so dead tired he could hardly keep his eyes open. But he kept them open somehow. The mate had told him, "Keep a sharp lookout, or heaven help you! And shout good and loud if you see another ship's lights."

When the mate's watch went off duty at midnight, the kid was pretty near all in, I guess, having been on the go since eight in the morning with practically no let-up. Since there wasn't a bunk for him, he lay down on the bare planks and slept there, curled up like a puppy; while the men snored in their bunks above him. At four in the morning he had to keep lookout again till daylight. It was five by then, and time to start the day's work. Back he went to his holystoning. But that day he worked watch and watch, working when the mate's men were on duty and going off when they went off. The cook found him an old, dented, tin plate and a rusty old pannikin, and the men left him a dollop of pea soup and a few mouthfuls of salt pork for dinner.

All day, every day, the kid holystoned the deck, and every night he took all the lookouts. If there was any work on the sails or with the ropes by day, he was never called from his holystoning to lend a hand. And at night, of course, a lookout man stays where he is, whatever happens; unless called away in some emergency. Never a bit of sailoring did he get a chance at. No one paid the least attention to him; except that when Monday came round he was served a little whack of margarine, same as the men.

You should have seen the way the kid filled out. I guess he'd never in his life had three meals a day of any sort. By the way he scoffed it, you could tell that ship's food was fine fare to him. His cheeks grew plump, and his ribs disappeared, and he got some color. One of the men gave him an old shirt that was three or four sizes too big for him. Another rigged him out with an old pair of dungaree trousers that would have held two and a half of him; for even now that he was plumping up he was not much but a runt. Another chucked him an old belt. He found a pair of discarded blucher boots that some young sailor who must have been about his size had left aboard when he quit the ship after her last voyage. One day when the ship was getting down toward the tropics, the mate gave him a battered old sundowner hat. "Put that on your head, or you'll be geting the blasted sunstroke. We don't want no loonies aboard," the mate said.

The ship had been roundabouts three weeks at sea when she came to the tropics and picked up the northeast trade wind. The kid hadn't done a blessed thing but holystone. Sometimes when the men were hauling on the ropes, or furling or setting a sail, he'd look at them with a longing sort of light in his eyes. But he never said a word. All you ever heard from him was now and then when he called to the mate at night from the lookout. "Light on the starboard bow, sir!" or "Light on the port bow, sir!" or "Light right ahead, sir!" He always sang out quick and shrill, in an excited sort of way, as much as to say, "I'm a sailor! Here I am!"

Soon as the ship came to the tropics, the crew sent down the strong canvas she'd come down the North Atlantic under, replacing it with old sails good enough for the trade winds. And then at last the kid was taken from holystoning. So as to have all hands for shifting sail, the mate sent him to the wheel. "Watch your steering!" the mate warned him. And you know how it is with helmsmen. It's always a green hand that steers best. Being scary, he keeps his eyes on the compass; whereas an old hand is apt to be careless and glance round now and then. The kid steered her straight as a die. And, losh, how tickled he looked! She was a hard ship to steer, but he held her true all through the four hours of the mate's watch. And he didn't look the least bit nervous either. But at the end of the four hours you could see how fagged he was. He tried to hide his tiredness, but couldn't. Not that anyone noticed it.

It took two days to get all the sails shifted, and then back went the kid to his holystoning. I guess he'd thought that he was going to be allowed to steer right along, for his eyes had a mighty sad look when he was no longer allowed to. He holystoned clear through the tropics, all down the northeast trades, across the line, and all down the southeast trades. And then, when the sails were being shifted again and the strong storm canvas sent up all ready for the bad weather that might be expected in the South Atlantic and off the Horn, he was allowed to steer again. He was plumped out all over by then. You'd hardly have known him. But he still lived all to himself, scarcely ever spoken to by any of the men; unless one of them told him to clean up the forecastle, or go get the scoff from the cook at mealtimes, or take the empty mess tin back afterward, or fill up a pipe. You know how it is with a lot of hard-case sailors. Though by now the kid would have passed for a pretty husky lad ashore, he was just a young lubber to them, and no more. The mates ignored him. The skipper never so much as saw him, I reckon. But now, while he was steering at the southern edge of the tropics, a ship appeared abeam first thing in the morning. The skipper had just come on deck, and saw her at once. And she was a rival ship that had left port on the same tide and was bound round the Horn for Vallapo. The skipper scowled at the kid and looked along the deck; meaning to call one of the able seamen to the wheel. He wasn't going to trust any kid to steer, with a rival close by. But the men were all aloft, and the mate was with them. "Watch your compass there!" he shouted, and strode to the kid's side. And the kid replied, "Watch the compass it is, sir! Aye, aye, sir!" He said it in regular sailor style, so that the skipper gave a bit of a start and took a sharp look at him. He was having to use every bit of his strength to hold her, but holding her he was. The skipper saw the sweat on his face and, as soon as the men came down from aloft, told the mate to send one of them to the wheel. You should have seen how disappointed he looked as he started forward. But when he came down to the main deck the men were starting to hoist another sail aloft, and it was dragging hard. He made for them, hoping to be allowed to lend a hand with some sailor work at last. No such luck. "Get back to your holystoning!" ordered the mate.

The rival ship was still in sight next day. So the kid got no more chance to steer. All he was was a sort of poor little sea housemaid, as you might say.

Well, after a time the ship came down to windy weather and rough seas. Over the side came the sprays. It was too wet on deck for holystoning now, so the mate sent him under the forecastle head to holystone there. While the crew got the ship all ready for the Horn, he stayed there day after day, unable to see anything of what went on on deck. It was cold on lookout now, and, having no oilskins, he shivered. But he said never a word. One of the men noticed him at last and went to the mate and said, "The kid ain't got no oilskins, sir. He's liable to freeze on lookout." So the mate told the skipper about it.

"It's mighty handy to have him on lookout all night, sir," the mate said. "It gives me the full watch for work on deck."

And the skipper gave the kid a suit of oilskins from the store that he kept in case any of the sailors might need any. "Maybe he's worth a suit of oilskins," he thought. "I bought 'em cheap anyway."

Well, the ship passed round the corner of Staten Island one black blowy morning. The Horn was only about a hundred miles away now. The seas were sullen and gray. The sky was dark, low-hung above the rolling mastheads. Albatross flew all about the ship, and cape hens, and mollymauks, and sea pigeons, and ice birds, and gulls of all sorts. Penguins swam beside and after her. Now and again a sea elephant lifted its whiskered head from the gray water and barked. There was snow on the black rocks of Staten Island, and it was cold as old misery.

The kid looked from under the forecastle head and saw all the crew, both watches, aloft furling the mainsail. "Oh, I wish they'd let me be a sailor!" he said aloud. And then in a few minutes there was a shout from one of the men, and in the driving mist, a half mile or so away, was the rival ship again. The kid jumped to his feet, left his holystoning, and ran out to take a look at her.

"Oh, I hope we beat her!" he cried. The second mate heard him, gave him a scornful look, and growled. "Get on with your job, you!"

Well, you know how it is off the Horn in June. Black, blowing, and cold as old misery always. The snow flew, the hail lashed, the graybacks thundered all over the rolling deck. Less than ever did anyone take any notice of the kid. Except for the cabin, the men's quarters and the cook's galley, the only place at all dry was under the forecastle head. And there the kid had to stay. Often it was too wet for him to work, even there. He stood, and flapped his arms, and stamped his feet, well-nigh frozen for want of exercise to make his blood flow. He wasn't even allowed to keep lookout at night now. The mate couldn't trust him there in such wild weather. The mate kept him up on the poop all through each night watch, just to have him handy to fill his pipe and go to the chart room and light it for him.

All day the sailors toiled on the masts, furling sail when the bitter black Horn gales yelled, or setting sail in the lulls that came now and then. 'Twas the same by night. It took the ship ten days to beat round the Horn, and during them the rival ship was sighted three or four times. The skipper scowled each time he got a glimpse of her in the scud and the sleet and the snow. He and his rival skipper had a bet of two hundred dollars on the race, and he didn't want to lose all that money, of course. Whenever he saw her, he strode to the wheel and shouted to the helmsman to watch out how he steered. He was like a bear on hot coals. The mate was like him, and so was the second. The men all cursed the other ship too. Except for the big Finn, there wasn't a man aboard who hadn't some money on the race.

Well, she got past the Horn at last, and stood away to the westward to get well clear of the South American coast before starting north up the Pacific. And as pretty nearly always happens, when a ship is well past the Horn, she fell in with a flat calm one day. There wasn't wind enough to lift a spider's web. The sea was level as the top of a marble table. The sky hung high and leaden above a black sea. Albatross, sea pigeons, cape hens, mollymauks and gulls sat motionless on the sea all about her; for when there isn't any breeze it's hard for them to fly. On his hands and knees, the kid pushed his holystone to and fro under the forecastle head. And the skipper and mates and men stared scowling away to the beam, where, her sails all hanging idle, lay the rival ship.

The kid looked out once, saw her, and said aloud, "Oh, I wish we could beat her!"

The mate heard him and growled, "None of your business! Get on with your work!" It was a mighty tough day on the kid, I guess.

Well, it was that day that the kid finished the holystoning under the forecastle head. He got it all done by eleven in the morning watch. He went up to the poop and he told the mate, "I'm all done under the forecastle head, sir."

The skipper was in the chart room and heard what the kid said. He looked out and glowered at him. "If it wasn't for that young devil, we'd be far ahead of the other ship," he muttered, looking over the sullen sea to his rival. "The young lubber's a Jonah. It's having him aboard that stops me running away from her." And he called to the mate, "Put that young whelp to holystoning up here on the poop, mister!" He was feeling mighty mean, and he figured it'd be fine punishment for the kid to have to holystone up there in the cold.

The kid holystoned till noon. He ought to have gone off duty then, but the skipper said to the mate, "Keep the young whelp at it all day, mister! It serves him right." The kid went to the forecastle for dinner at noon and came right back as soon as he'd eaten. His face was blue with cold. His fingers felt half frozen. Though the men had scraped him up a few old rags of winter underwear, his body felt like a lump of ice all over. But he said no word and made no sign. Only, now and then, when no one was near him, he looked anxiously over the sullen sea at the other ship. All afternoon he stayed on his hands and knees, and on his knees were big calluses from everlasting kneeling. The tips of his fingers had been sore for weeks from holding the sandstone day after day. His teeth chattered.

Well, you know how it is with those flat calms west of the Horn. They pretty nigh always end in a southerly buster. A wind comes up from the south pole, all in a twinkling—Whiff! Bang! A wind from due south, blowing for the north, whither a ship for Vallapo wants to go. Then, if a skipper dares, he runs his ship with the buster at her heels. It's the finest place on all the oceans for a tryout between two rival ships.

It was at just two minutes to four that afternoon that the skipper came from the chart room and looked at the rival ship. Then he looked astern, and there, close above the horizon, he saw a long, hard, white line in the sky, and beneath it a long, white line of broken water. A buster was coming. It'd be on the ship in two or three minutes.

"All hands on deck! Get everything off her but the topsails and foresail!" bawled the skipper.

Out came all hands on the run, and went to clewing up sail in a mighty hurry. And then, all in a jiff, as though a door had been suddenly flung wide open, along came the buster. Y-o-o-o-w-l! The wind blew the kid's bucket over and sent it rolling along the poop deck. It bumped against the skipper's legs and fell to the quarter-deck. And after it started the kid. But the skipper grabbed him. The seas were breaking over the bulwarks already, and already the main deck was thigh deep in foamy water. The ship was rolling hard already, in great seas that were every moment growing greater.

"Stay on the poop!" bawled the skipper. He didn't want even a stowaway washed overboard, of course. So the kid stayed on the poop. Clinging to the taffrail, he felt the raving wind tear at him. Dark began to fall almost at once. Losh, how cold it was! Wind straight from the pole! But it wasn't the cold the kid was worrying about. He could just see the light of the rival ship abeam, and what he said to himself was, "Now perhaps we'll run away from her!"

By half after four it was too dark to see anything plainly. By five it was black as a bishop's best Sunday hat. The kid could hear, now and then, above the roar of wind and smash of sea, the cries of the men aloft tying the sails down. "I wish they'd let me help," he thought. "I wish they'd let me be a sailor too." Now and again he had a glimpse of the other ship's light away on the beam, and he could tell that the two ships were racing neck and neck.

The big Finn was at the wheel. In front of the chart room, so that it kept a little of the wind from him, the kid clung to the taffrail. He could just make out the skipper's form a few feet from him. And presently he saw the skipper move away. Or, rather, the skipper disappeared. And then, next moment, he saw the skipper plainly as he passed by the open door of the lighted chart room on his way to the wheel to see if the helmsman was steering the ship true.

"I wish I were steering her now," thought the kid. And then he saw the skipper go back into the chart room.

The kid left the taffrail and started toward the wheel himself; eager to see how the helmsman was managing. He passed by the opposite side of the chart room to that where, just within the door, sat the skipper. And leaning against the screaming wind, he came to the wheel and peeped into the compass bowl. The wind had blown his sou'wester away. He was bareheaded. And then, feeling the ship give a terrific roll and dip her stern deep in the sea, he ran behind the man at the wheel and crouched close in under the weatherboard that long ago had been lashed all round the taffrail to keep the wild seas of the Horn from bursting onto the poop. Down went the ship's stern, down, and deeper down yet. And then, ere she could lift it quickly enough from the sea trough, over the weatherboard directly behind the helmsman thundered a wave of icy water. It passed clear over the kid, leaving him dry; just as one can be in the dry when close in under a waterfall.

The rising moon peeped for half a jiff through the flying clouds, just as that sea thundered onto the poop. And by its light the kid saw the big Finn swept bodily from the wheel and washed away forward as the ship lifted her stern and buried her pitching bows deep down in the sea smother ahead.

Most kids would have been too scared to move. But the kid darted like a flash to the wheel and gripped the spokes before the ship had time to take the bit in her teeth and get out of control.

The skipper had jumped to his feet when the sea came over the weatherboard. He looked from the chart-room door, but, his eyes being blinded for the moment from having been in the lamplight, didn't see the Finn swept bodily past within two or three feet of him. Aware that the man at the wheel had the ship under control still, he said to himself, "That fellow's a cracking good helmsman."

The wheel tore at the kid's arms and shoulders as, like a race horse flicked by its jockey's whip, the ship fought to get away from him. You know how it is when, with a gale dead astern, a big sea bursts onto the poop. She's liable to do what's known as "broaching to"—liable to rush up into the wind, bring it broadside on, have all her masts ripped out of her, spill over, and sink like a stone. Though, while she tried to broach to, the ship pretty nigh wrenched his arms from their sockets, the kid held her.

The big Finn picked himself up on the quarter-deck, all the wind knocked clear out of him. And as, wondering in his dumb mind why the ship hadn't broached to yet, he started back to the wheel, the second mate, just down from aloft, bumped into him. The second mate, who, but for the buster, should have been off duty, had no idea that the Finn had been washed from the wheel, and merely supposed that he was one of the men just come down from aloft.

The sails were not yet all furled. The mainsail, crossjack and staysails were still flapping wildly in their gear, threatening to blow to ribbons at any minute. "Get up to that mainsail!" bellowed the second mate to the Finn. The Finn stared at him in the gloom, in his usual dumb way. "Get up to that mainsail!" he bellowed again. And off went the big Finn; ready, as usual, to obey any order at all, no matter what it might be, once he got it clear.

It took all hands the best part of an hour to get the mainsail furled, and then it took them well over half another to furl the crossjack. By when the staysails were all made fast, the ropes cleared up, the swing ports lashed open to let the water run from the deck, and the life lines tightened up, it was close to eight o'clock.

From time to time the skipper peered out into the darkness. And each time that he did so he saw the light of the rival ship a little farther astern than the last time. "She hasn't got any such helmsman as I have," said he. "He's a cracking fine man!"

The mate came up to the poop to report to the skipper that all was well aloft and alow. The skipper looked from the chartroom door, and there wasn't a sign of the other ship's lights.

"All right, mister," said the skipper. "We'll let the crew have a tot of grog all round. We've run away from that ship and she'll never catch us again now." He was pleased as Punch, and grinning all over his face; and he added, "We've got a first-rate crew, and one topping, fine helmsman!"

"All hands to the poop!" shouted the mate, and up came all hands and gathered round the chart-room door. One by one they stepped into the lamplight to take a tot of grog from the skipper, while the mate stood by the door to count them as they came and see that nobody tried to come twice. "One, two, three, four, five," he counted, and when, presently, he came to "twelve," he let out a shout of amazement: "By gravy, who's at the wheel then?"

And at just that instant the newly risen moon broke clear from the scudding clouds.

The skipper jumped from the chart room and ran for the wheel. The mates ran after him, and the men ran after the mates.

The moon shone full in the kid's down-bent face. His eyes were fast on the compass. He didn't look up while all hands stared incredulously at him. They saw his shoulders heave, saw his hands gripping the kicking wheel spokes. They saw how tight the line of his set lips was. And they saw how ghost-white, how utterly weary, he was.

"Put another sailor to the wheel, mister!" shouted the skipper to the mate. And then, as one of the hard-cases stepped up and took the spokes from him, the kid looked up. His lips moved. There was a look of utter delight in his eyes. Everyone saw it, but nobody heard what it was that he said. He said, "Oh, he called me a sailor."

And then, before anyone could reach out a hand and grab him, the kid fell limp on the deck. He'd fainted clear away. They picked him up, carried him to the chart room and laid him on the settee. The skipper sat down and took the kid's head on his knee.

"Pass me that bottle, mister," said the skipper to the mate, and the mate passed him the rum bottle. "Here, sailor!" he said, and, setting it to the kid's lips, trickled a few drops in.

The kid's eyes opened. He sat up and stared round like a kid in a dream. Then, his eyes bright as twin stars, he looked square into the skipper's face.

"Please, sir, am I a sailor?" asked the kid.

"You're going to draw wages from the day she sailed," said the skipper; and, holding the rum bottle to the kid's lips again, added, "Take a good swig now, son! Sailors drink rum—and if a man's an extra good hand, he sometimes gets a double shot!"

Cargo of Gold

CHARLES RAWLINGS

THE OLD HELICOPTER, flopping her blades like a big, lonely bird cruising with her mind turned inward, was bound home to Key West on the northeast course from Mérida, Yucatán. She was running ahead of a norther that the morning weather reports warned would move into the Gulf of Mexico by night. She was a fine, expensive old bird—as she had to be to have a cruising range that would carry her across that stretch of water, rigged with pontoons that looked like big black sausages aloft in the afternoon sunlight. Once she had cost somebody a lot of money. Now, however, she was stony broke and glum and sad. Because she was broke, she was out in violation of regulations. There was a gaping void in her after bulkhead over the port passenger chair. The radio that had been there as recently as nine o'clock that morning had been removed by the Florida firm that owned it. Convinced that the trip to Mérida was a runaway junket to escape creditors, they had snipped with a pair of neat pliers and taken the radio away.

Her two crewmen, no runaways, were flying her home. The fare from Key West to Mérida, one way, from the quiet Englishman and his mousy wife who were going to get mosquito-bitten all over as they dug into the Yucatán Aztec ruins, was all the money they had in the world. They were going to keep that and quietly set the copter down on her squashy pontoons back in her home yard and walk quietly away from her forever. That was what the cancellation-of-charter-for-reasons-of-nonpayment papers that had been served on them this morning had said they must do as of a date that would be tomorrow. The fare to Mérida, evenly split, was safely in the right shoes of her two men. The older man's shoe was less the price of a bottle of Scotch whisky.

They were pleasant, peaceful, pathetic paupers. The head man, small, bald, middle-aged, was pathetic all the time. He was an old tramp flier who had done some brilliant and brave bomber flying in the turbulence over the New Guinea mountains in the Pacific war and some not very brilliant and very unlucky drinking afterward that had ruined him. His mate, a big yellow-haired conch boy, was only pathetic for the moment. He had worked his way through Princeton and now he was trying to get a money stake for a law degree. He would specialize in maritime law as a Key West conch boy named Thomas Pilot should. Much of the American writing on that branch of the law had come from the wrecks on the Florida reefs and the courts that had settled their cases. The youngster's great-grandfather had been the wreck master for three of the most famous strandings. His wisdom and discipline and courage had helped write much of the law.

Now, however, the last of the Pilots had to get some money in a hard, unromantic world that easily forgets grandfathers. The best part of the summer had gone for naught. Teaming up with old Bill Jenkins and chartering the plane had been a bad guess. There should have been more bone fishermen who wanted to be flown to Andros or Eleuthera or Cat Island or the other little choice places on Exuma Sound in the Bahamas than there had proved to be, or marlin fishermen who wanted to be set down in Nassau, or *bon vivants* who wanted suddenly to be ferried over to Havana for dinner. If Cuba had stayed peaceful and quiet in her Batista misery, instead of erupting into her Castro madness, things might have been different—different, too, if old Bill had not been visibly drunk too much of the time.

They were midway between Havana and Rebecca Shoal now, close to the axis of the Gulf Stream. Pilot was in the starboard seat doing the flying. The older man, cuddling the bottle of Scotch in his lap, slouched in the port chair.

"I can't tell you how lousy I'm feeling, Tommy boy," he said, "about what's happened. I don't matter. But you getting short-changed is very bad."

"Nothing but time. That's all I've lost," Pilot said. "I can't get to law school until next year. I resent that a little. I'll get a yacht job until something better turns up. Sailing's my great ability—if there was only money in it."

"You know," Jenkins said, "I've always wanted to send a boy of mine to college—the old and finished tossing the torch to the young and strong. All I lacked has been the boy and the torch."

Pilot turned and looked at him. He bit back the bitterness that was on his tongue. Poor old Bill—the old and finished. He had that part of his program well in hand. Pilot went back to his flying. He banked the copter suddenly and dropped her at a patch of sun glare on the Stream.

"Speaking of sailing," he said, "what's she doing out here? Look! Spars on deck! Isn't that a cradle trailing alongside? A little class-C ocean racer is what she is."

Jenkins sat up, pointed eastward. "Get over that," he said. "Something's just gone down here."

The flotsam that always survives when something goes down with suddenness was on the water. It was strung out over a mile—a hatch cover, two life rafts. Empty! There was an empty life boat trailing lines that had to be davit falls torn apart, because they were rotten as most davit falls always are. There were smaller objects that could have been human heads, but were buckets or deck swabs or a side lantern that winked its lens in the sunlight. They climbed straight up, and Jenkins circled the horizon with the copter's binocular. There was nothing. They came down and went up and down the wreckage three times more. There was no sign of any life. Jenkins tipped up the Scotch bottle and made it gurgle as he drank.

"Death by the dozen makes me sick," he said. "I still smell dead Japanese in heaps with the flies buzzin'. There's nothing even left to smell here. Maybe back on that hull."

They hovered over the little hull. She was nodding asleep on the low, even swell, waiting, holding her secret. A small pea-pod dinghy painted blue was lashed bottom-up atop her cabin house. Her aluminum mast and boom were lashed atop the cabin house, too, with their overhang supported on two low horses.

"What's that white floor in her cockpit?" Pilot said. "That's just raw wood. Some sort of temporary floor. A man couldn't stand and steer on that unless he was a midget."

He reached for the padded shoulder sling used in going downstairs on the copter's hoist cable.

"Take over," he said, "and drop me into her. I'll launch the dink. You set the copter down, and I'll bring over a line."

He went down like a monkey on a string and waved his arm. He splashed the dink overboard and tossed in a coil of white line. The copter settled on her squashy pontoons. The dink's oars flashed excitedly.

"Put the big pliers in your pocket," Pilot said, making the line fast to the copter's starboard-pontoon strut and holding the dink for Bill Jenkins to ease his small middle-aged bones aboard. "There's a padlock on the companionway slide that we'll have to twist off. She's a fine, tough little sloop."

They boarded her and made the line fast to one of her cockpit cleats, mooring her to the copter. The little brass padlock on the companionway twisted apart. There was nothing below but the smell of shut-up yacht cabin and the muskiness of fat sail bags that crowded it. They came back to the sunlit deck. Pilot had been right about the cockpit floor. It was naked pine boards, a shipping clerk's makeshift job hurriedly done. Driven in between the cracks of the boards was white cotton calking, making it tight. Two inches of water sloshed atop the boards. Pilot kneeled and wet his fingers and tasted them.

"Salt," he said.

The only wreckage was the cradle. It was a temporary, shipping clerk's job too, made of two-by-fours with a pair of two-by-sixes where the keel had rested. One side of it had been splintered and ripped apart. There was an envelope tacked to one of the broken uprights. Jenkins leaned out and carefully eased the soaked envelope free of its tacks. Pilot kicked the cradle loose, and it moved away. Inside the envelope was a bill of lading.

"'J. M. Gomez, General Delivery, Tampa,' for heaven's sake," Pilot said. "Thirty-five thousand dollars' worth of ocean racer, and the man's picking up his mail at the will-call window."

"Yeah," Jenkins said. "This is beginning to look juicy. How do you figure it?"

"She was deck cargo on whatever sank right here," Pilot surmised. "Probably heading for the Miami-Jamaica race which starts in two weeks, a Cuban entry. She came off with a splash. She shipped that salt water in the cockpit and cracked her cradle loose."

"She was meant to come off with a splash," Jenkins said. "Or somebody was afraid she might. Under that jackleg floor is open cockpit. It was made tight in a hurry. She's a displacement hull. She's got five or six tons of lead on her keel. She splashes overboard and, no matter how she hits, she rights herself. Calked up this way, she's as tight as a pirate's chest. Tommy boy, she *is* a pirate's chest. She's carrying something somebody did not want to lose."

They scrambled below. There were sails in the sail bags, linen napkins, towels, a man's shorts and T shirts neatly folded in the locker drawers, life preservers and folded blankets under the bunks, charts in the wide shallow chart drawer. In a small locker below the chart table was a box of distress-signal rocket shells and the big fat pistol for firing them.

The center floor board in the cabin had a bronze ring embedded in the wood, a lifting ring. Pilot got his finger through it and flopped up the board. Dry white sand was in the bilge. He burrowed into it and tipped up a small patty-cake of bronze-colored ballast metal. It was only nine inches across and bowl-shaped, but its weight pulled him off balance. He got both hands under it and thumped it on the naked port-side-bunk board. He tugged at his sheath knife and scratched. The cleaned place glinted like gold. It was gold. He said the word.

"Gold!" he squealed. "Bill, it's gold."

Jenkins floundered on his knees, and their hands scattered the dry sand. Neatly stowed, flat side down, were five more patty-cakes on the port side of the keelson and six more to starboard. Between the next set of frames the pattern was the same —and between the next set.

"Her whole bilge is cobbled with gold," Pilot said. "They traded her inside lead ballast for gold—hundreds of pounds of it."

"Melted down in a plumber's solder ladle," Jenkins said. "See the little pouring teat? *Cubanos'* smuggling job, hunting arms. *Cubanos'* revolution plot——"

As if the word "revolution" were a trigger, both men scrambled for the companionway. On deck they stared down the same bearing—south.

"There's where they'll come from, hunting her," Pilot said.

"And damned soon," Jenkins said. "If that was a time bomb in that freighter, they'll be coming soon. And it must have been a time bomb——"

He jumped for the cockpit and hauled on the copter's mooring line.

"Hey," Pilot said, "no need to run yet."

"Who's running? I can't think without a drink. We got to think."

He swung up into the copter and back on the sloop with his bottle. He gurgled it.

"Here! You drink for once. No? O.K. Young anti-Castro factions are a dime a dozen all over Cuba. All of 'em crazy for arms. Must be two of them sparring in this deal. Only it ain't sparring. Somebody just sunk a little sugar freighter. They're playin' for keeps. They'll kill you. What we do, Tommy boy, we've got to do fast."

"Haul in the chopper," Pilot cried, starting below deck. "We'll load all we can carry."

Jenkins grabbed his arm. "Wait," he said. "Sit down! We got to think. Gold! It drives men mad. We come in with patty-cakes of raw gold out of nowhere—gold and a crazy story. Even if somebody believes us, there's no legal market. We'd have to go underground. A couple of bartenders I know and the telephone numbers of a flamenco dancer or two on your list is all the underground we've got. We'd get our throats cut. We'd go to jail in Fort Knox. No sense to that, Tommy."

"But it's a chance," Pilot said. "And I'll take it. Nothing's too reckless a gamble right now for me. Don't try to stop me, Bill. You wanting to pass the torch. You've passed me a millstone around my neck all summer——"

"Whoa!" Jenkins said. He turned away and stood beside the spar, his back eloquent with deep hurt. "I'd do anything in the world to help you, Tommy," he said. "But I can't let you try highjackin'. You know better yourself." He turned. "Wreckin' master, what's really to do? What would your grandsire do right here?"

"He'd save this fine little sloop someway. If we only had some gas to spare, we could tow her somewhere. But we can't, and there's no time to get back here with something that can tow."

"Save ship—save all," Jenkins said. "That's an old wrecker's rule. Salvage is the word, Tommy. She's all ready to be salvaged."

"How? A jury rig would take too much time. Then two knots an hour. We'd be sitting ducks. Looting a couple hundred pounds of that pig gold is all that's left, Bill."

Jenkins tipped up the Scotch bottle then put back the cork and hammered it in with his fist in a strange gesture of finality. "Tommy, my boy," he said. "No jury rig. Racin' rig! A roaring getaway. I'll give it to you. The copter's sky hook, the winch—with me flyin' it. We'll sky-hook in this spar. Everything's here—riggin', all of it with the turnbuckles all greased and ready to set up, canvas by the acre in those bags below. I'll sky-hook in this spar. You get on the canvas and sail her in for wealth and glory. Salvage, you reef rat!"

"Gosh," said Pilot, "if we *could* get her stick in, we could save her so easy. Bill, do you think you can do it? You're pretty drunk."

"Just right," Jenkins said. "I'll bull's-eye that spar like a spear into a target. But how about you? Look at the sky. That norther's comin'."

"Let it come. Get this sloop rigged. I'll slide her in by dawn no matter what blows. But we gotta hurry. I can feel 'em comin' on the back of my neck. Get on up there."

"Got to think a little more," Jenkins said. "This riggin' will take time. Mustn't get caught flat-footed here. You get things ready downstairs for Jenkins's operation Sky Hook. I'll get upstairs and tow upstream. Whoever comes looking will search downstream first. Am I thinkin' straight?"

"No!" Pilot shouted. "Gas, you fool. We haven't got that much gas. You've got to get that helicopter in."

"Don't you worry about Old Bill gettin' in. Old Bill always gets in."

He reached for the line to the copter and hauled. Then he tipped back his head. "Wra-a-ack ashore!" he sang out at the top of his lungs, the ancient wreckers' cry. "Wra-a-ack ashore! Salvage or die, you reef rats! Salvage with Professor Jenkins's sky hook. Your grandfather never heard of that. Tommy's goin' to college, to get a lot of knowledge."

He stepped off on the copter's pontoon. "Always able to do the big things in life," he said with great gravity. "It was failure with the boring little things that made Mister Jenkins a failure and a drunkard. Now, Tommy, you walk that tin stick's butt up the deck when I take the weight off its forward end. When you get to the hole in the deck where the mast goes, you hold the mast down someway, and I'll start cranking up hoist. When she's straight up and down, start prayin' and stand clear. I'll spear her home. And"—he made a gesture of disdain—"forget about that gold. Spit on that drab dross. The ship's the thing. Save ship—save all. The gold just comes along for the ride."

They got under way smoothly. The copter dangled her hoist cable with its hook, and Pilot made it fast to the sloop's bow bitt. Jenkins, flying as he always did, drunk or sober, with the cautious surety of a master, hovered the copter while he payed out one hundred feet of slack in the hoist cable, then slowly flew it taut. Together they moved off, the copter's blades beating a steady rhythm, the little sloop squatting her stern and trailing a fast true wake, as straight as an arrow away from danger.

Pilot watched down it for a quick moment of elation, then beyond it to the southwestward horizon where all menace was lurking. Then he swung about to put all else from his mind save the all-consuming desperate task of the spar. He unlashed the rigging and stretched it out on deck as best he could. Its upper spliced loops had been left attached where they belonged on the spar.

Over the mast hole in the deck, where the spar must enter, was a tacked patch of painted canvas, making it watertight. With his sheath knife he pried loose the tacks and peeled the cover free. It was a trim snug hole, pear-shaped like the spar, with the fat curve of the pear forward. That was a blessing, for there was only one way for the spar to go in. He squinted, trying to see how the final target, the mast step, lined up below, but it was shrouded in the cabin's gloom. He needed to see it.

He swung into the cabin and squatted over the mast step. Like all the rest of the little sloop, it had been refined down to complete simplicity. It was a piece of white oak set atop the keelson. It was the same width as the keelson—nine inches. In its middle was a mortise. There was a metal tenon on the spar's foot to fit it. That was the target's bull's-eye. To hit it blind in a desperate chance was asking too much. A man on deck and a man below and the sloop in a quiet dock and a gin pole, with its slow windlass easing the spar down an inch at a time, was what this rig had a right to expect—not a blind stab in the dark. Fore and aft on the step was where he had a margin of error. A miss fore or aft, and the butt would still stay on the step's oak. But to miss to port or starboard! There was no margin of error there—only the thin mahogany planking of the sloop's bottom, her skin. If the spar dropped with any force, it would go through the planking like the spear, Bill called it, going through paperboard—a hole in the bottom with the spar hanging like a crazy centerboard and no chance to get it back, no chance to do anything. Down sloop—all lost! He'd have to shut his mind to that. The luck of the desperate and the half-drunken would have to see them through. Good luck it had to be.

The numbered mast wedges—to jam the spar tight with the mast hole in the deck—were hanging in a canvas ditty bag right where they should be, from a brass hook in the overhead. He pushed the bag up through the hole and let it sit on deck, ready on hand.

Now to get the sling rigged on the spar, ready for the copter's hoist. That had to be right the first time. He needed the strongest and best line he could find.

The door in the cabin's forward bulkhead opened into the chain locker with a little hand-pump toilet on the port side and open space forward of that. There was plenty of line. It was lovely cream-colored nylon, like all the line on the sloop—luxury cordage. He measured off what he would need. He reached for his knife and made the cut and spliced in the most painstaking eye of his life. Not a strand of it must slip. It would be holding the copter's hoist hook, lifting the full weight of the spar. He rolled the splice between his palms, working it down round and smooth. Gold! It came into his half-occupied mind. He was crouched in the head with his feet almost certainly over gold. He couldn't believe it. It was a dream. He started to move his feet to see, then jumped up. *Bill was right. Forget it.*

Remember Old Bill was up there burning gas. He gathered up the line and tossed it ahead of him up on deck and made it fast to the spar. He started six feet above the butt and went up the spar in a series of clove hitches drawn as tight as he could jam rope. He left the eye splice dangling just above the spar's spreaders. That was all he could do. He shut his eyes for a moment, making sure he had thought of everything.

Bill was hanging out the window watching him—still relaxed, still feeling just right, gambling gas, ready to gamble life and limb and a fine little sloop and just as contented about it as a child. Pilot threw up his arm. The copter's shadow drifted back across the sloop's deck. The hoist cable dangled slack. Pilot jumped for the hoist hook and transferred it from the towing bitt to his fine eye splice and scrambled aft to take station at the spar's butt.

Bill windmilled slowly and ground in hoist cable. He hovered at fifty feet, and Pilot could feel the wind off the blades. The cable tightened. His eye splice squeaked on the cable hook. The spar, limber as a huge tuna rod, lifted its tip. The butt jumped suddenly on its little sawhorse and started forward. He eased the cold metal log off the horse and down on deck. There he must straddle it, stay with it, keep it moving forward. Scuffing, straining, walking the sloop under him, trundling the thing, bumping it along, he went splashing through the tepid water on that white-pine cockpit floor, up over the cabin top and, none too soon for his arms and lungs, he came to the mast hole in the deck. It was just forward of the cabin. He could brace his quaking legs back on the cabin and catch his breath for a split second. Most of the spar now was out over the water, like a long, upward-sprung bowsprit with Bill's cable vibrating as it held the mast. The winch's motor began its whine overhead, and the whine was swallowed by the picked-up beat of the copter's blades. Bill was gunning for the big lift.

The butt tried to shove him aft now, but he braced and fought it and held it down. Then the thing stopped fighting him backward and lifted against all his strength. He took a stolen look up, and the mast was straight up and down. He swayed it over the mast hole. He got the pear of the metal and the pear of the hole lined up.

"Straight, Bill! Straight!" he screamed, as if Bill could hear him. "No cant to her, please! Now! Let her come!"

As if Bill could hear him, it came. It came like a plummet. There was a shriek of metal scraping wood as the thing rubbed the mast hole—and then a bouncing thump, a beautiful, bouncing thump, solid, solid as oak. The step had caught it. It was standing somehow, someway, on the good solid oak of the step —off center maybe, off side, but standing. He lifted his head to scream a cheer aloft, but it choked in his throat. The thin mask sticking straight up, unstayed and naked, was all alone now. Bill had eased off all tension, and it was a pitiful, swaying reed. Pilot fumbled for the key wedge and waited for the spar to sway and give him room and shoved it home. Then the others. That steadied the crazy thing to the deck.

He grabbed the dangling forestay and laid back on it, tracing it aloft. He ran with its end and clattered its shackle over the bronze eye waiting on the stemhead. He pinned through the shackle pin, caught the pin's thread and forced himself to screw it up tight. Then he screwed up the turnbuckle until he could feel the mast tugging on the wire like a hooked fish.

Then he scrambled aft and made fast the backstay. Now the spar was braced fore and aft. Its sideswaying could wait until he freed poor old Bill. Bill up there, still tethered by the winch hook, was burning gas he was going to have to have. Using the sling for a hand grip, Pilot went up the spar, and there was Bill across fifty feet of sky, not worried about gas or anything else, grinning, still just right.

Pilot unhooked the winch hook, hurled it and watched it splash. Then down the spar, freeing the sling, hitch by hitch, as he descended. When he dropped on deck, he discovered that somewhere he had knocked off enough hide to bloody his left pants leg—a skinned shin he had never felt, and no time to feel it now. He hooked the port shrouds in the chain plate on the rail waiting for them. There was just enough weather stain on the turnbuckle threads to show the spot they had been screwed down to before. He tightened down to that. The starboard shrouds would not come down to their weathered station. He knew what that meant—the spar was not perfectly set below. It was hiked up, riding on its tenon, cockeyed.

He scrambled below to see how cockeyed it was. One good swing of a six-pound maul would knock it home. He didn't have a six-pound maul. There wasn't anything to thump with save one of those patties of gold. It would be no good, be a finger breaker. Then he saw the sloop's second anchor, her bower, broken down and stowed neatly up in the very nose of the forward compartment. Tossing a jib in its bag against the spar for padding, and swinging the small anchor like a ram, he jolted the spar. He jolted again, this time with all his might, and the tenon made a royal lovely thump, dropping into place. Nothing could stop him now.

Up on deck, he saw Bill just setting the copter down. He'd been off wasting more gas somewhere. Pilot sank wearily on the cabin trunk. He was soaked with sweat. A draft made him shiver. The sun was going fast in a brassy-looking sky, and the breeze was not the soft easterly caress that had been the night wind for the past month. It was north and cold—the norther's first little chilly kiss.

"Drift down the dink," Bill called. "Flashlight! Water! Anything else you'll need?"

Pilot shook his head, payed out the dinghy painter and let the new breeze waft the corky little pea pod down.

"Get the mainsail ready," Jenkins cried as he jumped aboard. "I'll help you hist her. We've got to hurry, kid. I mean it this time."

"There's something back there?"

"Way off and working downstream—little gunboat or trawler. Dark will stop him. But get goin'."

Bill was beating the false floor in the cockpit to death with the biggest wrench in the copter's kit when Pilot came on deck with the Number One mainsail all rigged with the battens he had had to hunt for. Bill hurled the last piece of the shattered flooring into the sea.

"Where is it?" he screamed. "Why would a rich man who could afford it ship off a hull loaded just with gold? I knew a case of rum would be here. But nothing! Nothing but cypress floor slats and a compass set in the bulkhead. And now no binnacle bottle for poor lonely Old Bill."

The mainsail clattered aloft up its bronze trackway on the spar. The neat roller reefing boom that had fitted so swiftly into its gooseneck on the spar slatted its staccato hurried tune as the breeze strummed into the canvas. Pilot made the mainsheet blocks whine, threading through the fine nylon mainsheet. Bill came up out of the cabin.

"I'm scrammin'," he said. "I'm the one that will give them the tip-off, if they see me. Now listen, kid! Watch me when I get up there—hear? I'll wink my lights twice when I'm dead on magnetic north. Check that compass. It's been banged around plenty and may have error. Then I'll settle down for Key West. Northeast, a half east. You sail that course as close as ever you can. And you go straight for one of those big fat Navy moorings off the submarine base in Key West harbor. That's where I'm heading, and you look for me there. I'll tell the story right away. Maybe there will be something out to meet you even if you don't need it. The Navy! The Customs people! Then the best admiralty lawyer in town—Thomas Pilot, his assistant, sitting in on his first case in admiralty court. Salvage! Nice and legal loot—loot, loot. Thinkin' straight?"

"Straight and true," Pilot said, turning now.

Bill was tossing something up into the copter's cabin.

"You taking that gold chunk?" Pilot yelled.

"No. Honest. I'm borrowing something to comfort me a little. Something to light up and warm me, case I get cold."

"That little alcohol stove? Take it. How about gas? Tell me the truth."

"Wel-l-l," Bill said. "Come daylight, you might keep a little lookout. You'll be dead astern of me sailin' right. Just don't forget me. But Old Bill gets in. Even soberin' up, Old Bill flies home. Always has. Good-by, kid. Fond of you."

"Fond of you too," Pilot shouted after him, but the helicopter's winnowing blades swept all other sound aside as Bill went off with the lifting, shouldering way he could toss a copter aloft—that somehow had all the gallantry of D'Artagnan's sweeping, feathered hat.

Pilot realized how true his swept-away phrase was an hour later. It was after the search plane had come and gone and he was shaking with reaction from exhaustion and suspense. The plane, undoubtedly Cuban, had come in high, holding the last of the sun golden on its wings. It was a little land-based job, maybe with a radio. But it either did not see him or, seeing him, dismissed him because it was not looking for a sloop under sail. It carried straight on and vanished into the west.

The wind was cold now, straight from the north, but the sloop was balanced so evenly he could run below for some blankets. She was sailing beautifully, eating up knots through the clear night with its wiped-bright stars and whistling wind. Rail down, he was rigged just right with three rolls of reef in the mainsail and that little honey of a small genoa jib he had found in the smallest sail bag. He was hooked on to the norther perfectly in a close reach and he would stay just that way all night, all the way in—he would if he could ever get warm. He took two blankets from beneath a bunk mattress and swung the flashlight about the cabin. There was the little alcohol stove he thought Bill had taken. "Something to light up and warm me," Bill had said.

In a flash he guessed what Bill was covering up. He opened the locker under the chart table. The distress rockets and the pistol were gone. The old fool was really worried about gas. Start looking at daylight, Bill had said, but he wasn't really sure about getting even that far. Keep lookout for rockets in the night too. That's what he would have to do.

He rushed back to the cockpit and huddled in a tent of the blankets draped over his head. If Bill had to ditch, he'd pick him up. A wave of tenderness mixed with apprehension so intense it made his face screw up in agony flowed over him. The gallant old fool—risking his life. "Not that kind of torch," he whispered. "Not a distress torch, Bill." His eyes screwed into the blackness ahead. He was looking for lights now—the red bursting stars of distress rockets, the flash of Sand Key lighthouse, the first rosy light of dawn. Whichever came first, he would be ready.

Two hours later light found him. It was the scything blade of a powerful searchlight seeking. It found him and held. It closed on him fast. Mercifully it dipped and splashed on the wind-winnowed water, and its back-reflected glare lighted up what mounted it—a United States destroyer. Bill had made it. He had reported, and they knew about the gold. Gold! How completely he had forgotten the gold. It was as if it had been imagined, just a dream. But it wasn't a dream. The little sloop was lugging it. She was heavy with it, stiff with her gold. She liked it fine—sail her and let it ride.

The Ransom of Peter Drake

JACLAND MARMUR

IT'S GETTING ON DAYLIGHT along the Coast, but away out here it's the middle watch. I can see stars swinging past my hooked-back door when the ship rolls down, and the smell of the trade is sweet. It's quiet in the radio shack. The noisy wash of the ocean doesn't bother the stillness at all. Not in a liner. Not in the middle watch. And in just three minutes I got a traffic schedule with KPH. It'll be Joe Pagini over there, and Joe's an old-timer. The minute I open up, he'll know what kind of a transmitting key I use. He don't know why I use it, but he'll know right away it's me. Even before I give my sign, I'll hear him through the break-in relay, bustin' in from Frisco two thousand miles away.

"Good morning, MP," he'll say. "Got nine for you. Go ahead."

Then all the while I'm rapping out the code with the earphones tucked at my temples, I'll be thinking of Peter Drake. Till my message hook is clean. I wish it was Pete Drake's sideswiper I was using. But it couldn't be. So I did the next best thing. I made me one of my own, and I swore I'd learn to use it right. I hope I did. Because if it wasn't for him, I wouldn't be here.

He didn't belong to the afterguard. He didn't belong in the fo'c'sle, either. The devil only knows where he belonged. Not in the cargo steamer *Trintipal*, that's sure. But that's where he was, signed on as ordinary seaman for the voyage home to Seattle by way of Shanghai and Tsugaru Strait in the winter right after the end of the war. The Old Man picked him up in ruined

Manila because we'd sent two men ashore to hospital and the bos'n's crowd was short. You know how bos'ns are.

Me, I didn't even know he was on board. Not till the following day. The Trintipal was nosing the cobalt water of Manila Bay, and the third mate, Tony Fuller, was spilling tobacco ash on the settee of my boat-deck shack when we heard this voice.

"Give us a drink!" it said. I looked up. All I could clearly see was a face in the doorway's frame. The whisky sweat was beading out on it. His eyes were haggard, and his hair was a dusty gray. "Sparks," he whined, "for God's sake——"

He poured half a tumbler of my Scotch and he drank it neat. Then he went away. He never even said thank you or be damned, and I don't know yet why I did it. Except he needed that drink. He needed it worse than medicine. Tony Fuller laughed.

"That'll teach you," the third mate said. "Offering the bottle to one of those wrecks! Y'oughta know better, Sparks." Mr. Fuller snorted and stood up. "That's Pete Drake," he informed me, "and the mate is welcome to him. He says he don't know anything about ships. He's a liar. He knows his way around."

"Where the blazes did he come from?"

"Whoever knows where they come from—them shoreside bums? Or, for that matter, where they go?" Tony Fuller stepped over the weatherboard. "They live in a middle world all their own, halfway between the ocean and the land." He started aft for the ladderway, lean out there in the brilliant sun. "You better lock that bottle up!" he warned. "What's left of it, I mean." And the third mate laughed again.

Well, all right. They take you off your guard when their eyes peer out at you from the unlit caverns of their private agony. But I didn't intend it should happen again. All the way across the China Sea, whenever he shuffled along the boat deck with his narrow shoulders hunched and his head bowed down, he threw a quick sidewise glance toward the radio shack. I looked the other way. But you could tell from how he walked a tipping deck that he'd walked it once before. He was on the deck with the chief mate's crowd when the Trintipal hunted Steep Island Pass at the Yangtze River mouth in a cold, gray, drizzling mist. From the bridge he looked small and withered in his shabby reefer coat down there, peering against a windy distance with his gray head bare and his feet spread wide. Tony Fuller was right. He had a seaman's stance. They always stand like that. And while we lay moored off the Shanghai Bund I saw Peter Drake again. I saw him clearly enough that time. He was drunk. He was drunk as a cockeyed lord. But I couldn't throw him out.

He came into the radio shack. I had a small dry battery and a sounding buzzer hooked across my transmission key. A straight conventional key, it was. Same as most of the telegraph monkeys use ashore. I was beating out some five-letter cipher, practicing to get my ticket upgraded when the Trintipal got home. I didn't pay much attention when the door pulled open and slammed again. I thought it was Tony Fuller. He was always barging in. But it wasn't. It was Peter Drake.

"It's lousy, Sparks." He was standing over me, swaying a little, his head cocked over on one side, half a crooked smile on his lips. "It's lousy stuff," he said.

"What did you expect in Blood Alley? Fancy liqueurs? It was whisky, wasn't it?"

He uttered a bitter little snort at the hard, dry irony of my tone, and the crooked smile slipped the rest of the way across his lips. Then he looked around with a drunk's exaggerated care, his watery blue eyes taking all my equipment in.

"It sure has changed," he whispered.

Right then something clicked in my mind. He was turning away. I reached over and flipped my receiver switch on. A babble of code came pouring from the speaker. Peter Drake stopped short at once. He stopped swaying too. I was right. He was reading the stuff. All them old brass-pounders are alike. They never forget it. They can't. It gets into the blood. They never forget it to the day they die. It made Peter Drake spin savagely around. His eyes were ablaze.

"Turn that off! Turn it off, I say!"

I grinned at him. "Sure. So you think my fist is lousy, do you?"

He was breathing hard. It took him a while to quiet down. A fist is a radio operator's own peculiar characteristic of sending, like a man's handwriting and his signature. Drake knew what I meant, all right.

"I never liked a straight key," he mumbled. "Got no class to it. No class at all."

"Oh." I grinned again. I was having fun. "One of them old-time speed burners. A fancy bug man, hey?"

He shook his head. "No." Something seemed to be warning him he ought to get away from where he didn't belong any more. But the whisky kept churning his memory. He was doing fierce combat with both. A big soiled hand passed across his face, and he sagged suddenly down on my leather settee. "Got no use for a bug," his thick voice growled. "No use at all." He wagged his head and brushed shadows aside with the same big-fingered hand. "What is a bug? It works sideways, all right, instead of up an' down like a common key. One contact is solid, and the one opposite works against a vibrator rod y' can adjust for speed by moving the little controlling weight back or forward. All right. Y' hold the lever on one side an' y' got a dash. Y' thumb it the other way an' the weight of the spring rod rattles the dots off for you. No skill. No personal skill at all. Just a damn mechanical contraption! Now y' take a——"

"You must be one of them old-time sideswipe crackers!"

"One of the best!" The old buzzard's watery eyes began to glow. "We used to build our own." He leaned forward. "Y' make two contacts on solid vertical mounts about an inch apart. Your sending lever swings between. That's got to be good spring steel. Not too loose. Not too tight. Just right. Y' use your thumb an' forefinger on it. Side to side. Y' make your own dots an' dashes with a sideswiper. Y' space 'em the way y' want. Y' give the stuff your own personality. It's got class! It's you! It's no one else! A key like that is an artist's tool! In my day——"

"Hell!" I said, wanting to keep him wound up. "All you old-timers are alike. Just the same as windbag men. You think that broken-down gear you used to operate is still the only thing."

He looked around at all my modern tube equipment with a deep and drunken scorn. "You call this operatin'?" He snorted. "Short wave!" The crooked smile began to show again. "I suppose y' can work the Coast the minute you get outside. Copy your press around the world. Nuts!" he said. "Y' don't know what seafarin' is. I remember comin' home from the China Coast them days we used to get up in the middle watch, hungry to hear the first voice from home. Just before daylight was the best. The static dies down. Y' can hear things then. Maybe the old Matsonia, nosing round Diamond Head for Honolulu harbor an' clearin' KHK. Paul Snagg was chief in her. Snaggy used a bug."

Peter Drake wasn't looking at me any more. He was looking somewhere else, off where the shades of his old profession lived. He called them up for me, one by one.

"Next night you'd sit there all of a sweat, tuning the six-hundred-meter dials by a hair, hunting KPH. He used a rotary spark gap for his traffic calls. That old rock crusher had a deep, rich tone. The minute you heard it, you began to grin. You were coming home! Boy, it sounded sweet! Then KFS with his bubbling arc. It used to break every now and then, like a kid's voice when it's changing. An' maybe KSE from Wilmington, coming in with that fluting, quenched-gap note, like a young girl gettin' angry. That was Freddy Cugle, standing the graveyard watch, draggin' his dashes long. Freddy was a straight-key man. You'd hear 'em for maybe a minute just before daylight came, working the coasters, faint an' far away. You felt pretty fine that day. 'Heard Frisco this morning!' you'd tell the crowd at breakfast in the saloon. An' they'd all grin back at you. Even the engineers."

I grinned myself. But I let him rave. I just kept wondering when he'd stop. He didn't. He couldn't. Not yet.

"I used to run two days behind a tanker called Segundo," his voice growled on. "Rod Gibley was in her then. We used to clear half the Pacific traffic, Rod an' me, on a relay schedule with old PH. Y' talk about sideswipers!" His eyes began to glow again. "I never had to give my call. Not me. The minute I opened up, the whole damn ocean knew who it was. It was Drake! Pete Drake! It couldn't be no one else! They'd all come bustin' in right away. Better than if they heard my voice. That's what I mean. Y' take a key like that an' y' learn to use it right an'——" He broke off at last. He tried to get up. "Nuts!" he snarled. "What am I doin' here anyway?"

"I was going to ask you the same."

"Who? Me?" He made it to his feet this time, swaying. "Goin' home. Heard Helen died. Gotta see the kids."

"Kids? You mean you——"

"Hell, no!" He gave that drunken snort. "They ain't mine."

"Well, then what——"

"We was gonna get married, Helen an' me. She married someone else, though, an' I guess they're all grown up by now. But the way I figger it, kids is kids. They could 'a' been mine."

"Drake, you're nuts! I know that yarn myself. Any woman who won't marry a man just because he goes to sea has got no right to——"

"Who said she wouldn't? That's a lie! She begged me! It didn't make no difference to Helen. I told her I lost my ticket, an' still she——" He broke it off there, sharply. His eyes were suddenly wild. He thought it was me who'd betrayed him. "You!" he spat. "You——" He turned blindly away, groping for the door. But something savage took him by the throat, spinning him around. It wasn't the whisky, either. Whisky couldn't make a man's eyes burn like that. Not all the whisky in the world. "Yeah!" he said. "I lost my ticket. No inspector took it away from me. I took it away from myself! I was in the tanker Placenta when the gas exploded in her a thousand miles off the Flattery Cape. So I sent out the SOS. Sure! On my hot-shot sideswiper! Then I ran like hell for the boats."

"Look here, Drake; take it easy. What else could you do?"

He didn't hear me. He heard a voice, all right. But it wasn't mine. He'd been hearing it for twenty years. "I never cleared the hook!" he told it. "I just sent the SOS an' ran like hell for the boats. The position was off. Why wouldn't it be? No sun or star fix on the bridge for days with the North Pacific weather we'd had! Thirteen hours it took the liner Redondo to find us in the sleety fog. She was sixty miles away. She did fourteen knots! And it took her thirteen hours. I saw five men die in the boats in that time. I can hear them yet. Johnny, the little oiler—he's the worst. Johnny doesn't scream. Johnny only moans. No one blamed me. They never said a word. Why should they? I got the SOS off, didn't I? What else could I do? . . . I could have stayed where I belonged! I could have stayed till the hook was clean! Maybe I could have raised a couple of ships with direction finders. I could have sent them v's till they took cross bearings on my spark. They could have laid the Placenta's position down to a pin point on the chart! I never even froze the key! I just sent the SOS an' ran like hell for the boats. That's how quick it happened. Just like that. The first time Johnny moaned, I knew I'd lost my ticket. He took it away from me. Right there in an open boat. He was right! I never sailed on it again. But he keeps on moaning anyhow. He won't never stop!"

It poured out of him. Then he swayed there, panting. I never again want to see such a tortured fever in the eyes of any man.

"Drake!" When he turned half around in the doorway and saw the bottle I was offering, the crooked smile came back. "Why don't you build me a sideswiper?" What else could I say? "I'd like to give it a try."

"Sure!" He emptied what was left of the Scotch. He took it quick and neat. "Sure, I will," he said. "First thing when we get to sea."

Then he stepped to the boat deck over the weather coaming, into the darkness and the cold. He left the empty bottle where he'd tossed it on my settee. He left the smell of stale whisky and the echo of his voice. Funny. It wasn't bitter. It was full of a hollow scorn. And next morning the Trintipal sailed for home.

All right. I was only talking. You've got to talk the most when nothing you can say is any good. But Pete Drake kept his word. I guess he cadged what he needed from the first assistant and used the engine-room machine shop on his watch below. The first I knew about it, the Trintipal was pushing through the Japan Sea on the run to Hakodate. I came into the radio shack after supper for the usual evening watch, and there it was. He left it on my log table, this sideswiper he'd made, this precision transmitting key. He had good sense. He just left it while I wasn't there, and went away. The two polished vertical contacts glistened in the down-flung light. The sending lever between kept trembling gently from side to side with the vibration of the ship. It was good spring steel, all right. I knew he built it out of a whole lot more than good spring steel and polished contacts, though. So I didn't grin. I reached down. I let the small wooden finger piece come between my thumb and forefinger, and I gave it a careless whirl. That made me frown. I hooked on a dry cell and a sounding buzzer. I tried it again. It was awful. Like a fellow mumbling with mush in his mouth. Was I really as lousy as that?

"Now what the blazes have you got there, Sparks?" It was

Tony Fuller, barging in for a smoke on his way to the bridge, with half his mind on the weather. "Smells like it might be pretty dusty outside the Strait," he said. "What kind of a crazy gadget is that?"

"Sideswiper. A very fancy transmitting key. I never used one before. I was giving it a try."

"Sparks, all you birds are nuts. Always fiddling around. No wonder you can't sleep nights."

"Yeah." I grinned. "Takes lots of practice, Tony, to use one of these and use it right. The damn thing's got my goat."

That's all I told him. The rest belonged only to those of us who wore a different cut of the cloth. Then I put Pete Drake's precision key away. I thought maybe he'd come up there sometime, curious if nothing else, and give me a hint or two. He never did.

Meanwhile the Trintipal came snoring out of Tsugaru Strait, climbing the great Pacific circle toward the lightship on the Swiftsure Bank four thousand miles away. Tony Fuller was right. It was dusty enough. The westerlies were roaring up there. The ocean hills ran long and steep under lightless tatters of lower cloud. The Trintipal angularly climbed the white-veined flanks of the combers, hung there all of a shudder for a moment, and then plunged down, smashing green water all around her into acre-wide fields of foam. White cataracts gushed off the break of her fo'c'sle head, snarling across the forward well where the life lines were, and flinging icy sheets of spray as high as the weather cloth on the bridge. She was good in a seaway, though. She lifted clean and nice. She made you feel she was doing all right and knew all about this stuff. She had weathered gales before, tipping her funnel lip over whenever the sleet squalls came. I tried that sideswiper once or twice again. Then I gave it up in disgust. I just couldn't make the thing talk. The minute I touched it, it blubbered, that's all. I knew I'd have to get someone to show me the knack of it. In the end, it was Peter Drake who did.

We were four days out of the Strait and the gale was nearly spent. I was catching a little shut-eye on the bunk, wedged between the battery panel and the main transmitter stand. That much I know for sure. Then something exploded somewhere.

I remember that too. Something was roaring. Concussion took hold of the ship, hurling her aloft and then dropping her all at once. There was only a violent instant of consciousness between one dark sleep and another. Then the blackness closed again. But this one wasn't natural. It had to be struggled against. It was wrong. And the roaring went on. I don't know how long it went on. Then all of a sudden I recognized it. It was steam. And the ship was still. She was rocking in the water, but she was still. The engines weren't turning down there and the wheel was dead. The minute I knew that, the darkness began to shred away and a face was floating somewhere in the middle space. It kept getting closer all the time. Then the steam roar stopped. Abruptly. Suddenly the face belonged to Mr. Fuller, the Trintipal's third mate. And I wasn't in the bunk at all. I was on the deck, halfway across the shack. Pain stabbed my shoulder.

"I don't think it's broken. I got the bleeding stopped." He was strapping my arm against my side. "Hold still," Tony Fuller said.

That's how the nightmare began. It began up there near the fiftieth parallel toward the end of a heavy gale. It began with a floating mine. Some of it's blurred and fuzzy, like it happened to someone else. But things stand out, like things you see in a lightning flash, captured like that forever against surrounding blackness, frozen, immobile and crystal-clear. Pete Drake was a thing like that. All of a sudden, there he was, withered and small in the doorway's frame, peering in at the wreckage while Tony Fuller helped me stagger to my feet.

"Half an hour, Sparks," Fuller was saying. "An hour at the most. If we're lucky, the Old Man says. We're overhauling the starboard boats. She's filling up fast. Here's the position. You do what you can!" He turned and saw Drake. How would Tony Fuller know why Peter Drake was there? "You!" he ordered sharply. "You stay here! Give Sparks a hand! You do what he says!"

Drake didn't even look at him. "The antenna's okay," he told me. "I just checked."

He did what I told him. Something funny was in his eyes. Half the forward bulkhead was stove. You could see the ocean through the splintered hole. You could see it lifting under ragged clouds in the weird half-light of a sunless dawn, the long hills ribbed with foam and glinting bottle-green, hurrying away. Underfoot, the Trintipal rocked soddenly. She didn't rise. The voices of men at the boats and the creak of gear sounded far away. There was very little time.

He did what I told him. We heaved the wreckage aside. The power tubes and the generator looked all right, but you never can tell till you wind her up. It was broken leads I was worried about. We did a baling-wire job of splicing. My strapped-up arm wasn't numb any more. Pain kept knifing through it and across my chest. My right-hand fingers were thumbs, all thumbs. They wouldn't do what I wanted them to.

"All right, Sparks. Come along now." That was the Old Man, large in the doorway, blocking the ocean and the light. His voice was grave. "We are ready to launch," he said.

Ready to launch? That was nonsense. I had to get out on the air first. How long could men last in open boats in these latitudes? They could float around for days on that freezing wilderness of water if no one knew they were there. They wouldn't have a chance. I had to have more time. How did I know how long? Look at the wreck. I must have bellowed something like that at Captain Blandon. I was pretty groggy.

"I can't hold the boats any longer," he told me. I remember his voice. It was quiet and slow. "If the ship falls over any farther, we'll never get them away. There are badly hurt men to think about."

"Then launch them! I'll jump, sir! I'll jump as soon as I get an SOS out!"

"Very well. But you haven't got much time." And before Captain Blandon turned away, he added, "I'll stay too."

Sure he would! I knew damn well he would. It startled me to see Peter Drake still there, calmly finishing a cold splice on the leaded cable from the emergency-battery bank. Then he stood up. I'd forgotten all about him. Suddenly the shouted orders from the boat falls came very loud and clear. That and the deep overtone of moaning wind, the slapping noise and wash of the running seas. I started pulling the litter off the operating table.

"Clear out!" I remember barking that at Drake. "Get the blazes out of here now!"

"Sure," he said in the gentlest voice I ever heard. "Sure, I will. Right away." All in a moment it slashed across the back of my brain. My head snapped round quickly. And I heard him say, "It was just like this. It was almost exactly like this."

I suppose it was. But I didn't have any time for his miserable pangs of rum-soaked memory. Not now. I picked up what was left of my typewriter and heaved the broken mill aside. Then I groaned. The transmission key was smashed. I looked at the other one, and I groaned again. Then I flung open the tool chest—and there it was. The sideswiper. The precision key that Drake had built.

"Hook this up!" I sent it sliding on its base across the table to him. If he didn't have sense enough to get out of there, he might as well be useful. He didn't stir. He was in a daze. "Hook that damn thing up!"

He did. His fingers were trembling. They were trembling fearfully. I closed the main power line and the antenna circuit. I flipped the generator-starting switch, holding my breath. It was all right. It began its quick ascending whine. I reached over, pressing my thumb to the finger piece of that brand-new key, closing the contact on that side. But my eye was on the instrument panel. The needle on the radiation ammeter moved. The set was putting out.

"All right, Drake. Here's the position. The call is KPTS. Sit down. You're on the air."

He looked at me. He just stood there and looked at me, pleading. He half raised his trembling hands. "Me?" he said. "Me? With these?"

Then he sat down. I don't know what went through his mind. For an instant he looked around. The crooked smile slipped past his lips. In that wrecked place he saw the changes time and a war had wrought to a once-familiar trade. Through a jagged bulkhead hole he saw empty davits and the boat falls dangling. He saw the ocean, the long, wild-running hills, the tumbling hurry of the lower cloud rack, and maybe he heard the wind. Maybe he heard a whole lot else. Who knows what he heard? He was flexing his right-hand fingers.

"Twenty years," I heard him mumble. I heard him as plain as day. "Twenty years."

He reached out slowly. He touched the key. He tapped it again. Then his thumb came up to the finger piece and he sent off a trickle of v's. His eyes weren't pleading any more. His eyes were beginning to burn. Twenty years? What's twenty years to a man who ever pounded brass? What damage or harm can twenty years do to the language of your youth? They're all the same. They never forget it. It gets into the blood. They never forget it to the day they die. Drake's fingers stumbled a little. Then all at once the trembling stopped. They took hold. When they did, that sideswiper began to talk.

That's the clearest thing of all. That's the thing I remember best. It isn't blurred or fuzzy. It's sharp and shadowless. He had the earphones at his temples. He was braced against the sharp angle of the listing ship. And in that wrecked place, with a foundering deck beneath him, he didn't look old any more. I watched him, fascinated. And I listened. You think he was sending an SOS? Sure. But only with his fingers. This was Drake again. He was clearing Pacific traffic with a hot-shot sideswiper and a crummy old quenched gap. He was picking up relay stuff for KPH. Drake. Pete Drake! He never had to give his sign. The minute he opened up, the whole damn ocean knew who it was.

Maybe they did. Maybe even now they did. Maybe the restless shades of all the old brass-pounders heard him. If they did, then they knew. They knew right away who it was. Snaggy, somewhere off Diamond Head. Freddy Cugle, the straight-key man. They'd know. The instant they heard this fluting note, their heads would all come round and a wrinkling smile of recognition would suddenly touch their eyes. The stuff rolled off his fingers like a flowing song. I never saw fingers work a key like that. I never heard stuff like that before. Then the Trintipal lunged over. She teetered and hung there. She didn't rise. I looked up. Captain Blandon was back. His face was drawn. He was frowning severely at Drake. And at me.

"It's all right, sir." Speech sounded hollow. The ship was dead. It sounded like speech in an empty cave. "He knows his stuff," I said, giving Peter Drake the simple accolade.

"Well, come along! At once!" The Old Man's voice was brittle. "The boats are afloat. They're standing by. I've kept lines from them to the boat-deck rail. They'll haul us aboard when we jump. Can you manage, Sparks?"

"I'll manage, sir. We're—"

"Then I'll signal the mate."

"Yes, sir. We're coming right away."

"Hurry! She is on her beam ends now."

Then we were all alone again. Me and Drake. But not for long. "You listen to me! The Old Man won't leave till the last! I know!" I spat the words out at him. I knew what I had to do. "You tell him you can't swim. You're scared. Tell him anything you want. I can't help you in the water with this arm. He can. Get him over the side first. I'm coming back. You understand?"

"Sure. Sure, Sparks. I understand."

"I can use one side of that sideswiper. Good enough to be read. That position you sent don't mean a thing. We need compass bearings for a fix. Those boats will be floating around in a gale or a freezing pea-soup fog. You think I want to hear the things you hear? You think I want to wind up a damn drunken sousehead like you? Not on your life! Not me! I'm coming back!"

"Sure." He was moving ahead of me on the steeply slanted deck, his narrow shoulders and his gray head bent. "Sure, you are," he said. "And you're dead right, Sparks."

Then all in an instant he spun around. There was the funny look in his eyes. I saw it. That's all I saw. His fist smashed out at me. He had gathered up all his strength, leaping. My head rocked back with shock. I knew it. That's all I knew. I found the rest out later. I found out, huddled under a greatcoat in the stern sheets of Tony Fuller's boat.

He told the Old Man I fainted. I was cold, all right, out cold. That's how he got Captain Blandon to jump first. Then he lowered me into the water, a bowline under my arms, and waved all clear to the mate. They started to haul us across. And he stayed. He went back. He went back where he belonged.

That's how it was in the Trintipal. I saw her go down. We watched her from across a narrow space of ocean in that freezing, sunless dawn. The boats kept climbing to the white-flecked crests, rushing down to where the valleys glinted, ominous and green. I kept my eyes on the boat deck, on what was left up there of the radio shack. That's where Peter Drake was. I never saw him again, but I knew that's where he was. I knew what he was doing there. He was working the tool of his trade. The artist's tool. He was getting us plotted down to a pin point on the charts.

We saw the Trintipal shudder suddenly. Her leeside decks were awash. . . . *Whoever knows where they come from—them shoreside bums? Or, for that matter, where they go?* Stuff like that kept bubbling, without rhyme or reason, across the back of my brain. *I never even froze the key. I just sent the SOS and ran like hell for the boats.* There she was. She was going now. *The first time Johnny moaned, I knew I'd lost my ticket. He took it away from me. Right there in an open boat.* Steam gushed from the Trintipal's engine-room skylights. We heard the bulkheads inside her explode. The concussion was muffled. *Hell, no. They ain't mine. But the way I figger it, kids is kids. They could 'a' been mine.*

The Trintipal's wheel flung clear, the blades shining and motionless. Her head was sliding under already, dragging the rest of her down. There was nothing left but one great whirlpool on the ocean's face, and the broken debris swirling. She was gone. He went with her. But first he cleared his hook. He went back after twenty years and cleared his hook at last. He never expected a chance like that. It doesn't often come. He had an enormous good fortune. He saw his chance and he took it. I don't know yet where he came from, but I can tell Tony Fuller for certain where he went. He went back where he belonged. His smile isn't crooked any more. I know that for sure. And I know Johnny, the little oiler, doesn't moan. He's got his ticket back. He deserves it. I know that in all the ships who listened to him doing the Trintipal's last work, they tapped their keys for single dots when they heard Drake's set whine out and die. They were sending him their 73's—a brass-pounder's way of giving farewell. Farewell and godspeed. In my mind I sent him my own. He deserved that too. . . . We were picked up three hours later. We only lost one other man.

I told Dorothy all about it. I never would have seen her again if it wasn't for Peter Drake. Dorothy didn't think a girl ought to marry a man who went to sea. She had decided we ought to sign off for good. But I went back anyhow, and I told her. I told her all about it. She listened till I was done, the funny little wrinkles gathering between her eyes. Then she nodded.

Dot's gonna have a kid now. It's our first. I sure hope it's a boy. I'll get a deadhead message when it happens. Maybe I'll get it tonight. Because here I am in the middle watch with the earphones tucked at my temples. I'm waiting to meet a traffic schedule with KPH. It's Joe Pagini over there, and Joe's an old-timer. The minute I open up, he'll know what kind of a key I use. He don't know why I use it, but he'll know right away it's me. Then all the time I'm rapping out the code I'll be thinking of Peter Drake. Till my message hook is clean. I wish it was Pete Drake's sideswiper I was using. But it couldn't be. So I did the next best thing. I made me one of my own, and I swore I'd learn to use it right. I hope I did. Because if it wasn't for him, I wouldn't be here.

It's schedule time right now. I got my fingers on the key. I'm rolling the stuff off sweet. I'm calling for KPH. There he is. What did I tell you? I never even gave my sign. But here he comes through the break-in relay, bustin' in from Frisco two thousand miles away.

"Good morning, MP," he's saying. "Got nine for you. It's a girl. *K*—go ahead."

Port of Call

BUD HUTTON

THE FLYING DUTCHMAN came out of dirty weather around the Horn on the tail of a norther, picked up a good wind from almost dead astern that filled every sail, and began to reel off knots in the Pacific's long low swell. The wind was brisk and still held the chill of the Horn's ice floes as the Dutchman moved on a course almost into the setting sun, but almost overnight the weather turned tropical and every man not on watch came on deck to soak up the sun. They gathered in little knots, forward and aft, and they should have been happy to bring their unending arguments up from belowdecks and dispute them in the warm breeze, but they weren't.

For a while, Dewey and Sims tried to keep going their perennial debate with Lawrence and Jones over the merits of steam versus sail, and a few of the others paused to see whether anyone had thought of something new on the subject. Once they sounded like old times when Dewey made a point and Lawrence hollered, "Don't give up the fight, Paul!"

"Sir, I have not yet begun to argue," Jones answered, but his heart wasn't in it, and, after a rebuttal of sorts, he was silent.

Across the decks it was the same way. A couple of Roman admirals were arguing, as they always had, with two or three Carthaginians as to whether the extra power of a quinquereme's fifth bank of oars offset the added bulk and weight of that many more rowers and benches, but, as von Spee said caustically, those Mediterranean fellows lived so far in the past, nothing bothered them.

Even on the quarter-deck, where Nelson had the watch, the feeling of uneasiness communicated itself. Ordinarily, old Nelson would have had all hands holystoning the decks or mending sail, in weather so fine, but today he turned his blind eye on the decks as he paced behind the helmsman. Once or twice he looked over the man's shoulder at the compass, saw they still held a course just north of due west, and shook his head in bafflement.

Seated against a hatchway on the afterdeck, Jellicoe and Beatty tried for a while to interest some of the others in a game of crown 'n' anchor, but no one wanted to play. A single German admiral stood stonily staring at the crown-'n'-anchor board through his monocle. Ordinarily, lacking a game, Jellicoe and Beatty would have mentioned Jutland, just to hear the German start spouting the statistics of tonnages lost by the opposing fleets and trying to prove that it was really a victory for the Imperial Reich, *nicht wahr?* But today Jellicoe merely looked up and said, "Afternoon, *Graf*," because he had found it safe to call all those German chaps "*Graf*," and went back to staring emptily over the rail.

Inevitably, the glances of the men on the deck turned toward the admiral's cabin. The door remained shut, as it had been since the voyage began. Sometimes they could hear him pacing the cabin, back and forth, but he had all his meals brought in by the steward and hadn't once been on deck.

Even the usually jaunty Drake was depressed by the vague uneasiness, the strange feeling of something unknown and ominous, which hung over the ship. Dewey and de Grasse watched him turn away from a figure at the taffrail and come over to them.

"What do you hear, Frank?" Dewey asked.

Drake shook his head. "No one seems to know a thing," he replied. "I even tried asking that chap back there. Never can remember his name. You know, foreigner. Japanese fellow who crossed the T on the Russians at Tsushima Strait. But he just looked politely at me and hissed something or other." Drake frowned at the figure by the taffrail. "Odd bloke, anyway. Can't even speak English." He sat down by Dewey and the French admiral and watched the blue waters slip past.

"This is the queerest voyage yet," he said after a pause. "I've made plenty of them with the Old Man, but this one's different. Spooky, actually."

"Something is—how you say it?—yes, rotten in Denmark," agreed de Grasse, hastily adding, "No offense, monsieur," as an old sea dog from the Skagerrak turned at the words.

"Davy wouldn't even let da Gama navigate, the way he usually does," Dewey pointed out. "I asked Vasco if he knew where we were going, but he swore he didn't know a thing."

Drake pulled absently at his ear. "There was the time he got us all out of the locker room and aboard the Dutchman to go watch that affair at Hampton Roads," he recalled. "You know that Monitor-and-Merrimac business. Davy said that marked a turning point, and he wanted us all there to witness it. Of course, before we got Nelson with us, we always had to go for a critique on his shows, and there were a couple more. Finally, there was that trip we made in peacetime, just after the war in 1914–18, you remember, to watch some fellow fly an airplane off a ship's deck. Astounding thing, that; Davy said it was a turning point, too."

"Seems like every trip he's called us out of the locker room for was to watch some turning point or other," Dewey pointed out. "Maybe this is one."

"But there is no war now, messieurs," de Grasse interposed. "This last war is done, we know, and yet we sail into the Pacific, all of us, with such a feeling on board ship as I never have known."

"It's funny, all right, and the steward says the Old Man is acting like he's worried stiff, which isn't like Davy Jones," put in Mahan, who had come up just in time to hear the last phrase. They all stood up and went about the change of the watch as eight bells tolled.

Never had the weather been so fair for a voyage of The Flying Dutchman; never had the spirits of the men aboard her been so low. Once Eric the Red swore he had seen a black gull following them all through the sunrise watch, and every man aboard knew that was the worst possible luck.

On the next day they caught rainy weather, and that night the watch reported they had passed strange craft hove to. Finally the weather cleared again, and one morning all hands came scrambling on deck at sunrise when they heard the rumble of chains as the forward anchor was let go.

"Ships!" gasped Dave Farragut as he emerged into the sunlight. "Must be hundreds of 'em!"

"Battleships, cruisers, destroyers, some of those newfangled aircraft carriers, barges, tugs, transports and freighters!" Jellicoe exclaimed. "I say! Where in the world has Davy brought us this time?"

"Submarines, too," dryly remarked Simon Lake, "and I can't tell for sure about them, but, if you gentlemen will look closely, you'll notice as I just have that there isn't a man to be seen on a single craft."

The others looked. All across the huge fleet, which was anchored in a wide tropical lagoon, there wasn't a sign of human life. As they looked, they felt again the apprehension which had been with them throughout the voyage. The clear, bright day seemed falsely bright, and a faint wind in the rigging made a sad sound, like a violin playing far away. Even Nelson shivered.

The old seamen drew together on the midship decking, as if to find comfort in the presence of one another and present a solid front to the unnamed and intangible sense of doom which permeated the whole craft. They were standing like that when the door of the admiral's cabin opened, and, for the first time in the voyage, Davy Jones stepped on deck.

They were shocked at his appearance. The grizzled, hearty sea dog who had always seemed ageless to them looked tired, weary, as if he had not slept for nights. There was silence as old Davy's glance moved across his men. For a moment his eyes shone with pride, and then they clouded again and his face set in the lines of the worry that was in him.

Nelson broke the silence. "Begging the admiral's pardon," he said, "but we'd like to know where we are, and what we're here for, wherever it is."

There was a murmur of agreement from the admirals and captains around him. "This hasn't been a happy ship this trip, Davy!" someone called from the crowd. "Can you tell us why?"

Davy nodded, too occupied with his thoughts to notice the caller's lack of formality in address.

"As you all know," Davy Jones began, and the men fell silent under his words, "I've called you together for a voyage from time to time, one century or another, as the occasion demanded. This time—well, I've put off telling you as long as I could and——"

A far-off drone interrupted him. All heads turned toward the seaward sky. "Airplane," snapped Sims, who knew about such things. They turned back to Davy's words.

"I'm not certain yet. I won't be for"—Davy took a quick squint at the sky—"for a minute or two. But this, gentlemen, may be our last staff meeting."

"What?" The word went up from half a dozen throats.

"I'm not sure yet, mind you," the admiral went on, "but we'll——"

He broke off, staring. Everyone followed his gaze. Out of the hatchway scuttled a ship's rat. While they watched, he squeaked once, bared his long teeth, and with a rush was over the rail and swimming for the shore.

No one said a word. Davy Jones seemed to shrink inside his uniform. Wearily, almost with an air of resignation, he opened his mouth to speak again.

The sound of the ship's bell cut him short. It tolled twice, and before the third stroke there came to the men on the deck the sound of a hundred other ships' bells, borne across the water on the breeze.

One, two, three, four, five, six, seven——

The seamen looked quickly at the sun. It was a scant four bells, yet the sound tolled on, and it was Farragut who first noticed and shouted that The Flying Dutchman's bell was tolling with the rest, yet there was not a hand near it to strike clapper against bell.

Eight, nine, ten, eleven, twelve——

And still they tolled.

"Davy!" Paul Jones shouted. "No ship's bell tolls beyond eight bells! Davy, where are we? What is this?"

The admiral held up a hand. Overhead, the drone of the airplane seemed to be swelling, growing louder even above the sound of the bells.

"We're in mid-Pacific!" Davy called, and he had to shout because the ringing of the bells seemed louder, and the drone in the sky had become a thunder, and, though the sails hung almost limp and the water was still, the breeze in the rigging seemed to have become a full-blown gale, shrieking through the stays and whipping his words from his mouth.

"We're in mid-Pacific!" Davy repeated. "A place called Bikini Atoll! We've come—we're here to see if they'll need us any more!"

With the last sound of his voice, the roar of the wind grew to a wild, unending scream. The sound of aircraft engines beat and throbbed at their eardrums, and all across the lagoon of Bikini Atoll the bells of the ships went on tolling while the men of The Flying Dutchman looked to the high sky where an object had detached itself from a plane and was falling toward them.

The Sea Devil

ARTHUR GORDON

THE MAN CAME OUT OF THE HOUSE and stood quite still, listening. Behind him, the lights glowed in the cheerful room, the books were neat and orderly in their cases, the radio talked importantly to itself. In front of him, the bay stretched dark and silent, one of the countless lagoons that border the coast where Florida thrusts its great green thumb deep into the tropics.

It was late in September. The night was breathless; summer's dead hand still lay heavy on the land. The man moved forward six paces and stood on the sea wall. He dropped his cigarette and noted where the tiny spark hissed and went out. The tide was beginning to ebb.

Somewhere out in the blackness a mullet jumped and fell back with a sullen splash. Heavy with roe, they were jumping less often, now. They would not take a hook, but a practiced eye could see the swirls they made in the glassy water. In the dark of the moon, a skilled man with a cast net might take half a dozen in an hour's work. And a big mullet makes a meal for a family.

The man turned abruptly and went into the garage, where his cast net hung. He was in his late twenties, wide-shouldered and strong. He did not have to fish for a living, or even for food. He was a man who worked with his head, not with his hands. But he liked to go casting alone at night.

He liked the loneliness and the labor of it. He liked the clean taste of salt when he gripped the edge of the net with his teeth as a cast netter must. He liked the arching flight of sixteen pounds of lead and linen against the starlight, and the weltering crash of the net into the unsuspecting water. He liked the harsh tug of the retrieving rope around his wrist, and the way the net came alive when the cast was true, and the thud of captured fish on the floor boards of the skiff.

He liked all that because he found in it a reality that seemed to be missing from his twentieth-century job and from his daily life. He liked being the hunter, skilled and solitary and elemental. There was no conscious cruelty in the way he felt. It was the way things had been in the beginning.

The man lifted the net down carefully and lowered it into a bucket. He put a paddle beside the bucket. Then he went into the house. When he came out, he was wearing swimming trunks and a pair of old tennis shoes. Nothing else.

The skiff, flat-bottomed, was moored off the sea wall. He would not go far, he told himself. Just to the tumbledown dock half a mile away. Mullet had a way of feeding around old pilings after dark. If he moved quietly, he might pick up two or three in one cast close to the dock. And maybe a couple of others on the way down or back.

He shoved off and stood motionless for a moment, letting his eyes grow accustomed to the dark. Somewhere out in the channel a porpoise blew with a sound like steam escaping. The man smiled a little; porpoises were his friends. Once, fishing in the Gulf, he had seen the charter-boat captain reach overside and gaff a baby porpoise through the sinewy part of the tail. He had hoisted it aboard, had dropped it into the bait well, where it thrashed around, puzzled and unhappy. And the mother had swum alongside the boat and under the boat and around the boat, nudging the stout planking with her back, slapping it with her tail, until the man felt sorry for her and made the captain let the baby porpoise go.

He took the net from the bucket, slipped the noose in the retrieving rope over his wrist, pulled the slipknot tight. It was an old net, but still serviceable; he had rewoven the rents made by underwater snags. He coiled the thirty-foot rope carefully, making sure there were no kinks. A tangled rope, he knew, would spoil any cast.

The basic design of the net had not changed in three thousand years. It was a mesh circle with a diameter of fourteen feet. It measured close to fifteen yards around the circumference and could, if thrown perfectly, blanket a hundred and fifty square feet of sea water. In the center of this radial trap was a small iron collar where the retrieving rope met the twenty-three separate drawstrings leading to the outer rim of the net. Along this rim, spaced an inch and a half apart, were the heavy lead sinkers.

The man raised the iron collar until it was a foot above his head. The net hung soft and pliant and deadly. He shook it gently, making sure that the drawstrings were not tangled, that the sinkers were hanging true. Then he eased it down and picked up the paddle.

The night was black as a witch's cat; the stars looked fuzzy and dim. Down to the southward, the lights of a causeway made a yellow necklace across the sky. To the man's left were the tangled roots of a mangrove swamp; to his right, the open waters of the bay. Most of it was fairly shallow, but there were channels eight feet deep. The man could not see the old dock, but he knew where it was. He pulled the paddle quietly through the water, and the phosphorescence glowed and died.

For five minutes he paddled. Then, twenty feet ahead of the skiff, a mullet jumped. A big fish, close to three pounds. For a moment it hung in the still air, gleaming dully. Then it vanished. But the ripples marked the spot, and where there was one there were often others.

The man stood up quickly. He picked up the coiled rope, and with the same hand grasped the net at a point four feet below the iron collar. He raised the skirt to his mouth, gripped it strongly with his teeth. He slid his free hand as far as it would go down the circumference of the net so that he had three points of contact with the mass of cordage and metal. He made sure his feet were planted solidly. Then he waited, feeling the tension that is older than the human race, the fierce exhilaration of the hunter at the moment of ambush, the atavistic desire to capture and kill and ultimately consume.

A mullet swirled, ahead and to the left. The man swung the heavy net back, twisting his body and bending his knees so as to get more upward thrust. He shot it forward, letting go simultaneously with rope hand and with teeth, holding a fraction of a second longer with the other hand so as to give the net the necessary spin, impart the centrifugal force that would make it flare into a circle. The skiff ducked sideways, but he kept his balance. The net fell with a splash.

The man waited for five seconds. Then he began to retrieve it, pulling in a series of sharp jerks so that the drawstrings would gather the net inward, like a giant fist closing on this segment of the teeming sea. He felt the net quiver, and knew it was not empty. He swung it, dripping, over the gunwale, saw the broad silver side of the mullet quivering, saw too the gleam of a smaller fish. He looked closely to make sure no sting ray was hidden in the mesh, then raised the iron collar and shook the net out. The mullet fell with a thud and flapped wildly. The other victim was an angel fish, beautifully marked, but too small to keep. The man picked it up gently and dropped it overboard. He coiled the rope, took up the paddle. He would cast no more until he came to the dock.

The skiff moved on. At last, ten feet apart, a pair of stakes rose up gauntly out of the night. Barnacle encrusted, they once had marked the approach from the main channel. The man guided the skiff between them, then put the paddle down softly. He stood up, reached for the net, tightened the noose around his wrist. From here he could drift down upon the dock. He could see it now, a ruined skeleton in the starshine. Beyond it a mullet jumped and fell back with a flat, liquid sound. The man raised the edge of the net, put it between his teeth. He would not cast at a single swirl, he decided; he would wait until he saw two or three close together. The skiff was barely moving. He felt his muscles tense themselves, awaiting the signal from the brain.

Behind him in the channel he heard the porpoise blow again, nearer now. He frowned in the darkness. If the porpoise chose to fish this area, the mullet would scatter and vanish. There was no time to lose.

A school of sardines surfaced suddenly, skittering along like drops of mercury. Something, perhaps the shadow of the skiff, had frightened them. The old dock loomed very close. A mullet broke water just too far away; then another, nearer. The man marked the spreading ripples and decided to wait no longer.

He swung back the net, heavier now that it was wet. He had to turn his head, but out of the corner of his eye he saw two swirls in the black water just off the starboard bow. They were about eight feet apart, and they had the sluggish oily look that marks the presence of something big just below the surface. His conscious mind had no time to function, but instinct told him that the net was wide enough to cover both swirls if he could alter the direction of his cast. He could not halt the swing, but he shifted his feet slightly and made the cast off balance. He saw the net shoot forward, flare into an oval, and drop just where he wanted it.

Then the sea exploded in his face. In a frenzy of spray, a great horned thing shot like a huge bat out of the water. The man saw the mesh of his net etched against the mottled blackness of its body and he knew, in the split second in which thought was still possible, that those twin swirls had been made not by two mullet, but by the wing tips of the giant ray of the Gulf Coast, *Manta birostris,* also known as clam cracker, devil ray, sea devil.

The man gave a hoarse cry. He tried to claw the slipknot off his wrist, but there was no time. The quarter-inch line snapped taut. He shot over the side of the skiff as if he had roped a runaway locomotive. He hit the water head first and seemed to bounce once. He plowed a blinding furrow for perhaps ten yards. Then the line went slack as the sea devil jumped again. It was not the full-grown manta of the deep Gulf, but it was close to nine feet from tip to tip and it weighed over a thousand pounds. Up into the air it went, pearl-colored underbelly gleaming as it twisted in a frantic effort to dislodge the clinging thing that had fallen upon it. Up into the starlight, a monstrous survival from the dawn of time.

The water was less than four feet deep. Sobbing and choking, the man struggled for a foothold on the slimy bottom. Sucking in great gulps of air, he fought to free himself from the rope. But the slipknot was jammed deep into his wrist; he might as well have tried to loosen a circle of steel.

The ray came down with a thunderous splash and drove forward again. The flexible net followed every movement, impeding it hardly at all. The man weighed a hundred and seventy-five pounds, and he was braced for the shock, and he had the desperate strength that comes from looking into the blank eyes of death. It was useless. His arm straightened out with a jerk that seemed to dislocate his shoulder; his feet shot out from under him; his head went under again. Now at last he knew how the fish must feel when the line tightens and drags him toward the alien element that is his doom. Now he knew.

Desperately he dug the fingers of his free hand into the ooze, felt them dredge a futile channel through broken shells and the ribbonlike sea grasses. He tried to raise his head, but could not get it clear. Torrents of spray choked him as the ray plunged toward deep water.

His eyes were of no use to him in the foam-streaked blackness. He closed them tight, and at once an insane sequence of pictures flashed through his mind. He saw his wife sitting in their living room, reading, waiting calmly for his return. He saw the mullet he had just caught, gasping its life away on the floor boards of the skiff. He saw the cigarette he had flung from the sea wall touch the water and expire with a tiny hiss. He saw all these things and many others simultaneously in his mind as his body fought silently and tenaciously for its existence. His hand touched something hard and closed on it in a death grip, but it was only the sharp-edged helmet of a horseshoe crab, and after an instant he let it go.

He had been under water perhaps fifteen seconds now, and something in his brain told him quite calmly that he could last another forty or fifty and then the red flashes behind his eyes would merge into darkness, and the water would pour into his lungs in one sharp painful shock, and he would be finished.

This thought spurred him to a desperate effort. He reached up and caught his pinioned wrist with his free hand. He doubled up his knees to create more drag. He thrashed his body madly, like a fighting fish, from side to side. This did not disturb the ray, but now one of the great wings tore through the mesh, and the net slipped lower over the fins projecting like horns from below the nightmare head, and the sea devil jumped again.

And once more the man was able to get his feet on the bottom and his head above water, and he saw ahead of him the pair of ancient stakes that marked the approach to the channel. He knew that if he was dragged much beyond those stakes he would be in eight feet of water, and the ray would go down to hug the bottom as rays always do, and then no power on earth could save him. So in the moment of respite that was granted him, he flung himself toward them.

For a moment he thought his captor yielded a bit. Then the ray moved off again, but more slowly now, and for a few yards the man was able to keep his feet on the bottom. Twice he hurled himself back against the rope with all his strength, hoping that something would break. But nothing broke. The mesh of the net was ripped and torn, but the draw lines were strong, and the stout perimeter cord threaded through the sinkers was even stronger.

The man could feel nothing now in his trapped hand, it was numb; but the ray could feel the powerful lunges of the unknown thing that was trying to restrain it. It drove its great wings against the unyielding water and forged ahead, dragging the man and pushing a sullen wave in front of it.

The man had swung as far as he could toward the stakes. He plunged toward one and missed it by inches. His feet slipped and he went down on his knees. Then the ray swerved sharply and the second stake came right at him. He reached out with his free hand and caught it.

He caught it just above the surface, six or eight inches below high-water mark. He felt the razor-sharp barnacles bite into his hand, collapse under the pressure, drive their tiny slime-covered shell splinters deep into his flesh. He felt the pain, and he welcomed it, and he made his fingers into an iron claw that would hold until the tendons were severed or the skin was shredded from the bone. The ray felt the pressure increase with a jerk that stopped it dead in the water. For a moment all was still as the tremendous forces came into equilibrium.

Then the net slipped again, and the perimeter cord came down over the sea devil's eyes, blinding it momentarily. The great ray settled to the bottom and braced its wings against the mud and hurled itself forward and upward.

The stake was only a four-by-four of creosoted pine, and it was old. Ten thousand tides had swirled around it. Worms had bored; parasites had clung. Under the crust of barnacles it still had some heart left, but not enough. The man's grip was five feet above the floor of the bay; the leverage was too great. The stake snapped off at its base.

The ray lunged upward, dragging the man and the useless timber. The man had his lungs full of air, but when the stake snapped he thought of expelling the air and inhaling the water so as to have it finished quickly. He thought of this, but he did not do it. And then, just at the channel's edge, the ray met the porpoise, coming in.

The porpoise had fed well this night and was in no hurry, but it was a methodical creature and it intended to make a sweep around the old dock before the tide dropped too low. It had no quarrel with any ray, but it feared no fish in the sea, and when the great black shadow came rushing blindly and unavoidably, it rolled fast and struck once with its massive horizontal tail.

The blow descended on the ray's flat body with a sound like a pistol shot. It would have broken a buffalo's back, and even the sea devil was half stunned. It veered wildly and turned back toward shallow water. It passed within ten feet of the man, face down in the water. It slowed and almost stopped, wing tips moving faintly, gathering strength for another rush.

The man had heard the tremendous slap of the great mammal's tail and the snorting gasp as it plunged away. He felt the line go slack again, and he raised his dripping face, and he reached for the bottom with his feet. He found it, but now the water was up to his neck. He plucked at the noose once more with his lacerated hand, but there was no strength in his fingers. He felt the tension come back into the line as the ray began to move again, and for half a second he was tempted to throw himself backward and fight as he had been doing, pitting his strength against the vastly superior strength of the brute.

But the acceptance of imminent death had done something to his brain. It had driven out the fear, and with the fear had gone the panic. He could think now, and he knew with absolute certainty that if he was to make any use of this last chance that had been given him, it would have to be based on the one faculty that had carried man to his pre-eminence above all beasts, the faculty of reason. Only by using his brain could he possibly survive, and he called on his brain for a solution, and his brain responded. It offered him one.

He did not know whether his body still had the strength to carry out the brain's commands, but he began to swim forward, toward the ray that was still moving hesitantly away from the channel. He swam forward, feeling the rope go slack as he gained on the creature.

Ahead of him he saw the one remaining stake, and he made himself swim faster until he was parallel with the ray and the rope trailed behind both of them in a deep u. He swam with a surge of desperate energy that came from nowhere so that he was slightly in the lead as they came to the stake. He passed on one side of it; the ray was on the other.

Then the man took one last deep breath, and he went down under the black water until he was sitting on the bottom of the bay. He put one foot over the line so that it passed under his bent knee. He drove both his heels into the mud, and he clutched the slimy grass with his bleeding hand, and he waited for the tension to come again.

The ray passed on the other side of the stake, moving faster now. The rope grew taut again, and it began to drag the man back toward the stake. He held his prisoned wrist close to the bottom, under his knee, and he prayed that the stake would not break. He felt the rope vibrate as the barnacles bit into it. He did not know whether the rope would crush the barnacles, or whether the barnacles would cut the rope. All he knew was that in five seconds or less he would be dragged into the stake and cut to ribbons if he tried to hold on; or drowned if he didn't.

He felt himself sliding slowly, and then faster, and suddenly the ray made a great leap forward, and the rope burned around the base of the stake, and the man's foot hit it hard. He kicked himself backward with his remaining strength, and the rope parted, and he was free.

He came slowly to the surface. Thirty feet away the sea devil made one tremendous leap and disappeared into the darkness. The man raised his wrist and looked at the frayed length of rope dangling from it. Twenty inches, perhaps. He lifted his other hand and felt the hot blood start instantly, but he didn't care. He put this hand on the stake above the barnacles and held on to the good rough honest wood. He heard a strange noise, and realized that it was himself, sobbing.

High above, there was a droning sound, and looking up he saw the nightly plane from New Orleans inbound for Tampa. Calm and serene, it sailed, symbol of man's proud mastery over nature. Its lights winked red and green for a moment; then it was gone.

Slowly, painfully, the man began to move through the placid water. He came to the skiff at last and climbed into it. The mullet, still alive, slapped convulsively with its tail. The man reached down with his torn hand, picked up the mullet, let it go.

He began to work on the slipknot doggedly with his teeth. His mind was almost a blank, but not quite. He knew one thing. He knew he would do no more casting alone at night. Not in the dark of the moon. No, not he.

The Kid in Command

JACLAND MARMUR

ONE WAY OR ANOTHER, it has happened before. It will probably happen again. Maybe off the African coast, in Stephen Decatur's gunboat a hundred and fifty years ago, a seaman was faced with a choice like that. From Tripoli to Okinawa, one bloodstained beach is like another—they are all so far from home. So this doesn't belong to a time or a place. It belongs to the men of the fleet. To destroyer people, mostly. This kid was one of them.

They didn't know him in the USS James Blake. He didn't belong to that ship. She was lean and long, the Blake, sea-stained and battle-gray. Detached from Desron Twelve, she was steaming south and west along the rock-scarred Korean coast, coming down alone from bombardment missions in the north. Thin smoke haze trailed her funnel lips, her radar sweeping, westing sunlight washing all her starboard gun tubs. She was heeling in the ground swell, twin five-inchers midship trained, her signal yardarms bare when she stood past Yonte Cape, needing replenishment and rest. Tin cans are always overdue for replenishment and rest. This kid was too.

Russ Dobson saw him first. Dobson was on the fo'c'stle head, his chief's cap tipped far back. He was growling disapproval about the pelican hook and the cable stopper. Somebody soon would feel his wrath. Chickman and the others up there weren't worried, though. Bosun's mates were always growling, especially twenty-year chiefs. To hear them, these days nobody did things right. Chickman grinned.

"O.K.," said Chick. "We'll watch it, chief." And then, the wisdom of half a hitch behind him, he instantly picked the breeze up where they had left it off. "All right, you tell me, Pink. Your grandpa won a war. My old man too. And here we are again. You tell me why."

"I wouldn't know," admitted Pinkerton. "Ask Dobson here. The chiefs know everything."

"It ain't my trade," growled Dobson, one thick finger thrusting down to point the anchor cable at his feet. "This is!"

The ship's head slipped against a long green swell. The chief looked up in time to see a burst of spray collapsing, loudly hissing as it fell. The westing sunfire caught his cheek, his highboned face like scarred old leather. He kept standing that way, wrinkle-eyed and peering past the ground swell toward the land. It wasn't natural. His harsh wrath should have curled around them long ago, and when it didn't Chick said quickly, "People, Pink; it's people. Saw it in a book somewhere. Ten thousand years ago, all men were hunters. Had to be. It's in the blood. It's like an instinct. Now we're so civilized ain't nothing left for men to hunt—except each other. That's why every——"

"Bridge!" The voice was Dobson's. Hoarse. Explosive. They looked up, alarmed. The chief was facing aft, big head tipped up, four five-inch rifles in the forward gunmounts snouting at him. "Bridge!" he roared. "Man in the water! Starboard bow!"

Chick spun around. His eyes were young and sharp, but he saw nothing. Blue-green water, glitter of late sunlight. Nothing more. Then Pinkerton beside him, pointing, "There! Look there!"

Chick saw it then. Dark blob in shadow, halfway to the rocky shore, thin churn of foam behind. Chick thought he saw an arm lift, feebly waving. Man, all right. Hanging onto something, both feet thumping in the flood.

"What's wrong with all them topside lookouts? Someone ought to get chewed out!"

"Ditched pilot! Sometimes them jets go down like stone."

"In a kapok life jacket? That's no fly boy, Chick!"

It wasn't. Pinkerton was right. They could hear quick voices from the bridge. The Blake's bows tipped, knifed deeply over in the swell. Ensign Burnham was striding forward, Dobson already halfway down the weather deck to meet him.

When the chief came swaying back, his gravel voice was barking. "All right, sailors, let's get hot! They'll lay him alongside. Starboard bow. Won't use the whaler. Pink! Small line up here. Net ladder, too! He——"

"How about Wesley, chief?" Pinkerton didn't want to miss any part of a thing like this. He complained, "It ain't my watch."

"Maybe it ain't his, either, down there in the water! Move!" Dobson looked quickly out across the cold and glittering flood. What he saw made memory stab at him. His head shot back. "Corpsman up here, Chickman. On the double! Get the chief. And blankets. Move!"

They could see him clearly now. Mat of dark hair, his white face drawn, he kept dipping under, clinging to a half-washed timber with one arm. Every time his head came up, he gulped in air. He knew what he was doing, and his eyes were always open.

Dark eyes. Nothing hopeless in them. No despair. Not there. They kept glowing up at the lean tall hull, the noisy enormous bow wave bearing down upon him.

On the Blake's forecastle deck, they lined the chain rail, peering down. Dobson had the heaving line all ready in two skillful coils, his scarred brown cheek against the light, watching how the water narrowed in between. He was gauging speed, the distance, angle of approach. Only once he shot a quick glance aft. Looking upward, he could see Commander Rathbone's head and shoulders just above the splinter shield against the bridge wing. Dobson saw the captain's head turn, saw his lips in movement to his talker.

Something flicked across the chief's gray eyes, like pride or recognition. He looked back and down at the water again. He was reassured. The skipper had the conn himself. They wouldn't overrun. When he felt the Blake's deck shudder underfoot at all astern, he snaked the line out smartly. And the kid down there caught hold.

That's how he came aboard the USS James Blake. He couldn't make the rope rungs by himself. He tried. The best he could do was hang there, eyes uplifted, blue lips mumbling something no one heard. When they hauled him inboard, he did not collapse. Water draining from his tattered dungarees, he staggered. Then he turned his head. He didn't see Mr. Burnham. He saw Dobson first. He recognized the chief's cap.

"Commanding officer!" he chattered. "Chief, I got to see——"

"Sure, kid; sure." They were pulling the kapok life jacket off him. The corpsman's kit was open, a tube of morphine in his hand. "Shock," the medic was saying. "Bound to be. The blanket, Doyle! He'll——"

"Commanding officer!" The kid still chattered. "Got to see him! I——"

"Sure, kid; sure." The medic reached out, morphine needle bare. "Must have been rough," he soothed. "Tell us about it later."

"No!" The kid pulled his arm away. He wasn't chattering any more. "Commanding officer!" he cried again, his voice a little wild. "Now!"

He thrust them all aside. He was swaying aft. He must have been a tin-can man himself. He knew exactly where the captain was. He went staggering up all the ladders, past the signal bags. Ensign Burnham was mumbling vague apology up there about a dripping enlisted man bursting to the bridge like that. The kid didn't know it. Dobson's arm was around his shoulders, as much in support as in restraint. The kid didn't know that either. All he saw was Commander Rathbone, tall before him, binoculars against his chest. The kid shook off the chief's large arm. He came erect. He knew the captain right away.

"Hanford, sir," he said. "John Hanford, bosun's mate third. Captain, I need help."

"Well, son, you'll get it. There's no need to barge up here. The corpsmen know their trade."

"Not that, sir. I'm O.K. But I got fourteen men back on that beach, six of them wounded, two of 'em bad. I tried to signal with a mirror and some fire bursts. Couldn't reach you. They're my people. If I don't get 'em off, they'll fry! I need——"

"Do you mean to say you swam out here to intercept this ship?"

"Yes, sir. I did."

"Who is your commanding officer? Who sent you?"

"No one sent me. The way I figure, I'm in command myself."

"You!" Commander Rathbone snapped the word out and

stopped short. Eyes cold and narrow, he appraised the swaying youngster for an instant while above the chatter of the signal halyards and the sobbing of the sea the murmur swept through all the people on his bridge. Battle fatigue or shock, they thought. They thought the kid hysterical. Maybe the skipper of the James Blake thought so too. "Son," he was asking sternly, "what's your ship?"

"I was in the Talbot, sir. Took sick. I got detached to hospital. Contagious ward. I——" The kid must have seen the captain's black brows lift. "Mumps!" he spat out bitterly. "I had the mumps!" Then his voice rushed on. "I was rotting in the personnel pool at Pusan waiting orders when this mission came along. I volunteered." He took a forward step, eyes burning. "Captain, there ain't much time left. I got an hour. Maybe two at most. As soon as it closes down real dark, them people are gonna get slaughtered. Maybe the Gooks are bringing mortars up right now. I got to get 'em off that beach! I need——"

The captain's hard voice broke in, "Son, you need to make more sense."

"Sense? All right, sir, sense! We put an Army demolition team ashore to blow a tunnel and a bridge. Last night. I was in the landing party. We blew it. Then we got jumped. Must have been a whole platoon. Offshore, in the LCM, I guess they saw the fire fight. I saw Lieutenant Darby start her in to get us off, both motors open wide. Then the LCM blew up. Mine, maybe. I don't——"

The captain's voice cracked out, "Supporting ship! What name?"

"Code call was Dingbat Four. I think we were supposed to rendezvous with her tonight. I don't know when or where. We never had a chance to call her. Radios all smashed. The lieutenant, Sparks, and the chief got killed. The Army captain too. We knew we couldn't hold out where we were. Not as soon as it got light. Beach too exposed. No cover. So we had to leave the dead. We took our wounded with us. They kept sniping at us, but we made it. We dug in." The kid made a wild, vague gesture toward the land. "There!" Then his voice rushed on. "It's a good position, sir. Rocky. Right back against the beach. They can't reach us except across an open pass. Corporal and a Pfc have got it covered from a forward boulder. I got three men on each flank. Good cover. We got weapons, some grenades left. They tried to overrun us twice. They won't try again till dark. After that, they're cooked. I got an hour, captain. Two at most. If I don't get 'em off in time, they'll fry."

It poured from him. It drained him nearly dry. Dobson wasn't looking at the kid. The chief was looking at the captain, saw the glitter in Commander Rathbone's eyes. He heard the skipper's hard voice saying, "This ship is under orders for squadron rendezvous. Do you really expect me to——"

"Yes, sir, I do!" The kid's eyes glowed. He was a bosun's mate third, and he cut a three-striper short. He broke into a full commander's speech! Ensign Burnham blinked. Not Dobson. Something glowed inside the chief. He still kept looking at the captain, hearing that kid rush on: "I don't mean to be disrespectful, sir. The Navy put them people on the beach. When I saw this tin can standing down, I told them the Navy would get them off. I'm Navy, sir. Enlisted Navy. I was the only rated man left alive. The way I learned it, I took charge. I figure I'm in technical command. Those people are mine. I got to get 'em off! That's why I swam out here. I need your help. I need—"

The glitter was growing stronger in Commander Rathbone's eyes. "For a bosun's mate third," he murmured, "you have taken a lot for granted."

The kid's whole body sagged. An instant only, though. His dark eyes shot out toward the beach. His voice came taut, its calmness terrible. "I didn't shove out here to save my own skin. Lolly will think so for sure, when he sees this can steam off. And them people will fry." He made half a turn toward the after bridge. "I'm a pretty strong swimmer, sir. I'd just as soon fry with them. I request permission to leave the ship."

He meant it! He meant to rejoin his people the same way he had come. He meant to go back where he belonged. He was halfway to the signal bag when Commander Rathbone's voice snapped at him, "Hanford!" The kid turned slowly. "You will want the motor whaler, son," the skipper said. "How many men?"

"Five, six. No more. Be in the way, sir." The kid came striding back, excitement burning in his eyes. "Ammo, sir. And a medic. We got to have covering battery fire when we start to retire. I figure——"

"Simmer down now, son. You want dry clothes. . . . Mr. Burnham, get the gunnery officer. Have the whaler called away."

"Aye, aye, sir." Ensign Burnham's voice was dry. He didn't approve. He thought the captain's treatment of enlisted personnel entirely too unorthodox. "Captain, I would like to go," he said.

"No." Commander Rathbone shook his head. An odd smile touched his lips. "This seems to be an enlisted man's operation." He looked at Dobson sharply. The chief looked back. A flash of understanding passed between them. "Dobson," the skipper asked, "do you want to take the boat?"

"No, sir, I don't." Then Dobson grinned. "But I will."

"Good." The captain knew what Dobson meant. No one wanted to get himself killed. "You bring these people back."

That's how it was. The last cold light was draining from the water when the USS James Blake put her whaleboat smartly overside. The land looked dark, some sunfire still along its ragged peaks, white curl of surf along the rocky beach. Hanford, in the sternsheets with the chief, looked back and up. From down here where the sea noise was, the ship looked huge, sharp-angled, bristling with her armament. For moments he could see the shapes and faces of her topside people and he thought Commander Rathbone's cold blue eyes were boring at him from above the bridge wing splinter shield.

Fear touched him. He could feel the spasm of it at his stomach's pit. He felt the boat slide down along the steep flank of the ground swell, tossing sprays before she surged. Then he could see the Blake's three gunmounts stir. They turned together toward the land. The gun snouts lifted all in unison. Six rifle barrels, long and deadly, hovered up there, hesitated, lowered, and then suddenly hung still. The ship receded with them, gently swinging. But the rifles kept on pointing where he'd told them to. Lieutenant Gridley had it all triangulated. Hanford felt the spasm in his belly twist, hurl upward in sharp pain. Fresh rated. Third class. How much did he know? Suppose he'd told it wrong! He swallowed hard. He wanted to cry out. They ought to check again. They couldn't. They were halfway to the beach already, and they didn't have much time. The kid turned forward, swallowing again.

"We get two hundred yards offshore, they'll open fire," he said. Voice sounded funny. Was it really his? He tried again. "Spaced salvos. Call fire when we need it. The Old Man said we better do it fast."

"Damn right!" The voice was Pinkerton's. "Sure wish we had a walkie-talkie radio." Pink didn't have the watch, but he was there. "You got the right word on the signals, Flags?"

"I got 'em. You all better get 'em too." The quartermaster chuckled. "Maybe I'm just striking for a purple heart. If I make it, someone else has got to take these flags. Chick, you better say again."

"O.K., Buzz." Chickman started rattling off, "All horizontal, shoulder high and still—cease fire. Flags straight aloft and still, commence again. Aloft, both waving, raise the range. Both at the shoulder, waving downward, lower range. One flag out right and shoulder high, come right. And left the same. That right, Hanford?"

"Yeah, Chick, yeah. That's right." The kid could only hope his voice was sounding better now. He wasn't sure. "All spot calls are for fifty yards."

"Fifty? You nuts? Lieutenant Gridley can shoot, but you sure sliced it close!"

"He said he'd try."

"O.K. now. Better knock it off." The gravel voice was Dobson's. He spoke out at last. "That beach looks rocky foul. Where's your sandspit, Hanford? See it yet?"

The kid peered forward through the bow spray toward the land. It looked different from a landing boat. That tin can's cold-eyed skipper should have sent an officer. You had an officer, he told you what to do. The chief was here, though. He looked like he had his twenty in already. He looked tough. The kid was glad the chief was there.

Then suddenly his dark eyes narrowed and he flung his arm out, pointing, crying, "There! Between those offshore boulders, chief! Sandspit. Gravel bottom. We can——"

"Tell the coxs'n, son. Don't growl at me." Dobson's voice was gruff. "You got the conn."

The kid looked up. Swiftly. Dobson's big head never stirred, eyes on the beach, his cheek like saddle leather. What the devil was the matter with him! Wasn't he the chief? First twinge of anger stirred in Hanford. Then his eyes flew landward and he cried, "Come right! You see that sandspit, coxs'n? Bring her——"

"Got it, Hanford. We're on rails now. Shoreside liberty party! Here we go."

A ragged crackling reached them from the land. They stiffened in the whaler. Small-arms fire! The beach was in clear sight now, boulder strewn, reaching inland like a funnel narrowing. Up there they saw quick-licking points of orange fire, the smoke bursts punching out. Hanford thought dark shapes were stirring there. Twenty. Thirty. Panic touched him.

"You see 'em, chief? That's where they are! They see the ship. They see us too. In a minute they'll start screaming. They'll charge out. We got to pin 'em down! Lolly and the corporal are behind that forward boulder up there by itself. They only got five, six grenades left. They'll get overrun! Why don't the ship start——"

"Simmer down. You said two hundred yards." Dobson's gravel voice was calm. "Lieutenant Gridley knows two zero zero when he——"

Explosion cut him short. It came from far astern. Enormous sounding, its blast and concussion rocked the whaler. They could feel the air compress aloft. The kid's head spun around. He was in time to see six five-inch rifle muzzles drool out smoke. First salvo from the USS James Blake! Shells on the way. First shells to help his people. Low across the wine-dark water he could see the ship's slow heel and her recovery. Gray silhouette against the sky, sea-scarred and battle-gray, white feather of a bow wave at her eyes. Tin can out there! The kid belonged in tin cans. He could see her three twin-mounted guns all stirring down, then up in perfect unison, director holding on the target, compensating her slow roll. Then shell bursts crashed against the land. Fear welled up in him. If they'd struck too close! If he had told it wrong! His eyes flew shoreward just in time to see erupting dust and rubble.

"On!" he screamed. "Right on!"

"Then leave her be," growled Dobson. "Don't look back. She'll do what she's supposed to. Don't look back!"

"Sure, chief. O.K." The beach was rushing toward him now, black tide-washed boulders on each side. Astern he heard the second salvo crash out from the Blake's main battery. Clean-spaced shooting. Fire cover for the landing. Fire cover for the men. And Hanford told the chief, "I think we better get the wounded first. We better bring the medic, chief. I'll show you where——"

"Don't show me!" Dobson spat it out. "You told the Old Man you took technical command. That's fine!" Then all at once the chief's voice lost its harshness. When the kid looked at him, half a grin twitched past the muscles of that big, scarred face. "It's your show. Son, you name it and we'll do it. You're in charge."

He meant it. He was asking for his orders from a frightened bosun's mate third class. It wasn't fair! The kid had asked for help to help his people. He had never asked to carry the whole load. Resentment stirred in him. The big man kept on looking at him, eyes like steel. Then anger flamed in Hanford, anger drowning out the fear.

"O.K.!" the kid cried. "Cut the engine. Beach her, coxs'n!" Voice wasn't sounding funny to him any more. It was his own. It sounded savage, full of wrath. The chief's grin broke, but Hanford didn't see it. "Two of you stand by the whaleboat. Hit for cover, all the rest. Keep that ammo dry. You watch me, Flags. All ready? Jump then! Here we go."

That's how it was. The kid took charge. He had to. And he knew he had to do it fast. They brought the wounded to the whaleboat first. The kid remembered that. How could a man forget how wounded look along the shell-pocked beaches far from home? The rest was not so clear. It got mixed up in gunfire, in erupting shell bursts, in the nearer, deadly chatter of small arms and automatic fire. He knew the Blake was out there. Offshore, hovering in smoky sea haze, she looked gray and narrow, flame tongues spearing from her in slow rhythm.

Hanford heard the five-inch common whining overhead before each salvo slammed against the land in deafening explosions. They crashed where he'd told them to. Up past the narrow tip of this funnel-shaped and rock-strewn beach. Up past the boulders there where Lolly and the corporal were. Time they retired. What were they doing up there? Suddenly he knew. He saw the two shapes, dark against the land. They darted out from cover, two arms swinging back to hurl grenades, then instantly dived for the ground again. Salvo from the Blake slammed far beyond them. Flame bursts and erupting debris. Far. Too far! Before the hurled earth settled, dark specks leaped from cover, burp guns spurting. Lolly and the corporal were pinned down.

"Flags!" the kid cried. "Signal! Lower the range! Quick!"

The quartermaster leaped erect, flags at his shoulders, both out horizontal, waving downward rapidly. Next salvo from the Blake—where would it burst? Could the lieutenant, back there far away in the director, spot two flimsy buntings on a distant beach? Could he bring that deadly gunfire lower? Only fifty yards? Maybe Hanford wondered. Maybe not. He sprang up. He was crying, "When I get there, Flags, you watch me! We'll start back. You see us running, wave again. Down fifty more! I'll——"

"You nuts? You know what splinter bursts of five-inch shell can do?"

Maybe that was Dobson. Hanford didn't know. He didn't care. The anger swirled in him. Chief handed him the load. Too late to take it back. He had to pin those devils with the burp guns down for long enough to get the corporal out. And Lolly. Lolly, grinning slyly when he'd said he'd swim out to the ship for help. Lolly thought he'd save his own skin if he made it. Didn't like the Navy. Lolly never thought he would come back. Well, here he was.

"You heard me, Flags! You do it like I said!"

The kid's voice curled. Then he was racing over broken ground. He thought some others ran beside him. Pink and Chickman? Never asked them. What would they be doing here? And Dobson. Was that him, that big hulk, lumbering along and grinning with a carbine at ready? Hanford didn't know. He saw young Lolly on the ground behind a boulder, and the corporal kneeling. He dived in beside them.

"Well," said Lolly, looking upward, face all twisted. "Damn

if it ain't Navy!" Lolly tried to grin. "You did come back. Navy, I never thought——"

"Sure, Lolly; sure. You're hurt. We're shoving off. I'll carry you."

"Keep down! Blake salvo on the way!" The voice was harsh. The gravel voice was Dobson's, after all. Then shell bursts and eruption, deafening and close. That tin can out there gave you what you asked for! Maybe it would keep those devils quiet for a while. How long? Before the rain of debris ended, the harsh voice again. "Now! On your way!"

That's what the kid remembered best. Big, hulking man with gravel in his throat, half-crouching, Pink and Chickman on each side, all spraying bursts of automatic fire. Covering him. Moving backward with him while he staggered down a beach to where the whaleboat was. Lolly draped across his shoulder. Corporal limping. Salvo from the Blake again. Must have come down fifty more. Shellfire walking closer to the water's edge. Then stillness. Startling and abrupt. Who could believe such stillness? Voices murmured in it. Slap of water and an engine's drone.

Then suddenly he knew. The beach was fading into the distance. He could not remember clearly when they launched. He knew they must have, though. Gray shape ahead. Sharp-angled, full of gun tubs. Rocking on the ocean. Looming in the sea haze. Blotting out the dusky sky. Destroyer USS James Blake.

"Did we get 'em all, chief?"

"Yeah, son, all. Except Lolly. The Pfc is dead."

The kid said nothing. He just blinked his eyes. Someone has to pick the chit up. This time it was Lolly. Lolly didn't think the kid would ever make it. Lolly never thought he would come back. Hanford blinked again. Then at last he murmured, "Anyhow, he knew."

No one heard him. They were rounding to. Looming wall of gray steel towering above the whaleboat, faces peering down, the noisy slap and sob of water in between. Then they hooked on. Hanford staggered when he reached the deck. It was too solid underfoot. He kept babbling profound worry for his wounded. Man who took charge had to worry. If he didn't, who else would?

"Sir, we brought them all," the kid was saying. He was talking to a man with cold and Spartan eyes who had binoculars against his chest. He was giving his report to the commanding officer. It was correct and proper that he should. "All except the Pfc," he blurted. "Lolly got hurt bad. I carried him myself. I wanted him back most of all. I'm sorry, sir. He died. Beefy's hurt bad too. I wouldn't want to lose——"

"They are being cared for, son. They'll be all right."

"Thank you, sir."

"I am sending a signal to Dingbat Four. I thought you would like to know." The glitter showed again in the commander's eyes. He still remembered how a bosun's mate, third class, fished dripping from the water, fiercely asked his help for people pinned down on a hostile beach, demanding it because he was the man in charge. A slow smile touched the captain's lips. He spoke with clarity. "As one commander to another, son—you did all right." The kid just blinked his eyes. Commander Rathbone seemed to understand why he still stood there, swaying. "Son," he said with gravity, "you are relieved."

"Thank you, sir."

The kid's voice trailed off thinly. When he heard those last words, suddenly the load fell from him. When the burden dropped, he sagged. He thought someone supported him. It looked like Dobson, but he wasn't sure. It seemed to him the voices kept on murmuring, and he was sure he saw young Ensign Burnham frown. Couldn't help it. All the ladderways on this tin can were too unsteady. They kept rocking and he had to watch them with great care. Something told him he was in the wrong place. Chiefs' compartment? He didn't belong there. And the voices were still murmuring.

"Pretty crowded for'ard, sir. I put him in my bunk." Hanford recognized the gravel voice. Dobson didn't sound tough, after all. "Shut-eye's all he needs. He'll do."

Hanford thought he grinned. He'd keep awake. That's what he'd do. He knew the skipper was down there too. He'd lie there, listening. He'd play it cute. There was something funny between that tall three-striper and the big-faced chief. Now and then you saw it. Not too often. Mostly between old Navy CPO's and some scramble-egg-capped officer. Like Dobson here and this commander. When they looked hard at each other, something flashed between. Quick as lightning, cold as steel. Something they both recognized.

"Mr. Burnham seems browned off," the skipper said in a voice too still and quiet for a tin can's bridge. "The ensign is fresh from the academy, chief. He doesn't approve at all. He doesn't approve of you either, Dobson, letting that kid take charge." Commander Rathbone chuckled. It was a most astonishing thing to hear from that cold-eyed man. "Did you ever hear about the destroyer Perry, chief? The Perry was tied up at Mare Island Navy Yard in 1906. My father was an ensign then. After the earthquake, the whole Frisco water front was burning. My father says the commandant sent every man he could down bay to help. For several hours, on one of those days, there wasn't a soul on board the Perry except a Chinese wardroom steward. The mooring lines were in need of quick attention on the tide, and he took charge. Good job he did. The point is, chief, that for those hours a Chinese by the name of Sing Hoy had the honor of being in technical command of a fully commissioned ship of war of the United States Navy. I must tell Mr. Burnham about it." Commander Rathbone chuckled again. "If a Chinese steward's mate can pick up the chain of command—so can a bosun's mate third."

"Seems like when it's needful, sir, somebody always does."

"Yes. Let's hope somebody always will. Do you think I ought to fly Tare Victor George at the yardarm for him, chief?"

"Operation completed? No, sir, I don't." Dobson's voice was quick and flat. "Not on this lousy coast. They ain't gonna finish it here. They ought to, but they won't. It ain't completed at all. We're gonna have to do it someplace else. Someplace soon. We're gonna have to do it all over again."

"Maybe, Dobson, maybe." The skipper was looking down at the kid. "Name's Hanford," he was saying. "John Hanford, isn't it? Said he was waiting orders. I intend to ask for him. Make a good man for your division, chief. Be a good man for the ship."

"Yes, sir. He would."

"I wonder how old he is."

"Looks like maybe——" Dobson's voice cut short. When it spoke again, it sounded almost harsh. "Sir," it said, "I hope he's way past twenty-one!"

"Why?"

They were looking at each other now. Hanford should have seen it. Tall three-striper, tin-can skipper in fresh khakis, scrambled eggs along his cap peak. And the chief in dungarees, named Dobson, big man with the face like leather, scarred by conflict. They were staring at each other, blowers humming in the chiefs' compartment, sea noise sounding faint and muffled. They were silent for an instant. In that instant the quick lightning flashed between them. Hanford should have seen it. Tarawa and the 'Canal were in it. Saipan and the Okinawa picket line. Things half forgotten leaped up; all the perished comrades who were deathless rose, all crying glory and enormous tragedy. Respect was in it too. Respect for dignity and competence.

Then suddenly it passed. The lightning flickered out. And Dobson grinned. Dobson had three daughters, and no sons. Just like Commander Rathbone. Dobson didn't mind. The captain did. It was the first time in a hundred years no Rathbone son was at Annapolis or in the Line. The skipper was always prowling for some likely youngster he could sponsor. Dobson grinned again.

"I hope," he was repeating, "I hope he's way past twenty-one. Kid like that, sir, wouldn't feel right in a wardroom. Just like me. He'll ship over. Bound to. He's enlisted Navy. He'll——"

"And the first thing Stateside, Dobson," snapped Commander Rathbone, "you intend to introduce him to your youngest girl!"

"Yes, sir, I do. I sure do." Then Dobson's broad grin faded. "He will make a darn good chief, sir," Dobson's gravel voice said firmly. "Good chiefs ain't too easy nowadays to find."

The kid had never heard a word of it. The kid was fast asleep.

Troubled Voyage

WILLIAM HOLDER

WE WERE DUE TO SAIL AT NINE, but at eight o'clock, Simmons, the chief mate, slipped on the rain-glazed ladder leading to the boat deck and broke an arm. They took him off, and the Old Man roused someone at the company offices and told them to shake themselves and get a mate aboard, since he had no intention of spending the rest of his life tied to a pier in the North River.

He got a mate. The man came aboard at ten o'clock in a furious, driving rain, and three minutes later the tugs were hauling us away from the dock out into the stream, heading the bow of the Louise Vickers in the general direction of Cherbourg.

I had the watch and was standing in the wheelhouse, relaying to the helmsman the orders of the pilot, who was out on the bridge wing. The conversation taking place in the captain's cabin, just aft of the wheelhouse, came to me clearly. Captain Thompson was a thin old wisp of a man, but his voice was as sharp and penetrating as the blade of a well-honed knife.

"I don't know why they sent me you, mister, when I asked for a mate. I've been giving this company satisfactory service for years and certainly deserve better treatment."

The new mate's voice was low, even, controlled. "The situation is no more pleasing to myself than it is to you. Did I have more choice in the matter of ships, I'd not have accepted this one."

"You've master's papers, or so I've heard. Why do you sail as mate? There's no lack of ships."

"There's a lack of ships for me, as you well know."

I could almost see the captain smile, almost see him nod. Those things were in his voice, but no pleasantness. "Well, you know the sort of ship I keep, what I expect to be done. And try—try very hard—not to sink us. I've never lost a ship. That will be all, Mr. McCall."

And that name made part of the conversation understandable. McCall. Bad-Luck McCall. The man who had lost three ships in four years, but who, it seemed, would never get another. He was the son of misfortune, and no sailor or any steamship company wanted anything to do with him. He was a salt-stained nightmare to every man who rode the sea. He was bad luck.

It was a McCall run from the first moment. The night was as black as the inside of a cat and the rain was driving and chill. As soon as we cleared Sandy Hook we caught a heavy sea pushed by a freshening southeast wind, and the Vickers began to labor slightly. She was a fine big freighter and her virtues were many, but sea kindliness was not one of them. She did her work heavily, with a lack of that certain grace some ships possess. But tonight she seemed to be acting a bit more awkwardly than usual. Perhaps she had begun to feel the presence of McCall.

It really began when we dropped the pilot. The launch came alongside, rising swiftly, then dipping sharply into the trough, and we made a lee for her. The pilot went down the ladder, made the launch, and then it happened. The Vickers rolled slightly just as the launch rose on a swell and on the bridge I could hear the smash as her stem and forward frames splintered.

McCall was on deck. I recognized his voice, louder now, but even and unhurried. He took charge as if this happened to him every day. We had a bit of way on, and faster than I thought it could be done, he had a line on the launch. She swung with her stern to the sea, and her sternway served to keep her from taking water through her cracked bow. We held her like that until the pilot boat, summoned by our blinker light, came over and took charge.

The Old Man was on the bridge during the entire proceedings. When the pilot boat and the crippled launch were clear and we were under way once again, he walked through the wheelhouse to the chartroom. He was shaking his head, and I heard him say, "Whoever sent that man aboard——"

Mulligan relieved me at midnight. Mulligan was six feet two, had shoulders like a hatch beam, brought his favorite whisky aboard in five-gallon jugs. On our last trip to Oran, Mulligan had been arrested in a brawl in a shore dive and the Old Man wouldn't have allowed him to step foot on the dock the ship was tied to if Mulligan hadn't been one of the fine navigators of the world. He spoke five languages well and his voice was the gentlest I've ever heard. He was seventy years old.

"A fine night, Mr. Sherwood," he said. "A bit of breeze and a touch of rain and the faintest suggestion of a sea running, but all in all, a fine night."

"A fine night for McCall," I said.

He looked at me, then shook his great white head. "You're young, and superstition still in you, to think that weather recognizes the sound of a man's name. Sailors' tales and old wives' tales are both born to be ignored. And what's the course?"

I gave it to him as if it were news, and he accepted it with a pleased smile, as if he had not plotted it himself. I said, "Nevertheless, smashing that pilot launch was unusual. The Old Man said——"

Mulligan shook his head again, and said in his gentle voice, "The Old Man's not thinking of the launch, lad. He's got his mind on his daughter when he looks at McCall."

"His daughter? What's his daughter got to do with McCall?"

"Nothing," Mulligan said, "if the Old Man has his way."

I hadn't known there was a personal angle to the captain's evident dislike of McCall. "I thought it was just because he'd lost so many ships."

"Three," Mulligan said. "He was torpedoed once off Greenland, and his next ship hit a mine in the Irish Sea. Later, he was in collision with a tanker, in a big convoy that was creeping through heavy fog off the Banks, and if the tanker's skipper had lived, he would have lost his ticket."

It didn't sound bad when Mulligan recited it like that. Those things happened to ships. "But one man," I said. "Will anything decent ever happen to him?"

Mulligan nodded. "I think so. In the normal cycle of events, most of his fortune from now on should be good. Some men encounter trouble in its various forms all their lives. A man will fall and break a leg one year, lose his teeth another, and five years later his wife will run off with some young fellow with curly hair, and take the family savings with her. McCall's troubles are arriving in a crowd. He's having them now, having done with them, and the remainder of his life should be fortunate, does he survive them."

"Well, I hope he survives this trip," I said. "He, and us with him. I've got my fingers crossed."

"And your brains," Mulligan said.

But I wasn't alone in the way I felt. The thing ran through the ship quickly, and you could hear it and feel it and almost smell it. By morning, everyone on the Vickers knew that Bad-Luck McCall was aboard, and it was the sole topic of conversation.

Fletcher, the chief engineer, came into the saloon mess with a scowl on his face. He sat at the skipper's table and without preliminaries, said, "You should never have signed him on. The man carries ill luck with him like a ring that won't come off his finger."

The Old Man said, "You've forgotten something, Mr. Fletcher. The Louise Vickers isn't McCall's ship; it's mine."

"Which is no matter," Fletcher answered. "Bad luck followed him up the gangplank."

At ten minutes of eight I was on the bridge to relieve McCall. We carried but three deck officers, and the chief mate stood the four-to-eight watch. It was the first time I had seen him. I was surprised.

He was a tall, rangy man, and dark, about thirty, and when he turned to me, I saw that his features were strong almost to the point of harshness. His eyes were blue, and I could feel their cool, measuring impact.

I said, "I'm Sherwood, the third mate."

He nodded. "My name's McCall. Glad to know you." He gave me the course, showed me the log, signed for his watch. There was a tightness about him that was neither defiance nor apology, merely a flat statement of sufficiency. He needed no help, would accept neither a condolence nor an affront. I liked him at once.

When McCall had gone below, Lewis, the A.B. at the wheel, said, "And this'll be a fine trip. Watch the old bucket fall apart or blow up. I had a kid brother who sailed with McCall. He never came back."

"I had an older brother who was lost off the Florida coast," I said. "He was sailing with a skipper named Bishop. He never heard of McCall." I was a little surprised at myself.

But the ship had the fever. Everyone seemed to sit back and wait for something to happen. I knew how the deck gang felt. Every man on my watch had a story to tell about McCall. It seemed that they all knew someone who knew someone who had been touched by the shadow of the misfortune that trailed McCall like an ugly, shrewish but faithful mistress.

And the attitude of the engine-room crowd was reflected in the restlessness of Fletcher. He was waiting, almost anxiously, it seemed to me, for his engines to break down, for his shaft to crack. "Mark my words," I heard him say to Mulligan, "this will be the worst trip the Vickers has had, if not the last."

Mulligan laughed at him. "And now you've found an excuse to cover the neglect you've shown that heap of scrap below. If anything happens, if the whistle doesn't blow, it'll be all the mate's fault."

Which was not true. The Vickers' engine room was as tidy as a Dutch kitchen. The steel and the brass were shining and polished, and it would have been a day's task to find a spot of grease upon the gleaming decks. The huge pistons moved in their clean, unceasing rhythm that was the healthy pulse of a fine ship.

The rest of the big Liberty was like the engine room. The Old Man kept her looking like a yacht. The day men were skillful and fast and the watches made plenty of overtime. She used a lot of paint and was a proud if somewhat hippy lady.

As bad as the weather had been at the start, it improved hardly at all. The sky was continually filled with low scud and rain, and the seas ran long and high. We were heavy-loaded with a mixed cargo and we wallowed along before the weather, everyone blaming each gray dawn on McCall, everyone cursing him for the rain-lashed nights.

McCall worked hard, and in spite of the foul weather, the Vickers lost none of her handsomeness. The moment the weather broke for a few hours, he had his gang painting, and when the rain set in again, he turned them to, keeping the gear in shape.

It was the fourth day out before I got Mulligan talking again. I had just relieved the mate for supper. I came down from the bridge and passed Mulligan's cabin on the way to my own.

His door was open, and he called, "Come in, lad! Come in!" I entered the cabin, and he said, "And close the door, like a good lad." I closed it, and he reached into a closet and came up with one of his jugs. "A spot of the tea? A fine night for it."

I shook my head. I had to go on watch in a few hours.

He sympathized with me. "But it's a man of my own age that needs a bit of warmth in him on a night like this. You young fellows can well do without." He poured himself half a tumblerful, drank it and smiled happily. "It does take the curse off the weather."

I asked him about McCall and Captain Thompson's daughter. I'd been curious ever since he had hinted at some connection. Mulligan poured himself another huge drink, corked the jug and set it back in the closet. He placed his great bulk carefully in his chair, tasted the whisky and eyed me silently for a moment.

"You look like a man who can hold his tongue, Mr. Sherwood, so I've told you a little and I'll tell you the lot. But it would do no good were the story to get around the ship."

"I'm anxious to satisfy no curiosity but my own."

He nodded. "You're reasonable enough." The glass was tipped again, but not emptied. "Both Thompson and McCall are Newfoundland men. St. Mary's Bay men. There have been Thompsons and McCalls sailing out of St. John's for over a hundred years. They've been born near the water and bred to the sound of the wind, and there is sea spray in the blood of all of them."

"Then why," I asked, "is there this difference between them? Why does the Old Man dislike McCall?"

"He does not dislike him," Mulligan said. "He hates him. For, a bit over twenty years ago, Thompson's wife sailed on a ship skippered by McCall's father. It was late in the fall—St. John's to Boston, they were going—and the weather monstrous. The ship piled up on Cape Sable in the night and thirty-seven people were lost, including both Thompson's wife and old Jack McCall.

"But that's no reason——"

"A man's heart is sometimes an unreasonable thing," Mulligan said, "both in love and in hate. And when the two emotions are combined through circumstance, the result is rarely wisdom. Thompson believes old McCall was responsible for the death of his wife. He hates the name and any man who bears the name, and knowing all this, it's easy to see why he objects to McCall as suitor for his daughter. The two were children together, but once the worm entered Thompson's heart, he made certain his daughter did not see McCall." Mulligan finished his glass. "But when a man's at sea most of the time, he can't govern the actions of a spirited girl. Strength is in the young and love is in the young, and I think there's a bit of fear in the Old Man."

"It's an interesting story," I said.

Mulligan agreed with a nod. "It is that. And the end of it—whatever it may be—will be interesting too."

And when I relieved McCall at eight o'clock I looked upon the man with a new interest and a new sympathy. He bore the burden of his misfortunes with his own ships, and over him, like a cloud, hung the shadow of his father's tragedy. He carried the heavy load well. The broad shoulders were not bowed under it, and the only place the pressure showed was in his eyes. Doubt had unmistakably touched them, and a shadow that might have been fear. But these things had not stayed. They had touched him and somehow strengthened him, and were not a part of him now.

Captain Thompson rode him. He complained of the condition of the decks, of the ship's boats, of a trace of rust on the cargo runners. And the ship was tense, the Old Man's irritability reaching down through the crew like the fingers of a heavy fog. There was a savage fight between an oiler and an A.B. in the crew's mess that McCall had to stop, and on the seventh day out, in rotten weather, Chips went forward in the morning to sound the bilges. He slipped in a trickle of oil from a winch and lay there cursing with a broken leg. The very next day, the ordinary on the twelve-to-four lost a finger trying to secure an unfastened, swinging, watertight door.

It was that sort of trip. A McCall trip, everyone termed it.

Small incidents that occur every day, ordinarily, and which usually pass unnoticed, were lumped in a mighty mass of damnation against the mate. Mulligan and myself, I think, were the only ones aboard who spoke to him at all. The others raged at him behind his back, acccepted his presence with glowering silence.

The way he took it was an admirable thing, for the hostility of an entire ship is too great a burden for most men. It did not defeat McCall. He made no overtures, answered silence with silence, and his eyes were more direct, more forceful, than those of the men who strangely hated him for his own misfortune. His dignity was unassailable, and rode his wide shoulders like a magnificent cape.

I felt something for the man that was not pity, for that dignity was proof against pity. Sorrow, it might have been. Sorrow that a man should be forced to bear the solitude that was his. Admiration, I knew for him too. He was a sailor from the soles of his feet to the top of his head, and he showed me several navigational tricks that even Mulligan could not surpass.

We had trouble in the engine room, a pump breakdown which Fletcher, of course, ascribed to the influence of McCall, and we were a day late arriving in Cherbourg. The captain of the tug that handled us was sloppy and incompetent, and we slammed into the concrete wharf with a force that I thought would buckle half our plates. I, and I think everyone else on the ship, heaved a sigh of relief when the lines were finally ashore and we were tied up.

We unloaded our cargo in five days. They had cranes on the wharf again, and things moved swiftly.

McCall seldom left the ship. We were painting over the side, and he was busy with that, and he gave me a man to help with the lifeboats, to check the gear and make sure they were in order.

Captain Thompson didn't leave the ship. He hung on the bridge rail most of the day, examining proceedings with a cold and jaundiced eye. McCall gave him little opportunity for criticism. The work went quickly and it was well done.

I spoke to Mulligan one morning about the way Captain Thompson stayed on the ship. I'd noticed it in New York too.

He shrugged his huge shoulders. "The man has no interest

other than his ship. He regards it with the same affection another man would lavish on a wife. And that's the explanation of the thing. Since his wife died twenty years ago, his ships receive the devotion he once tendered her. He'll leave them only when necessary, and then for as brief a period as possible. I know for a fact that he's not been home in three years. He's been on the sea so long that I don't believe the man could sleep in a level bed."

When the holds were cleared, we took on slag for ballast. I was on the boat deck, and heard McCall and the Old Man talking on the bridge wing over my head.

"I'll take some men and secure that stuff," McCall said. "We've got some old cargo runners and a lot of dunnage, and——"

The Old Man didn't let him finish. His voice was thin, his words measured, "There is neither the time nor the necessity for that, mister. It's a late-spring crossing and the weather will be fine, and I can't spare a day to build a fence for that stuff. The owners would like the use of this ship. She makes no money carrying ballast, and I'd like to get back to the States for a cargo, if you don't mind."

I looked up, saw McCall nod and walk away. His face was set, his shoulders rigid. I wondered how tough that pride could be, how much punishment that dignity could take before it broke.

We sailed on time, and I wondered what the return voyage held for McCall, what new trials he would be forced to endure. The trip over had done nothing to moderate the harshness of his reputation. As a matter of fact, fresh wounds had been added to the old scars, and when this crew got ashore and their tales gained circulation, his stature as a jinx would have greatly increased.

I spoke of it to Mulligan, "How long can the man go on like this, having the blame for every miserable accident, every bit of foul weather, placed on his shoulders?"

Mulligan shook his head. "It's a hard question to answer, son. There is great strength in McCall, and a great patience. But in a situation like this there comes a moment when either the man or the legend must break. And the story that follows him is a powerful thing, gaining weight with every trip he makes, with every stupid, superstitious word that is spoken of him ashore." He shook his head again. "I pity the man and his future."

On the sixth day out, Captain Thompson fell ill. The weather was harsh and cold, for the season, and after one day in his cabin, when he saw no one, he sent for Owens, the purser, who was the medical man aboard. Owens came down to the dining saloon with a long face. The Old Man was running a high fever, and from the various signs and portents, Owens thought he might have pneumonia.

Mulligan said, "A good spot of the tea is what he needs, but he's not a drinking man."

Fletcher's face was lined with his frown. The chief engineer said, "I'd as soon carry a cargo of snakes as that McCall."

"And now you talk like a man whose head is stuffed with cotton waste," Mulligan told him. "What could McCall have to do with this?"

"He has only to come aboard a ship," Fletcher muttered, "and trouble is half a step behind him."

And everyone on the ship took the same attitude, of course. When anyone spoke of the Old Man's illness, McCall's name would be mentioned in the same breath.

It did not seem to affect McCall, though he was obviously aware of all that went on. His dignity was untouched; he went about his work with unchanging thoroughness. In his eyes there was no plea for quarter, and he was as aggressively remote as ever.

And I could see him going down the years like that, his world arrayed against him, the legend of his misfortunes growing, building up behind him, until finally it would break him, smother him by its very bulk. It was not a pleasant picture.

The next day the Old Man was worse. He was delirious, Owens said, from the fever raging within him. McCall went into the skipper's cabin, when I relieved him at eight o'clock that morning, and when he came out his face was grave. I wondered just how long it would be before the terrific pressure of opinion would convince the man himself that disaster was his ever-present twin.

The weather hit us the next day with only a two-hour warning. The glass dropped suddenly at noon, and by three o'clock, the Vickers was rolling heavily in a big sea pushed by a southwest wind that Mulligan logged as Force 7 on the Beaufort scale.

I ate at five o'clock and went up to relieve McCall. The glass was still falling.

I stood in the wheelhouse and watched her roll. She was high and light, and she was going fifteen degrees to either side as the big sea surged up to her, shoved her off balance, then swept underneath and let her roll back to meet the next. The rain was heavy, driven by the still-rising wind. I knew we had a miserable night in store for us.

When I took the watch at eight o'clock, the wind was up to fifty miles an hour. The roll was no longer amusing. She was bettering twenty degrees on every swing, heeling over until I thought she'd never stop, then coming back slowly and repeating the big dip on the other side. Down below, in the messrooms and in the galley, china crashed each time we hit the peak of the roll.

McCall stayed on the bridge. I wondered why he didn't change the course, swing the Vickers into this, so she'd ride more comfortably. Then he went into the Old Man's room, which was just aft of the wheelhouse, for a few moments, and I had the answer to that question. Every hour we saved was an important thing. That man needed care we couldn't give him.

At eleven o'clock the seas were huge, great rolling hills that swept up to the Vickers with a ponderous fury, heralded by the spray from their crests. She would heel to starboard under the vast pressure, then right herself with an effort and slide down into the trough.

McCall stood at one of the bridge ports, his weight shifting with the motion of the ship. He said, "We'll have to change the course, mister. She won't stand much more of this."

And at that moment she took her worst roll. She lay over on her side, and I fought for balance, holding to the rail along the forward bulkhead, waiting for her to come back. And I heard it, then, a great, slithering, rushing sound in the bowels of the ship. It lasted for ten seconds, ten eternities, and then the Vickers started the return roll.

She never had a chance. The next enormous sea was on her, pushing and surging with its incalculable thousands of tons of force. The ship went to starboard again, and I knew she'd go all the way, and fear was a terrible contraction in my stomach and a great cold hand on my throat. Over the panic that rose in me, I heard a repetition of that rushing, sliding sound in the hold.

She didn't go all the way. She lay over at a forty-five-degree angle and stayed there, her bow high, her stern low. The shifting ballast had piled up in the after starboard corners of the holds, and, being unable either to go any farther or to return to its former position, held the ship at that terrible list.

We did not roll now. The factors of balance had been destroyed, and we lay there like some great and grievously wounded animal. The seas lifted us, hammered at us, then left us stricken and near dead in the great valleys between the waves.

The engines stopped, and I knew what it must be like down below. I looked at McCall, but he was moving already, climbing the slope to the port side of the wheelhouse. The harshness of his voice jerked my numb body back into action, "Get all hands aft, mister. There's work to be done if any of us want to live another hour. Send a couple of men to get whatever shovels there are in the forepeak. Tell Mr. Mulligan to stand by, here on the bridge."

We went into the holds and worked. Everyone. We used shovels and buckets, and we carried the larger pieces of slag in our hands. It was a night conceived in hell. The Vickers lay sodden and helpless. The storm was at its height and we were part of it now, figures toiling through a mass nightmare.

And in the middle of the insane night, out of his mind with a raging fever, the captain came out on the starboard bridge wing and fell down the ladder leading to the boat deck. Someone grabbed him in time to prevent him from going over the side, but when they carried him back to his cabin, his right hip was broken.

McCall was everywhere. He drove fright out of men with his whiplash voice, turned fear into hatred of himself that found a release in the backbreaking work. He set men to building a rough fence out of cargo runners and dunnage, to restrain what ballast we reshifted. Half of us worked in the lower hold, half in the 'tween-decks. He kept us going at a pace that was insane, more than a mortal body could endure. I saw men cry and sob in their exhaustion that night, but it seemed that McCall was beside each one of us, and there was no moment given to rest.

And when, a little after dawn, the worst of the storm had passed us by, I saw him look around. The ship held a thirty-five-degree list still, but terror had gone from us now. The wind was dying and the seas had lost much of their power.

McCall said, "We should be under way in a few hours."

And we were. She waddled along like a drunk, heeled over at that absurd angle, and those men who weren't on watch were in the holds. Shifting fifteen hundred tons of slag by hand is more than a night's work. It was two days before we attained the relative safety of a twenty-five-degree list, and in comparison she seemed as level as a pool table.

The purser and McCall made the Old Man as comfortable as possible. I went into the cabin once, with a message for McCall, and I saw the captain. He was a small, hard shadow of a man now. The fever had passed, and it had taken his strength with it. His hip was splinted in an unprofessional manner. His eyes were closed, his breathing faint and labored. I looked at McCall, and his eyes told me nothing I did not know. Only the Old Man's toughness would keep him alive a few more days.

We made good time, considering the crazy angle we were canted at. I thought, and the idea must have occurred to McCall, of a Coast Guard plane. But the sea was too rough, and transfer of a man in the captain's condition would have amounted to murder. There was one way in which he could be removed from the ship—when she was tied to a pier and there were practiced hands to carry him off on a stretcher. And looking at him, I knew it would have to be soon.

A day out of New York he was still hanging on. In the saloon, the purser shook his head. "He isn't a young man, and he's taken a beating—is still taking it. In a hospital they could care for him, if they get him in time. His pulse is weak and half the time I don't know whether he's breathing or not."

Hynes, the first assistant engineer, said, "The man who signs McCall aboard a ship, after this, should have his head examined."

Fletcher nodded and was about to speak. But Mulligan got to his feet. I had never seen him angry before, but now he was massive in his controlled rage, his face pale with the intensity of his emotion.

"You're a bunch of drooling idiots, and I'm sick of listening to your gibberish, the while you ruin a man and steal from him his future! This ship would be at the bottom of the sea right now if it weren't for McCall, and if you had the brains God promised rabbits, you'd know it! No other man could have brought her back, that night she lay over! He drove you until you were bleeding in your souls, but he saved the ship, and your lives with it! Though to what purpose I cannot imagine! McCall is no bringer of trouble, you fools! But he can smell it! He has an acquaintance with it that amounts to kinship! He can seek it out and provide against it! And it can't defeat him!" He banged his great fist upon a table and coffee cups shot into the air. "And if you'd stop your moronic yapping long enough to think about it, you'd realize that there isn't a man aboard big enough to carry McCall's hat!"

He stalked from the room, and left a dead silence in his wake.

We were doing all of ten knots when we hit Ambrose Light. When we took the pilot aboard, the purser was on the bridge, talking to McCall, "He's conscious now, but I don't know how much longer he'll last. He needs oxygen, expert attention."

McCall nodded. "We'll have him ashore in two hours." His face was tight, his whole body seemed coiled with the unrelenting tension of the past week.

The pilot was a pleasant man with most unpleasant news. He eyed the ship, shook his head in sympathy, and said, "You needn't be in a hurry now. You'll have to anchor in the bay for a few days. The tugs are all on strike. Took effect this morning."

I looked at McCall. His head jerked and he seemed to falter for a moment. It was just a little too much, I thought. This was the straw. But then the line of his jaw hardened, and his voice was flat as he said, "We'll be at the dock in two hours, mister. We've a sick man aboard. We'll need no tugs."

We'd radioed ahead for an ambulance to meet us at the company docks, and we didn't stop at Quarantine. We had radioed asking for a modified pratique that would permit us to dock. McCall said, "We'll argue about it later."

It was noon, and Mulligan came on the bridge to relieve me. He said to McCall, "Ask for a tug, lad. Tell them your troubles. They'll send you help."

"Talk and talk," McCall replied, "while a man lies dying. They'll send a doctor out to confirm my statement, and that will take time. And then I'd wait for a tug. The hell with that. We have power and we have a rudder. We'll do without help."

I was up in the bow, taking care of the forward lines. The tide had changed an hour ago and was ebbing swiftly. He'd have one chance, and if he missed, the Vickers would go careening and smashing along the piers until we could get a hook to hold. It would be an unholy mess.

The men around me, I noticed suddenly, were relaxed. Morley, an A.B. on my watch, shook his head in admiration. "The man is tough. He don't scare easy."

"And why should he?" someone asked. "That guy has been in real trouble."

I looked at them, and it was hard to believe. I knew one thing. Mulligan's blast had been heard beyond the saloon.

We pushed against the outgoing tide, quartered up to our berth, which lay between two long piers. We were going too fast and our heading was wrong, and I knew that as sure as my name was Sherwood, we would smash the northern pier. We swung with agonizing slowness then, and I heard the jangle of the engine-room telegraph as the engines were stopped. We drifted in between the piers, carrying a great deal too much way. I thought those bells would never ring again, and then I heard them. There was an awful moment of silent drifting when I thought we'd ram the end of the slip, and then the engines turned and the screw bit frantically into the water. We were well between the piers now, out of the current, and the Vickers checked slowly, then hauled to a stop. We drifted ten feet, with our starboard side to the southern pier, and hit the pier with no more than a lusty thump as the telegraph jangled again and the engine stopped. The crew got the lines ashore with a roar. It had been a beautiful piece of work.

In a little while, Mulligan came forward to where they were getting a gangway up from the pier. His eyes sparkled. "Did you see it, lad? And do you get the feeling in the crew? They're a proud lot. They brought back a ship that should have sunk, and they've got a man who can put it up to a pier like a damned launch." He shook his head. "I've seen it before, but not often.

A moment in the scheme of things when a hoodoo becomes a hero. There's no change in him, but only in the minds of others. One single act can make them realize they've been wrong. It is difficult of understanding, but it is the nature of men."

The procession came down from the bridge then—white-uniformed attendants carrying the Old Man on a stretcher. McCall walked by his side. At the gangway, they paused. Captain Thompson's voice was weak, but his eyes were bright and alive, and I knew he'd pull through.

"Mister," he said, "sometimes a man is forced to change his mind."

McCall said nothing.

"I'll recommend you to the company for a ship," the Old Man said without graciousness, for the admission of a wrong is sometimes difficult. "You're a fine sailor," he muttered. And the rest was spoken almost as an afterthought, but was the most forceful admission of his guilt that he could make. "And if you're ever near St. Mary's Bay, you might stop in and see Margaret. It would please her, and you have my permission."

"I'll thank you for the one thing, but not for the other," McCall said, but there was a ghost of a smile on his face. "If you'd take the trouble to go home now and then, you'd find you have a grandson, two years old. Robert Brendan, his name is."

Mulligan nudged me and whispered, "A sly touch. The Old Man's name."

The Old Man did not smile, but as they carried him down to the pier, he said, "A rogue's trick, mister. A rogue's trick," and there was no trace of anger in his voice.

McCall turned from the gangway, and Mulligan touched him on the arm. He said, "Mr. McCall, I seem to remember that in my cabin is a small jug of something that you might find to your taste."

McCall looked at him for a moment, then a grin broke across his face. It was pleasant to see. "Mulligan," he said, "all in all, I consider that a very sound suggestion."

I stood there wishing that Mulligan would think to ask me along. I knew what I would drink to. To the passing of Bad-Luck McCall.

Captive Captain

John Paul Heffernan

When Jonathon Bailey fitted his brig *Nancy* for a privateer and put to sea in late 1812, there were deep-water sailors who wagged their heads and claimed that an education, a liking for fine clothes and a few years in the tiny United States Navy weren't enough to carry a man in the chancy business of privateering.

But there were some who gave him a second look and said that there was more to the man than his six feet, unruly black hair and his eyes with the look of the sea in them. "You can't tell," they said.

And they were right, for Jonathon Bailey had gone ahead to make fools of his detractors and, by the summer of 1813, virtual idiots of a number of British captains.

Half a cable's length under the *Nancy's* lee lay his latest victim, a British merchantman, ship-rigged and well laden, judging from the solid way she rode the gentle Caribbean swells. Prodded by superior gunnery from the American, her ensign had fluttered down only moments before, and with canvas clewed up she was awaiting a boarding party.

Bailey trained his glass on her and read the name *Countess of Pembroke* supported by ornate gilt scrollwork on her stern. She was a handsome ship, paint fresh and brightwork gleaming. Contrary to practice, he decided he would board her himself. Turning over the deck to Joshua Varney, his first officer, he descended to his gig and was rowed across to the *Pembroke,* followed by the *Nancy's* longboat carrying men who had been told off as a prize crew.

He went up a swaying ladder and through the merchantman's entry port, where he was greeted by a dour, puffy man who tried hard to be civil and made a poor job of it. He announced that he was Edward Pearson, the *Pembroke's* first officer, and added that it was he who had struck the ship's flag.

"I fired a shot across your bows," Bailey said, "and hoped you'd heave to without any nonsense. It's unfortunate that your captain chose to make a one-sided affair of it. I trust the captain hasn't been wounded?"

Pearson shook his head. "The captain refused to strike, so I assumed responsibility. Captain Smith is in the great cabin aft, surrounded by an arsenal of pistols and daring anyone to enter."

Every situation, Bailey reflected, had to be handled differently, but this was one he had not faced before. Shrugging it off as one of the facets of his dangerous calling, he said to Pearson, "If you'll come along with me, perhaps we may persuade your captain to be reasonable."

Pearson didn't move. "By your leave, I'd as soon remain here. The captain would probably shoot me on sight for striking our ensign. She's in a frightful temper."

"As you wish. I'll beard the lion alone." He took several paces aft before the impact of Pearson's words struck him. He wheeled. "You said 'she.' Do you mean the master of this ship is a woman?"

Pearson nodded heavily. "Aye—an Amazon you might say, though I don't recall that Amazons were seagoing."

Bailey heard his crew chuckle behind him. Mythological allusions were lost on them, he was sure, but the word "woman" was enough to titillate any sailor's imagination, and he could almost hear them chewing over the thought of anything in petticoats commanding a ship at sea—and making mental wagers as to what he would do to resolve the situation. He swore wordlessly. Some harridan, beyond a doubt—fat and besotted, with a cutlass in her teeth and a bottle of gin at her elbow. It was improbable, but Pearson appeared to be too unimaginative a man to weave the story on his own.

With five years of naval experience behind him, Bailey ran the *Nancy* Navy fashion and had given his officers and men Navy titles. More easygoing shipmasters thought it pretentious, but he had found it good for discipline and morale. He turned to the midshipman commanding his prize crew. "Get sail on her as soon as you've tidied up and repaired damage, Mr. Whitmarsh. How many dead?"

"Two, sir."

"Very good," Bailey said, giving the traditional answer that did not mean what it would imply to a landsman. "Have their sailmaker stitch them up. I imagine Mr. Pearson will want to conduct the service. I'll attend. Send someone aft for me when you're ready."

He paused at the entrance to the cabin, half drawing his sword, then he swore that nothing in skirts was going to panic him. He rammed the blade back in its sheath and opened the door.

She sat at a table facing him. He had been right about some things, wrong in others. There was a bottle at her elbow, a delicate decanter of wine, and beside it a half-filled glass. She held no cutlass in her teeth, but there was a rack of the weapons hanging behind her. And the table was heavy with pistols, neatly aligned and cocked. Each slender hand held a pistol as steadily as the gentle motion of the ship would allow.

And she was no harridan. His mouth narrowed in speculative admiration as he took in the greenish eyes, the startling red hair and the smoothly tanned skin dusted ever so lightly with freckles.

He made her his best bow. "Jonathon Bailey, master of the American letter-of-marque privateer brig *Nancy*," he said in the deceptively lazy tone that had charmed women from Malta to Maracaibo. "Upon my soul, you're a beauty."

The flashing eyes never wavered. "You didn't have to take my ship to pay an empty compliment. You're a pirate, and I'll thank you to get off my decks."

"Your eyes shoot green fires when you're angry. Could it be that this handsome vessel is named for your ladyship—and that you're the countess of Pembroke herself?"

"I'm nobody's countess," she snapped. "I'm plain Mary Smith and I'll thank you and your cutthroats to be on your way."

"Probably you haven't heard that the United States is once again at war with England."

"Oh, I've heard," said plain Mary Smith, "but it doesn't mean that any popinjay with letters of marque and reprisal is going to soil my decks. Get out!"

"Look," Bailey said, moving into the cabin, "can't we discuss this sensibly? I could have done with your pretty ship with a single broadside if I had wanted to. Now that I've seen her captain," he added, "I'm glad I told my gunners to be sparing with their fire." He indicated a chair opposite her. "May I sit?"

"No." She gestured with the pistol in her left hand. "Move over there and see what I have beside me."

Obediently he moved and saw an open powder keg beside her chair.

"I have only to snap a pistol into the keg," she said conversationally, "and we'll all disappear."

He tried to keep his tone light. "I doubt if you'd do anything so rash."

Mary Smith arched an eyebrow. "There are some things about me which, fortunately for both of us, you'll never need to learn. I'm not one of those fashionable females who swoon at the touch of a thistle. My father took me to sea when I was twelve, and I've seen a thing or two. Six weeks ago, before he died at sea on our way to Jamaica"—the husky voice faltered for only a breath—"I swore that this ship would always be sailed with honor."

A pistol butt rapped on the table for emphasis and upset the glass of wine. She gave a purely feminine cry of annoyance, dropped one pistol and hastily sopped the tablecloth with a napkin, never taking her eyes from his. As she picked up her second pistol, Midshipman Whitmarsh stuck his head in to announce that the committal service was about to be held.

"Would you care to attend?" Bailey asked Mary Smith. "They're your men."

"I'll stay here. Possibly a little fresh air on deck will clear your mind. Think about the powder keg."

Her injunction was unnecessary, and the mental image of the determined, greenish-eyed redhead stayed with him during the service. And it was only after two silent forms slid from beneath British ensigns and splashed into the sea that he had an idea. As soon as it was decently possible, he beckoned to Whitmarsh. "Send a man over to the *Nancy* and have him bring back Josiah Strong's cage of pets."

The midshipman goggled. "Strong's pets, sir?"

"Yes, Strong's pets! Must I draw pictures?"

Bailey was not given to growling at his subordinates, but he was uncomfortably aware that Whitmarsh must have felt he had taken leave of his senses. Well, let him. He didn't know about a determined girl sitting beside an open powder keg. Josiah Strong's pets, long a subject of amusement for the crew and an irritation to Bailey, might prove the solution.

Plain Mary Smith, as she styled herself, might be determined, but she was still feminine. The little cry of annoyance and the busy napkin mopping up the spilled wine had betrayed her. A man under similar strain would have ignored the tablecloth and kept his mind on the business at hand. It might work. If it didn't, Bailey had to admit to himself that he didn't know what would. Women, he told himself darkly, should never be allowed to do men's jobs. It was entirely too risky for the men.

He fretted away half an hour helping Whitmarsh organize damage-repair parties until a seaman climbed through the entry port carrying a cage of white mice. Strong was the best gunner Bailey had ever known, and it was because of that that he bore with white mice on his otherwise immaculate brig.

"Peake," he said to the seaman, "the captain of this ship is a woman, and it may be that Strong's mice may help us resolve a nasty situation."

If Peake thought that his captain was crazy, and he probably did, he gave no sign other than a slight wariness in his eyes.

"I'm going aft to her cabin," Bailey went on, "and I want you to follow me with the mice. I'll leave the door ajar. After I've been in there a minute or two, open the cage and shoo the mice into the cabin. Stand by until we see what happens."

Mary Smith still sat behind the table, lovely and determined as ever. "Well," she said coldly, "having disposed of the men you murdered, are you prepared to let a harmless merchantman resume her course?"

"As I pointed out, my angry beauty, we are at war, and you have fallen fair game. Quibbling will only prolong our association. The sooner my crew can get this ship under way, the sooner she'll reach an American port where arrangements can be made for your return to England."

"All very high-sounding," she sniffed, "but I've heard more than a little of your United States. My mother was an American and she told me tales of wild savages and hairy men who eat their meat raw. I suppose I'll spend the rest of the war in a smelly prison."

Bailey's patience was beginning to evaporate, but her remark prodded him into a short, hard laugh. "If you can show me a spot anywhere along the fine, clean coast of New England that smells anything like your precious London, then I'll give you back your ship and see you safely on your way. And we have no Dartmoor prisons, such as yours—where, I hear, a man hopes he will die quickly before he loses his mind and rots under his own eyes."

She reddened. "We're peaceful merchant traders and have no say in what the government does."

"Exactly the point we made when we decided to eschew your tender care nearly forty years ago."

As he was beginning to wonder if Peake had gone to sleep outside the door, he felt something cross his foot. He looked down carelessly, briefly, and saw that Josiah Strong's mice were on their way to his rescue. After three cruises aboard the *Nancy*, the small creatures were unafraid of humans and appeared eager to investiagate their new surroundings. Even as he glanced at the deck, three mice were hurrying under Mary Smith's table.

"This is a waste of words——" the girl started to say, and he almost laughed aloud as he saw her expressive features rapidly mirror puzzlement and mounting alarm. Then she gave an extremely uncaptainlike squeak of panic and moved back, darting a horrified glance toward the hem of her skirt.

It was the chance he needed, and he had only a second to spare. His long arms shot across the table, grabbed her wrists and forced her arms upward. Her pistols barked, and lead plowed into the fine oak paneling overhead. But there was still fight in Mary Smith. She freed one hand and tried to snatch a cutlass from the rack behind her. But he rounded the end of the table quickly and held her close against him, pinning both her hands behind her back.

Mice forgotten, she struggled like an imprisoned panther while Bailey shouted for Peake to secure the mice, her arsenal of pistols and the powder keg. As the seaman, puzzled but nimble, did as he was told, Bailey held the writhing girl, acutely aware of her nearness, the fires in her eyes and the rich red of her lips.

Then, when Peake made his final exit, carrying the open keg as tenderly as a young father carries a newborn son, Bailey, unable to resist, kissed Mary Smith soundly—and was bitten for his pains.

He released her, making sure that he placed himself between her and the cutlass rack. Lovely as she was, she was highly dangerous, and he found himself thinking that it was a good thing that men fought wars.

He shuddered mentally at what the casualties might be if a shipload of Mary Smiths ever came swarming over the *Nancy's* bulwarks, not even half as lovely nor half as angry.

The only weapon within reach was the decanter, and she sent it whizzing toward his head. It missed him by mere inches, and he laughed at her; but it was a hollow laugh, because the projectile hissing by reminded him too uncomfortably of a round shot that had passed his head in the same manner when he had fought an English brig only the week before.

She sat down, more exhausted from her own anger than from the tussle with Bailey. "A low Yankee trick," she panted. "What a brave captain who must take a ship by scaring a woman with a crew of mice!"

"But the shame of it was washed away with a kiss."

"Try it again and you'll lose a lip," she warned.

"I intend to," he said, removing an armful of cutlasses from the rack and prudently surveying the cabin for other weapons she might have hidden. "The reward is more than worth the risk."

It was then that Midshipman Whitmarsh came pounding down to report that a sail had been sighted. "There'll be time to get back to the *Nancy*, sir. Only her royals are sighted yet, but she seems to be setting a course for us."

"Royals, did you say? Then she'll be a frigate, likely, and there are none of ours in these waters."

"A fine, spanking British frigate," said Mary Smith with relish, "and on her deck a captain who will be happy to blow your puny brig right out of the water."

"She'll have to catch me first," Bailey said grimly, "and your ships are as lubberly as their captains. What are you carrying?"

"Rum, molasses and hardwoods from Jamaica—not that my cargo will ever realize you a shilling now."

Ignoring her, he shot rapid orders at Whitmarsh. "Clap on every rag she'll take. Get her under way first, then divide your crew and the English into two working parties. Put half on heaving up the molasses and rum and throwing it overboard. Have the others work on jettisoning the guns. Don't waste time rigging tackle to the yards to hoist 'em. Chop away the bulwarks and when the ship rolls to the proper side, chop away the gun tackles, and they'll pitch overboard on their own. I figure they weigh about eight tons all together, and the loss will bring her a little higher in the water. When that's done, send the men below to help the others unload cargo. Tell off two of our men to tap her water casks and see what can be pumped out. She hasn't been long out of Jamaica—she should be able to spare several tons. Every ton lost means speed gained."

Conscious of the passage of time, a commodity so precious now that he could almost hear it walking across the sea, he still had to pause for breath. And he thought, during the moment of silence he allowed himself, that he saw something resembling respect in the girl's green eyes. Could it be that she was beginning to see him as the captain of a fighting ship and not a pirate hiding behind his country's flag? But there was no time to speculate on what went on in a woman's mind, and he turned his attention to Whitmarsh, whose young eyes were dancing with eagerness to get away.

"Hoist her British ensign. We'll leave the *Nancy's* flag aloft, and I'll try to draw his fire while you haul away. If he's been in these waters or spoken any of his own ships, he'll have heard of the *Nancy* and may make a try for us if he can get within range." He clapped the midshipman on the back. "Get to it, lad, and good luck to you."

The midshipman scurried away, and Bailey said to the girl, "I'm taking you aboard the *Nancy*. Get a few things together and be above as quickly as you can. I can't allow you more than three minutes."

He was gone before she could reply and was deep in the business of helping Whitmarsh organize the working parties before he found himself wondering why he was taking Mary Smith along. If the *Pembroke* were to be recaptured—and there was a heavy chance she might be—the girl would be back in command of her own ship and on her way home. It puzzled a man who usually was in control of his own reactions; but when three minutes had elapsed, he found her standing by the entry port clutching a bundle, stray locks of hair fluttering like a scarlet mist in the wind.

His gig skimmed across to the *Nancy*, where Varney had men swarming up the shrouds to make sail the moment Bailey came alongside. He sent the girl below to his cabin, without a murmur from her, and felt the old thrill of danger mingled with delight as his little brig lifted her gray wings to the wind.

White water was beginning to boil around the *Pembroke's* forefoot too, and he was gratified to see two geysers spout along her larboard side. So much for the larboard guns. And when the ship rolled to starboard, Whitmarsh would take care of the pieces on that side, if he hadn't already. The midshipman was doing very well and would get an extra share of the prize money if he brought the *Pembroke* to a friendly port.

Whether the merchantman reached a safe haven depended a great deal on Jonathon Bailey, the *Nancy*, and whether the captain of the oncoming frigate recognized the privateer. In three cruises the *Nancy* had accounted for three Royal Navy gun brigs, all of which she had burned and scuttled, three topsail schooners and eleven merchant ships, eight of which had reached American ports with valuable cargoes. It was an enviable score, but it made her one of the most sought for of American privateers; and, as Bailey was well aware, there wasn't a Royal Navy captain in American waters who wouldn't have given a year's seniority to bring the *Nancy* under his guns and send her gurgling down to Fiddler's Green.

With the *Pembroke* under way, splashes indicating that Whitmarsh had his crew hard at their work unloading rum and molasses, Bailey worked the *Nancy* toward the frigate. He wanted her captain to have a good look at his vessel. He looked at the Englishman through his telescope and saw a knot of excited officers on her quarter-deck. He believed he had guessed correctly. The British captain, under the impression that he had caught the privateer in the act of capturing the *Pembroke,* was content to let the merchantman follow her course while he dealt contemptuously with the *Nancy.*

Even a cabin boy on his first cruise knew that a brig should never engage a thirty-two-gun frigate. The difference in number of guns and weight of metal was frightening to contemplate. Bailey had no intention of playing the fool, but the *Pembroke* was a fine ship and would realize a fancy price if Whitmarsh got her away. So Bailey would flirt with the frigate for a while to gain time. No wager, no return—that was the creed of a privateer.

The frigate put herself on a parallel course with the *Nancy,* trying to inch closer. And there were probably derisive officers aboard the Englishman asking one another if the celebrated brig had grown so cocky that she allowed her reputation to befog her common sense.

Bailey, fully aware that he could outrun and outmaneuver any frigate afloat, even showed the audacity to shorten sail and fire a mocking gun. As he bellowed out the order to Josiah Strong to fire, he heard a faint gasp beside him and turned to find Mary Smith shading her eyes with a slender hand to watch the result of the shot. Wind blew the greasy smoke away quickly, and they saw a splash about fifty yards short of the frigate's larboard beam.

"I'd far rather you stayed below," he told the girl.

"But this is folly," she protested. "If your carronades miss him by that small patch of water, it means his long guns can reach you easily. There's such a thing as being too bold."

He looked at her curiously. "Whose side are you on?"

She blushed furiously, her cheeks almost matching the color of her hair. "It was the excitement of the moment," she said. "I'm a foolish woman—as you proved when you let loose the mice."

He wanted to tell her that it wasn't so. He wanted to say that he had never seen greener eyes nor hair so softly red—but the frigate's larboard side disappeared suddenly behind billows of gray and black smoke pierced by flashes of orange flame. And he threw Mary Smith to the deck and covered her with his body. English gunnery was not of the best, he thought, but you could never tell. And then he thought of nothing.

It was a velvet blackness for a while, shot sometimes with flashing lights and pain—and strange dreams that made no sense at all. He would feel hot, and his dream would tell him there was a cool hand on his forehead. He would cry out that he was alone, and soft lips would brush against his—as in a dream.

Once he opened his eyes and was aware immediately of a pain in his right thigh and a pounding in his head. He mumbled something about changing the watch, or thought he did, but a soft voice told him that it wasn't time to awaken and that the watch had been taken care of. Like a small boy, drowsy and happy to know that it wasn't morning, he went down again into sheltering darkness.

When next he awoke, it was to find the *Nancy's* surgeon, Amos Peabody, and Joshua Varney standing beside his bunk. Both men broke into pleased grins, and Varney slapped the round little doctor on the back. "Doc," he said, "you're a great man. You brought him around."

Doctor Peabody looked pleased. "Aye, but don't forget I had very competent help. . . . A piece of splinter drove into your thigh," he told Bailey, "and a flying timber hit your head. It's a good thing your head's made of oak."

"Thanks to both of you," Bailey said. "You, doc, for bringing me through . . . and you, Josh, for saving the *Nancy*."

"'T wa'n't nothin'," Varney said. "He jest got in that one broadside that hurt you. After that, he must have got so mad at our impudence that his gunn'ry an' seamanship got turr'ble—plain turr'ble. We skipped out o' range, and when it come dusk, the wind jest died altogether. Not even a cat's-paw on the water. We put out the boats to haul her along, an' wet the sails so's they'd draw when a wind come. A little wind blew up after dark—caught us first, it did—an' his runnin' lights jest disappeared like fireflies blowin' out their lamps for the night. 'T wa'n't nothin' a-tall."

"Any word of the *Pembroke*?"

"No—not with her, that is. But we spoke the *Congress* frigate two days ago. On her way home, she was, and had all the *Pem-*

broke's prisoners aboard. Said she run down on the *Pembroke* two, three days before and took all them merchant Britishers aboard. *Congress* said this made Whitmarsh happy as a clam in high water. They hinted he should try to work her through the Chesapeake an' try for Baltimore or Annapolis. He'll get her through, that little Whitmarsh will. He's turnin' into considerable of a seaman."

"Aye," Bailey agreed, "and he'll have his own ship one day—as you will." Then he asked the question uppermost in his mind. "It seems I heard Captain Smith's voice near me—I heard so many. Is she——"

Doctor Peabody bobbed his head. "She's the competent help I mentioned. She's still aboard. There were eight others wounded besides you. I've been busy. She did most of the caring for you. Don't know what you would have done without her."

"Could I see her?"

Peabody gnawed at his lower lip with his teeth, his eyes twinkling a little. "Think I should allow it, Josh?" he asked Varney.

Varney was at his New England best. "Up to you, doc. My job's to work the *Nancy* home. Rest's up to you."

"All right, Jonathon," said the doctor, "but not for long. You're still a mite feverish, and it will be a time before you walk your own deck again. We'll come by later. . . . Come on, Josh."

She came in a few minutes later, looking not at all like the master of a merchantman, wearing a red dress of some soft material that matched the color of her hair and a bit of green ribbon at her throat that matched the color of her eyes.

She walked slowly across the cabin and stood beside his bunk. "It's good to see you awake," said the soft voice of his dreams. "It was a hard time for you."

He looked at her, trying to find his voice. And when it came, he said, "Doctor Peabody tells me that I owe you very much."

"Far less than I owe you. I might have been hit if you hadn't protected me." She paused, looking at her hands. "A woman couldn't bear what you've been through. I owe you my life."

"Then there is no debt involved. May we forget this and be friends—Mary?"

She held out her hand, and he found it was as soft as the hand that had cooled him in the darkness, not at all like the hand of a girl who could drive a tall ship through pounding seas, hurl a wine decanter at a bold Yankee or grab for a cutlass to defend herself.

His weak fingers curled around hers. She smiled, the first smile of hers he had seen. And it was like the promise of morning touching the edge of night. She bent over him, and her nearness assured him that they were on the threshold of something that would be as enduring as the sea that was rolling the *Nancy* home.

Without Warning

ROBERT MURPHY

THE GREEN-SHADED DESK LAMP was the only light burning in the cabin when the second mate, Corbeck, went in. Bartholomew, the radio operator, to whom the cabin belonged, sat on the bunk, shadowed and dim. Corbeck could see the line across his forehead where the sunburn stopped, and the whites of his eyes; the rest of him was almost invisible in the gloom. He seemed withdrawn and mysterious, even more withdrawn than he had been since they left England, not at all like himself; ordinarily he was a lively young man with a good deal to say.

Corbeck sat down with a murmured greeting and waited quietly for Bartholomew to speak; he thought the time had come for Bartholomew to say something about the very pretty girl he had been seen with in London, about whom the ship had been full of speculation.

But the silence went on, and presently Corbeck began to think that either the affair had been painfully serious or that there was more than the girl behind it. He moved his big body, and the chair squeaked loudly.

"Did they tell you about the fathometer?" Bartholomew asked. His tone wasn't that of a young man in love and ready to talk about it.

Corbeck raised his head quickly. "No," he said. "What's wrong with it?"

"It was after your watch, I guess," Bartholomew said. He was silent for a long moment. "It's deep here," he went on suddenly, "but half an hour ago they got a sounding of twenty-five fathoms on it."

"They couldn't," Corbeck said. "The thing's out of whack."

"I don't think so," Bartholomew said. "Curly was so surprised he hit it again, and got the same thing. He hit it the third time right away, and got bottom. They've been getting bottom ever since, right where it belongs. Something was under us, Corbeck."

A queer little feeling ran up Corbeck's spine. "A whale," he said.

Bartholomew got back into character. "Aye," he said sardonically, "or a school of chromium-plated gefüllte fish. Look," he said. "Three or four years ago there was a good deal of talk about them building big submarines. They knew they couldn't catch up with us with a surface fleet."

"Who?" Corbeck said.

Bartholomew leaned forward. "Now who could it be?" he said. "Don't you ever read the papers, you ignorant chicken farmer? When you get home to that two-by-four Jersey farm, I suppose you stick your head in a hencoop, so you won't know what's going on in the world."

Corbeck was nonplused. "What——" he began.

"Far be it from me," Bartholomew said, "to disturb you and bring you up to date. But didn't anybody in England tell you how bad things are?"

"Well," Corbeck said, and added unwillingly, "they didn't seem to like the way things were going very much."

Bartholomew looked at him for a moment in silence, with a sort of ironic admiration. "So," he said. "You certainly go in for understatement, Corbeck. You don't want any trouble, so there won't be any, huh?" He dropped into a serious and troubled tone. "They don't have to play fair just because we do. Even back in '47, a lot of people argued that we should bust them up, but we don't play that way. Maybe because we don't, we think they won't. What are they up to, Corbeck? You ought to understand them. You were born there, weren't you?"

"No," Corbeck said. "I was born in Brooklyn. My parents came from there. They Anglicized the name."

"You talk their lingo, anyway."

"We spoke it around the house sometimes," Corbeck said.

"You'd better practice it up," Bartholomew said, and returned to his bantering tone; it was grimmer now.

"I practiced it when I was in Germany with the Air Force," Corbeck said, feeling that he was saying a silly thing. "I sold a few watches."

"And got paid in Morgenthau's invasion marks," Bartholomew said. "I hope you saved them, friend. They might get you back from the far, far places they might send you. So you can't feel in your bones what your fine countrymen are up to, huh?"

"No," Corbeck said. He was disturbed now; Bartholomew's talk brought back the many things he had heard and the activity he had seen, all of which he had managed to push into the back of his mind. He didn't want his life disrupted again. He was married very happily; they had a little girl and the chicken farm. He hadn't had these things before. "You don't really think they'd do it, do you?" he asked.

"Everybody thinks we're safe because they can't invade us," Bartholomew said. "What do they have to invade us for? Why not an atom-bomb raid widespread enough to smash up everything important? And then, after a bit, another one? And another one? They can let us die on the vine that way."

Corbeck stared at him, seeing things in the gloom, unable to find words to answer.

"Maybe I'm a dope," Bartholomew said, "for not putting it on the air. We're only about five hundred miles off Washington. What do you think, Corbeck? Do you think I ought to go up and ask the Old Man? I've got a funny feeling, damn it."

Corbeck shuddered, and by a great effort of will forced the things he had seen in the shadows back into nothingness again. "No," he said. "It would be nonsense. You ate something or that girl in London did something to you. Go to bed, Bartholomew."

"I keep remembering the guy at Pearl Harbor," Bartholomew said. "The one that got something on the radar and nobody would pay any attention to him."

"Ah, damn it!" Corbeck said.

He got up, opened his mouth to speak, and closed it again. He walked out of the cabin, pulled the door shut behind him and started toward the stern. Nobody was on deck, but he could hear faintly an accordion being played in the crew's quarters. The three-quarter moon was clear and made a wide track on the calm sea; the ship rolled gently in her quiet progress, and nothing came within the wide, luminous circle of Corbeck's view.

He reached the stern, thought for a moment of going to his cabin, and gave the idea up. Bartholomew had disturbed him to an extraordinary degree. He knew that he wouldn't be able to sleep, and leaned on the rail. There was nothing, he tried to think, behind Bartholomew's talk. The fathometer, like any other instrument, was liable to aberration. The only trouble was that they had never had reason to complain about it; it had always been correct, and it was correct now. It had been correct ever since the two readings of twenty-five fathoms, and twenty-five fathoms was about the depth at which a submarine would cruise or lie.

Corbeck was not a very imaginative man, and he had fostered the habit of dismissing from his mind things which made him uncomfortable; the thought of another war had made him very uncomfortable indeed. He had so much disliked the reality of war at sea the last time that he had sneaked off and got a job as navigator in the Air Force, after some difficulty, and he wanted no more of that. He wanted no more of it, land, sea or air, and his reading about atom bombs, radioactivity and similar improvements had only helped foster the habit of shutting his eyes to possibilities.

But the things Bartholomew had said, the other things he had heard and read, the memory of the tenseness in the air of London and the great activities in the royal dockyards all came back to him again, and this time he couldn't dismiss them. He thought of the strong and cheerful Minnesota girl he had married, the little farm she managed so well while he was away, and the blond three-year-old who looked so much like her mother. Suddenly, as he looked over the empty, moonlit sea, he felt very forsaken and alone and, somehow, betrayed. A feeling of protest, which has arisen against aggression in every man of good will since history began, arose within him.

Nearly an hour later the engines stopped. Corbeck, still leaning on the rail, listened for a moment as the vibration of the screw ceased, then straightened up and hurried to the bridge.

The captain, in his pajamas, had just finished talking to the engine room as he reached the top of the ladder. He turned and frowned at Corbeck.

"Oil-line stoppage," he growled. "The fools must have taken the strainers out and forgot to put them back."

Corbeck felt an immediate and tremendous sense of relief. He took a deep breath and put out a hand to the bridge rail. "Shall I have a sea anchor put out?" he asked.

"Or forgotten altogether to clean them," the captain said. . . . "Eh? Sea anchor? No, not in this sea. They'll have it fixed in an hour or so."

He ran his hand through his sparse white hair, and began a nervous pacing up and down the bridge.

"Sparks was telling me about the fathometer," Corbeck said.

The captain stopped in the middle of a stride and turned to him. "Yes," he said. "I don't like it, but what can I do? What can anybody do?"

"Do you think it has any significance?" Corbeck asked. The relief began to run out of him.

"I don't know," the captain said. "I don't like to think about it. If I can get this ship into port——"

"Sparks thought——" Corbeck began.

"I know what he thought," the captain snapped, interrupting him, and then burst out, "Damn it, don't stand there staring at me, Mr. Corbeck! Can I help it if all hell's about to break loose all over again? I want to get to port; and those fools in the engine room——" He pulled himself up, looked at the quartermaster and dropped his voice, "Turn in, Mr. Corbeck. You can't do anything here, and I'd rather be alone. I'll call you if I want you." He swung back to the telephone. "Get me the chief again," he said, "and hurry up about it."

Corbeck descended the ladder and slowly walked back to the stern again. The momentary sense of relief he had felt had completely left him, and a profound depression had taken its place; it was not helped by the thought that Bartholomew and the Old Man might know something, some late radio news, that they hadn't shared with him. Presently he sat down, and after a while turned, put his arms on the damp rail, leaned his head on them and fell asleep.

He was a little stiff and cold when he awoke. They were still working in the engine room, for the vibration hadn't started again. The ship rolled a bit more than she had while under way, but still gently. From the moon's position, Corbeck estimated that he had been asleep for a little more than an hour. The ship was broadside on to the moon; there was nothing in the water on that side, and then he turned to the other.

He straightened up as though someone had put a knife blade into him. Off the ship's quarter a long black shadow lay on the water; Corbeck could see dimly the bulk of the conning tower. Automatically, without conscious thought, he estimated the submarine's distance, and by that her size. She was very large, his mind told him; outrageously large for a submarine. He wanted to cry out, to arouse the watch, who probably hadn't seen her because of her position, but the sound stuck in his throat. His throat refused to function, just as his legs refused to get themselves into action and carry him on a run toward the bridge or Bartholomew's cabin. *She didn't know we were here,* he thought; *she listened and couldn't hear us because we were lying dead in the water, and came up. And now—*

The "now" freed him, but too late. He had hardly taken a step when the torpedo struck a little forward of amidships. There was a tremendous roar and a tearing column of flame; the entire ship seemed to leap upward, and Corbeck became aware that he was trying to get to his feet in a strange silence, with the acrid smell of the explosive all around him. His guts hurt, and his legs. Sounds began again. Things were still falling around him, and a great flame sprang up between him and the bridge. The ship began to list.

Corbeck knew, without having to think, that the torpedo's war head was heavier than anything he'd ever heard about; there was no hope for the ship, and very little for anyone in her. She was already going down. Like a man in a dream, he got out of his shoes and most of his clothing, and went over the rail. The cold black water shocked him back to conscious thought. He came up treading water, and swam on his back away from the ship.

She was burning brightly and the list had increased until the deck was nearly awash. Corbeck swam desperately to get beyond the area of suction when she went down. A wave lifted him and he saw, for an instant, the submarine, tinted by the fire, and several men grouped on her conning tower. There was a confused and hollow rumbling from the ship, a column of steam and smoke arose high in the air and caught the light; her stern swung up and Corbeck could see her screw, black and stationary, against the pale sky, and then she slid out of his view.

His emotions had been in abeyance until then, but as soon as the ship was gone, they began to function again. He was alone in the water, and so far as he knew, there was nothing left to cling to. He was quite sure that Bartholomew hadn't got a message off, and that no one would come looking for survivors. These things didn't concern him very much. He was lost, a man with a little time before he died, and he recognized that and got beyond thinking of himself. *If I can only get aboard her*, he thought, *if I can only get aboard her and do something, anything; if I can only kill a single one of them.*

He didn't know what he could do, and he didn't dwell on that. He knew little of submarines; his thought went wildly around and then off into an incoherent and profane wordlessness full of hate and fury. He began to swim as quietly as he was able toward the submarine, hoping that they wouldn't start the engines and leave the vicinity to avoid any other ship which might have sighted the fire or the glow of it in the sky and come to investigate. He became obsessed with the idea that she might run away from him; he was a strong and enduring swimmer, and the obsession gave him additional speed.

He was fortunate that he managed to get so far astern of the ship, for the submarine had been lying parallel to her and he was enabled to come at it by the stern, too, out of the path of moonlight on the sea. He hoped that there wouldn't be a watch astern or that they wouldn't notice much of anything in that direction; he swam under water most of the time when he got near to her, coming up cautiously for direction and air. He stalked her as he would have stalked a seal asleep on a rock jutting out of the water—with grim and painstaking care.

After what seemed like an eternity of time and effort, he lay off her stern. The exhaust bubbled languidly and stank; he circled it, drifted across forward of it until his feet touched the plates, and stood up. The surface of the water just about came to his chin.

Forward, the conning tower loomed up as large as a house, flaring at the top; and Corbeck, after staring for a moment because of the sheer size of it, sank until he was belly down on the plates, and swam under water toward it. He knew the curve of the deck would bring him into view before he got under the flare, and he hoped luck was with him. He swam until the water wasn't deep enough for more swimming, got to his hands and feet and moved as quickly and as quietly as he could to the conningtower wall. There he crouched, back against the steel, and listened.

Several minutes passed as he held his breath, but there was no shouting or excitement. He had made it; he had been phenomenally lucky. He breathed again. A feeling of exultation, so strong that it took the strength from his legs, flowed through him. He sat down. The flared-out rim of the conning tower jutted out over him like the eaves of a roof; he could hear voices occasionally, but the lapping of the water against the hull covered and broke up the words.

The exultation in Corbeck let down a little. For a time it had covered everything, but now he realized how tired he was, how much alone, and how difficult things were going to be. He shivered, and looked out over the empty, restless ocean; it blurred a little on his sight, and he dropped his head on his arms. He was very tired. The voices drifted down from above him and grew fainter, and he fell into a doze.

He was shivering with cold when he started awake some time later, and every muscle in him was stiff; his legs and his belly ached from the shock the torpedo explosion had given him. He stood up and rubbed himself briskly until a wan glow of increased circulation was established. From the moon's position, it was getting on for morning, and the ocean looked inimical and black. He put his hands on the cold, damp steel of the conning tower and pushed against its unyielding surface, and thought of Samson pulling down the pillars of some heathen temple. It was the first time he had thought of the Bible or even of the religion in which he had been brought up, for many years. *Let me do it,* he thought, with a sudden and urgent humbleness. *Please let me do it.* He stood pushing against the steel with his head bowed, shivering a little and thinking confusedly of Samson and his wife and little girl and his own youth, and then stood back.

He took another look at the sky and judged that they would launch the planes soon, if they were going to launch them. There was room for five or six of them in the submarine—small planes, not bombers. Apparently they had got past the need for big bombers, too; they had also found the secret, before anyone thought they would. Corbeck recalled the pictures of Hiroshima and the people of Hiroshima, and stole around the faired corner of the conning tower.

Midway along the length of it he came to a deep bay with a five-inch gun mounted in it; the barrel was parallel to the submarine's long axis and secured by turnbuckles attached to eyes below the muzzle, like those used on the old French 75. There was a door in the middle of the bay, but it was closed and secured from within; he couldn't move it. He went on until he was under the front of the conning tower. It was very wide, curved slightly, and looked like a great barn door; they undoubtedly opened it, rolled the planes through and launched them down the long flat deck. The deck itself was longer than he thought it would be. It was long enough for a small carrier.

A voice above him broke the silence with undistinguishable words, and quiet fell again, and Corbeck got into action. He knew he couldn't wait until the great door was opened; there would be too many people, and no matter how much confusion his sudden appearance would cause, he wouldn't last very long. His only chance would be to get onto the conning tower, where there might be only two or three people. He moved around to the other side, sure that there would be a ladder, but there was no ladder. There was another gun, another door, and it was tightly closed. He couldn't get to the top; he couldn't get anywhere; he might as well have gone down with the ship. A feeling of utter defeat and helplessness took hold of him as he came back to the big door again.

There was a rumble from behind the door, and it slowly began to rise; Corbeck stared at the widening line of light along the bottom of it. For a long moment he was frozen in the attitude of watching, his muscles tense and his belly cold and tight, preparing to rush in and seize something with which to lay about him. His toes curled against the deck and his lips drew back; he crouched, and the door moved up several inches more. The feet of several men ran across the line of light, and one of them stopped, facing him. It was this man who took the tension, readiness to dash in, out of Corbeck. He had a swift mental picture of the two of them meeting like players on a football field, falling together and rolling about while the rest came running up. Even as the image moved violently across his mind, he straightened a little and ran around the corner of the conning tower and into the gun bay. His movements were involuntary, beyond his control, as though he had received an order that he couldn't repudiate, an order from someone who knew the future and sent him to await a better chance that was sure to come.

He didn't question it; even when he was in the gun bay and had a moment to think, he accepted it with a sort of fatalistic surety and trust. Looking around the corner of the conning tower, he saw them bring the first plane out and unfold the wings. The sky had started to pale, and it cut sharply against the horizon. Men moved and clustered darkly about it, and the two jet engines hung in nacelles from the wings began to grumble; their exhausts sent wavering, oily reflections down the wet deck. The four men of the crew came out in a body, walked around the port wing and got into the plane, and the handlers ran back out of Corbeck's view. The plane moved a little; Corbeck saw a wink of reflected light from the blister where the tail gun was housed, and then the pilot opened the jets. A blast of heat whirled past Corbeck, and when the plane was halfway down the deck the rocket boosters went off with a shower of fire and the plane was airborne.

They brought the next one out. Corbeck leaned forward and the beginning of doubt arose within him. His fingernails scraped the steel. They had the plane in position now, and the doubt grew stronger; then a man in bulky flying coveralls, with a light helmet on and his goggles pushed up, came around the corner and walked along the side of the conning tower. Corbeck crouched back against the rear of the bay. He couldn't hear the man walking in his flying boots; he crouched, staring at the corner, and then the man was between him and the sea. His face was slimy with sweat in the wan light, and his eyes were fixed. He was going to be sick, and at that instant he turned toward the water.

Corbeck moved swiftly. He leaped to the corner and looked around it; no one was watching, and he leaped again, smashing his fist down at the base of the man's skull. He caught the man around the middle as he crumpled, and dragged him back into the bay. There, with a fierce and terrible feeling of triumph, he broke the man's back over his knee and dropped him to the deck. He didn't look around the corner of the bay again; no purpose would be served by it. With the breath whistling between his teeth, he wrestled with the limp body and pulled it about in the wan light of dawn until he had the clothes off it, and put them on. He pulled the goggles down on his sweating face and walked around the corner toward the plane.

He was breathing hard, and he staggered a little. He found a scarf in the back pocket of the coveralls; it smelled of sweat and alcohol, and he held it up to his face. The three other men were waiting for him under the plane's wing. One of them, very broad and tall, was grinning, but the faces of the two others bore frowns. They were men, like himself, standing on their feet, with arms and heads and coveralls, and at the same time as strange and alien as though they had come from another planet or the Neanderthal age.

Corbeck halted and stared at them through the faintly fogged goggles, mopping his face and praying desperately for a hint as to where he belonged in the plane. His knees threatened to give way entirely, and his belly was thrusting at the back of his throat.

"You and that cursed gluttony of yours," one of the frowning ones said. "Get back to your gun before they call you back and send us off without you." He paused, and said in an aggrieved tone, "Why do you have to eat so much, even today?"

Corbeck needed no more. "Okay," he said through the scarf. "Okay." He turned to the door in the fuselage and made an attempt to get into it. It was high, and he failed. There were curses behind him; one of them stepped up and gave him a boost.

"For the love of God," the booster said, "take hold of something! Get in! They will be on us if you don't hurry, man!" He gave another heave and Corbeck landed on the floor. He pulled himself together and crawled on his hands and knees down the alley to the tail gun.

He fell into the seat and began to breathe again. Through the blister he could see the interior of the conning tower, dim in a sort of subaqueous light, with another plane waiting to come out and the men standing around it. A curtain swung across the opening and the pilot of Corbeck's plane opened his jets. They leaped forward and Corbeck saw the fiery trails of the exhausts streak past him; he was thrown face down on the gun, and when he had got up again, they were in the air.

His head buzzed from the blow on the gun, but was clearer for it; a sort of calmness descended upon him that was like walking out of a dark and violent nightmare into the cool light of morning. He found the earphones and put them on. There was a little talk between the others, and a question to him about his own condition, which he answered. After that he paid no more attention to the phones than he had to. He saw the wing lights of the plane which had gone up ahead of them, and several miniature splashes of light far down as other planes took off with the help of their rockets. Lights gathered as the other planes joined them in their circling; when the sixth came up, they fell into a hollow square, with a plane in the middle and Corbeck's plane leading, and swung off toward the coast.

He couldn't have been in a better position. The plane in the middle of the square, the burdened one, was immediately under his gun, and at that range impossible to miss. He investigated the firing mechanism of the gun and found it to be rather crude and easily managed. There was nothing to do then but wait for a little better light.

The light grew stronger slowly, running across the sea, bringing Corbeck's surroundings in the blister out of the gloom and hardening the outlines of the planes behind him; a great bank of cumulus clouds to the northeast took on a delicate and rosy glow. Corbeck saw the American insignia on the two nearest planes, took the earphones off his head and armed the gun.

As he settled the sights on the middle plane, he began to think again. It seemed to him that he hadn't thought for a long time. He remembered Bartholomew; a little of Bartholomew's irony touched him, and he realized that he had been phenomenally lucky, that he had been given every possible chance, only to fail. He had seen it all too narrowly, lost in his own frantic efforts in a single place and making no effort at all before that; for he and everyone else had seen the signs and carefully ignored them. He had got on the submarine and then on the plane by an unbelievable series of fortuitous circumstances, and was about to do what he had to do, but there were probably, very probably, many submarines, and they could well ignore the loss of this one. There would be enough without it; there were two oceans and the Arctic Circle, and many other methods as well.

He tightened his finger and the gun began to buck; the tracers drew swift lines of light into the middle plane and it started its long, twisting dive into the sea. The four others swung a little and the plastic blister before him shattered in their opening fire. The rosy cloud to the northeast vanished, and for an instant he saw the faces of his wife and the little girl turned up to him, tender and questioning and fading into the dark.

Treachery's Wake

Olaf Ruhen

Fresh out from the New Zealand port of Auckland in bright and dancing weather, the old bark *Jessie Seydon* wheezed and wallowed across the Tasman Sea, and young Amarillo knew that this, his first voyage in her, would also be his last.

He was her bosun; the skipper's ticket in its frame fastened temporarily to the underside of his sea chest's lid entitled him to a better job; but he had been keen to make for Sydney, the Australian port from which the little ships in these last days of the nineteenth century sailed for all the corners of the wide Pacific in feckless bids for fortune.

Young Amarillo—his first name was William—gave nothing away; neither his six feet of height, nor his great width of shoulder, nor yet his Spanish-sounding name hinted at his Cornish ancestry. His eye was uniformly steady, his expression seldom anything but pleasant, his curly hair inevitably disarranged. It would be hard to guess his capabilities. He looked cool and confident; but in fact he was full of misgivings over the voyage.

The *Jessie Seydon* had seen better days; her windmill sent a constant stream of bilge water over the side, and its efforts had to be augmented now and again by those of the crew. Her canvas was good, her standing rigging questionable; and that was a bad combination and pointed to an inefficient captain and careless owners. Above and below decks she carried a cargo of kauri pine for Sydney shipyards; and besides the bosun she had a complement of a skipper and two mates, a cook, seven seamen and a cabin boy, a lad of fifteen years or so. Then there were two passengers, two gentlemen he had seen but little; they spent their time aft with the captain.

Of his companions, thought Amarillo, the less said the better. Most of them had come aboard drunk just before sailing time; the cook was even now at the lee rail, retching, pale and wan, his unhealthy bulk ashiver in the sun. He had been there some time. Amarillo walked over to him.

"First time at sea?" he asked sympathetically.

The cook granted him a baleful glance. "I've had more water hit my oilskins than you're like to see, young fellow," he said. "I was born on a barge, and that forty years by."

"And you're still seasick?" Amarillo marveled.

"Seasick, is it? Seasick? I've never been seasick in my life, and by the grace of God I never will be. It's mustard is wrong with me, lad. Mustard. Forced down my throat in a pint of water near to boiling that ripped the lining out of me."

"Aye, mustard," a new voice said. It was Captain Stiles. He had come up behind them and was grinning in a malevolent way that Amarillo realized was characteristic. "Mustard. That's the medicine to make a man human, bosun. That's the stuff to make them stop crying 'sick.' I'll have no cook drunk in my galley, and now he knows it."

"I was sick, cap'n," the cook protested.

"Yes. Well, if you're not better yet, there's more of the same. Or I've got other remedies. If you're ready for a dose I'll lash you to the shrouds and let you have it."

He turned and walked aft. The cook spat and cursed him under his breath. A little later the captain must have been telling the story to his passengers—Amarillo saw them watching the cook, talking and laughing. One passenger was still in his early twenties; Amarillo supposed him to be the nephew of the other. When they were on deck they sat on cane chairs with the captain —and otherwise kept to themselves.

In any other ship it would have been a good voyage. The wind continued fresh and steady south and by west; they traveled close-hauled across the Tasman for a little better than two weeks with very little necessity to alter the setting of the sails. A clipper might have set a record passage, but speed was beyond the poor old *Jessie*. Amarillo, in charge of rope and canvas, was the busiest man aboard—most of the running rigging needed replacing; yet the stores were inadequate for the purpose, so that he had to be forever compromising between his materials and his needs. By the time the storm came that he feared, the gear for which he was responsible was dependable. But the forecastle walls sweated and worked; the state of the fastenings was such that the timbers groaned and creaked incessantly; the noise from sail and gaff above seemed never to stop; the men were dissatisfied and frightened of the captain; of the mates, one was weak and the other dour and remote; and the cook, a constant butt of the captain, seemed to retaliate by doing the worst he could with stores that had not been good in the first place.

They reckoned they were two days off the southeast coast of Australia and four from Sydney when the wind, veering to southeast, strengthened to a gale. Running ahead of it now, with canvas stripped to essentials and reefed to the storm points, the *Jessie Seydon* picked up her heels and, as far as it was in her, raced for the distant coast. Her cargo had put her low in the water; the newfangled Plimsoll mark had been next door to under as she had lain in harbor. The men, as they came down from the yards, were put immediately to the pumps, and one of the mates was fairly constantly at the well, measuring her intake. But there was no alarm; indeed the crew was jubilant that they would see the Sydney girls perhaps a day sooner than they had thought.

"The girls are on the tow ropes," they said; and they sang rude and happy little verses as they worked the pump handles.

So they ran into the dark night, with the boiling water plunging and curling round their quarters; and at an early hour in the morning, just before the false dawn raised a glow above their starboard quarter, they ran full tilt into the massive trunk of a heavy tree that rolled in the ocean where the offshore currents created a wild and stormy diversion.

Amarillo, in his thwartships bunk at the rear of the forecastle, was thrown to the deck. His first thought was that the ship had been driven on a rock; and as he reached for his trousers he was shouting, sending the awakened crew on deck. The secondary series of crashes, of cannonball reports and the thunder that followed testified that the sudden shock had broken away the masts. That was frightening. Even more ominous was the wash and surge of water within the ship.

While the rest of the crew ran past him and up the companionway to the deck, he fought a tendency to panic and opened the chain locker, striking a match for a quick assessment of the damage. At the level of his eyes the planks were sprung; somewhere below, the heavy stempost had broken, as he could judge from the angles of the timbers. The ship was lying well over on her starboard beam. The sea was free to enter her somewhere below the water line. Already water was round his ankles on the cabin deck and swiftly, swiftly rising.

There was obviously nothing he could do; the ship was gone. But he could make his report and he raced on deck. He found the most unutterable confusion. All three masts had gone, falling parallel, forward and to the right, their trucks still joined by the heavy jumper stay which, while it added strength to the normal rig, had ensured the totality of disaster. The masts were half under the black racing water, their butts pressing down on the broken starboard deck line, the remains of their rigging a fantastic web of stout line, weaving and snapping, that made progress on deck into that variety of obstacle race which is the stuff of nightmare. The thick darkness of the night, the rushing wind and the wash of ocean transformed the shouts of men into eerie croakings like the cries of distant gulls; and the new sounds, the grind and grate of wreckage, had replaced the pistol-crack noises, the whippings and the strainings of a ship under sail.

In one half of his mind, as he squirmed and struggled for the port rail at which he might reasonably expect to find a clearer passage aft, Amarillo was aware that the *Jessie Seydon* was still alive and responsive to the laws of wind and sea, swinging slowly on the new keel that the submerged canvas had formed, so that the port rail was now becoming the lee, sheltered from the main blast of the wind. That was good, he thought; the longboat on the port davits should be undamaged; in the new position of the *Jessie Seydon* its launching would be simplified. The bark was well down by the head now; the stern had hardly lifted, but the bow was almost under water.

He was the last to reach the afterdeck. Miraculously the whole complement had escaped death or being swept overboard; only the boy was clutching a shoulder from which a useless arm swung limp. Amarillo's eyes were used to the darkness now; the darkness itself was giving way to the promise of dawn.

"That you, bosun?" It was the captain.

"Aye, aye. I had a look at her, sir. Stempost gone, planks are sprung."

"No hope then?"

"None, I would say."

"Get three men and axes and clear the starboard davits."

That was it. He should have brought the ax from forward, and he had not. There were two axes socketed on the walls of the midships housing.

"Richards, Schmidt, Lane," he called.

The elder passenger was silhouetted against the glow in the East. His clenched hands were in front of his shoulders; he was lifting his face to the sky and crying like a woman. The younger man, bare legs appearing ridiculously under a knee-length greatcoat, was standing like a statue.

With his team Amarillo was making his tangled way for the axes and the boat davit, but he was aware of these things; as he was aware also of the captain's shouting to somebody to keep away from the longboat at the port rail. He mentally approved. Every minute they could afford to delay would make the longboat easier to launch. In his head, while he cut at the tangle in front of him, he worked out who would have been at the longboat—the second mate, the cook, and Martin Pilling.

The starboard boat was smashed to fragments; once they had cleared a little canvas from it it was obvious that no good could come of their further efforts. Ahead of it the small dory that they used for brief messages to the shore had one side broken out of it, the thwarts ending on air. By that time they were working knee-deep in water.

The *Jessie Seydon*, though, had leveled somewhat. Her stern was now little more elevated than her bows; the racing water had found an ample passage through her bilges to fill the after compartments too. It was now light enough to see the whole situation of the ship. The port side, now on the sheltered lee, was perhaps a couple of feet above the average level of the waves. It was difficult to tell; for the combers, under the pressure of wind, mounted the wreckage on the other side and raced wildly up the slope of the deck, creating a tangle and a swirl that made it doubly necessary to keep a handhold and a toehold at every shift of position.

Back at the stern the captain had left the ship's company and presumably had gone to make some last-minute requisition from his half-flooded cabin. The first mate took command.

"All right, lads. That's all we can do. Richards, Pilling, into the longboat. Stand to the blocks. The rest of you to the falls. Take it easy. Amarillo, watch the wash."

The normal exercise of launching the longboat from the davits was easier than usual: the only complication was the excitement of the men. They got her into the water and there was a scramble for places, a reasonably orderly scramble in which the mate kept some semblance of command. The boat seemed adequate. It was sixteen feet in length and beamy enough, but its load of men set it well down in the water. Still to come were the captain, the first mate and Amarillo.

Captain Stiles appeared from the still unsubmerged entrance to his quarters aft. Of all the men who had tumbled from their beds he was the only one wearing sea boots. The first mate, the two men and the boy of the starboard watch were shod; the rest were barefooted. From some still dry locker the captain had acquired a heavy coat, and he was walking even more deliberately than was his habit. He wore his captain's cap; indeed he was dressed as adequately as ever a man needed in the storm. And he was angry.

"Who gave the order?" he shouted. "Mister Mate, I'll have your skin. Off-load, the lot of you. Get back on board. And keep the ship until I tell you."

"There isn't much time, captain," Amarillo said, and the officer swung on him.

"I'm the best judge of that, bosun. . . . Now, Richards, ship the tiller. Stand by the forward tackle, you there. . . . You, gentlemen, remain seated. . . . The rest of you—out! And step lively."

Pilling leaped for the rail. The rest of the men stayed where they were. They looked uneasy, but sullen.

Very deliberately the captain reached inside the fastenings of his coat, fumbled a second or two and produced a heavy revolver. Just as deliberately he shifted the safety catch and cocked it. "I'm master here, and by God you'll know it. Get out!" he roared.

Hastily, as hastily as they had got on board, yet, as seamen, watchful for the trim of the little boat dancing by the half-submerged hulk, the men came over the rail and stood. Except the boy; he remained sitting at the point of the bows, crying aloud, still clutching his shoulder.

"Now jump to it," the captain roared at him.

"He has a broken arm," protested Amarillo.

"Aye. Well, he'll have a broken leg to match. Boy, you jump when I say." The captain leveled the revolver, and Amarillo gave voice to a half-articulate protest. The gun swung on him. But the lad, sobbing louder, was scrambling for the rail. Hands reached out to help him, and he made it, with a scream of pain.

"That's better," the captain allowed. "Now hear me. I give my orders. Before that boat puts off she'll be well found. What kind of way is that to put to sea?"

The first mate protested. "All found, sir. There's sail in the forward locker and the mast aboard. The coast isn't more than twenty-four hours. Not that, perhaps."

"Mister, I know where I am. . . . Amarillo—the spare sail from the starboard boat. And a spare pair of oars if they're whole. . . . You there, cook—what stores have ye? Bring them out. Whatever bread you have. Pork meat. And a flitch of bacon. Step to it. Lively now. . . . Schmidt, help him. And canisters, with sugar and tea. An iron pot."

Amarillo, looking over his shoulder, saw him wave the gun in an eloquent threat. The men scattered, the captain still shouting his requirements.

The small lugsail stacked under the canvas in the broken boat was easy to retrieve. The bark was still settling in the water, but much more slowly now, and Amarillo realized that the danger was not immediate. The timber cargo below decks was supplying flotation. But under the thudding pressure of the tethered masts and the heavy canvas in the sea the breakup of the ship was beginning.

Forward the chain lashings of the deck cargo had snapped: up there would be a wicked danger, for the timbers were tossing hither and thither, smashing at what construction was in their way. A few sticks had floated free in the wash, and some were caught in the tangle overside.

A wave washed clean over Amarillo as he gathered in the sail; another sent him flying as he turned with it in his arms.

The captain was silent, his gun leveled now to preside over the confusion. He had two men loading the growing pile of stores on board the longboat. He saw the arrival of the spare sail.

"She'll be carrying a big overload," the mate warned him.

"I'll see to it, mister." The captain suddenly raised his voice. Then his malevolent grin showed, and he added, "She'll ride high enough."

Amarillo stopped dead in his tracks as the horror of the captain's intention dawned upon him. The man proposed to ensure his own safety, even his own comfort, at the expense of his crew. He would take every facility for survival—and leave some men on the sinking hulk.

"There's no water here," the captain was saying. . . . "Cook, bring out a small keg. Filled, you hear me. And jump to it."

The galley must have been half-flooded; but the drinking water, for convenience, was kept high up. The cook disappeared again.

The confusion was resolved into stillness, a little at a time; a stillness that encompassed only the human element; a heavy stillness overlaid with fear, as though the men were beginning to realize what was in the captain's mind. Knee-deep in swirling water the cook staggered out of the galley door in the midships housing, carrying a keg of about five gallons' capacity. The men were silent while it was stowed with the rest of the gear in the boat.

"All right." The captain waved the gun. "Now Mr. Mate, you and Mr. Andrews get yourselves on board."

Both mates hesitated briefly and went over the rail. There were now in the longboat Richards, Lane, the two passengers and the two mates. One of the center thwarts was still vacant, and there was a space on the seat aft, where the rudder was already shipped.

"Two more men that can pull," the captain announced. "You, Amarillo . . . and Pilling. And that's the lot. The rest of you can take your chances."

Amarillo stopped short by the rail. "There's room for the lad," he said.

"You heard me, Amarillo. Get on board."

"He can have my place."

"What use is he, with a broken arm?"

"I'll stay."

"All right. You'll stay. . . . Schmidt, take his place."

Schmidt moved slowly forward, like a man in a dream, hesitated at the rail and looked round, but dropped over into the boat. The captain followed him, made for the vacant place by the tiller and sat down.

"Cast off!" he roared.

A few yards from the side, Richards and Lane unshipped the oars. On board the hulk the cook reached down into the rack below the broken mizzen shrouds and grabbed one of the spare belaying pins; but before he could throw it the captain's gun hand swept upward. The shot whistled over their heads. The explosion was no more than the snapping of a line in the noise of that violence of waters.

Amarillo stood with the rest and watched the longboat on its course. At a little distance he could see Schmidt and Pilling stepping the short mast forward. The longboat was handling the seas with ease; lightly loaded as she was there was little prospect of trouble.

With the waxing dawn the wind decreased. Amarillo stood a long time, conscious of the low-toned bitter cursing of his companions, a sound varied by the sobbing of the lad; then he turned and sized up the situation, realizing with a start that the others were looking to him, that he was in command.

There were six of them: a lad with a broken arm, a cook, three seamen and himself. The seamen were that by courtesy; they were the fag end of the crew. There was Anders Anderson, a Swede who seldom spoke and who acted most of the time as though he were half-witted. There were Swayth and Collins, neither one of whom he'd have picked if he'd had the signing on of crew.

"We can build a raft, maybe," Swayth now offered.

"Maybe."

Where did one begin? How did one act? What was there to do?

"Does anyone know anything about a broken arm? Anyone to strap young Charley's shoulder?" he asked, and to his relief the cook nodded.

"I'll take care of it."

"Then that's that."

The next concern was survival, and survival meant provisions. He sent Swayth and Collins to scour the galley, rescue everything that could be eaten or drunk and bring it aft to where the housing above the captain's cabin offered a dubious protection. With Anderson to help, he took the axes and went to clear the rail of the wreckage of the masts. It was a task for giants rather than for men. When the mizzenmast was freed elsewhere it still stubbornly clung in the socket it had smashed through the bulwark rail. Levering it with short gaffs, waiting till the water surged away and then bending every effort gave them no more than an inch or two, though they used all the cunning of seamen to enlist the power of the waves themselves. Eventually Amarillo stood in a constantly changing equilibrium, one foot on the half-floating mast, the other on the constantly submerged rail and chopped the timber through again over the water. The mainmast gave them the same problem; the foremast slipped out as easily as from a launching cradle. Once the wreckage was clear the *Jessie Seydon* came back to an even keel, and slowly enough drifted away from the tangle that had been her driving force.

She was level, but at her midships she was under water. Only fore and aft her castles lifted above the waves like connected islands. The butt of the mizzenmast reared up about six feet; the foremast had snapped at deck level and so had the main.

The boy Charley was lying on the deck, his arm strapped to his side.

"He'll do," said the cook. "It wasn't his shoulder; it was the arm up close. Have you got matches dry? There's pork and some bread—wet, it is; but I could light a fire——"

"Tonight we'll eat," said Amarillo. "Right now you're needed."

The hulk was floating; unless she broke she could be driven. Under forward way she stood a better chance of holding together. There was even a possibility that she yet might be brought to Sydney town.

Two spare booms were lashed inboard of the rail amidships. The biggest was short enough, but for a mast it was all the five of them could handle. With the bark lying level enough they cleared the loose timber, hammered broken lengths in place to make a rough socket against the forecastlehead, festooned the other end of the boom with blocks and stays, and led a line from it to the capstan on the foredeck. One man at the capstan, four at the stays, they raised it an inch at a time, working in water to their waists as often as not, with death threatening in every swing and plunge of the lifting boom. The men worked willingly enough, but without much hope; it did not seem that the poor old *Jessie Seydon* could long stay in one piece.

The sail locker was forward, reached from the flooded forecastle. There was an air space of a couple of feet between the mean water level and the deck, an air space that was cut across with the wash of water as the bark rolled soddenly. Stripped and waiting, Amarillo crouched on the companionway steps, watching his chance. He got the door open and an end of rope in his hand; and his companions above hauled it out. He had to repeat the whole procedure twice before he got a suitable sail—a spare foretop. The other two, though, they made fast on deck, against a later emergency, or lest they could jury-rig them somewhere to make use of more wind.

It was midafternoon before they had a sail hanging from a gaff at the head of the jury-rigged mast; they had not eaten since the night before. Charley, the boy, was still lying more or less where they had left him. He was shivering violently and in some sort of fever. But once Anders was sent to the helm and the sheets were made fast, the *Jessie Seydon* began to respond. She swung slowly, sluggishly, and headed into the northwest, where lay the port of Sydney.

Her pace was hardly to be distinguished. It amounted to no

more than a knot, or a knot and a half; it was certainly less than two. It was by the grace of God that the wind was now behind them; and Amarillo prayed that it might hold direction.

The cook had bundled the available provisions in a square of canvas with a pot or two and tethered the lot to the housing above the captain's cabin, where Charley also was sheltered. Now, with a meal to make ready, he called for matches; there were none dry. The captain's cabin was more out of water than the forecastle; with some difficulty Amarillo salvaged the captain's telescope from a locker above his bunk, and unscrewed its end for a burning glass. They split dry timber from the heart of one of the beams and lighted the fire on the deck itself; the teak would burn hardly, if at all, and the fire didn't offer much danger. They all ate well except the boy; the cook had made a kind of soup for him with a mash of bread for thickening; but it was too salty and he could not keep it down.

The wind steadied to a light breeze with the night, but they made some headway, and in the morning it continued fair. The food lasted them five days; the voyage went on for eleven, and the boy died and was consigned to the sea upon the eighth.

But on the night following the tenth day they saw lights ahead. In the morning the yellow sandstone cliffs of Sydney lay before them, and in no more than two or three hours after that a steam tug moved out toward them. It was overhauled and finally left far behind by a small launch from which, as it reached the *Jessie's* side, a small and dapper man, dressed in the height of fashion, jumped aboard with an agility incompatible with his city appearance.

"Waybrook, that's the name. Waybrook of the *Telegraph*," he said. "What ship is this, and who's in charge?"

"The *Jessie Seydon*, out of Auckland," Amarillo said. "And I guess I'm in charge. I shipped as bosun. Name of Amarillo."

The little man was staring at him. "But that's impossible," he said. "Not the *Jessie Seydon!*"

"The same."

"The *Jessie Seydon!* Mr. Amarillo, there's a mystery here. It's not a week ago I traveled down the coast myself to interview the captain, Captain Stiles. I had the words from his own mouth

—he saw the *Jessie Seydon* underneath the waves. He was the last man to leave."

"They made it then?"

"Aye, they made it. And a rough and terrible time they had. Six men, they said, were lost in the other boat—that would be yourselves? You made it back to the ship? Mr. Amarillo, you have a story here, an epic, if ever I heard of one. And the *Telegraph* I represent would like to have it exclusively—you'll find my principals not ungrateful. There's six of you here?"

"Five," said Amarillo. "The lad died."

The dapper man touched his hat in a perfunctory gesture of respect, but hesitated only a moment. "The story, Mr. Amarillo," he said. "The story."

Amarillo was thinking fast. "It would seem the captain has a different version from our own," he said. "I'll have to ask you to wait, Mr. Waybrook. I have a story, but it is for the owners. Perhaps if you apply to them——"

In any case he could no longer give attention to the journalist, for the tug was coming alongside. He went to deal with it, but the tugmaster, when he saw the condition of the bark's crew, put his own men on board. The ordeal was over.

And for all his disappointment the journalist played his part. His launch sped off ahead of them, back to the port, and before the *Jessie Seydon* could be berthed, the agent's launch had taken them all off, to good food and warm clothes and a quiet lodging at a waterfront hotel. The agents, Messrs. Piddington and Symes, were elated by the bark's delivery; Piddington, a large rotund man with a handle-bar mustache, listened to their stories again and again, and on the day following summoned Amarillo and the crew to a quayside office where clerks worked standing at chest-high desks.

"There'll be a Court of Inquiry, of course," he said. "As far as we are concerned, our judgment's made. Your stories are convincing; none more so than the story the bark itself tells. As for Captain Stiles, we'll come to a reckoning with him; he deserted a ship that could be brought home, and whatever way the court finds, he has done his last work for us. The *Jessie Seydon* goes to the shipwrights. Captain Amarillo—you have your ticket; we'll establish that—and if you'll accept command we'll put her in your charge as from today. We've wasted a lot of sympathy on Captain Stiles; he and those with him had apparently been through a terrible ordeal. They were in poor shape when they landed."

"It's hard to see why," Swayth offered. "'Twas a short-enough voyage they had to make, and the wind fair."

"It was the mustard," said the cook unexpectedly; and they all looked at him.

"I put it in their water barrel. A tinful of mustard—to send them off in the proper frame of mind."

"You might have been the death of them," said Amarillo.

"Maybe. And I'd have lost no sleep. There was no harm in it. Medicine, it is, to make a man human. The captain said so himself."

It was a long time afterward before Amarillo fell to marveling at the inventiveness of the vengeful cook; he was thinking of the *Jessie Seydon*. He'd promised himself never to sail in her again—but a ship under his own command? Well, that was something different. And besides, a man came to love a ship he'd taught to work miracles.

Dr. Blanke's First Command

C. S. Forester

Malcolm Blanke, M.D., was in a state of mental turmoil when he came back into the room where he had undergone his oral examination. Two stupendous things were happening to him at once. He was about to learn if he was to be granted a Ph.D., and he had just joined the United States Navy. About the Ph.D. he would hardly have worried at all if that had been the only factor in his present life. He had every confidence in his thesis on the Histology of the Peripheral Neural Plexuses.

It had broken new ground; it had disproved one theory and established another, and it opened the way to a fresh series of important researches. It had called for four years of hard work—four years of the most slavish concentration, the most accurate laboratory technique, the most painstaking observations and the most ingenious theorizing regarding the deductions to be made from them. The examining board could hardly deny him his Ph.D. now that they had studied his thesis.

Incidentally, it was more than likely that the end result of his work would be the alleviation of a good deal of human suffering, which was a strange thought in a world at war—Blanke could think that way now that he was emerging from four years of total abstraction and now that he had joined the Navy. In fact, as he went back into the room to hear the decision of the examining board regarding his Ph.D., another absurd human thought came up into his mind—at some rare frivolous moment in his youth he had read about the procedure at Naval courts-martial, and how the accused coming in to be told the finding was warned in advance by the position of his sword on the table; the sword point toward him meant a verdict of guilty. Blanke remembered this as he remembered everything he had ever read because he had the fantastic memory of the true scholar, but the clearest proof that he had been jolted out of a purely academic state of mind was that he actually found himself sparing a glance at the council table to see if there was a sword there.

"I must offer you my heartiest congratulations on your thesis, Doctor Blanke," said the chairman of the examining board.

"A very definite contribution to human knowledge," said another member.

"Thank you, sir. Thank you," said Blanke vaguely in acknowledgment.

"I understand we should address you as Lieutenant Blanke, and not as Doctor Blanke, in the future," remarked the chairman.

"I suppose that's so," agreed Blanke. "I've just received my orders."

"At any rate, you have your Ph.D.," said the chairman, "but I don't expect it will be much use to you in the Navy. Undoubtedly it's your medical degree that interests Uncle Sam at the present time."

The day the last word of the thesis had been typed, the last reference checked, Blanke had sent in his application to join the Navy. Less than a week later the Navy had asked for a copy of his M.D. degree, something he had almost forgotten about during four years of research. And now he was a lieutenant (j.g.) USNR—for years, he knew, that would be far more important than just being a Ph.D.

He went back to his home, and his mother awaited him as he let himself in at the door. She was Doctor Blanke, the same as he was; her vocation had been mathematics, but she had years ago reconciled herself to the fact that her son had chosen to be a mere scientist.

"Well, dear?" she said.

"It's all right, mother."

"I'm glad, dear," she said. "Of course, I never had any doubts."

She might have been expected to discuss his Ph.D. further,

but she was a woman as well as a Doctor of Philosophy, and there was something else she could hardly wait to mention.

"There are about a dozen big packages for you, dear," she said.

"My uniforms, I expect," Blanke said.

"Well, aren't you going to open them?" demanded his exasperated mother.

"Of course I will, mother," said he. "In fact, I seem to have heard somewhere that it's illegal for a member of the armed forces to wear civilian clothes now that there's a war."

"I'll help you, dear," said his mother.

Over some of the packages there was a shade of disappointment. "You didn't need any more underclothes, did you, dear?" asked his mother.

Blanke came over and looked at the contents. "That," he decided, "must be the 'six undershirts and six pairs of drawers' they spoke about."

"Your present things are much more suitable," sniffed his mother.

"Here's the khaki," said Blanke, opening another package. He unfolded the coat and held it up for inspection.

"Don't you think you'd better try it on, dear?" said his mother.

She left him while he put on regulation shirt and coat and trousers and tied the regulation tie. When he called her in again, he was standing before the mirror, trying to appear unconcerned at the first sight of himself in uniform.

"You look quite handsome, dear," she said, and only a mother could have thought that the gangling Blanke, with his laboratory pallor and scholarly shoulders, was "quite handsome." Blanke turned back to the mirror.

"Just a minute," said his mother, diving into one of the packages. "Here's something else you have to have." She produced the shoulder boards with their gold stripes.

"Yes, of course," agreed Blanke. "They show my rank. Let's put 'em on."

He buttoned them on his shoulders, and his mother handed him the regulation Navy cap. Blanke did not find much reassurance in the reflection that stared back at him out of the mirror. The United States Navy cap of 1942 did not sit well over a long, intellectual face; the coat was startlingly new and did not fit him very well. A more objective eye than Blanke's or his mother's would have thought he looked less like a naval officer than like a scarecrow that had oddly acquired a new naval uniform.

To be out in the street was a little disturbing; it seemed as if every eye were on him, even though he assured himself that by now naval officers were common enough to attract no notice. After he dismounted from the bus in the vicinity of the Naval District Headquarters, he realized that uniformed men were saluting him as they passed. As he entered the doors, he wondered if he should take off his cap. He knew that the Navy had odd customs to which he would have to conform, so he drew himself up to the full height of his gangling six feet three and spoke stiffly down to a seaman's stocky five feet four in what he decided was a peculiarly inefficient way of asking where he could find the transportation officer.

He said, "Thank you"—surely naval discipline did not ban that minor politeness—and turned away to follow the instructions given him. And then he entered into an encounter which was, in time to come, to save his life and the lives of fifty other men. A burly figure in khaki had intercepted him.

"Excuse me, sir."

"Yes?" asked Blanke.

"Could you spare me a minute before you go to the transportation desk, sir?"

"Yes, I suppose so." Blanke remembered to look at the shoulder boards; these were decorated each with a thin band of alternate blue and gold, and Blanke had no idea what rank this indicated, but he was reassured by the fact that he was being addressed as "sir," even though the man who spoke to him had snow-white hair. This individual looked around as if considering what action to take.

"This way, sir," he said, making up his mind. He led Blanke to a small office at the side of the entrance hall, and at a jerk of his thumb the three seamen sitting there at desks got up and left. When the door closed behind them, Blanke found himself being looked at with a sort of kindly forbearance that puzzled him.

"You've just joined, sir?"

"Yes."

"You haven't been to indoctrination school yet?"

"No," replied Blanke, who had never even heard of indoctrination school.

"Are you on your way there, sir?"

"No. I'm going to join my ship."

"Your ship, sir!" The astonishment was profound. "Well, you must excuse me, sir, but you can't go there like that."

"Why, what's wrong?"

"Everything, sir, if you'll excuse me. Those shoulder boards. You're wearing 'em the wrong way round, sir. You should have the points inward so the stripes aren't up under your neck. Here, let me do it for you, sir. . . . That's better. And these buttons—you keep them done up, all the time. And the pocket flaps should be out, not in."

By the time everything had been twitched into position, even Blanke was aware of the improvement.

"Thank you," he said with genuine gratitude. He knew he had much to learn, and this would be as good a time to start as any. "Who is it I'm thanking? What do those stripes mean?"

"Warrant bo'sun, sir. Warrant Bosun Dean. Thirty-seven years' service, but they won't let me go to sea now. You don't mind me speaking to you like this, sir?"

"Mind? I'm grateful to you, of course. I have to learn sometime."

"It's too bad they're sending you to sea without any indoctrination at all. But I know they're short of doctors. What ship, sir?"

Blanke had to stop and think, for one name meant no more to him than another. "The *Boon*."

"*Boon?* DD."

"DD?"

"Destroyer, sir."

Dean tried to conceal the pity he felt for a man who did not know what a "DD" meant and yet was going to be pitchforked into one.

"That's one of the smaller ships, I take it," said Blanke.

"You're darn right, sir," agreed Dean. "Let me show you the way to the transportation desk."

Blanke was learning fast; when he arrived at the desk he was much relieved that the glance the transportation officer gave him was very different from the glances he had received so far. He was looked at as if he were just one more raw lieutenant in the medical corps, and that was an immense step upward.

"Priority Four," said the transportation officer, examining Blanke's orders. "You could be here for weeks if we try to fly you out. But you've got to go. They want doctors."

He opened first one file and then another and ran through them without result. Then another idea struck him, and he reached for a third file.

"That's it," he said. "We can kill two birds with one stone. You're ready to go on board, I suppose?"

"Well, yes," said Blanke.

"Tonight?"

"Of course, if it's necessary."

"It's necessary, all right. *Wilhelmina*—Dutch registry, chartered transport, Dutch officers, Javanese crew. She's taking an anti-aircraft-artillery outfit out to Nouméa. They haven't an Army doctor with them, and we can fit you in all right. I'll get your orders endorsed. Come back in ten minutes."

Blanke walked away a little dazed, but trying to appear as if he were perfectly accustomed to being ordered to sail at a moment's notice with a Javanese crew to a place he had never heard of. He was grateful when bosun Dean appeared.

"Did they give you any orders, sir?" he asked, and Blanke told him. "*Wilhelmina*. She's a fast transport—one of the ships that got away when the Japs overran the Dutch East Indies. Look here, sir, would you care to come and wait in my office while they type out your orders?"

Blanke was glad to accept, was glad to take the proffered chair and the proffered cigarette. The transition was continuing. The eagle powers of observation that for four years had expended themselves down the tube of a microscope were beginning to devote themselves now to the human beings and the material things that constituted his new world. He was aware of the concern, almost paternal, with which Dean was regarding him.

"It's only now that they've decided to put doctors into every destroyer, sir," explained Dean. "Only one in four in peacetime. But now the DD's have twice as many men on board.

And those ships fight—more likely to fight than the battle wagons are."

"I see," said Blanke.

He would have to study the technique of naval warfare—and make plans how best to give rapid care to a crowd of wounded men in a shell-torn steel hull. Dean was shaking his head with something of sorrow—no, sympathy—in his expression.

"You don't know *anything*, do you, sir?" he said.

"I'm afraid I don't. I'll have to do some reading."

"I wish we was going to be in the same ship, sir," said Dean. "I could teach you a lot, quick."

"I wish we were," said Blanke with sincerity.

Dean's eyes strayed to something on the desk before him. Then he took the plunge.

"Look, Doc," he said. "I won't have the chance to make a Navy man out of you, but here's a book. Take it and learn something about the Navy." It was a largish, bluebound book that he offered.

"That's very kind of you," said Blanke, taking it; he did not know yet that his life depended on his taking it. It was the *Bluejacket's Manual*, and as he ran through the pages, all sorts of headings met his eye—"Uniform Regulations," "Types of Navy Ships," "Routines Aboard Ship" and more advanced subjects, like "Communications and Signaling" and "Boat Seamanship."

"Thank you again," said Blanke. "This must be just what I need."

"You're very welcome," said Dean. "I hope you find it useful. You'll have plenty of time for reading in the *Wilhelmina*—and your orders'll be ready by now, I expect, sir."

Those orders took Blanke on board the *Wilhelmina* that night. He walked down the gangway onto the first deck—except for ferryboats—that he had ever trodden in his life. There were soldiers and packing cases everywhere. Someone with dark skin —Javanese, Blanke guessed—passed him on to a harassed individual who said, 'Dis vay, pliss' and led him to a cabin where a fat Dutchman in shirt sleeves sat at a desk and read Blanke's orders and groaned.

"O.K.," he said at length. "You slip here."

"Here?"

The little cabin seemed to be completely full, with a desk and a bed and miscellaneous packages, but a wave of the fat Dutchman's arm indicated that there was an upper bed against the wall.

"I'm de purser," said the fat man. "I slip here." He indicated the lower bed, then said, "I am busy."

Blanke went quietly, nor was he averse to seeing something more of this first ship of his. As he entered a corridor, a door opened, revealing an Army officer who noticed his uniform and politely stood by the door for him to enter. It was a small room full of tobacco smoke and crowded with men who made him welcome and introduced themselves, the officers of the antiaircraft unit whose enlisted men thronged the deck.

"Glad to find we have a doctor with us after all," said one of the captains, and Blanke forbore to comment on the remark.

He was content to sit silent, for the officers, he was glad to observe, were as excited as he was and soon left him out of the conversation when he offered no contribution to it. After a time one of the lieutenants, at a nod from one of the captains, left for the purpose, as he said, of "seeing the boys into bed." Blanke saw his opportunity to say good night, made his way back by a miracle to the purser's cabin and entered it to find the purser stretched out on the lower bed, still checking through papers and not in the least inclined to conversation.

Blanke discovered how to lower his bed, just as he would have found out the principle of some novel piece of laboratory apparatus, and he climbed up and in. He glanced at the three books he had taken to bed with him, put down the *Bluejacket's Manual*, picked up and discarded *Wounds and Burns*, did the same with *Preventive Medicine in Tropical Climates*, and went back to the *Bluejacket's Manual* again. He was tired enough to go to sleep quite shortly, with the light on and the *Bluejacket's Manual* on his chest.

So it was in this way that Malcolm Blanke went to sea for the first time, a queer introduction to naval life, and yet one that early enough made plain to him the salient characteristics of life at sea in wartime—monotony, overcrowding, lack of privacy. In the *Wilhelmina* the United States officers shared the quarters of the Dutch officers, which meant that three men lived where one lived before; the sergeants shared with the ship's bosun and the stewards, about four men to one prewar berth, while the soldiers, 200 of them, could spread themselves where twelve passengers had once lived in comfort. And through all this the Javanese crew flitted like ghosts, going about the ship's business as if all these others did not exist.

There was little to do; there was very little that could be done in those cramped conditions. Twice a day there was boat drill and abandon-ship drill; there was physical drill; there were classes in the theory of antiaircraft gunnery, and not even the blue Pacific sky could brighten those. For twenty-four hours the prospect of arriving at the romantic Hawaiian Islands lifted the pall of boredom, but the pall closed down all the thicker when the *Wilhelmina* steamed out again into the endless Pacific after only eighteen hours' stay, during which not a soldier set foot on shore.

The one man in the ship who was free of boredom was, naturally, Blanke. He was a true scholar, and here he was congenially employed in study; and the tasks he set himself had the unusual quality of being planned for practical ends. He had to make himself ready for a new life; there would be fantastic demands made upon him, and he had to prepare himself to meet them. With the intense concentration of a scholar, he read the books he had with him; to achieve that concentration he spent most of his time stretched out in the upper berth of the purser's cabin, for the purser was a man of few words who left him alone and allowed him a privacy impossible to find in the crowded wardroom or on the noisy deck. He read his professional books with care, calling up memories of his life as a hospital intern to fill in the gaps. He would lay his book down, gaze up at the deck beams overhead and take himself, step by step, through an emergency appendectomy, for instance. That was easier than trying to picture himself handling casualties in a destroyer under fire, but he rigorously made himself visualize those possible situations as well.

Naturally he was methodical about all this; no one without method could have devised the scheme of research which had resulted in his Ph.D. thesis. He spent his mornings in study of his professional books, with a break for sick call, which he attended at the request of the officer commanding the troops, but at which nothing ever showed up which could not have been safely left to the medical corporal. Two hours in the afternoon he devoted to acquiring a tan, with nicely judged proportions of shade and sunshine, because he knew he would be much exposed to tropical suns in the future. And the rest of his time he read the *Bluejacket's Manual,* and this was the hardest work of his day. It called for an effort of will to concentrate on the thousands of new facts presented in those 800 crowded pages. But he made himself learn them, conscientiously setting himself to answer the quizzes at the ends of the chapters to test his knowledge.

Some of the knowledge was obviously advantageous; he learned about specialty marks and insignia, and in the few moments when he could be alone, he taught himself to salute in the prescribed method. He read about Personal Hygiene and First Aid to inform himself about what the Navy thought officially about these things; that was easier than the Manual of Arms and Close Order Drill, but he worked through those before applying himself to the more interesting chapters on Types of Navy Ships and Shipboard Routine. It was hard to study the technique of Cleaning and Painting, but the General Safety Precautions, of course, had a direct bearing on his future duties. He read everything and he conscientiously stored everything away in his remarkable memory. When he reached the glossary at the end, and admitted to himself that he knew the meaning of every term in it, from "abaft" to "yoke," he felt an actual sense of loss in that he had no further difficult work to occupy his mind—and the *Wilhelmina* was still not due to arrive at Nouméa for another four days.

That was when tragedy struck; that was when Blanke learned that those long periods of tedium that characterize naval life in wartime can be terminated in a single second.

Blanke was in his bunk dozing, his open book on his chest, when the torpedo exploded. He woke, only conscious that something violent had happened. The thundering noise he heard next second he could not explain to himself; it was the sound of the water, flung hundreds of feet into the air, bursting over the upper works of the *Wilhelmina.* Then there was a momentary silence, a dead, dead silence, in the midst of which the *Wilhelmina* lay suddenly over toward one side, rolling him against the bulkhead. He found the light switch and pressed it, and there was no result; he clicked it twice more before he realized that the electric power was off. Down below him the purser was talking volubly yet quietly in Dutch, and then Blanke heard a whistle blowing outside, its staccato notes bearing a message of great urgency.

He knew now that the *Wilhelmina* had been torpedoed, that she was lying helpless, without power, without even steam for the siren, and that she was heeling over in her death agony. He hauled himself up against the list out of bed. Those urgent whistle notes outside conveyed something of panic, and for two or three seconds that panic infected him; he was blundering frantically in the darkness of the cabin before he pulled himself together. He had learned by painful experience in the laboratory and operating theater that haste and carelessness brought disaster—that reaction came fast, and pride came only second. He was the only naval officer in the ship and he was not going to show fear. He forced his mind into its usual orderly way of thought, only incidentally observing—like a footnote to a thesis—the physiological symptoms of tension manifesting themselves as he found his shoes and his life jacket. Then he made his way up the sloping deck to the door on the heels of the purser, and out into the windy darkness toward his station for "abandon ship."

For many years after the torpedoing of the *Wilhelmina* he was able to recall clear-cut details of the abandoning of the ship; his mind, trained to observation, noted these details of a strange and new experience and stored them away. He learned about discipline. There were voices in the darkness; there was the tone of bravado in which unseen soldiers cracked jokes about their desperate situation, and there was the note of hysteria in other voices, and the stillness that ensued when the voice of one of the artillery lieutenants—cracking a little with strain and yet under control—ordered silence.

"Don't act like kids," added the lieutenant. "You're men." Blanke at thirty-one felt, even at that moment, an odd twinge at hearing someone of twenty-four speaking like that to soldiers of twenty.

The voice of the Dutch third mate, stumbling over his English, could now be heard.

"All right, thank you," said the lieutenant, and then to the soldiers, "Get into the boat."

Several flashlights made a pool of light in the darkness, and out of the pool the men climbed in, hastily but with hardly a sign of panic, although another rasping order from the lieutenant was necessary to impose silence again as the crowding began. Blanke stood waiting his turn beside the Army officers. He felt someone plucking at his sleeve. Someone—the second mate, he thought, but he could not be sure in the darkness—thrust a piece of paper into his hand.

"Position and course," said the man and then hastened off again toward the next boat before Blanke could reply. He put the paper into his pocket, ready to hand it over to whoever would be in command of the boat, and then there was a ridiculous moment of politeness as to whether he should climb in before or after the lieutenant. Then they sprang in together, pushing in among the soldiers, and after them came two of the Javanese deck hands, silent as always and insinuating themselves between the close-packed bodies on the thwarts.

There were Dutch orders shouted from the deck, and a clanking of machinery. The boat lurched and swung hideously in the darkness, crashed against the ship's side, swung and hit the invisible water with a splash amid yells from the soldiers, and then came soaring up on a black invisible wave and rolled horribly, as if she were going to turn over, righted herself at what seemed the last possible second, and then sank down again more unpleasantly than any elevator Blanke had ever experienced. Not until much later did he come to realize how fortunate they were to have reached the water at all without capsizing; the Javanese deck hands had done a neat piece of work at bow and stern.

It was the blackest overcast night anyone could imagine; the *Wilhelmina* was already out of sight, the more so as the soldiers who had flashlights in the boat were using them freely—one shone straight into Blanke's face and left him quite blinded.

"What do we do next, sir?" asked the artillery lieutenant beside him.

"I can't see a thing," was all Blanke could say at the moment.

The lieutenant lifted his voice in a bellow as he ordered the flashlights extinguished. "Save 'em until you need 'em," he said.

The boat lurched and rolled again, soaring up and then dropping down, the abrupt descent marked by wails from the soldiers. The Pacific swell which the *Wilhelmina* hardly noticed had free play on the small boat; moreover, the brisk trade wind was turning her round slowly in a series of circles, so that each successive swell met her at a different angle, and her rolling and lurching were unpredictable in the darkness.

"Parm me," said the lieutenant, with a blurry attempt at politeness, and then he was horribly seasick—so, judging from the sounds, were most of the soldiers. So was Blanke, after struggling with his symptoms for several minutes. He had never known such misery as overcame him then. The world was utterly pitiless, and he was hopeless and useless, and death would be welcome when it came, especially when the boat rolled wildly again, from far over to one side to far over to the other; a good deal of water slapped in, calling forth startled cries from the men it wetted.

Luckily for everyone concerned, that scientific mind of Blanke continued to function. It could not help analyzing the reasons for that uncontrolled and unpredictable motion of the boat. It was unpredictable simply because it was uncontrolled. The boat was spinning, slowly but helplessly, under the influence of the wind and should be brought under control so as to meet the rollers end on. Blanke's mind went back into the high-school physics and mechanics he had studied fourteen years before, picked out the relevant facts and proceeded to build up suggestions upon them. If something could be put up to catch the wind at the tail end— at the stern—the boat would turn like a weathercock and point into the wind and, presumably, into the waves. That would be a good idea, but he did not see how it could be done in the dark. Similarly, if something could drag in the sea at the other end— at the bow—the boat would trail back from it, with bows to wind and sea. That might work very well if it could be done, but Blanke was not too sure how to set about it; it was the crowding and the darkness, in other words, which prevented Blanke from reinventing the sea anchor that night.

The rudder, of course, would only function if the boat had

some motion of its own through the water. Of course! The boat had an engine. If that were set running, someone could hold the rudder and steer her so as to meet the waves properly. He remembered that while he was waiting his turn to get into the boat, he had heard one of the other boats, with an engine running, leaving the ship.

"Hadn't we better get the engine started?" he said to the artillery lieutenant and realized as he said it that the lieutenant was too far gone with seasickness to be rational.

Blanke would have to deal with it himself. With the need for instant action, he put aside the temptation to follow up a new line of thought regarding the effect of military discipline on the young men crowded into the boat; they were used to receiving orders and drilled into obeying them. No time for such thoughts now. Blanke got cautiously off his thwart and began to push his way in the direction in which one of the Javanese deck hands had disappeared when they got in the boat. He had to climb over shoulders; he trod on bodies lying in the bottom, bodies that hardly resented the pressure of his foot.

"Where's that sailor?" he demanded. "Where's that Javanese?"

"Here, sir—back here," croaked a voice.

Blanke shook the Javanese's shoulder. "Motor. Engine," he said.

The Javanese said something in reply. Blanke felt his wrist held and his hand guided; that was the tiller—he knew the word from the glossary in the *Bluejacket's Manual*—a short piece of iron or wood used to turn the rudder. It swung unresisting in his hand; of course, that would be the case if the boat had no motion through the water. The Javanese had left his side; Blanke had the impression that the seaman was climbing forward by the route he himself had followed, over the heads and shoulders of the crowded soldiers. He waited tensely; he heard the Javanese call out something to his compatriot, who answered. He heard noises and expostulations which indicated that soldiers were being heaved out of the way; he heard a clatter and clanking of metal—during this time the boat had pitched and rolled excruciatingly a dozen times, and three times water had slopped in over the sides.

There came a sudden roar of the engines, and Blanke felt

the rudder come to life under his hand. The roar ceased; the rudder died, but then the engine roared again, confidently, with every promise of permanence, and the water over the stern boiled, and the rudder bit. They were frightening, those first few seconds; it took Blanke that long to grasp the technique of turning the tiller the opposite way—during those seconds the boat slithered precariously along a crest and came nearer to capsizing than ever before, amid cries of dismay from the passengers. But by the time the boat had completed the circle, Blanke had matters almost under control. He met the next wave bows on; there was infinite satisfaction at first in doing so, in feeling the boat climbing the slope, but when they reached the crest and put their bows down and their stern up, and shot down the farther side, it was not so comfortable—in fact, it felt hideously dangerous.

He wanted to saw at the rudder, but restrained himself with the thought that that would be more dangerous still, but then his doubts were resolved by a sudden drop in the pitch of the engine's roar. He could feel the speed moderate, and the boat breasted the next slope more satisfactorily still and pitched over the crest in a manner quite restrained, so that some sort of small cheer came from the passengers capable of any sensation at all. Blanke guessed that the Javanese at the engine had throttled down, and he was grateful, even though he had little attention to spare for them; he had to concentrate on the feel of the wind on his face, on the lurch of the boat and on reminding himself to pull the tiller to the left—to port—when he wanted to head to the right—to starboard.

In a few minutes it was becoming second nature to him. Seasickness was forgotten; there was actually something exhilarating in handling the boat like this as she chugged valiantly forward in the dark. Where he was going he did not know, but he reconciled himself to that by telling himself that until daylight should come and new arrangements could be made, he was doing the only safe thing. Thinking along that line, he realized why there was no ship's officer in the boat—this was the chief engineer's boat, and he could guess what had happened to the chief engineer. The instant helplessness of the *Wilhelmina* after the torpedo struck told of a hit in the engine room; the chief engineer had died for his country.

That gloomy train of thought was interrupted by his overhearing a fragment of conversation among the soldiers just in front of him.

"There's lockers under these seats. Let's have your flash a minute, Joe."

"Leave those lockers alone," snapped Blanke; strain and excitement put an edge on his voice.

In four years of research he had had painful experience with overenthusiastic, or stupid, or inquisitive laboratory assistants, and he could guess at what disasters might ensue if prying fingers got to work on those lockers. But he was astonished at the intensity of his speech—he would never have snapped at technical assistants in that way, but then his life was not in danger.

The fact was that the steadying of the boat's motion and the comforting thought circulating among the soldiers that the Navy was now in charge, were encouraging the more active of the young soldiers to indulge their innate restlessness.

"Move over, can't you?" said a voice.

"Get off my feet, you big slob," said another.

"Wish I had a drink," said a third.

It seemed as if in no time at all the unseen passengers were beginning to surge about in the boat; Blanke, keyed up to the highest pitch, was acutely conscious of variation in the trim, even if he did not use that word to himself. He only knew that it felt dangerous when the boat went down on one side and that it was likely to interfere with his steering. He opened his mouth to expostulate—and then shut it again while he rehearsed what he was going to say. He had to give an order; he had to shout into the wind, so that he would have to use all his lung power. He took a deep breath, told himself that he must display no agitation and then let himself go.

"Sit still, all of you!" he yelled.

It was gratifying that he made so much noise, and the result was gratifying, too, in that there was quiet in the boat and that someone, presumably the lieutenant, endorsed his order.

"Sergeant, see that the men keep still over there."

"Yes, sir."

There was much to be said for discipline when it produced such results. But, on the other hand, the cessation of the bustling in the boat and his growing familiarity with the handling of the tiller gave Blanke an opportunity to think again. He began to wonder what would happen next, and what he ought to do—if anything. He was the biggest fraud who had ever held a tiller. When daylight came, decisions would have to be reached. They would have to set that course which was written on the paper in his pocket. "They"—whom did he mean by "they"? The Javanese? The artillery lieutenant? He had an uneasy feeling that by "they" he really meant himself.

There must be a compass in the boat—otherwise there was no reason for the paper with the course written on it. He presumed he could set a course. He had no idea where he was—the word had gone round the ship that they were four days from Nouméa, and four days would mean what? A thousand miles, fifteen hundred miles? There certainly would not be gasoline to last all that time. They would have to use the sails—he had seen masts in the boat and presumed that there were sails. He found himself hoping devoutly that the Javanese deck hands knew something about sailing a boat. There was a chance that daylight would reveal one or more of the other boats near them, but Blanke could guess how small a chance that was; he could work out in his mind how limited was the horizon from a small boat and how widely dispersed the boats could become during several hours with a brisk wind blowing.

As he reached that conclusion it became borne in upon him that he could now see something of the boat and its crowded passengers; he could see the heads and shoulders in front of him as dark masses in a lighter medium. Daylight was actually coming, and he stirred in his seat to discover he was horribly stiff, and his hand ached from its viselike grip on the tiller, and he was shivering with cold.

"Well, there it is, boys," said a voice in the boat, and everyone started chattering at once—at least, everyone who was not too cold or seasick to chatter. The light increased rapidly, and he could see the unshaven cheeks and the drawn features of the packed crowd. He could see the two Javanese crouching by the engine, and the young lieutenant perched on a thwart near them. The lieutenant rose with infinite stiffness and pushed his way to the stern of the boat and into a minute space beside Blanke.

"What do we do now, sir?" he asked, speaking in a muffled tone in an effort not to be overheard by the soldiers crowded all round.

The question, and the manner of asking it, confirmed Blanke in his certainty that the artillery lieutenant, although perfectly qualified to command an antiaircraft platoon, had not the least idea what to do when adrift in the Pacific with fifty castaways.

"Let's look round," said Blanke, temporizing.

The lieutenant agreed without making any move to follow up the suggestion, and Blanke knew he had to act. He caught the eye of one of the Javanese by the engine and beckoned to him. Then he handed over the tiller and prepared to stand up. It was not going to be easy.

"Prop me up," he said, coming erect on his aching legs and preparing to mount to the thwart. Half a dozen hands were raised to hold him as he stood, wobbling dangerously in the heaving boat. There was nothing to see; he shifted his feet precariously as he turned to sweep the horizon. There was only the sea, only the long rollers marching toward them. The motion of the boat became more pronounced, and Blanke saw that half, or more than half, of the soldiers, carried away by his example, were scrambling to their feet to look around too; he ought to have expected that. He nearly missed his footing and exclaimed loudly, and the lieutenant had the sense to appreciate the danger.

"Sit down, you men. Sit down, all of you!"

He was obeyed, and Blanke stepped down and reseated himself.

"Nothing in sight," he said, and now he had to think quickly—rather, he did not have to think, but had to implement the decisions which the meditations of the night had forced upon him. He took the scrap of paper from his pocket and studied what was written on it: "Course 222° True. Var 11°E." He could interpret that, all right, thanks to the *Bluejacket's Manual*.

"I have the course here," he said, "I think we'll have to get under sail."

He was painfully conscious that fifty pairs of eyes had him

under their scrutiny and that fifty lives might depend on his decisions. The Javanese beside him had caught the last word he said.

"Sail," said the Javanese and then pointed toward the engine. "Motor—stop."

The Javanese backed up his words with an eloquent gesture; he was clearly implying what Blanke had already thought of—that gas was likely to run short any moment.

"You see we'll have to——" said Blanke to the lieutenant; he was having to struggle against a curious constriction of the throat as he spoke. Then to the Javanese, "All right. Sail."

The Javanese nodded—he even smiled. He returned the tiller to Blanke, stood up and shouted in his own language to his fellow seaman. The two of them became immediately active, and Blanke was relieved to see that their movements were entirely purposeful and that they did not have to refer to him. They scrambled up and down the length of the boat, pushing the soldiers out of their way when necessary; the soldiers watched their actions with dull interest. There was a good deal of upheaval while the Javanese moved the soldiers off the lockers along the sides of the boat and dragged out grimy rolls of canvas and then busied themselves with the lines that came with them. There were two masts laid lengthways in the boat, and the Javanese raised first one and then the other—Blanke noted that they lay in opposite directions, sensibly, so as to call for the least movement to set them up. Each mast in turn had its base passed down through holes in the thwarts, and was settled down with comforting solidity into what Blanke knew—thanks to his scholar's memory—were called the "steps" below. The wire ropes attached to the tops of the masts were led out to the sides of the boat and hooked onto these; Blanke dived into his memory again to come up with the word "stays." Things were really moving too fast for his mental comfort. Already the Javanese were looking to him for orders, ready to set the sails. There must be a compass somewhere in the boat, otherwise he would not have been given that scrap of paper. Then before him he saw a small varnished trap door, which he raised in desperation, and underneath it was a compass. There were the words U. S. NAVY. BuSHIPS. No. 1 COMPASS, engraved on the ring—these lifeboats, of course, had been supplied by the Navy when the *Wilhelmina* had been chartered.

"I was wondering about a compass," said the artillery lieutenant, and Blanke forbore to say, "Not as much as I was." Instead he devoted himself, gratefully, to the deviation card inside the lid.

He plunged down into his memory again and, like the diver in the old ballad, came to the surface again with a pearl. "Can Dead Men Vote Twice?": Compass, Deviation, Magnetic, Variation, True—that was what the initial letters of those words stood for; the *Bluejacket's Manual* had told him so. He could perhaps have worked out the compass course from first principles, but the mnemonic saved time and trouble, besides reminding him forcibly of the need for correction. A few seconds' study of the deviation card revealed the huge importance of it, for it was a cumulative and not a self-canceling correction. He had to subtract no less than 27 from 222.

With the pencil he had taken from his pocket he wrote down the resultant figure 195, on his scrap of paper, and then checked through his working again, swallowing hard with excitement as he did so. An uncorrected error of twenty-seven degrees in the course could mean a difference of dozens of miles in their destination, the difference perhaps between life and a lingering death out in the wastes of the Pacific. It was almost inconceivable that a man should be facing that grim possibility when less than three weeks earlier his chief doubt had been whether he would be awarded a Ph.D.

Now everybody was waiting for him again. Now he had to reach fresh decisions. He pinned his faith on the Javanese and beckoned to one of them and then gestured toward the tiller; to his relief he received a nod in return. They switched off the engine, and the man he had beckoned to came scrambling aft, where they made room for him at the tiller. Blanke showed his written 195 and pointed to the compass, and was reassured again by a nod. The Javanese understood and shouted in his own language to his compatriot and was answered in a rapid-fire conversation.

It was a moment of tense excitement—now that the engine had ceased running, the boat was beginning to wallow aimlessly again over the rollers. The other Javanese was pushing his way through the crowd and putting ropes in the men's hands; and then with gestures he called on them to pull.

"Heave ho!" shouted someone, apparently thinking that was amusing.

With a creaking and groaning the sails began to rise up the masts. There was a moment of chaos, a moment when Blanke felt consuming doubt which later he realized was fear. The sails flapped with a thunderous din, and the boat lurched and pitched horribly. The Javanese at the sails was leaping about the boat, over heads and shoulders, attending to this and that. The boat lay over momentarily worse than ever, and then the Javanese at the tiller pulled it far over and she steadied herself. The sea bubbled round the rudder, and inconceivably, order emerged from the chaos. The Javanese at the sails was still leaping about, pulling at ropes, but obviously he was only making minor adjustments.

Blake looked at the compass, and there was the lubber's line swinging close about 195 degrees. He looked up at the sails, and they were bellying out, but under restraint, and the Javanese attending to them was hauling them in to a slightly closer angle, with the help of soldiers, into whose hands he was putting the ropes. He was pushing and gesticulating at some of the men to induce them to move across the boat and sit on the other side—that made an appreciable difference to the feeling of stability. For the boat was lying over, with the wind coming sideways at them; Blanke's mind promptly grappled with the deduction that on a course of 222 degrees True, in an area where the southeast trades prevailed, the wind would naturally come in over the side; he looked up at the sails again and down at the boat and thought about the triangle of forces at work which would drive the boat in a direction different from that of the wind.

And it was surprising, too, to see how differently the boat was behaving. Even though she was not heading directly into the waves, she was not lurching so wildly nor so menacingly as she did when not under control. Her behavior was actually purposeful; under the steadying influence of the sails, she was yielding to the rollers in a measured fashion, with a rise and a roll and a pitch that actually had some aesthetic quality about it. The water—the "wake," that was the word—bubbled behind him; a few fragments of spray were flying from the bows. Blanke was astonished at the discovery that this might almost be thought of as pleasant; and when, some moments later, the clouds parted sufficiently to allow the rising sun to shine on his back, he contrasted his previous feeling of despairing misery with what might almost be described now as well-being. He caught the eye of the Javanese at the tiller; busy though this man might be, darting vigilant glances up at the sails and down at the compass and over the side at the rollers, he yet could find a moment to grin at him in a sort of conspiratorial confidence.

There was a perceptible change in the soldiers too. Except for two unfortunates who were still far gone in seasickness, they were all talking at once. Cigarettes were being smoked in such numbers that the wind was carrying off a small trail of smoke—to "leeward," that was the word. And already there were cries of despair as cigarettes were counted up; there were men with none and men with a few and none with many. Every soldier in the boat was cursing the suddenness of the alarm which had set them adrift without a chance of gathering up precious possessions. Then, almost immediately, there were remarks made loudly by one and another, and questions asked of the sergeants, obviously intended to reach the lieutenant's ears. The soldiers were hungry and thirsty and they wanted to eat and drink.

The lieutenant turned to Blanke. "Any orders, sir?"

Blanke could not answer immediately. The difference in the size of his collar insignia—smaller than that of the Army—marked him as the only Navy officer in the boat. But that no more qualified him for the command than did his greater age. If by chance there had been present the lowliest, most newly joined seaman second class, that seaman would legally be in command. The oak leaf and acorn on Blanke's collar specifically disqualified him: the *Bluejacket's Manual* was quite definite about that. Yet, despite all this, Blanke could not close his mental eyes to the obvious fact that the course of previous events had conferred the command on him. And reluctantly he faced the next fact, which was that if he were to disclaim all responsibility and throw in his hand, the result might easily be disastrous for all on board.

There were many long difficult days ahead, and the occupants of the boat had come to look on him as possessed of all the technical knowledge necessary. That confidence, baseless though it might be, was an asset of supreme importance. He could not evade the trust reposed in him; yet he still longed to temporize.

The boat corkscrewed over a roller, and the water that had entered the boat surged over the bottom boards and slapped against his ankles—it had done that a hundred times already and had ceased to attract his notice until now, when he was looking for an excuse to evade decision. He seized on the chance; and that brought to his notice what the bottom of the boat was like, after that horrible night.

"Don't you think the first thing to do," he said mildly, "is to clean up? Look at all this."

The lieutenant might be a man who feared responsibility, but he was open to suggestion. "Quite right, sir," he said and then he lifted up his voice. "At ease!"

It was interesting how the commotion died away—interesting to notice the easy manner of the lieutenant, accustomed to command and expecting to be obeyed.

"We're going to get the boat cleaned up," the lieutenant went on. "Sergeant Schwartz, I want everyone at work."

Discipline, not too deeply rooted among those young soldiers, had a hard struggle against the complete novelty of the situation. The buzz of talk reasserted itself, but the lieutenant was ready for that.

"No breakfast until the boat's policed," he said. "Sergeant Schwartz, you heard my order."

So now, while the soldiers were at work bailing out and clearing up, the lieutenant turned to Blanke to discuss the next problem, which he had already raised by his last speech.

"What do we do about that, sir?" he asked. "What about food and water?"

Blanke was already turning over in his mind what the *Bluejacket's Manual* had to say about Survival Afloat and he supplemented that with what he had learned during his medical training. He opened the locker beside him and saw with relief that it was filled with small cans—he really had not doubted that it would be, but he was relieved, all the same.

"How long before we're rescued, sir?" asked the lieutenant.

Blanke felt acute irritation. He wanted to turn upon the lieutenant and point out that he did not know where he was, had only a vague idea of where he was going and could form no estimate of the speed between these points. The violence of his feelings surprised him; it was really shocking to find that there was something alluring about the prospect of losing his temper and flaring out, uncontrolled, in a wild outburst to compensate himself for the things life was doing to him and for the responsibilities piling on him.

The realization steadied him; it was the more easy to maintain his self-control because he was interested in the discovery that he was liable to such fits of rage even though he could not remember ever having had one before. Lastly, he remembered the *Bluejacket's Manual* again. There were a few lines there about the initial feeling of "relief and elation" when finding oneself in a lifecraft away from the sinking wreck, followed by a warning that these attitudes might "worsen into irritability and preoccupation." That book was certainly accurate. He almost smiled at the thought and, in consequence, could make himself talk with studied calm. He posed as if he had been accustomed all his life to dealing with problems of death and survival.

"We'll have to go carefully right from the start," he said heavily and unemotionally.

"Of course, sir."

"Each of these cans is a day's ration for one man. We'll have to halve that. Two meals a day—one can between four men at each meal."

"Yes, sir."

Blanke looked round again; his mind recovered another word from the glossary—those small barrels were called "breakers," but whatever their name, there were not too many of them.

"Of course, water's more important still," he said, in the same emotionless voice. "One pint a day—a quarter of a pint four times a day."

"Yes, sir. We'll start as we mean to go on," said the lieutenant helpfully.

That was indeed how they went on. By the second meal all novelty had worn off, and the healthy twenty-year-old appetites of the soldiers were insulted at the attempt to satisfy them with four sugar tablets and two malt tablets and one stick of chewing gum. A quarter of a pint of water went in two gulps, almost unnoticed. There were signs of that depression and reaction which the *Manual* warned against. The sun, which had so gratefully warmed them at dawn, turned into an enemy, fierce and unrelenting.

It was lucky for everyone in the boat that Blanke's orderly and active mind—the mind of a trained observer, seeking always a vent for its activity—was in charge. He noted at once that it would be impossible for the two Javanese to attend all the time to the tiller and the sails; moreover—grim thought—one of them might die. It was necessary to train replacements, so every half hour a fresh man came back to the tiller and studied how, under the grinning tuition of the Javanese (those Javanese stayed miraculously cheerful and were always ready with a polite grin as a substitute for words) to keep the boat steady on her course and to stand by what Blanke doubtfully called the "sheets"—he could not be quite sure of his memory regarding that word.

There was the horrible cramped discomfort of sitting up in the boat. Blanke realized that it was hardly necessary for the life jackets still to be worn. Removing them added considerably to the available room, and, as well, the life jackets could be used as a mattress in the one available space in the middle of the boat, whereon nine men at a time—nine out of fifty-four—could indulge themselves in the unspeakable luxury of stretching out straight and going to sleep.

Three hours of sleeping stretched out was very comforting and refreshing. Blanke chose that interval because then the cycle shifted through the day and gave everyone an equal chance of sleeping in the dark or in the daylight.

Naturally it was not very long before the survivors wanted to know how long the voyage would last, and Blanke, warned by his experience with the lieutenant, managed to decide upon an answer.

"Let's say a thousand miles," he said. "It may be more, but let's say that to start with."

At once everyone wanted to know at what speed they were traveling. No one could be sure, and even in the steady trade winds their speed was obviously variable. It took Blanke half a day to come up with the solution. Probably it was not an original reinvention of the old-fashioned ship's log; more likely some scrap of schoolboy reading had survived in Blanke's memory. At any rate, he took one of the long lines in the boat, knotted it at six-foot lengths (Sergeant Schwartz was just six-feet tall, he said), attached a couple of empty ration cans to the end and let it run out astern while timing it against the second hand of his watch.

So that was another item in the routine, one in which everyone was interested. Every half hour the log was cast, and the calculation made while everyone waited breathlessly. There were groans of despair when the speed was announced as being only 2.1 miles an hour; there was elation when it was 3.9—and another figure added to the column Blanke kept on the back of the deviation card, mounting up toward the arbitrary thousand that Blanke had selected, and only Blanke gave a thought to the fact that each result might easily be 50 per cent in error.

There were other breaks in the day. Early in the very first afternoon one of the Javanese rose hastily from where he was sitting, like a statue, in the middle of the boat, and called the attention of his colleague to something on the horizon. At the sight of what they saw, one of them came hastily back to the tiller while the other went to tend the sails. Blanke saw the squall approaching; he had seen similar ones from the deck of the *Wilhelmina* and had observed them with interest; but if it had not been for the Javanese, he would not have attached the importance to it demanded by an overcrowded small boat.

They dropped the big sail in the middle, which surely must be the mainsail, and they reduced the little triangular sail in front, leaving undisturbed the little rectangular sail on the mast in the stern. By that time, the squall was close upon them. When the boat rose on a wave, Blanke could see a gray line on the surface of the water, straight as if drawn with a ruler, advancing close upon them. Even before it reached them, preliminary gusts of wind roared at them, laying the boat over amid cries of alarm from the soldiers until the Javanese pulled the tiller over, turning the boat into the wind, and then she rode more steadily, while the wind howled about them, and the spray flew in sheets, and finally the rain came deluging down. The sail at the stern produced the weathercock effect that Blanke had already thought of. He ran through the glossary in his mind; what they had done was to "heave to"—an expression with an odd old-time flavor. Yet, with that wind howling and the sea screaming around them, to heave to meant to live; not to do so meant to die. He noted the rigidity with which he was sitting, the intensity with which he felt the greater gusts, his quickened heartbeat and the dryness of his mouth. This was fear again, intense physical fear.

There was a man over there—there was another—as frightened as he was, or even more. Fear could grip sturdy boys who had not completed high school just as much as it could Ph.D.'s. One of them was looking at him with staring eyes as if appealing to him, looking to him for safety or reassurance. Blanke made a huge effort. He told his muscles to relax, he forced his limbs into an easier attitude, he made himself turn toward the Javanese at the tiller with a nod and a smile which he hoped did not appear like the death's head grin he felt it to be. Then he glanced back at the scared soldier with every appearance of casual confidence he could manage. It seemed to help, even though at that moment the squall burst into its final paroxysm, changing direction several times, slightly but sufficiently to lay the boat over, horrifyingly, before she swung to it. Then a final roaring Niagara of rain, and the squall was over. On the far side of it the sun shone, and the sea was blue again, with the great rollers marching mechanically and predictably toward them.

"Say, cap'n," said a voice. "Cap'n."

Blanke realized with an effort that it was he who was being addressed by this title. "Yes?"

"That rain's salt. I've been trying to drink it."

Blanke tried to explain that with the spray flying, any rain would be tainted with sea water. He devoted thought to the question of devising a means to collect pure rain water during a squall, but in all that voyage he never succeeded. It never rained, as it happened, without wind and spray.

But the squall called more forcibly to his attention the problem of "leeway"—so he called it, self-consciously, to himself. The boat would move sideways to some extent with the wind over the side, and when they were hove to, she would drift considerably stern first before the wind. Allowance must be made for that. Blanke drew mental pictures of the triangle of forces at work on the boat, and arbitrarily selected ten degrees as a suitable correction. His announcement of the revised course was received without comment. The new course brought them closer to the wind, and that accentuated the odd aesthetic pleasure of thrashing along with the spray flying from the "weather bow." It was stimulating even to the most fainthearted and depressed of the passengers.

So depression and despair were combated during that voyage. There was the half-hourly relieving of the tiller and sheets, and the half-hourly heaving of the log, the three-hourly change-over on the life-jacket mattress and the occasional hasty heaving to when squalls approached. They had to heave to each evening as soon as it was too dark to have adequate warning of squalls. Sergeant Schwartz came up surprisingly with a remarkable plan during the dark evenings, for he started a spelling bee. Only a few men agreed to play, but the competition soon grew keen, and the onlookers were interested in spite of themselves. It was inevitable and highly significant that Blanke should be called upon as arbitrator over disputed points of spelling. There were language classes—in other words, attempts to teach English to the two Javanese, while the soldiers listened with amused interest to the polite efforts of the Javanese to explain to them the intricacies of their own language and of Dutch.

Any distraction was better than crouching idle in the boat, waiting for the moment when two sips of water per man was to be rationed out, waiting for four sugar tablets and two malted-milk tablets. Anything was better than to sit in black despair, in melancholy moodiness that might change at any moment into a flare-up of murderous rage. The pettiest, most trivial, most infantile distractions were of help.

Blanke came to learn quickly enough that the fifty young soldiers in the boat were fifty individuals, and not an undifferentiated mass of bristly faces. He came to know all of them, and in the long dark nights he came to know all the hoarse croaking voices, too, one distinct from another. Within a short time he knew the cheerful and the helpful, and the surly and the depressed.

Besides hunger and thirst, there was hideous physical discomfort, sitting eternally—with one blessed interval of stretching out on the mattress every eighteen hours—on unyielding seats. Damp salt on the skin and in the clothes as the spray dried made a man feel as if he would willingly tear off his skin. By the fourth day boils began to appear; nearly every man on board suffered from them. The sixth evening was marked by the presence of enough moon to make it possible to keep sail set for an hour and more after sunset and add a few more daily miles toward that absurd goal of a thousand miles which Blanke had set, and each successive night the period lengthened.

On the thirteenth day at noon they were still heading on their course. The sun was almost exactly overhead, blazing down upon them, the boat was maintaining its monotonous rise and fall, heel and pitch, with all the crowded heads and bodies swaying in unison as it did so. Then Private First Class Sanderson in the bow raised his head.

"Listen, you guys!"

They listened.

"What d'you think you can hear—harps?" croaked a voice.

"Listen!" repeated Sanderson.

Then another man heard it, and another.

"That's a plane!"

Everyone began to scramble to his feet, even the men on the mattress.

"Sit down! Sit down!" shrieked Blanke, his dry throat seeming to split with the effort.

It was one of the most dangerous moments of the voyage; it called for the united influence of the more levelheaded to restrain the excitement and to make the men sit down, fifty heads turning, fifty pairs of eyes searching the sky.

"There it is!"

The little speck was visible to them all.

"Maybe it's a Jap," said Marx the pessimist, but that suggestion could not prevail long with an antiaircraft unit trained in plane identification.

"It's a Kingfisher!"

"Is he going to see us?"

They watched with terrible intensity; some men were uttering prayers, and others blasphemy.

At 2000 feet the plane was heading a little away from them. Then the plane altered course.

"He's seen us!"

They tried to cheer; they started to stand up again.

"Sit down!" shrieked Blanke again—he had a memory of one piece of research wasted and ruined and necessitating restarting, all because of excited haste in the final technique. But if the boat overturned, there would be no restarting.

Straight for them came the plane. It dived and skimmed close about them, then wagged its wings and circled and made it obvious that they had been seen; it was also obvious that the plane would be unable to land on the rough water. Then it turned and headed back the way it had come; the prayers that followed it were prayers of thankfulness now, and the blasphemies were expressions of joy. Then every eye turned upon Blanke, the man who knew everything, to learn how soon they would be rescued.

"Not until tomorrow," said Blanke, doing hasty mental calculations based on the most fragile of data. "Not until tomorrow evening at the very earliest. But we can all have an extra ration of water this minute."

Seeing how utterly ignorant he was regarding the radius of action of a Kingfisher, and what shipping there might be at whatever base the plane had flown from, if it had flown from a land base, the guess was reasonably accurate—it was exactly twenty-four hours before the mine sweeper showed up on the horizon, and twenty-five hours before they were being helped up onto her deck, nearly twenty-six hours before Blanke was cautiously sipping at the cup of coffee which had haunted his unspoken thoughts for fourteen days.

"*Boon?*" said the mine sweeper's captain when Blanke gave the name of his ship in answer to the captain's question. "She's in at Tongatabu this minute—came in as escort to a torpedoed cruiser. You'll be able to join her at once."

Blanke was still too utterly weary to mention the fact that he had believed all this time that he was steering for Nouméa and had never heard of Tongatabu in his life until now. But he had sailed the lifeboat 400 miles straight toward Tongatabu all the same, 400 miles that made the difference between life and death.

So it was at Tongatabu that Blanke first set foot on the deck of a destroyer. It was there that he reported to the officer of the deck in the words he had rehearsed repeatedly after the mine sweeper's captain had taught them to him.

"Lieutenant Malcolm Blanke reporting aboard for duty, sir. I regret to report I have lost my orders while en route, sir."

The officer of the deck smiled politely and—to his credit—not the least broadly.

"We've been expecting you, doctor. But not in this condition. No baggage, I take it? Then I'll take you to the skipper right away."

The Kingfisher had spread the news of the sighted lifeboat the day before, and Commander Angell, captain of the *Boon*, did not need explanations of Blanke's presence. He made Blanke cordially welcome. Then he went on to say, "I'm certainly glad you've arrived, doctor. We've a plague of cockroaches on board, and I expect you to turn to right away to get rid of them."

The Cruise of the Breadwinner

H. E. BATES

As SHE WENT DOWN the estuary on the yellow tide between wintry stretches of salt-white marshland, The Breadwinner had the look of a discarded and battered toy. She was one of those small lug-sail fishing boats that in peacetime lie up the mud reaches of southern rivers, going out on one tide and back on the one after the next, indistinguishable from hundreds of her kind. Her once-blue deckhouse was now daubed with war gray, and her sail had been furled untidily to the mast like a copper umbrella. Aft she carried a Lewis gun that had never been fired in the twenty years between the wars, and that had now something of the appearance of a patent frying pan. She looked very old and very slow. Yet in ten minutes she had cleared the estuary and the long sandy point beyond and was well to seaward, heading due east up the Channel, rolling slightly and with invariable motion on the light westward crosswind of the early day.

Gregson stood at the wheel in the thirty-eight inches of space that separated it from the hatchway. He could just squeeze himself in. He had once been a man of six feet three, but now he had the slight downward curve of a man who is constantly about to stoop to pick something up, but sees only the eighteen-stone mass of his own flesh hiding whatever it was he was trying to find below. Sometimes when he held the wheel in one hand and turned his massive gray head first skyward, to look at the weather, and then downward, to bawl at the crew of two below, he was so enormous and he held the wheel so casually that it might have been a watch.

All day he bawled any amount of conversation into the hatch below. "Gittin' that tea ready, Snowy?"

"Yeh!" The boy's voice from below was drawled out and sometimes, when surprised, squeaky because it had not fully broken.

"Well then, git it ready!"

"Yeh!"

"Yeh what? What did I tell you?"

"I dunno."

"You dunno, eh? Well, I'll sure make you know! Ain't I allus told you call the skipper 'mister'?"

"Yeh."

"Yeh what?"

"Yeh, mister!"

"It don't matter now! Too late! Git that tea!"

If there was ever a smile on the face of Gregson as he yelled all this, the boy down below, warming the enamel teapot on the stove of a galley three feet by four, never saw it. It appeared to him always as if Gregson were a man of inexhaustible frenzy.

"How's that injun going, Jimmy?"

Gregson never succeeded in getting an answer to that question the first time. It was Jimmy's excuse that the noise of the eighteen-horse auxiliary drowned even what Gregson could say.

"Jimmy!"

"Hello."

Jimmy came and stood at the foot of the gangway, dark and pessimistic, looking up, mouth awry. He was a man given to violent depressions and upliftings of temper for no reason at all. "Hello?" he said again. The word had in it the slow challenge of a man full of all sorts of unknown and incalculable trouble. The voice was that of a man whose larger pleasure in life is the pleasure of grievance. It was inversely happy among the miseries of The Breadwinner. At home, Jimmy had a wife and three small children, and it was he who would fire the Lewis gun if ever it was fired.

"I said how's that injun?"

"I told you last time. And the time afore that."

"Don't tell me it ain't no good. I know different."

"It ain't so much it ain't no good. What I keep on tellin' yer is we oughta git two engines. Not one. We oughta git two fourteen-horse engines, instead of one eighteen-horse, so's we got a spare."

"And supposin' both go?"

"It ain't likely."

"No, it ain't likely. And it ain't likely I'll git the money either. Where's the money coming from?"

"Git the government to pay it! They got plenty. We're on government work, ain't we?"

Gregson did not care for the government. The government was some huge anonymous, thwarting, stingy, striking body empowered to frustrate the lives of ordinary men. Gregson felt for it a more positive enmity than he felt for any living person, enemy or friend. "Don't talk about no blithering government to me."

"Well, don't say I ain't told yer. One o' these fine days we'll get out there, forty miles from nowhere, and she'll go dead on you. And then what?"

"And then what?" Gregson roared. "What the bloomin' hell d'ye think wind and sail is for?"

Gregson stuck his belly harder than ever against the wheel, holding on with both hands, and was silent, looking at the day. The sun was rising dark red over the terraced and almost all empty white and crimson houses that lay under the line of hills on the English coast. It was from over these hills, becoming still farther eastward cliffs that came down to the sea like the carved edges of creamy glaciers, that Gregson saw the first patrol of the day.

"Snowy!"

"Yeh?"

"Planes!"

The boy Snowy came bouncing on deck like a blond and excited rabbit surprised out of a hole, carrying a teacup in one hand and blinking friendly blue eyes against the strong sea light. He looked about sixteen. His white-yellow hair was blown forward by the wind in one thick swath over his face as he turned to gaze at the land.

"Bunch o' Spits, ain't they, Snowy?" Gregson said.

"Hurricanes."

Gregson did not say anything. The boy knew everything that

flew, and a lot, Gregson thought, that had not yet begun to fly. He could name them at twenty thousand feet, and sometimes by mere sound, not seeing them at all. Without him, Gregson would have been utterly lost; The Breadwinner could never have done a single patrol.

"Looks like a nice day, anyway," Gregson said, as if that at least was something he could understand.

The boy stood watching the squadron of Hurricanes come over the cliffs, and then turn westward to follow the line of shore. The noise of engines was never loud enough to drown the noise of The Breadwinner's single auxiliary, but it was loud and beautiful enough to bring the engineer gunner on deck.

"Hurricanes," Gregson said, before the boy could open his mouth.

"Steady, steady. They might be Spits," Jimmy said.

"Ah, Spits your old woman," Gregson said. "Use your eyes."

"One missing," the boy said. "Man short."

"That they is, too," Gregson said. "I never twigged it. Snowy ain't half got a pair of eyes, ain't he?"

"Just as well," Jimmy said.

Gregson turned to look hard at the engineer, but Jimmy had even in that moment disappeared down the hatchway. On deck, the boy followed the course of the Hurricanes over against the thin line of shore with eyes that were lightly fixed in a dream. He was lost in the wonder of contemplation even when Gregson spoke again, "Tea ready yit?"

"Just made," the boy said.

"Ah, that's me old beauty. That's a boy. Bring us a cup up, Snowy. I got a throat like a starfish."

The boy was already going below.

"And you better stop on deck then and do your lookout. Looks like a flying day, don't it?"

The boy said yes, it was a flying day all right, and went down into the galley below and then came back, after a moment or two, with the tea. As Gregson drank, the boy went forward and stood in the bows, leaning forward and slightly over the boat's side, like a light figurehead. He went there every morning, irritated by the slightest recurrent grievance against Gregson.

Long ago, soon after the war had begun, when he had first

become boy on The Breadwinner, Gregson had promised him a pair of binoculars. Once a week, ever since, the boy had asked Gregson about the glasses. There was never any sign of them. It appeared to the boy as if Gregson forgot all about them not deliberately, but sometimes out of sheer ineptitude. And then sometimes it seemed as if he forgot them purely by reason of belonging to the larger, more preoccupied, more adult world. Then sometimes he found himself slightly afraid of Gregson, but it was a fear purely of size, of the enormity and noisiness of Gregson's flesh. It never matched the enormity of his disappointment at the constantly unfulfilled promise about the binoculars.

To have had the binoculars would have been the most exciting thing on earth—a greater thing than the sea rescue of a pilot, the wreck of a plane or even the firing of the Lewis gun. He had longed for all these things to happen on all the patrols of The Breadwinner, with a bright and narrow intensity that kept him awake at night and brought him down to the jetty in the mornings running and with bits of his breakfast still in his hands. But the realization of them would have been nothing beside the sight of Gregson coming down the street between the black fish warehouses carrying a brown leather case over his oilskins.

As he took up his place in the bows the air was so clear that he could begin to see the white relief of Northern France before the coast of England had begun to fade, with its dark bird patrol of Hurricanes, behind him.

He leaned on the bows and took in the whole of the smooth winter sea and sky for miles and miles about him and noted it, more or less unconsciously, as empty.

It was empty of sound too. For some time he had been practicing spotting by ear, so that now he could tell a Dornier, if ever one came, from a Heinkel, or a Spit from a Hurricane, even though he never saw them.

The Breadwinner had been cruising for a little more than an hour when he suddenly heard firing far across from the southwest.

"Machine-gunning!" Gregson yelled.

"Yeh! May be testing his guns!" the boy said.

"Too far out, ain't it?"

"Listen again!" the boy called.

They listened again, and then, as Jimmy came up the hatchway to listen, too, carrying his cup of tea in his hands, the burst came over the sea again.

"That ain't no gun testing," Gregson said. "Somebody's having a go."

The boy stood very intently, listening, his yellow head far forward.

"I can hear something out there!" the boy said.

"So can we. It ain't sea gulls either."

"I mean there's a plane out there. Two planes."

"Go on," Jimmy said. "Three planes."

"Ah, shut up," Gregson said. "You allus got your ears bunged up with injun oil."

"I tell y' it's gun testing," Jimmy said. "They were at it yesterday."

The boy had taken up an attitude of fierce excitement. He was balanced on the extreme forward edge of the bows, shading his face with his hands.

"There's only two planes," he said. "If Jimmy could shut the engine off, I could hear what they were!"

"Go on, Jim," Gregson said, "shut her off."

"Shut off? You want some trouble, don't you?"

"All right, all right, put her in neutral and keep her running."

In the half silence that came a minute later, the boy yelled frantically that he heard a Messerschmitt.

"Yeh! But can you see it?" Gregson said.

"No, but I can hear it! I can hear it!"

"What was the other?"

"I dunno. They both gone now. I can't see." It occurred to him suddenly that this was the moment in which he could throw at Gregson the subject of the binoculars, but his excitement soared up inside him in a flame that burnt out and obliterated in a moment all other thought. "We ought to have a look-see!" he shouted.

Gregson became excited too. "All right, why don't we?" The rolls of flesh on his throat were suddenly tautened in an amazing way as he lifted his head and strained to look westward.

"There's more firing!" the boy shouted.

"I'm turning her round, Jimmy," Gregson said, "as soon as you can git her away."

"Waste o' time. I tell y' it's practice firing," Jimmy said, and went below.

The boy felt in that moment the beginnings of a new emotion about Gregson. He felt that he loved him. And he felt also that he came very near despising the engineer.

Gregson cruised The Breadwinner at three-quarter speed for about half an hour. It was Gregson's impression, as they went farther west, that a haze was gathering low down against the horizon, but far beyond the possible limit of patrol. It was nowhere thick enough to have any color or any effect on the light of the sea.

Jimmy had come on deck. "I don't see much," he said. "I don't hear much either."

They were far enough westward now to be out of sight of land.

"You want so much for your money," Gregson said. "What's ahead, Snowy boy?"

"Keep quiet! Keep quiet!" the boy said.

"What is it?" Gregson roared.

"Can Jimmy shut off?" the boy said.

"What d'yer want shut off for?" Gregson yelled.

"I can hear something—a whistle or something—something like a whistle."

"A whistle!" Gregson said. "Shut her off, Jimmy! A whistle!"

In the interval of Jimmy going below and the engine being shut off in a series of choked bursts of the exhaust, The Breadwinner traveled about a quarter of a mile. It was far enough to bring within the boy's hearing the faint but madly repeated note of the whistle. He stood waving his arms as Gregson came blundering forward.

"Hey, what is it, Snowy? What is it? What yer twigged, Snowy, boy?"

"Can you hear it?" the boy said. "Can you hear it? The whistle?"

They listened together, Gregson leaning forward across the

bows of the boat, his face almost instantly lit up. "Snowy, that ain't fur off!" he said.

By now, the boy was not listening. He was mutely arrested by the conviction that far across the westward he could see something that might have been a floating cockle shell. He held his silence a little longer before he was quite sure.

Then he began shouting. "It's a dinghy!" he shouted. "It's a dinghy! I can see it! I can see it! A dinghy!"

"Where?" Gregson said. "Where, Snowy, boy?"

"Full ahead!" the boy said. "Full ahead!"

He heard his words go aft like a bellowed echo, so loud that in about twenty seconds an answer came in the noise of the engine.

Gregson marveled acidly, "We got going just bang! Don't say nothing, Snowy! Don't breathe, boy! We got going just bang!"

Two minutes later, the boy was shouting, "Now you can see it! Now Mr. Gregson, if you can't see it now, you're as—— Oh! If we had the binoculars, we would have seen it sooner!"

Gregson, seeing the yellow rubber dinghy at that moment, made no comment on the binoculars, and the subject, even for the boy, was instantly blown away by gusts of fresh excitement. He could see the man in the dinghy quite clearly now, and from that moment onward began to see him more and more sharply defined in the sunlight, until even Gregson, straining forward over the bows, could see him too.

The sight broke on Gregson with the effect of sublime discovery. "I see the bloke!" he roared. "I see the bloke, Snowy! I can see his head plain!"

"He's wearing his flying jacket," the boy said, "and a red muffler with white spots."

To that, Gregson had nothing to say, and three or four minutes later they came up with the dinghy and the figure which for the boy had long been so clearly defined. The young man in the dinghy had never stopped blowing his whistle. He was blowing it now, only taking it from his mouth at last to wave it at Gregson and the boy with a sort of mocking salutation.

"Mighty good whistle!"

"All right?" Gregson yelled over the side. "Ain't hurt or nothing?"

"Right as a pip. Wizard."

"Glad we seed you," Gregson said. "A coupla feet closer and we'll git y' in."

"Good show," the young man said.

As the dinghy came nearer, finally bumping softly against the boat side, the boy remained motionless, held in speechless fascination by the figure in the flying jacket. It grinned up at him with a sublime youthfulness that to the boy seemed heroically mature. The young man had a mass of thick light brown hair that curled in heavy waves and a light, almost corn-brown mustache that gave to his entire appearance and to whatever he did and said an air of light fancy. It proclaimed him as serious about nothing; not even about wars or dinghies or the menace of the sea; least of all, about himself.

Gregson and the boy helped him on deck. The boy, looking down, brought to the large muffling flying boots a little more of the wonder he had brought to the face.

"Sure you're all right? Cold?" Gregson said. "Cuppa tea?"

"Thanks," the youth said. "I'm fine."

Jimmy came up from below and walked forward, so that suddenly the small narrow deck of The Breadwinner seemed to become vastly overcrowded.

"Sort o' thing you don't wanna do too often," Gregson said, "ain't it?"

"Third time," the young man said. "Getting used to it now."

"Spit pilot?"

"Typhoon," the pilot said.

"There y'are, Snowy. Typhoons. . . . What was you gittin' up to?" he said to the young man. "Summat go wrong?"

"One of those low-level sods," the young man said. "Chased him all across the Marshes at nought feet. Gave him two squirts, and then he started playing tricks. Glycol and muck pouring out everywhere. Never had a clue and yet kept on, right down on the deck, bouncing up and down, foxing like hell. He must have known he'd had it." The young man paused to look round at the sea. "He was a brave sod. The bravest sod I ever saw."

"Don't you believe it," Gregson said. "Coming in and machine-gunning kids at low level. That ain't brave."

"This was brave," the young man said.

He spoke with the tempered air of the man who has seen the battle, his words transcending for the first time the comedy of the mustache. He carried suddenly an air of cautious, defined authority, using words that there was no contesting.

Gregson, pondering incredulously on this remark about the bravery of enemies, said, "What happened to you then, after that?"

"Pranged," the pilot said. "Couldn't pull out. Hit it with a bang."

"And what happened to him?"

"That's what I want to find out," the young man said.

"You better have a cuppa tea," Gregson said. "Never mind about jerry. If he's in the sea, we'll find him plenty soon enough. He'll wash up."

"I'd like to see what he's like," the boy said. "God, he was brave."

"You think you hit him?"

"I know I hit him."

"Then that's good enough, ain't it?" Gregson looked around, heaving his belly, with an air of heavy finality. . . . "Snowy, git us all another cuppa tea!"

The boy turned and went instantly down the hatchway. He lumbered about as if he were Gregson, partly stupefied with excitement, partly trying to listen through the cabin roof to whatever might be going on above.

He was astonished, coming up into the sunlight with the three cups of tea skillfully hooked by their handles into the crook of his first fingers, that even in those few moments a change had taken place. He came up in time to hear Jimmy saying, "I never knowed it was part of the game to go cruisin' round picking jerries up."

"I don't know that he's there to pick up," the pilot said. "He's probably dead. All I'm saying is he was brave."

"That suits me," Gregson said. "If he's dead, he's dead. If he ain't, he ain't. Have it which way you like, it's all I care."

The boy came with the tea and stood silent, fascinated, while each of the three men took a cup from him. He watched the young pilot, holding his tea in both hands, the fur collar of his flying jacket turned up so that the scarlet muffler on his neck was concealed, look away southward over the sea. It was very like a picture of a pilot he had once cut out of a Sunday paper. To see it in reality at last held him motionlessly bound in a new dream.

"How far do you cruise out?" the young man said.

Gregson had a superstitious horror of cruising down Channel to the west. Fifty years of consistent routine had taken him eastward, fishing in unadventurous waters somewhere between South Foreland and Ostend. He did not like the west for any reason he could name; he did not, for that matter, like the south either. There lurked within him somewhere the cumbrous superstition born of habit, never defined enough to be given a name.

"Well, we're out now about as far as we reckon to go. Don't you wanna git back?"

The pilot, not answering, seemed to measure the caution of Gregson as he gazed across the water. And it occurred suddenly to the boy, watching his face, that he knew perfectly that there were no limits to which Gregson, in human need, would not go. But eastward or westward it was the same as far as enemy pilots were concerned.

And then suddenly the boy remembered something. He spoke to the pilot for the first time. "How far out did you fire?" he said.

"Smack over a Martello tower," the pilot said, "on the shore."

"Then it wasn't you firing," the boy said. "What we heard was right out to sea."

"So it were," Gregson said. "So it were."

"You mean there was someone else having a go?" the pilot said.

"Sounded like gun testing," Jimmy said.

"Don't take no notice of him," Gregson said. "Was they any more of your blokes out?"

"A whole flight was up."

"There y'are then!" Gregson said. "What are we fooling here for? . . . Warm her up, Jimmy. Let's git on!"

As The Breadwinner swung round, turning a point or two southeastward, sharp into the sun, the boy went forward into the bows and discovered, a second or two later, that the pilot was there beside him, still warming his fingers on the teacup and sometimes reflectively drinking from it, balancing the two wings of the ridiculous corn-ginger mustache on its edges. It did not occur to the boy that he did not look like a fighting man; it occurred to him instead that he might be a man with binoculars.

"If we had a pair o' glasses, we might pick things up easier," he said.

"Never carry any," the pilot said.

If there was any disappointment in the boy's face, it was lost in the ardent gleam of steady and serious wonder which he now brought to bear on the sea. Gradually the sunlight everywhere was losing its lemon pallor, but it was still low enough to lay across the water the long leaf-broken path of difficult and dazzling light. The boy shaded his eyes against it with both hands. He desired to do something remotely professional; something to impress the man of battles standing beside him. He longed dramatically to spot something in the sea. They stood there together for about five minutes, not speaking, but both watching with hands framing their faces against the dazzle of sea light.

Suddenly far behind them Gregson called the boy, "I'm gittin' peckish, Snowy boy. Ain't peeled them taters yit, ayah?"

"No, mister," the boy said.

"Well, you better git in and peel 'em then. Peel a double dose. Pilots eat same as we do."

The boy said, looking up at the pilot, "I gotta git below now. I'll take your cup down, if you've finished."

Sometimes, as the boy sat peeling potatoes at the cabin table, he could hear the voice of Gregson from up above, always huge and violent, never articulate except for strong half words that the noise of the engine did not drown. He was driven, by the maddening isolation of this, to go and stand at the foot of the hatchway, and, one by one, peel the potatoes there. He stood there looking up into the shaft of sea light peeling his fifteenth potato when Jimmy came sliding down the hatch without any warning except a violent and wordless sort of bellow. The boy watched him disappear into the tiny and confined engine cradle that was not big enough to be called a room, and then bawled after him, "What's up, Jimmy? What's up now?"

"Somebody in the sea!" Jimmy said.

The boy went up the hatchway with a half-peeled potato still in his hands. The engine died behind him as he went, and Jimmy followed him a moment later.

On deck, Gregson and the pilot were up in the bows. Gregson was lumbering about in a state of heavy excitement. The pilot was taking off his white under sweater, and then began to take off his boots. He seemed to hesitate about his thick gray under socks and then decided to take them off too.

"Is he still coming in?" he said to Gregson; and Gregson, leaning heavily over the side, bawled, "He's floatin' on his back! He's a jerry all right, too!"

"Yes, he's a jerry all right," the pilot said, and stood ready, side by side with Gregson and the boy, watching, about sixty feet away, the floating and feebly propelling body of a man awkwardly moving across the face of the sea.

"Want a line?" Gregson said.

"Want a line?" the young man said. "I could swim to France."

He went over the side a moment later in a smooth and careless dive. He reached the other man, now moving with spidery feebleness parallel to the boat, in about twenty seconds, and rolled over beside him, coming up a moment later underneath and slightly to one side. The blue sleeve of his arm came up across the yellow, inflated, German life jacket, and then sleeve and jacket and the yellowish heads of both men began to move toward the boat.

The boy stood fascinated by the side of Gregson. The blob of yellow and blue coming in toward the boat sometimes receded and was lost for a second or two, like an illusion. When it reappeared, it seemed gigantic. The boy could then see clearly the water-flattened mustache of the pilot every time the head was thrown back, and he could see the upper half of the body of the rescued man. It seemed quite lifeless. But suddenly, as it came nearer, the boy could see, lying across the chest of it, a leather strap. It was attached to a leather case that appeared every second or so from below the sea and then was lost again. The boy, in a moment of painful and speechless joy, knew what it was.

At that same moment, Gregson, excited too, flattened him against the boat side, so that he could not move. And Gregson in that moment became aware of him again.

"What the pipe, Snowy! Git out on it!" Gregson bawled. "Git down and git some tea! They'll want it! Go on! Git crackin'! Git that tea!"

The boy put fresh tea into the teapot with his hands and then poured water on it and found two extra cups in the locker by the stove. He was filled with violent energy. His head rocked with the astonishing possibilities of the leather case slung across the body of the German. He had to be part of the world of men. Nothing like this had ever happened before; no pilot, no rescue, no jerry, no binoculars. He heard Gregson shouting again—this time much louder—something about a gun. The boy, standing with head upraised, listening, was swept by a torrent of new possibilities. Back in the pub at home, there were boys with the luck of the gods. They owned sections of air cannon guns, belts of unfired cartridges. He suddenly saw before him the wonder of incredible chances. He did not know what happened to the guns and binoculars of dead pilots or even captured pilots, but now, at last, he was going to know.

He poured tea into the two cups and was in the act of stirring sugar into them when he heard, from overhead, two new sounds. Somebody was running across the deck, and from a southeasterly direction, faint, but to him clear enough, came the sound of a plane.

He did not connect these sounds. He had momentarily lost interest in the sound of aircraft. Something much more exciting was happening on deck. Gregson was shouting again, and again there was the sound of feet running across the deck. They were so heavy that he thought perhaps they were Gregson's feet. But it was all very confused and exciting, and he had no time to disentangle the sound of voices from the sound of feet and the rising sound of the now not so distant plane. Nor did it matter very much. He had in that moment a fine and rapid impression that war was wonderful.

He picked up a cup of tea in each hand. He turned to walk out of the galley when he was arrested suddenly by the near violence of the plane. It was coming toward The Breadwinner very fast and very low. The roar of it obliterated the last of the voices on deck and turned the sound of feet into an echo. He ran out of the galley with the tea in his hands, and had reached the bottom step of the gangway when he heard the strangest sound of all. It was the sound of the Lewis gun being fired.

It fired for perhaps half a second, and then stopped. He did not know how he knew the difference between this sound and the sound of cannon firing directly afterward and for about two seconds from overhead, but he sprawled down the steps on his face. The hot tea poured down his arms, up the sleeve of his jacket and down his chest, but it did not seem hot and there was no pain. He did not look upward, but he felt the square of light at the head of the gangway darkened out for the space of a second as the plane went overhead. He was sure for one moment that the plane would hit the deck, but the moment passed, and then the plane itself passed, and there was no more firing, either from the deck or overhead. And at last, when the plane had gone, there was no more sound.

He waited for what seemed a long time before crawling up the gangway. He pulled himself up by his hands because his legs did not seem part of him. The small auxiliary of The Breadwinner had stopped now and it was dead silent everywhere.

The boy brought to the scene on deck a kind of ghastly unbelief. For a moment or two, he could not stand up. He lay with his head resting on the top step of the gangway, and became for some seconds quite sightless, as if he had stared at the sun. Shadowy and crimson lumps of something floated in front of him like bits of colored cloud, and then solidified, gradually, into a single object across the deck. It was some time before the boy brought himself to understand that this bundle had once been Jimmy.

He got up at last and walked away, forward, up the deck. All the forward part of the boat was hidden from him by the deckhouse. He suddenly felt alone on the ship. He felt the air very cold on his face and colder still on his chest and arms, where the tea had spilled, and then still colder on his eyes, shocked stiff by what he had seen of the engineer. This coldness became suddenly the frantic substance of a new terror. It was as if he had something alive and deadly in his hands and wanted to drop it.

He began to run. He ran like a blind man, away from something, careless completely of what lay before him. As he ran past the deckhouse, he began jabbering incoherent and violent words that were partly his fear and partly something to do with the need for telling someone of his fantastic discoveries. He had seen the dead.

He ran, in reality, about two yards beyond the deckhouse. The fear that had driven him forward from behind seemed to have got round in front of him, and now slapped him in the face. It stopped him dead. And as he stopped, the coherence of his speech came back with perfect shrillness. He was shouting, "Jimmy! Jimmy! Jimmy! Jimmy!" in a cry that was somewhere between anguish and a refusal to believe.

When this was over, he looked down on the deck. It seemed very overcrowded with the figures that lay there. They were the figures of the young pilot and the German, who lay side by side, together, and then of Gregson, who was lying half across them. There was something quiet and merciful in the tangle of limbs, and, though there was no blood, he was convinced of their being very dead.

Out of all this there emerged, suddenly, something very wonderful. He saw the enormous body of Gregson, on its hands and knees, heaving itself slowly upward, and then he realized several things. He realized that he was fantastically fond of the living Gregson, and he realized, too, that he must have run up from the galley and across the deck, in the silence after the shots were fired, in the space of a second or two. He caught for the first time the sound of the plane, quite loud still, receding across the sea.

"Mr. Gregson! Mr. Gregson! Captain, captain! Skipper!" he said.

"Snowy," Gregson said. He swung himself slowly round in the attitude of an elephant kneeling, and looked up at the boy blinking. "Rum'un," he said. "Where was you?"

The boy found that he could not speak. He wanted to tell of Jimmy. He made small, frantic and almost idiotic gestures with his mouth and hands.

Gregson, still on his hands and knees, groped forward like a man blinded by daylight. "You all right, kid?" he said. "All right y'self, eh?"

"Jimmy," the boy said. "Jimmy!"

"I heard him firing that thing. Wonder as it fired, first time. Like the bloomin' injun."

On the deck, the young pilot began suddenly to mutter repeated groans of agony, trying to turn himself over.

The sound and the movement woke Gregson out of himself. He crawled between the two pilots and leaned over the English one.

"All right," he said. "All right. Where'd it git y'?"

The young man was trying to push his heels through the deck, lifting his body with recurrent convulsions of pain.

Gregson turned and spoke to the German pilot, lying half on his side with his knees against his chest. "Mighty low flying. Is that the sort a bloomin' orders you git?"

There was no reply except a violent convulsive jerk that threw the German down on his face.

The English boy turned and looked up at the sky, rolling his head quietly from side to side. His body was still soaked from swimming, so that the clothes were shriveled on it.

"I'll git you down below," Gregson said.

"Don't move me," the pilot said. "Don't move me."

"Better down below. Git you warm. Git y' in a bunk. I can carry you."

"No," the pilot said. "Don't move me. It's wrong. Cover me over. Cover me over, that's all."

"Git them blankets, Snowy," Gregson said. "All of 'em. And the first-aid box. And tell Jimmy to come for'ard. Soon's he can."

The boy went down to the cabin in a cold daze of fright made worse by a determination not to look at Jimmy. He was hypnotized by the bloody tangle of flesh that lay on the deck; he could not pass it without looking that way. The sight of it drove him below with wild energy. He came up again, carrying the gray bundle of blankets, in a trembling terror of fresh sickness, determined this time not to look. But now, as he passed, he saw that Jimmy held something in his hands. It was the handle of the Lewis gun, severed from the rest of the frying-pan apparatus by the same curious miracle that had kept it in Jimmy's hands. It was painted harshly with coagulations of new blood.

It was the thought of Jimmy that kept him standing for some

seconds by the side of Gregson, holding the blankets and not speaking. Gregson was kneeling between the two pilots. The German was now turned over on his back. He was perhaps nineteen; he looked to the boy to be like the Englishman, wonderfully and terribly worn by the experience of battles. Pain had beaten deep hollows in his cheeks, so that the facial bones everywhere stood out.

But it was not this that fascinated the boy. He now found himself staring at the binoculars Gregson had unlooped and laid on the deck. It was clear now that they were binoculars; he had never seen anything that seemed so magnificent. They lay on the deck just above the German's head, the light brown leather dark and salty with sea water, the initials K.M. in black on the side. Gazing at them, the boy forgot the figure of the engineer in the stern.

Gregson took the blankets out of his arms as he stood there staring down at the leather case. He said something about "Ah, thassa boy, Snowy," but the boy did not really hear. He stood watching Gregson cover over first the English pilot and then the German, giving them three blankets each. A little wind had sprung up from the southwest and caught one of the blankets and blew it away from the German's feet. The boy bent down and pushed the feet back under the blanket, and the German screamed with pain.

It astonished both Gregson and the boy to hear the German break the silence after the scream and say, in English, quite quietly, "I think it is my leg. I think it is both my legs perhaps."

"I ain't much at first aid," Gregson said. "But we'll keep you warm. Git you back ashore quick. See? Hospital. See?"

"I didn't bring the first-aid box up," Snowy said. "I forgot."

No one seemed to notice this remark, and the English boy said, "How long before we can get in?"

"Depends," Gregson said. "Hour or more. Depends if the engineer can hot it up."

The boy stood rigid. It was his duty to tell Gregson that Jimmy would never hot it up again.

"Git some tea, Snowy," Gregson said. "Some brandy, ain't they, too? Put some o' that in. Four mugs. You have some brandy too. No, five. You'll want one for Jimmy too."

"Jimmy——"

"Go on, bring it up smart. Five mugs, Snowy, boy." He looked with powerful expansiveness and anger at the sky. "I wonder where that sod went? I thought Jimmy'd got him."

"He certainly made mincemeat of us," the English boy said.

"I'd mincemeat him!" Gregson said. "Next time I'll have that gun. . . . Jimmy!"

The violence of this shout drove the boy in fear from the deck and haunted him with constant terror as he made tea in the galley below. This time he put the mugs of tea on an iron tray, so that he could carry them in a single journey. He had filled them up with brandy. And for some reason he could not bear to go with four mugs only, and not five, and so there were five, as if perhaps the presence of the fifth would have some effect on the fact of death.

He carried the tray on deck and became aware, for the first time since the shooting, what change had come over the day. Low clouds had begun to come up from the west, in misty waves that had already in them a light spray of gray rain, and there was no light, except far eastward, in the face of the sea.

The position of Gregson on the deck had something at once awful and inevitable about it. It did not surprise the boy. It appeared fantastically exact. He stood a yard or two from where the gun had once been, legs apart, arms stiff and outwardly stretched down. It was only the color of these arms that shocked the boy; they were bright with blood. But where the body of Jimmy had been lying there was now only a brown tarpaulin.

Gregson looked at the boy as he came up with the tea. He was wiping the blood from his hands with a piece of engine rag. It seemed to the boy that his enormity had about it a shocked kindliness.

"Won't want five cups, Snowy," he said.

"I know," the boy said. He wanted to cry. "I saw it." He spoke of the engineer impersonally, in fear and respect.

"Got three kids," Gregson said. He stood with his vast body broken and deflated by thoughts of Jimmy. "Nice job. Nice thing." He wiped his hands with the oily rag until the fingers were a dull brown from the mixing of blood and oil. "He allus wanted to fire that gun. Allus wanted to fire it. Well, he fired it," he said, as if, perhaps, this thought would atone for all that was done. "Better take the tea along," he said, "while it's hot. Looks like rain."

The boy went forward with the tea, past the deckhouse. The two pilots were talking to each other, and the binoculars lay on the deck.

"That's a funny thing," the English boy was saying. "All the time I had an idea it was you."

"I don't think it was so funny."

"Teach you not to come fooling over on these low-level jobs anyway," the Englishman said. "There's no future in that."

They were both smiling.

"I got some tea," Snowy said.

"Good show." The English boy tried to lift his head, and relapsed in a paroxysm of pain that seemed to twist his entire spine. "God!" he said. "God!" He lay breathing deeply, his lips trembling. "God; oh, God."

Gregson came up and leaned over him. To the boy, his hands were white as paper. He had never seen them so clean. Gregson laid them quietly on the English boy's shoulders.

"You take it easy. I may have to get you below, after all. Looks like rain. Smoke?"

"I don't," the boy said. "Perhaps jerry does. His name's Karl Messner. Flies Messerschmitts. Should say flew Messerschmitts."

"I don't care if he flew archangels," Gregson said. "He's gittin' no fags o' mine."

"Ah, go on. He's the sod I shot down. The one I told you about."

"Is he? Pity his guts wasn't shot out. Like Jimmy's. The engineer. You saw him. Him with the gun."

Gregson looked from one of the pilots to the other, and then to the boy, in a single fierce glance of challenge to all of them. They did not speak. The German lay with eyes fixed upward, as if he were trying not to hear it all.

"Yeh, Jimmy's dead," Gregson said. "They bust him up all right."

The English pilot looked as if he were going to shake his head, and then, remembering the earlier pain, thought better of it, simply opening his eyes and shutting them again.

"I'm sorry," he said. "But he didn't do it. He's not the type. You give him tea anyway. What's the odds?"

"Ah, all right," Gregson said. "Go on. What's the odds? That's right. What's it matter? What's it matter now?" He furiously threw his cigarette packet and matches across to the German. They lay on the German's chest. He did not pick them up.

Gregson seized bitterly on this significant fact, making much of it. "Too proud to take 'em anyway. Lower yourself to give 'em all you got, and then they insult you. Makes me sick." He threw about him fresh challenges, now doubly embittered.

"Pull your fingers out, jerry," the English boy said. "No sulking. Take the captain's cigarettes when he offers them."

The German did not move.

"The captain wants to throw you overboard. He hates Germans. There's nobody to stop him, either, if he wants to."

The English boy was having fun; his face had a sad sideways grin on it as he spoke. But the German did not move.

"Throw him overboard, captain," the English boy said. "I shan't tell."

"All right," the German said. He moved his hands to the cigarettes. "Thank you very much. Very kind of you. Thank you very much."

"All that fuss for nothing," Gregson said.

"Behave yourself, Messner, old boy," the Englishman said. "You're just a POW now."

The boy, listening to these exchanges, felt the tremendous impact of the more serious, more curious, more important world of men. He set cups of tea down on the deck, one each by the pilots and one for Gregson. He took one for himself and left the odd one on the tray. This odd cup did not now impress him by its forlorn significance, nor any longer as being part of the dead engineer. He saw that there were attitudes in which it was possible to make light of pain, to be jocular about the impact of death. And part of the terror about Jimmy now receded in his mind.

"I don't think I can sit up," the English boy said. "Bad show."

"I'll hold you," Gregson said.

"No," the boy said. "Better give it to me in the spoon."

While Gregson cautiously lifted the English boy's head and held it slightly upward with one hand and then spoon-fed tea to him with the other, the German raised himself on one elbow. He held cigarette and teacup in the same hand, turning his face away and looking westward over the sea. He appeared to the boy as a person of sinister and defiant quality. The boy read into his silence, his gaze over the sea and the way he let his cigarette burn away without smoking it, a meditation on escape. He hoped that he would escape. If he escaped, Gregson would kill him. That would be a wonderful thing. If he was killed, the boy would take the binoculars. And when at last he reached home he would wear them slung on his shoulder, taking with him some of that same defiant quality of the man who returns with the trophies of war.

It began to rain as he stood there watching the German.

Gregson lifted his face to the sky. "All appearance on it," he said. "Better git you below."

"Get Messner down," the English boy said, grinning. "Guests first."

"You're a caution, you are," Gregson said.

Very gently he let the English boy's head lie back on the deck. "Snowy'll stay with you," he said. "I'll get the stretcher." Grinning, he seemed suddenly moved, for some reason, to extravagant praises of the boy. "Masterpiece of a kid for aircraft. Knows 'em all."

"Good show," the pilot said. "Good old Snowy." He smiled at the boy.

It was raining quite fast now, but the German, lying rigidly back, staring upward and swallowing his breath in rain and heavy gasps of pain, seemed glad to receive it on his face. He opened his lips, and as the drops fell into his mouth he licked them in relief with his tongue.

The stretcher was kept lashed to one side of the narrow skylight lying aft of the hatchway. Gregson unfastened it and carried it along the deck under one arm. "Job for you, Snowy," he said; "mind your backside." Gregson laid the stretcher on deck, parallel with the German, and in a moment the boy was on his knees, undoing the straps.

The German crushed his hands down on his face while Gregson and the boy carried him below on the stretcher. They laid him on the cabin floor below the bunks. The boy set down his end of the stretcher with a certain air of expansive and careless pride; it was the first time he had taken part in such things. He was no longer aware of the shock of seeing blood for the second time. He was elevated into a world of catastrophe and pain, bringing to it a taut and suppressed excitement.

Back on deck, it was raining fast. As Gregson and the boy arrived with the stretcher, the English boy grinned stiffly up at them.

"Collect up my things," he said to the boy. "The things I took off. Before they get soaked." And the boy went forward to where the pilot had kicked off his boots and socks on the deck.

When he had gone, Gregson leaned over the pilot. "Can you move?" he said. "A little bit. Just slide over while I take the weight?"

"How's old Messner?" the boy said. "Did you drop him?"

"Now," Gregson said. "Just gently. While I hold you."

"God!" the boy said. "God." He cried gently through his lips while he held them clenched with his teeth. Suddenly Gregson threw the blanket over his face, and then, just as the boy came back with the flying boots and socks, lifted him bodily, in a single smooth but desperate movement onto the stretcher. In that attitude, covered over and silent and never moving, the pilot lay on the stretcher while Gregson and the boy carried him below.

It was about five minutes before the boy reappeared on deck, coming to collect the tray and the five cups still half filled with tea. This time he did not look at the covered heap that had once been the engineer, and the blood where the two pilots had lain did not have on him any more effect than the blood he often saw on the floor of the fish market.

He was thinking only of the binoculars. The case was very wet from sea water, and he had some difficulty in getting them out. He pulled at them until the suction of water in the case was released, and then, when he had them out, he stood up on deck and looked through them, across the sea and through the gray and driving mass of rain. For some reason or other, either because the sea water had reached the lenses or because the lenses themselves were not adjusted for his sight, what he saw through the glasses was only a gray and misty mass of unproportioned light. It had no relation to what he had expected to see.

Trembling, he hastily put the glasses back into the case and gathered up the cups and hurried below.

Down below a new problem had arisen. He was startled by Gregson's voice muttering crustily from the box where Jimmy had so often been lost among the miseries of the auxiliary, "Know anything about injuns, Snowy?"

The boy put the tea tray and the binoculars on the cabin table, and went back to Gregson. Gregson, unable to squeeze himself into the hole containing the engine, was squatting half in and half out of it, regarding the engine with melancholy helplessness.

"Ought to be simple," the boy said, "if I can get it set."

"Wouldn't let nobody look at it," Gregson said. His grievances against Jimmy were not yet quite extinguished. "Wouldn't let nobody touch it. Kept it to 'isself. Wust on it. Allus knew best. You couldn't talk to him!"

The boy became aware of carrying a sense of responsibility arising from a succession of terrific events: the presence and sight of death, the fact of the binoculars, the business of carrying the wounded pilots below, and now the engine. He had come to think of the engine as sacred. It was not to be touched; it belonged to Jimmy; its faults and secrets were part of the man.

He squeezed himself in alongside the cradle and pressed the needle of the carburetor up and down, flooding it. He had watched Jimmy do these things. The engine was a mass of odd lengths of wire, strange extra gadgets devised by Jimmy, so that it had the look of an unfinished invention. One of these wires held the choke. It was necessary to pull it out, hook it back into fixed position by means of a piece of cord that slipped over a nail in the cradle, and release it only when the engine was running too fast. You turned her over twice before switching on.

Gregson, watching the boy do these things, said in a curious whisper, "We gotta git back fast. You know that, don't you?"

The boy nodded and said he thought he could get her started now. Gregson stood back a little, and the boy, with a sort of careless strength, pressed his weight down on the starting handle with his right hand.

"Think you can match it?" Gregson said.

The boy answered with something that was very near to tired contempt, "Can't start first time. You gotta get her swung over."

"Oh! That's it, is it?" Gregson said.

By the time the boy had swung the engine the fourth time, Gregson was sour with the conviction that it was never going to fire. The boy leaned his weight on the cylinder head, panting. "No spark in her," he said. He desired passionately to make the engine go, feeling that in doing so he would become in Gregson's eyes a sort of adult hero. But there was something queer about the engine. "No compression there," he said.

"Compression, compression!" Gregson said. "Let me have a go." He had not the faintest idea what compression was. He seized the engine handle rather as if it had been the key of a clock. When he swung it finally, it swirled round, under his immense strength, two or three complete revolutions, swinging him off his balance against the bulkhead.

"Thing never was no good!" he said. "Allus said so. Told him. Miracle it ever went." He leaned against the bulkhead in savage and heavy despair.

The boy did not answer. He was crawling back into the dark recesses behind the engine cradle, where there was just room enough for him to kneel. He did not know quite what he was looking for. Underneath the engine block lay pools of spent oil in which he knelt as he crawled. It suddenly occurred to him that these pools were too large. He put down his right hand and knew that they were pools of oil and water. Then he stopped crawling and began to run his hands over the engine block until he found the place where cannon shell had ripped it open in a single jagged hole. A little oil still clogged it there. The force of the shell had lifted up the head, warping it as it blew.

"We've had it," the boy called back to Gregson.

"Had what?" Gregson said. "Whadya mean? What's up?"

"We've had the engine," the boy said. "That's what. Cannon shell."

"Why'n't they bloomin' well sink us? Why'n't they sink us and have done?"

The boy, hearing the wind rising now with the sound of rain on deck, was sharply aware of a new crisis.

"What do we do now?" he said. He was aware that things

might, without the engine, be very tough, very desperate. He licked his lips and tasted the sickliness of oil on them. "What do we do now?"

"Git us a cuppa tea!" Gregson roared. "Git us a cuppa tea!" He bawled and raged up the companionway into the beating rain.

The English pilot opened his eyes with a sharp blink, as if he had been lost in a dream and the boy had startled him out of it into the cramped and gloomy world of the little cabin. Messner still lay with eyes closed, his face turned away. The only light in the cabin was from a single skylight, about a yard square, of opaque glass, over which rain had already thrown a deeper film. In this iron-gray light it was some time before the pilot could see clearly enough through the stupor of weakness to grasp that the boy was busy with an object that looked like a torch. This torch, though the boy held it upward, toward the skylight, and downward and sideways, toward himself and Messner, never seemed to light. He expected it to flash into his face, but after the boy had swiveled it around two or three times, he found himself dazed by angry irritation against it. It became part of the pain buried centrally, like a deep hammer blow, just above his eyes and extending, in a savage cord, to the base of his spine.

"What the hell are you doing?" he said.

The boy was surprised not by the abruptness of the voice, but by its softness. It seemed like a voice from a long way off. It made him feel slightly guilty.

"Not much," he said.

"Put that torch down," the pilot said. "Don't wave it about."

"Not a torch," the boy said. "Pair of glasses."

"Glasses?"

"Binoculars. The German's. I found them on deck."

"Oh," the pilot said.

"Can't make them work," the boy said. "Everything looks wrong."

"Let me look at them," the pilot said. "They ought to be good —German binoculars."

He held his hands upward, weakly, without extending his arms, and the boy bent down and gave him the glasses. He let them lie on his chest for some moments, and the boy saw it heaving deeply, as if the movement of reaching for the glasses had exhausted him. It seemed quite a long time before he slowly lifted them to his face. Then, when he held them there, it was without doing anything with them. His hands did not move on the adjustment screws. He rested the eyepieces lightly against the deep sockets of his eyes and simply held them there without a word, in what seemed a dream of tiredness, or forgetfulness, or pain. It did not occur to the boy that there might be in this long and silent inertia a savage struggle to behave with decent normality, without fuss, to accomplish the simple task of revolving the screws and say something about it without the shadow of even a small agony.

After some longer interval, the pilot let the glasses rest slowly back on his chest. To the boy, it seemed that he grasped them with extraordinary tightness. He gave a worried sort of smile. It was very quiet and strengthless, but quite calm, and seemed as if it were intended to be reassuring.

"Needs adjustment, that's all," he said. His words were hard, gasped out quickly. "I can do it. Quite easy. Nice pair."

He held the glasses hard against his chest and stared straight beyond the boy with a sort of lost vehemence. His eyes seemed to have difficulty in focusing on some point in very obscure and difficult distance far beyond the varnished pitch-pine walls of the cabin. They were terribly desperate.

But what worried the boy was that the glasses were held also with this same rigid desperation. He waited for some moments for the pilot to give them back to him. Then it became clear that they were not coming back. The pilot grasped them hard against the blankets which covered him and shut his eyes.

The boy stood gazing down for some moments, troubled and waiting for something to happen. Suddenly he knew that he was forgotten. It was no use.

He remembered the tea. He took a last look at the figure of the pilot lying absolutely still and rigid, grasping the binoculars as he had sometimes seen dying men in pictures grasping a cross, and then pushed the kettle on to the galley fire. He was sick of tea; he was tired of a succession of daily crises in all of which Gregson demanded tea, only to let it get cold without drinking it, and then demanded still more tea as another crisis created itself, letting it get cold again.

Reluctantly making fresh tea at last, the boy remembered that he ought to call Gregson. He went to the bottom of the companionway and shouted, "Mr. Gregson! Skipper, tea!" but there was no movement and no answering shout above the sound of rain. Also, as he looked upward and saw the rain flicking in steady drizzle across the section of dark sky, he felt there was something odd about The Breadwinner, and when he had taken two or three steps up the companionway, he saw what it was. He saw that Gregson had rigged a sail. The boy went slowly on deck and marveled at this strange brown triangle with a sort of reluctant wonder. He had never seen it before. It gave to the dumpy, war-painted Breadwinner an exciting loftiness; it made her seem a larger ship. It even seemed to dwarf the enormous figure of Gregson, pressing his belly rather harder than usual against the wheel, the peak of his cap rather harder down on his head.

"Tea, Mr. Gregson," the boy said. "Just made."

"Ain't got time!" Gregson roared.

The boy stood in the attitude of someone stunned on his feet; he was more shocked than he had been by the sight of the dead engineer. He stared at the face of Gregson pressing itself forward with a sort of pouted savagery against the driving rain, eyes popped forward, chin sunk hard into doubled and redoubled folds of inflamed flesh on the collar of his jersey. It was some moments before he could think of anything to say.

"Just ready," he said at last. It did not seem remotely credible that Gregson could reject tea. "I can bring it up."

"Ain't got time, I tell yer!" Gregson said. "Ain't got time for nothing! That wind's gittin' up! Look at that sea, too! Look at it! We gotta git them chaps in!"

The boy turned and saw, for the first time since the shooting, what had happened to the weather. Rain and wind beating up the Channel had already plowed the sea into a shallow and ugly trough of foam. The distances had narrowed in, so that the sky line was no longer divisible from the smoky and shortened space of sea. Overhead he saw lumpy masses of rain cloud skidding northeastward.

"Another hour and it'll blow your guts out!" Gregson said. "We went too far west! I knowed it!"

He had nursed the old superstitions in his mind, placing them against events. The boy remembered the desperate sarcasms of the dead Jimmy, appealing for a second auxiliary, but he said nothing. It was too late now.

"You git below," Gregson said, "and look after them two."

He went below and stood at the table and poured himself tea and drank it in hot, violent gulps. The boat had begun to sway a little, in short brisk lurches, still shallow. Already they were increasing, and he knew they would not stop now. Soon she would pitch forward, too, and if the wind rose enough she would fall into the regular violence of double pitch and roll that would not cease until she was within half a mile of shore.

The tea did something to dispel the horror of memory. He drained the cup before becoming aware that other things were happening in the cabin. The English pilot had stretched out one hand until he could reach the table leg. By grasping the leg, he had pulled himself, on the stretcher, a foot or two across the cabin floor. Now he could touch the German on the shoulder.

"Messner," he was saying. "Messner. I'm talking to you, Messner." He looked up at the boy. "He doesn't answer me," he said. "He's been coughing and groaning like hell, and now he doesn't answer." He pulled at the German's jacket. "Messner," he said. "Messner."

The boy bent down by the German, who had turned his face away from the English boy. It was clear that the German did not see him with his strange and pale, unfocused eyes.

"Blood coming out of his mouth," the boy whispered. "All over him. What shall I do?"

"Got your first-aid pack?"

"A box. Yes."

"Let's see what it's got."

While the boy found the first-aid box in Gregson's locker, the English boy lay rigid, eyes half closed, as if very tired. The German had begun to moan quietly again now, his head lolling slowly and regularly from side to side.

The boy opened the first-aid box and laid it by the side of the

English pilot on the floor. But the English boy ignored it, as if he had thought of something else.

"Look under his blanket," he said. "Loosen his clothes a bit. See if you can make him easy. Loosen his jacket and trousers."

He drew back the blankets and folded them down to just below the German's waist. A fantastic dark patch had spread itself all across the upper part of his legs and upward over the left groin. The boy stared at it with the blunted shock of weariness. It was something that did not ask for speculation. The fullness of its violent meaning swept over him for a few slow moments and then engulfed him with the terror of sickness. He felt his teeth crying against each other as he folded the blankets hurriedly back over the body, that now and then swayed slightly, helpless and a fraction disturbed, with the motions of the boat and the sea.

He sat on the floor between the two pilots, and could not speak for fear of the vast wave of sickness rising up in his throat.

"What is it?" the pilot said.

"Blood," the boy said. "Blood all over him. Legs and stomach."

"Keep him covered," the pilot said.

He spoke with brief finality, checked by his own weariness. He still had his hands on the binoculars, holding them tightly to his chest. He grinned at the boy with flickering, unexpected life.

"Bit bumpy."

"Freshening a bit," the boy said.

"Rain by midday, they said. Just time for one patrol. Quite a patrol too."

"Like some tea?" the boy said, and moved as if to get up, but the pilot grinned quietly again and said, "No. No more, thanks. Sit and talk to me."

The boy did not know what to say. It seemed to him it would be better if the pilot talked. He longed for him to speak of flying, of aircraft, of speeds; of battles especially. How did it feel up there? He supposed he must often have watched him come over the dunes and the marshes, going out to sea, this same man, and yet not thinking of him as a man, but only as something flying, terrific and untouchable, across the sky. He still could not grasp that that furious splendor had a reality now.

All the pilot said was, "It's getting hellish dark in here. Think so?"

"No," the boy said. "It's all right. It's not dark."

"Best of having white hair," the pilot said, and grinned in a very tired, old way at this joke of his.

"I could light the lamp," the boy said.

"Lamp?"

The pilot said the word slowly; he seemed to want to keep it on his lips, for comfort. He looked vaguely upward, as if desperately trying to see the boy in the small dark cabin. The boy got up. A pair of oil lamps was fastened into the bulkhead between the side lockers, and he now struck a match to light the one nearer the pilot. The dull orange flame hardly had any light at first. He turned it up. And then, when he moved away from it, his own shadow fell vast and somber across the body of the pilot, throwing into tawny edges of relief the yellow varnished paneling and the yellow face of the German beyond.

That shadow in some way discomforted him, and he crouched down. The face of the English boy came full into the oily glow; calm now, molded by the downward cast of light into a smoother, flatter shape of almost shadowless bone. The boy saw on it as he crouched down the first glimpse of death. It was so unagonized and silent that for a moment or two he almost believed in it. The eyes of the pilot were closed and his lips slightly open, as if the word "lamp" still remained only partly spoken from them.

Out of this deathly attitude, the pilot suddenly opened a pair of eyes that seemed blackened and not awakened by the light of the lamp. They were distorted by a dark and sickly brilliance, and the boy was startled.

"Better," he heard the pilot say. "Better."

The boy sat hugging his knees with relief.

"How's old Messner?"

"Quiet," the boy said.

"Messner," the pilot said, "how's things? How are you?"

Messner did not answer. He was not groaning now. He had turned his face away from the light of the lamp.

"Hell of a brave sod," the pilot said.

"Might not be him," the boy said. He was not handing out free bravery to any enemy yet.

"I think so," the pilot said. "He knows it was me too."

"You think so?"

"Certain."

"But you were faster, weren't you?" the boy said. "You could catch him easy, couldn't you? The English are faster, aren't they?" At last, in a rush, he had spoken his feelings.

"Being fast isn't everything," the pilot said.

"No?"

"Anyway, I wouldn't be as fast. He had a One-oh-nine. It was just luck." He grinned, tired, his eyes deadened again. "Smooth do, though, all the same."

A great quiver of pain suddenly came upward from his body as he finished these words, shaking his whole face with a great vibration of agony, and his eyes lightened bitterly with an awful flash of terror. They did a sudden vivid swirl in the lamp-light, like the eyes of someone falling suddenly into space and looking in final horror at something to cling to.

"Snowy," he said. "Snowy," and instinctively the boy caught hold of his hands. They were frantically fixed to the binoculars, glued by awful sweat, and yet cold, and the boy could feel the transmission of pain and coldness flowing out of them into his own.

The agony turned the pilot's finger tips to tangles of frenzied wire, which locked themselves about the boy's hands and could not release them. The Breadwinner lurched again, and the boy went hard down on one elbow, unable to save himself, and still, even in falling, unable to release himself from the frantic wires of the pilot's hands.

When he managed to kneel upright again, he was in a panic at the English boy's sudden silence. It was as if they had both been struggling for possession of the binoculars, and the pilot, tiring suddenly, had lost them.

"I'll get the skipper," the boy said. "I'll fetch Mr. Gregson."

He tried to get up on his feet, but discovered his hands still locked in the pilot's own.

"All right, Snowy. Don't go. All right now. Don't go."

"Sure?" the boy said. "I'd better."

"No. Don't go. Don't. How's old Messner? Have a look at old Messner."

Messner was quiet. The boy, still held by the pilot's hands, could not move. He told the pilot how Messner was quiet, how he ought to call Mr. Gregson. The pilot did not answer. The boy had long since lost count of time, and now the half darkness, the lamplight and the silence gave the impression that the day was nearly over.

He crouched there for a long time, imprisoned by the pilot's hands, waiting for him to speak again. He sometimes thought of the binoculars as he sat there. The strap of them and the two sets of fingers seemed inextricably locked together; he felt that they would never come apart. And all he could hear was the sound of the pilot's breath, drawn with irregular, congested harshness, like the pained echo of rain and sea washing against the timbers of the small ship outside. He shut his own eyes once, and let himself be swung deeply to and fro by the motions of the ship. He could almost guess by these motions how far they were from shore. At a point about five miles out they struck the current from the river mouth, faintly at first, but heavier close to land, and on days of westward wind, like this, there was always a cross swell and a pull that would take them up the coast. They still had some way to go.

"Messner all right?" The voice of the English boy, coming at last, was only a whisper. It seemed to the boy fantastic that there should be this constant question about Messner. He could not conjure any concern for Messner at all, beyond the concern for the binoculars, and he did not speak.

"Valuable bloke, Messner," the pilot said. "Might talk. If we get back."

He tried to grin, but the movement of his lips was strengthless, quivering and not very amusing.

"If we get back. That's the big laugh," he said. "Always is." When he spoke again, it was of quite different things. "The lamp's very bright," he said.

"I'll turn it down," the boy said.

"No." His voice had the distance of a whisper gently released in a great hollow. "Rather like it. Lean over a bit."

The shadow of the boy moved across and remained large and protective over the face of the young man. They still gripped each other's fingers tightly, the binocular case between. It seemed cold. There was no sound from Messner.

It seemed to the boy late in the afternoon when the pilot began to mutter and babble of things he did not understand. Once he opened his eyes with a bright blaze of fantastic vigor, and talked of a girl. The next moment he was saying, "Tell old Messner he put up a good show."

He did not speak again. The boy watched him dying in the vastness of his own shadow without knowing he was dying. It was only when he moved to get a better look at his face that he saw it without even the convulsion of breath.

After some moments he succeeded in getting his fingers out of the dead fingers, at the same time releasing the binoculars. He was cold and he moved quietly, crawling on the cabin floor. When he went over to Messner, he found that Messner had died, too, and now the lamplight was full on both of them, with equal brightness, as they lay side by side.

The Breadwinner came in under the shelter of rain-brown dunes and the western peninsula of the bay in the late afternoon and drove in toward the estuary, with the boy and Gregson on deck. Rain trembling across the darkening sky in gray cascades like spray hid all the farther cliffs from sight, and in the distance the hills were lost in cloud. The boy grasped the binoculars in his hands, pressing them against his stomach rather as Gregson pressed the wheel against his own, in the attitude of a man who is about to raise them to his eyes and see what the distances reveal.

"Just turned," Gregson said. "Bloomin' good job for us too. That tide'll come in as high as a church steeple with this wind."

As she came in full across the wind, lumping on the waves as if they had been crests of solid steel, The Breadwinner had more than ever the look of a discarded and battered toy. She bumped in a series of jolting short dives that were like the ridiculous mockery of a dance. Her deck, as it ran with spray and rain, gleamed like dirty yellow ice, so that sometimes when she heeled over and the boy was caught unawares he hung on to the deckhouse with one hand, his feet skating outward. With the other hand he held on to the binoculars. He gripped them with the aggressive tightness of a man who has won a conquest. Nothing, if he could help it, was going to happen to them.

At times he looked up at the face of Gregson. It was thrust outward into the rain with its own enormous and profound aggression. The boy sometimes could not tell from its muteness whether it was angry or simply shocked into the silences it held for half an hour or more. He wanted to talk to it. There rose up constantly in his mind, tired now and dazed by shock, images of the cabin below. They troubled him more each time he thought of them. Their physical reality began to haunt him much more than the reality of the dead engineer, who lay not ten feet before him, like a piece of sodden and battered merchandise, his blood washed away now by constant rain. He thought often of the conversation of the dead pilot. He thought less often of Messner. There were to him very subtle differences between the men, and death had not destroyed them. When he thought of Messner, it was with dry anger. He conceived Messner as the cause of it all. It was something of a low trick. Then he remembered Messner as the man who also carried the binoculars, and he remembered that the binoculars were the only things that had come out of the day that were not sick with the ghastliness of foul and indelible dreams.

He was very tired. The way the sea hit The Breadwinner also hit him in the stomach, a dozen times or more a minute, kicking him sore. He had not eaten anything since coming from the cabin. There had been no more shouts from Gregson, no more cups of tea.

When the boy had to talk to him again, he said, "When will we be in, Mr. Gregson, skipper?"

Gregson did not answer. He kept his face thrust forward into a gigantic pout, angered into a new and tragic sullenness. The boy had not known this face before. There were times when he had been afraid of Gregson; they were separated by what seemed to him vast stretches of years, by the terrifying vastness of the man. Now he was comforted by the gigantic adultness of Gregson. It shut him away, for even a little, from the things he had seen.

They were coming in toward the estuary now, Gregson giving the wheel a hard point or two to port, and then another, and then holding The Breadwinner hard down, her head a point or two west from north. The face of the sea was cresting down a fraction; the wind gave a suck or two at the sail as the boat turned and lay over, loosing it back as she straightened. The boy could see the shore clearly now, misty with rain, the dunes in long wet brown stripes, the only color against the winter land beyond. And suddenly, looking up at Gregson, he thought for a moment that he detected there a slight relaxation on the enormous bulging face. He saw Gregson lick the rain from his tired lips. It gave him courage to think that at last Gregson was going to speak again.

"Almost in, Mr. Gregson, skipper," he said.

The violence of Gregson's voice was so sudden that it was like the clamor of a man frightened by his own anger.

"Damn them!" he roared. "Damn them! All of them, damn them! Why don't they let us alone? Why don't they let us alone? Why don't they let us alone? How much longer? Why don't they let our lives alone? Damn and blast them—all of them, all of them, all over the world!"

Gregson finished shouting and gave an enormous fluttering sigh. It seemed to exhaust him. He stood, heavy and brooding, across the wheel, his body without savagery, his face all at once dead and old and colorless, the rain streaming down it like a flood of tears.

He put his hand on the boy's shoulder, as if he now suddenly remembered he was there. The sea was calming down at the mouth of the estuary and The Breadwinner was beginning to run lumpily in toward the narrow gap in the steel defenses, rusty for miles along the wild and empty shore. There were no lights in the dark afternoon, and the rain darkened a little more each moment the farther hills, the cliffs and the low sky. The boy did not move again. All the time he had wanted, at this last moment, to raise the binoculars to his eyes. For some reason he did not want to raise them now. There did not seem much use in raising them. He was not sure that there seemed much use in possessing them. As he stood there with Gregson's arm on his shoulder, he remembered the dead engineer; he remembered Gregson's violent outburst of words and he remembered the dead pilots, lying in the orange lamplight in the small cabin darkened by his own shadow, with their dead fair faces, side by side. And they became for him, just then, all the pilots, all the dead pilots all over the world.

At that moment they ran into the mouth of the estuary. Gregson continued tenderly to hold him by the shoulder, and the boy once more looked up at him, seeing the old, tired face again as if bathed in tears. He did not speak, and there rose up in him a grave exultation. He had been out to war and was alive and had come back again.